APPROACHING THE DIVINE

The Integration of Āḻvār Bhakti in Śrīvaiṣṇavism

APPROACHING THE DIVINE

The Integration of Āḻvār Bhakti in Śrīvaiṣṇavism

BHARATI JAGANNATHAN

PRIMUS BOOKS

PRIMUS BOOKS
An imprint of Ratna Sagar P. Ltd.
Virat Bhavan
Mukherjee Nagar Commercial Complex
Delhi 110 009

Offices at CHENNAI LUCKNOW
AGRA AHMEDABAD BENGALURU COIMBATORE DEHRADUN GUWAHATI HYDERABAD
JAIPUR JALANDHAR KANPUR KOCHI KOLKATA MADURAI MUMBAI PATNA
RANCHI VARANASI

First published 2015

ISBN: 978-93-84082-13-0

Published by Primus Books

Lasertypeset by Sai Graphic Design
Arakashan Road, Paharganj, New Delhi 110 055

Printed and bound in India by Replika Press Pvt. Ltd.

For
AMMA
and
APPA

Contents

Acknowledgements ix

A Note on Transliteration and Footnotes xiii

List of Abbreviations xvii

1. Introduction 1
2. The Hagiographical Accounts 47
3. The Ardently Loving Lord: A Promise of Salvation 95
4. Equal Before the Lord: Negotiating Caste 127
5. 'Whose God is the Greatest of All?' Engaging with Other Faiths 178
6. Bathing in Every *Tīrtha*: Patterns of Worship, Pilgrimage and the Saint Poets 224

APPENDICES

I. *Nālāyira Divya Prabandham*: Works with their Composers 281

II. Shrines mentioned in the Hymns/by the Āḻvārs

(a) The four *Antādis* of the *Iyarpā* and the *Tiruccanta Viruttam* 282

(b) Kulaśekhara, Pĕriyāḻvār, Āṇḍāḷ and Tŏṇṭaraṭippŏṭi Āḻvār 284

(c) Tirumankai Āḻvār 286

(d) Nammāḻvār 290

(e) The *Ciriya Tirumaṭal* and the *Pĕriya Tirumaṭal* 292

Other Compositions in the *Nālāyiram* 294

Bibliography 295

Index 329

Acknowledgements

How does one express, without the felicity of Āṇḍāḷ, Madhurakavi or Pĕriyāḻvār, one's love, gratitude and regard for family, teachers and friends? I have received so much from so many people that no thanks can suffice; I can only be grateful for this opportunity to mention some of them.

This book has emerged largely from my doctoral thesis submitted to the Centre for Historical Studies, Jawaharlal Nehru University, New Delhi. My research supervisor, Professor Kunal Chakrabarti, has been a friend, philosopher and guide in the true sense of the term. A scholar of immense range and depth who showed me how to ask diverse questions of my materials, a wonderful teacher whose engagement with and comments on my work made me believe in it, a careful supervisor whose attention to detail did not exclude even misplaced commas—when I did give him something to read, and an eternally patient one, understanding when I failed, time after time, to do so. But even more valuable than his supervision of my work has been Kunal da's friendship, easily my greatest reward from this project.

Guru Gobind dou khaḍe, kāke lāgoon pāy/ balihāri guru āpne, Gobind diyo milāy. Kabir's *dohā* juxtaposing God and Guru may be transposed in my case to Guru and Kumkum Roy. Gentle and generous, serene and sensitive, undemanding and ever-giving, like mother earth, Kumkum is someone I wish I were more like, but knowing I cannot be, feel blessed just to know.

So many people have touched my life in the years this project took shape: Tuni/Sharmishtha Roychowdhury, dearest of friends, who from across the oceans is as central to my life today as when we were roommates 25 years ago; Harish Dhawan and Shahana Bhattacharya who have given me the gift of the mountains; Naina Dayal, my dial-up Advanced-English Dictionary and Wren and Martin; Saswati Sengupta, who badgered me to write, write, finish; Deeksha Bhardwaj, companion on numerous wonderful journeys; Anant Gopal who supplied regular doses of philosophy; Kajal Sinha without whom I cannot imagine my time in Philly; Balwant Kaur, Bani Roy, C. Suvasini, Deepika Tandon, Chiku/Farah Kidwai, Hina/Rana Hafiz, Ira Singh, Jo/Jayeeta Sharma, Madhu, Meenakshi Khanna, Meeta Kumar, Monika Browarczyk, Radhika Chadha, Ranjeeta Dutta, Reema Bhatia, Rohini Muthuswamy, Shibani Bose, Snigdha Singh, Srimanjari, Tanika Sarkar and Yousuf Saeed who have all enriched my work or life or both in some way—thank you all. And thank you, Arun, Bhoop Singh, Rajvati, Rammurti, Sunita and Vimla for all that you do each day to make life so much smoother.

This work could not have been done without the help, inputs and advice of several scholars. The late Professor J. Parthasarathi, distinguished linguist and scholar of Śrīvaiṣṇavism, made the medieval Tamil-Maṇipravāḷa hagiographies accessible to me—but more of him later. Professor N.S. Sadagopan, Sanskrit scholar, read with me the *Rāmānujārya Divya Caritai* and the *Nālāyiram*, and patiently found me references from various Sanskrit texts. Professor K.K.A. Venkatachari who has been teacher and *mārgadarśaka* for two generations of scholars and researchers on Śrīvaiṣṇavism was characteristically generous with his vast knowledge. My thanks to his family too, which made me feel at home during the time I worked in his private library in Triplicane. Shrivatsa Goswami ji let me access his collection of rare books and journals in Vrindavan. Professor Kesavan Veluthat responded to endless questions with generosity and enthusiasm. The insightful comments of Professors K.M. Shrimali, Vijaya Ramaswamy, Rajan Gurukkal, Daud Ali, John Stratton Hawley and the anonymous peer reviewer, on different occasions, on parts or the whole of this work have helped refine my arguments. I owe a special debt to Daud, my mentor and host at the University of Pennyslvania—thank you for so much! I am grateful to Professors Upinder Singh, Archana Venkatesan, Mukul Kesavan, Farhat Nasreen, John Nemec, Ariel Glucklich, Aparna Vaidik, Richard Davis, Ramya Sreenivasan, Wendy Singer, Karen Pechilis and Indira Peterson for giving me the opportunity to share some of my work and benefit from comments and questions at their universities and for much beyond the confines of academics. Knowing Jack/John Stratton Hawley is as much a personal blessing as an academic one. I also want to record my gratitude to many teachers and students who have shaped me over the years.

My thanks also go out to the various libraries and their staff who made this research possible: the Kuppuswami Sastri Research Institute and the Adayar libraries in Madras; Miranda House (Geeta, Hanuman, Hasina, Kamlesh, Lateef, Om Prakash, Ramesh, Ratan Lal, Sunil and Y.K. Sharma), the Indian Council of Historical Research (Indu, Joshi, Krishnaji, Malvika, Nardev Sharma, Naresh, Noor, Mr Sahay), Sahitya Akademi (Mr Padmanabhan, best of librarians) and Jawaharlal Nehru University libraries in Delhi; the American Institute for Indian Studies (Mr Yadav and Mr Jagannath) in Gurgaon; and the Van Pelt Dietrich Library at UPenn, Philadelphia.

I thank Miranda House for the grant of three years of study leave to enable me to concentrate on my research. A fellowship from the Indian Council of Historical Research allowed me to take three months' further leave from teaching to finish the project. A post-doctoral research fellowship from ICHR enabled me to elaborate my work on the Śrīvaiṣṇava pilgrimage tradition. A Fulbright-Nehru Post-doctoral Research Fellowship in 2012-13 opened for me the wonderland of the American library system at UPenn.

During my fieldwork in Madras, I stayed with my grandmother Rukmini who, both as a practising Śrīvaiṣṇava with a deep interest in the intellectual traditions of her faith and from affection, took a keen interest in my work. So did her brother—my grand uncle Professor J. Parthasarathi, who, despite his 88 years, read the texts with me for several hours every day and discussed my work in exhaustive detail, while his family made me part of their household. As grandchildren themselves of the great Tamil savant and scholar of Śrīvaiṣṇavism, Professor Mu. Raghava Iyengar, they were particularly excited about a member of the 'younger generation' of the lineage returning to the study of the religious and literary tradition. I deeply regret that neither of them is around anymore to rejoice in the completed work.

My maternal aunt Komala was like a fairy godmother during my stay in Madras. I cannot thank her or my uncle Krishnamurthy enough for all that they did to ensure my comfort and also for making several pilgrimage/ field trips richer by their company. The home of my paternal aunt and uncle, Lakshmi and (the late) Sundararajan, was equally a home away from home. There I found, too, friendship and company of my own age in Kumar, Charu, Raghu and Uttara. While Appu/Preeti took an eager and amused interest in my work and found humour in the most unexpected places, Balaji's enthusiasm for my subject frequently surpassed my own. Thanks to Shruti, for making me feel brilliant, talented and wonderful. And Basant has been always present, even when absent.

My family. Simply put, I would not be able to do anything without the support, care and love of every one of them. What do I single out to mention among the great and small things that each one has done and continues to do for me each day?

Sundari and Kanya seem to have a fair degree of regard both for my work and for me while Kesu and Madhu keep me from taking either too seriously.

Kunju and Nitya, dearest on earth, you have brought joy and, indeed, meaning into my life.

Finally, Appa and Amma. There is no way to thank one's parents; I cannot even try. All I will note is that the only reason I ever finished this work was because Appa kept up the pressure relentlessly, so much so that I hid the novels I read inside textbooks like a truant teenager. Amma read, translated and explained the Tamil texts repeatedly. Their concern and involvement with this project has scarcely been less than my own. To them both, I dedicate this work.

New Delhi BHARATI JAGANNATHAN

A Note on Transliteration and Footnotes

In transliterating words from Sanskrit and Tamil, I have largely followed the standard format, and will point out only the exceptions.

I have not placed a dot above the *n* in words such as Sangam and Tirumankai.

The Tamil lexical system indicates the short vowels as *a, i, u, e* and *o* and long vowels by *ā, ī, ū, ē* and *ō*. Since Sanskrit does not have short vowels for *e* and *o*, one tends to read, in a text which has a sprinkling of both Sanskrit and Tamil words, *e* and *o* without diacritical marks as long vowels even when they happen to be Tamil words. I have, therefore, chosen to indicate the Tamil short vowels in these two cases by *ĕ* and *ŏ*. Plain *e* and *o* in Tamil words in my text connote long vowels as they do in Sanskrit.

Since Tamil has a large vocabulary borrowed from Sanskrit and words which are compounds of both languages, it is often difficult to decide whether to adopt Sanskrit spellings or Tamil ones for such words, especially when they occur in the Tamil context. I have largely chosen the Sanskrit spellings for wider intelligibility, as in *Divya Prabandham* in place of *Tivviya-p-Pirapantam*, Bhaṭṭar instead of Paṭṭar and Hṛṣīkeśa instead of Iruṭīkecan̲. Pūtattāl̲vār is rendered as the Tamil Pūtam, not the Sanskrit Bhūtam and *Tiruccanta Viruttam* has not been changed to a complicated *Tiru-chanda-vṛttam*, partly because these spellings have already acquired a fair degree of standardization in scholarly works, but also so that they remain intelligible to the Tamil reader! Similar considerations have governed my choice of spellings for the names of the Nāyan̲mārs Sambandar/Tirujñān̲a-Sambandar and Sundarar: neither the Sanskrit Sambandha and Sundara, nor the Tamil Campantar and Cuntarar, but really a rendering of the way the words are pronounced in

Tamil with the closest Sanskrit equivalent in spelling. Having known and loved Āṇḍāḷ as *iṣṭa devi* and confidante from long before I even thought of this research subject, I have retained the spelling I first knew, only decorating it with some diacritical marks!

I have retained the common spellings of well-known place names like Chingleput, Madurai, Sriperumbudur and Srirangam (which also features as Arangam), and made minor changes in others such as Tanjavur (for Thanjavur). Kanjivaram is spelt both as Kāñcīpuram and as the more colloquial Kāñcī. Lesser-known place names have been transliterated according to the above format. Since shrine centres often have Tiru prefixed to them, a town may be called both Per and Tirupper, or Āli and Tiruvāli in the same text. I have accordingly spelt such words when they appear with the prefix as TirupPer or TiruvĀli so that they can be easily identified when they appear in my text without the prefix. However, when the place name is part of the name of a person as in Tirukkoṭṭiyūr Nampi (Nampi of holy Koṭṭiyūr), I have not capitalized the letter from which the actual place-name begins mid-word. Nor have I in cases like Tiruppati or Tiruccirāppaḷḷi, which are never used without the prefix.

Spellings in quotations match their original text rather than mine.

As a native Tamil speaker, I tend to read, for example, Kaṭalmallai (correct transliteration) as Kaḍalmallai and fail to notice when I have *spelt* it as Kaḍalmallai. Words such as Devī and my own name, bhārati, end in the short *i* in Tamil though in their Sanskrit forms, they end in the long *ī*. Again, as a native Tamil speaker, but as one who has learnt Hindi through school, I seem to inhabit a zone of confusion, failing to notice when I have spelt such words in the Sanskrit fashion and when in the Tamil. I crave the reader's indulgence for these inconsistencies.

I have followed the standard format for footnotes with the exception of the inscriptional references from T.V. Mahalingam's nine-volume, district-wise compilation, *A Topographical List of Inscriptions in Tamil Nadu and Kerala States* (ICHR and S. Chand & Co., Delhi, 1985). I have footnoted all these (after the first in each chapter) as 'Mahalingam, 1985', followed by a sequence of alphabets and numerals. The key to decipher them is as follows.

'Vol. VIII, p. 220. Tp 998. Ref.: *ARE* 1936–7, no. 80; ibid., part ii, para 49, pp. 79–80; *EI*, xxiv, pp. 90–100; *SII*, xxiv, no. 266' should be read as volume VIII, page number 220, Tiruccirāppaḷḷi district 998 (as in, the 998-inscription from the Tiruccirāppaḷḷi district featuring in Mahalingam's compilation). Further, the reference is from the *Annual Reports of Epigraphy*, 1936–37, no. 80, featured in part ii, para 49, pages 79–80; in the *Epigraphica Indica*, volume xxiv, pages 90–100; and in *South Indian Inscriptions*, volume xxiv, page 226.

The nine volumes are arranged in the following fashion. The contractions are those that Mahalingam has chosen to identify the district-wise provenance of the inscriptions.

NA	Vol. I:	North Arcot District
SA	Vol. II:	South Arcot District
Cg	Vol. III:	Chingleput District
Cb, Dh	Vol. IV:	Coimbatore, Dharmapuri Districts
Kn, Md, Mdu	Vol. V:	Kanyakumari, Madras, Madurai Districts
Ng, Pk, Rn, Sm	Vol. VI:	Nilgiris, Pudukkottai, Ramanathapuram, Salem Districts
Tj	Vol. VII:	Tanjavur District
Tp	Vol. VIII:	Tirucchirapalli District
Tn	Vol. IX:	Tirunelveli District

Abbreviations

Agpp	*Ārāyirappaṭi Guruparamparā Prabhāvam* (Tĕnkalai)
DSC	*Divya Sūri Caritam*
Gpps	*Guruparamparā Prabhāvams*
Mgpp	*Mūvāyirappaṭi Guruparamparā Prabhāvam* (Vaṭakalai)
NDP	*Nālāyira Divya Prabandham/ Nālāyiram*

ONE

Introduction

'What she said'

Evening has come
but not the Dark One.

The bulls
their bells jingling,
have mated with the cows
and the cows are frisky.

The flutes play cruel songs,
bees flutter in their bright
  white jasmine
and the blue-black lily.

The sea leaps into the sky
  and cries aloud.

Without him here,
  what shall I say?
  how shall I survive?

—A.K. RAMANUJAN, *Hymns for the Drowning: Poems to Visnu by Nammālvār*, 1993, p. 33.

This could well be a classical love poem from the Sangam Tamil collection, *Akanāṉūru*, the poems of the 'interior landscape', made familiar to us by A.K. Ramanujan's excellent translations. And it does share many features with the poems of that anthology—for one, this poem is also originally from Tamil, and has also been translated by Ramanujan.

Though the similarity does not end there, it is actually a product of careful reworking of the older idiom, the established conventions of Sangam poetry, to convey a new sensibility.[1] This new poetry breaks a cardinal rule of the *akam* genre—that none of the protagonists be named. For here, the beloved, the one causing the heroine the sufferings of love-in-separation, is, as in the *puram* genres, identified, as The Dark One. And to the initiated, this clue tells all—it is not a generic dark lover but the Cosmic Lord who swallowed the seven worlds and then lay as a baby on a banyan leaf; who smote the demon Hiraṇyakaśipu as a man-lion; who killed Rāvaṇa in his *avatāra* as Rāma; who, as Kṛṣṇa, held aloft the mountain Govardhana as an umbrella to protect his cowherd community from torrential rains; who sleeps on the hooded serpent in the milky ocean, and in Srirangam. He is also Māyoṉ of classical Tamil, the dark lord of the *mullai tiṉai*, the pastoral landscape.

Māyoṉ or Māl of the Sangam poems already exhibits features of the northern Kṛṣṇa; in fact, it is difficult to always tell which elements of the composite god are Dravidian and which draw on northern sources. His early identification with Kṛṣṇa, Viṣṇu, and, indeed, with Nārāyaṇa, the supreme aspect of Viṣṇu,[2] in the *Cilappatikāram*, a late Sangam text, must certainly owe to northern influence. But a more important element from our point of view was the localization, the 'fixing' of the transcendental god. 'The universal god becomes a personalized god, almost "visible", his presence must be tangible, almost physical, "here and now", contrasting with aniconic Vedic worship. . . . A person with whom one may enter into an individual, highly personal, intimate, exclusive relationship and close contact.'[3] The immanence of the deity in the landscape—Murukaṉ/Cĕyyoṉ in the *kuriñci tiṉai* and Māyoṉ in the *mullai*—that seems to have been fundamental to the Tamil ethos, and the relationship with this rooted deity, were to become significant for the trajectory of development of religious ideas in early medieval Tamil Nadu.

The sixth to ninth centuries CE in Tamil Nadu saw the emergence and flowering of a deeply devotional form of religion which, as it acquired a distinct character, came to be called bhakti.[4] Bhakti devotionalism which

[1] Friedhelm Hardy, *Viraha Bhakti: The Early History of Kṛṣṇa Devotion in South India*, New Delhi: Oxford University Press, 1983, pp. 266, 315–24; Kamil Zvelebil, *Tamil Literature*, Leiden: EJ Brill, 1975, p. 103.

[2] Kamil Zvelebil, 'The Beginnings of Tamil Bhakti in South India', *Temenos: Studies in Comparative Religion*, vol. 13, 1977, p. 248.

[3] Ibid., p. 249.

[4] These are the most commonly accepted dates for the Āḻvārs and Nāyaṉmārs.

was eventually to become one of the most important aspects of the religious landscape of much of the subcontinent was focused primarily on either of the two gods, Śiva and Viṣṇu (or his *avatāras*), who came to be elevated far above the rest of the fairly extensive contemporary pantheon, and indeed above each other, in the minds of their respective devotees. The Śaiva tradition recognizes sixty-three saints called Nāyaṉmārs,[5] while the Vaiṣṇava tradition reveres twelve Āḻvārs. While many of the Nāyaṉmārs may have been legendary, since only a few have left behind compositions, the twelve Āḻvārs have usually been thought to have been historical figures, as there are hymns attributed to all of them.[6]

The Śrīvaiṣṇava community based largely in Tamil Nadu and in parts of Karnataka and Andhra Pradesh venerates the Āḻvārs as saints and devotees par excellence of Viṣṇu. Needless to say, Viṣṇu is the supreme godhead for the Śrīvaiṣṇavas who designate themselves so, first, in order to distinguish themselves from other Vaiṣṇava sects and second, because of a crucial theological belief in the inseparability of Viṣṇu and Śrī, the latter signifying both the god's *śakti* and the mediatrix between the god and his devotee. This theological position was elaborated between the eleventh and fourteenth centuries by brahmanical *ācāryas*.

The Śrīvaiṣṇava corpus of scriptures comprises the following:

1. The hymns of the Āḻvārs in Tamil collected as the *Nālāyira Divya Prabandham* (henceforth *NDP*);[7]
2. Philosophical works in Sanskrit, including commentaries such as Rāmānuja's *Śrībhāṣya* and *Gītābhāṣya* expounding authoritative

Tradition naturally places them in a long bygone age, and even till the beginning of the twentieth century, numerous traditional historians tried to prove the early date of the Āḻvārs with evidence from scriptures. One example will suffice. In explicating verse 8.9.10 of the *Tiruvāymŏḻi*, the *Īṭu* records this: Nammāḻvār described TirupPuliyūr as a spot blessed with abundance. Bhaṭṭar (a medieval *ācārya*), jestingly remarked, 'How could our saint describe this place as blessed when its inhabitants are racked by rents and debts?' Ref.: A. Govindacarya, *The Divine Wisdom of the Dravida Saints*, Madras: CN Press, 1902, p. 172. Govindacarya reads this as proof of the great interval of time between the Āḻvārs and the *ācāryas*, the Āḻvārs' time naturally having been a 'golden age' of plenty.

[5] Tamil singular: Nāyaṉār; plural: Nāyaṉmār. I shall, however, add an s to the plural, i.e. spell the word as Nāyaṉmārs so that it reads better in English.

[6] See discussion later in the chapter.

[7] Literally, 4,000 Sacred Compositions.

texts, and independent treatises such as Vedānta Deśika's *Samkalpa-sūryodaya*;

3. A vast body of commentarial literature on the *NDP* in Tamil and in Maṇipravāḷa developed from the eleventh century onwards;
4. Hagiographies of the saint-poets and the early *ācāryas* of the community composed in Sanskrit and in Maṇipravāḷa; and
5. *Stotras* (praise-poems) composed by various *ācāryas* in Tamil, Sanskrit and Prākṛt.

In addition to these, the *sthalapurāṇas* of about a hundred shrines also constitute the bases of the belief and worship patterns of the community, though they do not have the same kind of canonical status as the five categories listed here.

The Śrīvaiṣṇavas believe that there is a direct preceptorial line from Lord Viṣṇu through the Āḻvārs, particularly Nammāḻvār, to Nāthamuni, the first of the Śrīvaiṣṇava *ācāryas*. Orthodox Śrīvaiṣṇava scholars also, therefore, believe in the continuity of the religious tradition from the Āḻvārs to the *ācāryas*. This position draws directly from the *ācāryas*, beginning with Nāthamuni, who saw themselves as direct spiritual descendants of the Āḻvārs. In 1966, Robert Lester disputed the authorship of the *Gadyatrayi*,[8] on the grounds of its theological orientation. He also suggested that Rāmānuja, traditionally considered the third major *ācārya* in the line of Śrīvaiṣṇava preceptors,[9] was post-facto appropriated by the devotional Tamil tradition.[10] In 1983, Friedhelm Hardy further challenged age-old assumptions in his path-breaking *Viraha Bhakti*, arguing that the *ācāryas* of the Śrīvaiṣṇava tradition reinterpreted the hymns of the Āḻvārs to fit their contents into their own theological positions, in the process more or less erasing the deeply emotional content of the hymns,[11] at least some of which draw on the rich erotic–emotional *akam* genre of Sangam literature. This position, thus, implies a decisive break between the Āḻvār *bhakti* tradition and Śrīvaiṣṇavism as a religious system that developed in the early centuries of the second millennium. Critical scholarship in the field has since concentrated on marshalling textual

[8] The three prose compositions of Rāmānuja are *Śaraṇāgati Gadyam*, *Śrīranga Gadyam* and *Vaikuṇṭha Gadyam*.

[9] Rāmānuja is actually sixth in the line; the first two major *ācāryas* are Nāthamuni and Yāmunācārya.

[10] Robert Lester, 'Ramanuja and Srivaisnavism: The Concept of Prapatti or Saranagati', *History of Religions*, vol. 5, 1966, pp. 226–82; Robert Lester, *Ramanuja on the Yoga*, Adyar Library and Research Centre, Madras, 1976.

[11] Hardy, *Viraha Bhakti*, pp. 46, 480.

evidence either to support or to refute these theses. Few scholars still doubt Rāmānuja's authorship of the *Gadyatrayi*. Regarding the second, I believe that while the traditional claim that the *ācāryas* were faithfully following the Āḻvārs in both letter and spirit needs modification, there being significant departures from the themes of the saint-poets in their writings, it is equally incorrect to posit a radical break in the tradition. Indeed, I propose to show the *ācāryas* engaging, through the compositions of hagiographies and commentaries, in a creative project to integrate Āḻvār bhakti into Śrīvaiṣṇavism.

Also, the traditional view of continuity has had important consequences for modern historians' understanding of the phenomenon of bhakti in the Tamil context. The arguments that have been made about the role of the Āḻvārs and Nāyaṉmārs in their contemporary society have often been chronologically inaccurate, being based on substantially later sources. In other words, the picture we have of the *bhakti* movement in the Tamil land is one that is frequently refracted through the eyes of the hagiographers of the twelfth to fifteenth centuries.

In this study, which spans the period from the late sixth to the early-mid-fifteenth century, I shall examine the source materials closely to distinguish elements of continuity between the Āḻvār and *ācārya* traditions as well as differences between the two. This examination will also bring out the ways in which the latter tradition addresses contemporary concerns through the medium of hagiographies and interpretation of the hymns of the saints, 'creates', as it were, the bhakti movement, carefully weaving older elements, popular legends and details available in the hymns of the Āḻvārs themselves with the theological and social vision of the brahmanical *ācāryas*.

The hymns of the Āḻvārs and Nāyaṉmārs express a religious consciousness which seems to privilege profound emotionalism over formal ritual, and yet, itself establishes a system of ritual worship popularly known as *pūjā*.[12] There certainly were devotees of the two High Gods of brahmanical Hinduism among different social groups: kings and queens as well as ordinary persons belonging to diverse castes have left ample testimony of their piety in inscriptions recording gifts to temples of Śiva and Viṣṇu, and to *brāhmaṇas* engaged in their worship. Did the '*bhakti* movement' in the Tamil country invite fisherman and farmer, hunter and housewife to a devotional milieu shorn of hierarchy? Or did it merely call out, in deeply moving language, for them to renounce long-held faiths

[12] Suvira Jaiswal, *Origin and Development of Vaiṣṇavism*, Delhi: Munshiram Manoharlal, 1980, p. 138.

in 'false gods' if those were incompatible with their own, to embrace one where they might become members of a community of the faithful (Śaiva or Vaiṣṇava), equal perhaps spiritually, but distinctly nailed to a hierarchical, unequal social system? While lay *bhaktas* obviously came from all castes, I will explore whether the bhakti 'movement' itself was one that challenged the caste hierarchy or was an agency for the spread and consolidation of hierarchical brahmanical religion in the south, or if its social philosophy lay somewhere between these two extremes. I will also examine how the Śrīvaiṣṇava hagiographies wove in motifs from the hymns of the Āḻvārs to express antipathy towards the heterodox faiths and the rival 'orthodox' bhakti sect, i.e. Śaivism. Lastly, I will examine how the Śrīvaiṣṇava tradition as it developed in the second millennium elaborated the theme of pilgrimage found in the poetry of the Āḻvārs to create an elaborate religious complex centred around and spread out over nearly a hundred temples in the Tamil land.

(i) Political Background

The development of the religious tradition called bhakti took place against the background of profound political changes in the Tamil land. The period just prior to the flowering of bhakti saw the Kaḷabhra dynasty in control of large parts of Tamil Nadu. Believed to be supporters and patrons of the heterodox religions,[13] the Kaḷabhras are reviled as enemies of civilization by conservative historians.[14] Accyuta Vikkanta of the Kaḷabhra *kula* is denounced by later Tamil literary tradition for having kept in confinement the three Tamil kings, Cera, Coḻa and Pāṇṭiya.[15] K.A.N. Sastri's contention that their rule was a 'long historical night'[16] seems to be based on the above and on the Kaḷabhras having supposedly abrogated *devadāna* and *brahmadeya* rights,[17] though the evidence for this is scarce. The prejudice against these *kali aracars* (evil kings) runs

[13] Indeed, it has been surmised that the reason for the rise of bhakti religion in the Tamil country was to overcome the oppressive Jain and Buddhist faiths imposed upon the populace by their rulers. See S. Vaiyapuri Pillai, *History of Tamil Literature and Language*, Madras, 1956, p. 100.

[14] K.A. Nilakanta Sastri, *A History of South India*, Madras: Oxford University Press, 1955, p. 139.

[15] Ibid., p. 139. One cannot but wonder at this criticism, for wasn't vanquishing their enemies and extending their own power what kings were traditionally supposed to do?

[16] Ibid., p. 139.

[17] Ibid., p. 139. K.A. Nilakanta Sastri, *The Culture and History of the Tamils*,

so deep, however, that the period of their rule is referred to as the 'dark period' in the history of Tamil Nadu,[18] or as the Kaḷabhra 'interregnum', suggesting that it was considered merely an unpleasant interruption of an otherwise continuous 'Hindu' political domination.[19] The later Sangam works, including the great Tamil epics, the *Cilappatikāram* and the *Maṇimekalai*, composed in this age attest to the spread and influence of Jainism and Buddhism.[20] Available inscriptional and literary records only allow a patchwork picture of the political history of Tamil Nadu between the fourth and sixth centuries to emerge.

The early Pallava rulers of Kāñcī had started as a political power in south India in the beginning of the fourth century CE.[21] It was, however, in the last quarter of the sixth century that Kaḷabhra rule in northern Tamil Nadu was brought to an end by the Pallava Simhaviṣṇu. About the same time, Kaṭunkoṉ and his son Māravarmaṉ Avaṉicūḷāmaṇi put an end to Kaḷabhra power in the Madurai region and re-established Pāṇṭiya power there. Political records from this time onwards are less obscure but no less confusing, for the next two centuries were an age of repeated conflicts between the three major regional powers—the Cālukyas of Bādāmi, the Pallavas of Kāñcī and the Pāṇṭiyas of Madurai. Towards the middle of the eighth century, the Rāṣṭrakūṭas took the place of the Cālukyas in the main triangular conflict, though the two branches into which the Cālukya family had split and the Gangas of Mysore took sides

---

Calcutta: Firma KL Mukhopadhyay, 1963, p. 19 also mentions the ninth-century Veḷvikuṭi grant of the Pāṇṭiyas making a statement to this effect.

[18] Sastri, *A History of South India*, p. 139.

[19] Ibid., p. 142 speaks of a 'many sided religious revival that checked the growth of Jainism and Buddhism'. In *The Cōḻas*, University of Madras, Madras, 1935–7 (revd edn., repr. 1975), he refers to 'the battle against heresy' (p. 637), and records his appreciation of the 'pious exertions of the Āḻvārs and Nāyaṉmārs who led a great Hindu revival...[so that] the spread of the protestant faiths was stopped and the orthodox creeds restored to their place of dominance' (p. 107).

[20] B.G.L. Swamy, 'Kaḷabhra Interregnum—A Retrospect and Prospect', *Bulletin of the Institute of Traditional Cultures, Madras*, vol. 20, no. 1, pp. 81–148, 1976, argues on the basis of the Veḷvikuṭi copper plate inscription that the 'so-called 'Kaḷabhra interregnum' was only of an extremely short duration lasting for a couple of years during the period of Rājasimha I (about the middle of the eighth century)'.

[21] T.V. Mahalingam, *Readings in South Indian History*, Delhi: BR Publishing Corporation, 1977, p. 1. Also, R. Champakalakshmi, 'Introduction', *Studies in History*, vol. 4, no. 2, 1982, pp. 164–5, suggests that the Pallavas were confined to parts of the Andhra region between the fourth and sixth centuries.

in it, sometimes with decisive results. The Co<u>l</u>as of the Sangam era seem to have disappeared altogether unless they survived in the Telugu Coḍas in Rayalaseema.[22]

The conflict-ridden accession of Nandivarman II Pallavamalla of the junior branch of the Pallava family in *circa* 733 CE is narrated in sculpted panels in the Vaikuṇṭha-p-Pĕrumāḷ Temple at Kāñcīpuram.[23] Tirumankai Ā<u>l</u>vār, in his hymn on the temple of Aṣṭabhuja Svāmi in Kāñcīpuram, mentions Nandivarman's son and successor, Dantidurga (*c.* 795–845 CE),[24] also known as Vairamegha,[25] who was related to the Rāṣṭrakūṭas from his mother's side.[26] Interestingly, the period from the seventh century inaugurated a great age of temple building in both the Pallava and Cālukya realms,[27] which gained momentum and reached its culmination in the Co<u>l</u>a period.[28] After a brief fall from glory, the Pallavas were again in the ascendant in the mid-ninth century under Nandivarman III (844–866 CE). A Tamil inscription of this ruler mentioning a Viṣṇu temple and a tank called Ava<u>n</u>ināraṇam after one of his titles has been found in Takua-pa in Siam,[29] attesting to his vigour in propagating the Vaiṣṇava faith.

The middle of the ninth century saw the emergence of Co<u>l</u>a power.[30]

[22] Sastri, *A History of South India*, pp. 139–41.

[23] C. Minakshi, *The Historical Sculptures of the Vaikuṇṭha Pĕrumāḷ Temple, Kāñchī*, Memoirs of the ASI, no. 63, Manager of Publications, Delhi: Government of India Press, 1941.

Mahalingam, *Readings in South Indian History*, pp. 25, 37–8. An inscription of Nandivarman II Pallavamalla in the Vaikuṇṭha-p-Pĕrumāḷ Temple at Kāñcīpuram describes the historical events relating to the coronation of the king. Ref.: T.V. Mahalingam, *A Topographical List of Inscriptions in Tamil Nadu and Kerala States*, vol. III, ICHR and S. Chand & Co., Delhi, 1985, pp. 118–19. Cg 490. Ref.: *ARE*, 1888, no. 37; *SII*, iv, no. 135, *MASI*, no. 65, pp. 54–5.

[24] Date from Sastri, *A History of South India*, p. 151.

[25] *Pĕriya Tirumŏ<u>l</u>i* 2.8.10.

[26] Mahalingam, *Readings in South Indian History*, p. 41. Hardy, *Viraha Bhakti*, p. 264 cites K.A.N. Sastri (book not mentioned, publication year given as 1966, p. 156), to say that Dantidurga alias Vairamegha was a Rāṣṭrakūṭa ruler who 'went down to Kāñcī, and after a demonstration of force, struck up an alliance with Nandivarman II Pallavamalla to whom he gave his daughter Reva'.

[27] Sastri, *A History of South India*, pp. 147–8.

[28] K. Meenakshi, 'The Siddhas of Tamil Nadu', in *Tradition, Dissent and Ideology: Essays in Honour of Romila Thapar*, ed. R. Champakalakshmi and S. Gopal, New Delhi: Oxford University Press, 1996, p. 122.

[29] Sastri, *A History of South India*, pp. 153–4.

[30] Ibid., p. 165.

For over three centuries from this time, the Co̱las were to dominate the region of modern Tamil Nadu, despite some significant setbacks and gradual diminishing of their territory from the late eleventh century onwards. The Pāṇṭiyas were defeated in the first quarter of the tenth century, but the period of real glory of the Co̱la rule dates from the accession of Rājarāja I in 985 CE.[31] The Co̱la dominions passed into the hands of the Eastern Cālukyas with the accession of Kulottunga I in 1070 CE,[32] but the elements of continuity in polity and, indeed, even in the family name adopted,[33] were significant enough for the empire to still be called Co̱la. Disintegration set in from the twelfth century and by the mid-thirteenth, the Co̱la empire had disappeared. The Pāṇṭiyas who had continued in the Madurai region, albeit as a minor power during the period of the imperial Co̱las and had engaged in several wars with them during that time, rose to power again in the early thirteenth century.

After the final collapse of Co̱la power in 1279 CE, the resurgent Pāṇṭiyas had to contend with powers such as the Kākaṭiyas and Hoysalas attempting to establish a foothold in the Tamil land. To the ever-shifting balance of power among these and the changing political scenario must also be added the arrival of a new force, the armies of Allaudin Khilji under the generalship of Malik Kafur in 1310, and again in 1324–5. Eventually, the brothers Harihara and Bukka laid the foundations of the future empire of Vijayanagara at modern Hampi in 1336.[34] After the Madurai sultanate was overthrown (as a result of several campaigns between 1365 and 1371), Vijayanagara power was extended to most of the Tamil region. This century of warfare introduced two new elements in the social fabric of the macro region—Muslims and Telugu warriors.[35] The integration of new people into established local societies was not a new feature in itself, for migration and conquest have a long history in this region. What is crucial is that besides the well-recorded movements of *brāhmaṇa* specialists from the Andhra region to the Kaveri basin or ritual specialists from one temple to another to install and maintain

[31] Ibid., p. 171.

[32] This is considering the strictly patrilineal succession, for Kulottunga I's mother was a Co̱la princess and the Co̱las and Eastern Cālukyas had been intermarrying for several generations.

[33] They continued to call themselves Co̱las, no doubt because of the prestige the name had acquired.

[34] Sastri, *A History of South India*, pp. 217–34.

[35] Burton Stein, *Peasant, State and Society in Medieval South India*, New Delhi: Oxford University Press, 1979, p. 366.

a particular bhakti ritual form, there were also movements of lower groups accompanied by their 'progressive inclusion in the expanding agrarian and trade systems of the macro region'.[36]

(ii) Religious Background

We have already seen that the cult of *bhakti* to a personal god came to flower in south India about the same time as the Pallavas uprooted the Kaḷabhras and established themselves in Tŏṇṭaimaṇḍalam. *Bhakti* has been traced by different scholars to various earlier sources. The word finds its first mention in the *Śvetāśvatara Upaniṣad* where something akin to unique devotion to Īśvara is elaborated.[37] Much confusion arises, however, from the broad range of meanings that are read into the word *bhakti*, with the result that, as in much of 'Hinduism', nearly anything can be proved to be like everything else. Bhakti as devotion to a personal god is perhaps the most common and partial definition, for evidence for such devotion can be traced in much of the religious history of India, or indeed even elsewhere in the world. In fact, Krishna Sharma does state that it constitutes a part of every religion,[38] arguing against the explanation of bhakti as a religion, cult or doctrine. She believes that bhakti means devotion to god only in a general sense, with no implication of any particularized image or conception of god.[39] Holding that bhakti can be both *nirguṇa* and *saguṇa*, she believes that the genesis of *nirguṇa bhakti* can be traced to the *Bṛhadāraṇyaka Upaniṣad*, the *Kaṭhopaniṣad* and the *Muṇḍakopaniṣad*.[40]

Many later Vedic texts are, with better justification, considered devotional in character. Jalauka, grandson of Aśoka, the Mauryan Emperor, is known to have been a devotee of Śiva. The *Gītā*, often dated to the two centuries preceding the beginning of the Common Era, is usually seen as the first text to speak of *bhakti* in a meaning similar to how it came to be understood. It has also been argued that the bhakti *yoga* spoken of in the *Gītā*, though a possible source for the later movement,[41]

36 Ibid., p. 368.

37 Jan Gonda, *Viṣṇuism and Śivaism: A Comparison*, London: Athlone Press, 1970, pp. 21–2.

38 Krishna Sharma, *Bhakti and the Bhakti Movement: A New Perspective*, Delhi: Munshiram Manoharlal, 1987, pp. 40–1.

39 Ibid., p. 41.

40 Ibid., pp. 46–7.

41 Gonda, op. cit., p. 22.

is very remote from the kind of emotionally charged religiosity that is implied in the context of the Nāyaṉmārs and the Āḻvārs of Tamil Nadu, and of the bhakti saints of north India a few centuries later. Then again, the *Tirumurukāṟṟupaṭai*, a late Sangam poem devoted exclusively to one deity, Murukaṉ, has been considered the earliest textual evidence of *bhakti* in India.[42] In the *Paripāṭal*, a roughly contemporary anthology, we find fine examples of a mature expression of the exclusive worship of Māl or Viṣṇu, interspersed with poems devoted exclusively to Murukaṉ.

Though Murukaṉ, the deity par excellence of the Tamils, never suffered a complete eclipse, his cult was put rather in the shade from about the sixth–seventh centuries by the rise of the cults of devotion to Śiva and Viṣṇu. Both these monotheistic streams were deeply sectarian, hostile to not only Buddhism and Jainism, commonly perceived as heterodox for denying the authority of the Vedas, but often to each other as well. In fact, it has been argued that the *bhakti* movement, despite being commonly perceived as opposed to the hierarchies of caste, was really directed against the heterodox cults.[43] Tirujñāṉa-Sambandar, one of the major Nāyaṉmārs, devotes one stanza in each of his 400 hymns to expressing his contempt for and hostility towards Buddhists and Jainas.[44] Appar, another of the three major Nāyaṉmārs, famous in the tradition for converting the Pallava ruler Mahendravarman from Jainism to the worship of Śiva, often pours scorn on the 'false doctrines' of the Jainas, perhaps with an insider's perspective, having been a Jaina monk before he turned to Śiva.[45] Tirumankai Āḻvār, glorified in the hagiographies for abstracting and melting a golden idol of Buddha to embellish the Viṣṇu temple at Srirangam, takes issue with Śaivism too.[46]

It has been argued that in the 'early days of the [Pallava, Pāṇṭiya and Coḻa] monarchies, the monarch may have found the support of these movements quite useful. The movement in its turn derived much benefit from royal patronage, especially in making use of state power for winning

[42] Zvelebil, 'The Beginnings of Tamil Bhakti', p. 250.

[43] R. Champakalakshmi, 'The City in Medieval South India; Its Forms and Meaning', in *Craftsmen and Merchants: Essays in South Indian Urbanism*, ed. Narayani Gupta, Chandigarh: Urban History Association of India, 1993, p. 17; also, R. Champakalakshmi, *Trade, Ideology and Urbanization: South India 300 BC- 1300 AD*, Oxford University Press, 1996, pp. 395–6.

[44] Indira Viswanathan Peterson, *Poems to Śiva: The Hymns of the Tamil Saints*, New Jersey: Princeton University Press, 1989, p. 10.

[45] See Chapter 2-xi of the present work.

[46] See Chapter 5 of the present work for detailed discussion.

their conflicts with rival sects in a physical way'.[47] The examples cited in support of this contestation are the above conversions and that of the Pāṇṭiya Neṭumāraṉ from Jainism to Śaivism by Kulaiccirai Nāyaṉār. These stories are, understandably, very popular in the hagiographies, but while the legend regarding Appar may have some historical basis, there is no evidence for the second. Besides, the relation of emerging royal power with the bhakti movement is unclear despite the use the Coḻas later made of the Śaiva bhakti ideology. The fact that there was a partial chronological overlap between the two (and again here, the equation is frequently made with the Coḻas, though the accepted dating of the Āḻvārs and Nāyaṉmārs places almost all of them in the pre-Coḻa age or, at best, the last among them in the early Coḻa phase) does not automatically mean that the ideology of bhakti was particularly suited to validate royal power. It has not been explained why Buddhism and Jainism were unsuited to perform the same task. The above argument, of *bhakti* religion serving as a better tool for legitimation of royal power, requires the assumption that Śaivism (or Vaiṣṇavism) had a wider popular base. However, the evidence suggests that Buddhism and Jainism were popular in the Tamil land in the late Sangam age, especially among merchant communities.[48] The hostility towards Buddhists and Jainas expressed in many of the hymns of the Āḻvārs and Nāyaṉmārs points to their continued prominence in the later period too. While there can be no doubt that Śaivism was carefully used by the imperial Coḻas to project their own sovereignty,[49] I would like to underline that it only holds true for the period beginning from the second half of the tenth century.

What also emerges from the earlier evidence is that these saints were not located in a religious vacuum, nor were they mystics far removed from the rough and tumble of ordinary life. I believe that mystics too need to be firmly located in the contexts of time and space for their expressions to be properly understood. This context is early medieval Tamil Nadu where brahmanical Hinduism was in the ascendant and aggressively attempting to counter the influence of the heterodox religions. Thus, the post-Kaḷabhra period naturally saw *brāhmaṇas* keenly striving for patronage, and all means, including decrying the Buddhists and the Jainas as deceivers and propagators of false doctrines,

[47] Kesavan Veluthat, 'Religious Symbols in Political Legitimation', *Social Scientist*, vol. 21, nos. 1–2, January–February 1993, pp. 25–6.

[48] Both the late/post-Sangam Tamil epics, *Cilappatikāram* and the *Maṇimekalai* had Jaina/Buddhist authors and themes.

[49] R. Champakalakshmi, '*Patikam Pāṭuvār*: Ritual Singing as a Means of Communication', *Studies in History*, vol. 10, no. 2, July–December 1994, p. 200.

were deemed fair. That a number of evidently inspired men (and some women) chose at such a time to sing, in highly emotive language, of their love for Śiva or Viṣṇu, was an interesting coincidence.

Implicit in the above statement is my belief that these saints did not form a 'movement' in their lifetimes. The hagiographical accounts make at least some of these saints contemporary to each other. For instance, the Nāyaṉār Tirunāvukkaracar is said to have been a senior contemporary of Tirujñāṉa-Sambandar[50] who is said to have addressed the former as 'Appā' out of respect, thus giving him the name by which the saint is known to Tamils (Appar). A musician of the *pāṇar* caste named Tirunīlakaṇṭayāḻppāṇar is said to have accompanied Sambandar on his travels and set his hymns to music.[51] Sambandar and Tirumankai Āḻvār are said to have met and engaged in a poetical contest.[52] The two Nāyaṉmārs—Ceramāṉ Pĕrumāḷ and Sundarar—are said to have been friends and companions during their extensive pilgrimages.[53] Pŏykai, Pūtam and Pey, the three *mutal* Āḻvārs, are supposed to have been born on three consecutive days and met in TirukKovalūr.[54] Further, they are said to have travelled for some time together to sacred shrines of Viṣṇu and met Tirumaḻicai Āḻvār during their peregrinations.[55] All the same, with the exception of Pĕriyāḻvār and Āṇḍāḷ, the two Vaiṣṇava saints who were father and daughter, as is clear from the hymns of the latter who frequently signs herself as Kotai[56] of Viṣṇucitta of the Veyar *kula*,[57] temple priest in Śrīvilliputtūr, which we know the former to have been from his own songs,[58] most of the other instances of contemporaneity may be largely legendary. The two other prominent exceptions must

[50] Sastri, *The Culture and History of the Tamils*, p. 109; Peterson, op. cit., p. 19.

[51] Peterson, op. cit., p. 20.

[52] *Ārāyirappaṭi Guruparamparā Prabhāvam* (henceforth *Agpp*), *Mūvāyirappaṭi Guruparamparā Prabhāvam* (henceforth *Mgpp*), Tirumankai Āḻvār *vaibhavam; Divya Sūri Caritam* (henceforth *DSC*), Śrī Parakāla Sūri *vaibhavam*. See Chapter 2-viii of the present work.

[53] Sastri, *The Culture and History of the Tamils*, p. 111. Also Peterson, op. cit., p. 21.

[54] *Agpp, Mgpp, Mutal Āḻvārkaḷ vaibhavam; DSC*, Kāsārayogi *avatāra*, Śrī Bhūta Sūri *avatāra*, Śrī Mahadāhvaya Sūri *avatāra*. See Chapter 2-i of the present work.

[55] *Agpp, Mgpp*, Tirumaḻicai Āḻvār *vaibhavam; DSC*, Śrī Bhaktisāra Sūri *avatāra*. See Chapter 2-i and ii of the present work.

[56] Āṇḍāḷ is the honorific by which the saint-poetess, Kotai, is known in the Śrīvaiṣṇava community.

[57] *Nācciyār Tirumŏḻi* 6.10, to take just one example.

[58] *Tiruppallāṇṭu*, 11 (*Pĕriyāḻvār Tirumŏḻi*, 1.11), for instance.

also be pointed out. Madhurakavi Āḻvār speaks of Kurukūr Nampi, i.e. Nammāḻvār, as his preceptor.[59] While traditional scholarship takes this claim literally, it has been doubted whether Madhurakavi was referring to a living person or the idol of the saint which he revered.[60] The Nāyaṉār Sundarar speaks of the lineage of *bhaktas* in which he includes Appar, Sambandar and even his own parents; in fact, it is his hymn known as the *Tiruttŏṇṭar Tŏkai* (literally, the anthology of the holy servants)[61] that forms the kernel of the stories of the 63 Nāyaṉmārs later elaborated in the *Pĕriya Purāṇam*. This does suggest that by the time of Sundarar, there was a consciousness of a community of exceptional devotees beyond the common folk among whom the saints lived and sang their hymns and exhorted to join in their worship. It must, however, be remembered that Sundarar's list of 62 predecessors is largely legendary, based on folklore and remembered history. Though modern historiography seems to suggest that the saints had a common mission, it is difficult to trace in the hymns of the saints themselves, Śaiva or Vaiṣṇava, any distinct connecting thread other than ecstatic devotion to their chosen god. The facts that several of the saints reviled the Jaina and the Bauddha ascetics, or called to the community of devotees to join them in their singing and in worshipping Śiva/Viṣṇu, are to be traced to the socio-religious context in which they were operating rather than to a well-formulated agenda.

While completely accepting the rootedness in society, and even a distinctly social mission of these saints, I do not deny them an individual, exclusive inspiration. In other words, I do not accept that the bhakti saints were recruits, as it were, in a proselytizing campaign. I believe that personal spiritual endeavour and emotionally surcharged devotion were the moving forces behind the saints, but saints are human too, and they reflect the ideas and prejudices of their times. In doing so they became, both consciously and unconsciously, agents of a certain kind of change that might, in retrospect, seem orchestrated in multiple ways. As products of their time and as individuals with natural egos—notwithstanding the claims of abject humbleness they make in their

59 *Kaṇṇinuṇciruttāmpu* 1-10.

60 Friedhelm Hardy, 'The Tamil Veda of a Śūdra Saint: The Śrīvaiṣṇava Interpretation of Nammāḻvār', in *Contribution to South Asian Studies*, ed. Gopal Krishna, New Delhi: Oxford University Press, 1979, pp. 28-87. I, however, incline to the view that Madhurakavi was an actual disciple of Nammāḻvār. See Chapter 6-iii of the present work.

61 *Tevāram* 39.

songs—they were very likely fired by a missionary zeal. To regard Appar's conversion of the Pallava ruler, Mahendravarman, from the Jaina faith to Śaivism, or Sambandar's similar conversion of the Pāṇṭiya ruler, Arikesari Parānkusa Māravarman, as blatantly mercenary acts, intended to divert the royal coffers from Jaina monasteries to Śiva temples, would surely be to reduce these saints to mindless cogs in a juggernaut, but to see these as acts of devotion with exclusively other-worldly concerns would be equally inappropriate.[62] In fact, much is made in the hagiographies of such startling and important conversions by both traditions, Vaiṣṇava and Śaiva, indicating their real-world importance.

Hawley has suggested that the notion of a bhakti 'movement' is a 'cultural step-child of the nationalist movement' and dates to perhaps no earlier than the fourth decade of the last century.[63] Indeed, it has been convincingly argued that the idea of a coherent movement owes to Hazari Prasad Dwivedi's translation of Grierson's notion of *bhakti* as a religious revolution into the Hindi phrase, *bhakti āndolan*.[64] There is evidence of a self-consciousness of bhakti being a unique religious idea with a specific chronological and geographical progression from about the early eighteenth century.[65] While I will continue to use the phrase, '*bhakti* movement' for reasons of convenience, I believe that the unity of purpose that the phrase conveys was one that was only constructed, in the Tamil case at least, by the *ācāryas* composing hagiographies between the twelfth and fourteenth centuries.

The extensive pilgrimages undertaken by some of the saints need also to be contextualized in a tradition of pilgrimage that had already come into being in the Tamil land, as is evident from late Sangam works. The *Tirumurukāṟṟupaṭai*, being a text in the *āṟṟupaṭai* genre of

[62] My examination of the Vaiṣṇava material will show that the veracity of both these acts of conversions is open to doubt as they are first mentioned in the Śaiva hagiography composed by Cekkiḻār in about the twelfth century.

[63] John Stratton Hawley, 'The Bhakti Movement: Since When?', Lecture delivered at the India International Centre, New Delhi, 23 March 2009.

[64] John Stratton Hawley, 'The *Bhāgavata Māhātmya* in Context', in *Patronage and Popularisation, Pilgrimage and Procession: Channels of Transcultural Translation and Transmission in Early Modern South Asia; Essays in Honour of Monica Horstmann*, ed. Heidi Rika Maria Pauwels, Wiesbaden: Harrasowitz Verlag, 2009, pp. 81–100.

[65] The *Bhāgavata Mahātmya*, 1.48–50, records this answer from a beautiful maiden asked by the sage Nārada about her identity, 'I was born in Drāviḍa,/ Grew mature in Karnāṭaka,/Went here and there in Mahārāṣṭra,/Then in Gujarāt I became old and worn./... For long I went about in weakened condition/... But on reaching Vṛndāvan I was renewed...' John Stratton Hawley's translation. Ibid.

puram poetry which advises poets about munificent patrons, directs pilgrims to the sacred spots, the 'residences' of Murukaṉ.[66] The *Paripāṭal* describes pilgrimage to the mountain shrine of Mālirunkuṉṟu.[67] In the *Cilappatikāram*, Kovalaṉ and Kaṇṇaki are said to have met, while journeying from Pukār to Madurai, a *brāhmaṇa*, native of Mānkāṭu in the region of Kutamalai or the western hills, travelling to feast his eyes on the lord reclining on his serpent bed in the island shrine.[68] He further describes the beauty of Nĕṭiyoṉ (the tall one/great one) on the peak in Venkaṭam hill[69] and, after praising TiruMālirunkuṉṟam, advises them to journey there. Indeed, the *brāhmaṇa* even tells them that he intends to go to the sacred places of the Lord 'who measured the earth'.[70]

The Tamil pilgrimage tradition, though reflective of the larger medieval emphasis on *tīrtha* that is elaborated in the Purāṇas, has some unique features which derive from the ancient Tamil concept of the immanence of divine powers or of specific deities in the landscape. The Tamil land itself is considered holy as is clear even from several Sangam poems. Specific sites came to be associated with specific incidents in the Purāṇas which had, by the early medieval centuries, obviously achieved considerable popularity. *Sthalapurāṇas*, popular texts which detail the mythic greatness of specific shrines and the merits accruing to pilgrims at the shrine, were produced in great numbers from about the sixteenth century.[71] It has been suggested that the saints sang about the feats

[66] R. Champakalakshmi, 'From Devotion and Dissent to Dominance: The Bhakti of the Tamil Alvars and Nayanars', in *Tradition, Dissent and Ideology*, R. Champakalakshmi and S. Gopal, Delhi: Oxford University Press, 1996, p. 137 dates the *Tirumurukāṟṟupaṭai* and the *Paripāṭal* to the fifth–sixth centuries. These are the most commonly accepted dates. However, Peterson, op. cit., p. 4, footnote 7, dates the texts to the sixth–seventh centuries.

[67] The word means the mountain where Māl resides. Mālirunkuṉṟu is identified with modern TiruMāliruñcolai/Aḻakarmalai near Madurai. The modern names of the place mean the 'sacred grove of Māl' or the 'mountain of the beautiful lord'.

Paripāṭal, v 15. Cited in Katherine Young, *Beloved Places (Ukantaruḷina nilankal): Praise of Tamil Nadu and the Making of Indic Civilization*, Unpublished Manuscript, p. 2. Also quoted with a translation by Norman Cutler in Norman Cutler and A.K. Ramanujan, 'From Classicism to Bhakti', in *Essays on Gupta Culture*, ed. Bardwell L. Smith, Delhi: South Asia Books, 1983, pp. 177–214.

[68] Likely to be a reference to Srirangam.

[69] Modern Tirumalai/Tiruppati.

[70] *Cilappatikāram*, canto XI. Cited in Katherine Young, *Beloved Places*, p. 18.

[71] David Dean Shulman, *Tamil Temple Myths: Sacrifice and Divine Marriage in the*

of Viṣṇu and the legends connected with him without any particular reference to the deities enshrined in the temples they visited and that this localizing of the myths might itself have been a product of the age which produced these *sthalapurāṇas*.[72] It was, accordingly, in the later Cola and Pāṇṭiya ages that certain hymns became the inspiration for entitling particular deities. While this was true in several instances, some of which I shall examine, many hymns themselves give ample evidence of territorially locating the Lord and his activities, of 'singing temples into existence'.[73]

The Vaiṣṇava Āḻvārs and the Śaiva Nāyaṉmārs sang in Tamil, the language of the masses, not in Sanskrit, the usual language of erudition and scholarship and, consequently, of the privileged elites. The later, north Indian *bhakti* saints also expressed themselves in the vernacular but, while noting this parallel, the contrast needs to be established as well. Though Sanskrit did, even in the Tamil country, carry prestige and was associated with the priestly elite, and though the Tamil tradition also mythically traces its origins to the north through the Vedic seer Agastya, the earliest origin myths also place Tamil on a level of equality with Sanskrit. Tamil itself boasts a literary tradition of about 600 years by the time of the earliest *bhakti* saints. Analysis of the hymns of the Āḻvārs demonstrates clearly their familiarity with the conventions of Sangam poetics which, as suggested by various scholars, was far from rustic.[74] Not only are Sangam motifs strewn throughout the corpus of the devotional poetry of the Āḻvārs, the *Nālāyira Divya Prabandham*, the *akam* genre of classical Sangam poetry is, as has been pointed out earlier, elaborated and creatively reworked in the devotional love poetry of some Āḻvārs, notably Āṇḍāḷ and Nammāḻvār. In fact, the unknown poet of the *Muttŏlāyiram*, a sixth-century anthology of perhaps 900 poems of which only 130 have survived, had already experimented with a fusion of the *akam* and *puram* genres.[75] The occasional, tangential references to Kṛṣṇa/Viṣṇu in the *Muttŏlāyiram*, in contexts where a love-sick girl addresses the Coḻa/Cera/Pāṇṭiya ruler with the epithets of the god,

South Indian Śaiva Tradition, Princeton: Princeton University Press, 1980, p. 32.

72 R. Champakalakshmi, *Vaiṣṇava Iconography in the Tamil Country*, New Delhi: Orient Longman, 1981, p. 188.

73 Phrase borrowed from Ramanujan, *Hymns for the Drowning*, op. cit., p. 107.

74 A.K. Ramanujan, *The Interior Landscape: Love Poems from a Classical Tamil Anthology*, New Delhi: Oxford University Press, 1995, pp. 97–115.

75 M.L. Thangappa and A.R. Venkatachalapathy, *Red Lilies and Frightened Birds: Muttolayiram*, Delhi: Penguin Classics, 2011, p. xii.

may be the precursors of the more elaborate love poetry of the Āḻvārs directed to the god himself.[76] These continuities with the earlier literary tradition of the Sangam age might have formed the foundation for the Āḻvārs' hymns finding reception in an audience well-attuned to its resonances. The Sangam poems composed in a language far removed from daily speech may not have been accessible to the lay Tamil speaker unlikely to be versed in classical literary conventions; the hymns of the bhakti saints, on the other hand, make a point of being close to the Tamil spoken during their time.[77] At the same time, this reinforces the hymnists' own superior familiarity with the classical tradition, and a distinct presence of 'craft' as opposed to literary naiveté. Tamil itself was a 'divine gift', a boon, and despite its closeness to the speaker as mother tongue, worthy of reverence.

Though some poems of the Sangam corpus are designed as soliloquies, they often address a listener, usually a stereotyped other such as the girlfriend or the mother. Bhakti poems expand this audience to include the world of devotees of the lord. The audience is invited to join in the worship, indeed, in the joy of looking upon and serving the lord in his temple. The natural world, woven into the emotional heart of Sangam literature, serves yet another purpose in bhakti poetry—glorification of the lands where the lord resides. That these poems were meant for a wide audience is made clearer still by the promise held out in numerous poems that faultless, loving, meditative recitation or singing of the same would secure happiness in this world and hereafter.

I have already stated that I do not believe that the *ācāryas* and the Āḻvārs constitute one seamless, homogenous tradition. There appears, rather, a well-woven synthesis, one deeply emotional and based firmly in a this-worldly tradition, and another highly intellectual, owing a substantial debt to a philosophy of world negation (though substantially modifying the notion of *māyā* or illusion). The Āḻvārs' devotion seeks union with the object of adoration, the lord's feet, not just post-mortem, but in a palpable, corporeal sense. This found expression often as a desire for service to or union with the temple idol. However, as Hardy points out, the ultimate empirical impossibility of corporal union with the transcendental divine gave birth to a poetry of exceptional emotional intensity in the *viraha bhāva*,[78] seeming, in its most despairing cry of separation, to exult in the depths of ecstasy it could plumb. As David

[76] Ibid., pp. 7, 69, 110.

[77] Cutler and Ramanujan, op. cit., pp. 191–2.

[78] Hardy, *Viraha Bhakti*, pp. 364–9.

Shulman puts it, 'Having inherited the goal of world renunciation from an earlier stage of Indian religion, bhakti stands it back on its head and directs man back to life on earth'.[79] The *ācāryas,* however, while not dismissing worldly existence as mere illusion, do not see the body as a vehicle for achieving their ultimate destination which, for them, as for the Āḻvārs, is the lord. However, there remains a subtle difference here as well—the hoped-for bliss that lies firmly in the afterlife for the teachers is eternal service at *paramapada*—the feet of the lord; this life is a mere preparation of the soul by focusing on the lord and providing service to him in the temple. Interestingly, we find in some of the Āḻvārs' hymns, the celebration of a human life as one in which service to the Lord is possible—in the temple—and thus as good as what can possibly be attained later, and certainly better than what even the *devas* (minor divinities) can enjoy. These differences, which mark critical departures from the Āḻvār bhakti tradition while seeming to reiterate it, are central to the way the incipient community imaged itself.

N. Jagadeesan contends that the *bhakti* movement was a response to the challenges of the heterodox (he calls them heretical) organizations of the Buddhists and the Jainas. It was, like the temple and the later *maṭhas*, one of the ways of resistance and reformation of 'Hinduism', and an agency for the overthrow of religions with a proselytizing mission. He believes that Śankara approached Buddhist metaphysics insofar as a personal god was irrelevant to both, whereas Rāmānuja approximated to the Buddha in his (mildly) democratic predilections.[80] Interestingly, the first part of this position concurs with the Śrīvaiṣṇava criticism on Śankara: Vedānta Deśika, the thirteenth-fourteenth century theologian-scholar, revered later as the greatest of the Vaṭakalai *ācāryas*, often reviles the followers of Śankara as *pracchanna* Bauddhas (Buddhists in disguise).[81] The latter argument is again based on tradition: the hagiographies tell us that Rāmānuja broadcast from the balcony of a temple in TirukKoṭṭiyūr a particular esoteric teaching that his own preceptor had imparted to him on the condition of absolute secrecy. On being questioned on this unforgivable lapse, i.e. disrespect to the *guru*, he is supposed to have expressed his willingness to bear the worst punishment possible—eternal damnation, if only it would secure the salvation of the multitudes.[82] The

[79] Shulman, op. cit., p. 21.

[80] N. Jagadeesan, *History of Srivaisnavism in the Tamil Country, Post Ramanuja*, Madurai: Koodal Publishers, 1977, pp. 148–9, 173.

[81] Varavaramuni, *Yatirāja Vimśati*, ed. Satyamurti Svami.

[82] *Agpp, Mgpp,* Iḷaiyāḻvār *vaibhavam*. See Chapter 2-x of the present work.

hagiographies make much of this incident. I suggest that this careful modulation of the caste order was common to both the saints and the teachers: neither wishing to topple the established structure of society, and both offering limited caste mobility. Whether the Āḻvārs were comparatively more radical than the *ācāryas*, as is suggested by some scholars, can only be ascertained after determining how much we know of the Āḻvārs that is not viewed through the prism of the *ācāryas*. While I do not wish in the least to suggest that the society of the sixth to ninth centuries in Tamil Nadu was egalitarian, I would like to explore how the rigidly stratified society of the twelfth to fourteenth centuries chose to represent the religious past, carefully preserving *varṇāśramadharma* even while suggesting transcendence, if only in the afterlife, or on the spiritual plane.

(iii) Sources and Hypotheses

The sources for my study are both literary and archaeological. About 16,000 inscriptions from the earliest times to the fourteenth century have been recorded from the states of Tamil Nadu and Kerala.[83] Approximately 9,000 inscriptions belonging to the Coḻa period alone have been reported and copied by epigraphists.[84] The great majority of Coḻa inscriptions have been found on the walls of temples and are concerned with religious gifts.[85] I will use this wealth of inscriptional material to test any hypothesis and to bolster any argument I formulate about the development of the Śrīvaiṣṇava community and the ways in which it engages with Āḻvār bhakti. Where the inscriptional evidence directly challenges accepted positions regarding important issues—as it sometimes does—I shall argue for a revision of conventional wisdom. In fact, I will make use of the inscriptional evidence in the present chapter, the Introduction, itself, to make some significant points and to engage with certain debates about the sources.

The literary sources of this study comprise selected critical texts from the vast body of scriptural literature of the Śrīvaiṣṇavas. The earliest of these is the *Nālāyira Divya Prabandham*, the corpus of 4,000 hymns of the twelve Āḻvārs. These 4,000 hymns are, to be precise, 4,000 stanzas, about 3,000 of which make up a few hundred poems, usually of 10 or 11 stanzas, though longer ones are not uncommon. The last stanza in a majority of

83 Mahalingam, 1985, Introduction.

84 Y. Subbarayalu, 'The Cola State', *Studies in History*, vol. 4, no. 2, 1982, p. 265.

85 Ibid.

these poems is a combination of signature verse and *phalaśruti*. There is some dispute regarding the origin and meaning of the word 'Āḻvār', several scholars supporting the formation of the word from the root, '*āḻ*', which means depth, and hence denoting those who plunged or immersed themselves deep in the ocean of devotion.[86] Since '*aḷ*' means 'to rule', some linguists understand Āḻvār to mean leader or ruler.[87] Despite the poetic appeal of the first etymology, the second derivation seems to stand on much stronger ground. It finds support from the fact that the term for the contemporary Śaiva saints, Nāyaṉmārs, also means 'leaders'. It is significant in this context that the Śrīvaiṣṇava tradition in the earlier phase recognized only ten Āḻvārs.[88] This can be understood to mean that Āṇḍāḷ and Madhurakavi were not considered Āḻvārs till a slightly later period.[89] The word 'Āṇḍāḷ' means 'she who ruled' and can thus be considered a feminine equivalent for Āḻvār in the sense of a lord or a ruler.[90] It thus follows that, as a woman, she was not called an Āḻvār.[91] Madhurakavi might have been excluded from the early classification of Āḻvār as he himself professed to be a disciple of Nammāḻvār; it was only later, as the preceptorial tradition developed, that his crucial position as the link between the Āḻvārs and *ācāryas* came to be underlined.

A great number of inscriptions suffix the word Āḻvār to the name of the god in a Vaiṣṇava temple just as in numerous Śiva temples, the deity

86 Ramanujan, *Hymns for the Drowning*, p. ix; John Carman and Vasudha Narayanan, *The Tamil Veda: Pillan's Interpretation of the Tiruvaymoli*, Chicago: The University of Chicago Press, 1989, p. 3.

87 Hardy, *Viraha Bhakti*, pp. 250–1 favours this view.

88 An inscription of the 25th regnal year of Vijayarājendradeva, i.e. Śaka 1153=1231–2 CE, from the Utamalpet *tāluk*, Sankarāmanallūr village, Coimbatore district in the Karivaradarāja-p-Pĕrumāḷ Temple records gifts of land for offerings to the *ten* Āḻvārs̱ in the temple of Aḻakar at Tirumāliruñcolai in Kīḻiraṇiyamuṭṭanāḍu, a subdivision of Paṇṭimaṇḍalam. The grant also provides for a festival in the temple called Vijayarājendraṉ sandi. See Mahalingam, 1985, vol. IV, p. 153. Cb 737. Ref: *ARE*, 1909, no. 135. Ibid., part ii, para 40.

89 Vedānta Deśika in the *Guruparamparāsāram*, p. 7, speaks of 'the ten Āḻvārs'. Cited in K.K.A. Venkatachari, *The Śrīvaiṣṇava Maṇipravāḷa/The Maṇipravāḷa Literature of the Śrīvaiṣṇava Ācāryas: 12th to 15th Centuries* AD, Bombay: Anantacharya Indological Institute, 1978, p. 13. Also see Sastri, *The Culture and History of the Tamils*, p. 112, 'The Vaiṣṇava movement . . . is represented by the ten Āḻvārs—some reckon them as twelve including Āṇḍāḷ and Madhurakavi'.

90 Hardy, *Viraha Bhakti*, pp. 250–1, also argues for this meaning.

91 Many Śrīvaiṣṇavas even today speak of 'eleven Āḻvārs and Āṇḍāḷ'. Personal observation.

has the suffix, Nāyaṉār. For instance, a Pāṇṭiya inscription of 1236 CE in the TiruvĀlīśvaram Temple in Kiḻappavūr, Tĕnkāśi *tāluk*, records a gift of land by purchase for offerings to the temple of Tirukkavilīśvaramuṭaiya Nāyaṉār.[92] From the temple of Kariyamāṇikka-p-Pĕrumāḷ in Iṭaikkāl, Ambasamudram *tāluk*, comes the record, dated 1192 CE, of a gift of one *accu* for burning a twilight lamp in the shrine of Senāpati Āḻvār in the temple of Jayatŏnka Viṇṇagar Ĕmpĕrumāṉ of Vaṭattalaikkalam.[93] A Pāṇṭiya inscription of 1134 CE from the Venkaṭācalapati Temple in Kiḻappavūr, Tĕnkāśi *tāluk*, records gift of land for daily expenses of the temple of Muṉaikatimokar Viṇṇagar Āḻvār.[94] In fact, even the presiding deity in a Śiva temple or a Jaina *paḷḷi* may be addressed as Āḻvār as is seen from the following examples.[95] One dated 953 CE from the Pipīlikeśvara Temple in Tiruvĕrumpūr registers a gift of land by purchase from the Pĕrunkuri *sabhā* of Śrīkaṇṭha *caturvedimangalam* for the maintenance of four persons who were singing *Tiruppatiyam* hymns in the Tiruvĕrumpiy-āḻvār Temple with *uṭukkai* (stringed musical instrument) and *tāḷam* (beat/rhythm) during the three services.[96] Another inscription of the same date from the same temple refers to it as the temple of Tirumalaimēlāḻvār.[97] An inscription of the third year of the reign of Coḻa Parakesarivarman in the Otavaneśvara Temple in TirucCāturai, Tanjavur *tāluk*, refers to the temple as that of TirucCoṟṟuturaiyāḻvār, while earlier and later inscriptions from the same site speak of TirucCoṟṟuturai Mahādevar and TirucCoṟṟuturai Uṭaiyār.[98] Such interchangeable use of the terms Āḻvār, Mahādevar and Uṭaiyār, (meaning lord/owner/possessor), can scarcely be ignored. A record of 995 CE in the Ujjīvanāthasvāmi Temple in Uyyakŏṇṭāṉ Tirumalai, Trichy *tāluk*, says that a gift of a gold diadem (*śrīmuṭi*) was made by Cĕmpiyan mādeviyār, the mother of Kaṇṭan-Madurāntakadeva-Uttamacoḻadeva, to the deity of Tirukārkuṭiyāḻvār

[92] Mahalingam, 1985, vol. IX, p. 173. Tn 823. Ref.: *ARE*, 1917, no. 390.

[93] Mahalingam, 1985, vol. IX, p. 16. Tn 72. Ref.: *ARE*, 1916, no. 514.

[94] Mahalingam, 1985, vol. IX, p. 173. Tn 822. Ref.: *ARE*, 1917, no. 396; ibid., part ii, para 43, p. 153.

[95] This is merely a sample selection from several dozen inscriptions.

[96] Mahalingam, 1985, vol. VIII, pp. 297–8. Tp 1348. Ref.: *ARE*, 1914, no. 129: *SII* xiii, no. 51, pp. 23–4.

[97] Mahalingam, 1985, vol. VIII, pp. 297–8. Tp 1347. Ref.: *ARE*, 1914, no. 123: *SII* xiii, no. 50, pp. 22–3.

[98] Mahalingam, 1985, vol. VII, p. 642. Tj 2834. Ref.: *ARE*, 1930-31, no. 166; *SII* xix, no. 76.

in the *brahmadeya* of Nandīpan̲mangalam.[99] On a rock below images of Tīrthankaras in Kal̲ukumalai are a set of Vaṭṭĕl̲uttu inscriptions of the eighth century recording the names of several persons (including women, nuns and teachers) who caused the images to be made; one mentions worship of Araimalayāl̲vār.[100] An early thirteenth-century inscription from Jina Kāñcī records a sale of land free of taxes to the god Tirupparutikkun̲r̲āl̲vār.[101] An eleventh-century inscription from Kīl̲cāttamangalam, North Arcot district, records a gift of tax-free land for offerings to Āl̲vār Vimala Śrī Āryatīrthapaḷḷi.[102] Yet another, dated 1148 CE, from Cittamūr in South Arcot district, records a gift of a village as *dīrghamānya* to the deity Pārśvanātha in the temple of Paḷḷiyāl̲vār by a *devaraṭiyār.*[103] A thirteenth-century inscription in the central shrine of the Kuntu-Tīrthankara Temple in Karantai, North Arcot district, registers a gift for a perpetual lamp in the temple of Arukadevar (Arhat) Virarājendrapĕrumpaḷḷiyāl̲vār.[104] Even more tellingly, an inscription from Pullalūr village in Chingleput *tāluk*, after recording a donation for a perpetual lamp to a temple, says that if the Śivabrāhmaṇas failed to maintain the lamp service, the *ūrāl̲vār* and the members of the *vāriyam* of the year were authorized to collect a fine and maintain the charity.[105] Clearly here, the *ūrāl̲vār* were the leaders or lords of the *ūr*. One can scarcely overlook such overwhelming inscriptional evidence.

The hymns of the Āl̲vārs have been gathered together in four books called the *Mutal Āyiram* (first thousand), *Iraṇṭām Āyiram*, (second thousand),[106] *Iyarpā* and *Tiruvāymŏl̲i.*[107] A brief discussion about the authorship of the hymns is in place here. The Śrīvaiṣṇava tradition reveres twelve Āl̲vārs who are usually considered to have been historical figures in that they have all left behind compositions, unlike most

[99] Mahalingam, 1985, vol. VIII, p. 311. Tp 1408. Ref.: *ARE*, 1892, no. 95; *SII* iv, no. 542, p. 180.

[100] A. Ekambaranathan and C.K. Sivaprakasam, *Jaina Inscriptions in Tamil Nadu: A Topographical List*, Research Foundation for Jainology, Madras, 1987, pp. 74–5, Ref.: *ARE*, 68/1894; *SII*, vol. V, no. 357.

[101] Ibid., p. 41, Ref.: *ARE*, 99/1923.

[102] Ibid., pp. 236–7, Ref.: *ARE*, 224/1968–9.

[103] Ibid., p. 344, Ref.: South Indian Temple Inscriptions, vol. I, no. 28.

[104] Ibid., p. 223, Ref.: *ARE*, 130/1939–40.

[105] Mahalingam, 1985, vol. III, p. 229, Cg 930. Ref.: *ARE* 1923, no. 49: *SII* xii, no. 152.

[106] The numbers of hymns in the first two books are, however, 947 and 1134 respectively.

[107] See Table no. VI in the Appendices.

of the Nāyaṉmārs, who are known to us only through hagiography and are consequently considered legendary. While Books I and III are anthologies of the compositions of several saint-poets, Books II and IV comprise the works of Tirumankai Āḻvār and Nammāḻvār respectively. However, it needs to be pointed out that of the 22 separate compositions that comprise the *Nālāyiram*, 11 do not bear any clear signature verse allowing us to identify the composer. This can have two potential implications, namely, that the unsigned hymns might have been the work of any one or more of the seven known 'historical' Āḻvārs or that, there might have been eleven other saints whose *bhakti* songs have been anthologized besides those of the named seven. In other words, were there only seven Āḻvārs or were there eighteen instead of the twelve that we are familiar with from the hagiographical records?[108] I think the first possibility unlikely as poets who carefully embedded their names in some of their compositions would not have neglected to do so in others. Further, there seems to be a definite chronological gap between the first four *Antādis* of the *Iyarpā* that are widely accepted as the earliest compositions, and the other hymns. The Śrīvaiṣṇava hagiographies hold that the three *mutal* Āḻvārs, i.e. Pŏykai, Pūtam and Pey, and Tirumaḻicai were the earliest Āḻvārs; indeed, the word *mutal* means first. We will see too that the 'life stories' of these four Āḻvārs are either the sketchiest[109] or the most fantastic and incredible.[110] A perusal of the hymns ascribed to these four, collected as the *Mutal Tiruvantādi*, *Iraṇṭām Tiruvantādi*, *Mūṉrām Tiruvantādi* and *Nāṉmukaṉ Tiruvantādi* in the third book *Iyarpā*, shows that there is no reason they could not have been the work of a single composer. And yet, there is equally little reason why the *Tiruccanta Viruttam*, a highly esoteric work of 120 stanzas that forms part of Book I, should be ascribed to the author of the *Nāṉmukaṉ Tiruvantādi.* I agree with Hardy that the *Tiruccanta Viruttam* is different in tone from much of the rest of the *NDP*; Hardy even suggests that it anticipates Viśiṣṭādvaitic philosophy.[111] The last two compositions in the *NDP*, the *Ciriya Tirumaṭal* and the *Pĕriya Tirumaṭal*, also appear entirely different in texture from the other hymns;[112] indeed, they read in part like lists of

[108] In fact, the number could be anything in between the two limits if more than one of these works were composed by a single individual, either from among the historical Āḻvārs or an anonymous poet.

[109] See Chapter 2-i of the present work.

[110] See Chapter 2-ii of the present work.

[111] Hardy, *Viraha Bhakti*, pp. 439–42.

[112] Two examples will illumine the point. Hymns in the *NDP* usually assume

pilgrimage centres.[113] It is possible that these two were comparatively later compositions that were added to the collection to make up the round figure of 4,000.[114]

Modern historians[115] have largely accepted the traditional relative chronology of the Āḻvārs, placing the first three in the sixth–seventh centuries, i.e. around the beginning of Pallava domination of Tŏṇṭaimaṇḍalam. The reasons for the same may be adduced from the fact that the four *antādis* in the *Iyarpā* seem to constitute a stage in the religious development that falls between the devotionalism of the *Paripāṭal* and the bhakti of the later Āḻvārs. Also, they exhibit a special form of theistic yoga combined with temple worship and indications of the composite Hari-Hara conception that was eventually abandoned in favour of the belief in Māyoṉ as the sole, absolute lord.[116] Another important aspect to note is that the number of shrines mentioned in the four *antādis* of the *Iyarpā* are comparatively fewer than those mentioned by the other Āḻvārs.[117] More significantly, a majority of the temples mentioned by them are in Tŏṇṭaimaṇḍalam, whereas the later Āḻvārs have sung of many more temples in Coḻanāḍu and Pāṇṭiyanāḍu.[118] In fact, only eight sacred places in the Cola and Pāṇṭiya *nāḍus* have been mentioned in these four works, of which Arangam, TirukKoṭṭiyūr,

---

that the context of a Puranic story will be known to the listeners and refer to the 'lustful woman of the *rākṣasa* clan' or the 'sister of the *arakkaṉ* (*rākṣasa*) whose nose was severed by the lord' and almost never by name (*Pĕriya Tirumŏḻi* 3.7.3, 3.9.4, *Tiruvāymŏḻi* 2.3.6). The *Pĕriya Tirumaṭal* 76/144, surprisingly, takes her name Cūrppaṇakā (Śūrpaṇakhā) while speaking of the incident, and thus appears closer to the later tradition which was more pedagogic. The *Pĕriya Tirumaṭal* 7/13 statement that 'the *Vedas* extol *dharma*, *artha*, *kāma* and *mokṣa* as the fourfold path of virtue', seems equally uncharacteristic of the *NDP*.

[113] There is remarkable similarity in the two works besides a fair degree of correspondence of the sacred centres mentioned in them. See Table II e.

[114] The counting of the 'stanzas' in these two works is rather unconventional, and varies according to whether the *Rāmānuja Nūṟṟantādi* is to be counted as part of the *NDP* or not.

[115] Hardy seems to be one of the few sceptics, *Viraha Bhakti*, pp. 247–56.

[116] Ibid., pp. 281–3.

[117] However, Tiruppāṇāḻvār (also one of the 'ascribed' Āḻvārs), mentions no shrines except Arangam (Srirangam) and Venkaṭam, and Tŏṇṭaraṭippŏṭi restricts himself to singing of just Srirangam. Madhurakavi's devotion is directed entirely towards Nammāḻvār whom he calls Kurukūr Nampi.

[118] See also, Hardy, *Viraha Bhakti*, pp. 256–61 for an excellent argument for placing the early Āḻvārs in the Venkaṭam-Kāñcī environment.

Kuṭantai[119] and Māliruñcolai seem to have acquired pan-regional fame by the late Sangam period itself.[120] It can be argued, thus, that the initial locus of the bhakti cult was in the northern part of the Tamil region and that in the middle period it moved towards the Kaveri delta. Finally, the Āḻvārs placed last chronologically, i.e. Pĕriyāḻvār, Āṇḍāḷ and Nammāḻvār, focus more on sacred sites in Pāṇṭiyanāḍu, though they do sing of shrines in Coḻanāḍu and in the northernmost parts of Tamil Nadu as well.[121] The fact that the northern part of Tamil Nadu was the first to be brought under the political sway and settled rule of kings inclined towards patronage of brahmanical institutions[122] lends some credibility to this hypothesis. None of this militates against the possibility of the four *antādis* in the *Iyarpā* being the work of one hand. The hagiographies, however, preserve a legend which is difficult to ignore considering that inscriptional evidence attests to its popularity in the period before their composition.[123]

The question of the other seven compositions is more vexed. The fact that the hagiographical tradition has chosen to attribute authorship of one of these unsigned poems to one of the historically unverifiable *mutal* Āḻvārs, i.e. Tirumaḻicai Āḻvār, another to a 'new' poet, i.e. Tiruppāṇāḻvār, and the other five to two of the Āḻvārs known from their other compositions is, therefore, significant. It is fairly clear that the hagiography of Tiruppāṇāḻvār serves some important purposes in communicating to the larger community the theological and social vision of the Śrīvaiṣṇava *ācāryas*, which I shall investigate in the second and third chapters. The hagiography of Tirumaḻicai also serves

[119] Śrīvaiṣṇava name for Kumbhakoṇam/Kuṭamūkku.

[120] See above, quotes from *Paripāṭal*, *Cilappatikāram*, etc.

[121] See Appendix, Tables VI b and VI d.

[122] The Kailāśanātha Temple in Kāñcīpuram, the rock-cut cave temples and the shore temple in Mahabalipuram are all dated to the Pallava period. Other rock-cut temples bear inscriptions of the seventh century, such as the one which says that Guṇabhara excavated a spacious temple of Murāri named Mahendra Viṣṇugṛha out of the rocks on the banks of the Mahendra *taṭākai* (Sanskrit: *taḍāga*) in the city of Mahendrapura. (See Mahalingam, 1985, vol. I, p. 10. NA 46. Ref.: *ARE* 1896, no. 13; ibid., 1943–4, no. 83.) Also, the first inscriptional mention of the singing of *Tiruppatiyams*, belonging to the eighth century, is dated in Pallava regnal years and comes from Tŏṇṭaimaṇḍalam (see below). Rock-cut shrines to brahmanical deities were also created in the eighth century in Pāṇṭimaṇḍalam (See Mahalingam, 1985, vol. VI, p. 426. Sm 52 and 53. Ref.: *ARE* 1960–1, no. 291; *EI* xxxvi, no. 18 (A), 137 and *ARE* 1906, no. 7; *EI* xxxvi, no. 18(D), 138).

[123] See Chapter 6-ii of the present work.

to underline various issues important for the Śrīvaiṣṇava community. Coming to the other five compositions, it seems unlikely that either Nammāḻvār or Tirumankai Āḻvār, the two most prolific Āḻvārs who have left behind 1,202 and 1,134 signed hymns respectively (generally in the last stanza of every set of ten or eleven), would have neglected to affix a signature verse to their other compositions. And yet, it is these two saints that the hagiographers have chosen to credit with the authorship of the other five works.[124] To what degree did the medieval *ācāryas* rely on oral tradition in the composition of the hagiographies? Had popular memory failed to preserve any traditions of some other saints whose songs had also been recited and handed down the generations, as had those of the remembered saints so that the *ācāryas* decided to invest these hymns with the sanctity that already belonged to the two most prolific saint-poets? Why did they not 'invent' other saints and suitable life histories for them, as they did for Tiruppāṇāḻvār, and ascribe these songs to them? This, of course, begs the question as to whether even the story of Tiruppāṇāḻvār was already a part of folklore—early epigraphic evidence documenting it is yet to be found—when the *ācāryas* wove it into the *Guruparamparās*.

A literary examination of the unsigned compositions to substantiate or refute the traditional ascription of authorship is beyond the scope of this work. In quoting from any of these said texts, that is, the four *Tiruvantādis* in the *Iyarpā*, and the *Amalaṉādipirāṉ*, I will go by the traditional ascription, i.e. refer to a particular verse as having been sung by Pŏykai, Pūtam, Pey, Tirumaḻicai or Tiruppāṇāḻvār as the case may be, despite my reservations about their authorship. In other words, since the poems exist and one ahistorical name is as good as another, I will follow the tradition in the names of the poets. In the event, however, of quoting from the *Tiruccanta Viruttam* also attributed to Tirumaḻicai,[125] the *Tiruvāciriyam* or the *Pĕriya Tiruvantādi* attributed to Nammāḻvār, and the *Tiruvĕḻukūṟṟirukkai*, the *Ciriya Tirumaṭal* or the *Pĕriya Tirumaṭal* attributed to Tirumankai, I shall only take the name of the composition referred to. It is important to note here that the Śrīvaiṣṇava hagiographies especially relate the context in which Tirumankai Āḻvār is supposed to have composed the *Tiruvĕḻukūṟṟirukkai*.[126]

124 Three are ascribed to Tirumankai and two to Nammāḻvār. Interestingly, Tirumankai has three separate signed works and Nammāḻvār two. See Table I.

125 The *Tiruccanta Viruttam* appears entirely different in style and focus from the *Nāṉmukaṉ Tiruvantādi*, leading us to doubt that they could be the works of the same composer. See also Hardy, *Viraha Bhakti*, pp. 439–42.

126 The Āḻvār is said to have composed the poem 'structured like a chariot'

The problems in dating the Āḻvārs will be brought out further by a brief comparison with the dating of the Nāyaṉmārs. The saints Appar and Sambandar are thought to have lived between 570 and 670 CE, while Sundarar is the placed around the end of the seventh and the beginning of the eighth centuries.[127] Zvelebil believes that Sambandar's mention of the Pallava general Ciruttŏṇṭar, who destroyed the Cālukya capital of Vātāpi in 642 CE, gives us some idea of his date. Appar is presumed to have been a contemporary of the Pallava king, Mahendravarman I (580–630 CE). Sundarar is seen as a contemporary of the Pallava king, Narasimhavarman II (690–710? CE).[128] It has been noted that the Tamil Śaiva cult was born and flourished in the Kaveri delta, the richest rice-growing region in the Tamil country.[129] On the other hand, the focus on and placement in the milieu of Tŏṇṭaimaṇḍalam, presumed to have been the early focus of the bhakti cult is, as we saw earlier, crucial to dating the early Āḻvārs in the sixth–seventh centuries. There is clearly an unresolved contradiction here which demands attention.

All three major poets of the *Tevāram*, i.e. Appar, Sambandar and Sundarar, speak of King Koccĕnkaṇāṉ as a great temple builder; indeed, Sambandar identifies at least two specific temples as those built by him.[130] Koccĕnkaṇāṉ is also known from Tirumankai's hymns on TiruNaraiyūr[131] where the Āḻvār too speaks of him as one who raised 70 temples to Śiva. While this ruler is mentioned in the past tense by both the *Tevāram* trio and by Tirumankai Āḻvār,[132] he would have to have lived about two centuries previous to Tirumankai if the seventh century dates for Sambandar are admitted. The other problem arises from Sundarar's mention of the ruler as a Coḻa,[133] for the Nāyaṉār should have, according to the traditional chronology, lived long before the age of the imperial (and temple building) Coḻas. If it is admitted that the reference to the dynasty owes merely to the prestige that the name continued to enjoy in the Tamil land long after the Sangam era, and that

---

during a poetical contest with the Nāyaṉār Sambandar. See Chapter 2-viii-c of the present work.

[127] Peterson, op. cit., p. 18.

[128] Zvelebil, *Tamil Literature*, pp. 141–2.

[129] Peterson, op. cit., p. 39.

[130] Sambandar, III. 276 and 277.

[131] *Pĕriya Tirumŏḻi* 6.6.3–9.

[132] The references in *Pĕriya Tirumŏḻi* 6.6.3–9 admit reading in both the simple present and the past tenses.

[133] Sundarar, VII. 98. Translation by Peterson, op. cit., p. 196. I do not know if the other two Nāyaṉmārs also speak of him as a Coḻa king.

this king was merely mythical, the references to him in Tirumankai's poem become more problematic. If this was merely a legendary patron of Śaiva temples, there would be little reason for the Āḻvār to single him out from among the numerous Nāyaṉmārs as a worshipper of Viṣṇu at TiruNaraiyūr. Moreover, the tone of the entire poem combined with the specific reference to his victory over his enemies in a battle at Aḻuntūr[134] suggests that this was a historical person, possibly one of the chieftains of the Kaveri region who claimed to be descendants of the ancient Coḻas. Koccĕnkaṇāṉ has, besides, been identified as the grandfather of Vijayālaya, the founder of the imperial Coḻas, by the discovery of the Velañceri Copper Plate of Parāntaka I.[135] I suggest that this presents an argument for a downward revision of the dates of the *Tevāram* trio to the eighth-ninth centuries.[136]

Tradition holds that the hymns of the Āḻvārs were all but lost for many millennia till the *ācārya* Nāthamuni recovered them after meditating 'on the feet of Nammāḻvār', the most revered among the Āḻvārs, in the village of the Āḻvār's birth, Kurukūr. Nāthamuni was the priest of the temple of Maṉṉaṉār in Vīranārāyaṇapuram. Some pilgrims arrived 'from the western country'[137]/TirukKurukūr[138] and recited eleven extraordinarily moving stanzas,[139] the last of which indicated that they were part of a larger work of a thousand stanzas. Upon being questioned they said they knew no more, but Nāthamuni was inspired to try and discover the rest. He repaired to Kurukūr,[140] the birthplace of Nammāḻvār,[141] where

134 *Pĕriya Tirumŏḻi*, 6.6.9.

135 R. Champakalakshmi, 'Religious Conflict in the Tamil Country: A Reappraisal of Epigraphic Evidence', *Journal of the Epigraphic Society of India*, vol. 5, p. 76 and footnote 75.

136 This would also agree better with the dating of most of the Āḻvārs, with the geographical distribution of the temples in the *Tevāram*, and with the inscriptional evidence. The story connecting Appar with the Pallava ruler Mahendravarman is, in any case, a late one and can scarcely be an argument for an early date for the Nāyaṉār. I do not, however, support tenth century dating for the three Nāyaṉmārs suggested by B.G.L. Swamy, 'The Date of the Tevaram Trio: An Analysis and Reappraisal', *Bulletin of the Institute of Traditional Cultures, Madras*, vol. 19, no. 1, 1975, pp. 119–80.

137 *Agpp*, Nāthamunikaḷ *vaibhavam.*

138 *Mgpp*, Nāthamunikaḷ *vaibhavam.*

139 *Tiruvāymŏḻi* 5.8.1–11.

140 Modern Āḻvār Tirunagari.

141 *Tiruvāymŏḻi* 5.8.11 is the signature verse giving his name as Kurukūr Caṭakopaṉ.

disciples of Madhurakavi Āḻvār taught him the *Kaṇṇinuṇciruttāmpu*,[142] which was all that they knew. By repetition of the sacred poem 12,000 times, Nāthamuni obtained, as a divine gift, the hymns of not only Nammāḻvār but also all the other Āḻvārs, which he then proceeded to classify and compile, to set to music and to teach his disciples so that they should be preserved for posterity.[143] The Śaiva tradition preserves a parallel story of the passing into oblivion and miraculous recovery of the hymns of the Nāyaṉmārs. According to the fourteenth-century composition of Umāpati Śivācārya, the *Tirumuraikaṇṭapurāṇam*, literally the story of the discovery of the *Tirumurai*, the Coḻa king, Rājarāja, is said to have been moved to tears upon hearing a few verses from the poems of the *mūvar*.[144] He searched far and wide for the rest without success till he heard of an Ādiśaiva *brāhmaṇa* boy Nampi Āṇṭār Nampi, whose extraordinary devotion caused the image of Vināyaka to actually consume the offering of bananas he brought him. Nampi put the king's request to Vināyaka who revealed that the sacred hymns were hidden in a chamber in the great temple at Chidambaram. The Coḻa king reached the chamber only to discover that it was locked, and its door marked with the hands of the three saint-poets. When the temple priests said it could be opened only if the three saints came in person, the king arranged for the celebration of a great festival in which the *utsava mūrtis* (processional idols) of the three saints were ceremonially brought to the chamber. Within were found the manuscripts of all the hymns buried under an anthill, most destroyed beyond recovery. A divine voice, however, informed Rājarāja that whatever the world required had survived, upon which he had the hymns of the *mūvar* arranged in seven volumes (the *Tirumurai*) while those of other saints were compiled in four more volumes.[145]

These legends have usually been thought to signify the temporary loss and rediscovery of these sacred hymns,[146] the miraculous features of the process of recovery serving to justify and enhance their sanctity.[147] The Śaiva legend serves the additional purpose of underlining the centrality

142 Madhurakavi Āḻvār's poem of 10 stanzas devoted to Nammāḻvār.

143 *DSC, sargaḥ* 16; *Agpp, Mgpp*, Nāthamuṉikaḷ *vaibhavam*.

144 'The three', i.e. Appar, Sundarar and Sambandar.

145 David Dean Shulman, 'Poets and Patrons in Tamil Literature and Legend', in *The Wisdom of Poets: Studies in Tamil, Telugu and Sanskrit*, ed. Shulman, New Delhi, 2001, pp. 81–2. Also Peterson, op. cit., pp. 15–16.

146 Venkatachari, op. cit., pp. 14–15.

147 Peterson, op. cit., p. 16.

of the shrine at Chidambaram. In the context of the Śaiva canon, the *Tevāram*, François Gros says:

We have to assume that the meticulous arrangement was *a posteriori* and came in to replace the mysterious chaos of history with a formal classification, and scattered manuscripts with a definitive version, proof against variations and alterations. Leaving aside the chronology and factual history which exist only in vestigial form, there remains a coherent grouping within the boundary of its premises, the cultural environment constituted by the apogee of the Tamil middle ages.[148]

According to the traditional Śrīvaiṣṇava hagiographies, the dates of the Āḻvārs range from the *Dvāpara yuga* to the first four centuries of the *Kali yuga* (whose fifth millennium we are in), which we can of course dismiss. The only Āḻvār to be dated with some confidence is Tirumankai, owing to references in his hymns to Nandivarman II Pallavamalla, the ruler who constructed the Vaikuṇṭha-p-Pěrumāḷ Temple in Kāñcīpuram, as the one who defeated the southern Pāṇṭiya king in the decad dedicated to the said temple[149] and to his son Dantidurga alias Vairamegha in the decad dedicated to Aṭṭabuyakaram.[150] Tirumankai can, therefore, be placed in the second half of the eighth and the early ninth centuries.[151] It has been argued that references to Māmallai[152] were not possible before the town had been established by the Pallava ruler Narasimhavarman I, alias Māmalla, in the second half of the seventh century;[153] Pŏykai

[148] François Gros, 'Towards Reading the Tevaram', in *Tevaram Hymnes Sivaites du Pays Tamoul*, ed. F. Gros and T.V. Gopala, Pondicherry: Publications de l'Institute Françoise d'Indologie, no. 68.1, 1984, p. xxxvii.

[149] *Pěriya Tirumŏḻi* 2.9.1–10 dedicated to Parameccura Viṇṇagaram.

[150] *Pěriya Tirumŏḻi* 2.8.1–10.

[151] A set of five copperplates of Paṭṭataṉmangalam discovered in TirutTuraipūṇṭi *tāluk*, Tanjavur district, dated to the sixty-first year of the reign of Ko Vijaya Nandivikrama who, it is argued, refers to Nandivarman Pallava II, refers to a grant of land to the *brāhmaṇas* of the place by a Mangalanāṭāḻvāṉ, who appears from the Sanskrit portions of the plate to be a Viṣṇu *bhakta*. The epithets used to describe him seem to agree with those Kaliyaṉ gives himself in *Pěriya Tirumŏḻi*. The grant refers to him as Pallava *bhṛtya*, a vassal of the Pallava. That Kaliyaṉ spent his early years in service of this king is shown in *Pěriya Tirumŏḻi* 1.9.7. It is argued that this donor was none other than the Āḻvār. Ref.: S.V. Varadaraja Ayyangar, 'The Date of Tirumangai Āḻvār', *Journal of Indian History*, vol. 26, no. 2, 1948, pp. 131–4.

[152] *Mutal Tiruvantādi* 70, *Pěriya Tirumŏḻi* 2.5.1–10, 2.6.1–10.

[153] T.A. Gopinatha Rao, *The History of the Srivaisnavas*, Madras: Madras University, 1923, p. 16.

cannot, therefore, be earlier than this date. The occurrence of the name Madhurakavi, son of Māṟaṉ, as a minister in Pāṇṭiya records of 770 CE, in connection with the excavation of some shrines for Viṣṇu is interpreted as referring to the last Āḻvār.[154] Nammāḻvār's mention of the temples of Śrīvaramangalam and Varaguṇamankai may be more reliable pointers to his date as the temples derive their name from the Pāṇṭiya ruler Varaguṇavarman (also called Jaṭila Parāntaka Nĕṭuñcaṭaiyaṉ) whose reign is dated 765–815 CE.[155] Nammāḻvār's placement in some part of the ninth century would give us a mid-late ninth century date, at the earliest, for Madhurakavi. Dating Pĕriyāḻvār on the basis of his reference to Pallavamalla is less certain, especially as the word '*mallāṇṭa*' in the *Tiruppallāṇṭu* hymn offers the possibility of another interpretation.[156] Some modern scholars have tried to work out the dates of the Āḻvārs by deciphering the astronomical references in the hymns and interpretation of epigraphic evidence.[157]

Though we are far from possessing accurate dates for the Āḻvārs, we can be fairly certain that there was probably less than a century between the last of the Āḻvārs and Nāthamuni. The Aṉbil plates of the fourth year

[154] Ibid., pp. 18–20. Two inscriptions of Jaṭāvarman Parāntaka, one in Sanskrit and the other in Tamil, were found by Rao on Ānaimalai hill near Madurai. The identification of the minister with the Āḻvār is, however, disputed by Krishnaswami Aiyangar, *Early History of Vaisnavism in South India*, London: Oxford University Press, 1920, p. 46, and Hardy, *Viraha Bhakti*, pp. 255–6 footnote 55.

[155] Dating from Sastri, *A History of South India*, p. 164.

Hardy, *Viraha Bhakti*, pp. 255–6 footnote 55, chooses an earlier date for Nammāḻvār despite acknowledging this evidence. A date in the ninth century is both more reasonable and in concord with the evidence. See Chapter 6-iii of the present work.

[156] *Pĕriyāḻvār Tirumŏḻi* 1. '*Mallāṇṭa tiṇ toḷ maṇivaṇṇā*' may mean 'the gem-coloured, great shouldered One who ruled over Malla' (i.e. Pallavamalla) or 'the mighty gem-coloured One with shoulders like a wrestler'.

[157] On the basis of a reference to the setting of Jupiter and rising of Venus in *Tiruppāvai* 13, M. Raghava Iyengar has postulated that Āṇḍāḷ's *Tiruppāvai* was composed in 731 CE or, less probably, in 885–6 CE (M. Raghava Iyengar, 'The Date of Sri Āṇḍāḷ', *Journal of Oriental Research*, vol. 1, no. 2, 1927, p. 157) which K.G. Sankar has strongly disputed offering 850 CE as the exact date. (K.G. Sankar, 'The Date of Tiruppavai', *Journal of Oriental Research*, vol. 1, no. 2, 1927, pp. 167–9). Similarly, astrological calculations based on the details given in the *Guruparamaparās* combined with the inscriptional data from the Madras Museum plates, the Veḷvikuṭi plates and the Ciṉṉamaṉṉūr plates lead him to give Nammāḻvār a precise birth date, 4 November 798. (K.G. Sankar, 'Contemporaries of Pĕriyāḻvār', *Journal of Oriental Research*, vol. 1, no. 4, 1927, pp. 336–49).

of Sundara Coḻa alias Parāntaka, dated to approximately 960 CE, have yielded material of immense interest to scholars of Śrīvaiṣṇavism. The document records a grant of land to a minister of Sundara Coḻa, a learned *brāhmaṇa* named Aniruddha, a native of the village of Premāgrahāra.[158] A devotee of God Ranganātha of the temple at Srirangam, he is said to have made rich donations to the temple at Srirangam for feeding a large number of *brāhmaṇas* during the *Pankuni* festival. His parents, grandfather and great grandfather[159] are all described as great devotees and generous donors to the temple of Ranganātha. Aniruddha is said to belong to the Jaimini *sūtra* and to the Āveṇi *gotra*. The last verse in the Sanskrit *praśasti* portion informs us that the composer of the document was Mādhava Bhaṭṭa Yajvan, son of Bhaṭṭa Datta of the Parāśarya *vamśa* and that he was a very learned man and a disciple of Śrīnātha.[160]

The epigraphist, Gopinatha Rao, who also happens to have authored *The History of the Śrīvaiṣṇavas*,[161] points out that the *gotra* Āveṇi is often mentioned in south Indian inscriptions in connection with the names of Śrīvaiṣṇavas as also in their literature. Further, he draws attention to the Vaiṣṇava names of the ancestors of Aniruddha, and the astronomical calculations of Mr. Svamikkannu Pillai which date the births of Nāthamunikaḷ and Āḷavantār to 823 CE and 916 CE respectively.[162] Śrīnātha is accordingly identified as the Śrīvaiṣṇava *ācārya* Nāthamuni and it is suggested that the composer Mādhava Bhaṭṭa was a student of Nāthamunikaḷ who is reputed to have had a very long life.[163]

Considering that the hagiographies themselves claim a wide, appreciative contemporary audience for the hymns of the saints, the legends of loss and recovery do not seem credible. Besides, inscriptional evidence gives the lie to these legends. We hear of persons who had to

158 Sanskrit rendition of An̲bil. The village is in the Tirucchirapaḷḷi *tāluk* of Tirucchirapalli district, and hence very close to Srirangam.

159 Father's name is Nārāyaṇa, grandfather's Aniruddha, and great grandfather's Ananta.

160 *Epigraphica Indica*, vol. XV, pp. 44–57.

161 Rao, op. cit.

162 I believe these dates are excessively early; in fact, if the Śrīnātha mentioned in the inscription is indeed Nāthamuni, he can reasonably be placed in the tenth century which would agree with all our evidence. Besides, I find that the attribution of nearly 120 year-long life spans to all the three major early *ācāryas*, Nāthamuni, Yāmuna and Rāmānuja, rather strains credibility. Also, the astronomical dating is based on the hagiographical evidence which is late. The inscriptional evidence is, however, compelling.

163 A. Gopinatha Rao, *Epigraphica Indica*, vol. XV, pp. 53–5.

sing the *Tiruppatiyam* in the Bilvanātheśvara Temple at TiruMallam, North Arcot district, from an inscription of Nandivarman III Pallava's time.[164] While the term *Tiruppatiyam* has come to refer to the verses of the first three Nāyaṉmārs, it seems to have been used for the Vaiṣṇava hymns too during the tenth and eleventh centuries,[165] as is made evident from an inscription of the sixteenth regnal year of Rājendra Coḻa I (1028 CE) from the Venkaṭeśa-p-Pĕrumāḷ Temple in TiruMukkūṭal. Apparently, certain *vaikhānasas* of the temple reached an agreement regarding the recitation of *Tiruppatiyams* therein.[166] Again, according to an inscription of the third year of Rājendra I (1015 CE), the Śrīvaiṣṇavas who recited the *Tiruppatiyam* in the presence of Rāghavadeva in the Sundaravarada-p-Pĕrumāḷ Temple in Uttiramerūr were to receive the food that was offered to the deity.[167] Two other inscriptions in the same temple, of the nineteenth and twenty-sixth regnal years of the same ruler record the creation of endowments of land for the maintenance of three Śrīvaiṣṇavas who were to recite the *Tiruvāymŏḻi* in the temple.[168] It seems unlikely in these contexts that the term, *Tiruppatiyam*, could refer to the hymns of the Śaiva saints. Inscriptional evidence till at least the thirteenth century is certainly more bountiful from Śiva temples and regarding Śaivite material, but offers important clues for the reconstruction of Vaiṣṇava

[164] *SII* vol. III, part 1, pp. 92–3.

C. Minakshi, *Administration and Social Life under the Pallavas*, Madras: University of Madras, 1938, p. 178 dates Nandivarman III to 710–755 CE; François Gros believes this inscription belongs to 863 CE. See Gros, op. cit., p. xl. Gros' dating of Nandivarman III agrees with Sastri, *History of South India*, p. 163 and Mahalingam, 1985, vol. 1, pp. 123–4, NA 531. Ref.: *ARE*, 1890, no. 1(A). The record may, thus, be said to belong to the second half of the ninth century. Further epigraphic evidence of the recitation of the *Tiruppatiyam* in temples is dated to 911 CE, 921 CE, 944 CE, 948 CE, etc. (Mahalingam, 1985, vol. VIII, p. 152. Tp 716. Ref.: *ARE*, 1903, no. 373 (A); *SII*, VIII, no. 687, pp. 345–6; Mahalingam, 1985, vol. VIII, pp. 159–60. Tp 745. Ref.: *ARE*, 1903, no. 358; *SII*, viii, no. 139, p. 285; Mahalingam, 1985, vol. VIII, pp. 62-3. Tp 294. Ref.: *ARE*, 1928-9, no. 99; Mahalingam, 1985, vol. VIII, p. 165. Tp 770. Ref. *ARE*, 1936-37, no. 149).

[165] B.G.L. Swamy, 'The Four Samayacaryas of the Tamil Country in Epigraphy', *Journal of Indian History*, vol. 50, no. 1, pp. 97–8.

[166] Ibid., p. 98; *SII*, no. 183 of 1915.

[167] Ibid., p. 98; *SII*, no. 185 of 1917. Also Mahalingam, 1985, vol. III, p. 288, Cg 1140. Ref.: *Are*, 1923, no. 181.

[168] *SII*, no. 176 of 1923. Also Mahalingam, 1985, vol. III, p. 291. Cg 1151 and 1152. Ref.: *ARE*, 1923, nos. 176 and 194. Also cited in Sastri, *The Cōḻas*, vol. II, part I, pp. 479–80.

history too. We hear of provision for the recitation of *Tiruppatiyams* during the time of Āditya I,[169] Parāntaka I[170] and Rājarāja I.[171] Indeed, there are at least ten inscriptions of the tenth century which refer to the singing of *Tiruppatiyams* in various temples pointing clearly to the fact that at least some of the hymns were not only widely known, but that singing them was also popular as a meritorious, devotional practice during the late ninth and through the tenth centuries. Two inscriptions of the reign of Uttama Co<u>l</u>a (accession 970 CE) from the Mahālingasvāmi Temple in TiruvIṭaimarutūr, Kumbhakoṇam *tāluk*, record endowments of land for the maintenance of a musician to sing before the deity, *deśi* songs[172] which are likely to refer to the hymns of the Tamil bhakti saints. A tenth-century inscription dated to the thirteenth year of Sundara Pāṇṭiyadeva found in the Saumya Nārāyaṇa Temple in TirukKoṭṭiyūr village,[173] TirupPattūr *tāluk*, registers an order of the assembly to the temple authorities to give two *prasādas* and betel every day to the *śrīkāryam* (temple manager) as an act of appreciation (*sanmānam*) for his having arranged for the recitation of *Tirumŏ<u>l</u>i* before the deity during the ten day festival in Mārka<u>l</u>i. An inscription of 1012 CE from the A<u>l</u>akiya Narasimha-p-Pĕrumāḷ Temple in Ĕ<u>nn</u>āyiram in Vi<u>l</u>uppuram *tāluk* records a substantial gift for a variety of things including appointment of four persons for the recitation of the *Tiruvāymŏ<u>l</u>i* and for the maintenance of an institution for Vedic study.[174] An early eleventh-century record from the Trivikrama-p-Pĕrumāḷ Temple in TirukKoyilūr registers a gift of 96 sheep for a perpetual lamp for the deity and the sale of land to Kausika<u>n</u> Aṇṇāva<u>n</u> (mentioned in another inscription of same temple dated to 1008 CE) by the *sabhā* of TirukKovalūr for offerings of 100 *appam* (a sweetmeat), betel leaves, etc., to the deity on the occasion of Tiruvoṇam Tiruveṭṭaiṇāḷ (a festival) in the month of Aippaci. A payment of one *kācu*

[169] Swamy, 'The Four Samayacaryas', p. 99; *SII* 129 of 1914, 349 of 1918.

[170] Ibid., p. 102; *SII* 149 of 1936–7.

[171] Ibid., p. 99; *SII* 423 of 1908.

[172] Mahalingam, 1985, vol. VII, pp. 134–5. Tj 586. Ref.: *ARE* 1907, no. 234; *SII* xix, no. 181; ibid., xxii, no. 234, and vol. VII, p. 136, Tj 592. Ref.: *ARE* 1907, no. 231; *SII* xxiii, no. 233.

[173] This is a very important sacred site mentioned by Pĕriyā<u>l</u>vār in the *Pallāṇṭu* hymn and, in the hagiographies, said to be the hometown of an important *ācārya* from whom Rāmānuja learned the *rahasya granthas*. See Chapter 2-x of the present work.

[174] Mahalingam, 1985, vol. II, pp. 452–3, SA 1946. Ref: *ARE*, 1917, no. 33; ibid., part ii, para 28, p. 145f.

was to be made for the person singing the *Tiruněṭuntāṇṭakam*.[175] The *vaikhānasas* of the *sthānam* agreed to maintain the charity.

In 1028 CE, the *vaikhānasas* of the Venkaṭeśa-p-Pĕrumāḷ Temple in TiruMukkūṭal, Madhurāntakam *tāluk*, entered into an agreement with certain officers to use the surplus paddy due to them, which had been discovered by an enquiry into the accounts of the temple, for reciting the *Tiruppatiyam* in the temple for the first time.[176] A few decades later, an inscription of 1070 CE in the Srirangam Temple records the purchase of land from some persons and its endowment for services to the God Anantanārāyaṇasvāmin of TiruvArangam and for the recitation of the *Tiruvāymŏḻi*.[177] Another epigraph of 1085 CE from the same temple provides for the recitation of *Tiruppaḷḷiyĕḻucci–Tiruvāymŏḻi* during the wake-up ritual of the deity.[178] An inscription from Srirangam dated to 1088 CE says that a hymn by Kulaśekhara Āḻvār beginning with the phrase, *Teṭṭaruntiral* was to be recited before the deity during the course of a three-day festival.[179] As early as 998 CE, the lord in one of the three shrines in the Viṣṇu temple in Ukkal in the Chingleput district is called *Tiruvāymŏḻideva* in an inscription of the thirteenth regnal year of Rājarāja I.[180] Inscriptional records of the twelfth and thirteenth centuries continue to register donations for the maintenance of the singing of the hymns of the Āḻvārs.[181] A record of 1203 CE from the Rāmasvami Temple, TirukKoyilūr, records the provisions made for offerings to the god while *Tiruppāvai* was being recited.[182]

[175] Mahalingam, 1985, vol. II, p. 371. SA 1597. Ref.: *ARE*, 1900, no. 126; *SII* vii, no. 139.

[176] Mahalingam, 1985, vol. III, pp. 335–6. Cg 1310. Ref.: *ARE*, 1915, no. 83.

[177] Mahalingam, 1985, vol. VIII, p. 200. Tp 924. Ref.: *ARE*, 1947-48, no. 120; *SII*, xxiv, no. 60.

[178] Mahalingam, 1985, vol. VIII, p. 182. Tp 848. Ref.: *ARE*, 1892, no. 61; *SII*, iv, no. 508, pp. 146-7; xxiv, no. 57.

[179] Mahalingam, 1985, vol. VIII, p. 183. Tp 853. Ref.: *ARE*, 1892, no. 62; *SII* iii, no. 70, pp. 148–52; *SII* xxiv, no. 63.

[180] Mahalingam, 1985, vol. I, p. 105. NA 456. Ref.: *ARE*, 1893, no. 20; *SII* iii, no. 2. Also cited in Champakalakshmi, *Vaiṣṇava Iconography*, p. 221.

[181] Mahalingam, 1985, vol. VIII, p. 189. Tp 877. Ref.: *ARE* 1947–8, no. 119; *SII* xxiv, no. 87; Mahalingam, 1985, vol. II, p. 377. SA 1616. Ref.: *ARE*, 1921, no. 343; Mahalingam, 1985, vol. VII, pp. 440–1. Tj 1897. Ref.: *ARE* 1922, no. 503; ibid., part ii, p. 107; Mahalingam, 1985, vol. III, pp. 188–9, Cg 771. Ref.: *ARE* 1919, no. 557.

[182] Mahalingam, 1985, vol. II, p. 380. SA 1630. Ref.: *ARE* 1921, no. 354, CE 1203.

Tiruvāymŏḻi is the name given to the collection of the 1102 hymns of Nammāḻvār. *Tiruněṭuntāṇṭakam* is Tirumankai Āḻvār's composition. *Tirumŏḻi* is

In light of this overwhelming evidence for the awareness, not to say popularity, of the Tamil hymns of the Āḻvārs and Nāyaṉmārs, the legends of the rediscovery of the hymns must be examined for the multiple messages they encode. The miracle tales, weaving in divine intervention in this process of the rediscovery of the hymns, would have helped establish them as revealed scripture. Indeed, this is how these miracle tales have been understood by modern scholars.[183] But is it not equally likely that the later Śrīvaiṣṇava tradition claimed these well-loved hymns in order to acquire the prestige of tradition? I propose that it was not the hymns which needed to be invested with sanctity, but the Śrīvaiṣṇava community, probably initially a small, brahmanical one, which was seeking, through association with the well-loved songs of the Āḻvārs, to address a larger audience and weld together a greater community—a theme I will explore in detail in the last chapter.

In 1202 CE, a record was made in the Kirikṛṣṇa Temple in Kalliṭaikuricci, Ambāsamudram *tāluk*, recording a gift of land to the temple of Nālāyira Viṇṇagar Ĕmpĕrumāṉ.[184] From 1204 CE, we hear of Nālāyira-Iśvaramuṭaiyār in the Tirunelveli district.[185] From a Pāṇṭiya inscription of 1209 CE in the Kulaśekhara Āḻvār shrine in the Gopālasvāmi Temple in Maṉṉārkoyil, Ambāsamudram *tāluk*, we learn, among other things, that King Jaṭāvarmaṉ alias Tribhuvanacakravartiṉ Kulaśekhara, on the occasion of his presence at the Nālāyira-vaṉ-tirumaṇḍapam to hear the *Tiruppāvai*, remitted all the taxes on certain grant lands.[186] These inscriptions of the early thirteenth century where the adjective *Nālāyira* is applied to the temple/the Lord in a temple/canopy, establish that the hymnal canon was certainly ordered and well-known by the said name by the twelfth century, if not long before as claimed by the hagiography.[187]

One of the most important innovations of the period of the early

---

a name given generally to the songs of the Āḻvārs; suffixed to the honorific of an Āḻvār or some defining adjective, it signifies a particular composition such as *Pĕriyāḻvār Tirumŏḻi, Pĕrumāḷ Tirumŏḻi, Nācciyār Tirumŏḻi* and *Pĕriya Tirumŏḻi. Tiruppaḷḷiyĕḻucci* is the wake-up hymn to the lord, composed by Tŏṇṭaraṭippŏṭi Āḻvār. *Tiruppāvai* is the name of the collection of 30 songs of Āṇḍāḷ.

183 Sastri, *The Cōḻas*, pp. 637–40.

184 Mahalingam, 1985, vol. IX, p. 18. Tn 78. Ref.: *ARE*, 1907, no. 104.

185 Mahalingam, 1985, vol. IX, pp. Tn 79. Ref.: *ARE*, 1907, no. 97.

186 Mahalingam, 1985, vol. IX, pp. 33–4. Tn 154. Ref.: *ARE* 1916, no. 402.

187 I tend to accept the hagiographic claim in this case since the absence of inscriptional evidence to attest the literary sources does not mean that the latter necessarily lie.

ācāryas was that the *Nālāyiram* came to be acknowledged as scripture on par with the Sanskrit *śruti.*[188] This is a radical step in that it is the first and (with the exception of the Śaiva canon a little later)[189] perhaps the only time a claim is made that a language other than Sanskrit can express revealed truth and can possess the sanctity and authority of the Vedas.[190] The name given to the hymns of the Āḻvārs is, accordingly, *Drāviḍaveda*, i.e. the Tamil *Veda*. It can be argued that this unusual claim was first put forward by Madhurakavi Āḻvār in the *Kaṇṇinuṇciruttāmpu.*[191] Madhurakavi, in this remarkable poem in praise of and devotion to his preceptor says quite clearly that Caṭakopa<u>n</u>/Kāri Māra<u>n</u>[192] graced the Vedas and rendered their inmost meaning in his thousand songs.[193] The Śrīvaiṣṇava tradition believes that the four works of Nammāḻvār are the Tamil equivalents of the four Vedas,[194] that it is, therefore, the inheritor of a two-fold Vedic heritage, in two languages, and puts forth this belief in its claim of *ubhaya Vedānta*. Doubtlessly too, the *ācāryas* explicating the hymns saw 'confirmation' of this claim to *śruti*-hood in Nammāḻvār's utterance that it was the lord himself who sung his own praise though his mouth.[195]

The problem of how the canon came to comprise the particular hymns it did, doesn't admit easy solutions. Let us consider, for example, an

[188] Venkatachari, op. cit., p. 4.

[189] Peterson, op. cit., p. 52 says that the Nāya<u>n</u>mārs' hymns were referred to thus by the twelfth century hagiographer, Cekkiḻār.

[190] Venkatachari, op. cit., p. 4.

[191] *Kaṇṇinuṇciruttāmpu*, vs. 7–8.

[192] 'Nammāḻvār' is an honorific, meaning simply, 'our Āḻvār'; he signs himself Māra<u>n</u>/Kāri Māra<u>n</u> and as Caṭakopa<u>n</u>. Madhurakavi Āḻvār's *Kaṇṇinuṇciruttāmpu* verses 7 and 9 refer to Kāri Māra<u>n</u> as Caṭakopa<u>n</u>. The meaning of the word Caṭakopa<u>n</u> remains unclear though various interpretations are offered.

[193] It must be clarified that the *Tiruvāymŏḻi* comprises 1,102 stanzas, but since the refrain in every eleventh stanza says 'these ten of a thousand', they are loosely considered a 'thousand songs', though not in the tabulation of the corpus.

[194] Sometimes only the equivalence of the *Tiruvāymŏḻi* with the Veda is claimed. On the other hand, the compositions of the other Āḻvārs are considered the *angas* of the *Vedas* and meticulous numerical equivalents between the *angas* and *upāngas* of the Vedas and the Tamil works of the Āḻvārs are drawn. Various conflicting equivalents happily coexist.

Also, two of these are Nammāḻvār's signed compositions while the other two are attributed to him.

[195] *Tiruvāymŏḻi* 7.9.1–10.

inscription from a ruined Viṣṇu temple in Tirumālpuram in Arakkoṇam *tāluk*. Dated in the tenth year of Rājakesarivarman 'who destroyed the ships at Kantalūr Śālai', i.e. Rājarāja I (accession 985 CE), it records a gift of gold by Kulakkuṭaiyān̲ Arun̲ilai Śrīkṛṣṇan̲ alias Mūventa-Piṭavūr-Veḷān̲ and stipulates that a *Tiruppatiyam* beginning with the words, *Kolanār kul̲al*, composed by the donor's father in praise of Govindapāṭiyāl̲vār, was to be sung on the occasion of a festival.[196] Since this hymn does not feature in the *NDP*, it seems reasonable to assume that the formal codification of the hymns of the saint-poets had already been completed and that tampering with the canon was not acceptable. On the other hand, the Śaiva canon, which was arranged in the reign of Rājarāja I by Nampi Āṇṭār Nampi, was added to till the middle of the twelfth century.[197] It would appear, therefore, that the Śrīvaiṣṇava *Guruparamparās* are correct in recording that Vedic status was claimed for the *Prabandham* from the time of Nāthamuni himself.

The question I am asking, in other words, is whether there were other devotional songs besides these few thousand hymns that have been canonised. There must have been a process of selection, perhaps partly a product of natural survivals in and erasures from popular memory, but also in part of what may be called an editorial choice. It also remains possible that the abovementioned hymn was one of many in praise of Viṣṇu which, despite popularity in their respective localities, had less of a supra-local reach and were, accordingly, unknown to the compilers at the moment of codification. This question raises other interesting issues: not all the hymns that have been preserved in the corpus fit neatly with the theological or philosophical vision of the *ācāryas*. I will, indeed, show how such hymns were interpreted creatively, or 'allegorized', as Hardy puts it, to achieve a pattern of overall harmony. But the fact remains that the *NDP*, and the Śaiva *Tevāram* for that matter, may not necessarily be either the sum of the devotional literary output of their times, nor necessarily belong in their entirety to the time to which they are purported to belong. As has already been pointed out, the *Tiruccanta Viruttam* seems so unlike the other bhakti hymns that it could well belong to a date much closer to the *ācāryas*, or even be an early acaryic contribution to the corpus. The same could be said for the *Ciriya Tirumaṭal* and the *Pĕriya Tirumaṭal* as well; indeed, they seem to share the concerns of the hagiographical and commentarial literature in their focus on pilgrimage. They were, however, perhaps assimilated into

[196] Mahalingam, 1985, vol. I, p. 33. NA 143. Ref.: *ARE*, 1906, no. 333.

[197] Sastri, *The Culture and History of the Tamils*, p. 115.

the hymnal canon before the actual composition of the hagiographies. The incorporation into the *NDP* of the *Rāmānuja Nūṟṟantādi*, a *praśasti* on the lineage of spiritual preceptors beginning with the earliest Āḻvārs and concluding with Rāmāṇuja, probably sometime late in the twelfth or early thirteenth century, may point to the flexibility of the canon till at least that date. On the other hand, the complicated system of counting the lines in the *Ciriya Tirumaṭal* and the *Pěriya Tirumaṭal* by the Tĕṉkalais in order to include the 108 stanzas of the *Rāmānuja Nūṟṟantādi* and still add up to the count of 4,000 may indicate that the corpus had already been largely standardized by this time. Either way, it is beyond doubt that after the early twelfth century, no surreptitious deletion or addition was possible to the hymnal corpus.

I have used epigraphic evidence extensively to trace the beginnings of recitation of the sacred songs in temples. The words *Tevāram* and *Tiruppatiyam*, standing as they do today for the songs of the Nāyaṉmārs, have been uncritically taken to have been used in the same sense more than a thousand years ago as well. We have seen too that when the same word is used in the context of a Viṣṇu temple, the meaning is expanded to include the compositions of one or the other of the Āḻvārs. Could they have referred to other songs which we no longer know? At least in one instance, a hymn by the Nāyaṉār Sambandar, unknown to the *Tevāram* canon, was found inscribed on a temple wall, by archaeologists in the twentieth century.[198] Was it accidentally left out in the past, was it simply not known to the compilers, or is it indicative of a process of careful inclusions and exclusions? Or have we borrowed an older word for an entirely different set of religious poetry? I believe the last to be unlikely, but this discussion should sensitize us to the fact that what we believe to be the production of the Tamil *bhakti* saints has itself come down to us in a mediated fashion. Part of the problem is related to the fact that popular memory may have preserved only a fraction of the songs that had circulated in the *bhakti* devotional milieu; this would indicate an even greater range of engagement of *bhakti* devotionalism in the period between the sixth and ninth centuries. It is important to keep in mind that the corpus available to us was part of a larger, popular oral tradition, and may have acquired its present shape due partly to the intervention of the brahmanical *ācāryas* who, in pruning and elaborating it, gave it what it did not have: Sanskritic acceptability and a wider reach.

Modern literary theory recognizes that literary form needs to be thought about not merely in terms of rhyme and meter but also as a

[198] Sastri, *The Cōlas*, p. 637 (footnoting *ARE* no. 8 of 1918).

structure of communication between author and audience. This has been traditionally true in the case of the Tamil devotional hymns, as Tamil Hindus have always turned to the legends of the saints' lives to illuminate their poems.[199] Our primary source of information about the Āḻvārs is, other than the incidental biographical details scattered in the hymns, usually in the signature verses, the *Guruparamparāprabhāvams* (henceforth *Gpps*), i.e. the Śrīvaiṣṇava hagiographies (literally, the splendour of the succession of teachers),[200] composed between the twelfth and fifteenth centuries. In this study, I will consider three major hagiographies, the *Divyasūricaritam* (henceforth *DSC*), a Sanskrit *kāvya* composed in Srirangam by Garuḍavāhana Paṇḍita, and two Maṇipravāḷa texts, the *Ārāyirappaṭi Guruparamparā Prabhāvam* (henceforth *Agpp*) composed by Piṉpaḻakiya Pĕrumāḷ Cīyar and the *Mūvāyirappaṭi Guruparamparā Prabhāvam* (henceforth *Mgpp*) by Tṛtīya Brahmatantra Svatantra Cīyar.

Maṇipravāḷa, literally gems and coral, is a language composite of Sanskrit and Tamil with a Tamil syntactical base.[201] It has been called a 'situational language in that it developed in specific circumstances (to expound *Ubhaya-Vedānta* to a diverse religious community whose mother tongue was Tamil) and was used in specific contexts (religious instruction involving the larger tasks of writing *vyākhyānas* [commentaries] and *sampradāyagranthas* [works concerning the tradition])'.[202] The first text to be composed in Maṇipravāḷa was the *Ārāyirappaṭi,* a commentary on Nammāḻvār's *Tiruvāymŏḻi* by Tirukkurukaip-Piräṉ Piḷḷāṉ,[203] between 1100 and 1150 CE, apparently at the instance of Rāmānuja himself. The *Gpps,* which falls in the category of *sampradāyagranthas* had, therefore, a clear purpose. While meaning to be 'histories' of the preceptors, stretching backwards from the contemporary *ācāryas* to the saint-devotees of a long-bygone age, whose near mythical lives are meant to serve not only as models and as inspiration but also as objects of devotion in their own right, they also sketch out a conception of the community in the vision of its leaders and articulate a well-defined ideology.

199 Norman Cutler, *Songs of Experience: The Poetics of Tamil Devotion,* Bloomington: Indiana University Press, 1987, p. 6.

200 Carman and Narayanan, op. cit., p. 4.

201 Maṇipravāḷa denotes a number of composite languages such as Sanskrit–Tamil and Sanskrit–Malayalam. This study is concerned only with texts in the Sanskrit–Tamil combine.

202 Venkatachari, *The Śrīvaiṣṇava Maṇipravāḷa*, p. 40.

203 Ibid., p. 61.

One must reiterate the interval of approximately three centuries between the last Āḻvār's earthly existence according to the most commonly accepted dates and the composition of the first hagiography. The *DSC* is often considered the earliest, owing to a reference to Rāmānuja, the revered founder *ācārya* of the community, in the present tense, and the narrative ending before Rāmānuja's death in 1137 CE. B.V. Ramanujan, however, assigns it to the fifteenth century, arguing that a chapter considered by most scholars a late interpolation is integral to the text.[204] Archana Venkatesan, too, argues for a fifteenth century dating, owing to the very divergent treatment of the Āṇḍāḷ story in the *DSC* and in the Maṇipravāḷa hagiographies.[205] Its frequently awkward translations of Tamil names and terms into Sanskrit also points to it being a later work. Reasons for assigning an early date to the *DSC* are the *Agpp* mentioning the *DSC* and quoting it as its source in at least twelve places,[206] and the absence in the *DSC* of a popular episode in the life-story of the preceptor Rāmānuja which is elaborated at some length in the *Agpp* and the *Mgpp*, not to speak of later chronicles. The *Agpp*, and the *Mgpp* (dated to the late thirteenth–fourteenth centuries), and later temple records like the *Koyil Ŏḻuku* from Srirangam credit Rāmānuja with having travelled to Delhi to recover the processional idol of the deity of the temple Rāmānuja established in TiruNārāyaṇapuram in Karnataka.[207] This idol is said to have been taken away by Muslim invaders. The first Muslim invasion of the Tamil land took place in 1310 CE, and was followed by others in the course of the century. The story is necessarily fictional as Rāmānuja could naturally not have been involved in any attempt to reclaim an idol looted by Muslim invaders.[208] What is likely, however, is that after a series of invasions, popular memory began to project them into the distant past as well. The authors of the *Agpp* and the *Mgpp*, perceiving the past through the eyes of the present, wove in the tales of the historic invasions in recent times into the hagiography of Rāmānuja.

204 B.V. Ramanujan, 'The Divyasūricaritam', *Journal of Indian History*, vol. 13, no. 4, 1934, pp. 181–203.

205 Archana Venkatesan, *Āṇṭāḷ and her Magic Mirror: Her Life as a Poet in the Guises of the Goddess. The Exegetical Strategies of Tamil Śrīvaiṣṇavas in the Apotheosis of Āṇṭāḷ*, Unpublished Ph.D. thesis University of California, Berkeley, 2004, pp. 21, 42, 60, 83–94.

206 Hardy, 'The Tamil Veda of a Śūdra Saint', p. 78.

207 V.N. Hari Rao, Madras: ed. and trans., *Kōil Oḻugu: The Chronicle of the Srirangam with Historical Notes*, Madras: Rochouse Sons, 1961, p. 105. *The Koyil Ŏḻuku* does not, however, connect Turuṣkas/Muslim rulers with the episode.

208 See Chapter 2-x of the present work for the story.

Though the *DSC* speaks of Rāmānuja's flight to TiruNārāyaṇapuram, which in the other texts is the frame-context for the story referred to earlier, it makes no reference to any 'Tulukka/Turuṣka'[209] in any way, thus strengthening the hypothesis that it is an earlier text. A third point which has bearing on the case will be discussed later. Since my examination of the hagiographies prioritizes the *Agpp* and *Mgpp* over the *DSC*, it is not critically affected by the dating of the Sanskrit hagiography. I will, however, wherever the context demands, specify any different readings available from the *DSC*.

The Śrīvaiṣṇava community seems to have split by the eighteenth century into two sects, the Tĕṉkalai and the Vaṭakalai. While eighteen points of difference in the philosophical conceptions are elaborated,[210] and the history of difference is traced to late fourteenth-early fifteenth centuries, the period of the *ācāryas* Maṇavāḷa Māmuṉi and Vedānta Deśika, who came subsequently to be venerated as the founding *ācāryas* of the Tĕṉkalai and the Vaṭakalai sects respectively, it appears that the actual split may have had to do as much with control of temples and resources as doctrinal differences.[211] One of the consequences of this split is that the lineage of preceptors after Rāmānuja differs in the case of each sect. Equally important from the point of view of this study is that owing to the markedly different positions of these two sects of the Śrīvaiṣṇava community on such key issues as caste status of devotees in the community, the means to and eligibility for salvation and the role of the *guru*, the sectarian concerns are woven into the fabric of the life-stories of the saints in the texts produced by each sect. I have accordingly chosen the earliest of the Tĕṉkalai and (available) Vaṭakalai[212] *Gpps*, the *Agpp* and the *Mgpp* respectively. A fairly reliable way of dating these hagiographies is by computing the dates of the latest of the preceptors

[209] Corruption of 'Turk'; generic term for Muslim in the southern Indian vernaculars.

[210] Alkondavilli Govindacarya, 'The Astadasa Bhedas: 18 points of Doctrinal Difference between the Tengalais (Southerners) and Vaḍagalais (Northerners) of the Viśiṣṭādvaita Vaiṣṇava School in South India', *Journal of the Royal Asiatic Society*, 1910, pp. 1103–12.

[211] Ranjeeta Dutta, 'Community Identity and Sectarian Affiliations: The Śrīvaiṣṇavas of South India from the Eleventh to the Seventeenth Century AD', Unpublished Ph.D. Thesis, Jawaharlal Nehru University, New Delhi, 2004.

[212] The *Mgpp* composed by Tṛtīya Brahmatantra Svatantra Cīyar claims that it is an abridged version of the earlier *Pannirāyirappaṭi Guruparamparā Prabhāvam* composed by the Dvitīya Brahmatantra Svatantra Cīyar which, however, is lost to us.

mentioned in each. The proper lineage of teachers is absolutely crucial in the Śrīvaiṣṇava notion of salvation, one's association with one's own teacher stretching backwards to Rāmānuja who, by his paradigmatic *śaraṇāgati*, secured the redemption of all his followers. An *ācārya's* role is said to be that of a mediator and unifier (*ghaṭaka*) between the *jīvas* and the *paramātmā*.[213] The *Gpps* are, therefore, meticulous in recording the lineage: indeed, the very name of these scriptures indicates the same. Pi<u>n</u>pa<u>l</u>akiya Pĕrumāḷ Cīyar, the author of the *Agpp*, claims to be the disciple of Pĕriyavāccā<u>n</u> Piḷḷai whose birth is dated to 1228 CE.[214] The composition of the *Agpp* is accordingly placed in the late thirteenth or the first half of the fourteenth century.[215] In the case of the *Mgpp*, internal evidence is substantiated by epigraphic evidence as well. An inscription of 1359 CE in the Varadarāja Svāmi Temple in Kāñcī mentions a Brahmatantra Svatantrar as the head of a *maṭha*.[216] This points to a date in the late fourteenth or early fifteenth century for the third Brahmatantra Svatantrar, the composer of the *Mgpp*. Since no critical editions have been prepared for either of these texts, making it very difficult to identify later interpolations, inscriptional evidence will be my primary basis for any dating.

Later hagiographies of each sect relied heavily on the earlier ones, omitting or elaborating specific details in accordance with the circumstances of their composition. I will occasionally draw on some of these sources, especially the *Vārttāmālai*, an anthology of the sayings of the *ācāryas* compiled by Pi<u>n</u>pa<u>l</u>akiya Pĕrumāḷ Cīyar, the author of the *Agpp*, the *Yatirāja Vimśati* of Varavaramuni and the *Rāmānujārya Divya Caritai* of Piḷḷai Lokā<u>n</u> Cīyar. I will also consider supplementary evidence from such *vyākhyāna* texts as the *Īṭu* of Vaṭakku-Tiruvīti-Piḷḷai, the *Śrīvacana Bhūṣaṇa* of Piḷḷai Lokācārya and the *Ācārya Hṛdayam* of A<u>l</u>akiya Maṇavāḷa-p-Pĕrumāḷ-Nāya<u>n</u>ār whenever necessary to complement an argument or to test a proposition.

The *sthalapurāṇas* are a later genre of literature and usually less authoritative than the sources discussed earlier here. However, they constitute an important source of information about the myths and

[213] S. Sampathkumar, 'Bhagawad Ramanuja and Visistadvaita Vedanta', *Visistadvaita: Philosophy and Religion: A Symposium by Twenty Four Erudite Scholars*, Madras: Ramanuja Research Society, 1974, p. 43.

[214] Venkatachari, op. cit., p. 77.

[215] I incline to the latter date to accommodate Malik Kafur's invasion of 1310 CE.

[216] *Epigraphica Indica*, vol. XXV, no. 34.

legends associated with the numerous shrines. Many of the temples dotting the Tamil land derive their status, if not sanctity, from the Āḻvār and Nāyanār saints having sung the praise of their chosen deity in specific shrines and thus mapping what has come to be called a sacred geography.[217] The Tamil pilgrimage tradition, both Śaiva and Vaiṣṇava, has received a degree of scholarly attention. It would be interesting to examine how the pilgrim map, as it appears in the *NDP*, compares with the frequent elaborations in the hagiographies and to discover the germs of the standardized medieval network.

Few modern Śrīvaiṣṇava scholars[218] have questioned the veracity of the hagiographic accounts or pointed to the absence of any contemporary documentation of the lives of the Āḻvārs. The different tellings in the three major hagiographical texts are assumed to represent either multiple oral traditions or the natural embellishments and changes that occur in oral traditions.[219] It is evident on examination, however, that many of these 'differences' are purposeful and reflect the differing viewpoints of the two major sects over crucial sectarian issues. Significantly, the *DSC* seems comparatively innocent of these confrontational issues, but in one central issue of establishing the proper lineage of the preceptors, it seems to bolster the Tĕṉkalai viewpoint in suggesting that Rāmānuja appointed Parāśara Bhaṭṭar as his successor.[220] This might suggest one of three things: (1) the *DSC* is a later text, of the Tĕṉkalai persuasion; (2) it is contemporaneous with Rāmānuja, and that Parāśara Bhaṭṭar was the successor appointed by Rāmānuja, in which case the Vaṭakalai sect patently changed the order of succession; and (3) the *DSC* is contemporaneous with Rāmānuja and the two verses which speak of the succession being passed on to Bhaṭṭar are a later interpolation. Indeed, the verses in question don't seem to agree with the few that follow, in that the latter of the two speaks of Rāmānuja's imminent end, whereas the last few verses indicate his continued pontificate—technically possible, but stylistically clumsy. On the other hand, the representation of Viṣṇu's divine world as a royal court prefigures Tamil courtly poetry and the theological parallels that it draws between Āṇḍāḷ and Sītā following the

[217] Ramanujan, *Hymns for the Drowning*, p. x.

[218] That is, scholars who are personally Śrīvaiṣṇavas.

[219] Professor K.K.A. Venkatachari expressed this viewpoint in conversation. However, see, Venkatesan, op. cit., for an excellent discussion of the various tellings of the Āṇḍāḷ story.

[220] *DSC*, *sargaḥ* 18, verses 14–15.

exegetical tradition established by Pĕriyavāccan̲ Piḷḷai, a Tĕn̲kalai *ācārya*, make it likely that it did belong to the Tĕn̲kalai stables, so to speak.[221]

If the *DSC* is an older text than either the *Agpp* or the *Mgpp*—which is by no means certain—it is not necessarily closer to the 'truth'. Any searcher for the 'truth' of the lives of the Āl̲vārs would do well to remember Kurosawa's *Rashomon*.[222] Merely bringing the saints down from the almost uncorrupted *Dvāpara* age and the very beginnings of the *Kali* age when darkness had not gathered so thick, to a more mundane time as the late first millennium CE will not restore historical accuracy to them. Nor will simply stripping these tales of the fabulous and the miraculous.

The *ācāryas* have, to be fair, scrutinized the verses of the Āl̲vārs with immense care to glean whatever detail can be obtained about the saint's lives from their own words, and then embellished the same. I shall examine these details in the hymns against the stories woven around the lives of the saints to discover the areas where the imagination of the hagiographers has been at work. Needless to say, this creativity was purposeful. It is not fairy tales that have emerged as the final product but texts which enunciate a specific vision of the community. I propose to examine aspects of Śrīvaiṣṇava theology, the Śrīvaiṣṇava position on caste, the relationship of the Śrīvaiṣṇavas with Śaivas, Buddhists and Jainas, and the Śrīvaiṣṇava conception of pilgrimage as woven into the hagiographies. While the hymns of the Āl̲vārs sometimes bolster the conceptions of the *ācāryas* in these issues, they speak at other times in slightly different registers, and occasionally in startlingly different terms too. I hope that my examination of the hagiographic literature against the evidence of the Tamil hymns will allow us to understand the processes of historic change in religious ideas and to achieve a more nuanced view of early Tamil bhakti.

221 Venkatesan, op. cit., argues for a later dating for the *DSC* on this basis. Also, it must be reiterated that the formal split between the sects occurred much later.

222 Akira Kurosawa, *Rashomon*, 1950.

TWO

The Hagiographical Accounts

In this chapter, I will present the narratives of the twelve Āḻvārs, and the *ācārya* Rāmānuja in the traditional chronological order,[1] both for reasons of narrative consistency and cross-referencing, and examine them thematically in the chapters that follow. As my analyses only occasionally draw upon the hagiographical accounts of the *ācāryas* Nāthamuni and Āḷavantār, I have referenced them directly to the primary sources and have not presented them here. I have also included very brief versions of the accounts of five Śaiva Nāyaṉmārs from the *Pĕriya Purāṇam*. While I have tried to be as faithful as possible to the traditional accounts, these should not be treated as translations, as the following narration is interspersed with my own comments and glosses.

The *Mgpp* accounts use more Sanskrit and are, being largely devoid of decorative embellishments, usually far tighter than those of the *Agpp*. Indeed, they are on occasion so cryptic that they would make little sense if the 'stories' they purport to tell were not already familiar to us. Since the *Agpp* is known to have been composed prior to the *Mgpp* and the *Mgpp* itself claims to be a *précis* version of an earlier hagiography (now lost), composed by the second Brahmatantra Svantra Cīyar,[2] it is possible that some of the missing details may have been assumed to be common knowledge, in no need of repetition. The *Agpp* accounts reproduce at the outset of each saint's hagiography, Sanskrit verses from the *DSC* that describe the astrological and environmental details of the time of the

[1] *Agpp, Mgpp* and *DSC* are agreed in their chronology; the *Agpp*, however, presents Nammāḻvār and Madhurakavi at the end. All translations from the hagiographies have been done jointly by (late) Professor J. Parthasarathi and me.

[2] See Chapter 1-iii of the present work.

Āḻvār's birth, followed by the same in Tamil prose, while the *Mgpp* gives the same details in Sanskrit-dominated Maṇipravāḷa prose. The *DSC* account is embroidered with numerous poetic conventions, and in doing so, differs in several details from the two Tamil hagiographies. Not all of these differences in tellings are critical for my analysis; I shall pass over minor differences as well as those embellishments in the tales that do not impact my examination of the hagiographies. I shall, however, point out any significant variations in the three accounts.

An examination of the hagiographic accounts reveals a peculiar fact—there is practically no detail about the lives of the three *mutal* Āḻvārs. The account of the fourth Āḻvār, Tirumaḻicai, which is as long as the first three are short, tells us little about a real person, being replete with miraculous happenings. Interestingly, none of these four have a proper name; in fact, the names of the first three mean, simply, a pond (Pŏykai, from his birth in a pond), and ghost/ghoul (Pūtam and Pey—equivalent to the Sanskrit *bhūta* and *preta*, perhaps signifying their god-madness). TiruMaḻicai is simply a place name, supposedly the saint's birthplace.

(i) Mutalāḻvārkaḷ vaibhavam *(glory)*

The *Agpp* tells us that Brahmā performed an *aśvamedha yajña* in which Viṣṇu appeared. Since Brahmā is '*ka*', the spot of his sacrifice came to be known as Kāñcī. The *Mgpp*, however, informs us that of the seven places that grant *mokṣa*, Kāñcī is the best. In this holy Kāñcī, during the *Dvāpara yuga*, in the month of Aippaci, under the Tiruvoṇa asterism[3] was born the saint Pŏykai,[4] the first of the *mutal* Āḻvārs in the womb of a lotus in a tank. He was an *amśa* of Pāñcajanya, the conch of Viṣṇu. Pūtattāḻvār,[5] an *amśa* of Kaumudiki, the Lord's mace, took *avatāra* next day, in a *mādhavi* flower grove (*Agpp*)/*nilotpala* (*Mgpp*) in Māmallapuram by the sea in the Aippaci month under the asterism of Aviṭṭam.[6] An *amśa* of Nandakam, Viṣṇu's sword, was born on the third day in the heart of a red *alli* flower in the tank of the temple of Ādikeśava-p-Pĕrumāḷ in Mayūrapuri,[7]

[3] Sanskrit Śrāvaṇa.

[4] Pŏykai means tank; the name derives from his birth in one. The Sanskrit *DSC* calls him Kāsārayogi.

[5] (Sanskrit) Bhūtam+ (Tamil) Āḻvār= Pūtat-t-Āḻvār. The *DSC* calls him Śrī Bhūta Sūri.

[6] Sanskrit Dhaniṣṭa.

[7] Mayilai or Mylapore in modern Madras.

in Caṭaya *nakṣatra*.[8] Being filled with the madness of Viṣṇu bhakti, he became '*pey*'.[9]

The three *ayonija* saints, i.e. of immaculate births,[10] without *rajas* or *tamas guṇas* and filled with deep devotion, would not stay more than one night in any place.[11]They wandered (each separately) from one shrine of the lord to another. Desiring to bring his three great devotees together, the lord caused a *mahā andhakāra* (great darkness) and thunderstorm one day in TirukKoyilūr/TirukKovalūr, forcing the three to take shelter in a narrow vestibule.[12] The three Āḻvārs then felt the presence of a fourth among them, the lord being inseparable from his devotees just as Hari is present wherever there are *tulasi* gardens and light where there is Bhāskara. The lord 'pressed them as sugarcane in a cane press'[13] to make *rasa stotra* flow out in the form of *antādi.*

In oral tellings, the story has greater drama. The first Āḻvār to reach the passage is said to have lain down there. When the second Āḻvār arrived, they sat down together but the arrival soon thereafter of the third seeking refuge from the storm forced them to stand up huddled against each other. As they stood thus, they felt further crowded by the presence of a fourth, unseen one, whom they perceived with their inner eyes and celebrated in their songs.

The *Mutal Tiruvantādi* attributed to Pŏykai begins with the words, 'The earth is my lamp, the ocean the oil, the sun the flame, I offer this 'garland of song. . .'. The *Iraṇṭām Tiruvantādi* opens with, 'With love as lamp, passion as oil and my heart as wick, I light this flame and offer this garland of songs. . .' and the first stanza of the *Mūnrām Tiruvantādi* attributed to Pey is, 'Today I have seen Tiru (Śrī), today I have seen the golden body of my ocean-hued Lord. . .'. Śrīvaiṣṇavas have traditionally understood these lines as representation of the Āḻvārs' meeting with the Lord in the *iṭaikali*[14] in TirukKoyilūr.

[8] Sanskrit Śaṭabhiśā.

[9] Tamil form of Sanskrit *preta* (ghost). The Āḻvār's name, therefore, is Peyāḻvār. The *DSC* calls him Mahadāhvaya Sūri.

[10] See discussion of their caste in Chapter 4.

[11] This detail comes from the *Agpp*, Mutalāḻvārkaḷ *vaibhavam.*

[12] *Iṭaikaḻi/reḻi* in Tamil, *dehali* in the Sanskrit text.

[13] *DSC, sargaḥ* 2, verses 18–19. Interestingly, Vedānta Deśika uses the same image in his poem, *Dehalīśastuti.*

[14] Passageway/aisle.

(ii) Tirumaḻicai Āḻvār (Agpp/Mgpp)/*Mahadāhvaya Sūri* (DSC) vaibhavam

In the year named Siddhānta in the *Dvāpara yuga*, on a Sunday during the dark phase of the moon, under the Makha asterism in the month of Tai was born a son of the Ṛṣi Bhṛgu in the town of Mahisāra (Tamil Maḻicai) as a partial incarnation of the Lord's discus.

Bhṛgu, Vasiṣṭha and other sages went to Brahmā to ask him which the holiest spot on earth was, for them to meditate in. On the scales, Maḻicai tipped the balance against all other holy spots put together, and Bhṛgu *ṛṣi* began his penances there. Eventually, his wife (in the *Agpp*) gave birth, after a twelve month pregnancy, to a mass of flesh which she abandoned under a bamboo bush. In the *DSC* and *Mgpp* accounts, Indra, troubled by the sage's austerities sent an *apsarā* to disrupt his penance—and having successfully done so, the celestial damsel abandoned the fruit of the union—a mass of flesh, which eventually sprouted limbs and became a human child.

When the child cried from hunger, the lord graced him with his vision, satisfying it. Eventually, a childless hunter/bamboo-worker (*Mgpp/Agpp*) and his wife adopted the child which, being supremely detached due to innate knowledge, and having been fulfilled for all time by the grace of the lord, neither ate nor drank anything. Hearing of this miracle, an old, wise, childless *śūdra* accompanied by his wife began to bring an offering of milk for the baby every morning. Eventually, the child, divining their wishes, condescended to accept the offering. The couple drank the remainder themselves, acquired youth and in course of time, a son. This boy, Kaṉikaṇṇaṉ, became learned in all the *vidyās*, and dedicated himself to the service of the Āḻvār.

At the age of seven, the Āḻvār started *yogābhyāsa*. Over the next 400 years he learnt all that the *bāhya* (heterodox faiths, enumerated in the *Agpp* as Śākya, Ulūkya, Akṣapāda, Kṣapaṇa, Kapila and Patañjali) and the *kudṛṣṭi* (incorrect philosophies, including, in the *Agpp* text, Śaiva, Māyāvāda, Nyāya, Vaiseśikha, Bhaṭṭa and Prabhākara) *samayas* had to say, and discarded them all as useless. Deciding that the Śramaṇas knew nothing, the Bauddhas missed the truth, that the Śaivas were *alpa* (mean), and that these philosophies were transient took him, according to the *Agpp*, another 700 years. The *Mgpp* has the Āḻvār begin his meditation on Śrīyaḥpati Nārāyaṇa (Nārāyaṇa as the Lord of Śrī which subtly bolsters the Śrīvaiṣṇava understanding of the inseparability of the lord and his consort),[15] without this second interval, a meditation which lasts in both versions, another 700 years.

Once when Śiva and Pārvati were riding on their bull in the skies, the Āḻvār, engaged in sewing some rags, moved slightly to keep their shadow from falling on him. Impressed by his single-minded devotion, the divine couple alighted and Śiva offered the Āḻvār a boon. Though the Āḻvār was indifferent, on Śiva's pressing him, he asked for the grant of *mokṣa*—if he could. Śiva declared it beyond his powers. The Āḻvār then asked in jest that Śiva thread the needle he was using. Insulted, Śiva opened his third eye to let fire pour forth, but the Āḻvār opened one in his right toe which blinkered Śiva's own fire. The incendiary contest escalated rapidly. Finally, the enemy of Kāma acknowledged defeat and Viṣṇu sent down torrential rain to put out the conflagration.

Once, the three *mutal* Āḻvārs going on a pilgrimage were astonished at a divine light emanating from a cave. On approaching, they perceived Tirumaḻicai meditating within. Rejoicing at their meeting, they all meditated together awhile before the other three proceeded on their travels. Tirumaḻicai then left for Vĕhkā in Kāñcī where he spent another 700 years, while Kaṉikaṇṇaṉ attended to his needs. In time, a pious old woman took upon herself the task of keeping the place clean. Once, the Āḻvār opening his eyes, saw her and blessed her with unfading youth and divine beauty. The Pallavarāyaṉ (Pallava ruler)[16] who soon fell in love with and married her, asked her after some years how it was that she never aged. On learning her secret, he asked Kaṉikaṇṇaṉ to fetch his master so that he could revere him. On Kaṉikaṇṇaṉ's loftily refusing, for his master would go nowhere, nor be bid by anyone but the lord, the king banished him from his kingdom. The Āḻvār left with his disciple, asking the Lord of Vĕhkā as he did so, if he would stay where his devotee was not welcome. So, rolling up his serpent bed the lord, and following him, the populace of the town, left too. Trees dried up. The repentant king then

[15] See Chapter 3-ii of the present work.

[16] Noboru Karashima, Introduction, *History and Society in South India: The Colas to Vijayanagar*, New Delhi: Oxford University Press, 2001, p. xxi, mentions Pallavarāyaṉ among important official titles under the Coḻas. The twentieth century Śrīvaiṣṇava understanding of this has been 'Pallava king', especially as the early historians of south India knew the Kāñcī region to have been under the Pallavas during the presumed period of the *mutal* Āḻvārs. However, since these hagiographies were composed during the late Coḻa period when the term may have carried the meaning Karashima gives, it is possible that our sources may have been using this term in the latter sense. The analysis presented below is not affected by either usage.

came to the village the party had camped in for the night, and begging the Āḻvār's forgiveness, asked them to return. Back in Vĕhkā, the lord lay down again on the serpent Ananta, supporting his head now on his left hand to show that he had gone and come back. The lord in the temple is accordingly known by the names of Yathoktakāri (yathā+ukta+kāri, i.e. the one who did as told) and its Tamil equivalent, Cŏṉṉa-vaṇṇam-cĕyta Pĕrumāḷ.[17]

Tirumaḻicaip-pirāṉ then embarked on a pilgrimage to Kumbhakoṇam. En route, he passed the village of Pĕrumpuḷiyūr[18] where some *brāhmaṇas* were engaged in *Vedādhyāyana*, i.e. study of the Vedas. On seeing the *śūdra*, they abruptly stopped, but when they wished to resume after the Āḻvār had passed, they found that they could not recall the point in their recitation that they had stopped at. The priest in the temple saw the *arcā vigraha* turn its head to watch the progress of the Āḻvār down the village, and told the Vedic *brāhmaṇas* of it. Realizing their mistake, they begged his pardon for their *bhāgavata apacāra* (disrespect to a Viṣṇu worshipper). Tirumaḻicai wordlessly scratched a grain of black rice with his nail, and the *brāhmaṇas* remembered the phrase they had stopped at: '*kṛṣṇānām vrīhīnām nakhanirbhinnam*'.[19]

One of the *brāhmaṇas* desiring *yogaphala siddhi* took him to an assembly where a *yajña* was being performed, causing others to object to a *śūdra* being honoured. The Āḻvār then revealed the Sudarśana *cakra* (Viṣṇu's discus) enshrined in his chest, causing the wrongdoers to fall at his feet. Then the Āḻvār taught them that followers of Viṣṇu were always worthy of worship. Finally reaching Kuṭantai,[20] he worshipped Ārāvamutaṉ,[21] meditated in that most holy of *kṣetras* for 2,300 years, and recorded his experience in the *Nāṉmukaṉ Tiruvantādi* and the *Tiruccanta Viruttam.*

The *Agpp* and the *DSC* feature another small, but interesting anecdote.

[17] In the reclining posture, Viṣṇu invariably rests his head on his right hand. The peculiar iconography at Vĕhkā seems to have inspired this legend. The 'campsite' of the legend is a village known to date by the name Orirukkai, a contraction of *orurāvu irukkai*, i.e. 'one night's stay'. See Chapter 6-ii of the present work for discussion of the legend.

[18] Literally the *ūr* of the great tamarind tree.

[19] The words mean exactly what the Āḻvār's action indicated.

[20] Vaiṣṇava name for Kumbhakoṇam.

[21] Name of the lord in Kumbhakoṇam, meaning, 'nectar that never cloys/ satiates'. The lord is in a partially reclining posture here. The ten stanzas of Nammāḻvār (*Tiruvāymŏḻi*, 5.8.1–11) which Nāthamuni is supposed to have heard some pilgrims recite, and which inspired him to discover the rest, start with the word, 'Ārāvamutaṉ'.

In Kuṭantai, the Ā̲lvār is supposed to have asked the reclining lord which tiring cosmic act of His, He was resting after, and to speak 'even as He lay as though He was rising'[22]—an allusion to the image which is partly risen from the regular reclining posture. (The lord is said to have risen to answer the Ā̲lvār.)

(iii) *Kulaśekhara Ā̲lvār* vaibhavam

In an army camp in Kŏḷḷinagar[23] (*Agpp*)/Vañcikaḷam[24] (*Mgpp*)/ Kukkuṭakuṭa[25] (*DSC*), in the twenty-eighth year of *Kali yuga*, was born the hero Kulaśekhara in the royal Cera clan, as an *amṣa* of the Kaustubha, in the month of Māci under the Punarvāsu asterism, on the twelfth day of the bright half of the moon.

Having learnt all the arts of warfare, he conquered Kŏḷḷi, Kūṭal, Koḻi, and protected with his sharp lance, *bhāgavatas* and *sādhus* (religious mendicants). He delighted in hearing expositions of the *Rāmāyaṇa* and the *mahātmyas* of the various *divya deśas* (glories of the holy places of the lord), and grew indifferent to the pleasures of the palace. One day, while listening to a recital of the *Rāmāyaṇa*, he was distressed to think of Rāma having to face the 16,000-strong *rākṣasa* force alone, and impulsively summoned his fourfold army to set out to Rāma's help. His flustered advisors at once recited the next verse wherein Vaidehi (Sītā) embraces the victorious hero, thus healing all his battle wounds.

Another time, his ministers, annoyed with the king's partisanship towards *bhāgavatas*, hid the jewels of his *gṛha arcā*[26] and blamed the Śrīvaiṣṇavas for the theft. Refusing to believe ill of Śrīvaiṣṇavas, Kulaśekhara thrust his hand into a pot writhing with snakes, calling for his hand to be smote if the allegation were true. When his hand emerged unbitten, the frightened *mantrīs* confessed and craved pardon. The king was calmed, but life among those immersed in the ways of the world had become distasteful to him. He longed to live in Srirangam in the

[22] *Tiruccanta Viruttam* 61. The poet asks the lord if he is tired from lifting the earth (in his *avatāra* as a boar) or from traversing the worlds (as Trivikrama). However, we have seen that the ascription of this poem to Tirumaḻicai is questionable.

[23] Kŏlli is identified with Uraiyūr, near modern Srirangam.

[24] Vañcikalam is identified with modern Cranganore. Geographically, Vañcikalam and Kŏlli are fairly distant.

[25] Presumably Sanskritization of Kŏlli.

[26] Icon for domestic worship.

company of devotees of the lord. So he crowned his son king and left for Srirangam where he remained absorbed in contemplation of the lord. He recorded his experiences in the *Pĕrumāḷ Tirumŏḻi* and the (Sanskrit) *Mukundamālā*.[27]

The *DSC* has an interesting addition to this largely consistent narrative. It says that Kulaśekhara Āḻvār had a daughter, an *amśa* of Nīlādevi, (the third, Tamil spouse of the lord), whom he 'gave' to the lord of Srirangam along with all his wealth as dowry.

(iv) Pĕriyāḻvār vaibhavam

In the month of Āṉi under the Svāti asterism, 46 years after the beginning of the Kali *yuga*, on a *śukla ekādaśi* Sunday, was born, in a family of pure *muṉkuṭumi*[28] Vedic *brāhmaṇas* of the Veyar clan, in Śrīvilliputtūr, an *amśa* of Garuḍa. After learning the Vedas and *Vedāngas* of the *Yajurveda Śākhā*, Viṣṇucittar began to perform the *kainkarya* (service) of stringing flower garlands for the lord. He was especially devoted to the lord in his form as the baby Kṛṣṇa.

About this time, Vallabhadeva the ruler of Madurai, heard a religious man recite the following *śloka*: 'One must strive for eight months for a few months of rain, during the day for the night, for one's old age during youth and for the next life in this one'. He asked his priest, Cĕlva Nampi, for advice and was told to summon a *vidvat-goṣṭhi* (an assembly of scholars). The king did so after having a bag filled with gold hung up as *vidyā-śulka* (fee for learning) in the *sabhā maṇḍapa* of the palace. Many Vaiṣṇavas feared that the debate might reflect negatively on the glory of the Lord. Vaṭapĕrunkoyil-uṭaiyāṉ[29] appeared in Viṣṇucittar's dream and asked him to establish the identity of the supreme lord in the royal court

[27] The *Mukundamālā* is not included in the *Nālāyiram*; its authorship by the Āḻvār is also disputed.

[28] A *brāhmaṇa* clan where the men wear their hair in a top knot just above the forehead.

[29] The Lord of the Great Banyan Temple—so called because the Lord takes the form of Vaṭapatraśāyi, baby sleeping on a banyan leaf, there. Pĕriyāḻvār/ Viṣṇucittar was supposed to have been a priest of this temple. Interestingly, however, the actual representation of the deity in this temple is the familiar one of Viṣṇu reclining on Ananta—personal visit. Dennis Hudson, 'A New Year's Poem for Kṛṣṇa: The Tiruppallāṇṭu by Villiputtūr Viṣṇucittan ('Periyāḻvār')', *Journal of Vaishnava Studies*, vol. 7, no. 2, 1999, p. 100, explains this feature thus: 'Because each story of Vasudeva easily refers to all others, the reclining stucco icon in New Town [i.e. Villiputtūr] could be viewed as Madhusūdana; or as

and collect the reward. He appeared in Cĕlva Nampi's dream too, and the latte,r therefore, arranged for Pĕriyā̲lvār to be received with appropriate honour. This, however, angered the other *vidvāns* gathered and they prepared for a hair-splitting examination of Pĕriyā̲lvār's words. But as he expounded the *Puruṣasūkta* along with the *Smṛtis* and the *Purāṇas*, the prize bag tore itself and fell into his lap. Everyone present acknowledged the truth of his exposition and the Pāṇṭiya king bestowed upon him the title of Bhaṭṭar Pirā̲n,[30] had him seated on a caparisoned elephant and taken in procession to the accompaniment of musical instruments. Just as parents come to witness and rejoice in the success of their children, Ĕmpĕrumā̲n (the Lord) and his consort came riding on Garuḍa, like a cloud-laden golden mountain, to bless him for having established His supremacy in the world of men. Even as the Ā̲lvār worshipped the lord, he began to worry—like a father would about a ṣon—that He should have left his heavenly abode and come down to the world in this *Kali yuga*. Using the elephant's bell as cymbals for rhythm, he sang *mangalāśāsana* to Nārāyaṇa.[31]

Eventually, he returned to Villiputtūr and devoted himself to the lord's service, and growing increasingly attached to His *Kṛṣṇāvatāra*, sang his experiences of the Lord's *bāla-līlā* in the *Pĕriyā̲lvār Tirumŏ̲li*.

(v) Āṇḍāḷ vaibhavam

In Śrīvilliputtūr in the Pāṇṭiya land, Kotai was born in the month of Āsāḍha/Āṭi, in the *Pūrva phālguni* asterism, the fourth day of the waxing moon, on a Tuesday in the ninety-eighth year of *Kali yuga* called Nala.

The earth goddess in the form of a baby was discovered, we are told, by Pĕriyā̲lvār (literally, the Great Ā̲lvār), also called Viṣṇucitta, as he was digging the soil for a *tulasi* plant, even as Janaka discovered Sītā. She was named Curuppārkul̲al Kotai by her foster father. Viṣṇucitta, the priest of the temple of Vaṭapatraśāyi (the lord as a baby reclining on a banyan

Krishna growing up disguised as a cowherd; or as Mārkaṇḍeya's baby lying on the banyan branch in primordial Darkness'.

30 Prince among Bhaṭṭas/Lord of Bhaṭṭas (learned men). Pĕriyā̲lvār frequently signs himself thus.

31 This is the famous *Pallāṇṭu* hymn with which the *Nālāyira Divya Prabandham* opens wherein Pĕriyā̲lvār blesses the Lord, His consort and His appurtenances with everlasting glory. It seems, too, to be the model for numerous *mangalāśāsanas*, composed in both Sanskrit and Ṭamil, over the following centuries and which have become an integral part of Śrīvaiṣṇava worship in both domestic shrine and temple.

leaf), used to string flower garlands to offer the lord each day. As Kotai was growing up, bedecking herself in all her finery, she would try on the garlands in her father's absence, to see if she would make a fit bride for the lord, if he would accept her. Viṣṇucitta saw her in the act one day and was distressed that the offering to the lord had been polluted thus. That day he offered no garland, and craved the lord's pardon for having offended him unknowingly in the past. However, the lord appeared in Viṣṇucitta's dream to tell him that he preferred the garlands worn in and made fragrant by Kotai's hair. The Āl̠vār, her father, wondered if his daughter was Śrī, Bhūmidevi or Nappin̠n̠ai. She came henceforth to be known as Cūṭikŏṭutta Nācciyār, literally, the lady who gave the lord what she had worn.

Even as the *tulasi* plant is imbued with fragrance, the Nācciyār grew through the stages of infancy, childhood and youth with *para* bhakti, and *para jñāna* leading to *parama* bhakti. As she came of age, her attachment to the Lord grew so much that Kṛṣṇa *viraha* became intolerable to her. She then performed the Mārkal̠i *nompu*, a traditional vow performed by maidens during the month of December–January,[32] involving rising early in the morning, bathing in the river and abstaining not only from wrong-doing, but also from milk, ghee, decorating the hair with flowers, and lining the eyes with kohl. She then prayed to Kāma to grant her Kaṇṇan̠ (Tamil name for Kṛṣṇa).

As Āṇḍāḷ came of age, Pĕriyāl̠vār worried about her marriage even as Janaka had worried about Sītā's. Āṇḍāḷ, however, declared that she would not live to hear of her marriage with a mortal, and would look at none other than the Lord Māyan̠ of Tirumāliruñcolai.[33] The Āl̠vār then asked Āṇḍāḷ which of the 108 lords she would marry, and on her request, recited the specific glories of each of the lords.[34] The *DSC* account waxes eloquent at this point; in fact the verses—in the best style of Sanskrit flowery *kāvya*—that describe the beauty of a few temple towns and shrines, and the specific attributes of some of the 108 Viṣṇus, the love-yearnings of the lord and of Āṇḍāḷ for each other and their eventual marriage, constitute over two chapters of the eighteen that comprise the *DSC*.

[32] C. Minakshi, *Administration and Social Life under the Pallavas*, Madras: University of Madras, 1938, p. 204, says, 'The *pavai nombu* is equivalent to Katyayani *vratam*. The *pavai* represented Katyayani and was made of sand on the riverside'.

[33] An important temple of Viṣṇu on the outskirts of Madurai.

[34] Only a few shrines/gods are actually named and described.

Āṇḍāḷ finally decided to wed Aḻakiya Maṇavāḷaṉ, (the name of the *utsava mūrti* or processional idol at Srirangam; literally, the bridegroom-lord), a choice which won her father's approval. The lord relieved the Āḻvārs' worry about how the marriage was to be accomplished by appearing in his dream to tell him of his acceptance. The lord then sent his attendants to Śrīvilliputtūr with fitting paraphernalia, to bring the bridal party to Srirangam. Āṇḍāḷ was carried in a covered palanquin to the accompaniment of music and chants of praise. On reaching Srirangam, she feasted her eyes on the beauty of the lord, and pressing the coils of the serpent bed of the lord, she climbed up, and in front of the astonished eyes of all including the Pāṇṭiya king, disappeared into the lord. The lord graciously announced that the Āḻvār was now his father-in-law, even as was the king of the milk-ocean,[35] and presented him with all the due honours. Then bidding the lord farewell, Pĕriyāḻvār returned to Śrīvilliputtūr with a father's sadness over the parting.

I must point out at this juncture, a curious, but frequent collation of the names of the processional idol and the *mūla mūrti*, the immovable icon, made often of stone, though occasionally of other materials like stucco, or even wood. While it is Aḻakiya Maṇavāḷaṉ that Āṇḍāḷ is said to have chosen to marry and, indeed, upon whom she gazed, on finally arriving at Srirangam, it is the *mūlavar*, Ranganātha/Pĕriya Pĕrumāḷ, who in this instance is not named, who reclines on a serpent bed, and into whom she presumably merged. The Śrīvaiṣṇava tradition recognizes both the distinct individuality and the identity of the two, i.e. *mūlavar* and *utsavar*, even as it recognizes the identity and distinctiveness of the Viṣṇus of the different shrines. I shall explore the implications of the same in a later chapter.

The *DSC* has an additional section on Āṇḍāḷ's *viraha* where she is described as wasting away with secret love for the lord.[36] 'Was not the *kankaṇa*[37] he took from Bali as Vāmana sufficient for him that he now covets my *kangana* (bracelet)? Why does he who crossed the sea as Rāghava for Janaka-Nandini not think of me? He dived in the ocean to rescue the earth, does he not see me drowning in the ocean of sorrow now?' A *sakhi* finally induces her to share her secret and, learning that it is the lord she has lost her heart to, draws the pictures of the 108 lords. Āṇḍāḷ

[35] According to Puranic mythology, Śrī, the consort of Viṣṇu, is believed to be the daughter of the Ocean of Milk.

[36] *DSC, sargaḥ* 10, verses 52–84.

[37] The Hindi translation glosses this as a drop of water.

lowers her face in shyness on seeing the picture of Ranganātha.[38] Finally, the *DSC* account makes some interesting connections with the lives of some other Āḻvārs. In the *svayamvara*, which is located in Kurukāpuri (the birthplace of Nammāḻvār), all the Āḻvārs except Nammāḻvār and Tirumankai/Parakālaṉ take part as uncles of the bride, being as it were, brothers of her father due to their kinship through the lord. The Āḻvārs then praise Śaṭhakopa, hear his *prabandhas* and recite theirs and Godā's[39] to him. Sages and celestials arrive for the wedding as do the 108 Viṣṇus. Śaṭhakopa then asks Godā to make her choice, announcing the suitors, '40 gods from Coladeśa, 18 from Pāṇḍyadeśa, 13 from Keraladeśa, 22 from Toṇḍir, 2 from the Madhyadeśa and 11 from the north.'

(vi) Tŏṇṭaraṭippŏṭi Āḻvār vaibhavam

In the 289th year of *Kali yuga* called *Prabhava varṣa*, on a Tuesday under the Keṭṭai asterism of the *kṛṣṇa caturdaśi* (fourteenth day of the dark half of the lunar cycle) in the month of Mārkali, was born in Maṇṭankuṭi, an *amśa* of the lord's garland in a *brāhmaṇa* family of the *Yajurveda śākhā.*

Named Vipranārāyaṇa, the boy soon learnt all the Vedas and *Vedāngas*, and being deeply devoted to Aḻakiya Maṇavāḷaṉ, started performing the *kainkarya* (service) of weaving and offering flower garlands for the lord of Srirangam everyday. One day, as he was engaged in his usual task of tending to his flower garden, a beautiful *varastrī/devastrī* named Devadevi rested awhile with her friends in the bower, and was surprised at his complete indifference to her. The *Mgpp* adds that Vipranārāyaṇa was so detached from worldly affairs that Pirāṭṭi (the divine consort) asked the lord if he could ever be interested in material things. The lord, in sport, decided to make him attached to sensory objects and sent Devadevi with her friends to his garden. Piqued at his indifference, Devadevi laid a wager with her friend that she would enslave the man within 6 months. She cast off her rich jewels, and in the garb of a simple woman, she approached the *brāhmaṇa* and asked to be allowed to share in the service to the lord. After six months, during which she worked beside Vipranārāyaṇa, weeding and watering the plants, there was a heavy downpour. Upon Vipranārāyaṇa inviting her into his cottage for shelter, she seduced him, making him lose himself entirely in her. From this moment, he lived only for the pleasure of her embraces and

38 Rather inconsistently, this section follows Pĕriyāḻvār's recital of the 108 Viṣṇus and Āṇḍāḷ's asking him how she could obtain Ranganātha for husband.

39 *DSC*'s Sanskrit spelling of Tamil 'Kotai'.

forgot his dharma, spending all he had on her. Devadevi (predictably) abandoned him when he ran out of wealth, but Vipranārāyaṇa, unable to bear separation from her, lay unconscious in the street outside her door. The lord and his consort passing by saw this, and the goddess asked her husband to restore their devotee to his former self.[40] Accordingly, the lord arrived at Devadevi's door carrying the golden water-pot used for the deity's ablutions, and giving his name as Aḻakiya Maṇavāḷaṉ,[41] said he had brought her a gift from Vipranārāyaṇa. Delighted, Devadevi welcomed her distraught lover back. The next morning, however, the temple functionaries discovered the theft and reported the matter to the king. The vessel was soon traced and Vipranārāyaṇa was accused. After a suitable interval in which he protested his innocence, and came to repent his long folly, the lord appeared in the king's dream (*Agpp*)/spoke *arcaka mukhena* (through the temple priest) (*Mgpp*) that he himself was responsible for the deed, and had Vipranārāyaṇa punished in order to cleanse him of his accumulated karma. The Āḻvār went back to stringing *Tirumālai*[42] for the lord with steadfast devotion and became a servant of the servants of the lord.[43]

(vii) Tiruppāṇāḻvār vaibhavam

In the month of Kārttikai, on the second day of the dark phase of the moon in the Rohiṇi asterism, a Wednesday, in the year 343 of *Kali yuga* was born an *amśa* (part *avatāra*) of the Śrīvatsa (Viṣṇu's chest mark), in Uraiyūr. Beyond this, since the *DSC*, *Agpp* and *Mgpp* accounts differ rather drastically on major points, three separate retellings are in order.

Along with the other details of the birth, the *Agpp* adds that the Āḻvār was born in the *pañcama varga*, i.e. as an outcaste. It then continues the 'Tiruppāṇāḻvār *vaibhavam*' by telling us that the lord bestowed his grace upon the newborn child, filling him with *sattvaguṇa* (pure qualities). It quotes next, a story from the *Kaiśika Purāṇa* where a bard, Nampāṭuvār, of TirukKurunkuṭi, was spared by a bloodthirsty *brahma-rākṣasa* (a demon

[40] Both the *Mgpp* and *Agpp* feature this intercession by the goddess, but the *Agpp* labours the point. See Chapter 3–iv of the present work.

[41] This is the name of the processional deity in the Srirangam temple. Many ordinary folk would have been named after the lord, as they still are.

[42] *Mālai* means garland; *Tirumālai* is also the title of one of Tŏṇṭaraṭippŏṭi's compositions.

[43] The name Tŏṇṭaraṭippŏṭi means 'dust of the feet of devotees'; this is how the Āḻvār signs the *Tirumālai* and the *Tiruppaḷḷiyĕḻucci.*

who was a *brāhmaṇa* in a previous birth) for singing songs in praise of Viṣṇu. After further likening him to Nārada for his proficiency in music, the *Agpp* tells us that the Āḻvār never stepped inside the area between the rivers Kaveri and Kŏḷḷiṭam as befitted his caste. Rather, he stayed on the southern bank of the southern river, in front of the *ghāt* facing the shrine, and sang the lord's praise with *vīṇai* (lute) in hand. Just as the lord was himself drawn to Bhīṣma when the latter lay on his bed of arrows meditating on him, Pĕriya Pĕrumāḷ himself was attracted to the Āḻvār.

At this point, some manuscripts add that the goddess asked her consort how he could allow his *bhakta* to stay out thus. The lord agreed, but when he called him, the Āḻvār refused because of his humility and low birth. As the Āḻvār was engaged in meditating on the lord one morning, a temple priest named Lokasārangamuni brought the pot for the lord's ablution waters to the river. Seeing the outcaste, he commanded him to remove himself, but the god-absorbed Āḻvār didn't hear. Lokasārangamuni flung a stone, drawing blood from the Āḻvār's face, and rousing him. The Āḻvār, profoundly sorry for having distressed a *bhāgavata* (worshipper of Viṣṇu), went away. After having duly bathed and ritually recited the daily prayers—the *nityakarmānuṣṭhānam*—the priest carried the water pot back to the temple with all the paraphernalia of umbrella, fly-whisk, drums and instruments. In his shrine, the lord was deeply disturbed that his *bhakta* should have suffered so. Pirāṭṭi (literally, the lady) too added that the bard so intimate to them could not be allowed to suffer, or remain outside. When Lokasārangamuni entered, the lord closed the doors of his shrine and remonstrated with him in private.

This episode, very central in popular retelling of the Āḻvārs' lives, is apparently not found in some manuscripts,[44] which simply state that the lord appeared in the priest's dream and instructed him to bring the bard to him on his shoulders.

Lokasārangamuni came to the bathing *ghāt* where *brāhmaṇas* bathed, and bowing to Tiruppāṇāḻvār praying at a respectful distance, conveyed the lord's message. The Āḻvār protested that having been born in a caste outside of the four castes, and having no redeeming personal qualities himself, he could not place his feet in the hallowed grounds of Srirangam. The priest then asked him to climb onto his shoulders; the Āḻvār obeying the lord's bidding did so. Thus, he carried the Āḻvār into the presence of Aḻakiya Maṇavāḷaṉ just as *ādivāhakan*, the primordial carrier/vehicle, transports souls across Vaitaraṇi, the river of forgetfulness, to the lord's

[44] *Agpp*, p. 65. The editor specifies that this is found only in some manuscripts.

abode, Vaikuṇṭha. The Āl̲vār then drank in the beauty of the lord—which is described in the hagiography through quotations of Sanskrit verses and from hymns of other Āl̲vārs—beginning with his sacred feet, and poured out his overflowing love in a beautiful poem of ten stanzas beginning with the phrase (and hence called the) *Amalan̲ādipirān̲*—the flawless, primordial lord. As he was singing thus, the lord absorbed into himself the Āl̲vār in his bodily form, even as those who wear fragrant roots in their hair do so with the mud sticking to it.

In the *Mgpp* version, a baby abandoned in the fields was found by a childless couple who, despite being performers of good deeds, were born in the *caṇḍāla* caste due to misdeeds in previous lives. They brought the child up on cow's milk, so that the (future) Āl̲vār would be unpolluted by the consumption of impure foods. As soon as he began to speak, he began to sing praises of the lord to the accompaniment of the *vīṇai*. His upbringing in a *caṇḍāla* family prevented him from entering the temple; following custom therefore, he stayed at the banks of the Kaveri, focusing on the lord.

Pĕriya Pĕrumāḷ, pleased by his devotion, instructed Lokasārangamuni in a dream to fetch the Āl̲vār to him on his shoulders. When the priest approached the devotee with the lords' instruction, the Āl̲vār replied that he was of an unapproachable caste and unfit to enter the sacred shrine. Interestingly, the text even adds that he said this for the hearing of common folk lost in crass customs! While the rest of the tale is similar to the *Agpp*'s, the *Mgpp* pronounces that even if one is pure by birth, one must follow the customs of the world, and gives the example of Kṛṣṇa who grew up among cowherds—that it became apparent when the young Kṛṣṇa went to the sage Sāndipani for Vedic learning, that he was a cowherd only by upbringing, and not by birth.

The brief *DSC* account[45] says that the child born in an *antima kula* (last caste), never even cried, but was ever immersed in singing the lord's praises with *vīṇā* in hand, on the southern bank of the Kaveri. Pāṇanātha Sūri[46] was superior to even a devotee of yore called Kaiśika who had been born in the *svapaca jāti*. Lakṣmī and her lord rejoiced at his singing without thought of sleep till Lakṣmī asked that their devotee be brought close to them. The lord then commanded Lokasārangamuni/Śuka to do so, and the Āl̲vār, carried despite his protests on the *muni*'s shoulders into his presence, sang of the glory of the lord from toe to head.

[45] *DSC*, *sargaḥ* 7, verses 18-28.

[46] Sanskritized name of Tiruppāṇāl̲vār.

(viii) Tirumankai Āḻvār vaibhavam

In the 398th year of *Kali yuga*, on a Thursday, in the month of Kārtika, under the Kṛttika asterism, on a *purṇimā*,[47] was born in TiruvĀli-TiruNagari, to Nīlan̲, a man of the fourth *varṇa* (*Mgpp*)/*mleccha varṇa* (*Agpp*)/*śūdra* (*DSC*), an *amśa* of Śārnga, Viṣṇu's bow. The child was named Nīla-nirattar (blue-complexioned).

The boy became proficient in *dhanuṣa śastra*, his *kula vidyā* (the art of warfare which was the traditional art of his clan) and was appointed an *adhikāri*[48] (official), by the Coḻa king. With the support of four loyal followers, one of whom could walk on water (Nīrmel Naṭappān̲), another who cast no shadow/whose stepping on the shadow of a person rendered the latter powerless (Niḻalai Mitippān̲), a third who could blow locked doors open (Tolūtuvān̲), the fourth who could argue endlessly (Tola Vaḷakkan̲), and his horse, Āṭalmā, he was invincible.

Meanwhile, in TiruvĀlināḍu, an incarnation of an *apsarā* (*Agpp*)/*divya kanyā* (*DSC*)/*amśa* of Bhūmi (*Mgpp*), appeared as a baby girl in a lotus pond, and was adopted by a devout Vaiṣṇava *vaidya* of TiruNānkūr. Here the *Agpp* gives a long story of her previous life and the curse which caused her to take human form, including her predestination to be the wife of Parakālan̲.[49] The baby girl was named Kumudavalli on account of her having been found in a tank of *kumuda* flowers. When she reached marriageable age, her father began to worry, especially as her *kula-gotra* were unknown. Parakālan̲ heard of her immense beauty and approached her parents for her hand, bringing suitable presents of clothes and jewellery. Her father was agreeable, but the girl said that she had vowed to marry only a true *bhāgavata*, who would moreover pledge to feed a thousand Vaiṣṇavas everyday. The love-smitten Parakālan̲ thereupon went immediately to the sacred spot of Tirunaraiyūr[50] where he received the *pañcasamskāra*, i.e. got himself branded with the marks of Viṣṇu, the *śankha, cakra*, etc.[51] Following his marriage to Kumudavalli, he engaged himself in feeding Nārāyaṇa's devotees everyday, using up the

[47] Full moon day.

[48] Inscriptions show that the *adhikārī* was an important official in the state administration. See Karashima, op. cit., Introduction, p. xxi.

[49] The *DSC*'s name for Tirumankai Āḻvār meaning 'death to his enemies'; the *Mgpp* and *Agpp* also frequently refer to him by this name.

[50] Tirumankai devotes 100 stanzas in the *Pĕriya Tirumŏḻi* to Tirunaraiyūr.

[51] The *sthalapurāṇa* of TiruNaraiyūr also claims that it was the Lord of Naraiyūr, Tirunaraiyūr-Nampi/Śrīnivāsa/Vyūha Vāsudeva, who gave Tirumankai the *pañcasamskāras* and converted him to Vaiṣṇavism. See A. Etirajan, *108 Vaiṇava*

royal funds given in his keeping for this task. Hearing of it, the Co<u>l</u>a king summoned him, but Parakālan̲ simply fobbed off the messenger with an excuse. The commander of the royal forces was then despatched with infantry, cavalry, elephant corps and chariots, but Kalikan̲r̲i,[52] mounted on his Āṭalmā, managed to completely ravage the Co<u>l</u>a army. The king himself came to battle next and was similarly dealt with. The DSC, in true *kāvya* style, expends dozens of verses in descriptions of the battle and the heroism of the combatants, while the *Agpp* tells us that the *jagadeka dhanurdharan̲* (the foremost archer of the world) churned the king's forces as the *devas* and *asuras* had of yore churned the mount Mandara in the ocean. Finally, the Co<u>l</u>a ruler, pretending to be impressed by Parakālan̲'s valour, accepted defeat and invited him to the court where he imprisoned him by deceit. He also asked the Ā<u>l</u>vār to make good the losses he had inflicted on the royal treasury. Being unable now to feed Śrīvaiṣṇavas everyday, the Ā<u>l</u>vār too began to fast.

Moved, Lord Varadarāja (≈Peraruḷāḷar) of Kāñcī appeared in the Ā<u>l</u>vār's dream and said that he had a great treasure in Kāñcī to enable Parakālan̲ to pay off his debts. (Some manuscripts of the *Agpp* say that Parakālan̲ was imprisoned without food in the *devālaya* [temple] of Tirunaraiyūr.)[53] The distressed Nācciyār (goddess) told Nampi (here, the lord) that they could not let their son starve so,[54] and induced him to intervene—yet another instance of the mediation of the goddess which, we will see, is a central tenet of Śrīvaiṣṇavism. When the Ā<u>l</u>vār told the Co<u>l</u>a *rājā* of his dream, he was allowed to go to Kāñcī under escort. The lord there revealed to him substantial wealth, out of which he gave the royal servants the king's due, and then re-engaged himself in the service of feeding Śrīvaiṣṇavas. Back in the Co<u>l</u>a court, when his servants recited the miraculous tale to the king, he repented, recognized the Ā<u>l</u>vār's greatness, and himself employed the funds obtained for feeding devotees of the lord. Meanwhile, Parakālan̲ rapidly ran through the treasure. Since he could not discontinue feeding *bhāgavatas*, he took

---

Divya Deśa Stala Varaḷāru, Vaiṇava Siddhānta Nūrpatippuk Ka<u>l</u>akam, Kāraikkuṭi, 2003, pp. 108–15.

[52] Destroyer of Kali, yet another name of Tirumankai Ā<u>l</u>vār.

[53] The *Agpp* text I used specifies that another version holds so. Also, in *Pĕriya Tirumŏ<u>l</u>i*, verses 6.6.1–9, Tirumankai says that the valorous Co<u>l</u>a ruler Cĕmpiyan̲ Koccĕnkaṇān̲ worships at the temple here.

[54] Again, the *sthalapurāṇa* of Tirunaraiyūr claims this for the goddess enshrined in that temple, which is also called Nācciyār Koyil. See Etirajan, op. cit., pp. 108–15.

to highway robbery—a sort of Robin Hood plundering non-Vaiṣṇavas to feed Vaiṣṇavas. Here the *DSC* comes into its own, describing with great relish and gore, the numerous successes of the hunter-saint, but adds a curious caveat—apparently, Parakāla Sūri only killed *hinsak mṛga* (violent/carnivorous beasts)! The lord, seeing his single-minded devotion, decided to bestow His special grace on the Āḻvār. He appeared with his consort and retinue in the forest disguised as a bridegroom and his party. In the *Agpp* version, Kaliyaṉ[55] succeeded in removing the jewellery of the party, except for the lord's ring which was too tight to be removed. It was when he tried to pull it off with his teeth that he realized that this was the great Lord himself. According to the *Mgpp*, Parakālaṉ stashed the loot in a box which, however, proved impossible to lift. Suspecting the workings of magic, he asked for the spell that would move the box. The lord then whispered the *Aṣṭākṣaram* in his ear and the enlightened Āḻvār performed *śaraṇāgati* at the feet of the divine couple. The lord favoured the Āḻvār with his *divya mangala vigraha* (transcendental auspicious form) and then advised him to journey to all the *divya deśas*. Tirumankai-maṉṉaṉ did so and sang of his experiences in the six *prabandhas*, viz., the *Pĕriya Tirumŏḻi*, *Tirukkuruntāṇṭakam*, *Tirunĕṭuntāṇṭakam*, *Tiruvĕḻukūṟṟirukkai*, *Ciriya Tirumaṭal* and the *Pĕriya Tirumaṭal*, which are the six *angas* of the four Vedas.[56]

While in the *Agpp* and the *Mgpp* accounts, this incident is integral to the account of Tirumankai Āḻvār, the *DSC* makes the wedding party that of Ranganātha and Āṇḍāḷ's. In fact, it suspends the account of Parakāla Sūri midway, launches into that of Pĕriyāḻvār and Āṇḍāḷ, and returns to Parakāla at the end of the latter, with his robbing the bridal procession of Āṇḍāḷ's and the lord. One could almost say that the narratives of Pĕriyāḻvār and Āṇḍāḷ are an inset within the Parakāla Sūri *vaibhava*.

After he had journeyed to the north and south, he reached KāḻicCīrāma Viṇṇagaram,[57] where his titles, Kaliyaṉ, Ālināṭan (Lord of Āli), Aruḷmāri (Rain-cloud of Grace), Kŏṟṟavel-Parakālaṉ (Sharp-speared One who is Death to his Enemies), Kŏnku-malar-kuḻaliyar-vel (Lover of Women with Fragrant-Flower-Adorned Hair), Mankai-ventaṉ (Conqueror of Mankai), Parakālaṉ, Paravādi-matta-gaja (a Destructive Elephant to other Doctrines) and Nālu-kavi-p-pĕrumāḷ (master of the four kinds of

[55] Warrior, yet another name of Tirumankai Āḻvār.

[56] In the Śrīvaiṣṇava understanding, Nammāḻvār's four *prabandhas* are considered the Tamil equivalent of the four Vedas, and Tirumankai's *prabandhas* the *Vedāngas*.

[57] Modern Cīrkāḻi, said also to be the birthplace of Tirujñāṉa-Sambandar.

poetics) were announced.[58] The followers of the Nāyaṉār Tirujñāṉa-Sambandar opposed the last saying that no one could announce himself with that title where Sambandar[59] was present. The Āḻvār's disciples challenged Sambandar to debate with their master. But the Āḻvār's own speech could not flower in that town which, being entirely Śaiva then,[60] had not a single Bhagavat *vigraha*. Finally, spotting a Vaiṣṇava woman, Tirumankai asked her for her *arcā vigraha*. A battle of skills between the Āḻvār and Sambandar ensued. The latter composed a verse which the Āḻvār pointed out as being faulty. He, in his turn, sang a hymn in seven divisions that could be arranged as a chariot[61] and left Sambandar speechless. I shall reproduce a little further below the *DSC* version, which differs significantly from the Maṇipravāḷa *Guruparamparās*.

The Āḻvār proceeded to Srirangam to worship the reclining lord therein and found the temple in sad disrepair. In order to obtain money for the task of renovation, he decided to plunder the Buddhist *vihāra* in Nāgapaṭṭinam which was fabled to possess a golden image of the Buddha. While the *Mgpp* restricts itself to saying that he managed—with the help of his four remarkable companions—to steal the idol, melt it and use the money to fortify the third *prākāra* (rampart/enclosure wall) and build

[58] Interestingly, Tirumankai Āḻvār who usually signs himself with one or two titles, uses a number of titles including most of above (excepting Paravādi-matta-gaja and and Nālu-kavi-pĕrumāḷ), and also Araṭṭa-mukki (He who Subdues the Wicked) and Aṭaiyār-Cīyam (Lion to His Opponents) in the decad devoted to KāḻicCīrāma Viṇṇagaram, *Pĕriya Tirumŏḻi*, 3.4.10.

[59] The *DSC* calls him Trikavi, which is not a generally known name for Sambandar. Nor are his Śaiva followers or his own devotion to Śiva mentioned. The identification is made possible because of the correspondence with the accounts of the *Agpp* and the *Mgpp* and from the reference to his having 'drunk the milk of Girijā'—a popular episode of the Nāyaṉār's life story. Here as elsewhere, it gives preference to poetics, depending on a prior understanding of its content, which might suggest that it was addressing an audience familiar with most of the tales recounted in it.

[60] KāḻicCīrāma-Viṇṇagaram, known today as Cīrkāḻi, is the birthplace of the Nāyaṉār Sambandar. While it is better known for its Śiva temple, there also are eleven Vaiṣṇava *divya kṣetras* in the vicinity, situated very close to each other. In fact, all eleven shrines have *divya kṣetra* status owing to Tirumankai's hymns alone.

[61] The reference is to the *Tiruvĕḻukūṟṟirukkai*, one of the six *prabandha*s attributed to Tirumankai Āḻvār; it does not bear his signature. The only sacred centre mentioned in this composition is Kuṭantai. It is surprising that the *ācāryas*, usually so careful in their elaboration of the hymnal material, should have decided to locate the composition of this poem in Cīrkāḻi.

the fourth *prākāra* of the temple, the *Agpp* and the *DSC* give delightfully colourful accounts of the expedition.

Upon reaching Nāgapaṭṭinam and finding that the idol's hiding place was a secret known to none but the goldsmith who had fashioned the statue, Tirumankai, disguised as a Buddhist, proceeded with his accomplices to the goldsmith's house. There he began to lament that the Muslims had destroyed the town and abstracted the idol of the Buddha. The dismayed goldsmith, who wondered aloud how they could have reached the secret cellar where the idol was fastened under the *vimāna* with a chain to the façade of a water spout outside, was tricked thus into betraying its location. When the Āḻvārs' party entered this secret sanctum, the gold idol perceiving the impending theft, bemoaned its being made of such a precious metal. In the *DSC* version, the other icons started to proclaim their own unworthiness as being made of base metals and to point to the gold idol as the only one fit to steal. Interestingly, it adds that the Buddha perceiving that it was the gold which had brought this fate upon him, left the idol as a bee flies from a plucked flower.[62]

The *Agpp* account credits this distinctly daredevil Āḻvār with yet another fraud during the course of his short sojourn in Nāgapaṭṭinam. Having learnt the idol's whereabouts from the goldsmith (and with time to spare till it grew dark enough for the robbery, presumably), Tirumankai and his four companions went to the seashore where they asked a ship-owner to take them aboard his ship. This merchant, Dharmavāṉ, was carrying a load of arecanuts. Once aboard the ship, Tirumankai asked for half a betel nut, which the hospitable merchant naturally proffered. Then he asked the merchant to accept that half *a*[63] betel nut in the ship was his. Needless to say, he got the same written down carefully, and once back ashore, demanded that half *the* cargo on the ship belonged to him.[64] Lamenting his 'debt of a previous life', the hapless merchant parted with half the profits from the sale of the betel nuts.

In the *DSC*, the episode of Tirumankai's meeting with Sambandar is narrated after the expedition to Nāgapaṭṭinam to rob the *vihāra*. Parakālaṉ's having become renowned for his victory over the Buddhists, the boy Nāyaṉār Sambandar surrounded by people singing his praises,

[62] *DSC, sargaḥ* 14, verse 47.

[63] English syntax unlike Tamil demands an article here; the choice of one of the two articles, 'a' or 'the' gives the pun away.

[64] This episode has given rise to a popular proverb in Tamil. Literally, 'Half the betel nut in the ship is mine', to ridicule one who claims to have contributed much more than he/she actually has to a spot of work.

set forth from Kālipura[65] to meet Parakāla. But when he saw Parakāla himself approaching, he promptly dismounted from his horse and inquired about his welfare. He then invited Parakāla into the town and expressed his desire to hear the latter's compositions. Parakāla, however, replied that he would not enter a town where there was no image of Viṣṇu whereupon Trikavi disclosed that the town had indeed had an ancient temple of the lord which the *avaidikas* had destroyed. The Lord of Kālinagara was ever since being worshipped by an *arcaka* in his dwelling. Parakāla accordingly entered the town and sang of the lord of the place in a remarkable composition called the Saptavati[66] impressed by which Sambandar composed a poem in praise of the Āḻvār.[67] Parakāla left Kālinagara after making arrangements for the ruined Viṣṇu temple to be renovated.

Two very popular episodes[68] of the unscrupulous Āḻvār's eventful 'life' are surprisingly not found in the *Mgpp*. The Buddhists of Nāgapaṭṭinam, on discovering the theft, traced the Āḻvār's party by their footsteps all the way to Srirangam, where, with their proof and the backing of the king, they demanded their idol back. The Āḻvār who had already begun to melt parts of the idol and sell them gave them a written commitment that he would return 'even the little finger' of the idol after a year. After precisely a year, the Buddhists returned, to be given, not surprisingly, a little finger of gold. The Buddhists did take the case to officials for judgement, but the Āḻvār's promissory note was well worded, besides which, he had as we saw at the outset, the support of an indefatigable disputant! The *DSC* adds some other interesting details that are recounted separately below.

Another time, when the labourers engaged in the construction project asked for their wages, Parakālan promised to pay them on the other bank of the river. Reasoning that even a *pāpa* performed for the lord's service

[65] K.A.N. Sastri, *The Cōḻas*, Madras: University of Madras, 1935–7, p. 636 reads this as Ālinagar, Tirumankai's hometown. However, it can be easily identified with KāḻicCīrāma Viṇṇagaram, Sambandar's hometown. Indeed, the *DSC* offers an explanation of a close translation of the latter Tamil place name: since Rāma had rested here briefly on his way to Lanka, it was called Rāmaviyat-pura (*DSC, sargaḥ* 14, verse 94).

[66] See footnote 63 above.

[67] *DSC, sargaḥ* 14, verses 89–99.

[68] I have frequently heard these episodes retold with chuckles, but without any disapproval.

becomes a *puṇya*,[69] he had the boat carrying all the hopeful workers sunk midstream.[70] Later he told the outraged families that their grief was misplaced as their drowned loved ones had all earned the blessed feet of the lord.[71]

Each of the three accounts relates different stories before concluding the section on this very colourful saint. The *DSC* tells us of his returning to his wife Kumudavalli, to apprise her of his numerous adventures. She, along with her father, then entered the pond wherefrom she had first emerged. Seeing them both ascending heavenwards in a jewelled chariot, Parakāla retired to the service of Ranganātha before finally entering perfect *samādhi*.[72] The *DSC* makes an oblique reference to an important episode which, strangely, is mentioned only in the otherwise concise *Mgpp*. Its omission from the *Agpp* is curious as the narrative explicates the origins of a ritual performed predominantly by the Tĕn̲kalai sect at Srirangam.

(a) An episode from the Parakāla Sūri vaibhavam *in the* DSC

The *Divya Sūri Caritam* account, while less involved in the controversies between the Tĕn̲kalai and Vaṭakalai sects, seems to be more deeply disputatious with regard to non-Vaiṣṇava, and especially, 'heterodox' faiths. Thus, when the Tamil hagiographies close their accounts with the Āl̲vār's success in procuring the image, the *DSC* elaborates the legal dispute that ensued when the Buddhists returning after a year to claim their property against the promissory note, got a mere finger of gold. The Buddhists are said to have dragged Parakāla to the king of Niculāpuri[73] who was displeased with him and feared that his kingdom would not prosper (if he allowed injustice). Parakāla, however, convinced him that no sin incurred on one who destroyed an image in a temple established by non-Vedic means. When the king countered that it was the lord who had appeared in an *avatāra* as the Buddha, Parakāla agreed that he had

[69] *DSC, sargaḥ* 14, verse 78.

[70] The two branches of the Kaveri circling Srirangam are called Kaveri and Kŏḷḷiṭam; the latter translates into 'the site of robbery'.

[71] Eternal service at the lord's feet is the ideal destination for the soul.

[72] *DSC, sargaḥ* 14, verses 100–3.

[73] Site of Uttamar Koyil, one of the Vaiṣṇava *divya deśas*, just outside Tiruccirāppaḷḷi.

indeed done so, in order to destroy the *maṇḍala* of Tripurāsura.[74] The lord, he stated, inheres in everything even as oil inheres in *tila* (sesame seed). Further, the relationship of the lord to *Vedabāhya mata*, i.e. faiths outside the pale of the *Vedas*, was as that of a household fire to a corpse and of a menstruating mother to a son. The lord, Parakāla continued, had said that those who worship him in temples made by non-Vedic means disobey his command[75]—a rare (and significant) display of assertion indeed, from an otherwise easy-going and forgiving god! Finally, Parakāla engaged in debate with the Buddhists and routed them using the sharp weapons of pure *śāstra*.[76]

(b) An incident from the Parakāla Sūri vaibhavam *in the* DSC[77]

Once on his way to Venkaṭam, Parakāla and his retinue were hungry and thirsty. At that time they encountered an old Vaiṣṇava who bore on his forehead the *ūrdhva puṇḍra*, or mark of Viṣṇu. Parakā̱la asked him if he could tell him from his holy books what destiny held for him, and to give them what food he had on his person. (Evidently, the Āl̲vār had no scruples about depriving a Vaiṣṇava of food if he himself was hungry!) The old Vaiṣṇava, who was Viṣṇu himself in disguise, told him that his future would be *harimaya* (filled with the lord), and then distributed the delicious food he was carrying to the Āl̲vār's party—a mere handful each of which satisfied them entirely. Parakāla then asked the *brāhmaṇa* who he was. Here the text says significantly, 'Since the Lord is always in the *vaśa*, bondage, of Vaiṣṇavas, He gladly answered.'[78] Thus, the *brāhmaṇa* replied that he was a resident of western Kāñcī, by the name of Aṣṭabāhu Narasimha,[79] and so saying, vanished.

[74] The reference is unclear; it is Śiva who is supposed to have destroyed Tripurāsura. Not only are no Vaiṣṇava associations known, these hagiographies come too late in the day for the Hari-Hara amalgam that is seen occasionally in the hymns (*Mutal Tiruvantādi* 5, *Mūn̲rām Tiruvantādi* 63, *Tiruvāymŏl̲i* 1.3.7, etc.), where the deeds of both gods are praised, Śiva being seen as a manifestation of Nārāyaṇa, and his glories, therefore, devolving on the latter.

[75] *DSC*, *sargaḥ* 14, verses 79–86.

[76] *DSC*, *sargaḥ* 14, verse 87.

[77] *DSC*, *sargaḥ* 14, verses 6–16.

[78] *DSC*, *Sargaḥ* 14, verse 12.

[79] The reference is to a *divya kṣetra* in Kāñcī, that of Aṣṭabhujasvāmi, where the lord is imaged with eight arms.

(c) *An episode from Parakāla Sūri* vaibhavam *in the* DSC

Hearing the *stotras* of Parakāla, the lord grew eager to hear the songs of Śaṭhakopa.[80] Accordingly, he sent summons to the *divyasūri* (the Āḻvār) through his *parijanas* with all the appropriate honours such as sandal paste and garlands. Śrī Śaṭhakopa immediately set out and in the thousand-pillared hall in Srirangam, Lord Ranganātha heard the *Veda pārāyaṇa* along with the *Drāviḍa Veda* over 20 days in the month of Śravaṇa.[81] Thus, every year, all the *divyasūris* leave their hometowns and their disciples to go and participate in such festivals.

While all the three major Nāyaṉmārs seem to have travelled from one shrine of Śiva to the other, most of the Āḻvārs seem to have made far more restricted pilgrimages. Nammāḻvār, the second 'most–travelled' saint, has sung of 34 holy places of Viṣṇu, while Tirumankai Āḻvār's major work, the *Pĕriya Tirumŏḻi*, praising 68 shrines, is almost a pilgrims' manual, not unlike the *Tevāram* hymns.

(d) *Variant telling of the above from the Tirumankai Āḻvār* vaibhavam *in the* Mgpp

It is curious that this tale of Tirumankai Āḻvār which forms the basis for the popular understanding of the origin of a very important Śrīvaiṣṇava festival should be omitted by the *Agpp*,[82] especially as it is the Tĕṉkalai sect which is intimately connected with the worship and rituals at the Srirangam Temple. Once during the Kārttikai festival, during the *tirumañjanam* (sacred bath of the divine couple), Tirumankai asked the Lord to grant the status of the Veda to Nammāḻvār's *Tiruvāymŏḻi*. The recitation of the *Tiruvāymŏḻi* was established alongside *Veda pārāyaṇam*. As Pĕrumāḷ consented to the arrangements, the *Tiruvāymŏḻi* was sung on the ten days following the *śukla ekādaśi* (eleventh day of the bright

[80] Since this is a translation from the Sanskrit *DSC*, I am using the Sanskrit spelling for Caṭakopaṉ.

[81] In the present time, the *adhyayana* festival in which the hymns of the Āḻvārs are sung (and performed where resources and availability of skilled *araiyars* [traditional performers] allow) is conducted in the month of Mārkaḻi, i.e. December-January.

[82] The text which establishes this connection is the *Koyil Ŏḻuku*, the remarkably detailed chronicle of the Srirangam Temple from circa fifteenth century. See, V.N. Hari Rao, ed. and tr. *Kōil Oḻugu: The Chronicle of the Srirangam Temple with Historical Notes*, Madras: Rochouse & Sons, 1961, pp. 9–11.

half of the moon) of the month of *Mārkaḻi*.[83] The *vigraha* (image) of Nammāḻvār was duly brought from Tirunagari to Srirangam, and established opposite that of Aḻakiya Maṇavāḷaṉ, the processional idol of Srirangam, in a *maṇḍapa* called the *paramapada vācal* (gateway to heaven) that Tirumankai Āḻvār had built for the purpose. The festival, called *adhyayanotsava*, was made an annual feature.

(e) *An incident from the Tirumankai Āḻvār* vaibhavam *in the* Agpp

The lord himself instructed the Āḻvār's companions[84] to build a temple, complete with *gopuram*, *prākāram* and *maṇḍapam*[85] in TirukKuraiyalūr,[86] the town where the Āḻvār was born, and to establish his image therein. The followers did so, and established a *vigraha* of Kumudavalli Nācciyār as well. Regular festivals were then performed, and the couple in their *arcā rūpa* blessed all devotees.

(ix) *Nammāḻvār and Madhurakavi Āḻvār* vaibhavam

(Since the hagiographies recite a part of the tale of Nammāḻvār under the section on Madhurakavi, I shall recount them together.) On the forty-third day of *Kali yuga*, on the full moon day of the month of Vaikāci under the Viśākha asterism, on a Friday, in the holy town of TirukKurukūr[87] was born in a family of *sat śūdras*, who had been Vaiṣṇavas for seven generations, a boy of faultless birth. The *DSC* goes so far as to say that all residents of Kurukāpuri,[88] of all four castes, were aglow with *bhakti*, the *śūdras* especially so. While the *Mgpp* narrates the story of Nammāḻvār in the order of his 'appearance' on earth, the *Agpp* reserves his story for the last, as 'he is the *avayavī*, all the other Āḻvārs his *avayava*'.[89] The word Nammāḻvār is itself an honorific, meaning 'Our Āḻvār', but easily his most popular name among Śrīvaiṣṇavas.

[83] December-January.

[84] A loose translation since the meaning of the Tamil word is not entirely clear.

[85] Familiar architectural features of Coḻa temples.

[86] Since the same account began with saying that the Āḻvār was born in TiruvĀli-Tirunagari, this reference to TirukKuraiyalūr as his birthplace is strange unless these are alternate names for the same place.

[87] Today known as Āḻvār Tirunagari.

[88] Sanskrit rendition of TirukKurukūr.

[89] *Avayava*= parts, *avayavī*= the owner of the parts.

While the loquacious *Agpp* gives the names of the Āḻvār's forefathers for seven generations as well as the details of the selection of a bride for his father (from a *bhāgavata* family), even the *Mgpp* gives us the names of his parents—Kāri and Uṭaiya-nānkiyār. Interestingly, while we are told the names of Tirumankai Āḻvār's wife and the courtesan with whom Tŏṇṭaraṭippŏṭi Āḻvār was infatuated, this is the only Āḻvār whose mother is named. The child was named Māraṉ which, from the *Agpp* account, appears to have been also his grandfather's name.[90]

The child who was an incarnation of the lords' *senāpati* Viṣvaksena was no ordinary baby.[91] It neither cried, nor took breast milk. The parents then worshipped the deity of their local temple, Pŏlintu-niṉṟa-pirāṉ,[92] and left the baby under a tamarind tree which incidentally was itself an incarnation of Ananta, the serpent-couch of the lord, come down to shield the Āḻvār from the elements. And under this tree sat the Āḻvār in complete silence for 16 years. The lord was his food, drink and betel leaf.[93] Seeing that the child was supernatural, the parents named him Caṭakopaṉ.[94]

At this time, Pĕriya Pirāṭṭi, Mother of the World, said to the lord that they must teach the world the way of salvation.[95] Agreeing, the lord asked Viṣvaksena to give Nammāḻvār *sakala rahasya*, i.e. the sum of all esoteric knowledge. The divine commander then instructed Nammāḻvār (who was, properly, his incarnation) in the *tirumantram, dvayam, mantrārtham*

[90] It was, till very recently, a common practice among Tamils to name children after their grandparents or great-grandparents.

[91] There is an inconsistency in the *Agpp* account for it mentions the Āḻvār's mother praying to the lord of TirukKurunkuṭi for a son and being promised by the lord that he would himself incarnate in her womb. Hardy suggests that the unresolved contradiction might indicate tensions between two traditions regarding the Āḻvār. Friedhelm Hardy, 'The Tamil Veda of a Śūdra Saint: The Śrīvaiṣṇava Interpretation of Nammāḻvār', in *Contribution to South Asian Studies*, ed. Gopal Krishna, New Delhi: Oxford University Press, 1979, pp. 29–87.

[92] One of the 108 Viṣṇus.

[93] The hagiographers probably derived this motif from *Tiruvāymŏḻi* 6.7.1.

[94] Nammāḻvār frequently signs himself thus, for example, *Tiruvāymŏḻi* 5.9.11. The exact meaning of the word is debated, especially since its etymology is traced by some scholars from Tamil roots and by others from Sanskrit, and all attributed meanings are unsatisfactory. See Chapter 1 of the present work, discussion on sources.

[95] See Chapter 3 of the present work for the role of Śrī in the salvation of souls.

and the *Drāviḍa Veda*,[96] besides branding him with the discus and conch, the Vaiṣṇava emblems.

In the closing years of *Dvāpara yuga*,[97] on the fourteenth day of the waxing moon in the month of Citra, in TirukKolūr[98] in Pāṇṭiyanāḍu, was born an *amśa* of the *kumuda*[99] in a *pūrvaśikhā brāhmaṇa vamśa*[100] of the *Sāmaveda* branch.[101] Having learnt the sixteen *vidyās*, he embarked on a pilgrimage. One night near Ayodhya, he perceived a great light towards the south and set out to discover its source. Even when he reached Srirangam, the holiest of holy lands, he saw that it was further south. Eventually, having passed Tirunagari, and finding that the light was now to his north, he retraced his steps to its epicentre—where the beacon disappeared. Under the sleepless tamarind tree,[102] he found a 16 year-old in meditation, and asked, 'If from the womb of the small one, the large one is born, what will it eat and where will it stay?' (*Mgpp*)/'If in the womb of the *acit* (i.e. one without consciousness) is born the little one, what will it eat and where will it stay?' (*Agpp*). The Āḻvār broke his long silence to reply, 'That it will eat and there it will stay'. The *Mgpp* explains this mysterious exchange thus: 'If the all-pervading One is born in the *aṇu* (atom), It will experience Brahman. It will not have heavenward aspiration, but become *prakṛt*, i.e. self-individuated'. And the *Agpp*, 'It will have the body for abode, It being the *ātmā* (soul)'.[103] Madhurakavi then asked the Āḻvār to accept him as his disciple.

[96] While this term in popular Śrīvaiṣṇava understanding sometimes refers specifically to the *Tiruvāymŏḻi*, at others, the entire corpus of Nammāḻvār's compositions bear this title. Śrīvaiṣṇavas believe that the *Tiruvāymŏḻi* is divine revelation, merely transmitted by the Āḻvār through Madhurakavi to the people of the world, just as the Vedic *Samhitās* were 'heard' by the *ṛṣis* of yore. See Chapter 1–iii, of the present work discussion on sources.

[97] The *yuga* before the present one, i.e. *Kali yuga*.

[98] Village near Āḻvār Tirunagari.

[99] Lotus flower that adorns the lord.

[100] This is a reference to *brāhmaṇa* families who wear their (partially shaved off) hair in a knot just above the forehead. Pĕriyāḻvār is supposed to have belonged to such a *brāhmaṇa* clan too.

[101] Vedic *brāhmaṇa* families usually specialize in one of the four Vedas, and its corresponding *angas*.

[102] Tamarind trees usually fold their leaves at night, i.e. 'sleep'. This miracle tree naturally did not!

[103] This esoteric exchange between the two Āḻvārs, master and disciple, is a favourite among Śrīvaiṣṇavas, as an expression of the deep mysticism of the former.

The lord accompanied by Śrī and his retinue granted Nammāḻvār a vision of his *divyarūpa* (divine form). This experience overflowed in the *Tiruviruttam*, *Pĕriya Tiruvantādi*, *Tiruvāciriyam* and the *Tiruvāymŏḻi*, the first three of which contain the essence of the *Ṛk*, *Yajus* and *Atharvan* while the last is the essence of the *Sāmaveda*.[104]

In the *Kaṇṇinuṇciruttāmpu* Madhurakavi, who was the *ādi-prapanna*, i.e. the first Śrīvaiṣṇava to take refuge with a *guru*, sang of the glory of Kurukūr Nampi, Caṭakopan̲/Kāri Māran̲[105] as his only god, for it was he who gave him the Veda in a way that could be apprehended by him.

Madhurakavi is known as the pupil who received the essence of the Vedas from Nammāḻvār, i.e. the master's *prabandhas*, and gave them in his turn to the world. He is also said to have established, after Nammāḻvār attained Vaikuṇṭha, an *arcā vigraha* of his master, and conducted regular worship of the same. While the *Mgpp* tells us that when Madhurakavi spoke the words, 'Nampi of southern Kurukūr', his mouth was filled with nectar—a clear reference to the first verse of the poem of ten stanzas,[106] the *Agpp* relates, as usual, another interesting tale about the hymns of Nammāḻvār himself. Once during a temple *utsava*, when the Āḻvār's titles were being announced, students of the Tamil Sangam objected to the glories claimed for him and challenged him to the 'Sangam test'. Madhurakavi then went to Madurai, the seat of the Sangam, and wrote the opening line of a verse from the *Tiruvāymŏḻi*[107] on a chit which the scholars of the hallowed academy placed on the 'Sangam plank' along with the works of 300 other poets. The plank immersed all the other compositions (in a body of water, presumably),[108]and righting itself, brought up only the work of the Āḻvār. The assembled scholars were naturally awe-struck and repentant, and their chief expressed his wonder

[104] The *Sāmaveda* is considered the greatest/holiest of the Vedas by Śrīvaiṣṇavas.

[105] *Kaṇṇinuṇciruttāmpu*, 1–10. Kurukūr Nampi= lord/priest of Kurukūr. Kāri Māran̲= Māran̲, S/o Kāri.

[106] Reference to *Kaṇṇinuṇciruttāmpu* 1.

[107] *Tiruvāymŏḻi* 10.5.1

[108] Other legends, about the 'Sangam test' such as the contest between the Śaiva saint Appar and the Jainas relate that inferior works were drowned in the Vaigai, Madurai's river. Evidently, there remained a strong sense of the tradition of the Sangam in Madurai long after the 'Sangam age'; certainly, till as late as the thirteenth-fourteenth centuries, acceptance by the Madurai scholars was seen as the acid test of good literature.

in verse: 'Can one word of the verses of Vākulābharaṇa[109] be equalled by the songs of worldly poets? Can a house-fly look up at Garuḍa, a glow worm at Sūrya, or a dog at a roaring tiger? Can a jackal walk before a lion or a *preta* dance before Ūrvaśi?' Thus did Madhurakavi spread the glory of his master in town and country, and redeem the world.

The account of Rāmānuja is by far the longest in all the three hagiographies, in fact longer alone than the stories of all twelve Āḻvārs put together. I will naturally present it here in a highly condensed form.

(x) *Iḷaiyāḻvār*[110] vaibhavam

Pĕriya Tirumalai Nampi, a close disciple of Yāmunācārya, had two sisters. The elder of them, Bhūmi Pirāṭṭiyār was married to Āsuri Keśava-p-Pĕrumāḷ of Sriperumbudur, a *dīkṣitar* (Vedic *brāhmaṇa*), of the Somayāji branch and the younger, Pĕriya Pirāṭṭiyār,[111] to Kamalanayana Bhaṭṭar of Madhuramangalam.[112] Just as the lord was born to Kausalyā and Devaki, so Ananta, the serpent in whose coils the lord sleeps in the milk ocean, was born to Bhūmi Pirāṭṭi to destroy the darkness of the Kali age, in Śaka 939 (1017 CE). All the prescribed *samskāras* were performed for the child who was named Lakṣmaṇa. Meanwhile, Pĕriya Pirāṭṭi gave birth to a baby boy too, named Govinda Bhaṭṭar. The cousins began their study of *Vedānta* in Kāñcīpuram under a reputed Advaitin scholar called Yādava Prakāśa. Once, explicating the phrase, '*satyam jñānam anantam brahmā*' from the *Taittiriya Upaniṣad*, the tutor said *satyam* was that which denied momentary nature, *jñānam*, that which was not soulless, *anantam*, that which was not limited, and that these were characteristic of the *cetana vyāvṛtti*, i.e. sentient beings. He was offended when Rāmānuja asked him for the meaning of *brahmā*. Another time, when Rāmānuja was massaging his guru with oil, Yādava, in explaining the phrase, '*yathā*

[109] Title of Nammāḻvār, literally, 'He garlanded by the blossoms of *Vākula*' (Latin: Mimesops elengi).

[110] Rāmānuja. The hagiographies refer to the greatest of the Śrīvaiṣṇava preceptors by a number of names, but Iḷaiyāḻvār and Uṭaiyavar are the commonest. Iḷai means younger, and Āḻvār, as we have seen above, is a term of reverence; the name is a reference to Lakṣmaṇa, the younger brother of Rāma, literally, Rāma+anuja, who is also believed, in Tamil tradition, to have been an incarnation of Śeṣa/Ananta. Uṭaiyavar means 'He who possesses'.

[111] Bhūmi Pirāṭṭiyār and Pĕriya Pirāṭṭiyār are Tamil forms of Bhūmi devī and Śrī devī.

[112] Both Sriperumbudur and Madhuramangalam townships are close to Kāñcīpuram and Madras.

kapyāsam puṇḍarīkam evam akṣiṇi' bisected the conjugate word, *kapyāsam*, to mean 'monkey-like'. Rāmānuja was deeply grieved, and his hot tears fell on the guru's thigh. On being asked what the matter was, he offered that the correct *padayojana* (division of phrase), was *kam+ pibati= kapi* (i.e. the drinker of water= sun), and that *āsa* was an *upaveśaṇa*, so that the word *kapyāsam* meant, 'lotus dependant on the sun'.[113] The teacher was angered at the student's questioning his omniscience and ordering Rāmānuja to leave, collected his other disciples to plot Rāmānuja's end. This was imperative as Rāmānuja's interpretation would threaten the very basis of Advaita. Though many plans were proposed for doing away with Rāmānuja, they were all attended with sin. Hence, Yādava decided to take his students on a pilgrimage to the north and have Rāmānuja drowned in the holy Maṇikarṇikā Ghāṭ in Varanasi. During this journey, the disciples of Yādava made sure that Govinda did not get to speak with his cousin, Rāmānuja, alone. But the opportunity did present itself at some point while they were crossing the Vindhya forests, and Rāmānuja accordingly managed to separate himself from the group. Alone in the wilderness, he found himself facing a daunting prospect. Just as he was beginning to despair, a hunter couple appeared and said they were going to Kāñcīpuram. That night, when the huntress was thirsty, her husband said he would show her a well of sweet, flawless water the next morning. Rāmānuja was saddened at not being able to help immediately. When he woke the next morning, he found the couple gone, but walking on, soon reached a well and a grove with some people. On asking them where he was, they pointed ahead and asked if he did not know the famous *Puṇyakoṭi vimāna*.[114] Rāmānuja was as delighted as Rāma on hearing Hanumān's words, 'Sītā *dṛṣṭā*' upon his return from the exploratory trip to Lanka (*Agpp*)/as Sītā had in the Aśoka *vana* when she saw Rāma's signet ring (*Mgpp*). He realized that the hunter and his wife were none other than the Peraruḷālar and Pĕrundevittāyār.[115] From that day, he

[113] I am elaborating the details of this argument because it forms the basis of the Viśiṣṭādvaita understanding of the divine; indeed, it marks what Śrīvaiṣṇavas consider their crucial difference from Advaita.

[114] Every temple tower has a 'proper' name; Puṇyakoṭi *vimāna* is the name of the Kāñcīpuram–Varadarāja-p-Pĕrumāḷ Temple's tower. Whether the temple tower existed at the time of Rāmānuja is a moot question.

[115] The name of the lord and his consort in the Kāñcī Varadarāja-p-Pĕrumāḷ Temple.

began the *kainkarya* (service) of taking water from the well near which he had found himself,[116] for the lord's ritual bath each morning.

Meanwhile, Yādava and his party reached their destination. One day, when bathing in the Ganga, Yādava floated a *linga* towards Govinda. Suddenly finding a *linga* in his palm, he naturally felt he had been specially graced. Upon their return to the south, Govinda went first to his birthplace to establish the *linga* there and then proceeded further to serve Śiva at his great temple in Kālahasti. Yādava, however, returned to Kāñcī, and was astonished to see Rāmānuja there. He had assumed Rāmānuja had lost his way in the forests and died. Hearing Rāmānuja's account of his miraculous delivery by the divine couple, he invited him to rejoin his *goṣṭhī* (group of disciples).

At this time, two Śrīvaiṣṇavas from Srirangam happened to visit Kāñcī on pilgrimage. On their return home, they told Āḷavantār,[117] the current *darśana pravartaka* (preceptor of the faith), about the lord having bestowed his *viśeṣa kaṭākṣa* (special grace) on Rāmānuja. Yāmunācārya rejoiced, and wondered if Rāmānuja was intended by the lord to be the next *darśana pravartaka.* Taking permission from Pěriya Pěrumāḷ,[118] he went with his retinue to Kāñcī to worship Peraruḷālar. While in the temple precincts, he saw Rāmānuja in Yādava Prakāśa's party, and though refraining from speaking to him then as he was with his teacher, he gazed at the tall, well-formed youth with his lotus-eyes.[119] He then prayed to Peraruḷālar to bring Rāmānuja to the Vaiṣṇava fold.

Around this time, the ruler's daughter was possessed by a *brahma-rākṣasa*[120] which refused to budge despite the efforts of the best sorcerers. Hearing that Yādava Prakāśa was a great master of mantra, the king sent for him. Yādava sent the royal messengers back with the message, 'Tell the *brahma-rākṣasa* that I command him to leave.' When this was relayed to the *brahma-rākṣasa,* he retorted that he ordered Yādava Prakāśa to go away instead. The enraged Yādava then set out for the court with his retinue and chanted mantras. The *brahma-rākṣasa* replied that he was not

[116] This is the well to which the hunter presumably meant to lead his wife in the morning.

[117] Honorific for Yāmunācārya.

[118] Literally, Great God, name of the lord of Srirangam, also called Ranganātha.

[119] This point is stressed by all the Śrīvaiṣṇava hagiographies. Since Rāmānuja was not a direct disciple of Yāmuna, and the continuity of the lineage of preceptors is crucial, this physical link between the two preceptors is of great significance.

[120] A demon who was a *brāhmaṇa* in his previous birth.

to be frightened off by mantras he knew well himself. 'You don't know your previous birth or mine.' Yādava asked him if he knew, and the demon replied, 'You were a reptile living on the banks of the Madhurāntakam *eri* (pond). Some Śrīvaiṣṇavas from Srirangam on their way to Kāñcī stopped there to bathe and eat. You consumed their leavings spilt on the ground, and were thus blessed with birth as a *brāhmaṇa* with some *vidyā*. I was a *brāhmaṇa*. An error during the performance of a *yajña* caused me to be reborn as a *brahma-rākṣasa*.' Yādava asked him then whose word he would obey, and the demon said that he would leave if so commanded by Rāmānuja. Rāmānuja did so on Yādava's instruction, and the demon fell at his feet saying his sins had now been removed.

When Rāmānuja again objected, some time later, to certain Advaitic explanations of the Vedānta given by Yādava, the teacher told him to leave. Rāmānuja went home and asked his mother for advice— one of the rare instances where the hagiographies give such importance to a mother.[121] Feeling that he had studied enough, she instructed him to perform *kainkarya* (service) to Peraruḷāḷar. The *Agpp* adds that his mother told him to take guidance from Tirukkacci Nampi, a *vaiśya*: a detail that the *Mgpp* omits.[122]

About this time, Āḷavantār fell ill, and anticipating his end, summoned his immediate disciples, Tiruvaranga-p-Pĕrumāḷ Araiyar,[123] Pĕriya Nampi and Tirukkoṭṭiyūr Nampi and instructed them to be steadfast in their discipline. He asked some pilgrims from Kāñcī for news of Rāmānuja and was pleased to learn that the latter had quit Yādava Prakāśa and was now engaged in the service of the Lord. Grateful that the lord had granted his wish, he despatched Pĕriya Nampi to Kāñcī to fetch Rāmānuja to Srirangam.

Upon reaching Kāñcī, Pĕriya Nampi placed himself strategically on the route from the sacred well to the shrine and, as Rāmānuja came along, he recited the *Catuḥśloki* and the *Stotraratna* of Āḷavantār. Moved, Rāmānuja asked Nampi who had composed such extraordinary songs and expressed his desire to pay obeisance to him. Nampi immediately offered to take him to Srirangam to meet Āḷavantār. When they reached Srirangam, however, they were deeply grieved to find that Āḷavantār was

121 We can safely assume Rāmānuja's father was no more. Another such example of a strong woman is Kūrattāḻvā<u>n</u>'s wife, Āṇḍāḷ, not to be confused with the saint-poetess.

122 See Chapter 4 of the present work for discussion on the relative positions of the *Agpp* and *Mgpp* on the caste question.

123 Āḷavantār/Yāmunācārya's son.

no more. Prostrating before the body which the disciples were preparing to lay in *samādhi*, Rāmānuja noticed that three of the master's fingers were bent. He asked the disciples if they had always been so, and on learning that they had not, inquired further if he had had any unfulfilled wishes. The disciples said they he had been devoted to the works of Vyāsa and of Parāśara and had wanted to render homage to them. They had also heard him speak of his wish for a *vyākhyāna* (commentary) of the *Brahmasūtras*. Rāmānuja pledged that with the grace of Peraruḷāḷar and Yāmunācārya, he would fulfil these wishes. The three fingers immediately straightened.[124] Rāmānuja returned to Kāñcī to resume his *kainkarya* there.

Noticing Peraruḷāḷar's particular fondness for Tirukkacci Nampi,[125] Rāmānuja wished him to put his questions before the lord.[126] The lord answered in six points, five of which constitute some of the fundamental philosophical beliefs of the Śrīvaiṣṇava community. The sixth was an injunction to Rāmānuja to take Pĕriya Nampi for his guru.

The details of how Rāmānuja, having taken *sannyāsa*, came eventually to reside in Srirangam, and began to acquire the teachings that Yāmunācārya had entrusted to five of his disciples will be recounted in Chapter 4 as they are directly relevant to the narrative there.

Meanwhile, Yādava Prakāśa's mother decided to take refuge at Rāmānuja's feet. Her decision was attended by good omens which she communicated to her son, urging him to do the same. Yādava was dismayed, aware that as an *ekadaṇḍa sànnyāsi*, lacking *śikhā* and *yajñopavīta*, he was unfit.[127] The atonement for these sins, he knew, was *bhū-pradakṣiṇā*.[128] Peraruḷāḷar, however, appeared in his dream to

[124] Rāmānuja's major works are these commentaries that he is said to have promised at this time. This is another way by which the Śrīvaiṣṇava tradition links the two preceptors.

[125] The lord is supposed to have favoured Tirukkacci Nampi with *viśeṣa kaṭākṣa* and *kṛpā dṛṣṭi.*

[126] The details of the interaction between Rāmānuja and Tirukkacci Nampi and the different representations of the incidents in question in the *Agpp* and *Mgpp* will be discussed in Chapter 4.

[127] Śrīvaiṣṇava ascetics are *tridaṇḍi sannyāsis*, i.e. their staff is three- forked, unlike Advaita *sannyāsis*'. Advaita *sannyāsis*, moreover, give up all marks of caste, such as the forelock of hair and sacred thread, whereas Śrīvaiṣṇava *sannyāsis* continue to wear the same.

[128] *Bhū-pradakṣiṇā*: circumambulation of the earth. Note the sanctity of the marks of brahmanism to the Śrīvaiṣṇava faith such that giving them up should be considered such a grave sin.

say that circumambulating Rāmānuja was equivalent to going around the earth. Rāmānuja accepted Yādava as his disciple and gave him the new name of Govinda Cīyar. Eventually, Govinda Cīyar composed the *Yatidharma Samuccaya* reconciling the statements in the *Śāstras* which are apparently but not actually contradictory.

Established as the pontiff at Srirangam, Rāmānuja sent some messengers to TiruMalai[129] with a mission for his uncle, Pĕriya Tirumalai Nampi, who was engaged in the worship of Tiruvenkaṭamuṭaiyāṉ.[130] Nampi immediately left for Kālahasti[131] with a group of disciples, and came upon Govinda Bhaṭṭar, now known as Uḷḷankai Kŏṭunta Nāyaṉār,[132] collecting water from a tank for *rudrākṣa abhiśekha*,[133] reciting hymns in praise of Śiva. Nampi asked Nāyaṉār what fruit could be obtained by worshipping the one with matted hair, but Nāyaṉār only smiled in reply. A brief debate[134] proved inconclusive too. The next day, Nampi placed himself strategically where Nāyaṉār, up in a tree plucking flowers for Śiva's worship, could hear him recite and explicate the *Tiruvāymŏḻi* to a group of his disciples. The hymns chosen were those that described Nārāyaṇa's creating the worlds including Śiva, Brahmā and Indra. Moved, Govinda threw away the *linga* and *rudrākṣa* beads and fell at Nampi's feet regretting that he had wasted his time worshipping the one with a stinking skull in his hand. Though the other priests at the shrine of Kālahasti tried their best to dissuade him (presumably with warnings about the consequences), Govinda replied that he had no need to fear mere *piśācas* when the great magician himself was beside him.[135]After serving Pĕriya Tirumalai Nampi for some years, Govinda became devoted to Rāmānuja, and was known by the name of Ĕmpār.

Rāmānuja commenced studying the esoteric learning Āḷavantār had commended to five special disciples with instructions to eventually pass them on to him. From Pĕriya Nampi, Rāmānuja acquired the *darśārtha*, i.e. the essence of the (Viśiṣṭādvaita) philosophy. He would later learn

[129] Another name for Tiruppati.

[130] He who 'owns' the holy mountain, Venkaṭam, i.e. the Lord of Venkaṭam.

[131] Kālahasti is fairly close to Tiruppati; about an hour's journey today. It may have been a day's journey in older times.

[132] Literally, the leader who found (a miracle) in the palm of his hand.

[133] Ritual bathing of *rudrākṣa*, beads sacred to Śiva.

[134] For want of a more suitable word. We get an exchange of esoteric phrases, on Nampi's part intended to impress Govinda with the superiority of Viśiṣṭādvaitic principles; on Govinda's rather non-committal. Scarcely a debate.

[135] *Piśācas* and *pretas* are the *anucaras* (followers) of Śiva in the *śmaśāna*, i.e. cremation grounds; the great magician would be Rāmānuja.

the *rahasya granthas*, or esoteric texts from Tirukkoṭṭiyūr Nampi. From Tiruvaranga-p-Pĕrumāḷ Araiyar, skilled in the recitation with music of the *Tiruvāymŏḻi*, Rāmānuja learnt Nammāḻvār's hymns, and Tirumālaiyāṇṭāṉ expounded the meanings of the same. Eventually, he made a pilgrimage to TiruMalai where Pĕriya Tirumalai Nampi taught him the *Rāmāyaṇa*.[136]

Once a *brāhmaṇa*, Yajñamūrti, who had debated with and defeated various scholars in Kāśi, came to Srirangam in pursuit of *digvijaya*.[137] He challenged Rāmānuja to debate, saying that if the latter could establish his *siddhānta* (philosophy) against his own, he would become Rāmānuja's disciple. If not, Rāmānuja would have to become his. They debated for eighteen days without either giving a quarter. On the seventeenth day, Yajñamūrti's side seemed stronger. At night, Rāmānuja worshipped his *gṛhārcā* (personal icon) of Peraruḷālar, saying, 'This *darśana* gave birth to me, will it be defeated because of me? Oh Lord, You were[138] *saguṇa Brahman*.[139] If you now wish to wipe away, through this perpetrator of falsehood, all the proofs[140] and engage in *līlā*, it is Your will.' He fasted that night. The lord appeared in his dream and asked him why he despaired and if he had forgotten Āḷavantār's compositions. The next morning, Rāmānuja brought to the debate what he had learnt from Āḷavantār, and easily trounced his opponent. Yajñamūrti recognized the superiority of Rāmānuja's system, and became his disciple, assuming the name of Aruḷāla-p-Pĕrumāḷ Ĕmpĕrumāṉār. His *Jñānasāra* and *Prameyasāra* are said by the *Agpp* to have made the essence of the entire Vedānta comprehensible even to women and the illiterate.[141]

Rāmānuja continued to expound the *darśana* in the temple at Srirangam, and composed the *Śrībhāṣya*, the *Gītābhāṣya*, the *Vedāntadīpa*, the *Vedārthasamgraha*, the *Gadyatrayi*, etc. The hagiographies describe a number of pilgrimages that he made. One of his earlier pilgrimages was to Kashmir where he was able to read Bodhāyana's *Vedānta Sūtras*, which his disciple Kūrattāḻvāṉ memorized within a day and thus helped

[136] When he left Tirumalai, Pĕriya Tirumalai Nampi 'gifted' Govinda to Rāmānuja.

[137] World conquering.

[138] That is, 'You *were* to this day, recognized as being.... Because of my defeat in debate, it may not be recognized any longer...'

[139] The Supreme Lord with attributes. This is the fundamental difference between Viśiṣṭādvaita and Advaita; the latter denies that the Supreme Being has any qualities, i.e. it is *nirguṇa*.

[140] Proofs of being *saguṇa*

[141] The accessibility of sacred knowledge for these groups is hereby underlined. See Chapter 4-iii of the present work.

Rāmānuja write his commentary on the same. An interesting pattern emerges from one of the most important of these pilgrimages. He is said to have worshipped the lord in the *divya deśas* of TiruMāliruñcolai, TirukKuṭantai, etc., in Colanāḍu, proceeded to Pāṇṭiyanāḍu where he visited not only the shrines of the lord but also the birthplace of Nammāḻvār in Āḻvār Tirunagari, and thence to the sacred spots in Malaināḍu. He is said to have journeyed along the western coast to the north where he worshipped the lord at Mathura, Śāligrāma, Dvārāvatī, Ayodhya, Uttara Badarīkāśrama, Naimiśāraṇyam, Puṣkaram, Āyppāṭi (literally, cowherd hamlet), Govardhana giri, Vṛndāvana, etc. He is also said to have visited the Sarasvatī *bhaṇḍāra* where the goddess herself graciously received him, and after getting from him a satisfactory answer to a query on the meaning of a stanza of *śruti* that had long puzzled her, honoured him with the title of Bhāṣyakāra and presented him with an idol of Hayagrīva.[142] He returned via Varanasi where he bathed in the Ganga. The *Agpp* adds that his bathing in the river rid her of *kapāli-sparṣa-dośa* (the sin of having been touched by the skull-bearer). From Devaprayāg he went to Puri where he worshipped Jagannātha. Returning by way of Śrīkūrma, Ahobila and Venkaṭam, Rāmānuja stopped with his retinue at Tiruppati. Here the Śaivas were claiming that Tiruvenkaṭamuṭaiyāṉ was actually a form of their God.[143] Rāmānuja had the symbols of both deities, i.e. the conch and discus of Viṣṇu, and the trident and drum of Śiva, placed inside the god's chamber at night and the doors securely locked. In the morning, the lord was found wearing the *śankha* and *cakra*, while Śiva's symbols were lying at his feet.[144] Back in the Tamil land, he worshipped at the sacred shrines of Tŏṇṭaināḍu and Naṭunāḍu before returning to Srirangam. One can distinguish that this clockwise route charts out a *pradakṣiṇā patha* in a pan-Indian context. The texts stress the dual purpose of these extensive peregrinations: pilgrimage and debate

142 In Śrīvaiṣṇava understanding, this is the form of Viṣṇu that gave the Vedas to the world.

143 The idol at Tiruppati is probably an anthropomorphic deity of pre-Vaiṣṇava or Śaiva origin which the early bhakti saints probably claimed as a representation of their god. Peyāḻvār has praised the lord in Tiruppati as the one bearing both discus and axe, wearing both snake and sacred thread, matted hair and crown. Ref.: *Mūṉrām Tiruvantādi* 63. This can be seen as proof either of its being a composite image, or as an instance of a bhakti saint praising his lord as one encompassing the other, rival deity.

144 The identification of the Tiruppati icon as a Viṣṇu figure is certainly late. The hagiographies might be recording the memory of an actual conflict. Some manipulation must have been at work to prove the Vaiṣṇava identity of the idol.

with scholars of other faiths, often specified as Māyāvādīs (Advaitins), Śākyars (Buddhists) and Śramaṇas (Jainas). Needless to say, Rāmānuja is said to have defeated all his opponents.

Envious scholars of other persuasions who lacked the courage to debate with Rāmānuja carried tales to the Co̱la ruler[145] who was himself

[145] Unidentified so far. Since Rāmānuja is said to have lived for 120 years, this could be any of several rulers. Sastri, *The Cōḻas*, p. 644, identifies the ruler as Adhirājendra (reign: 1068–70 CE), the last Co̱la ruler of the Vijayālaya line who, he says, lost his life in a popular revolt. He himself has, however, pointed out (*The Colas*, p. 643), on the basis of inscription SII 205 of 1904, the rebuilding in stone in the short reign of Adhirājendra, of the brick shrine of Varadarāja-p-Pĕrumāḷ in TiruvAkkārai originally built by Kocco̱la.

It has also been suggested that the ruler who persecuted the Śrīvaiṣṇavas could have been Kulottunga I or II, though the most widely accepted dates for Rāmānuja's life (1017–1137 CE) make it unlikely that the latter king (who only ascended the throne in 1133 CE) could be the cause of his troubles. Second, inscriptions dated to the reigns of both kings have been found in several temples attesting to patronage and thus belying this tale of persecution. An inscription in the Srirangam Temple dated to the fifteenth regnal year of Cōla Kulottunga I= *c.* 1085 CE registers a gift of land by purchase, by Rājarāja Madhurāntakan, alias Vatsarājan, for worship and offerings to the God A̱lakiya Maṇavāḷa-p-Pĕrumāḷ on the day of his natal star Mṛgaśīrśa, and for feeding Śrīvaiṣṇavas in the Madhurāntaka̱n *maṭha* during two festival days. (Ref.: T.V. Mahalingam, *A Topographical List of Inscriptions in the Tamil Nadu and Kerala States*, ICHR, S. Chand and Co. Ltd, Delhi, 1985, vol. VIII, p. 182, Tp 849. Ref.: *ARE*, 1892, no. 15; *SII* xxiv, no. 58). An inscription of 1091 CE, dated to the twenty-first regnal of year of Kulottunga I from the Ranganātha Temple at Srirangam registers a gift of a *cauri* with a gold handle for service to God Anantanārāyaṇasvāmin, by the Malayāḷa officers belonging to the Pĕruṇṭanam and Ciruṇṭanam of the king. (Mahalingam, 1985, vol. VIII, p. 184, Tp 856. Ref. *ARE*, 1938–9, no. 130; *SII* xxiv, no. 66). Rājarājan Arumŏ̱liyār, alias Tĕ̱ṉṉava̱n mādevi, Queen of Kulottunga I, endowed in 1095 CE, the twenty-fifth regnal year of the same king, land towards feeding *bhagavatar* in the temple of Srirangam. (Mahalingam, 1985, vol. VIII, p. 186, Tp 863. Ref.: *ARE*, 1947–8, no. 126; *SII* xxiv, no. 73). Another inscription in the Aruḷāla-p-Pĕrumāḷ Temple, Cinna Kāñcīpuram, of 1113 CE registers a gift of a perpetual lamp to God Tiruvattiyūr Ā̱lvār in Eyil *nāḍu* in Eyil *koṭṭam* by A̱lakiya Maṇavāḷeni Mantaiyālvār who was the wife of Karuṇākara̱n, alias Tŏṇṭaimā̱nar of Vaṇṭalañceri, the latter being known to us as the generalissimo of the Co̱la army who led the expedition to Kalinga in 1110 CE on behalf of the King, Kulottunga I (accession date, 1070 CE) (Mahalingam, 1985, vol. III, p. 158, Cg 644). Two other records (1090 CE and 1104 CE) from the same temple are actually orders of the king himself for grants of land to the temple of TiruVĕhkā (Mahalingam, 1985, vol. III, pp. 156–7, Cg 640–1). Yet another grant from the Varadarāja/Aruḷāla-

a staunch Śaiva. He commanded all the scholars in his realm to sign, on pain of death, the declaration, '*śivāt parataram nāsti*', i.e. nothing is greater than Śiva. Some signed out of fear, others from greed. But a court official, Nālūrā<u>n</u>, impressed upon the king that unless he could make Rāmānuja and Kūrattā<u>l</u>vā<u>n</u>[146] accept it, the signatures of all others were worthless. When the king's messengers reached Koyil,[147] Kūrattā<u>l</u>vā<u>n</u>, who was drawing water from the well for Rāmānuja's bath heard the news first. Dressing himself in his master's *kāśāya*[148] and *tridaṇḍa*,[149] he

---

p-Pĕrumāḷ Temple in Kāñcīpuram dated to Kulottunga II (accession date, 1133 CE) registers a sale of land for maintaining a lamp in the *maṭha* attached to the temple and a gift of land for feeding Śrīvaiṣṇavas who come to witness the festivals of Māci and Vaikāci (Mahalingam, 1985, vol. III, p. 161, Cg 657, Ref.: *ARE*, 1919, no. 406). And in 1129 CE, the Co<u>l</u>a ruler Cakravarti Vikramaco<u>l</u>adeva set up the image of Vikramaco<u>l</u>a-Viṇṇagar-A<u>l</u>vār in the same temple and made provision for its daily worship by a gift of land as *devadāna* in the village of Vilvalam. (Mahalingam, 1985, vol. III, pp. 160–1, Cg 654, Ref.: *ARE*, 1919, no. 590). These sample inscriptions alone cover most of the rulers contemporary to Rāmānuja. Such patronage seems incompatible with the tale of persecution. On the other hand, it seems difficult to believe that such a detailed story involving royal personages and harm to senior *ācāryas* could be entirely fabricated. Even the *DSC*, believed to be contemporary to Rāmānuja, speaks of the persecution of Vaiṣṇavas and of Rāmānuja's fleeing to the western country.

A hint of troubled times—though of an entirely different nature from that indicated in the hagiographies—may be had from an inscription in the great temple at Srirangam dated to 1080 CE (Co<u>l</u>a Kulottunga I, regnal year 11). It states that the temple of Mummuṭico<u>l</u>a-Viṇṇagar-Ā<u>l</u>vār at Rājamahendra *caturvedimangalam*, a *brahmadeya* in Kāntāra *nāḍu*, a subdivision of Nittavinoda *vaḷanāḍu*, was unable to safeguard its property owing to burglary of its treasury during the conflict between the right and left hand castes in the 2nd year of the king's reign. The assembly of Rājamahendra *caturvedimangalam*, therefore, received a lump sum of 50 *ka<u>l</u>añcu* of gold from the temple and exempted certain lands belonging to it from paying taxes (Mahalingam, 1985, vol. VIII, pp. 180–1, Tp 843. Ref.: *ARE*, 1936-37, no. 31; *SII*, xxiv, no. 53).

[146] One of Rāmānuja's intimate disciples, but a householder, not a *sannyāsi*.

[147] Literally, temple, but also used in Śrīvaiṣṇava parlance to mean Srirangam, Viṣṇu's temple town par excellence. I have followed the traditional Śrīvaiṣṇava texts such as the *Gpps* in using this word here to convey both meanings simultaneously.

[148] The saffron robes of an ascetic.

[149] Three-pronged staff characteristic of Vaiṣṇava *sannyāsis*, as against the single staff of Śaiva ascetics.

prepared to leave with them without informing Rāmānuja. Pěriya Nampi accompanied Āḻvāṉ. When Rāmānuja emerged from his bath and asked for his *tridaṇḍa-kāśāya*, Mutaliyāṇṭāṉ[150] told him what had happened and urged him, as did his other disciples, to flee Srirangam. Rāmānuja donned the householder's white clothes Kūrattāḻvāṉ had left behind, and fled with a group of disciples to the western country. At the foot of a mountain, the party came across a group of hunters who were disciples of Tirumalainallāṉ, himself a disciple of Rāmānuja. The hunters brought the escapees honey and raw corn that they could pound and roast themselves, so that they could consume ritually pure food. They eventually escorted them to a *brāhmaṇa* household where they could be properly fed. However, Rāmānuja asked his disciples to secretly watch the cooking, and only when satisfied both on account of its ritual purity and on the housewife's *Bhagavat*-bhakti, did he allow them to eat.

Eventually, the travellers reached Tŏṇṭanūr, where the daughter of the king, Viṭṭhala Deva Rāya, was possessed by a *piśāca* that none had been able to drive away. The king proclaimed that he would become the disciple of whoever cured his daughter. Tŏṇṭanūr Nampi[151] told Viṭṭhala Deva Rāya of Rāmānuja's success with the *brahma-rākṣasa*, and he immediately invited Rāmānuja. Needless to say, the girl was soon well. Rāmānuja gave the king the new name of Viṣṇu Vardhana Rāya.[152] At that time, 12,000 Jainas, the former teachers of the king, appeared to rebuke Rāmānuja for having lured away their follower and to challenge him. Going behind a screen, Rāmānuja assumed the form of the thousand-headed Ananta[153] and answered all their questions simultaneously.

[150] Another of Rāmānuja's intimate disciples; also his nephew.

[151] Presumably, the priest of Tŏṇṭaṉūr.

[152] Viṣṇuvardhana was king from 1110 to 1152 CE. He seems to have had this name from the beginning of his reign. See John Braisted Carman, *The Theology of Rāmānuja, An Essay in Inter-Religious Understanding*, Bombay: Ananthacharya Indological Research Institute, 1981, p. 45. However, it has also been pointed out that an inscription belonging to the reign of Viṣṇuvardhana, the Hoysala king, found at the Lakṣmīnārāyaṇasvāmi Temple in Tŏṇṭūr mentions a grant to the Rāmānuja *maṭha* and, in his early inscriptions, Viṣṇuvardhana is called Biṭṭi Hoysala Deva, the name found in the *Guruparamparā*. See K.V. Raman, 'Śrī Rāmānuja in Epigraphy', *Studies in Rāmānuja: Papers Presented at the First all-India Seminar on Śrī Rāmānuja and his Social Philosophy at Śrīperumbūdūr*, Madras: Sri Ramanuja Vedanta Centre, 1979, p. 134.

[153] Rāmānuja is supposed to be an *avatāra* of Ananta.

Some of them converted to Śrīvaiṣṇavism; Rāmānuja had the king grind the rest in a stone mill.[154]

Soon afterwards,[155] the Lord Tirunārāyaṇa-p-Pĕrumāḷ appeared in Rāmānuja's dream to tell him that he was languishing in a pit in a corner in the *tulasi* grove there. When the pit was dug, a golden shrine appeared from the earth. This was in the Śaka year 1012.[156] After consecrating the temple with great pomp (and devotion) under the auspices of Viṣṇu Vardhana, Rāmānuja found that the *utsava mūrti* (processional idol) necessary for celebrating temple festivals was missing. Pĕrumāḷ appeared in his dream again to tell him that the *utsavar*, named Rāmapriya, was then performing *līlā* in the Turuṣka *rājagṛha*,[157] and asked him to fetch it. Rāmānuja immediately proceeded to Dillipuram (Delhi) where the Turuṣka ruler honoured him and invited Rāmānuja, on the ascetic's asking for their *kuladeva* (family deity) to be returned to them, to look for it in their stores. When their search proved fruitless, Rāmānuja learnt, again through divine agency, that the idol was in the princess' chambers. The king conducted him therein. On Rāmānuja's beckoning, the idol

[154] This episode in the hagiographies is traditionally believed to mark the penetration of Śrīvaiṣṇavism into Karnataka. However, there is evidence of the presence of the sectarian faith in Karnataka before the time of the great preceptor. Two inscriptions of Rājarāja I's reign dated to 1014 CE and 1021 CE from Chennapatna near Bangalore district and Mysore district respectively mention Śrīvaiṣṇavas (*Epigraphica Carnatica*, IX, Ch. 129-AD 1014 and EC XIV, Tn./34-AD 1021. Ref: R. Vasantha, 'The Colas and the Introduction of Srivaishnavism in Karnataka', *Quarterly Journal of the Mythic Society*, no. 64, 1973, pp. 32–3.

[155] While the *DSC* also speaks of the wicked 'Coḻa' ruler and of Rāmānuja's flight to Tirunārāyaṇapuram and his establishing a temple therein, it makes no reference to the episode that follows. Indeed it has Rāmānuja propound the *darśana* for a while in Tirunārāyaṇapuram and then return to Srirangam soon after the evil Coḻa king's being struck by disease and dying. See Chapter 1 of the present work for discussion of dates of the hagiographies.

[156] Gives us an almost accurate date, i.e. 1090 CE. Needless to say, several historians have tried to match the events related in the hagiographies with known political ones, without any success. Besides, the first Muslim invasion of south India, by Malik Kafur, General of Allaudin Khilji, took place in 1309–11 CE. Almost every single aspect of the anachronistic story that follows defies credibility.

[157] The palace of the Muslim king. Turuska= Turkish. Generic in Tamil for Muslim. See also Richard H. Davis, *Lives of Indian Images*, Princeton: Princeton University Press, 1997, p. 119.

jumped into his lap in the presence of all, all its ornaments tinkling.[158] The astonished Dilli-*purīndra*[159] presented the idol to Rāmānuja with all due honours. Returning to the south, Rāmānuja established the *utsava vigraha* in the temple, and named the town Tirunārāyaṇapuram.[160] He gave the *caṇḍālas* who had helped him during his crisis the name of Tirukkulattār (those belonging to a holy clan), and the rights to bathe in the temple tank, circumambulate the temple and receive *tīrtha* (consecrated water) on the occasion of the chariot-procession festival.

A significant annexure to this story is found in the *Mgpp*, the *Rāmānujārya Divya Caritai*, a later hagiography,[161] the *Koyil Ŏluku*,[162] the remarkable chronicle of the Srirangam Temple, and several other later texts. Equally significant is its absence from the *Agpp* and the *DSC*.[163] In the *Mgpp* and the *Rāmānujārya Divya Caritai*, the princess, whose plaything the idol had been by day, and lover by night, could not bear the separation and followed Rāmānuja to Tirunārāyaṇapuram, while in the *Koyil Ŏluku* and later chronicles,[164] the princess does follow the idol but Rāmānuja does not feature in the Delhi/Muslim ruler episode.[165] Besides, it is to Srirangam that she comes, not to Karnataka in the latter texts.[166] It is various local people—whose tribal/community identities

[158] Rāmānuja is said to have fondly addressed the icon as 'Cĕlvapiḷḷai', i.e. 'my dear boy'—the name by which the *utsavar* is known to this day.

[159] King of Delhi.

[160] In modern Karnataka. Also known as Melkote.

[161] Carman, op. cit., p. 279, refers to it as a late text. Robert Lester, 'The Sāttāda Śrīvaiṣṇavas', *Journal of the American Oriental Society*, vol. 114, no. 1, 1994, p. 40 dates the author to *c.* 1550 CE.

[162] *Ŏluku* means a record or register. The *Koyil Ŏluku* that weaves in details of ritual and practices in the Srirangam Temple with older myths and ongoing records of donations to the temple belongs to the larger category of *sthalapurāṇas*.

[163] Ranjeeta Dutta states that this is a popular story from the hagiographies. We have seen, however, that it is absent from the *DSC* and from the *Agpp*. See Ranjeeta Dutta, 'The Politics of Religious Identity: A Muslim Goddess in the Śrīvaiṣṇava Community of South India', *Studies in History*, vol. 19 no. 2, 2003, pp. 157–84.

[164] Ibid., pp. 157–84. Also see Richard H. Davis, 'A Muslim Princess in the Temples of Viṣṇu, *International Journal of Hindu Studies*, vol. 8, nos. 1–3, 2004, pp. 137–56.

[165] In the seventeenth-century *Prapannāmṛta*, for instance, the setting for the Tughluq attack on Srirangam is the period of Piḷḷai Lokācārya.

[166] The *sthalapurāṇa* of Tirunārāyaṇapuram and some late poetical works from Karnataka understandably bring the princess to Melkote.

are specified—who are involved in the recovery of the idol.[167] The silence of the *DSC* on this entire episode despite featuring Rāmānuja's exile to Śrī Nārāyaṇapuri[168] in Karnataka, establishment of a temple there, and his eventual return to Srirangam seems to argue in favour of its being an older text.[169]

According to the *Mgpp* and the *Agpp*, Rāmānuja's exile in Karnataka lasted 12 years. A visiting Śrīvaiṣṇava from Srirangam once brought him news of events back in Koyil. Kūrattāḻvān and Pĕriya Nampi had been dragged to the Coḻa court where the wicked ruler had demanded that they sign the statement proclaiming the greatness of Śiva. The Vaiṣṇava saints gave numerous proofs to show the proposition was untenable, but finding the Coḻaṉ[170] unwilling to listen to reason, responded by recourse to pun. Accordingly, they countered the original statement, i.e. '*śivāt parataram nāsti*' with one of their own, '*droṇam asti tataḥ param*': a clever interpretation, since *śivam* in Tamil also means a measure, which is a fraction of another called *droṇam*. The enraged Coḻaṉ ordered the *ācāryas* to be blinded before being thrown out. Pĕriya Nampi, already ripe in years, died of the pain, while the blinded Kūrattāḻvān made his way back to Srirangam with the help of Pĕriya Nampi's daughter, Attuḻāy. Deeply saddened, Rāmānuja performed *Śrīcūrṇa paripālanam* (a rite for the deceased) for Pĕriya Nampi, and sent a disciple, Ciriyāṇṭāṉ, to Srirangam to comfort Kūrattāḻvān. At this time, the wicked Coḻaṉ was struck by a mortal disease—worms infested his neck—and died. (In Śrīvaiṣṇava texts such as the *Gpps*, the ruler is consistently called Kṛmikaṇṭha Coḻaṉ, literally, the worm-necked one.) Ciriyāṇṭāṉ took this news back to Rāmānuja who then returned to Srirangam. Both the Tĕṉkalai and Vaṭakalai hagiographies elaborate the steps he took to standardize worship at the temple he had established at Tirunārāyaṇapuram, besides leaving, for his soon-to-be-bereaved disciples there, an image of himself invested with his very essence.

As is often the case with these narratives, the texts also lay down in detail, the roles and rights of various groups of people, belonging to separate caste groups, in the daily and the annual ritual cycles of the temple. This is also the first record of the apotheosizing, in iconic form,

[167] See Davis, 'Muslim Princess', op. cit., and Dutta, op. cit., for discussions of this narrative.

[168] *DSC*'s Sanskritized version of Tirunārāyaṇapuram.

[169] See discussion on dating the *DSC* in Chapter 1-iii.

[170] Coḻa ruler.

of any of the *ācāryas*. Upon his return to Srirangam, Rāmānuja is said to also have enshrined images of Nammāḻvār, the other Āḻvārs and some venerated early *ācāryas*. The texts of course frequently speak of the *ācāryas* venerating the images of the Āḻvārs, but since they reflect the circumstances of the late thirteenth–early fourteenth centuries at the earliest, it is not to them but to archaeological evidence that we must look for confirmation of the worship of the Āḻvārs in images.[171]

Rāmānuja is also credited with standardizing the practices, rituals and organization of the Srirangam Temple. This was, understandably, productive of conflict especially where Rāmānuja's arrangements interfered with established practices and older interest groups. Some of these find reflection in the hagiographies in stories of some jealous temple priests trying to poison Rāmānuja, and in the oral tradition preserved by the family of Pĕriya-Koyil Nampi, the *arcaka* displaced by Rāmānuja's reorganization.[172] Pĕriya-Koyil Nampi himself, however, seems to have finally become a disciple of Rāmānuja's with the name of Tiruvarangattu Amutaṉār[173] and is credited with composing a 100-stanza poem in praise of his preceptor, the *Rāmānuja Nūṟṟantādi*, which is, according to some calculations, considered part of the *NDP*.[174]

[171] See Chapter 6-ii of the present work for inscriptional evidence for worship of the Āḻvārs.

[172] Carman, op. cit., pp. 34–6.

[173] 'The holy nectar of Srirangam'.

[174] This poem devotes a verse each to the Āḻvārs and the earlier *ācāryas* in the line of preceptors. It is possible that the germ of some of the elaborate stories of the Āḻvārs may be found in the *Rāmānuja Nūṟṟantādi*. As the poet is said to be one of the disciples of Rāmānuja, the poem may be considered contemporary with Rāmānuja. It has also been argued that it must be a later composition, not contemporaneous with Rāmānuja at all. See Friedhelm Hardy, *Viraha Bhakti: The Early History of Kṛṣṇa Devotion in South India*, Oxford University Press, New Delhi: 1983, p. 250, footnote no. 9. The poem is mentioned in the *DSC*, but if the *DSC* itself is considered a later work as has been argued (see Introduction), this work could be later too. Yet, the accounts of Rāmānuja found in the *Rāmānuja Nūṟṟantādi* and the *DSC* are comparatively believable, being less replete with miracles. Rāmānuja himself is considered an *avatāra* of Ananta—but it can be argued that in a developing tradition of venerating preceptors as incarnations of Viṣṇu's appendages and attendants, the same could be done of a living preceptor as well. The *Gpps* are not only generally very careful about the lineage of preceptors, they were also composed in the context of establishing the rival lineages of the Tĕṉkalai and Vaṭakalai traditions respectively and 'meddling' with chronology would have attendant complications. The teachers

About this time Rāmānuja also made a trip to Tiruppati whence the *utsava mūrti* of TiruCitrakūṭam[175] had been secretly transferred when the evil Colan̲ had gone about desecrating the Vaiṣṇava shrine of TiruCitrakūṭa.[176] Rāmānuja formally established the displaced *utsavar* in the shrine at the foot of the hill,[177] and laid down the order of worship at and the administration of the temple.[178]

Since Rāmānuja had innumerable disciples, he wished to impose some *nibandhanam* (arrangement), to which end he established 74 *simhāsanādhipatis* (leaders) and various functionaries (of different castes) to take care of different aspects of the temple administration. The Tĕn̲kalai and Vaṭakalai *Gpps* diverge vastly from this point regarding the succession; sometimes even important preceptors of a sect, whose works, compositions and biography are elaborated in great detail in the sectarian *Gpp* fail even to find mention in the *Gpp* of the rival sect.

After 120 years of untiring service to the lord, Rāmānuja renounced the world and returned to his original form as Śeṣa so as to be forever united with him in Vaikuṇṭha.

(xi) Incidents from the Account of Appar/Tirunāvukkaracar from the Pĕriya Purāṇam[179]

The saint Appar was born Maruṇīkkiyār in a *veḷāla* family. As a young man, he became a Jaina monk, took the name of Dharmasena and became

---

who feature in both *Gpps* are likely to be early *ācāryas*, not rejected by either sect. It appears unlikely, therefore, that a later *ācārya* could have been made a contemporary of Rāmānuja. Finally, it appears unlikely that the *NDP*, which had acquired canonical status by at least the twelfth–thirteenth centuries, would have been modified later by the addition of a new poem, especially in so prolific a scriptural tradition.

175 The Vaiṣṇava shrine at Chidambaram. See further discussion below.

176 Sastri, *The Cōḻas*, pp. 644–5 believes the ruler involved in displacing Govindarāja from Chidambaram to have been Kulottunga II on the basis of inscriptions.

177 There are two temples in Tiruppati: one on top of the hill and another at its foot, known in Śrīvaiṣṇava parlance as upper and lower Tiruppati(s). Though only the mountaintop shrine is counted as a *divya kṣetra*, the pilgrimage to the shrine is considered incomplete without a visit to the lower one.

178 Rāmānuja is credited with the establishment of the formal procedures of temple ritual and administration in several places including Srirangam.

179 Taken from G. Vanmikanathan, *Periya Puranam by Sekkizhaar: Condensed English Version*, Madras: Ramakrishna Math, 2004, pp. 272–316; Minakshi, op. cit.,

the head of a monastery in TirupPātiripuliyūr. A terrible colic which the medicines and ministrations of his fellow monks could not cure made him turn to his elder sister, Tilakavatiyār. A devout worshipper of Śiva, she bade him take refuge in the lord. Filled with remorse for his years of apostasy, Appar prayed to Śiva at TiruvAṭikai Vīrattānam and was cured miraculously. Pleased with the hymn he sang, the lord bestowed upon him the title, Tirunāvukkaracar.[180] The Jainas of the place accordingly instigated the (Jaina) Pallava ruler Mahendravarman to torture Appar by having him incarcerated for a week in a limestone kiln, poisoned, bound with a granite boulder and flung into the sea and trampled underfoot by a mad elephant. Needless to say, Śiva protected his devotee all along and indeed, the elephant instead of crushing him bowed and garlanded him and turned its fury on the hapless Jainas. Mahendravarman, after his re-conversion to Śaivism under Appar's influence, destroyed the Jaina monastery and with that material had a temple to Śiva built at Tiruvaṭi.[181]

Eventually, Appar embarked on pilgrimage in the course of which he met the child saint, Sambandar, who is said to have addressed him as 'Appa' and thus given the older Nāyaṉār the name by which Tamil Śaivas have since referred to him. At one point, Appar is supposed to have visited Paḻaiyarai where the temple of Śiva had been walled up by the Jainas. He pledged to fast till he could worship Śiva there, upon which the lord directed the king of the land in a dream to his temple which had been falsely converted into a Jaina shrine. After restoring the original temple, the king too worshipped the lord with proper ceremony.

(xii) Incidents from the Account of Tirujñāna-Sambandar from the Pĕriya Purāṇam[182]

The Pāṇṭiya king, Kūṉ Pāṇṭiyaṉ,[183] had strayed from the righteous path and had become a Jaina. His queen, Mankaiyarkkaraci, and minister, Kulaicciraiyār, both ardent Śaivas, (and counted among the 63 Nāyaṉmārs) requested Sambandar, one of the three major Nāyaṉmārs, to bring the king back to the true faith. When Sambandar arrived in Madurai, the Jainas tried all kinds of vile tricks and black magic to destroy

pp. 223–30; Indira Vishwanathan Peterson, *Poems to Siva: The Hymns of the Tamil Saints*, Delhi: Motilal Banarsidass, 1991, pp. 19–20

180 King of the holy tongue/lord of speech.

181 Minakshi, op. cit., p. 230.

182 Vanmikanathan, op. cit., pp. 218–71.

183 Hunchbacked Pāṇṭiyaṉ. Identified with Nĕṭumāraṉ.

the child saint,[184] but without any success. Instead, the king was gripped by a deadly fever which the Jainas, despite their best attempts, failed to cure. Sambandar (naturally) succeeded but the Jaina monks, not wishing to concede defeat so easily, challenged him further. Accordingly, the Nāyaṉār and the Jaina monks submitted their respective faiths first to a fire ordeal, and then to a water-test. While the palm leaves containing the essential principles of the Jaina creed were burnt, Sambandar's, needless to say, emerged unscathed, and while the Jaina manuscript was washed downstream by the torrential river Vaigai, Sambandar's hymn on Śiva floated gently upstream. Realizing that their game was up, the Jaina monks impaled themselves en masse as the royal party and the Nāyaṉār looked on.[185] The ruler's hunched back miraculously straightened. Sambandar proceeded to Kāraikkāl where the abbot of a Buddhist monastery at Bodhimankai challenged him to a debate—in which he was routed. At Taḷicceri near Kŏṭṭappāṭi, he debated with and converted Buddhanandi and Sariputta.[186] In Tiruvoṟṟiyūr,[187] a humble Śaiva complained that he was the object of ridicule for the local Jainas as all the palm trees in his grove were male and didn't yield any fruit. Sambandar sang a hymn which, to the delight of Śiva's devotees and the consternation of the Jainas, miraculously transformed the palm trees into fruit-yielding female ones. In Mayilāpūr, a rich merchant, Śivaneśa, was hoping to arrange a wedding between his only daughter and Sambandar. The girl, however, died from snake bite just before Sambandar's arrival. The fond father, however, preserved the girl's ashes in an urn, convinced that the Nāyaṉār would be able to revive her. The residents thronged to watch, the denizens of the heavens crowded the skies, and the faithless Jainas jeered as Sambandar had the merchant place the urn outside the walls of the temple of Kapālīśvara and sang a hymn to the lord. Even as he sang, 'The unbelieving Jaina and Buddhist monks will declare such

[184] Sambandar.

[185] K.A.N. Sastri, *The Culture and History of the Tamils*, Calcutta: Firma KL Mukhopadhyaya, 1964, p. 110, 'Even now Madurai conducts an annual festival in the temple commemorating the incredible impalement of eight thousand Jainas at the instance of the gentle boy-saint'.

[186] Minakshi, op. cit., p. 225.

[187] A suburb of modern Madras/Chennai.

a deed impossible',[188] the girl's hand decked in bangles rose out of the pot.[189]

(xiii) *Account of Mūrti Nāyaṉār from the* Pĕriya Purāṇam[190]

Mūrti, a *vaiśya* who lived in Madurai, ground sandal paste for adorning the body of the temple image. At this time, the country was invaded and conquered by the Vaṭuka Karunātar, a tribe from Karnataka. Their chief, now king of the Pāṇṭiyanāḍu began, under the influence of Jainism, to harass the devotees of Śiva in every way possible. Declaring all sandalwood forests the property of the state, he sought to impede the proper worship of Śiva. Mūrti, however, proceeded to rub his own arm against the grinding stone to obtain paste for the adornment of the lord. Even though blood flowed out, and his bones split to the very marrow within, he did not shrink from his task. Touched by his devotion, Śiva caused the wicked Jaina ruler and his dynasty to die out. When the people sent an elephant around the country to pick out a successor, it chose Mūrti Nāyaṉār who ruled with the sacred ash for his anointment, *rudrākṣa* beads for jewellery and a coil of matted locks for his crown.

(xiv) *Account of Taṇṭiyaṭikaḷ Nāyaṉār from the* Pĕriya Purāṇam[191]

In the holy city of TiruvĀrūr, the Jainas, who were very numerous, had trespassed into the very temple of Śiva and encroached upon the banks of its tank, the Kamalālayam. A blind devotee, Taṇṭiyaṭikaḷ, decided to compensate for the loss of the tanks' width by increasing

[188] The legend seems to have been inspired by a hymn of Sambandar's describing the festival cycle in the temple of Kapālīśvara in Mayilai (Mylapore). In every stanza in this hymn, Sambandar addresses a beautiful girl (Pūmpāvai), asking her if she would go [presumably die—though it could simply mean go elsewhere from Mayilai] without seeing the (different) festivals of the temple. The tenth verse, as is customary in Sambandar's hymns, refers to the great festival of purification in the said temple as the one 'slandered by the naked Jainas and base Buddhists in voluminous robes'. *Tevāram*, Book II, no. 47, verses 1–10, cited in Vidya Dehejia, *The Sensuous and the Sacred: Chola Bronzes from South India*, New York: American Federation of Arts, in association with Mapin Publishing, Ahmedabad, 2003, p. 240.

[189] Sambandar didn't marry the girl finally, claiming that he stood in the relationship of a father to her, having brought her to life.

[190] Taken from Vanmikanathan, op. cit., pp. 468–70.

[191] Ibid., pp. 476–9.

its depth. Having groped his way to its centre, he erected a pole there which he tied with a rope to another planted on its bank. Making his way to and from the centre of the tank by way of this rope, Taṇṭiyaṭikaḷ began to dig at the centre. The alarmed Jainas raised an uproar about the innumerable creatures buried in the soil that would be killed by this action. They pulled up the poles and rope and abused Taṇṭiyaṭikaḷ, mocking him for being blind and asking if he had gone deaf too that he refused to heed their righteous words. The enraged 'slave of the Lord' responded by calling the Jainas men of uncertain dogma and devoid of perception, and saying that it was they who were blind; he could see the lord who burnt the three cities,[192] which was all that was worth seeing. The Jainas challenged him saying that if his god could restore his sight, they would leave the city. In response to his devotee's prayer, Śiva not only restored his eyesight, but also caused the Jainas to lose theirs and who then shamefacedly tottered out of TiruvĀrūr.

(xv) Account of Naminandi Nāyaṉār from the Pĕriya Purāṇam[193]

Naminandi, a *brāhmaṇa* devotee from Emapperūr, walked to the holy temple town of TiruvĀrūr,[194] prayed awhile, and as evening came on, wished to light lamps for the lord. The house from which he happened to beg for some ghee was a Jaina one; the inhabitants mocked him saying he should burn lamps for his lord with water. Chanting the names of Śiva, Naminandi filled lamps with water from the temple tank, and lit them. Lo and behold! The lamps burnt all over the temple with a bright flame.

[192] Śiva as Tripurāntaka.

[193] Vanmikanathan, op. cit., pp. 462–5.

[194] About two and a half hour's walk, says Vanmikanathan, ibid., p. 463.

THREE

The Ardently Loving Lord
A Promise of Salvation

(i) Hypothesis

Devotion, or *bhakti*, was not a new element in Vaiṣṇavism; it held a major place in the *Bhagavad Gītā* and earlier works, and it was already accepted as one of the ways of salvation along with *karma* and *jñāna*. In its earlier form, however, *bhakti* was primarily meditation or concentration of one's thoughts on the deity. In the *Bhāgavata [Purāṇa]*, as for the Āḻvārs, it is a passionate devotion of one's whole life in complete surrender to the Lord, a way of life that is not one among many, but the only way to true salvation'.

—THOMAS HOPKINS, 'The Social Teaching of the *Bhāgavata Purāṇa*', in *Krishna: Myths, Rites and Attitudes*, ed. Milton Singer 1966, p. 6.

This immersion in the lord was not, however, a consistently joyful experience, if the hymns of the Āḻvārs are any indication. The songs of the earlier Āḻvārs express a submissive devotion to a supreme and sublime god,[1] meditation upon whom is its own end. However, Nammāḻvār, Tirumankai, Pěriyāḻvār, Āṇḍāḷ, and to a lesser degree Kulaśekhara, often speak in more intimate voices to their lord. While the motif of the girl in love with her divine beloved is the most striking one, there are poems in the parental voices of Yaśodā,[2] Devakī[3] and Daśaratha.[4] Despair

[1] *Mutal Tiruvantādi* 11, 13, 14; *Iraṇṭām Tiruvantādi* 10, 11, 12.

[2] *Pěriyāḻvār Tirumŏḻi* 2.1.1–10; 2.2.1–11; 2.3.1–13; 2.4.1–10; 2.5.1–10; 2.6.1–10; 2.7.1–10; 2.8.1–10, etc.

[3] *Pěrumāḷ Tirumŏḻi* 7.1–11.

[4] *Pěrumāḷ Tirumŏḻi* 9.1–11.

fights with ecstasy, and hopelessness is seen as often as expressions of fulfilment upon a meeting in the classical lover–beloved poems. Clearly, the saints despite the overwhelming bhakti that allowed them to scold the beloved could not take their divine lover for granted.

There is, however, a sense of determinism that informs the hagiographical accounts of these saints. Let us take an example from the epic, *Rāmāyaṇa*. The story of Rāma's killing of Rāvaṇa exists on numerous planes, first as the actual occurrence in the story as Rāvaṇa's punishment specifically for abducting Sītā and generally for embodying evil, and second as the logical conclusion of Viṣṇu's ridding the earth of the scourge who had secured miraculous boons from Śiva as a result of meditation, and therefore as the reason and justification for Viṣṇu's *avatāra* as Rāma. There is a third level too: Rāvaṇa and Kumbhakarṇa are, as Hiraṇyakaśipu and Hiraṇyākṣa in an earlier epic episode and Śiṣupāla and Jarāsandha in a later one,[5] the incarnations of Jaya and Vijaya, the faithful guards of Viṣṇu's palace who would not let the sage Durvāsa in when the lord was resting. On being cursed to separation from the lord, they chose, against a thousand *dhārmic* lives devoid of His presence, three short lives of evil redeemed by death at the hands of the lord. The past, the present and the future are all linked in a cosmic scheme, and the lives on earth and netherworld are in a piece with otherworldly ones. The Śrīvaiṣṇava hagiographies similarly speak of the Āḻvārs on three different planes. At the outset, they are incarnations of one or the other attributes, accoutrements or companions of the lord; second, they are human devotees with the occasional human failing but super-humanity often lingering just below the surface. Their human trials and tribulations may be merely for the enlightenment of common folk, though they may sometimes result from the lord's *līlā*. Besides, the lord becomes tangibly present on one or more occasions in their human lives. Finally, there is no doubt about their eventual destiny as *nityasūris* blessed with the joy of dwelling in the eternal presence of the lord in Vaikuṇṭha.[6]

Had the Āḻvārs this certainty themselves, we would certainly never have heard Nammāḻvār in his lovesick sleeplessness asking the ocean with its

[5] Earlier and later here refers simply to their popular Puranic sequence.

[6] See Archana Venkatesan, 'Āṇṭāḷ and her Magic Mirror: Her Life as a Poet in the Guises of the Goddess. The Exegetical Strategies of Tamil Śrīvaiṣṇavas in the Apotheosis of Āṇṭāḷ', Unpublished Ph.D. thesis, University of California, Berkeley 2004, pp. 27–41, for a discussion of the apotheosis of Āṇḍāḷ.

restless tides if, like himself, it had also lost its heart to the faithless lord[7] or Āṇḍāḷ's threat to pluck her breasts from their roots and fling them at the 'thief' if he failed to unite with her.[8] But the early Śrīvaiṣṇava *ācāryas* assured the community of the faithful that the lord shall not fail to unite with the devotee, indeed he could not, yearning as he himself was for the redemption of his *bhakta*. They expressed this conviction in a variety of media: in *stotras* (poems of praise), in commentaries, in esoteric treatises and in the hagiographies. The hagiographies, as *anubhava granthas*,[9] by definition draw their reader/listener into savouring, re-experiencing the experience of the Āḻvārs,[10] and thus illustrate for the lay devotee the theological vision of the Śrīvaiṣṇava *ācāryas* which was also elaborated in esoteric and philosophical texts with few frills for popular taste. I will examine how this unity of purpose was achieved in the different strands of literary and philosophic composition, especially through the hagiographical accounts of Āṇḍāḷ and Tiruppāṇāḻvār and indeed, episodes in the lives of the other Āḻvārs.

(ii) Some Aspects of Śrīvaiṣṇava Philosophy

Śrīvaiṣṇavism is composed of three major strands: a long-standing tradition of Viṣṇu bhakti, embodied most profoundly in the Tamil context in the hymns of the Āḻvārs; the ritual precepts of the *Pāñcarātra Āgamas*; and the philosophical system of *Viśiṣṭādvaita*, qualified non-dualism, the philosophical doctrine propounded by Rāmānuja. The Śrīvaiṣṇava hagiographies credit Nāthamuni, a Vedic *brāhmaṇa* attached to the temple of Vīranārāyaṇapuram, with the 'discovery' and compilation of the hymns.[11] We have already seen that there is sufficient reason to doubt this claim.[12] From the earliest levels of Śrīvaiṣṇava literature, an attempt to knit in these streams of the tradition is apparent. Outside the *Nālāyiram* itself, the earliest instance of the *Tiruvāymŏḻi* being equated with the Sanskrit Veda is a *taṉiyaṉ* (a free-standing stanza of praise) on Nammāḻvār, attributed to Nāthamuni.[13] While it is possible that this

[7] *Tiruvāymŏḻi* 2.1.3.

[8] *Nācciyār Tirumḍi* 13.8.

[9] The hagiographies and commentaries are traditionally referred to in Śrīvaiṣṇava parlance as *anubhava granthas*, i.e. texts of enjoyment.

[10] Venkatesan, 'Āṇṭāḷ and her Magic Mirror', p. 64.

[11] *Agpp*, *Mgpp*, Nāthamunikaḷ *vaibhavam*.

[12] See Chapter 1-iii of the present work.

[13] K.K.A. Venkatachari, *The Śrīvaiṣṇava Maṇipravāḷa/ The Maṇipravāḷa Literature*

stanza is a later composition,[14] it must be remembered that the same claim was made perhaps a century earlier, in the Tamil *Kaṇṇinuṇciruttāmpu*,[15] by Madhurakavi, in praise of his preceptor Nammāḻvār as the author of the Vedas in Tamil. This claim is made again in the first commentary on the *Tiruvāymŏḻi*, the *Ārāyirappaṭi* of Tirukkurukaip-Piraṉ Piḷḷāṉ, the first *ācārya* in the Vaṭakalai apostolic succession after Rāmānuja, who is said to have composed it on the express instructions of Rāmānuja himself.[16] In the Sanskrit language, this claim is first made in a composition by Parāśara Bhaṭṭar,[17] the first *ācārya* after Rāmānuja in the Tĕṉkalai *Guruparamparā*. Whether or not the hagiography is accurate in recording the wishes of Rāmānuja, it cannot be denied that the Vedic equivalence of the *Tiruvāymŏḻi* was accepted within the Śrīvaiṣṇava community in Rāmānuja's own lifetime. Despite the absence of all reference to the Tamil hymns in Rāmānuja's own works, one may therefore safely accept the centrality of the *NDP* to the early Śrīvaiṣṇava community.

The extant writings of Yāmunācārya, Nāthamuni's grandson, and predecessor of Rāmānuja in the lineage of preceptors, are all in Sanskrit. There emerges clearly from these the attempt to forward Nāthamuni's programme of establishing the Vedic orthodoxy of the devotional literature.[18] The *Pāñcarātra Āgamas* received their first (extant) defence in the *Āgama Prāmāṇya* of Yāmunācārya, where the *ācārya* argues that the *Pāñcarātra* is as authoritative as the Vedas since it has a divine origin like the Vedas.[19] Since the Śrīvaiṣṇava philosophical tradition which adopted the *Pāñcarātra Samhitās* considered their theological portions inessential, they were lost when the former was established.[20] Accordingly, the *Pāñcarātra* texts came to be regarded as manuals of ritual for Vaiṣṇava

of the Śrīvaiṣṇava Ācāryas, 12th to 15th Centuries AD, Bombay: Anantacharya Indological Institute, 1978, p. 15.

14 Ibid., pp. 11–15.

15 *Kaṇṇinuṇciruttāmpu* 2.

16 *Agpp*, Iḷaiyāḻvār *vaibhavam*.

17 Nancy Ann Nayar, *Poetry as Theology: The Śrīvaiṣṇava Stotra in the Age of Rāmānuja*, Weisbaden: Otto Harrassowitz, 1992, p. 43.

18 John Carman, *The Theology of Rāmānuja: An Essay in Interreligious Understanding*, Bombay: Ananthacharya Indological Research Institute, 1981, p. 26.

19 Swami Adidevananda, 'Pancharatra and Visishtadvaita', in *Visistadvaita: Philosophy and Religion: A Symposium by Twenty Four Erudite Scholars*, Madras: Ramanuja Research Society, 1974, p. 225.

20 M. Matsubara, *Pāñcarātra Saṁhitās and Early Vaiṣṇava Theology*, Motilal Banarsidass Publishers Pvt. Ltd., 1994, p. 40.

initiates.[21] There is a good deal of agreement in the treatment of these subjects between the *Samhitās* and two Śrīvaiṣṇava texts, the *Tattvatraya* by Piḷḷai Lokācārya (a senior contemporary of Vedānta Deśika) of the Tĕṉkalai school and the *Yatīndramatadīpika* by Śrīnivāsadāsa of the Vaṭakalai school.[22]

While the Sanskrit writings of Yāmunācārya do not appeal for scriptural authority to the Tamil hymns as they do to the Vedas, the influence of the former is marked. Devotion to Viṣṇu is evident in his *Gītārthasamgraha*, a brief verse summary of the *Bhagavad Gītā*, the *Stotraratna*, and the four verses in praise of Śrī.[23] The Vedic *brāhmaṇa* status of Nāthamuni's family with its Sanskrit learning was important for the pan-regional prestige of the nascent community oriented towards Viṣṇu worship. In fact, the word 'Śrīvaiṣṇava' occurs in an inscription in the TiruVenkaṭam temple at Tiruppati as early as 966 CE,[24] implying the existence of at least a small community by this name by the mid-tenth century. Rāmānuja gave this devotional tradition the seal of Vedic authority by his theological interpretation of Bodhāyana's *Vedānta Sūtras*, traditionally considered the essence of the teachings of the *Upaniṣads*, in his major work, the *Śrībhāṣya*. The refutation of Śankara's Advaita and the establishment of *Viśiṣṭādvaita*, a Vedantic system on theological principles was largely the handiwork of Rāmānuja, considered the greatest *ācārya* by the community of the faithful. Rāmānuja is credited with nine treatises, the authorship of some of which has been contested by some modern scholars.[25] The arguments of Robert Lester and Pandit Agnihotram Ramanuja Thatachariar against Rāmānuja's authorship of the three *Gadyas* and of the *Nityagrantha* rest on their assumption that the *Śrībhāṣya* alone is the key to understanding Rāmānuja, and that views which do not strictly conform to those expressed in the former are those of later Śrīvaiṣṇavas. However, Carman has convincingly shown that

[21] Ibid., p. 35.

[22] Ibid., p. 39. Śrīnivāsadāsa is, however, placed in the seventeenth century.

[23] Carman, op. cit., p. 26.

[24] Vasudha Narayanan, *The Vernacular Veda: Revelation, Recitation and Ritual*, Columbia, SC, University of South Carolina Press, 1994, p. 2.

[25] Robert Lester, 'Rāmānuja and Sri-Vaiṣṇavism: The Concept of Prapatti or Śaraṇāgati', *History of Religions*, vol. 5, no. 2, 1966, pp. 266–82. Pandit Agnihotram Ramanuja Tatachariar is apparently the first to have raised doubts about the authorship of the three *Gadyas*, which Lester followed up—personal communication from Professor K.K.A. Venkatachari. See also, Agnihotram Ramanuja Tatachariar, 'Vaisnava Tradition', *Bulletin of the Institute of Traditional Cultures, Madras*, vol. 20, no. 2, 1976, pp. 43–62.

most of the passages or doctrines to which Lester and Pandit Agnihotram have taken exception are equally removed from the trajectory of the development of those doctrines in both the Vaṭakalai and Tĕṉkalai sects.[26] Even earlier, van Buitenen, despite some questions regarding the authorship of the three *Gadyas*, had concluded in favour of Rāmānuja's authorship, arguing that Rāmānuja was not only a philosopher but also a theologian and officiating priest, as is evident from even his *Gītābhāṣya*.[27]

Though Rāmānuja was primarily a Vedic *brāhmaṇa* of the Vaṭama sect, there can be no doubt of his deep devotional orientation. The accounts of the *Agpp* and the *Mgpp*[28] describe his natal family as both *Somayāji* and as being devoted to Viṣṇu. Even if these accounts were to be dismissed as inherently biased, we have the evidence of his own writings. There are a number of passages in the context of meditation, devotion, or commitment where Rāmānuja's emphasis shifts to god's gracious and loving nature and his desire to bring his devotees to a state of eternal communion with him.[29] Indeed, devotion to Viṣṇu could be confidently said to be one of the predominant motifs of Rāmānuja's thought. Though Rāmānuja refers to the *Pāñcarātra Āgamas* only rarely, it is important to note that he considers them sanctioned by orthodoxy.[30] In fact, Daniel Smith calls him a champion of the *Pāñcarātra* cause.[31] Besides, Rāmānuja positioned himself strongly in the tradition of Nāthamuni and can thus be considered an adherent of the *Pāñcarātra* system. Rāmānuja continued the policy of fusing the two great traditions, Vedic and Vaiṣṇava; his cultic life is, in fact, said to have been the most creative factor in the formation of his Vedānta.[32] Having said this, let us now look at the broad outlines of Śrīvaiṣṇava doctrine. It must be kept in mind that the tradition is not frozen in time at the point of the merger of the three streams mentioned

[26] Carman, op. cit., pp. 212–17, 231–3.

[27] J.A.B. van Buitenen, *Rāmānuja's Vedārthasamgraha*, Deccan College Monograph No. 16, Madras, GS Press, 1956, p. 32, and J.A.B. van Buitenen, *Rāmānuja on the Bhagavadgita*, S. Gravenhage: H.L. Smits, 1954, p. 27 cited in Lester, 'Rāmānuja and Śrī-Vaiṣṇavism', p. 273.

[28] *Agpp*, pp. 140–1, *Mgpp*, pp. 50–4. See Chapter 2-x of the present work.

[29] Carman, op. cit., p. 72.

[30] Nayar, op. cit., p. 105.

[31] Daniel Smith, 'Pancaratra Literature in Perspective', *Journal of Ancient Indian History*, vol. 12, 1978–9, p. 50.

[32] Eric Lott, 'Iconic Vision and Cosmic Viewpoint in Ramanuja Vedanta', in *Proceedings of the Seminar on Temple Art and Architecture*, ed. K.K.A. Venkatachari, Series no. 10, Bombay: Ananthacharya Indological Research Institute, Bombay, 1980, p. 32.

earlier—indeed there is no such point in time when such a merger neatly took place—but that the interweaving was a process that was carried on over some generations, mainly through the continuous interpretation of the Tamil hymns.

The great majority of the *Pāñcarātra Āgama* texts have not yet been sufficiently studied. The literature spells out the ritual framework of worship, elaborating the principles of construction of temples and shrines, and the format of worship. Some of these features such as worship with fragrant flowers and leaves seem to have been common to the Āḻvārs' devotional expression too. Dennis Hudson asserts that the Āḻvārs were deeply influenced by the *Pāñcarātra*;[33] in fact, he reads the poems of Āṇḍāḷ and Viṣṇucitta as illustrations of *Pāñcarātra* principles.[34] Though his interpretation offers an interesting new perspective from which to examine the bhakti hymns, I believe it to be unjustifiably reductionist, especially considering the many layers of meaning that have been read into the hymns by medieval *ācāryas*, themselves heir to the *Pāñcarātra* tradition.

The *ācāryas*, as we have seen, wrote their theological treatises in Sanskrit. Being not only inheritors of a Brahmanic-Upanisadic tradition, which used Sanskrit exclusively, they were also consciously positioning themselves in a continuing discursive philosophical tradition. They were drawing on the *Upaniṣads*, commenting upon and elaborating (each in his own light) Upanisadic ideas. One of the most important, indeed, among the earliest to interpret the *Upaniṣads* was Śankarācārya in the eighth-ninth centuries. His commentary on the *Bhagavad Gītā*, and on the Upanisadic philosophical systems can almost be said to have promoted the system of *Vedānta* (also called *Uttara Mimāmsa*) to the supremely pre-eminent position. It would be no exaggeration to say that the *Upaniṣads* considered principal today are those that Śankara chose to comment on. Indeed, after Śankara, it was impossible for any philosopher who wished to interpret the ancient scriptures differently to bypass Śankara's interpretation. The original Vedantin had to be engaged with, and at least partially refuted before any other hypothesis could be presented. It is, thus, in this convention that we must place

[33] Dennis Hudson, 'Early Evidence of the Pāñcarātra Āgama', in *The Roots of Tantra*, ed. Katherine Ann Harper and Robert L. Brown, Albany: State University of New York Press, 2002, pp. 135–60.

[34] Dennis Hudson, 'A New Year's Poem for Kṛṣṇa: The Tiruppallāṇṭu by Villiputtūr Viṣṇucittaṉ ('Periyāḻvār')', *Journal of Vaishnava Studies*, vol. 7, no. 2, 1999, pp. 93–129.

Rāmānuja and the later Vaiṣṇava thinkers like Nimbārka, Vallabha and Madhva. Several modern scholars have, in fact, concurred in their view that Śankara put artificial constructions on the *Vedānta Sūtras.*[35] Some of the later philosophers could speak without reference to Śankara only because they placed themselves largely in the philosophical tradition of Rāmānuja, who was seen as having already refuted Śankara sufficiently. A number of Śrīvaiṣṇava scholars after the thirteenth century composed philosophical treatises exclusively in Maṇipravāḷa,[36] since they were addressing, and debating with, only other scholars within the larger Śrīvaiṣṇava community itself. There seems to have developed at least in Srirangam, a tradition of exposition of the verses of the Āḻvārs to a wide public, presumably composed largely of lay Śrīvaiṣṇavas. The interpretations of the hymns were based on the philosophical treatises studied by the smaller circle of *ācāryas*, and the numerous, elaborate and extensive commentaries that were composed from the twelfth century onwards. The hagiographies written in Tamil, as comparatively less abstruse texts, and consequently accessible to a larger segment of the populace, could have then served as vehicles for a dissemination of this theological vision. Even specific ritual practices exclusive to Śrīvaiṣṇavas, though possibly evident in the daily life of the temple, were reinforced and given sanctity by their inclusion within the hagiographies, as having been practised by the Āḻvārs and *ācāryas* of yore.

In the *Vedāntasāra*, considered to be Rāmānuja's earliest work, he stressed the idea basic to the theology of Vedānta that god is the material cause of the universe and the efficient cause of its periodic origination, continuing existence, and eventual dissolution.[37] Both his *Bhagavad-Gītābhāṣya* and Yāmuna's *Gītārthasamgraha*, which the former follows closely, regard *jñānayoga* and *karmayoga* as only preparatory stages which result in contemplation of the *ātman* but not in the attainment of god, which is the final goal. God can only be attained through bhakti to which the disciplines of *jñāna* and *karma* are indispensable means.[38] J.A.B. van Buitenen believes that in the *Gītābhāṣya,* Rāmānuja 'loves to dwell upon the devotional and emotional aspects of the continuous representation

[35] Carman, op. cit., p. 53. Also, pp. 199–202, where he puts forth the arguments of A. Govindacarya, Rudolph Otto, J.A.B. van Buitenen and K.D. Bharadwaj, among others.

[36] See Chapter 1–iii of the present work.

[37] Carman, op. cit., p. 59.

[38] Ibid., p. 61.

of god'.[39] The aspects of god's nature that are important in redeeming the devotee and bringing him into communion with him are those that receive the greatest praise from Rāmānuja in this text.[40]

To Rāmānuja, the notion that 'God has a particular name, Nārāyaṇa, implies that god has a particular bodily form about which the scriptures inform us, a form not only in His phenomenal manifestations or descents (*vibhava* or *avatāra*) but also in His supreme state'.[41] There are numerous passages in Rāmānuja's writings in 'the context of meditation, devotion or commitment in which there is a noticeable shift in emphasis to stress God's gracious and loving nature and his desire to bring His devotees into a state of eternal communion with Him'.[42] He believed that although the immediate occasion of the lord's descents was to relieve the earth's burden of evildoers, their deeper intention was to provide a refuge for those who resort to him by becoming a visible object to all mankind and accomplishing such tasks as would win the hearts and eyes of all creatures.[43] Despite his belief that god who is inaccessible to men and even gods like Brahmā has made himself accessible to his worshippers in the phenomenal realm, Rāmānuja never uses the term *saulabhya*, for he holds that attainment of god is anything but easy.[44] Rather, the lord's accessibility is a gift of staggering magnitude. By the time of the later commentators, however, the doctrine of the divine grace and the attributes expressing divine *saulabhya* had become widely accepted and indeed fundamental to Śrīvaiṣṇava theology.[45] In fact, Rāmānuja's immediate disciple Kūrattāḻvāṉ expresses his relish, in the *Sundarabāhustava*, at the condescension of the inaccessible Supreme Being in manifesting himself in Tirumāliruñcolai to be accessible to humanity.[46]

[39] J.A.B. van Buitenen, *Rāmānuja on the Bhagavadgīta*, p. 22, cited in Carman, ibid., p. 61.

[40] Carman, *The Theology of Rāmānuja*, op. cit., p. 61.

[41] Ibid., p. 167.

[42] Ibid., p. 72.

[43] Ibid., p. 78.

[44] Ibid., p. 79.

[45] Ibid., p. 87.

[46] Cited in Vasudha Narayanan, 'Arcāvatāra: On Earth as He is in Heaven', in *Gods of Flesh, Gods of Stone*, ed. Norman Cutler and J.P. Waghorne, Chambersburg: Anima Publications, 1985, p. 62.

More openly expressed in Rāmānuja's Vedantic writing than the conception of *saulabhya* and *paratva* is the *śarīra-śarīrī bhāva.*[47] The universe is the great body of the lord, of which he is the inner controlling self. Though Rāmānuja wrote little about the *prapatti* aspect of the god-man relationship, the devotees' utter dependence on the lord, just as the body is dependent upon its controlling self, is a persistent theme.[48] The self-body analogy most directly and richly explicates the meaning of the dependent relationship.[49] The picture that emerges from the works of Rāmānuja is that the Supreme Brahman, the primeval person, is Viṣṇu, consort of Śrī, possessed of all auspicious qualities and entirely free of impurities.[50] Śrīvaiṣṇava doctrine allows every individual, male or female, and among the Tĕṉkalais, high-born or low, access to the lord's grace. *Prapatti* has radical potential, being an 'existential act on the part of the individual which qualitatively changes his life from being a *sansārin* to a *prapanna*'.[51] In the three *Gadyas*, Rāmānuja expressed his devotion and surrender (*śaraṇāgati*) to the lord.[52] The act of *prapatti* itself was eventually formalized into a ritual one, with the individual *prapanna* surrendering to his preceptor and being initiated in the three esoteric mantras mentioned above. Among the Tĕṉkalais, Rāmānuja is believed to have performed the act of *prapatti* on behalf of his whole community; this paradigmatic *prapatti* is repeated by every individual *ācārya* taking on the faults of his followers, and securing his/ her redemption. That such surrender assures liberation is made explicit by Vedānta Deśika,[53] though it may be delayed if (1) the devotee sins frequently, (2) is attached to worldly objects and (3) has contact with other deities. The human response to god's loving and redemptive action is typically designated by the term bhakti.

One of the most important and characteristic, though infrequently

[47] Eric Lott, 'Iconic Vision and Cosmic Viewpoint in Ramanuja's Vedanta', pp. 36–7.

[48] Ibid., p. 42.

[49] Eric Lott, 'Śrī Rāmānuja's Śarīra-Śarīri Bhāva: A Conceptual Analysis', *Studies in Ramanuja: Papers Presented at the First all-India Seminar on Sri Ramanuja and his Social Philosophy at Sriperumbudur*, Madras: Sri Ramanuja Vedanta Centre, 1979, p. 21.

[50] Carman, op. cit., p. 67.

[51] Katherine Young, 'Dying for Bhukti and Mukti: The Śrīvaiṣṇava Theology of Liberation as a Triumph over Death', *Studies in Religion/Science Religieuses*, vol. 12, no. 4, 1983, p. 390.

[52] *Śaraṇāgati Gadyam, Śrīranga Gadyam, Vaikuṇṭha Gadyam* by Rāmānuja.

[53] Vedānta Deśika, *Śrīmad Rahasyatrayasāram* 193.

used, ideas in Rāmānuja's theology is the *śeṣa-śeṣi* concept; his definition of the soul-body relationship hinges on them.[54] He defines the terms in the course of a debate with one school of the Karma-Mīmāmsakas. *Śeṣa* for Rāmānuja is 'an object possessed, whereas the possessor is *śeṣi*', while in the thought of his followers, the idea that it is the function of the *śeṣi* (the master) to look after his *śeṣa* becomes of prime importance, for it is on this that the confidence of the *prapanna* in his salvation hinges.[55] Vedānta Deśika defines the lord as *śeṣi*, the one for whose purposes material things exist and the master whom intelligent beings are obligated to serve.[56] The Śrīvaiṣṇava tradition does not 'obligate' god to save his dependants but has tended to assume that He would eventually save those who surrender themselves to him.[57] This fundamental doctrine of Śrīvaiṣṇava theology has, however, two variant interpretations, i.e. whether continued effort is required on the part of the individual soul after the surrender or if it is entirely the grace of the lord which is salvific; the difference is one of the eighteen points of distinction between the Tĕṉkalai and Vaṭakalai schools.

The role of Śrī in the salvation of the individual soul is one of the critical points of difference between the northern and southern sects. The earliest reference to Śrī in specifically Śrīvaiṣṇava writings is in the *Catuḥślokī* of Yāmuna. In Rāmānuja's own writings, there is acceptance of the doctrine of inseparability of the lord and Śrī. Later commentators on his *Śaraṇāgati Gadyam* interpreted his surrender to Śrī at the beginning of the composition as illustrative of the goddess' role as *puruṣakāra* (intercessor). Her role as mediatrix in salvation was developed intensively in the doctrinal compositions of Śrīvaiṣṇava *ācāryas* who succeeded Kūreśa and Bhaṭṭar, Rāmānuja's immediate disciples.[58] Pĕriyavāccāṉ Piḷḷai explicating stanza 19 of the *Tiruppāvai* makes the necessity of a mediatrix explicit by showing that the *gopīs* are Piṉṉai's dependants, because she is the only one who can make Kṛṣṇa available to them.[59] In the further development of the concept of the centrality of the divine consort, Śrī in the Vaṭakalai understanding is inseparable from and infinite like the lord himself, acting both as *upāya* and *upeya*,

[54] Carman, op. cit., p. 147.
[55] Ibid., pp. 148–9.
[56] Ibid., p. 150.
[57] Ibid.
[58] Nayar, op. cit., pp. 222–3.
[59] Dennis Hudson, 'Radha and Pinnai: Diverse Manifestations of the Same Goddess?', *Journal of Vaishnava Studies*, vol. 10, no. 1, 2001, p. 1135.

whereas for the Tĕṉkalai, she is the first among finite souls, ranking above an ordinary *jīva*, yet lacking the lord's autonomy, lordliness and supremacy.[60]

The 4,000 hymns of the Āḻvārs take us on a multidimensional emotional-devotional journey. This is not the place to examine the complex hues of the mystic poetry; I shall, accordingly, focus on only some aspects of the same. Though a deep sense of *viraha* frequently informs this poetry, it is equally easy to find verses that speak of the (experienced) joy of union with the divine, or of *viraha* intensified after, and due to, an experience of union. Equally, numerous verses speak of the bliss of serving the lord in his shrine—the Śrīvaiṣṇava word for beholding the image in the temple[61] is *sevai* (=Hindi/ Sanskrit *sevā*) carrying the connotation of service. This seems to be a reflection of the Āḻvār tradition of interchangeably speaking of 'seeing the Lord' in any of his shrines and of offering worship with flower garlands, etc. Indeed, in the hymns, this life that offers the opportunity of serving the lord in his temple shrine is often spoken of as superior even to heaven.

The rich pilgrimage poetry of both the Āḻvārs and the Nāyaṉmārs underscores the fact that Āḻvār bhakti was rooted in this world. Bhakti rarely aims at renunciation as the ultimate goal[62] and is radically opposed to the strand of classical Hindu thought which would reduce the world to mere *māyā* (divine illusion).[63] The Tamil bhakti tradition is rooted in realism; human life is seen as offering greater opportunity for the soul to commune with the lord. In the penultimate verse of the *Tiruppāvai*, Āṇḍāḷ asks not for *mokṣa*, final liberation, but entanglement with Kṛṣṇa in life after life, continuous service to him for seven lives to come.[64] He is both the goal and the means to the goal,[65] a point to which I will return later. The intensity and depth of *viraha* may itself arise from the final, actual

[60] See *Mumukṣuppaṭi* of Piḷḷai Lokācārya with Maṇavāḷamāmuni's Commentary, Translation by Patricia Y. Mumme, Ananthacharya Indological Research Institute Series no. XIX, Bombay, 1987, pp. 19–20.

[61] The equivalent of Hindi *darśana*.

[62] David Dean Shulman, *Tamil Temple Myths: Sacrifice and Divine Marriage in the South Indian Saiva Tradition*, Princeton: Princeton University Press, 1980, p. 21.

[63] David Dean Shulman, 'Divine Order and Divine Evil in the Tamil Tale of Rāma', in *Studies of South India*, ed. G.W. Spencer, 1985, pp. 56–7.

[64] *Tiruppāvai* 29.

[65] Dennis Hudson, 'Bathing in Krishna: A Study in Vaiṣṇava Hindu Theology', *Harvard Theological Review*, vol. 73, nos. 3–4, 1980, p. 547.

impossibility of union with the Divine in this corporal existence.[66] While the emotions expressed in the hymns themselves alternate between joy and despair, the commentarial tradition tried to impose uniformity through interpretation. The hagiographies record an early instance of the same.[67] Rāmānuja is said to have been tutored in the *Tiruvāymŏli* by Tirumālaiyāṇṭāṉ, one of the five disciples of Yāmuna to whom the old preceptor had imparted the sum of his teachings in order to be passed on to Rāmānuja. When Āṇṭāṉ was explicating a certain verse of the *Tiruvāymŏli*,[68] Rāmānuja is said to have objected to it on the grounds that the Āḻvār's statement in that verse, according to that interpretation, seemed inconsistent with the verses immediately preceding and following it. When Āṇṭāṉ remonstrated with his disciple for dissenting from the views of Āḷavantār (Yāmuna's honorific in the community), terming his interpretation a 'creation of Viśvāmitra', (i.e. baseless fabrication, a reference to *Triśanku svarga*), another disciple mentioned having once heard Āḷavantār give the alternate interpretation.[69] While this incident is important in the hagiographies for establishing Rāmānuja's instinctive apprehension of Yāmuna's own ideas, and thus his position in the *guruparamparā*,[70] it is important for us as a record of the centrality of creative and constant interpretations of the hymns. It is crucial too in demonstrating that Rāmānuja's interpretation was in the interests of logical consistency: devotion in his view must consist of unremitting remembrance of the perfections of god.[71] Few later commentators dared—unlike Rāmānuja—to dissent from the opinions of their predecessors; what we see in the growing commentarial literature is the aggregation of interpretations. Each commentator elaborated on the views of earlier ones. While uniformity was often, therefore, imposed at the expense of the more turbulent emotional landscape through

[66] Friedhelm Hardy, *Viraha Bhakti: The Early History of Kṛṣṇa Devotion in South India*, New Delhi: Oxford University Press, 1983, pp. 353–4, 366, 443.

[67] *Agpp*, pp. 193–9.

[68] *Tiruvāymŏḻi* 2.3.3.

[69] *Agpp*, pp. 193–9.

[70] Rāmānuja was not Yāmuna's direct disciple; in fact, they never 'met' each other—it seems a point so well established and well remembered that the hagiographies do not attempt to gloss it. This might explain the emphasis on detailing Yāmuna's desire to see Rāmānuja established at the pontificate in Srirangam, and elaborating instances of Rāmānuja having apprehended the unspoken wishes of Yāmuna. The incident mentioned above thus further 'legitimises' Rāmānuja's succession.

[71] Carman, op. cit., pp. 210–11.

which the hymns meander, ambiguity remained in a number of aspects. While this life remains important in the opportunity it offers for service to the temple icon, there can be no doubt that in the formulations of the *ācāryas*, final liberation was obtainable only in the afterlife.[72] Rāmānuja describes the glories of Vaikuṇṭha, the Lord's celestial abode, in the *Vaikuṇṭha Gadyam*.[73] Āl̲vār devotionalism, however, was frequently focused on particular images in particular shrines. This absorption in the *arcā* (image-incarnation) finds indirect support in a key concept of early Śrīvaiṣṇavism, viz., the parity of the different forms of the lord.[74] *Pāñcarātra* doctrine envisages the Lord in five forms— *para*, i.e. transcendental lord in his supreme heaven, *vyūha*, emanations, *vibhava* or incarnations such as Rāma and Kṛṣṇa, *arcā*, and finally, *antaryāmi*, the indweller in all creation.[75] The concepts of *antaryāmin*, *avatāra* and *arcā* are modes of god's approach to the human self for its salvation, and thus the principle of initiating grace.[76] Piḷḷai Lokācārya's analogy of the five forms of water is telling: a man thirsting for water is similar to the soul thirsting for salvation; the *antaryāmi* is like water underground, the *para* form like water surrounding the world-egg, the *vyūhas* like the milk-ocean, the *vibhavas* like seasonal rivers while the *arcā* is like standing pools in these rivers.[77]

The emphasis upon transcendence in Nammāl̲vār's thought is believed to establish god's supremacy; the emphasis upon immanence his condescending grace. If god were merely transcendent mystery, there could be no personal relationship and no self-understanding which would be adequate for living; if he were merely immanent, one would

[72] There are exceptions, however. Vedānta Deśika says in *Varadarāja Pañcāśat* 49, 'Oh lord of Varaṇaśaila! As I constantly visit your beautiful form, the place that is untainted by anxiety, I have no desire even for Vaikuṇṭha—by truth, I swear!' (Translation by Katherine Young, 'Dying for Bhukti and Mukti', op. cit., p 395). The influence of the poetry of the Āl̲vārs is discernible here.

[73] One of the works whose authorship is disputed by Lester.

[74] Nayar, op. cit., pp. 105–33.

[75] Ibid., p. 105; Carman, op. cit., p. 179; Matsubara, *Pāñcarātra Saṁhitās*, op. cit., pp. 117–44.

[76] R. David Kaylor and K.K.A. Venkatachari, *God Far, God Near: An Interpretation of the Thought of Nammalvar* no. 5 (supplement), Bombay: Ananthacharya Indological Research Institute Series, 1981, p. 37.

[77] *Śrīvacana Bhūṣaṇa* 39, cited in *Mumukṣuppaṭi* of Piḷḷai Lokācārya with Maṇavāḷamāmuni's Commentary, Translation by Patricia Y. Mumme, op. cit., p. 201.

have no assurance of the ground of faith.[78] Unlike later commentators who developed a contrast between the *paratva* and *saulabhya* of the Lord, i.e. His transcendence and accessibility,[79] Rāmānuja did not; rather, he maintained their simultaneity (though, as we have seen, he did not use the specific term *saulabhya*). The Lord, in Rāmānuja's thought, does not give up his essential nature even during his partial descents, i.e. as *avatāras*.[80] Rāmānuja himself does not mention the word *arcā*, though his *Śrīranga Gadyam* is devoted to the image of the lord at Srirangam.[81] In their Sanskrit *stotras*, Kūreśa and Parāśara Bhaṭṭar express their enjoyment of the tension inherent in the polarity between the lord's supremacy and his accessibility. Several of Bhaṭṭar's verses actually suggest that the lord prefers to dwell in the accessible and worshippable temple icon over even Vaikuṇṭha.[82] Indeed, the lord is thought to desire his devotees as ardently as they desire him. Returning from a visit to the temple of the lord in TiruvAhīndrapuram, Vedānta Deśika came upon a glorious vision of the Lord Devanāyaka in the middle of the night. The deity wanted to know why he was leaving without composing songs in his honour. Deśika sang, 'You never turn from your devotees, O Acyuta,/ whose minds/ like moonstone that sweats/ under shining moonlight/ melt into a flood of tears at the sight of your face.'[83] Says Nayar, 'The mutuality of the relationship between Viṣṇu and his devotees is a distinctive element of the Śrīvaiṣṇava tradition, and as such, represents an important point of continuity between the Ālvārs and *ācāryas*'.[84] Indeed, this finds expression in Rāmānuja's *Bhagavad Gītābhāṣya*[85] in his gloss of Kṛṣṇa's words to Arjuna, 'You are dear to me'. Rāmānuja represents the lord as being unable to bear separation from his devotee, thus causing him to attain him.

Meditation upon and recitation of three esoteric stanzas are central

[78] Kaylor and Venkatachari, op. cit., p. 36.

[79] Carman, op. cit., p. 251. Also, the above statement by Kaylor and Venkatachari reflects a conscious attempt to look at Nammālvār's thought from outside the prism of the commentaries.

[80] Carman, op. cit., p. 251.

[81] This, the devotion to an *arcā* form, is the main reason for Lester's rejection of the authorship of this text by Rāmānuja.

[82] Nayar, op. cit., pp. 131–2.

[83] Steven Paul Hopkins, *Singing the Body of God: The Hymns of Vedāntadeśika in their South Indian Tradition*, New Delhi: Oxford University Press, 2002, pp. 3–4. The translation of Deśika's hymn is also Hopkins'.

[84] Nayar, op. cit., p. 197.

[85] *Bhagavad-Gītābhāṣya*, 18.65.

articles of Śrīvaiṣṇava faith.[86] These three are: (1) the *aṣṭākṣaram*, i.e. *Om namo nārāyaṇāyaḥ* (2) the *dvayamantram*, i.e. *Śrimad nārāyaṇa caraṇau śaraṇam prapadye, Śrimate Nārāyaṇāya namaḥ*, and (3) the *carama śloka*, i.e. *sarvadharmān parityajya, māmekam śaraṇam vraja/ aham tvā sarvapāpebhyo mokṣayiṣyāmi mā śucaḥ*. The last *śloka* is from the *Gītā*. It is considered by the Śrīvaiṣṇava community to be the essence of the teaching of the lord, hence, the appellation *carama*. It is interpreted by the community as the promise of the lord to grant salvation to all who take refuge in him. I will now examine the hagiographic material to see how these key Śrīvaiṣṇava philosophical tenets are brought out in the lives of the Ā<u>l</u>vārs.

(iii) Painting the Ālvārs into the Picture

Āṇḍāḷ has a unique position among the twelve Āḻvārs by virtue of being the only woman among them. From the *Tiruppāvai*, a poem of 30 stanzas, emerges the picture of a young woman intensely devoted to Kṛṣṇa. Her other composition, the *Nācciyār Tirumŏḻi*, comprising 143 stanzas that make 14 poems, is among the earliest literary pieces suffused with 'bridal mysticism'. The early *ācāryas* and commentators accorded a special status to Āṇḍāḷ, not merely because of the impassioned quality of her verse but owing perhaps to her gender too. Other Āḻvārs, notably Kulaśekhara, Nammāḻvār and Tirumankai have also composed verses in the voice of a woman yearning for her divine beloved, but as Piṉpaḻakiya Pĕrumāḷ Cīyar, the author of the *Agpp* phrases it, the love of a man for a man is like water flowing uphill whereas that of a woman for a man and of a man for a woman is as natural as water flowing downhill. Āṇḍāḷ came to be considered variously an incarnation of Bhūmi, the earth-goddess who is one of Viṣṇu's two chief consorts, or of Nīlā/ Nappiṉṉai, the Tamil bride of the lord.

The 'life-story' of Āṇḍāḷ is evidently based on a careful reading of the hymns of Āṇḍāḷ.[87] Let us try and retrace some of the steps that the hagiographers must have taken—for it is first in his commentary on the *Tiruppāvai*, in contextualizing her verses, that Pĕriyavāccāṉ Piḷḷai, the teacher of Piṉpaḻakiya Pĕrumāḷ Cīyar, is said to have first elaborated the

[86] It is difficult to tell when they became important. Certainly, the hagiographies represent Yāmuna as having reposed their esoteric meanings in his disciples, and Rāmānuja as having taken particular pains to obtain the meaning of the *dvayam* from Tirukkoṭṭiyūr Nampi—a particularly popular incident. See Chapter 2-x of the present work.

[87] *Agpp*, pp. 47–50.

legend of Āṇḍāḷ.[88] The *Tiruppāvai* begins with a call to maidens to join in the *pāvai* vow, and promises that careful observance of the same would lead to such boons as a bountiful monsoon, golden heaps of paddy, and plentiful milk from their cows.[89] Māṇikkavācakar, a Śaiva hymnist-saint, takes a similar penance for the theme of the *Tiruvĕmpāvai*, a poem that forms part of the Śaiva canon. It appears that our present knowledge of this custom of the *pāvai vrata* is based essentially on these two poems. The *Bhāgavata Purāṇa* interpreted the *pāvai*, a sand figure or mother goddess central to the vow, as the goddess Kātyāyani;[90] a statement that must be accepted in the absence of other evidence. Āṇḍāḷ turned its focus to the worship of Kṛṣṇa. Āṇḍāḷ frequently alludes to various feats of Viṣṇu in his various incarnations—measuring the worlds in three strides,[91] killing Rāvaṇa and Kumbhakarṇa,[92] etc.,— but references to events from the Kṛṣṇāvatāra doubtlessly predominate. Āṇḍāḷ, like the other Āḻvārs, is familiar with the legends of Viṣṇu (as is further evinced in the *Nācciyār Tirumŏḻi*), and is conscious of the identities of Viṣṇu's different forms, even when concentrating on any one specific form, either as *avatāra* (incarnation), or as *arcā* (iconic incarnation).[93] Indeed, when speaking of the lord installed in any of the numerous shrines dotting the Tamil land, or the dozen or so beyond the borders of modern Tamil Nadu, the Āḻvārs regularly allude to his residence in other shrines, and even address the lord in a particular shrine as the one who dwells in another. However, I will return to this subject in a later chapter.

Āṇḍāḷ frequently speaks of 'northern Mathura', and the banks of the Yamuna,[94] but not only as distant holy places of the lord. The voice in such verses is that of one of the *gopīs* of the cowherd clan who addresses some hymns[95] to her friends and cousins, rousing them to join in the early morning rituals of the vow and, in others,[96] addresses Nappiṉṉai as Nandagopa's daughter-in-law—showing an interesting amalgam in the southern mythic imagination of the identification of the Tamil bride of

[88] Hudson, 'Bathing in Krishna', p. 553.

[89] *Tiruppāvai* 3.

[90] Hardy, op. cit., p. 416.

[91] *Tiruppāvai* 3.

[92] *Tiruppāvai* 12.

[93] I owe the term to John Carman and Vasudha Narayanan, *The Tamil Veda: Piḷḷāṉ's Interpretation of the Tiruvāymoḻi*, Chicago: The University of Chicago Press, 1989, p. 89.

[94] *Tiruppāvai* 5.

[95] *Tiruppāvai* 9, 10.

[96] *Tiruppāvai* 18, 19.

the lord with his specifically northern persona. Finally, numerous hymns are naturally addressed to Kṛṣṇa himself. While in some verses Āṇḍāḷ asks for various boons, such as prosperity for the land,[97] forgiveness for past sins,[98] or even for the ritual implements necessary for the performance of the vow itself, the penultimate verse expresses the running theme—the grant of eternal service to the lord.

The *Nācciyār Tirumŏḻi* is more complex in its organization than the *Tiruppāvai*. In the opening poem of ten stanzas, Āṇḍāḷ asks Kāma, the God of Love, to unite her with Kṛṣṇa. She details the rites she has performed for securing her beloved. It is in this poem that Āṇḍāḷ speaks the words[99] considered decisive by the Śrīvaiṣṇava community: that she would not live if there were even talk of marrying her to a mortal, indeed, that it would be such sacrilege as jackals sniffing at the (Vedic) sacrificial oblation meant for the gods. In the sixth poem,[100] she sings of her dream of her wedding with the lord. It is interesting as a window to marriage rituals in the eighth–ninth centuries, almost all of which (with the exception of the elephant-back ride of the newly-wedded couple) continue to feature in the modern Śrīvaiṣṇava wedding, not least because of the sanctity in which the *Divyaprabandham* has been held since at least the eleventh century. Both medieval and modern scholars of the Śrīvaiṣṇava persuasion have, however, treated this dream as indicative of a prophetic revelation, an eventual fait accompli as it were. In the hymns spoken in the voice of a lovelorn maiden, Āṇḍāḷ asks to be united with (1) Kṛṣṇa (or one of the other names of Viṣṇu such as Govinda, Hṛṣikeśa, Vāmana, Tirumāl, etc.), or the Lord of Vṛndāvana[101] and of Tuvārai[102] (Dvārakā), and (2) the deity in specific shrines in the Tamil land. Since the former are generic, I shall concentrate here on the latter, particularly due to their significance to our hypothesis. Though Āṇḍāḷ mentions the lord's presence in Venkaṭam, Kaṇṇapuram,[103] Villiputtūr,[104] Māliruñcolai,[105] and Kuṭantai,[106] impassioned hymns

[97] *Tiruppāvai* 3.
[98] *Tiruppāvai* 5.
[99] *Nācciyār Tirumŏḻi* 1.5.
[100] *Nācciyār Tirumŏḻi* 6.1–6.10.
[101] *Nācciyār Tirumŏḻi* 14.1–14.10.
[102] *Nācciyār Tirumŏḻi* 1.4.
[103] *Nācciyār Tirumŏḻi* 4.2.
[104] *Nācciyār Tirumŏḻi* 5.5.
[105] *Nācciyār Tirumŏḻi* 4.1.
[106] *Nācciyār Tirumŏḻi* 13.2.

are addressed only to the lord in Venkaṭam,[107] Māliruñcolai[108] and Srirangam,[109] apart from Āyppāṭi (literally, cowherd-hamlet, which in Śrīvaiṣṇava lore has acquired the status of one of the 108 sacred places of the lord).[110] The emotion of *viraha* predominates in the penultimate song;[111] but the last,[112] structured as a dialogue between two *gopīs*, is strangely an anticlimax to this set of extraordinarily intense poems.[113] It may perhaps be explained by the fact of the compilation being much later than the actual composition of the hymns, when considerations other than gradation in emotional intensity might have predominated. Hardy holds, in fact, that the erotic-emotional content of the poems was anything but significant in the Śrīvaiṣṇava circles where the compilation is likely to have occurred.[114]

Tai is the Tamil month that follows Mārkaḻi (Sanskrit Mṛgaśīrsa), which falls between mid-December and mid-January. Mārkaḻi is traditionally considered inauspicious for the performance of weddings, and the fact that this seems as true of northern India as of the south may indicate its origin in some hoary past. There remains the fact of the *pāvai nompu* being performed in the month of Mārkaḻi, with the attainment of good husbands as one of the stated objectives.[115] After the austerities of the coldest month of the year, Kotai speaking as a *gopi* and thus by definition a lover of Kṛṣṇa, asks for no more than the pleasure of service in life after life. Tai (harbinger also of spring in Tamil Nadu), allows expression of love and longing, besides holding out the promise of the grant of the desired boons. Is it stylistic and ritualistic considerations—the fact that the *Tiruppāvai*, an internally ordered unit, begins with the words, '*Mārkaḻit tingaḷ*'(literally, month of Mārkaḻi)—that was critical in the choice of the poem beginning with the phrase '*Tai ŏru tingaḷ*' (the month of Tai) as the first of the other collection by the saint-poetess?[116]

107 *Nācciyār Tirumŏḻi* 8.1–8.10.

108 *Nācciyār Tirumŏḻi* 9.1–9.10, 10.1–10.10.

109 *Nācciyār Tirumŏḻi* 11.1–11.10.

110 See Chapter 6-ii of the present work.

111 *Nācciyār Tirumŏḻi* 13.1–13.10.

112 *Nācciyār Tirumŏḻi* 14.1–14.10.

113 See Venkatesan, 'Āṇṭāḷ and her Magic Mirror', for a discussion of this.

114 Hardy, op. cit., p. 480.

115 While in popular understanding, this is considered the primary objective of the vow, unmarried girls being encouraged to recite the *Tiruppāvai* through the month of Mārkaḻi, it is markedly absent in the poem itself.

116 See also Katherine Young, 'The Spirit and the Bride say "Come!" Continuing a Hindu-Christian Dialogue', *Journal of Vaishnava Studies*, vol. 6,

Since Āṇḍāḷ often describes her own youthfulness, physical beauty, and dense black tresses adorned with flowers when asking the lord to join her, the early Śrīvaiṣṇava *ācāryas* often read her hymns as autobiography; indeed at times, it seems difficult not to do so.[117] Combined with the details in the signature verses: that she is the daughter of Putuvai/Villiputtūr's priest, Viṣṇucitta of the Veyar clan, who is well known to us from his own 400-odd hymns, the hagiographical account shorn merely of the miraculous—particularly the incident at the end, of Āṇḍāḷ's merger with Ranganātha—seems almost entirely believable. Yet, the fact remains that a substantial portion of what the hagiography tells us is entirely unverifiable, and it is some of these aspects that will engage our attention.

While hymns 11.1 to 11.10 are dedicated to the Lord of Srirangam, and are composed in the erotic-emotional mode, Āṇḍāḷ does not specifically ask to be united with him. It is important to remember that it is to the Lord of Venkaṭam (and once to Tuvārai) that Āṇḍāḷ repeatedly asks Kāma to deliver her.[118] The *Agpp* says that when Pĕriyāḻvār desired to know whom Āṇḍāḷ wished to marry, she answered that she would look upon no one but Māyaṉ of Māliruñcolai.[119] This temple town is geographically closer to Śrīvilliputtūr than Srirangam, and thus likely to be more familiar to Āṇḍāḷ than the former. The impression is strengthened by the hymns themselves—unlike those on Srirangam, Āṇḍāḷ's twenty stanzas on Māliruñcolai are rich with descriptions of the landscape. Why then did the *ācārya*-hagiographers choose to make her the bride of Aḻakiya Maṇavāḷaṉ (literally, the beautiful bridegroom) of Srirangam, particularly when it is inconsistent with Āṇḍāḷ's purported statement?

Srirangam, Venkaṭam and Māliruñcolai seem to have attracted pilgrims as early as the fifth–sixth centuries CE. In the *Cilappatikāram*,[120] Kovalaṉ and Kaṇṇaki meet, while travelling from Pukār to Madurai,

---

no. 1, 1998, pp. 99–116, for an interpretation of the *Nācciyār Tirumŏḻi* as a coda of the observance of a fourteen-day ritual performed in the month of Tai.

117 Venkatesan, 'Āṇṭāḷ and her Magic Mirror', and Archana Venkatesan, *The Secret Garland: Āṇṭāḷ's Tiruppāvai and Nācciyār Tirumoḻi*. Translated with Introduction and Commentary, New York: Oxford University Press, 2010, offer many excellent insights into how we may read Āṇḍāḷ. Since this chapter was originally written before I could read or profit from Venkatesan's analyses, and also because my very lack of awareness then of Venkatesan's work allows yet another window of exploration into the subject, I have left it largely unaltered.

118 *Nācciyār Tirumŏḻi* 1.1–1.10.

119 *Agpp*, pp. 47–9.

120 *Cilappatikāram*, Canto V.

a *brāhmaṇa* from the western hill country. He tells them that he is travelling to see the great lord in Venkaṭam and the lord reclining on the serpent in the island: an evident reference to Srirangam. Further, he praises Mālirunkuṉṟam (Māliruñcolai), advising the couple to go there. These sacred centres continued in importance in the centuries to come, but Srirangam certainly grew to be the pre-eminent sacred shrine. It has been pointed out[121] that the three early Āḻvārs focused on shrines in Tŏṇṭaināḍu— the Venkaṭam-Kāñcī environment,[122] while Nammāḻvār sings of far more temples in Malaināḍu (the modern Kerala region) than does any other Āḻvār. A greater number of temples in the neighbourhood of their respective hometowns, including smaller ones, feature in the hymns of most Āḻvārs, though almost all sing also of some major shrines, irrespective of which region they hail from. While Venkaṭam is mentioned by ten Āḻvārs, eleven laud Srirangam. This island shrine became the pontifical seat of the Vaiṣṇava *ācāryas* from the time of Nāthamuni onwards, and though important teachers hailed from towns such as TirukKoṭṭiyūr, Kacci (Kāñcī), etc., Srirangam remained the epicentre. Rāmānuja himself, though based in Kāñcī before assuming the leadership of the community, moved to Srirangam after the demise of Yāmunācārya. While Kāñcī, and specifically the shrine of Hastigiri therein, became important in the medieval centuries as the centre of the Vaṭakalai or northern sect, Srirangam, despite its greater association with the Tĕṉkalai stream, continued to remain *the* temple, so much so that in popular Śrīvaiṣṇava parlance as well as in the medieval Śrīvaiṣṇava texts, the word '*koyil*' (literally, temple) unqualified by any adjective or place name refers to Srirangam.

It is, thus, only natural that the prime importance of this shrine should be enhanced by the hagiographical literature. While, according to the theology, all the Viṣṇus are equally the great lord himself—the lord evidently suffering no diminution from his simultaneous presence in numerous shrines—and though even the terrestrial Viṣṇus are absolutely at par with the eternal lord reclining in the milkocean, or in Vaikuṇṭha surrounded by the celestials, Āṇḍāḷ's *svayamvara* would have less significance if it were not to underline the centrality of Srirangam.

The acme of spiritual progress in Śrīvaiṣṇava theology is *parama* bhakti, the apogee of devotion, which Āṇḍāḷ is said to have been imbued with. But the path to this pinnacle is through devotion to and knowledge of the divine lord—*para* bhakti and *para jñāna*. There is disagreement between

[121] Hardy, op. cit., pp. 257–61.
[122] Ibid., p. 258.

the two sects about the relative importance of devotion and knowledge for the attainment of the goal of salvation, the northern school with its Vedic-Sanskritic tilt stressing more on the individual's ritual capability and textual learning and the southern on *prapatti*, surrender. The latter is a means not denied but qualified by the Vaṭakalai sect.

A second and theologically pregnant issue emerges from the story of Āṇḍāḷ, and is mirrored in the story of Tiruppāṇāḻvār, the only Āḻvār said to belong to a *pañcama* caste.

In the case of Āṇḍāḷ, we saw how the hagiography draws upon the material available in her hymns. The singer of the *Amalaṉādipirāṉ*, however, gives us not the least clue about himself. There isn't even a signature verse. The tradition recognizes it to the degree that the name given to the hymnist is merely generic—Tiruppāṇāḻvār literally means the bard-saint. It remains almost impossible to discover his identity unless some hitherto unknown text is discovered. However, some features of the poem itself can be considered. The ten stanzas of great lyrical beauty are composed with first syllable rhyming, a style often met with in classical Tamil poetry. The poet shows awareness of various acts of Viṣṇu in his *avatāras* as Narasimha, Vāmana-Trivikrama, Rāma and Kṛṣṇa, and of some other cosmic acts of his. While the poem is specifically in praise of the physical form of the lord of Srirangam, he twice mentions the lord's residence in Venkaṭam. The descriptions of Venkaṭam are minimal and stereotyped, allowing the supposition that the Āḻvār's knowledge of the place was based on hearsay—something which the hagiography too implies by its insistence that he spent his entire life singing on the southern bank of the Kaveri, across from the shrine of Ranganātha. Perhaps the sense of wonder at the beauty and the rich adornments of the lord that the poem expresses may have also led to the formulation that the singer was in the presence of the *arcā* for the first time.[123] The poem ends with the impassioned declaration that the eyes (of the Āḻvār) which have feasted on the nectar that is the lord of Srirangam will see nothing else.

It is of course possible to read this as poetic hyperbole, but the Śrīvaiṣṇava community evidently chose not to do so. Again, a literal interpretation of the rapturous expression could equally easily have lead to the story ending with the Āḻvār becoming blind after the 'divine vision', maybe a blindness made glorious by an unending vision of the

[123] I am not arguing for the veracity of the hagiographic account, but merely presenting the plausibility—after all, good poetry can well convey a sense of childlike wonder even at the familiar.

lord in the 'inner eye'. Indeed, the roughly contemporary *Pĕriya Purāṇam* relates the story of a blind Nāyaṉār Taṇṭiyaṭikaḷ, who was compensated for his sightlessness by *jñānakkaṇ*, the eye of knowledge or gnosis.[124] The more dramatic ending in the Śrīvaiṣṇava hagiography is not, however, an arbitrary choice; rather, it embodies a coherent theological vision of the community.

(iv) The Integration

As we have seen earlier, Āḻvār poetry oscillates between expressions of the bliss of union and the despair of *viraha*. The Āḻvārs speak of the changeling lord—bestowing his grace and tormenting by denying union—as Māyiṉ (possessor of *māyā*, illusion); his *māyā* explaining the inexplicable, as it were. Nammāḻvār cries out, 'You seem to come to me, my radiant Lord, but never stay. Now how can I join You, if you do not stay and give me strength?'[125] Āṇḍāḷ asks in despair, 'O dark monsoon clouds! I sing the praise of the Lord of Venkaṭam who emerged victorious from the battlefield. I fall apart like withered Calotropis milkweed leaves in the rain. Alas! Will he never send a word of hope?'[126] In the highly elliptical *Tiruccanta Viruttam* we find, 'I have no thoughts but of you, no kith nor kin but you. Oh! You of countless *māyā*,[127] you must promise never to forsake me.'[128] But a little further down, this poet expresses his confidence that, 'The Lord will grant eternal goodness: freedom from return to the earth',[129] and finally ends with, 'Pursuing me through countless births, the cloud-hued Lord has now come into my heart and revealed his endless glories. My old sins cut away, my blessed soul has found its home.'[130] Tirumaḻicai says, 'O Lord, you have decided that the faithless ones should fall into the throes of fourfold birth. But you also wait for an occasion to relieve them of their curse. Did you not free the waning moon of his curse? Did you not send your discus spinning and

124 G. Vanmikanathan, *Periya Puranam by Sekkizhaar: Condensed English Version*, Madras: Sri Ramakrishna Math, 2004, pp. 476–7. See also, Chapter 2-xiv of the present work.

125 *Tiruvāymŏḻi* 3.2.5.

126 *Nācciyār Tirumŏḻi* 8.8.

127 The Tamil word used is *māya*.

128 *Tiruccanta Viruttam* 91.

129 *Tiruccanta Viruttam* 112.

130 *Tiruccanta Viruttam* 120. Also, the *Tiruccanta Viruttam* approximates mature Śrīvaiṣṇava theology far more than other works in the *NDP*. See Hardy, op. cit., pp. 439–41.

relieve both elephant and crocodile of their curses?'[131] Not all the Āḻvārs possess this assurance, however, or when they seem to, it doesn't last. Nammāḻvār rejoices, 'The Lord is easy to reach for devotees through love. His feet are hard to get for others, even for the lady of the lotus. Oh, how easily he was caught and bound to the mortar, pleading, for churning butter from the milkmaid's churning pail!'[132] But the dejection of separation is never far away. 'Māyakkūttaṉ (the one who dances the dance of *māyā*)[133] of southern Kuḷantai surrounded by groves and tall mansions, the discus-wielder went away, borne on his dancing bird. I followed him and lost my heart, my bangles, my all. Now I stand shamed before my bangle-decked friends, what more can I lose?'[134] Kulaśekhara Āḻvār expresses this dependence on the lord starkly, 'O Lord of Vittuvakkoṭu surrounded by fragrant groves! If you do not help me overcome the obstacles you place in my path, I have no refuge but you. A child beaten by the mother cries to be pacified by the mother alone.'[135]

Even this small selection of hymns demonstrates the untenability of Burton Stein's belief that the hymns (of the *NDP*) expressed the central ethos of the bhakti faith: divine and redemptive grace conferred by a merciful god upon a loving devotee.[136] What emerges rather is the

131 *Nānmukaṉ Tiruvantādi* 12.

132 *Tiruvāymŏḻi* 1.3.1.

133 Today, the name of the *utsava mūrti* in the temple town of Kuḷantai. See Chapter 6-ii of the present work.

134 *Tiruvāymŏḻi* 8.2.4.

Two separate editions of English translations of this hymn, one of which also gives detailed exegesis in Tamil, claim on their respective front pages that they are based on the 'commentaries of *pūrvacāryās*'. Neither glosses the word with the meaning that springs forth as the most obvious. While one merely reproduces the word as a proper noun in English, the second does not even do so. Instead, in the Tamil exegetical section, we find that the lord is said to be riding Garuḍa who is described as dancing with the intoxication of being the carrier of the glorious lord with his discus and conch, *like* one who has consumed *madhu*.

References: *The Sacred Book of Four Thousand: Nalayira Divya Prabandham rendered in English with Tamil Original*, by Srirama Bharati, Sri Sadagopan Tirunarayanaswami Pathasala, Chennai 2000, p.566; *Āḻvār Tiruvuḷḷam: Nammāḻvār Aruḷiccĕyta Tiruvāymŏḻi*, by Vankipuram Navanītam Vedānta Deśikaṉ, Śrī Viśiṣṭādvaita Research Centre, Madras, 1994, pp. 765-766.

135 *Pĕrumāḷ Tirumŏḻi* 5.1.

136 Burton Stein, 'Social Mobility and Medieval South Indian Hindu Sects', James Silverberg (ed.), *Social Mobility and the Caste System in India: An Interdisciplinary Symposium*, Paris, 1985, p. 288.

degree to which modern historiography has accepted the medieval *ācāryas*' valuation and representation of the bhakti saints and their compositions. Considering that for every verse that declares, 'O lord Nārāyaṇa, you may grace me today, or tomorrow, or some time later, but your grace is definitely coming. I cannot be without you; nor can you without me',[137] there are others that express the fear of rebirth and endless karmas,[138] it is difficult to postulate that Āḻvār bhakti was grounded in an assurance of salvation. Rather, it was the acaryic tradition beginning with Nāthamuni, most strongly shaped by the theology of Rāmānuja, and further elaborated, defined and, in the process, modified in the succeeding generations, that made the redemptive intention and qualities of the lord its central feature. Indeed, it is these elaborations and the gradual modifications that they entailed, particularly in the two different environments of Srirangam and Kāñcī, such that the Srirangam *ācāryas* were more deeply involved in writing commentaries on the hymns of the Āḻvārs and explicating these to mixed audiences[139] while the *ācāryas* in the more cosmopolitan Kāñcī were concerned to defend Rāmānuja's system against rival philosophies (which involved their continued engagement with proving the Vedic compatibility of Viśiṣṭādvaita) that eventually led to the formation of two distinct theo-philosophical systems within the larger umbrella of Śrīvaiṣṇavism.

The importance of the commentaries in shaping the understanding of the Āḻvārs' hymns is seen from the fact that within 60 years of Rāmānuja's death, two commentaries had been written on the *Tiruvāymŏḻi*, using the ideas of Viśiṣṭādvaita Vedānta to interpret Nammāḻvār's hymns.[140] The commentaries try to impose a certain degree of uniformity over the hymnal expressions of the Āḻvārs, at least when dramatic emotional swings occur repeatedly within the same hymn.[141] In her analysis of the *stotras* of the early *ācāryas*, Kūreśa and Bhaṭṭar, Nayar shows that the latter, despite closely following the Āḻvārs in their devotional expressions, 'integrating Āḻvār devotionalism into their Sanskrit poems',[142] carefully

[137] *Nāṉmukaṉ Tiruvantādi* 7.

[138] *Pĕriya Tirumŏḻi* 11.8.1–5.

[139] The audiences would have been mixed in terms of caste and gender.

[140] Patricia Mumme, *The Śrīvaiṣṇava Theological Dispute: Maṇavāḷa Māmuṉi and Vedānta Deśika*, New Era Publications, 1988, p. 4.

[141] The hagiographies record Rāmānuja's insistence on a new interpretation of certain hymns of Nammāḻvār.

[142] Nayar, op. cit., p. 207.

eschewed expressions of Viṣṇu as Māyin̲.[143] In his arguments against Śankara's conception of the Supreme Brahman as *nirguṇa* (without qualities), Rāmānuja emphasizes the lord's infinite auspicious qualities. For Rāmānuja, there can be no ambiguity in the nature of the lord. Nammāḻvār, on the other hand sees god both as poverty and wealth, heaven and hell, enmity and friendship, poison and ambrosia, joy and sorrow, confusion and clarity, punishment and compassion, town and country, wisdom and ignorance, incomparable light and deepest darkness, good and evil, unity and separation, remembering and forgetting, crookedness and straight-forwardness, black and white, truth and lie, youth and old age, shadow and sunlight, smallness and greatness, shortness and length, mobility and immobility.[144] However, a lord capable of evasiveness or confusing his devotees, as he often is in Nammāḻvār's thought, would be to 'play into the hands of those philosophical schools for whom a God-with-attributes (*saguṇa* Brahman) was lower than the unqualified Brahman, and is Himself a effect of *māyā*'.[145] The lord is characterised by *nirmalatva*, blemishlessness, freedom from all taint—this is brought out in the well-known episode of Rāmānuja's life where he breaks with his Advaitin teacher, Yādava Prakāśa. Explicating a certain Upanisadic passage, Yādava is supposed to have described the eyes of the lord as being red like a monkey's behind. Deeply saddened, Rāmānuja explained the passage as describing the lords' eyes as beautiful like a blossoming red lotus.[146] That this should form, in the understanding of the Śrīvaiṣṇava community, the basis of its greatest preceptor's break with the Advaita tradition rather than such issues as the oneness of or distinction between Brahman and created beings, speaks as much of the community's self-perception as of its specific, theological orientation. Thus, when *ācāryas* like Vedānta Deśika composed poetry of separation following the Āḻvār tradition, they carefully attributed this inability to achieve union to their own inferior bhakti or lack of good qualities.[147] The Āḻvārs, however, are considered *parama bhaktas*, their devotion wanting nothing.

[143] Ibid., p. 207.

[144] *Tiruvāymŏḻi* 6.3.1 to 6.3.5.

[145] Nayar, op. cit., p. 207. See also, Bharatan Kumarappa, *The Hindu Conception of the Deity*, Delhi: Inter-India Publications, 1979 (first published 1934), pp. 196–205, for Rāmānuja's refutation of the doctrine of *māyā*.

[146] *Agpp*, pp. 142–4.

[147] See Hopkins, *Singing the Body of God*, op. cit., passim, for translations of poems by Vedāntadeśika, and Friedhelm Hardy, 'The Philosopher as a Poet: A

The lord, in the Śrīvaiṣṇava understanding, enjoys his creation, and the service and devotion of his worshippers. Indeed, he delights in the sight of them in his temples.[148] For the Āḻvārs, whose lord arbitrarily unites with and forsakes his devotees, the motif of Kṛṣṇa's relationship with the *gopīs* was symbolic. For the *ācāryas,* however, the central erotic relationship of the Divine is not Kṛṣṇa and the *gopīs* of Vṛndāvana; it is the inseparable union of Viṣṇu with Śrī.[149] In fact, Śrī acquires a significant ontological status in the developing theology of the community, with important differences in the perception of the two sects. It has been pointed out that Piḷḷāṉ and later commentators used categories that were not intrinsic to the poems, but borrowed from Sanskrit. Where the hymns merely hint at an idea, the commentators use formulaic phrases from Sanskrit to explain the theme. Thus, if Śrī is mentioned in a hymn by one of the Āḻvārs, the commentators take it as a symbol of divine intercession.[150]

I will return here to the point raised by the *carama śloka*—the command of the lord to eschew all other dharma and to resort to him alone, and tie in some of the points I have made earlier. The interpretation of the manner of taking refuge in the lord forms the basis of some of the crucial points of dissent between the Vaṭakalai and Tĕṉkalai sects of the Śrīvaiṣṇava community. These are, briefly: (1) Does *śaraṇāgati* or *prapatti* constitute the sole means or is it one of the means to salvation? (2) Does the devotee have agency in the action of taking *prapatti,* or is it too the result of the grace of god? (3) Is Śrī, who serves as mediatrix between the *prapanna* and the lord, an essential part of the Supreme Lord, or merely the first among created beings, and in a position far elevated above all other created beings? The debates that have engaged Śrīvaiṣṇavas for about 500 years need not detain us here; our purpose is merely a familiarity with the theological framework.

What emerges clearly is the salvational nature of Śrīvaiṣṇava theology, the promise of the lord to save his devotees. The *Rāmāyaṇa* in Śrīvaiṣṇava understanding is essentially a *prapatti stotra.* Rāma's offer of asylum, protection and perennial love to Vibhīṣaṇa is central to the Śrīvaiṣṇava doctrine of *śaraṇāgati* and the lord's boundless grace is seen as reflected in his declaration to Sugrīva that his grace was open to all

Study of Vedāntadeśika's Dehalīśastuti', *Journal of Indian Philosophy,* vol. 7, 1979, pp. 277–32, where he brings out Deśika's deep sense of his own sinfulness.

[148] Nayar, op. cit., p. 209.

[149] Ibid., p. 217.

[150] Narayanan, *The Vernacular Veda,* op. cit., p. 111.

supplicants, even Rāvaṇa if he sought it.[151] We saw the emphasis in the *DSC* account of Tirumankai Āḻvār's pilgrimage to Venkaṭam on the lord's compulsively responding to his devotee's hunger.[152] The theme is further developed in legends from specific shrines. The *sthalapurāṇa* of TirukKaṇṇamankai recites the story of a devotee, Lakṣminārāyaṇasvāmi. This *bhakta*, who had no family, spent all his time doing *kainkarya* at the temple. When the temple doors were opened on the morning after the devotee's death, not only were *darbha* grass and sesame discovered in the shrine, but the lord's *veṣṭi* (lower cloth) was found to be wet and his sacred thread in the reverse position (signifying the performance of *tarpaṇa* and last rites). The lord who had become kinsman to his devotee is accordingly called Bhaktavatsala.[153] As the lord delights in the service of his devotees and is so eager for their salvation, he is ever looking for an excuse to save them. The act of *prapatti* gives him the excuse. While both schools believe that the devotees' faults are not impediments to salvation, the northern sect holds that the lord in his love, is blind to the devotees' faults, while the southern goes so far as to say that he relishes the faults of his devotees, the better to express his mercy and grace. In their exegesis of the *Rāmāyaṇa* episode of Sītā meeting Rāma after the war in Lanka was over, Tĕṉkalai scholars say that Rāma was displeased that Sītā had bathed before coming to him even though she had acted merely as he had instructed, because he really wanted to see her at once and as she was.[154] Indeed, the merits of the devotee do not endear him/ her to the lord any better. The Tĕṉkalai *ācāryas* take the example of Rāma asking Sītā during their stay in the forest not to wear even a necklace as it would interfere in their lovemaking, to argue that one's merits, instead of increasing the lord's pleasure in communing with the soul, may actually obstruct it.[155] Both Tĕṉkalai and Vaṭakalai positions will, however, be answered by the very telling phrase in the Tiruppāṇāḻvār *vaibhavam*, 'the Lord absorbed into Himself the Āḻvār in

[151] K.V. Rangaswami Aiyangar, 'Govindarāja', *Annals of the Bhandarkar Oriental Research Institute*, vol. 23, 1942, pp. 30–1.

[152] See Chapter 2-viii-b of the present work.

[153] A. Etirajan, *108 Vaiṇava Divya Deśa Stala Varaḷāru*, Karaikkuti: Vaiṇava Siddhānta Nūrpatippuk Kaḻakam, 2003, pp. 101–2.

[154] Patricia Mumme, 'Ramayana Exegesis in Tenkalai Srivaisnavism', in *Many Ramayanas: The Diversity of a Narrative Tradition in South Asia*, ed. Paula Richman, New Delhi: Oxford University Press, 1994, p. 209.

[155] Ibid., pp. 208–9.

his bodily form, even as those who wear fragrant roots in their hair do so with the mud sticking to it'.

The lord here is, as we know from the hagiography, the accessible *arcā* at Srirangam; equal to the transcendent lord who resides in Vaikuṇṭha, eternal service to whom is the goal of the *ācāryas*' devotion,[156] itself expressed as *nitya kainkarya* (daily service) to the temple icon.

It is again Lord Ranganātha of Srirangam who decides, as a matter of sport, and in response to a question from his consort, to throw in the way of his devotee, Vipranārāyaṇa, the courtesan, Devadevi, and thus gets the story of Tŏṇṭaraṭippŏṭi Āḻvār going, so to speak. While the main outline of the 'life-story' seems stereotypical, with its tropes of obsession with a courtesan leading to pauperism and dishonesty, eventual disillusionment—in every sense of the word—and return to the righteous path, the interventions of the lord mark this tale out as distinctly Śrīvaiṣṇava. Most important, however, is the point that the lord says he had put his devotee through all this pain in order for him to repent and thus cleanse him of his accumulated karma.[157]

The Āḻvārs, who repeatedly sang about their surrender and looked to him alone for protection, are, for the Śrīvaiṣṇava, the ideal *prapannas*. Their exemplary devotion is brought out in different ways throughout the hagiographies. Their births being described as *avatāras* of different aspects of Viṣṇu, such as his discus, mace or Śrīvatsa (chest mark/hair tuft), or of one or the other of his eternal attendants, may have served to establish their worship-worthiness in the community of believers; certainly by the time of the early *ācāryas*, the practice of installing the images of Āḻvārs in temples is known.[158] Then again, the lord is often

[156] There are, however, instances in the writings of the *ācāryas* where they state that worshipping the lord in a particular temple icon, they have no desire for even Vaikuṇṭha. See, for example, Vedānta Deśika, *Varadarāja Pañcāśat*.

[157] See Chapter 2-vi of the present work.

[158] An inscription of 1021 CE from the Kulaśekhara Āḻvār shrine in the Gopālasvāmi temple, Maṉṉārkoyil, Ambāsamudram *tāluk*, mentions the setting up of the shrine of Kulaśekhara-p-Pĕrumāḷ. See T.V. Mahalingam, *A Topographical List of Inscriptions in Tamil Nadu and Kerala States*. ICHR and S. Chand and Co., Delhi, vol. I, 1985, vol. IX, pp. 28–9. Tn 134. Ref.: *ARE*, 1916, no. 400; ibid., part ii, para 2. Another from 1082 CE in the Caurirāja-p-Pĕrumāḷ Temple in TirukKaṇṇapuram, Naṉṉilam *tāluk*, records a gift of land as *arcanā bhoga* to the shrine of Tirumankai Āḻvār. See Mahalingam, 1985, vol. VII, pp. 437–8. Tj 1886. Ref.: *ARE*, 1922, no. 510; ibid., part ii, p. 105. Inscriptional evidence for images of the Nāyaṉmārs is more plentiful, the earliest dating to 995 CE. See Mahalingam, 1985, vol. VII, p. 21. Tj 96. Ref.: *ARE*, 1917, no. 299. The formal consecration of the images of the

said to have specially graced the new-born infant.[159] More relevant than these instances of miracles, however, are the descriptions of the exalted *bhakti* of the Āḻvārs. Of the twelve Āḻvārs, four are placed according to the traditional dating in an earlier *yuga*, while eight belong to the Kali age. This suggests that they may be religious models for those living in this, the most degenerate of all *yugas*.[160] Despite their doctrinal differences over the relative merits of bhakti and *prapatti* for salvation, both schools recognize three stages in the evolution of the devotee, the last of which brooks no questions regarding its sufficiency for salvation. These three are, *para* bhakti, spiritual perception of the lord, *para jñāna*, intimate spiritual knowledge of him, and *parama* bhakti, the apogee of devotion that will never tolerate separation from him.[161] It may be recalled that the *Agpp* mentions Āṇḍāḷ having grown through these three stages. Bhakti is considered by Rāmānuja as both the goal of the religious life and the means to the goal.[162] Service is natural to the human soul who is, as we have seen, the *dāsa* (servant) or *śeṣa* (disposable property, remainder) of god who is the *Śeṣi* (possessor, of all).[163]

The Śrīvaiṣṇava theological position distinctly differs here from the Āḻvārs' more diverse pronouncements. The devotion of the saint-poets was entirely directed towards the lord; his accoutrements such as the discus, conch shell and lotus, and even his consort serving only to glorify him. While they often praise their chosen deity as the lover of the lotus-born one and/or lord of the earth goddess[164] or as he who bears the 'lady' on his chest,[165] they do not ask his consort to intercede with the lord on their behalf. Indeed, it seems to be the lord alone who has not merely the power to save but the grace to will the salvation of his devotees. Pĕriyāḻvār expresses this succinctly, 'Even if Lakṣmī[166] herself were to give adverse reports about his devotees, he would say, "My devotees would never do that and if they did, they did well." Will anyone

63 Nāyaṉmārs in the Rājarājeśvara Temple in Tanjavur (1004–14 CE) is, of course, well-known. See Mahalingam, 1985, vol. VII, pp. 598–619, Tj 2636 to 2732.

159 *Agpp, Mgpp*, Tirumaḻicai Āḻvār *vaibhavam*, Nammāḻvār *vaibhavam*. See Chapter 2-ii, 2-ix of the present work.

160 Hudson, 'Bathing in Krishna', p. 548.

161 I am using Dennis Hudson's translation/ interpretation of these concepts. Ibid., p. 548.

162 Carman, op. cit., p. 222.

163 Ibid., p. 214, citing Rāmānuja's *Vedārthasamgraha.*

164 *Pĕriya Tirumŏḻi* 8.10.4.

165 *Pĕriyāḻvār Tirumŏḻi* 1.1.2; *Pĕriya Tirumŏḻi* 3.1.2.

166 The expression used is 'lotus-lady'.

choose to serve a master other than my Lord of TiruvArangam?'[167] It would be inaccurate to postulate a distinct theological vision of the Āḻvārs on the basis of this verse. I reiterate my argument that the great degree of variety in the hymns of the saint-poets were systematized and streamlined by the commentarial tradition.

It is in the lives of his *bhaktas par compare* that the lord can demonstrate what is true for every devotee, the promise to redeem. What can only be assumed for even the greatest of preceptors, Rāmānuja, believed by the faithful to be an *avatāra* of Ananta, the serpent upon whose coils the lord reclines in his transcendent abode, can be visibly perceived in the lives of two Āḻvārs, Āṇḍāḷ and Tiruppāṇāḻvār. The lord does not fail to answer the *bhakta*'s call to unite with him. It is indeed possible for the lord to not save, as theologians of both schools struggle to explain in their debates on the sufficiency or otherwise of the means to salvation, his lordliness, and his unfettered freedom to act as he pleases. To say that the lord *must* save is to confine him, to deny his ultimate agency. So, while the lord *may* choose to not redeem the *prapanna*, Śrī, the mediatrix, will ensure, from her motherly compassion and her eternal closeness to the lord, that he does.

It was Śrī who interceded with the lord on behalf of Tŏṇṭaraṭippŏṭi when he lay distraught after being rejected by Devadevi, and Śrī again who could not bear to see Tirumankai starve when he was incarcerated by the Coḻa king in the temple of TiruNaraiyūr.[168] In the case of Tiruppāṇāḻvār too, it was Śrī who urged the lord to not let the bard-saint remain separated from them. Āṇḍāḷ being considered herself an incarnation of (one of) his consorts could approach him through her own devotion and be absorbed into him—where she belongs. The earthly lives of both Āṇḍāḷ and Tiruppāṇāḻvār ended with bodily merger in the icon at Srirangam, perfect illustrations of the ultimate union of individual souls with the Supreme One, who is, in Śrīvaiṣṇava thought, completely incarnated in the consecrated image.

The integration of the Tamil tradition was a consistent creative project, carried out largely by the interpretation of the verses of the Āḻvārs in the light of Viśiṣṭādvaita principles. The vast commentarial literature in Maṇipravāḷa was not merely an academic exercise limited to the scholarly, but formed the basis for regular discourses to lay followers. The Tamil hymns, meant from the outset to be sung and experienced—being considered *anubhava grantha*—and from at least the

[167] *Pĕriyāḻvār Tirumŏḻi* 4.9.2.

[168] See Chapter 2-viii of the present work.

twelfth century, also elaborated in commentaries and expounded to an audience of devotees in the temple complex, were not, however, the only means of this integration. The very stories of the lives of the saints, while serving for the edification of the community and constituting examples of the ideal life of *bhaktas*, underlined and reinforced this vision.

FOUR

Equal Before the Lord
Negotiating Caste

(i) Hypothesis and Historiography

A subject of much debate in south Indian historiography is the nature of the bhakti movement: whether it was a radically egalitarian one, seeking through religious discourse to question, if not completely destroy the hierarchies of caste, or itself the agent of brahmanization, and consequently of the establishment and strengthening of hierarchies. I will argue on the basis of the Śrīvaiṣṇava sectarian literature that the idea of the egalitarian 'bhakti movement' is itself a creation of the post-bhakti centuries, the period to which growing rigidity in caste hierarchies is commonly imputed. Was the hierarchical ordering of society abandoned in this egalitarian programme? I believe that the *varṇa* order was never lost sight of and that contemporary socio-economic realities made it expedient for the brahmanical *ācāryas* to evolve a more inclusive if not genuinely egalitarian system. It may be incorrect to generalize from the evidence for all of Tamil society, but I believe that this formulation will bear testing against wider evidence, such as the Śaiva Siddhānta material and the context of the creation of the *Pĕriya Purāṇam*, i.e. the hagiography of the Śaiva Nāyaṉmārs.

In Chapter 3, we saw that Śrīvaiṣṇava theology offers salvation to the devotees of Viṣṇu even though they be of the *pañcama* caste. I will now attempt to show that there was a consistent reiteration that the 'lowest' castes have equal (and occasionally, even greater) access to salvation as the 'highest'. In analysing how the story of Tiruppāṇāḻvār served to reinforce certain points of Śrīvaiṣṇava theology, I argued that the 'life-story' itself is a careful construct of the era in which it was composed, a position I shall now examine by an analysis of the aspect of caste.

The hymns of the Āḻvārs do often show evidence of indifference to caste, and of treating all devotees of the lord as one's superiors.[1] I will examine how the Śrīvaiṣṇava tradition wove these sentiments of the saint-poets into their life stories and the *vyākhyānas* and imputed to them, a greater degree of egalitarianism than they, i.e. the hymns themselves, display.

Much of the theorizing on the nature of the state in medieval Tamil Nadu has resulted from research on the temple and its pivotal role in the society and economy of the region from early medieval times. The conclusions about the nature of bhakti have been related to the larger assumptions about the state system, and indeed, have themselves served as arguments in support of the same. Since it is against these formulations that my own examination of the bhakti material is situated, I will briefly retrace the historiography on bhakti. I will, next, examine the assumptions that underlie the construction of the life stories, and analyse these along with examples from the commentarial tradition.

R.N. Nandi holds that (Śaiva) monasteries and temples served as the institutional bases of the bhakti concept, which encouraged the doctrine of servitude, of unstinted loyalty and unpaid labour to an absolute superior. The slave attitude (*dāsatva*) of the bhakti ideology was seen as especially relevant in forming the basis of the relationship between the monastic superior, i.e. the pontiff, and the subordinate staff, particularly the *ryots* (*sic*) and essential artificers attached to the temple or the monastic estate. The Nāyaṉmārs are said to have 'used the *dāsatva* sentiment with profit and obliged the low-born to render compulsory service to the Nāyaṉmār priesthood'.[2] The complete surrender to the will of god advocated in the lyrics of the fourth Āḻvār, Tirumaḻicai, and the element of divine grace that informs the poetry of Nammāḻvār are seen as examples of the same sentiment.[3]Needless to say, much of this is simply fantastic, especially as the Nāyaṉmārs (or the Āḻvārs) were not an organized priesthood but peripatetic saints belonging to different castes.

[1] *Pĕrumāḷ Tirumŏḻi* 2.2.

[2] R.N. Nandi, 'Origin and Nature of Saivite Monasticism: The Case of the Kalamukhas and Pasupatas', in *Indian Society, Historical Probings: In Memory of D.D. Kosambi*, ed. R.S. Sharma, New Delhi: ICHR and People's Publishing House, 1974, pp. 191–2.

[3] R.N. Nandi, 'Some Social Aspects of the Nalayira Divyaprabandham', *Proceedings of the Indian History Congress*, 37th Session, 1976, pp. 118–19.

In fact, the hagiographies stress the fact that many of the saints hailed from the lowest and 'untouchable' castes. I will return to this point later.

Veluthat points out, 'What was achieved was to ensure the acceptance of differentiation by all sections of society. The stories of Nandaṉar who was a *paraiya* and Tiruppāṇāḻvār [who was a *pāṇar*] apparently showed that even people belonging to the lowly castes could reach the highest rung in *bhakti* hierarchy, but it really showed what the position of the ordinary *paraiya* or *pāṇa's* place was.'[4] Though conceding that the movement was unlikely to have started as a conscious one,[5]Narayanan and Veluthat take the hagiographic accounts of the origins of the saints literally; thus, Tŏṇṭaraṭippŏṭi, Madhurakavi, Pĕriyāḻvār and Nammāḻvār are said to have been *brāhmaṇa*, and Kulaśekhara, a *kṣatriya*. 'Other Āḻvārs belonged to *Kaḷḷar* and even *Pāṇa* communities of the *śūdra* caste.'[6] I shall show that while the hagiographic attribution of caste status is verifiable in some cases, it is clearly not in several others. Besides, the inclusion of Nammāḻvār among the *brāhmaṇa* Āḻvārs is strange—since all our primary sources, i.e. both the hagiographies and the signature verses in Nammāḻvār's own hymns, represent him as a village chieftain, likely a *veḷāḷa*.[7]None of the texts assign Tirumankai Āḻvār to the *kaḷḷar* caste.[8] Further, the leaders of the bhakti movement in south India are said to have been leading a temple movement where devotion to Viṣṇu or Śiva was 'reduced to devotion to the deity consecrated in a particular temple'.[9] The popularity of the temple resulting from the bhakti movement is seen as leading to the popularity and acceptance of all that the institution represented including its religion, its norms of social differentiation and the peculiar organization of the forces and relations of production.[10] The conviction about this character of bhakti is so

[4] Kesavan Veluthat, 'Religious Symbols in Political Legitimation', *Social Scientist*, vol. 21, nos. 1–2, January- February 1993, p. 27.

[5] M.G.S. Narayanan and Kesavan Veluthat, 'Bhakti Movement in South India', in *Feudal Social Formation in Early India*, ed. D.N. Jha, Delhi: Chanakya Publications, 1987, pp. 348–75.

[6] Ibid., p. 352.

[7] A *sat śūdra* caste of cultivators/landowners.

[8] Kaḷḷaṉ simply means thief. Though Kaḷḷar suggests an occupational category, it is also a caste name. In fact, members of this caste have special privileges in the Śrīvaikuṇṭham Temple in Tirunĕlveli. See Chapter 6-ii of the present work. Though the hagiographies 'credit' Tirumankai with numerous robberies, they maintain that he was born a chieftain.

[9] Kesavan Veluthat, 'Religious Symbols in Political Legitimation', pp. 24–5.

[10] Ibid.

rooted that the word *bhakta* is said to have been originally employed to denote a servant, as one who enjoyed a share in the wealth of his master, and came eventually to denote a devotee imbued with *dāsya bhāva* or the attitude of service,[11] while the word, Āḻvār is stated to be a literal translation of the word, *bhakta*.[12]

Though R.S. Sharma curiously refers to 'some *heterodox sects* (emphasis mine) such as Vaisnavism' which tried to improve the position of the lower orders, he aptly surmises that the 'Vaisnavite teachings were not meant to upset the *varṇa* system, but were capable of being interpreted as such'.[13] Narayanan and Veluthat aver that 'although the element of protest and reform are clear in this movement, these aspects are subordinated to the overall pattern of a greater movement—the consolidation and extension of classical Hindu society in early medieval India'.[14] Brahmanism with its institutional base in the temple-centred agrarian settlements is seen as the dynamic force behind the opening up of river valleys and corresponding agricultural expansion, which led to the formation of clear-cut divisions in society.[15] The existing social structure, thus, got the necessary sanction and validation from the temple-based religion of Agamic–Puranic Hinduism, eminently spread by the bhakti movement.[16] This movement began from Tŏṇṭaimaṇḍalam in northern Tamil Nadu, and expanded southwards to include the Pāṇṭiya and Cera territories. By the ninth century, the Kaveri valley itself became the core region of a new kind of monarchical state. 'It is significant that the identical trajectory is followed in the spread of the *bhakti* movement.'[17] It is noteworthy that while this geographic concordance of the bhakti movement agrees with the accepted chronology of the Āḻvārs, it throws

[11] Veluthat and Narayanan, 'Bhakti Movement in South India', p. 349. It must be pointed out that such a derivation is not indicated by any etymological source.

[12] See discussion on the etymology of the word Āḻvār, in Chapter 1-iii of the present work.

[13] R.S. Sharma, 'The Kali Age: A Period of Social Crisis', in *Feudal Social Formation in Early India*, ed. D.N. Jha, Delhi: Chanakya Publications, 1987, p. 55.

[14] Narayanan and Veluthat, 'The Bhakti Movement in South India', p. 348.

[15] M.G.S. Narayanan and Kesavan Veluthat, 'The Temple in South India', paper presented in the Symposium on the Socio-Economic Role of the Religious Institution in India, *Proceedings of the Indian History Congress*, Bodhgaya, 1981, p. 44.

[16] Veluthat, 'Religious Symbols in Political Legitimation', p. 27.

[17] Ibid., pp. 25–6.

into doubt the traditional dating of the major Nāyaṉmārs and paves the ground for a revision of the same by a century or two.[18]

While early medieval Tamil society was certainly hierarchically stratified, with some castes and classes clearly exploiting others,[19] the assumption that bhakti played a central role in propagating it needs to be re-examined. In this context, one could 'ask whether religion is simply a reflection of material reality... if religion and caste are always in the service of, and ultimately answerable to the economy... Are they destined to consolidate and reproduce the relations appropriate to the economy?'[20]

Champakalakshmi has shown that '*bhakti* ideology... helped in the transformation of Vedic brahmanism into the sectarian religions of Vaiṣṇavism and Śaivism, both of which evolved out of older beliefs of popular worship and cult practices'.[21] Stein notes that examples of social mobility in India in medieval times are widespread and persistent, and constitute one of its most dynamic elements.[22] This mobility was usually not corporate mobility of the contemporary sort, especially as there were sufficient opportunities for individual family mobility. Large tracts of marginally settled lands suitable for cultivation and permitting the establishment of new regional societies set limits on the amount of tribute in the form of agricultural surplus that local warriors could extract, or for other arbitrariness. Besides, floods, droughts, excessive tribute demands or the denial of existing or claimed privileges could spur families or groups of families to move to more remote settlements. Many branches of the *veḷāḷa* community, a powerful and respected cultivating class, are seen to have developed in this manner.[23] Stein's view of the bhakti movement as being both based on folk traditions and related to

[18] See Chapter 1-iii of the present work.

[19] Narayanan and Veluthat, 'The Bhakti Movement in South India', pp. 359–60, p. 371.

[20] P.K. Basant, 'Review of R.S. Sharma: Early Medieval Indian Society', *Studies in History*, vol. 19, no. 1, 2003, p. 141.

[21] R. Champakalakshmi, 'Religion and Social Change in Tamil Nadu AD 600-1300', in *Medieval Bhakti Movements in India, Sri Caitanya Quincentenary Commemoration Volume*, ed. N.N. Bhattacharyya, Delhi: Munshiram Manoharlal, 1989, pp. 164–5.

[22] Burton Stein, 'Social Mobility and Medieval South Indian Hindu Sects', in *Social Mobility and the Caste System in India: An Interdisciplinary Symposium*, ed. James Silverberg, Paris: Mouton, 1985, p. 78.

[23] Ibid., p. 79.

brahmanical religion is surprisingly ignored by many later historians.[24]

Narayanan and Veluthat believe that from the tenth century, when the place of the Nāyan̲mārs and Āl̲vārs was taken by *ācāryas*:

> all of whom were *brāhmaṇas* and scrupulous ritualists. . . there was a return to orthodoxy in all walks of life, especially in the field of culture. The temples with their enormous landed property and established positions in society became the conservative custodians of power and wealth. In the new context, there was no place for the aberrations of the devotee although the exploits of the earlier saints were sung and cherished. *Maṭhas* headed by *brāhmaṇa ācāryas* increased in numbers and championed the cause of *varṇāśramadharma*. Kings depended no more on the prop of *bhakti* for consolidating their political power.[25]

The historical evidence points differently. While religious leadership in the Śrīvaiṣṇava community remained in the hands of *brāhmaṇas* in the period after the tenth century, Śaiva *maṭhas* in the second millennium were firmly in the hands of non-*brāhmaṇas*. Also, temples seem to have become central in the Tamil religious landscape in the time of the bhakti saints themselves. Finally, I will argue that it was in the later scriptures, i.e. the commentaries and the hagiographies which were composed in the period of the brahmanical *ācāryas* from the time of Rāmānuja onwards, that a less orthodox perspective on *varṇāśramadharma* was most clearly and consistently articulated.

Champakalakshmi has shown that in the later Col̲a period, Śaivism strengthened itself by 'more direct involvement of non-*brāhmaṇa* elements in temple administration, establishment and maintenance of monastic organisations and by controlling the functions of collection and distribution of resources'.[26] I propose that contemporary Vaiṣṇavism in the Tamil macro-region, organized by then into a distinctive sect called Śrīvaiṣṇavism, also consolidated its ranks by opening its doors to non-*brāhmaṇa* members and giving them specific ritual and administrative responsibilities in the temple. This was no doubt necessitated, at least in

[24] Burton Stein, 'Brahman and Peasant in Early South Indian History', *The Adayar Library Bulletin*, vols. XXXI–XXXII, 1967–8, pp. 256–7, '(An) aspect of the complicated interplay of religious activities and power relations through the Coromandel plain during the pre- and early Pallava period is that of the *bhakti* movement. The Śaiva and Vaiṣṇava saints were from all social strata from *brāhmaṇa* to untouchable. At the same time when Śiva and Viṣṇu worship was apparently still dominated by *brāhmaṇa* votaries of the *jñānayoga* tradition, these works reflect an important folk devotionalism.'

[25] Narayanan and Veluthat, 'The Bhakti Movement in South India', p. 372.

[26] Champakalakshmi, 'Religion and Social Change', p. 170.

part, by the growing economic and social importance of certain groups like the *veḷāḷas.*

What emerges clearly is the gradual but distinct difference in the social formations of the period between the sixth and ninth centuries and that between the tenth and fourteenth. The earlier period saw the beginnings of royal patronage for religious establishments and the extension of agriculture under the aegis of *brāhmaṇa* donees both in the Pallava territory in the northern Tamil lands and the Pāṇṭiya in the south. From the second half of the tenth century, Co̲la imperial policy encouraged the accommodation of different social categories in the fabric of what became almost a 'state religion'.[27] The canonization of the *Tevāram* hymns and the composition of the Śaiva hagiography, the *Pĕriya Purāṇam*, were both undertaken directly under royal authority. The development of Vaiṣṇavism is thus doubly interesting, as it did not follow royal diktat or compulsion. That the *Nālāyira Divya Prabandham* was canonized and the *Gpps* composed at roughly the same time—independent of royal involvement—indicates a more substantial social reality, one into which the Co̲las were tapping, to consolidate their rule. If social stratification was heightened by the consolidation of brahmanism, the greater economic reach and social prestige of agricultural groups like the *veḷāḷas* and prosperous merchant groups like the *Ticai-āyiratti ainnū̲r̲r̲uvar*[28] challenged the hierarchy. As patrons of the brahmanical sectarian religions, Śaivism and Vaiṣṇavism, expressed through temple worship, these groups claimed greater visibility and prestige in the religious organization.[29]

[27] While using this term, I do not at all imply a theocracy, nor draw any parallels with modern states that have a specific state religion or where scripture forms the basis for the constitution. My reference is to the Co̲la use of Śaivism as a cohesive ideology.

[28] R. Champakalakshmi, *Trade, Ideology and Urbanisation: South India 300 BC-1300 AD*, New Delhi: Oxford University Press, 1996, p. 210.

[29] T.V. Mahalingam, 1985, *A Topographical list of Inscriptions of the Tamil Nadu and Kerala States*, ICHR and S. Chand and Co; vol. II, pp. 513–14. SA 2192. Ref.: *ARE*, 1903, no. 21, *SII* viii, no 291. The inscription of 1168 CE records the assembling of members of the Citrame̲li guild in the Sukhāsīna-p-Pĕrumāḷ temple and contains a eulogy of the guild. It further records the assembling of the members of the Citrame̲li Pĕriyanāḍu of 79 *nāḍus* and the *Ticai-āyiratti-ainnū̲r̲r̲uvar* at Tittaikuṭi alias Tiruci̲r̲r̲ambāla-caturvedimangalam and the consecration of the images of Bhūmi pirāṭṭi and decoration of the *melitoraṇam*. Thereafter, they agreed to make annual contributions towards the expenses of the temple as follows: a *patakku* of paddy per plough, a *kuruṇi* of paddy per head, five *kācu* from each

Privileges and duties in the routine of temple worship and ritual apportioned to various caste groups were some of the evident methods of accommodating these claims. I believe that the hagiographies and commentarial texts express another important response to this demand for inclusiveness. It must be noted, however, that inclusion does not necessarily mean egalitarianism; indeed, it can lead to minute stratification. A look at the hagiographies of some of the Āḻvārs and indeed of the 'biography' of Rāmānuja that forms the longest section in all the *Guruparamparās* will clearly show how this process was actualized. It will also be seen how the bhakti movement acquired the 'egalitarian character' it is so known for.

(ii) Weaving in the Āḻvārs

The tale of Tiruppāṇāḻvār, the bard-saint who belonged to the *pañcama* caste is indeed one of the most striking ones in the hagiography, and in oral retellings is, along with that of Nammāḻvār, the most popular even in *brāhmaṇa* Śrīvaiṣṇava households to establish that all are equal in the eyes of the lord.[30] Here, it will be useful to take a look at the caste status of the twelve Āḻvārs. It must be remembered that in Tamil Nadu, the four-fold *varṇa* classification is largely inapplicable, owing no doubt to the brahmanical *varṇa* order being imperfectly superimposed on a social system with its pre-existent hierarchies. We see, thus, a two-fold classification between *brāhmaṇas* and *śūdras*, the latter category being divided into the right- and left-hand castes.[31] Groups such as the *veḷāḷa*, to whom Nammāḻvār is said to have belonged, are classified as *sat śūdra*. With rare exceptions, only royal lineages are classified as *kṣatriya*, no

flower vendor, two *kācu* from each of the servants (*paṇimakkal*), and four *nāḻi* of ghee per family of the shepherd community.

[30] Personal experience. True particularly among Tĕṉkalais.

[31] Numerous studies on the left- and right- hand castes, such as that of Arjun Apppadurai, 'Right and Left Hand Castes in South India', *The Indian Economic and Social History Review*, vol. 11, nos. 2–3, 1974, pp. 216–59 and Burton Stein, *Peasant, State and Society in Medieval South India*, New Delhi: Oxford University Press, 1979, pp. 173–215, suggest a difference in status between the two, but different lists based on field studies disagree as to which caste a particular occupational group belongs to. Y. Subbarayalu, *South India under the Cholas*, New Delhi: Oxford University Press, 2012, p. 6, points out that 'in the early centuries of its [the right-hand/left-hand division] development was just a case of two contesting landholding groups, the traditional agriculturists (Veḷḷāḷa) versus the newly emerging, martial people turned landholders'.

doubt because of fabrication of genealogies for rulers by *brāhmaṇas* in return for patronage. Similarly, the trading communities which would, in the *Dharmaśāstra* scheme, be classified as *vaiśya*, are, in the Tamil land, also grouped under either the left- or right-hand *śūdra* castes.

	Name	*Caste ascribed by tradition*	*Caste known from hymns*
1	Pŏykaiyāḻvār	None	None
2	Pūtattāḻvār	None	None
3	Peyāḻvār	None	None
4	Tirumalicaiyāḻvār	*brāhmaṇa* birth, but *śūdra* upbringing	None
5	Nammāḻvār	*sat śūdra* (*veḷāḷa*)	Village chief or official
6	Madhurakavi	*brāhmaṇa*	None
7	Kulaśekhara Aḻvār	*kṣatriya*	*kṣatriya*
8	Pĕriyāḻvār	*brāhmaṇa*	*brāhmaṇa*
9	Āṇḍāḷ	*brāhmaṇa*	*brāhmaṇa*
10	Tŏṇṭaraṭippŏṭiyāḻvār	*brāhmaṇa*	*brāhmaṇa*
11	Tiruppāṇāḻvār	*Pāṇar*, outcaste	None
12	Tirumankaiyāḻvār	*śūdra* (occupation: *kaḷḷar*, i.e. robber)	Chieftain, warrior

It is clear from the table that in some cases, there are significant discrepancies between the statements made in the signature verses by some Āḻvārs and the castes ascribed to them. The difference is not very pronounced in the case of Nammāḻvār or even Tirumankai Āḻvār as the ascribed and stated categories may partially overlap, and yet, they are critically important to the imaging of a community. Besides, though the hagiographies do not attribute any specific caste status to the three *mutal* Āḻvārs (i.e. Pŏykai, Pūtam and Pey), in popular modern perception at least, they are all *brāhmaṇas*.[32] Insights from anthropology suggest that such elements of traditional oral culture can serve as guidelines for an understanding of the past in the absence of other evidence.

32 Their births are considered 'perfect'. (See Chapter 2-i of the present work). Friedhelm Hardy, *Viraha Bhakti: The Early History of Kṛṣṇa Devotion in South India*, New Delhi: Oxford University Press, 1983, p. 402, footnote 1, states that tradition believes the early Āḻvārs to not have been *brāhmaṇa*. Our informants evidently differ. However, Professor K.K.A. Venkatachari, a scholar of the Tĕṉkalai persuasion, believes that the story of the *ayonija* birth of these Āḻvārs was meant to gloss over their low-caste status (personal communication).

The *Tiruccanta Viruttam* attributed to Tirumaḻicai Āḻvār is a highly esoteric poem of 120 stanzas which offers practically no clue about the poet. The *Nāṉmukaṉ Tiruvantādi*, a poem of 96 stanzas is also attributed to Tirumaḻicai. Some of the verses in the latter speak of Śiva not only as inferior to or worshipping Nārāyaṇa but also as a part of the composite/ universal lord, Nārāyaṇa. The *Nāṉmukaṉ Tiruvantādi* may, thus, be seen to belong, along with the other three *antādis* in the *Iyarpā*, to an older stratum of religious thought[33] when the Hari-Hara concept probably still had some validity. The geographical range of the *Nāṉmukaṉ Tiruvantādi* and the *Tiruccanta Viruttam* are similar: roughly an equal number of shrines each in Tŏṇṭaināḍu and Coḻanāḍu finding reference in both poems.[34] The *Nāṉmukaṉ Tiruvantādi* mentions Venkaṭam twelve times,[35] Srirangam thrice,[36] and seven other shrines once each. The *Tiruccanta Viruttam* mentions seven shrines: Venkaṭam (twice),[37] three shrines in the region of Kāñcī, and three in Coḻanāḍu, among which Srirangam is mentioned nine times[38] and Kuṭantai five times.[39] Clearly, the focus of the saint who composed this poem was the Srirangam Temple, unlike that of the composer of the *Nāṉmukaṉ Tiruvantādi* whose major focus was Venkaṭam. For the present purposes, however, I will only examine how the *ācāryas* having, for reasons I cannot determine, ascribed these compositions to the same Āḻvār, proceeded to construct a story that blended elements from both these.

While frequent references to the Vedas or their essence—which are both said to inhere in the Lord Nārāyaṇa—do not necessarily indicate *brāhmaṇa* caste, the mention of the 'sweet sound' of the Vedas or of the number of consonants and letters that make up the *Ṛk*, *Yajur* and *Sāman*[40] is probably more suggestive, considering the *dharmaśāstric* injunction against the 'low-born' hearing the Vedas—for the power and the sanctity of the Vedas are believed to inhere in its sound. Some of the cryptic passages which are understood by the Śrīvaiṣṇava tradition to imply

[33] Hardy, op. cit., pp. 281–93, suggests that the early Āḻvārs belonged to a different devotional milieu from the later ones.

[34] With the exceptions of the major shrines Arangam, Venkaṭam, Kuṭantai and Vĕhkā, however, which are common to both poems, the shrines mentioned in each are different.

[35] *Nāṉmukaṉ Tiruvantādi* 34, 39, 40, 41, 43, 44, 45, 47, 48, 53, 54, 90.

[36] *Nāṉmukaṉ Tiruvantādi* 3, 36, 60.

[37] *Tiruccanta Viruttam* 60, 81.

[38] *Tiruccanta Viruttam* 21, 49, 51, 52, 53, 54, 55, 93, 119.

[39] *Tiruccanta Viruttam* 56, 57, 58, 59, 60.

[40] *Tiruccanta Viruttam* 4.

various esoteric concepts may also indicate familiarity with different philosophical traditions, justifying, at least partly, the Āḻvār's reputation as a student of numerous philosophies. Again, the longer poem shows a thorough grasp of a wealth of legends connected with Viṣṇu, both from the Tamil and the Sanskritic–Puranic traditions. Though the majority of the verses of the *Tiruccanta Viruttam* are highly elliptical, a fair number specifically posit Viṣṇu in a hierarchical relationship with other gods, specifically Śiva.[41] These slighting references to Śiva seem to be the only common factor between this poem and the *Nāṉmukaṉ Tiruvantādi*[42] besides the description in both of the four *yugas* by the colours, white, yellow, red and black.[43] Some virulent stanzas condemning Śramaṇas, (i.e. Jainas), Buddhists and Śaivas clearly lie at the root of the story of the Āḻvār's long study of these rival religious systems before rejecting them all as worthless.[44] The descriptions of the lord in various shrines, unlike in the *Amalaṉādipirāṉ* which mentions only Venkaṭam apart from Srirangam, convey a sense of the familiar—indicative of easy access into the sanctum, and thus an argument against the low caste status of its composer.

What is thus amply clear is the lack of basis for the Āḻvār's upbringing by a hunter/bamboo worker—a detail that *could* have been omitted by the hagiographies especially since his purported biological father, a sage, was in all likelihood, a *brāhmaṇa.* That it wasn't, and that this 'confusion' of caste forms the basis for further sub-plots in the story is significant. In fact, this theme is played out from the very outset whereby the Āḻvār, despite his upbringing in a clearly low-caste family, refuses all nourishment except a devotee's offering of milk. Food taboos are the most important of restrictions for the maintenance of ritual purity. That this is scrupulously adhered to, even as the texts place the Āḻvār in a lowly social environment, reflects more than ambiguity regarding caste status. The *Mgpp* account of Tiruppāṇāḻvār also has a foundling brought

41 *Tiruccanta Viruttam* 42, 53, 70, 71, 72, 87, 113.

42 *Nāṉmukaṉ Tiruvantādi* 1, 4, 9, 10, 20, 31, 42, 43, 56, 73, 75, 78, 82 express the superiority of Viṣṇu over Śiva, Brahmā, etc.

43 *Tiruccanta Viruttam* 44 and *Nāṉmukaṉ Tiruvantādi* 24.

44 *Nāṉmukaṉ Tiruvantādi* 6 slights Buddhists and Jainas. Stanza 14 disparages those who do not take the name of Nārāyaṇa. Stanza 38 says that the six schools of thought are for those without the heart to seek him. In Stanza 63 the poet says he learnt the mysteries of astrology, and all about the lord through writings, by word of mouth and by prayer. Stanzas 66, 84, etc., express his refusal to worship Śiva.

up by a *caṇḍāla* couple on nothing but cow's milk[45]—ritually pure food. There appears a clear intent to draw in diverse social groups into the community of Viṣṇu worshippers, and to promise them grace. It is, however, an attempt fraught with tension, and anxiety to not destabilize the established patterns of hierarchy. Thus, Tirumaḻicai Āḻvār's deep familiarity with the Vedas, demonstrated by his recalling to the errant *brāhmaṇas* the point in their recitation they had stopped at, underscores that a *bhāgavata* is beyond brahmanical hierarchies, and that knowledge of Nārāyaṇa is superior to, indeed, encompasses knowledge of the Vedas, which are but of him. On the other hand, even this *bhāgavata* among *bhāgavatas* does not break the absolute taboo of *pronouncing* a phrase of the Veda;[46] he only makes the physical gesture of scratching a grain of rice with his nail. Thus, the very limits are reached, tested, briefly shown to be invalid, but finally reiterated! Similarly, Lokasārangamuni carrying Tiruppāṇāḻvār on his shoulders into the Srirangam Temple oversets established norms of caste hierarchy, but is preceded by the Āḻvār's refusal to soil the hallowed portals of the temple with his presence. And no less important, this act of transcendence, even though by god's own orders, is unrepeatable by any other *bhakta*—Tiruppāṇāḻvār never returns to mundane human existence. One act of transcendence thus leads to another; and the startling nature of one is emphasized by the finality of the other.

The hagiographies are on comparatively surer ground with Kulaśekhara Āḻvār who speaks of himself as lord of Kŏlli,[47] Kūṭal,[48] Koḻi[49] and Kŏnku,[50] as a sharp-spear wielder and commander of an army. The three places to which the poet lays claim have a deeper significance: Kŏlli, Koḻi and Kūṭal were associated with the Sangam Ceras, Coḻas and Pāṇṭiyas respectively.[51] Equally significantly, he speaks of himself as one with a parasol/heir to the parasol[52] which indicates royal status. Since Kulaśekhara is known to be the title of some Cera kings, the Āḻvār is said to have been of the Cera royal lineage.[53] The Kerala region had come to

[45] See Chapter 2-vii of the present work.

[46] The power of the Veda is said to inhere in its sound.

[47] *Pĕrumāḷ Tirumŏḻi* 2.10, 6.10, 7.11.

[48] *Pĕrumāḷ Tirumŏḻi* 1.11, 2.10, 6.10. Kūṭal is modern Madurai.

[49] *Pĕrumāḷ Tirumŏḻi* 9.11, 10.11 Koḻi is identified as modern Uraiyūr.

[50] *Pĕrumāḷ Tirumŏḻi* 3.9.

[51] The association was pointed out to me by Professor Kesavan Veluthat.

[52] *Pĕrumāḷ Tirumŏḻi* 1.11, 9.11.

[53] Elamkulam Kunjan Pillai identified the Cera rule from the ninth century as the 'Kulaśekhara empire' believing that Kulaśekhara was the *abhimāna nāma* of

be identified with the rule of the Ceras from the ninth century onwards. The fame of this medieval dynasty which took its name from the Sangam Ceras, undoubtedly to gain legitimacy and prestige, continued even after the decline of the dynasty in the early-mid twelfth century.[54] What we see here is the hagiographies transposing contemporary/near contemporary reality on to an earlier period by speaking of the Āḻvār as a Cera ruler,[55] and by grouping the compositions of this Āḻvār as the *Pĕrumāḷ Tirumŏḻi*, i.e. the sacred words of Pĕrumāḷ, Pĕrumāḷ being the title that the (later) Cera kings took. This follows the pattern that the compilers of the *Nālāyiram* have generally followed, i.e. prefixing the honorific by which name the Āḻvār is known in the Śrīvaiṣṇava community to the word *Tirumŏḻi*, to refer to the collection of his/her compositions. To read this backwards and posit that the composer of the *Pĕrumāḷ Tirumŏḻi* bore the title Pĕrumāḷ, would, therefore, be anachronistic. Further, the name Kulaśekhara was by no means unfamiliar in the Tamil land. A number of Pāṇṭiya kings bore the title Kulaśekhara, as can be seen from numerous inscriptions.[56] There is an attempt to fix Kulaśekhara Āḻvār with exactitude[57] based on the assumption that he was a crowned king of Kerala. However, our evidence does not permit this confidence, especially as none of the above-mentioned sites can be reliably placed in Kerala; rather, they seem to be located around present-day Madurai and Uraiyūr. Even Kŏnku, which is suspect only because of having been the realm of the Sangam Ceras,[58] is specifically said to comprise Coimbatore and parts of Salem, Tirucchirapalli and Madurai districts.[59]

---

the rulers of the dynasty. Ref: Kesavan Veluthat, 'State Formation in Early South Indian History', Paper presented at the Centre for Historical Studies, Jawaharlal Nehru University, 28 March 2009.

[54] Personal communication from Professor Kesavan Veluthat.

[55] The hagiographers have clearly chosen to ignore the references to Koḻi and Kūṭal in his hymns for the purpose of declaring him a Cera king.

[56] Mahalingam, 1985, vol. VI, p. 263. Rn 229. Ref: *ARE*, 1924, no. 33; ibid., part ii, p. 106; Mahalingam, 1985, vol. IX, p. 18. Tn 78. Ref.: *ARE*, 1907, no. 104; Mahalingam, 1985, vol. VI, p. 106. Pk 426. Ref.: *IPS*, no. 583.

[57] Kesavan Veluthat, 'The Socio-Political Background of Kulasekhara Alvar's Bhakti', *Proceedings of the Indian History Congress,* 38th Session, Bhuvanesvar, p. 138, cites M.G.S. Narayanan in order to identify the Āḻvār with Sthāṇu Ravi Kulaśekhara, 844–83 CE.

[58] Ibid., p. 138.

[59] Brenda E.F. Beck, 'The Authority of the King: Prerogatives and Dilemmas of Kingship as Portrayed in a Contemporary Oral Epic from South India', in *Kingship and Authority in South Asia*, ed. J.F. Richards, Delhi: Oxford University Press,

If Kulaśekhara Āḻvār was indeed a king of this territory, he should be known to us from other sources, for the eighth–ninth centuries are by no means a dark page in historical records.[60] It is remarkable that so devout a ruler does not appear as a generous donor to any Viṣṇu temple in the epigraphic records of the age of the Āḻvār.[61] Further, it has been pointed out that in a medieval astronomical treatise from Kerala, the *Laghu Bhāskarīya Vyākhyā*, the employment of the literary device of double entendre allows the opening verse to be read as praise of both Śiva and the patron of the poet, Sthāṇu Ravi Kulaśekara.[62] Would a *bhakta* devoted exclusively to Viṣṇu have appreciated a work that could be a panegyric to Śiva, scarcely respectable in his eyes?[63] Indeed, in the *bhakti* environment charged with sectarianism, would he have borne the name, Sthaṇu?

Kulaśekhara Āḻvār has sung of five shrines, besides referring once to Ālinagar[64] and a few times to Ayotti (Ayodhya)[65] which, as the mythological realm of his chosen deity, must have been especially sacred for him, but is likely to have been notional rather than a physical, geographical reality. The five south Indian shrines are Venkaṭam,[66]

1998, p. 189, and footnote no. 1 on pp. 212–13. Also, K. Meenakshisundaram, 'A Brief Study of the Marriage System of the Kongu Vellāla Gounder Community', *Bulletin of the Institute of Traditional Cultures, Madras*, vol. 18, no. 1, 1974, p. 1.

[60] Kesavan Veluthat, 'Imagining a Region: Kerala in Medieval Literature and Historiography', Paper presented at the Centre for Historical Studies, Jawaharlal Nehru University, 18 March 2009, interactive session, specified that no inscription of the Ceras of the ninth to twelfth centuries have been found east of Palghat.

[61] Two inscriptional records mention Sthānu Ravi Kulaśekhara. The earlier, dated in his sixth regnal year, is the Syrian Christian copper plate grant which gives certain trading rights to the said community. The second, dated in his eleventh year, is a resolution of a temple community. I am indebted to Professor Kesavan Veluthat for the information.

[62] Kesavan Veluthat, 'Ideology and Legitimation: Early Medieval South Asia', in *Mind over Matter: Essays on Mentalities in Medieval India*, ed. D.N. Jha and Eugenia Vanina, New Delhi: Tulika Books, 2009, p. 8.

[63] See Chapter 5 of the present work for the conflicts between Śaivas and Vaiṣṇavas.

[64] *Pĕrumāḷ Tirumŏḻi* 8.7.

[65] *Pĕrumāḷ Tirumŏḻi* 8.6, 8.7, 10.1.

[66] *Pĕrumāḷ Tirumŏḻi* 4.1-10.

Srirangam,[67] TirukKaṇṇapuram,[68] Tillai-TiruCitrakūṭam (Chidambaram),[69] and TiruVittuvakkoṭu,[70] with a clear focus on Srirangam. The geographic distribution is as follows. Vaṭanāḍu: 1; Co̱lanāḍu: 3 and Malaināḍu: 1. I wish to point out here that Tirumankai of TiruvĀli in Co̱lanāḍu has sung of three temples in Malaināḍu whereas it is from the hymns of Nammāḻvār, who hailed from Kurukūr in Pāṇṭiyanāḍu, that twelve of the thirteen shrines in Malaināḍu get their status as *divya deśas*; three of these twelve are also hymned by Tirumankai. While this evidence is not conclusive, for Tirumankai and Nammāḻvār were in any case more oriented towards pilgrimage than was Kulaśekhara, one would expect that a crowned king who was also a staunch devotee would have chosen to glorify more abodes of his chosen deity in his own realm. More pertinently, Kulaśekhara's concentration on sacred sites in the Kaveri delta point to his greater familiarity with this region than with Kerala. It is known that prior to the rise of the imperial Co̱las, numerous chiefly families were in control of different parts of the Tamil land outside the area of influence of the Pallavas and Pāṇṭiyas. I suggest that this Āḻvār hailed from any one of these clans with royal aspirations and appurtenances.[71] Undoubtedly familiar with the Sangam poetical conventions,[72] this saint-poet was drawing on the historical tradition of Sangam to boost these royal claims and for legitimation.

B.V. Ramanujam seems to be correct in suggesting that Vittuvakkoṭu was not a Malaināḍu shrine at all, especially as Nammāḻvār has not sung of it. Further, he points to a Viṣṇu shrine on the banks of the river Āṉporuṉai in Karūr which is even today called Vittuvakoṭṭagrahāram. Having crowned Kulaśekhara king of the western littoral tract, the Śrīvaiṣṇava hagiographical and pilgrimage traditions seem to have invested a place in the Malayāla country with the name of a shrine that the Āḻvār had sung about. Ramanujam further points out that Vañci,

[67] *Pěrumāḷ Tirumḏi* 1.1–10, 2.1–10, 3.1–10.

[68] *Pěrumāḷ Tirumḏi* 8.1–10.

[69] *Pěrumāḷ Tirumḏi* 10.1–10.

[70] *Pěrumāḷ Tirumḏi* 5.1–10.

[71] See George W. Spencer, *The Politics of Expansion: The Chola Conquest of Sri Lanka and Sri Vijaya*, Madras: New Era Publications, 1983, p. 13 for a picture of the ninth-century Pallava and Pāṇṭiya dynastic kingdoms as 'regional spheres of hegemony' which included, beyond their heartland, a 'broad and ambiguous hinterland' with 'local power centres under the control of chiefs or other locality leaders'.

[72] Hardy, *Viraha Bhakti*, pp. 231–81 discusses the influence of Sangam traditions on the poetics of the Āḻvārs.

the purported birthplace of Kulaśekhara Āḻvār, is the classical usage of Karūr on the banks of the Kaveri, an association strengthened by the archaeological evidence of the Ciṉṉamaṉṉūr plates.[73] It appears we have sufficient proof to relocate the historical poet-devotee Kulaśekhara from modern-day Kerala to the western Tamil region. An interesting corollary is that while Malaināḍu should have one less *divya deśa*, the *real* Vittuvakkoṭu/Vittuvakoṭṭagrahāram would mean the presence of a *divya deśa* in a region practically barren of them![74]

While all the Āḻvārs praise the lord by mentioning his deeds of grace and valour performed in the course of various incarnations, *Kṛṣṇāvatāra* is the greatest favourite, especially for the poetic scope it gives. Kulaśekhara is perhaps unique in his focus on Rāma,[75] which is no doubt the basis for the delightful legend about the Āḻvār. The tale also underscores the accessibility of the lord[76] as one towards whom mere humans may be solicitous as towards a friend in need, or as a mother towards her baby.[77]

Even to one only marginally familiar with Tamil poetry and literature, the power and beauty of the *Tiruvāymŏḻi* is immediately apparent. It is easy to see why Nammāḻvār is regarded by the tradition as the sum of which the other Āḻvārs are but parts.[78] Nammāḻvār refers to himself as

[73] B.V. Ramanujam, *History of Vaishnavism in South India upto Rāmānuja*, Annamalainagar: Annamalai University, pp. 184–194.

[74] See Chapter 6-ii of the present work for further discussion of the pilgrimage network.

[75] However, *Pĕrumāḷ Tirumŏḻi* 6.1-10 and 7.1-11 are devoted to Kṛṣṇa.

[76] See Chapter 3-iv of the present work.

[77] Pĕriyāḻvār has composed a number of songs purportedly sung by Yaśoda for Kṛṣṇa. In fact, they are structured as folk songs that any mother could sing about/to her child, weaving in references to the divine child. Kulaśekhara Āḻvār sings lullabies to the baby Rāma, laments in the voice of Daśaratha after Rāma has left Ayodhya, and in that of Devaki who hasn't had the joy of bringing up the baby Kṛṣṇa. These form part of a genre known as *Piḷḷaittamiḻ*, specifically devoted to the glorification of childhood/miraculous children. Paula Richman dates the first extant *Piḷḷaittamiḻ* to the twelfth century. (Paula Richman, *Extraordinary Child. Poems from a South India Devotional Genre*, Honolulu: University of Hawai'i Press, 1997, p. 3). It is likely that this genre had its beginnings in Āḻvār poetry. See also, Lynn Marie Ate, 'Periyāḻvār's Tirumŏḻi—A Bālakṛṣṇa Text from the Devotional Period in Tamil Literature', Ph.D. thesis, Madison: University of Wisconsin, 1978, for Pĕriyāḻvār's hymns to the baby Kṛṣṇa.

[78] See hagiographic reference to *avayava* and *avayavī*.

Vaḻuti-vala-nāṭan,[79] (lord of the fertile Pāṇṭiya land)[80] and as *Nagarāṉ.*[81] As the term *valanāḍu* technically refers to the administrative division above the village level, Hardy believes that he may have been a provincial administrator, possibly of noble descent.[82] Madhurakavi however calls him *Nagara Nampi,*[83] a term which in the case of Pĕriyāḻvār denotes a temple *brāhmaṇa.* Considering the acute analysis that was brought to bear upon the *prabandhas* by the medieval Śrīvaiṣṇava *ācāryas*, it is hardly likely that this reference could have escaped them. Hardy suggests that Madhurakavi may have never actually met Nammāḻvār, but was perhaps referring to his temple icon.[84] The earliest epigraphic evidence of the installation of images of the bhakti saints is from the late tenth century[85] which of course does not rule out the existence of images of the saints in a slightly earlier period. However, to picture Madhurakavi as revering merely an image of Nammāḻvār would imply a substantial time gap between the actual lives of the two, which would present immense difficulties in the chronology of the Āḻvārs.

Certainly, Madhurakavi was deeply impressed by the poetry of Nammāḻvār, which he considers the Tamil Veda. If he did not learn the hymns directly from the composer (and, by implication, was not influenced by the *presence* and teachings of the master), but only acquired them from the oral tradition, is it likely that he would have preferred to concentrate his devotions towards the image—assuming that an image existed—of the singer of such songs alone, neglecting even the lord to whom those songs were addressed? Though there are no easy answers, I think it unlikely. It also reopens the question of Nammāḻvār's

[79] *Tiruvāymŏḻi* 2.8.11, 3.6.11, 5.6.11.

[80] Translation- Hardy, *Viraha Bhakti*, p. 254.

[81] *Tiruviruttam* 100, *Tiruvāymŏḻi* 4.10.11.

[82] Hardy, *Viraha Bhakti*, pp. 254–5.

[83] *Kaṇṇinuṇciruttāmpu* 3.

[84] Hardy, *Viraha Bhakti*, p. 255, footnotes. In fact, this is his reason for discarding a ninth century dating for Nammāḻvār and placing him earlier despite acknowledging the difficulty in the early date presented by Nammāḻvār's reference to two temples that owe their name to a Pāṇṭiya ruler of the ninth century.

[85] Mahalingam, 1985, vol. VII, p. 21. Tj 96 and 97. Ref.: *ARE*, 1917, nos. 275 and 299. Several more references to the installation of the saints' images come from the Rājarājeśvara temple in Tanjavur, dated 1014 CE. (Mahalingam, 1985, vol. VII p. 603. Tj 2654. Ref.: *ARE*, 1888, no. 96; *SII* ii, no. 38, pp. 152–61. The images were of Nampi Ārūrāṉ, Nankai paravaiyār, Tirunāvukkaraciyār and Tirujñāṉa-Sambandar, among others.)

caste and occupation; could Madhurakavi in his reverence have referred to his teacher as *Nampi* in the more diffuse sense of leader?[86] Why, when there was a possibility of picturing Nammāḻvār as a *brāhmaṇa*, did the hagiographers choose to give the 'greatest' Āḻvār *satśūdra* parentage?

The numerous legends about Tirumankai Āḻvār defy clear-cut analysis, unless the message is simply that single-minded devotion to Viṣṇu excuses, indeed overrides, the worst of wrongdoings—a message often apparent in the *Pĕriya Purāṇam* as well. A life of piety is perhaps to be considered outside the pale of the laws governing normal social life. At least one example from the *Īṭu*,[87] relevant in this context, is meant to demonstrate the supremacy of the lord. A holy man is said to have once complained to the lord of Tiruppati that Tirumankai Āḻvār's hymns were full of self-adulation. The lord thereupon replied, 'There was no self-adulation before he declared his loyalty to Me. After he declared his allegiance, all self-adulation acquires the virtue of praise offered to Myself.'[88] This is supposed to show that god cannot be praised by uninspired men.[89] I believe that this passage also reinforces the notion of the lord's unfettered *paratva* and his promise to redeem,[90] not to speak of such allegiance being sufficient effort for salvation. Here, however, I shall concentrate on only those aspects which have a bearing on the social status of the Āḻvār or his associates.

Since most of the epithets by which the hagiographies refer to Tirumankai Āḻvār are derived from his own signatures, it is very likely that he was a warrior chieftain or an official of some royal overlord[91]—who is invariably said to be Coḻa, reflecting the hagiographers' contemporary reality. He regularly refers to the mansions, fertile fields and fortifications of his native Ālināḍu/Mankai,[92] his own generosity, his

[86] A. Appan Ramanujam, 'Non-Vedic basis of Srivaisnavism', *Bulletin of the Institute of Traditional Cultures, Madras*, vol. 26, no. 1, July–December 1982, pp. 45–8. Ramanujan believes that the word *nampi* denotes a non-*brāhmaṇa* priest and argues that before *brāhmaṇas* took over, south Indian temples had non-*brāhmaṇa* priests. He concludes, therefore, that Pĕriyāḻvār was non-*brāhmaṇa* too. This is arguable as in at least one of his signature verses, *Pĕriyāḻvār Tirumŏḻi* 2.8.10, the poet speaks of himself as '*Veda*-knowing'.

[87] The largest commentary on the *Tiruvāymŏḻi*.

[88] A. Govindacarya, *The Divine Wisdom of the Dravida Saints*, Madras: CN Press, 1902, p. 70, quoting *Bhagavad Viśayam*, Book 4, commentary on *Tiruvāymŏḻi* 4.9.1.

[89] Ibid., p. 70.

[90] See Chapter 3-iv of the present work.

[91] He styles himself usually as 'lord'.

[92] Both places are situated near each other in the vicinity of TiruNānkūr

valour, his horse Āṭalmā, and his conquering spear. It is interesting that Kumudavalli, the woman responsible for bringing him to the Vaiṣṇava path,[93] was brought up by a *vaidya*— we have seen the importance of foster parentage in previous stories. Indeed, her father is shown to have worried about the girl's marriage as her *kula* and *gotra* were unknown. On a lighter note, I suggest that since the brahmanical scheme permits a marriage of desire (*gandharva vivāha*) for the warrior classes, Tirumankai Āḻvār might have seemed a desirable *parti* in the eyes of Kumudavalli's father, who may have suspected that she was of *apsarā* extraction.[94]

Marriage/sexual union is strictly controlled along caste lines, and the hagiographies allow no breach of the same. True, Tŏṇṭaraṭippŏṭi Āḻvār is said to have been besotted with a *gaṇikā*, but the story is clearly a trope on the power of women to lead potential *bhaktas* astray. Indeed, many of the Āḻvārs lament that they had wasted their youth pursuing beautiful women and advise their listeners to reject such worthless pursuits and devote themselves to the lord of Vaikuṇṭha without delay. We often hear that ancient India was the 'land of the *Kāmasūtra*' and free of the notion of 'original sin'. And that contemporary India, however, is fettered by the shackles of sexual repression introduced only as recently as the nineteenth century by our colonists, while the actual descendants of the Victorians have rid themselves of the same. I contend that this is an oversimplification. Despite the absence of a notion of original sin, and despite the inclusion of desire (and its fulfilment) among the four legitimate goals of human life,[95] sexuality was fraught with tensions in the religious and semi-religious literature.[96] While love and sexuality have been celebrated in numerous contexts and also been given a semi-divine status, as in the context of Kṛṣṇa's amorous dalliances, it remains equally true that desire and sexuality have given rise to much remorse and self-flagellation. It has been pointed out that while the Āḻvārs visualized the erotic relationship of the divine couple as that of Kṛṣṇa with the *gopīs* in general, and with Nappiṉṉai in particular, the *ācāryas*

[93] This aspect belongs only to the hagiographies; there is no mention of Kumudavalli in his compositions.

[94] After all, it is such a familiar Puranic theme that, as a learned man, Kumudavalli's father *should* have presumed that some unfortunate *apsarā* was having to live out some curse through an earthly life!

[95] *Dharma, artha, kāma, mokṣa.*

[96] Women are frequently condemned as snares for spiritual aspirants (always assumed to be men). Any number of Puranic legends or *Jātaka* tales can be adduced to prove this point.

'legitimized' it by singing strictly of the perfect mutual love of Viṣṇu and Śrī.[97] The ambiguity over desire is brought out beautifully in the verses of Tirumankai himself. While he frequently repents his wasted years when he was entranced by women with 'round breasts' and 'lightning-like waists',[98] he also signs himself with a flourish as 'lover of many wide-eyed women' and 'desirable to women with flower-adorned tresses'![99] The hagiographies do not, however, make much of this in the case of this Āḻvār, assigning to him a 'legitimate' attachment to a single, semi-divine, devout Vaiṣṇava woman. I suggest that this transmutation of the self-confessedly 'woman-entranced' Āḻvār into a faithful spouse in the hagiographies is further evidence of the same trend, i.e. of subsuming the concept of erotic love within the conjugal framework.

This discussion clarifies that there is a clear match in the caste status as mentioned in the hymns themselves and in the hagiographies in the case of four Āḻvārs, i.e. Kulaśekhara, Pĕriyāḻvār, Āṇḍāḷ and Tŏṇṭaraṭippŏṭi. The given and ascribed statuses are not seriously in conflict in the case of two others, i.e. Tirumankai and Nammāḻvār. Thus, the caste status of six Āḻvārs, i.e. exactly half the number of the Vaiṣṇava saint-poets, is actually unknown and merely ascribed. The case of the first three Āḻvārs, said to have had immaculate births, may also be left out of the picture for the present. This leaves us with Tirumaḻicai, Tiruppāṇ and Madhurakavi, the first two of whom are, in any case, not even historical. Madhurakavi is said to be a *brāhmaṇa* even though a reference in his hymn to the scholars of the Vedas regarding him as lowly could indicate low social status.[100] Tirumaḻicai's status is more ambiguous, and Tiruppāṇ is firmly classed as belonging to the lowest of the low.

An analysis of the *Therīgāthā* and the *Theragāthā* suggests that the ascription of caste status to the Buddhist nuns and monks regarded as the composers of these works may encode important messages for the audience of the texts.[101] While a fair number of these renunciants are

[97] See Chapter 3-iv of the present work.

[98] *Pĕriya Tirumŏḻi* 1.1.1–4.

[99] *Pĕriya Tirumŏḻi* 6.10.10, 3.4.10.

[100] *Kaṇṇinuṇciruttāmpu* 4. Hardy, 'The Tamil Veda of a Śūdra Saint', pp. 29–87, believes this stanza indicates that Madhurakavi's revering Nammāḻvār as the one who had rendered the Vedas in Tamil must have been regarded with disapproval by the *brāhmaṇa* establishment. This reasoning, however, can hardly account for the medieval hagiographers' accounts.

[101] Kumkum Roy, 'Of Theras and Theris: Visions of Liberation in the Early Buddhist Tradition', in *Re-searching Indian Women*, ed. Vijaya Ramaswamy, Delhi: Manohar, Delhi, 2003, pp. 75–96.

pictured as hailing from *brāhmaṇa* families, the low caste status of others is also highlighted. The compilers and commentators of these texts, thus, pointed to the comparatively egalitarian character of Buddhism, but simultaneously stressed that the Buddhist faith was not merely the refuge of the socially inferior but attracted members from even the highest rung of the social hierarchy.[102] It is possible to see similar factors operating in the case of the Śrīvaiṣṇava hagiographers. The low caste status of certain Āḻvārs was balanced by the *brāhmaṇa* status of others, and in an interesting reflection of the Buddhist situation seen from the *Therī-* and *Thera-gāthās*,[103] there is a preponderance of saints from the *brāhmaṇa* caste, reinforced by others from those of comparatively high social standing.

Nammāḻvār is the composer of the largest number of verses in the *NDP* (1,202 hymns), followed by Tirumankai (1,134 hymns).[104] Here, I am including only the hymns in the *Pĕriya Tirumŏḻi*, the *Tirukkuruntāṇṭakam* and the *Tirunĕṭuntāṇṭakam* that carry Tirumankai's signature and not the *Tiruvĕḻukūṟṟirukkai*, the *Pĕriya Tirumaṭal* and the *Ciriya Tirumaṭal* which are only ascribed to him. Tirumankai also appears to have travelled to more shrines of the lord than any other Āḻvār, even assuming that the poems on shrines in northern India are based on hearsay than on actual pilgrimages. Clearly, such an important Āḻvār deserved—in the eyes of the hagiographers—a sufficiently gripping life-story. Thus, stereotyped laments about a life of sin and wrongdoing[105] that can only be redeemed by the special grace of the lord were embroidered to create the extraordinary bildungsroman. However, I believe that this suggestion that the grace of Viṣṇu is available to every true devotee, irrespective of his deeds, subtly reinforces the notion of the lord's grace being available irrespective of a person's birth. This insistence on the centrality of bhakti, and of belonging to the community of *bhaktas* over and above ones' caste-community was crucial to the emergent Śrīvaiṣṇava community, as will be brought out by examples from the sectarian scriptures.

[102] Personal communication from Professor Kumkum Roy.

[103] Roy, op. cit., pp. 81–3.

[104] Tirumankai is considered the most prolific by addition of the poems ascribed to him, for two of which, two systems of counting are in vogue. According to one, Tirumankai's hymns add up to 1,351 while according to the other, the sum is 1,253. Nammāḻvār's compositions, including the traditionally ascribed songs, add up to 1,296.

[105] *Pĕriya Tirumŏḻi* 1.1.5, 'I was a thief. I sinned. Now I am reformed. . .'. *Pĕriya Tirumŏḻi* 7.4.9, 'I am false, wicked, constantly living in misery. Yet I have received His grace . . . .'

Here, however, a qualification is necessary. The Śrīvaiṣṇava scriptural tradition began, within about two centuries after Rāmānuja, to exhibit two different doctrinal orientations, the gap between which deepened till they came eventually to be crystallized into two distinct sects, the Tĕn̲kalai and the Vaṭakalai. The animosity that came to characterize their relations is, however, not seen until much later. There are eighteen points of doctrinal difference between the two sects, but the crucial issue dividing them is undoubtedly their position on caste; the Tĕn̲kalai stance being far more radical than the Vaṭakalai.

(iii) The Integration

The Viṣṇu temple at Srirangam had become the focus of the Śrīvaiṣṇava community at an early date thanks to the early *ācāryas* having established their pontifical seat there. Though Nāthamuni hailed from a small temple town called Viranārāyaṇapuram, it was in Srirangam that his grandson Yāmunācārya established the early tenets and practices of the faith. Yāmuna is supposed to have desired Rāmānuja, a young man whose prodigious philosophical knowledge he had heard of and whom he had seen but never actually met,[106] to succeed him as the *darśana pravartaka* (propagator of the doctrine). Some time after the *ācārya's* death, Rāmānuja, who had been based in Kāñcī, moved to Srirangam and spent most of his long and eventful life thenceforth in that temple town. Kāñcī, which had long been the pre-eminent site of religious learning, not only of the orthodox faiths but also of Buddhism and Jainism, continued to attract Vaiṣṇava scholars. As we know, Śrīvaiṣṇava theology bases itself on two sets of scripture—the Sanskrit Vedas and the Tamil hymns of the Āl̲vārs. It appears that the early Vaiṣṇava scholars were called upon to defend their faith against accusations of heterodoxy—in this context, misinterpretation of the Vedas rather than non-acceptance of its principles— for Yāmuna's *Āgama Prāmāṇya* carefully sets out the Vedic basis of the *Pāñcarātra Āgamas*[107] which were central to Vaiṣṇava ritual practice. His other work, the *Gītārthasamgraha*, similarly interprets the *Gītā* in the light of Vaiṣṇava bhakti.[108] After Rāmānuja's *tour de force*,

[106] See Chapter 2-x of the present work.

[107] K.K.A. Venkatachari, *The Srivaisnava Manipravala, 12th to 15th Centuries AD*, Anantacharya Indological Institute, 1978, p. 18. Also *Āgama Prāmāṇyam of Yāmunācārya*, Sanskrit Text and English Translation with Introduction by J.A.B. van Buitenen, Madras: Ramanuja Research Society, 1971, pp. 4–5.

[108] See Chapter 3-ii of the present work.

the *Śrībhāṣya*, established Viśiṣṭādvaita as a genuine Vedantic school, Śrīvaiṣṇava scholars did not, presumably, feel the need to re-establish the Vedic orthodoxy of their faith. Rather, their focus moved towards an in-depth study of the canonized scripture itself i.e. the 4,000 hymns of the Āḻvārs, and the philosophical treatises of their own early *ācāryas* which, understood to contain the entire teaching of the Vedas, formed the basis of study in their own right.

The definition of the hymns of the Āḻvārs as the Tamil Veda was in itself revolutionary. Venkatachari asserts that this claim regarding the '*Drāviḍa Veda*' was relatively unknown outside Śrīvaiṣṇava circles for very long, especially as occasions for public debate were rare.[109] While the Sanskrit Veda is *śruti*, eternally revealed, and by implication *anādi*, i.e. without beginning, the Tamil hymns were considered to be *śruti* which has *ādi*.[110] Vaṭakku-Tiruvīti-Piḷḷai says in the *Bhagavad Viśayam*, his massive commentary of 36,000 stanzas, more popularly known in the Śrīvaiṣṇava community as the *Īṭu*, that the Sanskrit Veda is like the *paratva* form of the lord, the *Itihāsas* and *Purāṇas* like his *avatāras*, and the *Tiruvāymŏḻi* like the *arcāvatāra*.[111] This must be understood in the light of Śrīvaiṣṇava theology, where the five forms of the lord are considered equal, but the *arcā* form is dearer for being accessible.[112] As inheritors of two Vedic traditions, orthodox Śrīvaiṣṇavas claim the title of 'Ubhaya Vedantins'. We have already seen that the very first reference to the Tamil Veda occurs within the *NDP* itself: twice in his poem of eleven stanzas, Madhurakavi says that Nammāḻvār rendered the Vedas/the essence of the Vedas in sweet Tamil.[113] To that extent, the almost extraordinary claim to equality with the Vedas for scripture in a vernacular language was not an innovation of the Śrīvaiṣṇava *ācāryas*. However, the continuing reiteration of this claim also gives us a clue to how the community imaged itself. The 'Tamil Vedas' were accessible to all irrespective of caste not merely because of the Tamil language, but also because, unlike the Sanskrit Vedas, they were seen as inherently meant to bring divine revelation to all. Aḻakiya Manavāḷa-p-Pĕrumāḷ Nāyaṉār[114] says that the *Tiruvāymŏḻi* is like a golden pot that

[109] Venkatachari, op. cit., p. 18.

[110] Ibid., p. 18.

[111] Ibid., p. 21.

[112] See Chapter 3-ii of the present work.

[113] *Kaṇṇinuṇciruttāmpu* 8 and 9. Also see Chapter 1-iii of the present work.

[114] This is not one of the Śaiva Nāyaṉmārs, but the name of a Śrīvaiṣṇava *ācārya*, the word Nāyaṉār meaning leader.

everyone may use, whereas the (Sanskrit) Vedas are like a mud pot.[115] This statement is to be understood against the southern Indian notions of purity-pollution, whereby certain items (like mud pots) are thought to transmit pollution, and must therefore be guarded against the same, whereas other materials (like gold) remain pure irrespective of who touches them.

While scholars based in Srirangam gradually began to concentrate on the Tamil scripture, those in Kāñcī eventually developed a separate specialization within the domain of Śrīvaiṣṇava studies—study of the Sanskrit texts. This bias may have been partly due to the personal predilections of the scholars, but was partly due to a tangible social reality. Srirangam was the hub of an emergent community of the faithful while Kāñcī was the seat of philosophers. The needs of the nascent community meant that the Tamil hymns of the Āḻvārs, easily understood and emotionally appealing, were the preferred tools of propagation of the faith. Generations of scholars in Srirangam devoted themselves to expounding the Āḻvārs' poetry, delving into the canon for insights that previous *ācāryas* may have by-passed. A vast commentarial literature was built up in Maṇipravāḷa. The Śrīvaiṣṇava term for the commentaries, *anubhava grantha*, i.e. works of enjoyment, is instructive of how the community views/viewed the hymns of the Āḻvārs. The emphases in the commentaries were thus on 'teaching the community and the purely intellectual pleasure of understanding the rich heritage of the *ubhaya Vedānta*'.[116] The first Tamil-Maṇipravāḷa text, the *Ārāyirappaṭi*, a commentary on Nammāḻvār's *Tiruvāymŏḻi* by Tirukkurukaip-Pirāṉ Piḷḷāṉ, has a heavy Sanskrit component, but over the centuries, the Tamil content grew steadily in relation to the Sanskrit. The very reasons which had privileged the Āḻvārs' hymns in Srirangam over the Sanskrit philosophical treatises also influenced the direction in which these hymns were interpreted. Inscriptions attest to the substantial contribution of merchants, artisans, landowning groups and royal officials to the institution of the temple. To retain the patronage of these groups, indeed, to draw in as many social groups as possible into the life of the temple, and to create a broad-based community was undoubtedly an important preoccupation for the *ācāryas* at Srirangam. I shall examine how the commentarial literature reflects these concerns.

Piḷḷai Lokācārya, regarded as the key figure among the *ācāryas* of the

[115] *Ācārya Hṛdayam*, Surnai 73. Cited in G. Damodaran, *Acarya Hrdayam: A Critical Study*, Tirupati: Tirumalai Tirupati Devasthanams, 1976, pp. 40–4.

[116] Venkatachari, op. cit., p. 87.

Tĕn̲kalai or the southern sect— so called for both its geographical location vis-à-vis Kāñcī and for its concentration on the scripture of the southern language as opposed to the Vaṭakalai or northern sect with its focus on Sanskrit—was the first to write independent treatises interpreting the Vedānta in a vernacular language.[117] Lester believes that the 'style and content of his writings show him to be especially concerned to communicate Vaiṣṇavism to the uninitiated masses of South India. . . Given. . . his views on caste...he can be considered something of a social revolutionary'.[118] Lokācārya argues that the *bhāgavata* transcends caste, and even though he or she may be of the lowest caste, such a one is to be given the highest honour and service. Apparently, after the composition of the *Śrīvacana Bhūṣaṇa*, some prominent Śrīvaiṣṇavas objected to his teachings regarding the *bhāgavatas*. The story goes that Al̲akiya Manavāḷa-p-Pĕrumāḷ Nāyan̲ār (a contemporary *ācārya*) took the complaint to the lord who, through his priest (*arcaka mukhena*), himself vindicated Lokācārya in front of the community.[119] Indeed, it is easy to understand why orthodox *brāhmaṇas* would have objected to the contents of the *Śrīvacana Bhūṣaṇa*. Let us look at some examples from the text.

There is no condition of place, time, manner, fitness or fruit for *prapatti*.... Three kinds of persons are fit to perform *prapatti* to the *arcā*: the ignorant, the one having superior knowledge, and the one who loses himself in devotion. People like us are *prapannas* on account of ignorance, the *ācāryas* of yore are *prapannas* on account of their superior knowledge and the Āl̲vārs by the ecstasy of devotion... Offences against *bhāgavatas* are of many kinds. One of these is inquiry about their birth. This indeed is more cruel than thinking about the material stuff of (which) the *arcāvatāra* (is made). Verily, inquiry after the birth of a *bhāgavata* is like a man inspecting the reproductive organs of his mother. The very sacred thread of such a person becomes a leather strap, like that of Triśanku, a *caṇḍāla* by *karma*.

These startling pronouncements are bolstered by references to older texts as well.[120] We learn of a legend from the *Udyoga parva* of the *Mahābhārata*, of Garuḍa, who was punished with the loss of plumage and inability to fly for thinking ill of the place where Śāṇḍilya, a female sage,

[117] Robert Lester, *The Śrīvacana Bhūṣaṇa of Piḷḷai Lokācārya*, Madras: The Kuppuswamy Sastri Research Institute, 1979, p. 3.

[118] Ibid.

[119] Ibid., p. 4.

[120] I do not know if the quotations are genuine. Suffice it to say that the *Śrīvacana Bhūṣaṇa* claims these quotes.

was staying. And unambiguously, 'The price of brahmanism is acceptable if as a result of the Vedas and the like, there is attainment of the Lord; if that indeed is a detriment, then it is to be renounced'. Further, the *Śrīvacana Bhūṣaṇa* states that for a low-born one, humility is consistent with his birth while the high-born must cultivate humility. Therefore, a humble birth is better than a superior one. The *Bhāgavata Purāṇa* is quoted to establish that even one 'who cooks dogs, (*svapaca*), but has Viṣṇu *bhakti* is better than a twice-born one without *bhakti*'. The lord himself is shown to have never distinguished between castes. 'Though Rāvaṇa abused Vibhīṣaṇa as a disgrace to his clan, Rāma embraced him as one of the Ikṣvākus. Rāma performed the *brahma medha* ritual (last rites) for Jaṭāyu, and Yudhiṣṭhira for Vidura.' Besides these assertions of the primacy of bhakti, all Vaiṣṇavas who have received the sacred mantra are declared to be equal.[121]

The *Īṭu* explains and elaborates the hymns with examples from older texts, the epics and popular mythology. Its very interpretations of these popular episodes are interesting. That the text is a product of discourses to the community is brought out by delightful anecdotes about well-known previous Srirangam *ācāryas* who are, as elders in the revered *guruparamparā*, models to be emulated. Explicating *Tiruvāymŏḻi* 1.10.2, wherein Nammāḻvār says that the lord who unfolds himself as earth, water, fire, wind and sky, enters and fills his heart when he worships him with love, the *Īṭu* gives us the following story. Velvĕṭṭi Nampiyār is said to have asked Nampiḷḷai[122] if *prapatti*—reliance on god alone and ceasing of self-effort—demanded some conditions. Nampiḷḷai replied:

> Vibhīṣaṇa who suggested to Rāma the expediency of petitioning the ocean, did not himself, when he came to Rāma as his refuge, bathe in the ocean as previous preparation. What do we infer from this? It was meet for[123] Rāma to adopt preliminary observances, becoming the race of Ikṣvāku, whereas the circumstances of birth as one of the *rākṣasa* race did not warrant any previous ceremony (for Vibhīṣaṇa). Thus each one must do what is proper to his station in life.[124]

While this statement seems to reinforce the status quo in a manner familiar to us from numerous brahmanical texts,[125] its opposite import

[121] All the examples featured above are from Lester, *Śrīvacana Bhūṣaṇa*, op. cit., citing *Śrīvacana Bhūṣaṇa*, pp. 20, 39–40, 60–62, 65, 67.

[122] Both are Śrīvaiṣṇava *ācāryas*.

[123] Old usage for 'suitable'.

[124] Govindacarya, op. cit., pp. 34–5, quoting *Bhagavad Visayam*, Book 1.

[125] In the *Bhagavad Gītā*, canto 4 verse 13, for example, each person is

can be grasped when look at some other examples from the same text. In a conversation between the ācāryas Nañcīyar and Bhaṭṭar, Nañcīyar is said to have asked the latter what qualifications were needed to be able to recite god's names. Bhaṭṭar replied:

Son, when a man stumbles on the road, he involuntarily cries out, 'Ammā'. (What qualification is required for this?) He who goes to bathe in the Ganga need not cleanse himself beforehand by dipping into a salt water pond. So, when we wish to be saved, what more qualification do we require than the desire to be saved? A saviour who is fit to save can also render us fit for salvation.[126]

It is clear that the purpose is to demonstrate that *prapatti*, the sole and sufficient means of salvation according to Tĕṉkalai doctrine, is open to all, regardless of caste.

The doctrine of *prapatti*, complete surrender to the lord, is central to Tĕṉkalai belief. In their insistence that *prapatti* requires no effort, nor any qualification, on the part of the individual, the Tĕṉkalai *ācāryas* challenge the Vaṭakalai who believe in a measure of self-effort, a qualification which embraces ritual worthiness. While performance of prescribed duties in accordance with *varṇāśramadharma* is perfectly compatible with the Vaṭakalai programme of salvation, any self-effort, including such ritual ones is, in the Tĕṉkalai view, to doubt the lords' all-embracing capability to save and hence to actively oppose his omnipotence.[127]Though this doctrinal position does seem to make caste a redundant category, there can be no doubt that tensions remained. The following example reveals the tensions in accommodation of older religious traditions.

Nammāḻvār describes TirucCenkuṉūr as the abode of Vedic seers performing sacrifices.[128]In glossing this, the *Īṭu* frames a question about how people of the new faith, i.e. of loving devotion to the lord, could perform ritual acts prescribed in the Vedas, and answers it thus: the

---

enjoined to perform the duty proper to his caste. See also, D.D. Kosambi, 'Social and Economic Aspects of the Bhagavad-Gītā', in *Myth and Reality: Studies in the Formation of Indian Culture*, ed. D.D. Kosambi, Bombay: Popular Prakashan, 1962, repr. 2000, pp. 12–41.

[126] Govindacarya, op. cit., pp. 202–3, quoting *Bhagavad Viṣayam*, Book 10, commentary on *Tiruvāymŏḻi* 10.2.5.

[127] Patricia Mumme, 'Jīvakartṛtva in Viśiṣṭādvaita and the Dispute over Prapatti in Vedānta Deśika and the Tenkalai Authors', in *Prof. Kuppuswami Sastri Birth Centenary Commemoration Volume, Part 2*, ed. S.S. Janaki, Madras: The Kuppuswami Sastri Research Institute, 1985, pp. 114–16.

[128] *Tiruvāymŏḻi* 8.4.5, 8.4.10.

ritual of the old law is observed by votaries of the new faith merely to prove their obedience to the divine decree, but not to reap the rewards attached to their performance. If they produce any effects at all, it would be to the benefit of the world in ridding it of its ungodliness.[129]

The *ācāryas* of old are frequently shown to be indifferent to caste. 'A woman had filled her water pots by the riverside of the Kaveri, but there was no one around to help lift the pots on to her head. Kūrattāḻvān̲, noticing it, helped her, forgetting his high caste and her low one.'[130] Another time, Piḻḻai Akalanka Brahma Rāyan̲, a disciple of Kūrattāḻvān̲, unwittingly offended his guru's son Bhaṭṭar, who, as a consequence, left Srirangam for TirukKoṭṭiyūr. Anxious to conciliate him, Rāyan̲ asked Irukai Maṭa Vāraṇan, weaver-in-chief of the lord, known to be an intimate servant of Bhaṭṭar, to mediate. The placated Bhaṭṭar then said of the servant that his natural (inborn) humility could not but conquer all.[131] Of course, such examples of the inherent nature of servitude of the low-born making *prapatti* natural cut both ways. In another illustration, Mutaliyāṇṭān̲[132] and Vankīpurattu Nampi went to worship Ranganātha. There was a great gathering there of the high and the low, the learned and the illiterate. While Dāśarathi[133] took his place among the Śrīvaiṣṇavas, Nampi joined the humble cowherdesses. Observing Nampi's unusual conduct, Āṇṭān̲ asked him the reason; Nampi replied, 'We are swelling with the pride of our caste; these folk are humble and ignorant.' He then quoted from the *Rāmāyaṇa* to prove that the lord looks more graciously upon the low and humble than on those puffed up with their birth and learning, and said he had hoped, by standing among them, to be thus favoured by the lord. Nampi then described, on Āṇṭān's questioning him, how the cowherdesses had prayed. They had said, 'Dear Lord, eat fruit, drink milk, wear warm robes', while Nampi had praised the lord, '*Vijayasva, vijayī bhava*', (Victory be to thee, Victory be thou). Āṇṭān is reported to have then said, 'Brother, even in their ranks, you did not think of discarding your stiff Sanskrit. We are we and they are they how

129 Govindacarya, op. cit., pp. 165–6, quoting *Bhagavad Viṣayam*, Book 8, commentary on *Tiruvāymŏḻi* 8.4.5.

130 Ibid., pp. 85, quoting *Bhagavad Viṣayam*, Book 4, commentary on *Tiruvāymŏḻi* 4.9.1

131 Ibid., pp. 188–9, quoting *Bhagavad Viṣayam*, Book 9, commentary on *Tiruvāymŏḻi* 9.4.10.

132 Kūrattāḻvān̲ and Mutaliyāṇṭān̲ are said to be among Rāmānuja's closest disciples. Mutaliyāṇṭān̲ was also Rāmānuja's nephew.

133 Another name for Mutaliyāṇṭān̲.

much so ever you may forget and conceal our differences. Come, join our ranks as usual.'[134] This anecdote can indeed be read in two ways. On the one hand, it seeks to demonstrate, like the earlier one, that the low-born are dearer to the lord for their simple devotion, and better candidates for *prapatti*, being naturally free of pride. But in its reiteration of caste status and distinction, it resembles numerous brahmanical treatises and could well have served as a tool for maintaining the poor in subjection, while promising them a glorious afterlife. What is remarkable, however, is the self-perception and honest acknowledgement of the differences that persist despite their stated goals, especially since these stories were meant to be recounted to large, mixed audiences. It also is clear that worshippers of different castes had access to the sanctum, even if they assembled in largely segregated groups.

One day, the washerman of Srirangam brought particularly well-washed clothes to Rāmānuja who led him by the hand into the presence of Ranganātha, and recommended him to the lord. Pleased, the lord said that for this service, he would condone the offence of the washerman of *Kṛṣṇāvatāra*.[135] This anecdote about the rather mysterious forgiveness of sins long-ago committed[136] is interesting in other respects. While it may have meant to demonstrate the accessibility of the lord and his condescension towards the humble, as also the benefits of intercession by an *ācārya*, here the great Rāmānuja himself,[137] the idea that the sin of one washerman could be vicariously expiated several aeons hence by another washerman (i.e. a member of the same caste group) demonstrates that caste/birth remained central to the *ācāryas*' imagination. I suggest that it might also have reinforced the practice of making offerings or performing penances on behalf of one's deceased ancestors, a ritual mediated generally by *brāhmaṇas*.

A̱lakiya Maṇavāḷa-p-Pĕrumāḷ Nāyaṉār is said to have composed the *Ācārya Hṛdayam* to 'reveal the essence of Nammāḻvār's *Tiruvāymŏḻi* to

[134] Govindacarya, op.it., pp. 183–4, quoting *Bhagavad Viṣayam*, Book 9, commentary on *Tiruvāymŏḻi* 9.2.8.

[135] Ibid., p. 65, quoting *Bhagavad Viṣayam*, Book 4, commentary on *Tiruvāymŏḻi* 4.3.5.

[136] Properly speaking, *that* washerman should have experienced the fruits of his karma ages earlier!

[137] Intercession by the *ācārya* is again a key Tĕṉkalai concept. The *ācārya* takes on the sins of the disciple and recommends ḥim/her to the lord. Indeed, Śrīvaiṣṇavas believe that Rāmānuja performed a paradigmatic *prapatti* on behalf of all Śrīvaiṣṇavas. (See Chapter 3 of the present work). It offers an interesting parallel to Jesus' crucifixion on behalf of all humanity.

all devotees without any distinction of *varṇa*'.[138] This is especially so as Nammāḻvār himself is stated to have been born a non-*brāhmaṇa*. 'The *Ācārya Hṛdayam* attempts to establish that in spite of his birth, Nammāḻvār gained a position unequalled among the Āḻvārs due to his piety, devotion and erudition.'[139] The very reason for Nammāḻvār's birth in a lower order was to raise the status of the group even as Kṛṣṇa was born and lived among cowherds to save the world.[140] Aḻakiya Maṇavāḷa-p-Pĕrumāḷ Nāyaṉār believes that Nammāḻvār was greater than Veda Vyāsa who composed the *Mahābhārata*, and Kṛṣṇa who gave the *Bhagavad Gītā* to the world, and supports his argument as follows. Veda Vyāsa was an illegitimate child of Matsyagandhī, a fisherwoman, who abandoned him at birth. Kṛṣṇa was separated from his mother at birth and brought up by Yaśodā, a foster mother. Nammāḻvār, however, was brought up by his own loving parents[141] and the grace of god! Aḻakiya Maṇavāḷa-p-Pĕrumāḷ Nāyaṉār adds that Veda Vyāsa was born in a place reeking of fish, Kṛṣṇa in the putrid atmosphere of prison—from where he was transferred to another steeped in the rancid smell of butter, while Nammāḻvār was born amid the freshness of holy *tulasi* groves.

It is interesting indeed that immediately after rejecting birth as a criterion for worthiness, the *ācārya* claims the superiority of Nammāḻvār using the very same category, albeit those of the circumstances of birth. Veda Vyāsa's low birth is presumably not a handicap, but his illegitimacy is, and so is Kṛṣṇa's separation from his biological parents. So too, the accident of their surroundings. There can be little doubt then that the Śrīvaiṣṇava *ācāryas* striving to create a comparatively egalitarian community could not completely escape the larger conditioning of a hierarchical society of which they were part, and whose prejudices they were imbued with to a far greater degree than they themselves acknowledged.[142] This inherent caste distinction is nowhere better illustrated than in notions of purity-pollution. The example of the mud pot given earlier has meaning only in a hierarchical society where caste-based taboos on commingling and commensality are a lived reality. All

138 Venkatachari, op. cit., p. 38.

139 Ibid.

140 Ibid.

141 This commentarial argument is rather curious for Nammāḻvār was, according to the hagiographies, deposited by his parents under a tamarind tree soon after birth. See Chapter 2-ix of the present work.

142 The fundamental restrictions of caste in 'Hindu' society have never been transgressed, even by the most radical of the medieval bhakti saints.

the same, its radical potential must also be recognized— it is this very tension between a hierarchical society and a limited egalitarian sphere within it that informs the efforts of the Śrīvaiṣṇava *ācāryas*.

Two arguments can be presented against my hypothesis. First, all the examples I have chosen are from texts composed by *ācāryas* of the Tĕṉkalai sect. Vaṭakalai Śrīvaiṣṇava scholars, while unlikely to deny the commentarial literature status as scripture will, no doubt, point out that many of the views propagated and endorsed by the Tĕṉkalai *ācāryas* were 'innovations' or departures without the sanction of the 'true' *ācāryas*— indeed, it has been argued that the Tĕṉkalai *guruparamparā* or sequence of preceptors is itself fabricated,[143] that Rāmānuja appointed Tirukkurukaip-Pirān Piḷḷān (the first *ācārya* according to the *Mgpp*) and not Parāśara Bhaṭṭar (the first *ācārya* of the Tĕṉkalais) as his successor. Second, it may be argued that it was not the Śrīvaiṣṇava *ācāryas* but the Āḻvārs themselves who laid the basis for a broad-based, non-hierarchical society. The low-caste background of numerous Nāyaṉmārs and some Āḻvārs is seen as proof of the wide social base of the movement, not to speak of their choosing to sing in the tongue of the people. In fact, many scholars studying different aspects of the bhakti movement in Tamil Nadu have seen it as a clarion call against brahmanical hierarchy. Trying to understand the role of the royal patron and the importance of patronage to the notion of royalty, Peterson says, 'In the *egalitarian vision* of the Tamil *bhakti* movement, kings and commoners were alike servants of Śiva. The Śaiva devotee bowed to Śiva and to all of Śiva's devotees irrespective of their social status'[144] [Emphasis mine].

It is true that the more radical prescriptions regarding caste do come from the Tĕṉkalai stream of the Śrīvaiṣṇava tradition.[145] The *Ācārya*

[143] V. Rangachari, 'The Successors of Rāmānuja and the growth of Sectarianism among the Srī-Vaishṇavas', *Journal of the Bombay Branch of the Royal Asiatic Society*, no. 24, 1914–15, pp. 102–36.

[144] Indira V. Peterson, 'In Praise of the Lord: The Image of the Royal Patron in the Songs of Saint Cuntaramūrtti and the composer Tyagarāja', in *The Powers of Art: Patronage in Indian Culture*, ed. Barbara Stoler Miller, New Delhi: Oxford University Press, 1992, p. 129.

[145] Professor K.K.A. Venkatachari (author of *The Śrīvaiṣṇava Maṇipravāḷa*), a distinguished scholar of the Tĕṉkalai persuasion, believes that the stories of the Āḻvārs said to be foundlings were attempts by the hagiographers to disguise their low-caste status. He explained it thus: caste status was irrelevant in the time of the Āḻvārs but brahmanical hierarchy was strengthened in the ensuing centuries which is why the *Guruparamparās* had to hide the 'innocent' facts of low-caste birth by stories of miraculous births. Personal communication.

Hṛdayam, a Tĕn̲kalai text, gives the examples of the sage, Viśvāmitra, who despite being born a *kṣatriya* became a *brāhmaṇa*, and of Triśanku of the Ikṣvāku dynasty who became a *caṇḍāla* through the curse of Vaśiṣṭha's sons, to show that birth and caste have lesser significance than deeds.[146] On the other hand, Vedānta Deśika, the renowned Vaṭakalai *ācārya*, is said to have taken the example of the temple cow which despite being worthier than other cows in that its milk and butter are used to make offerings to the lord does not, in the final analysis, cease to be a cow![147] Even Surabhi, the Kāmadhenu, whom all desire, he points out, remains a cow. The Tĕn̲kalai school holds that a gifted *śūdra* who becomes a *prapanna* can be a teacher of a *brāhmaṇa* and that such a one may recite the *mūla mantra* with the *praṇava*.[148] Deśika, however, cites the cases of Vyādha and Tulādhara who, though born in a lower *varṇa* and thus ineligible to study the Vedas or teach them, were still able to clear the doubts of *brāhmaṇas* who approached them for clarification on some points of the *Vedas*. Deśika says they were like guides who direct travellers who have strayed into the forest. But though important as guides, they could not become members of a higher *varṇa*. Deśika makes an exception for the Āl̲vārs, considering them a special category, not to be classified with mortals. In his *Guruparamparāsāram*, he calls the 10 Āl̲vārs the *navīna daśāvatāra*, i.e. ten new incarnations of the Lord.[149] Deśika follows the Āl̲vārs' expressions in acknowledging that a devotee (of Nārāyaṇa) born in a lower *varṇa* is superior to one without devotion though born in a higher *varṇa*, but refuses to believe that *varṇa* status can change.[150]

146 *Ācārya Hṛdayam*, stanza 87 quoted in Damodaran, *Acarya Hrdayam*, op. cit., pp. 55–6.

147 Ibid., pp. 55–6, citing Vedānta Deśika, *Rahasyatrayasāram*.

148 K.V. Rangaswami Aiyangar, 'Govindarāja', *Annals of the Bhandarkar Oriental Research Institute*, vol. 23, 1942, p. 31.

Om namo nārāyaṇāyaḥ. Though Deśika denies women and *śūdras* the right to enunciate the *praṇava*, he says that they would get the rewards attached to it. Vedānta Deśika, *Rahasyatrayasāram*, pp. 928-31, cited in Friedhelm Hardy, 'Tiruppāṇ Āl̲vār The Untouchable who Rode Piggy Back on the Brahman', in *Devotion Divine: Bhakti Traditions from the Regions of India*, Diana L. Eck and Francoise Mallison, Groningen: Egbert Forster, 1991, p 151.

149 S. Satyamurthi Ayyangar, *Tiruvaymoli English Glossary, Volumes I and II*, Ananathacharya Indological Research Institute, Bombay, 1981, pp. xv–xvi. Also, Vedānta Deśika, *Śrīmad Rahasyatrayasāram* 1.3 and 1.7, cited in John Carman and Vasudha Narayanan, *The Tamil Veda: Pillan's interpretation of the Tiruvaymoli*, Chicago: The University of Chicago Press, 1989, p. 260.

150 Satyamurthi Ayyangar, ibid., pp. xv-xvi.

As we have seen earlier, this difference in attitude to caste is partly related to the course of development of the nascent community in Srirangam. Another factor which must be considered here is the contemporary political reality. It has been pointed out that Śaivism became almost the royal cult of the Co̱las. '*Patikam* [ritual hymn] singing represents a regional cultural form in the evolution of the temple as the channel of communication and the chief mechanism of ideological consolidation for the emergent Co̱la state, the ideology itself being derived from the *bhakti* of the Śaiva Nāyaṉmārs... The *bhakti* ideal was consciously adopted by the Co̱las to integrate the Tamil macro-region into a regional polity with a distinct regional culture'.[151] The 'recovery' of the 'lost' hymns of the Nāyaṉmārs,[152] their compilation and canonisation, and finally, the composition of the hagiographies of the Nāyaṉmārs was all under the aegis of the royal Co̱las. The apotheosis and worship of the *Tevāram* trio, which had begun by 945 CE also seems to have begun under Co̱la auspices. The metal images of Appar, Sundarar and Sambandar were consecrated by Rājarāja I (985–1014) in the great temple at Tanjavur.[153] Inscriptional evidence from other, older Śaiva temples attests to consistent patronage in the mature Co̱la period.

The trajectory of development of Vaiṣṇavism was parallel to that of Śaivism, but it occurred under very different circumstances. Vaiṣṇavism had received royal patronage under the Pallavas, and continued to do so under the Co̱las, albeit on a smaller scale. The Co̱las, despite their predilection for Śaivism were too astute empire builders to ignore Vaiṣṇava institutions. However, the period of greatest glory for Vaiṣṇavism in Tamil Nadu lay in the future—in the Vijayanagara period. For the greater portion of the period of this study, therefore, Vaiṣṇava institutions developed without any marked royal patronage or interference.[154] This can have one of two important implications, viz., that institutional developments in Śrīvaiṣṇavism were direct engagements with and responses to the contemporary social reality, even more than those of Śaivism, and can therefore offer a window towards understanding the developments in Śaiva institutional structures in Tamil Nadu during the

[151] R. Champakalakshmi, '*Patikam Pāṭuvār*: Ritual Singing as a Means of Communication in Early Medieval South India', *Studies in History*, vol. 10, no. 2, 1994, p. 200.

[152] See Chapter 1-iii of the present work.

[153] Champakalakshmi, '*Patikam Pāṭuvār*', op. cit., p. 207.

[154] See Chapter 2-x of the present work for the major exception: the persecution of Rāmānuja and Vaiṣṇavas by an unidentified Co̱la ruler.

tenth to thirteenth centuries. In other words, if it was exigencies of state that partially influenced the radical social philosophy of Śaiva Siddhānta, it might be the very lack of state support that made it important for the authors of Śrīvaiṣṇavism to conceive as broad a social base as possible for the nascent sectarian community. However, it is also possible to see some of these developments as arising from mutual competition between two closely related devotional sects, both of which were trying to establish their bases among similar social groups. As I have pointed out earlier, both the Śaiva and Vaiṣṇava hymnal canons were compiled and the hagiographies composed around the same time despite their very different 'political fortunes'. It is important to remember that the later Cola and early Vijayanagara periods saw the rise to political and economic power of several new groups whose patronage was, no doubt, crucial to both the Śaiva and Śrīvaiṣṇava establishments.

Though Srirangam eventually became the epicentre of Tĕṉkalai Śrīvaiṣṇavism, important Vaṭakalai groups and lineages continued to be attached to the temple. Second, the earliest *ācāryas* were all based therein, irrespective of which sect claimed them in the subsequent period. The attempt to create a broad-based community which seems, from our twentieth-century perspective, to have been a concern of only the Tĕṉkalai sect, can be seen from the period of the early history of the community. Though it has been contended that Rāmānuja's true successor was Tirukkurukaip-Pirāṉ Piḷḷāṉ,[155] even the most partisan Vaṭakalai scholar will not deny that Parāśara Bhaṭṭar, Kūrattāḻvāṉ, etc., were important early *ācāryas* associated with Rāmānuja. Though Piṉpaḻakiya Pĕrumāḷ Cīyar, the author of the *Agpp*, clearly places himself in the Tĕṉkalai succession, as the first composer (or compiler) of the hagiographies of the Āḻvārs, he set the agenda for future hagiographies.[156] Even assuming that the now-lost antecedent of the *Mgpp* was much older, the fact remains that the available Vaṭakalai hagiography includes details pertaining to caste which it might easily have omitted. I believe that these inclusions are evidence of accommodation and acceptance of what were concerns of the undivided community, and which were eventually marginalized in the development of a sectarian position. Nowhere is this

[155] Rangachari, op. cit., pp. 112–28.

[156] I have presented, in Chapter 1, arguments regarding the date of the *DSC*; if it were the earliest, it could be said to have been the text that 'set the agenda'. Even so, as a 'Srirangam text', it may be considered as illumining the agenda of the early Srirangam *ācāryas*. Considering the *Agpp* earlier will not in any way change the argument here.

better reflected than in the tale of Tiruppāṇāḻvār. Considering medieval Vaṭakalai emphasis on Sanskrit scripture, and the entire debate on the means of salvation where birth/caste assumes centrality, the *Mgpp could have* pictured the poet of the *Amalaṉādipirāṉ* very differently.[157] It might be the fact that the *Agpp* version was already well-known and popular that the *Mgpp* retains it,[158] with, however, the important clarification that the Āḻvār was not *born* in, but only *brought up* by a *caṇḍāla* family and, of course, nourished entirely on milk. So also the retention of the tale of the adoption of the abandoned baby, Tirumaḻicai Āḻvār, by a low-caste couple, and the insistence on the baby needing no food, having been nourished for all time by the grace of the lord.

I shall now consider the second possible argument against my hypothesis. I will also take examples from the *Pĕriya Purāṇam* to show how the later, institutionalized religious systems created the 'bhakti movement', or rather, endowed it with such characteristics as have since come to be seen as its defining features. First however, I will examine the hymns themselves.

As Pĕriyāḻvār, Āṇḍāḷ, and Tŏṇṭaraṭippŏṭi were *brāhmaṇas*, it is reasonable to expect references to brahmanical ritual practices in their hymns. Interestingly, however, the poetry of Pĕriyāḻvār, a temple *brāhmaṇa*, and of his daughter, Āṇḍāḷ, are rich in folk elements; indeed 'in language and idiom, Pĕriyāḻvār comes closer to ordinary people than any other Āḻvār'.[159]

Kulaśekhara Āḻvār sings of the lord of Srirangam as the One praised by Brahmā with the chants of the Vedas,[160] and as the substance of the Vedas.[161] He speaks of the lord as the One spoken of in 'sweet Tamil' and in the 'northern tongue',[162] i.e. the Vedas. Though a king, he repeatedly expresses his desire to be united with the throngs of devotees in the temple towns of the lord, particularly Srirangam. He wishes to 'worship

[157] Two *taṉiyaṉs*, i.e. stanzas of praise, were composed by two disciples of Yāmuna, Pĕriya Nampi and Tirumalai Nampi and are, accordingly, dated to the tenth or early eleventh centuries. The former, a Sanskrit verse, refers to him as *munivāhana*, while the latter, in Tamil, speaks of him as *pāṇar* and also has an elliptic reference to his being carried by a priest to be shown the figure of Viṣṇu in the temple. See Hardy, 'Tiruppāṇ Āḻvār', p. 133.

[158] Perhaps the legend was borrowed from popular tradition. See Chapters 2-vii and 6-ii of the present work.

[159] Hardy, *Viraha Bhakti*, pp. 411–12.

[160] *Pĕrumāḷ Tirumŏḻi* 1.5.

[161] *Pĕrumāḷ Tirumŏḻi* 4.8.

[162] *Pĕrumāḷ Tirumŏḻi* 1.4.

their holy feet', 'bathe in the dust of their holy feet', and 'to apply the dust from their feet on his forehead'.[163] Nammāḻvār says that those who praise the people who praise the lord who churned the milk ocean for the *devas*, and those who serve the servants of the devotees of the lord who wears yellow vestments are his masters.[164] Though the sentiment expressed may be perfectly genuine, the motif of calling oneself the servant of the servants of the lord was an accepted way of expressing renunciation of pride;[165] indeed, we know one Āḻvār only from his title, Tŏṇṭaraṭippŏṭi, i.e. the dust of the feet of (the lord's) devotees. Apart from this profession of humility, this *brāhmaṇa* Āḻvār[166] has little patience with those who do not share his faith. Indeed, he declares that men learned in the *Śāstras* proclaim the cowherd lord/Rāvaṇa's killer the only god.[167] The *Tiruppaḷḷiyĕḻucci*, Tŏṇṭaraṭippŏṭi's wake-up song for the lord, despite its lyrical beauty, could hardly have been a popular song, meant as it was for a specific temple ritual. Many of Tirumankai's and Kulaśekhara's hymns could, however, be sung by the common people, as were many of those of Pĕriyāḻvār and Āṇḍāḷ.[168] A verse of Nammāḻvār's expressing the familiar exaltation of the devotees of the lord that says, 'If even a *caṇḍāla* from among the lowly *caṇḍālas* below the four castes were devoted to the discus-bearing lord, I would consider as my masters,

163 *Pĕrumāḷ Tirumŏḻi* 2.2, 2.3, 2.4.

164 *Tiruvāymŏḻi* 3.7.5 and 3.7.4.

165 This motif abounds in the hymns of the *Tevāram* as well.

166 He tells us that he is the *tulasi* garland weaver for the lord at Srirangam; the occupation, and his song for the lord's ritual reveille indicate his caste. More directly, he regrets his misdeeds that have caused him to forfeit the rights of priesthood and of feeding the three fires (*Tirumālai* 25). These, and a stereotypical lament for his past when he was a wicked thief and a rogue and 'caught in the net of fish-eyed beautiful women' (*Tirumālai* 16) lie at the root of the rather stereotypical story about the Āḻvār.

167 *Tirumālai* 6 and 9.

168 Pĕriyāḻvār's songs for the infant Kṛṣṇa continue to be sung by mothers and grandmothers and have a special ritual role during life-cycle ceremonies like naming the child, ear-boring etc. The popularity of the *Tiruppāvai* remains undiminished to date. Kamil Zvelebil, *The Smile of Murugan: On Tamil Literature of South India*, Leiden: EJ Brill, 1973, p. 185, says that the 'Saivite and Vaisnavite hymns have played, since the very days they were composed until the present time, an immense, indispensable and often decisive role in the religious, cultural and social life of the entire Tamil people'.

the servant's servants of such a one'[169] is a radical reorienting of the social hierarchies.

In the verses of Tirumankai, nearly all the holy places of Viṣṇu are described as being inhabited by multitudes of learned Vedic *brāhmaṇas.* Temple towns are extolled for their skies thick with the smoke from Vedic sacrifices.[170] The lord is praised for having come, in the days of yore, as Hayagrīva to give the flower-born one (Brahmā) the four Vedas that he had lost (to the Asuras).[171] When the earth and the sky had not appeared, and darkness enveloped all, the lord came as a swan and lit the world with the gems of the Vedas.[172] He came as a beautiful manikin to Mahābali's auspicious Vedic sacrifice.[173] He is the beautiful One who overpowered the horse (Keśin), who is the husband of Śrī, the Lord of gods, the radiance of coral, the indweller of the seven worlds, time, and the learning of Vedic seers.[174] The lord resides in Nānkūr where the chanting of the four Vedas, the six *Angas*, and the seven *svaras* reverberates through the eight quarters of the wealthy city.[175] In the temple town of Vaṇ-purusottamaṉ, among seers who tend the three fires, recite the four Vedas, perform the five sacrifices and master the six *Angas*, lives the lord who as a cowherd climbed the *kadamba* tree and danced on the hoods of the poisonous snake.[176] These references to Vedic rituals—which number many dozens—point to the brahmanical orientation of this Āḻvār's devotions.

However, mere reverent references to the Vedas or *brāhmaṇas*—and these can be found in almost every section of the *NDP*—do not prove that the Āḻvārs were trying to introduce, spread or stabilize brahmanic worship and superiority in south India. We have seen the consistent reiteration of the superiority of bhakti, consuming devotion, over other, traditional forms of worship. Yet, despite their envisaging a community of devotees who throng the streets of temple towns,[177] mingling without regard for caste, the Āḻvārs reflect the prejudices of their society: one cannot imagine a hymn that praises a sacred centre as one where

[169] *Tiruvāymŏḻi* 3.7.9.
[170] *Pěriya Tirumḍi* 5.4.7.
[171] *Pěriya Tirumḍi* 5.3.2.
[172] *Pěriya Tirumḍi* 5.1.9.
[173] *Pěriya Tirumḍi* 4.4.7.
[174] *Pěriya Tirumḍi* 7.10.6.
[175] *Pěriya Tirumḍi* 4.4.8.
[176] *Pěriya Tirumḍi* 4.2.2.
[177] *Pěrumāḷ Tirumḍi* 2.1–2.9.

numerous *caṇḍālas*, *pulaiyas* or for that matter, even *veḷāḷas* or *vaṇiyas* live. Tirumankai Āḻvār's *Pĕriya Tirumŏḻi*, which is almost a pilgrimage manual, justifies Veluthat's assertion that 'the leaders of the *bhakti* movement in South India were leading a temple movement... The *bhakti* movement went a long way... in popularising the temple'.[178]

Certainly, temple worship was deeply rooted in the Tamil country by the ninth-tenth centuries; indeed, it seems well established even in the earlier period. The Kūram plates of the seventh century CE record donations by the ruler Pallavādhirāja Vidyāvinīta of *devadāna* and *brahmadeya* in favour of the temple of Vidyāvinīta Pallava Parameśvara to provide for the worship, bathing (of the idol), flowers, perfumes, incense, lamps, oblations, conches, drums and the recitation of the *Bhārata* at this temple.[179] An inscription in the Laksmīnārāyaṇa Temple in Kāvāntaṭalam, Chingleput *tāluk*, of 883 CE, the fourteenth regnal year of Pallava Kampavarman, records the construction of the said Viṣṇu temple and the grant of two *patti* of land and a flower garden at Oṭṭankāṭu village to the temple as *arcanā bhoga* by a certain Mānacarppaṉ of Kuḷanūr in Venkaināḍu.[180] In the twenty-fourth regnal year of Pallava Nṛpatungavarman, i.e. 893 CE, a certain Arikkanta Pĕrumāṉer made a gift of 30 *kaḻañcu* of gold for a perpetual lamp to the temple of Viṣṇu Bhaṭāra at TiruMukkūṭal.[181] An inscription of 922 CE (of the fifteenth regnal year of Parāntaka I) near the entrance into the central shrine of the Raghunāthasvamin Temple in Erode records that the people of EḻukkaraitTiruVāyappāṭināḍu agreed to pay certain taxes for the worship of Vĕṇṇaikūtta Nāyaṉār in the temple of Paḷḷikŏṇṭa Āḻvār. The fees were ½ *paṇam* on each tenant, 1/8 *paṇam* from the bridegroom and 1/8 *paṇam* from the bride in each marriage ceremony and one *kuṉṟi* and one *mañjaḍi* of gold as *cūtukāṭṭupaṭṭam*.[182] In 934 CE, the *sabhā* of Tiraimūr recorded in the Mahālingasvāmi Temple in TiruvIṭaimarutūr that the temple officer and the *patipātamūlam* met in the *nāṭaka śālai* of the temple and assigned some land of the temple to a person who played

[178] Veluthat, 'Religious Symbols in Political Legitimation', pp. 24–5.

[179] Mahalingam, 1985, vol. III, pp. 210–11, Cg 859. REF.: *SII*, i, no. 151l *EI* xvii, no. 22, pp. 340–4.

[180] Mahalingam, 1985, vol. III, pp. 206–7, Cg 847. Ref. *ARE*, 1901, no. 207; *SII* vii no. 420.

[181] Mahalingam, 1985, vol. III, pp. 332–3. Cg 1299. Ref.: *ARE* 1915, no. 179; *SII*, xiii, no. 75.

[182] Mahalingam, 1985, vol. IV, p. 101. Cb 489. Ref.: *ARE*, 1910, no. 167; Ibid., part ii, para 20: *SITI* 1 no. 247, pp. 228–9.

the *uṭukkai* during the three daily services.[183] In the Vaikuṇṭhavāsa-p-Pĕrumāḷ Temple in Nĕn̲mali is engraved an inscription dated to 973 CE which records the gift of sheep by Āttirayan̲ Nārāyaṇan̲ Vāsudevan̲ for a lamp in the temple called Ticai-āyiratti-ainnūr̲r̲uvan̲[184]—a reference to the famous mercantile community, 'the 500 of the 1000 directions'. Another from the Vedanārāyaṇa-p-Pĕrumāḷ Temple in Āmūr, Chingleput district, dated to 999 CE, registers a gift of land by the *mahāsabhā* of An̲iyūr in Kālattūr *koṭṭam* as *bhaṭṭavṛtti* to a *brāhmaṇa* of the village well-versed in a *Veda* besides the *Sāmaveda*, in the Pāṇini grammar, in the *Mimāmsa*, etc., without detriment to the money income due therefrom to the Subrahmaṇya temple at TirutTaṇi, to which the land had been originally assigned, to teach these subjects to four pupils and feed them daily. There are three more fragments of the inscription, one of which seems to record provision for playing musical instruments during the various temple services.[185]

Inscriptional evidence in the succeeding centuries showing the involvement of diverse social groups in the life and ceremony of the temple is plentiful.[186] Not only did people belonging to different caste and occupational groups make a great number of donations and gifts

[183] Mahalingam, 1985, vol. VII, p. 125. Tj 550. Ref.: *ARE*, 1895, no. 157; *SII* v, no. 721.

[184] Mahalingam, 1985, vol. III, pp. 488–9. Cg 1932. Ref.: *ARE*, 1942–4, no. 149.

[185] Mahalingam, 1985, vol. III, pp. 2–3. Cg 10. Ref.: *ARE*, 1932, no. 76; ibid., part ii, para 22, p. 65.

[186] Mahalingam, 1985, vol. II, p. 504. SA 2146. Ref.: *ARE*, 1928–9, no. 271; ibid., part ii, para 32, p. 75. Varadarāja-p-Pĕrumāḷ temple, Vṛddhācalam *tāluk*. Sanskrit Grantha, Co̲la Jayadhara, i.e. Kulottunga I regnal year 38= 1108 CE, states that Māliruñcolai of Pūvan̲ūr who is described as Co̲lendramantri (minister of the Co̲la king), the foremost among *śūdras* and a devout worshipper of Viṣṇu, erected a *maṇḍapa* in front of the Pĕrumāḷ temple. Also, Mahalingam, 1985, vol. II, p. 474. SA 2025. Ref.: *ARE*, 1904, no 207: *SII* xvii, no. 229. On the north base of the *maṇḍapa* in front of the Varadarāja-p-Pĕrumāḷ shrine in the Candramaulīśvara temple, Vi̲luppuram *tāluk*. 1126 CE. Registers gift of 12 sheep by Ceṭṭan Tiruvārai, a shepherd of Gangaikŏṇṭaco̲lapuram situated in the Naṭuvirkūru of Co̲lamaṇḍalam for a *sandhi* lamp to the God Ā̲lvār at TiruvAkkarai in Mattūr *nāḍu* in Jayakŏṇṭaco̲lamaṇḍalam. The gift was received by the Kulankilavan̲, Ātreyan̲ Tirunāḍuṭaiyān̲, a lease holder of the temple. See also Mahalingam, 1985, vol. III, pp. 42–3, inscriptions nos. Cg 189, 190, 191 from Cinka-p-Pĕrumāḷ Koyil, tenth century, recording gifts of land, sheep etc, and Mahalingam, 1985, vol. III, pp. 92–9, inscriptions nos. Cg 392–8 from the Varāha-p-Pĕrumāḷ Koyil, TiruvIṭavĕntai.

of land, sheep, cattle and gold to temples,[187] they were also frequently involved in the conduct of various temple festivities and ceremonies. For instance, an inscription of the seventeenth regnal year of Rājarāja I, corresponding to 1002 CE, from the temple of Varāha-p-Pĕrumāḷ in TiruvIṭavĕntai records the dedication of 12 fishermen's families (*paṭṭinavan kuṭi*) for conducting a seven-day festival called *Rājarāja devan tirunāḷ* which fell on the *nakṣatra* Śaṭabhiśai (evidently the king's asterism) in the month of Āvaṉi. The fishermen were required to pay a tax of ¾ *kaḻañcu* per head earned by them either by weaving or by venturing on the sea, and to render also physical assistance in celebrating the festival. This arrangement, it is stated, was engraved on stone under orders of the two (named) state officers, one of whom was evidently the overseer of the district (*nāḍu kaṇkāṭci*) and the other who was performing the duties of district settlement (*nāḍu vakai*). The *brāhmaṇas* came in for a major share of the enjoyment of the charities made by devotees.[188] In 1004 CE, i.e. the nineteenth regnal year of Rājarāja I, a merchant of TiruvOṟṟiyūr in Pulankoṭṭam gifted 30 *kaḻañcu* of gold to the temple of Varāhadeva in TiruvIṭantai.[189] Further, the record says that the residents of Taiyūr, on receiving this amount, agreed to pay interest in oil and paddy to the assembly of TiruvIṭantai for burning a lamp in the temple and feeding 35 *brāhmaṇas*.[190] In 1099 CE, the twenty-ninth regnal year of the Coḻa ruler, Kulottunga I, provision was made for burning two lamps in the temple of Śrīrangadeva in Srirangam by a person (name lost) who was the Kannada *sandhivigrahi* and *daṇḍanāyaka* of Mahārājādhirāja-parameśvara-parama-bhaṭṭāra-satyāśraya-kulatilaka-tribhuvanamalla (i.e. Vikramāditya VI, the western Cālukya king). Some (named) shepherds undertook to supply the required quantity of ghee for burning the lamps. The inscription also refers to the application of lime mortar to the shrine of Senāpati

[187] Mahalingam, 1985, vol. III, pp. 133–4. Cg 549. Ref.: *ARE*, 1893, no. 17; *SII* iii, no. 68. This record from the Pāṇḍava-p-Pĕrumāḷ Koyil in Kāñcīpuram dated to 1075 CE records the donation by a merchant named Aruḷāladevan alias Kumāra Peruvaṇiyan Devan Ĕriñcoti, resident of Arumoḻidevappĕruntĕruvu in Kāñcīpuram provided the temple of Tiruppāṭakam with a flower garden and purchased some land from the *ūr* of Orirukkai in order to maintain gardeners and their families. The *ūr* apparently sold the land after declaring it tax- free.

[188] Mahalingam, 1985, vol. III, p. 95. Cg 401.Ref: ARE 1910, no. 274; ibid., para ii, para 21, p. 70.

[189] Same as TiruvIṭavĕntai.

[190] Mahalingam, 1985, vol. III, p. 96. Cg 402. Ref.: *ARE*, 1910, no. 267: ibid., part ii, p. 70

(Viśvaksena) caused to be done by the same donor.[191] Another record of 1216 CE, from the Kariyamāṇikka-p-Pĕrumāḷ Temple in Vijayamangalam in Erode tāluk refers to the temple itself as Tirumerkoyil-Cittirameḻi-Viṇṇagar-Aḻvār, i.e. the western temple of the Lord Viṣṇu of the Citrameḻi, an important guild. Interestingly, the gift was placed under the protection of 99 persons belonging to the left-hand castes.[192] In 1232 CE, a gift of 32 cows and a lamp stand was made for burning a lamp in the Varadarāja-p-Pĕrumāḷ Temple, Kancipuram, by (named) a resident of Mayilāppūr, of the weaver caste.[193] In 1252 CE, a (named) *kutirai cĕṭṭi* (horse trader) of Malaimaṇḍalam purchased land to gift to the temple of Srirangam.[194]

The 'great' temples of southern India[195] are nearly all brahmanical temples, associated with the worship of one or the other of the 'great' gods of the Puranic pantheon. This forms the basis for the argument that in 'popularising temple worship', the bhakti saints were instruments of brahmanization. However, considering the fact that all the extant *Agama* texts seems to have originated in southern India, it is possible that worship at shrines in the manner known to us today may itself have originated in the south. In that case, the Āḻvārs and Nāyaṉmārs may be considered the medium of integrating the prestige of pan-Indian Vedic brahmanism with an indigenous form of worship. The Tamil notion, known from Sangam texts, of the immanence of divinity in specific sites, supports this hypothesis.

The picture of co-existence of belief in the primacy of bhakti or god-absorbedness as the religious goal irrespective of social status with acceptance of the hierarchical ordering of society is reinforced by an analysis of the hymns and the hagiographies of the Nāyaṉmārs. The roughly contemporary Śaiva saints too display familiarity with Puranic religious themes and Vedic praxis. Unlike the Āḻvārs, all of whom are considered historical figures,[196] numerous Nāyaṉmārs seem to be

[191] Mahalingam, 1985, vol. VIII, p. 186. Tp 865. Ref.: *ARE*, 1941–2, no. 204; *EI*, xxxvi, no. 25 (a); SII xxiv, no. 75. Srirangam.

[192] Mahalingam, 1985, vol. IV, pp. 117–8. Cb 569. Ref.: *ARE*, 1905, no. 546.

[193] Mahalingam, 1985, vol. III, Cg 718. Ref.: *ARE*, 1919, no. 460.

[194] Mahalingam, 1985, vol. VIII, Tp 992. Ref.: *ARE*, 1953-54, no. 361; *SII*, xxiv, no. 264.

[195] The adjective is not meant to convey any ritual superiority. It simply means the larger, wealthier, more visible temples.

[196] Here, 'historical' is used in the sense of their having left written records. See Chapter 1-iii of the present work. It has been pointed out that the number of Nāyaṉmārs was a response to the Jaina concept of *salākāpuruṣas*, ideal religious

legendary. It is significant that these legendary Nāyaṉmārs were 'placed' in various castes and occupations from the 'highest' to the 'lowliest'. The stories of some of these devotees of Śiva reinforce my argument that it is not in the compositions of the Āḻvārs but in the teachings of the *ācāryas* that we must look for the formulation of the radical idea of bhakti.[197]

Iyarpakai Nāyaṉār, having promised a Śaiva ascetic (who was Śiva himself in disguise) whatever the latter desired, gladly gave him his wife; this Nāyaṉār was a merchant.[198] Manakkañcaṟṟaṉar, who, for a similar request of another Śaiva ascetic (again, Śiva in disguise), cut off his daughter's exquisite tresses even as she was being readied for her wedding, was a *veḷāḷa*.[199] Tirunīlakaṇṭhar, the second Nāyaṉār on Sundarar's list of 62 Nāyaṉmārs, so called because the name of the blue-necked lord was ever on his lips, was a potter who lived in the city of Tillai.[200]

Ciruttŏṇṭar, a physician, who was also a successful commander of the Coḻa armed forces, would not eat without feeding at least one devotee of Śiva everyday. He and his wife were blessed with a child only after many years of prayers to Śiva. One day, when Ciruttŏṇṭar, literally, small devotee, had gone out to look for a devotee to feed, none having landed at his door despite his fame as a generous host, Śiva arrived in the guise of a devotee, and left on learning that the master of the house was away. Ciruttŏṇṭar, on returning empty-handed, rushed to the temple whereto his wife said the devotee had repaired. The devotee said, however, that it would be impossible to feed him as he had pledged to eat nothing but the flesh of a child not older than five years, slaughtered by his own parents. The Nāyaṉār (to-be) was delighted that the devotee's wish was not beyond his means, and proceeded to, with the perfect cooperation of his wife, slaughter, cook and serve his only son to the ascetic. Not only that, the ascetic insisted that Ciruttŏṇṭar join him in the gruesome meal, and after the father had done so, asked him to call his son to join

---

men. However, a few Nāyaṉmārs besides Appar, Sundarar and Sambandar, like Kāraikkāl Ammaiyār, are historical.

[197] See Glenn E. Yocum, 'Tests of Devotion among the Tamil Saiva Nāyaṉmārs', *Journal of Oriental Research*, vols. 42–6, 1972–7, pp. 66–71, for an interesting discussion of the same Nāyaṉmārs cited here. Yocum also stresses that the model Nāyaṉār is one who surrenders totally to Śiva in all His unpredictability.

[198] G. Vanmikanathan, *Periya Puranam by Sekkizhaar: Condensed English Version*, Madras: Sri Ramakrishna Math, 2004, pp. 348–50.

[199] Ibid., pp. 347–52.

[200] Ibid., pp. 378–85. Tillai is the Tamil name for the sacred town of Chidambaram.

them. The Nāyaṉār replied that he no longer had a son. On the ascetic's insistence however, he did call out, to be rewarded by the boy running in to the arms of his delighted parents![201]

The story of Kalikkampar, a merchant who fed a number of devotees of Śiva everyday, has strong resonances of the Śrīvaiṣṇava insistence on the primacy of bhakti over the more customary marks of social status. An old servitor of the family who had left after a quarrel had apparently become a Śiva worshipper. One morning, when the couple was, as was their custom, engaged in washing the feet of their guests, the wife pouring water from a jug as the husband scrubbed their feet, the wife noticed that the man her husband was serving thus was their former servant, and stopped. When the flow of water abruptly ceased, Kalikkampar looking up and perceiving the reason, simply severed his wife's hand with a sword, and taking the jug, proceeded to wash the guest's feet by himself.[202]

One of the most startling stories of devotion is told of Kaṇṇappa Nāyaṉār, a hunter by caste. Named Tiṉṉappaṉ by his parents, he roamed the hillsides of Kāḷahasti in search of game. Once, out on a hunt, he strayed onto a hillock where a natural *linga* of rock commanded his adoration. Kaṇṇappar was concerned that there was no one to feed the lord, and proceeded to get meat to offer the *linga*. Being completely ignorant of the ways of worship, he chewed the pieces of boar he had killed to pick the most tender ones for offering.[203] Then he ran down the hill to a stream below, and filled his mouth with water (having nothing to carry it in). Back on the hilltop, he brushed off the withered flowers and leaves on the *linga* with his shoes, spewed out the water in his mouth over the shrine to wash it, and adorned it with the flowers he had, en route, tucked in his hair! He then stood guard over the *linga* all night, quitting his post only in the morning. A *brāhmaṇa* priest, Śivakośaṉ, who served the shrine, arrived after his departure to be shocked by the desecration—meat around the *linga*, and strange flowers and shoe marks on its crown. Kaṇṇappar arrived after he had left, having cleaned the shrine and worshipped it ritually, and proceeded with his own unorthodox worship. After this had gone on for five days, the distraught *brāhmaṇa* asked Śiva to punish the offender. The lord asked his priest to hide and watch his devotee. That day, when Kaṇṇappar arrived, he saw blood flowing from the eye of the *linga*. His efforts to staunch the

[201] Ibid., pp. 354–64.

[202] Ibid., pp. 495–8.

[203] The similarity to Śabari first tasting the fruit she offered Rāma is apparent.

flow with medicinal herbs from the forest failing, he simply plucked out with his spear, his own eye and stuck it into the rock. He had hardly had time to rejoice over his success when the other eye of the *linga* began to bleed. Never hesitating, Kaṇṇappar proceeded to pluck out his other eye as well, taking only the precaution of marking with his foot, the bleeding spot which he would not be able to see once he had lost his sight.[204]

The legend of Kaṇṇappar seems to have enjoyed popularity well before the composition of the *Pĕriya Purāṇam*, as Appar, Sundarar and Sambandar have all sung about him. While this story emphasizing the value of true devotion over mere rite and form is an old one, a number of the tales of the Nāyaṉmārs[205] must have been the creation of the age of the hagiographers.[206] While the saint-poets do esteem bhakti above caste, and express their willingness to be servants of the lord's servants,[207] the only examples from the Āḻvār's hymns that can be adduced for actual veneration by one *bhakta* of another are those of Madhurakavi for Nammāḻvār, whom as we have seen, he calls *Nagara Nampi*,[208] an epithet designating high status. It is perhaps our modern preoccupations that seek from the saints, further critique of the hierarchies of their society; it is evident, however, that they did not.[209]

[204] Ibid., pp. 520–30. The saint's name, Kaṇṇappaṉ, owes to his extraordinary sacrifice: *kaṇ*= eye (Tamil). See also, David Dean Shulman, 1980, *Tamil Temple Myths, Sacrifice and Divine Marriage in the South Indian Śaiva Tradition*, Princeton: Princeton University Press, pp. 135–6, for an interpretation of the legend as a myth of the sacrifice of the deity.

[205] Yocum, op. cit., pp. 66–71, argues that the tests undergone by the Nāyaṉmārs are not real tests at all but displays. 'When Śiva wants to make known to the world his *bhaktas*' unswerving devotion, he 'tests' them knowing full well that they will meet the test—another one of the god's many sports (*vilaiyāṭal*) to show other humans how to live without ego.' p. 71. This agrees with my argument.

[206] Interestingly, an inscription, date unknown, in the Tālapurīśvara temple, Tiruppāṉankāṭu, Cĕyyār *tāluk*, North Arcot district, makes a reference to this story. The record states that some hunters who claimed to belong to the family of Tirukkaṇṇappar made a gift for the merit of Sambuvarāya. See Mahalingam, 1985, vol. I, p. 91. NA 401. Ref.: ARE, 1906, no. 247.

[207] *Pĕriyāḻvār Tirumŏḻi*, 1.1, *Tiruppaḷḷiyĕlucci* 10.

[208] Madhurakavi Āḻvār *vaibhavam*.

[209] We do have evidence of radical questioning of the caste ordering of society in the works of Jñāneśvar from Maharashtra, but interestingly, he is closer to the period of the *ācāryas* than of the Āḻvārs or Nāyaṉmārs.

Some anecdotes from the life of Rāmānuja bolster my argument that it was the needs of the nascent Śrīvaiṣṇava community at Srirangam that led to the formulation of a (relatively) egalitarian theology. The hagiographies were much closer in time to the preceptor than to the hoary Āḻvārs—as is clear even from the fanciful dates that are ascribed to the saints. While the extraordinary place Rāmānuja acquired in the community must have—and did—led to the creation of apocryphal tales about him, the reverence in which the community held him and the fact that the hagiographers were only about three or four generations removed from him has led to the preservation of an astonishing amount of factual detail. This alone can explain why contentious anecdotes and an occasional one that shows Rāmānuja as less than ideal[210] have been preserved. In some instances, however, memory of more recent events has led to thorough garbling and anachronisms, as in the extraordinary story of Rāmānuja's going to Delhi to retrieve the icon of the lord from the Sultan whose armies are said to have plundered the Srirangam Temple.[211]

After Rāmānuja had broken with his Advaitic teacher Yādava Prakāśa, he began, on the advice of his mother, to perform the *kainkarya*, service, of fetching from a sacred well, the oblation water for Lord Varadarāja at Kāñcī, and placed himself under the guidance of Tirukkacci Nampi.[212] Lord Varadarāja was in the habit of regularly conversing with Tirukkacci Nampi, a *vaiśya*, who performed the *kainkarya* of constantly fanning him. Rāmānuja noticed the particularly fond gaze (*viśeṣa katākṣa*) that the lord inevitably bestowed upon Nampi, and desired to become his disciple. The *Agpp* elaborates that Rāmānuja prostrated at Nampi's feet while making the request, and quotes a *śloka* to establish that there is no need to examine the *kula* and *gotra* of truly great persons—details that do not, understandably, feature in the *Mgpp*. In both versions, however, Nampi refuses on the grounds that it was inappropriate according to *varṇāśramadharma* for Rāmānuja, a *brāhmaṇa*, to take a *vaiśya* for his *ācārya*. The *Mgpp* has Nampi relate to Rāmānuja, an

[210] *Agpp*, pp. 218–22. Rāmānuja is said to have lost his temper with Kūrattāḻvāṉ when the latter refused to take down a part of the dictation of *Śrībhāṣya*. Kūrattāḻvāṉ was well within his rights to do so as the agreement was that the disciple would not write anything he disagreed with. Eventually, Rāmānuja reflected on the *vākyārtha* that he had dictated, realized Kūrattāḻvāṉ was right, and apologized.

[211] *Agpp*, Iḷaiyāḻvār/Ĕmpĕrumāṉār *vaibhavam*.

[212] *Agpp*, Iḷaiyāḻvār/Ĕmpĕrumāṉār *vaibhavam*.

anecdote from the life of Nāthamuni. The *ācārya* had once been deluded into seeing the king and his queens as a party of Kṛṣṇa with his *gopīs*, and had begun to reverentially follow them— an act that earned him a reprimand from Uyyakŏṇṭār.[213] He then said that for one who had not, unlike Tirukkaṇṇamankai Āṇṭāṉ, renounced food, sleep and even the *nityakarmas* (the daily rituals), transgression of Śastraic injunctions against caste was not permissible.[214]

Wishing to clear some doubts about his future course of action, Rāmānuja asked Tirukkacci Nampi to place his questions before the lord.[215] Before doing so, however, he asked Nampi to come home for a meal. As it happened, the two took different routes to his house, and by the time Rāmānuja reached after performing his *kainkarya* for the lord, Nampi had already eaten and left to fan Varadarāja. Worse, he found that his wife had swept and washed the place where Nampi had eaten, and bathed again to purify herself after the *vaiśya's* visit.[216] Rāmānuja's desire to honour the holy man and to eat his leavings was thwarted. He was deeply grieved that his wife did not understand the true nature of *kainkarya* and *bhagavat*-bhakti. Eventually, the lord did answer Rāmānuja's questions through the agency of Tirukkacci Nampi, who had apparently taken no offence over the incident.[217]

Among the six points of advice of the lord was the injunction to Rāmānuja to take discipleship under Pĕriya Nampi, a *śiṣya* of Āḷavantār.[218] Rāmānuja accordingly left for Srirangam. At about the same time, the chief disciples of the recently deceased Yāmunācārya, recalling their master's desire to instate Rāmānuja as the *darśana pravartaka*, agreed that Pĕriya Nampi must go to Kāñcī to fetch him. The two met midway

[213] Another *ācārya*.

[214] *Agpp, Mgpp*, Iḷaiyāḻvār/Ĕmpĕrumāṉār *vaibhavam*.

[215] Tirukkacci Nampi is believed by the Śrīvaiṣṇava tradition to have had the unique privilege of holding conversations with the lord. In general, when the lord wishes to convey something, he appears in a person's dream; occasionally he speaks '*arcaka mukhena*', i.e. through the priest—a sort of Delphic oracle!

[216] Traditionally, women of the household are supposed to scour with their hands, the place where a respected person has eaten. Sweeping is considered sacrilege.

[217] *Agpp, Mgpp*, Iḷaiyāḻvār/Ĕmpĕrumāṉār *vaibhavam*.

[218] Literally, 'the one who has come to redeem'. The queen in whose court Yāmuna established the superiority of his philosophical system in the course of a debate is said to have addressed him thus. It is the traditional name by which Yāmunācārya is known among Śrīvaiṣṇavas.

at Madhurāntakam,[219] where Rāmānuja insisted on being given *dīkṣā*, initiation,[220] immediately. Both then returned to Kāñcī; Pĕriya Nampi and his wife established a household in a part of Rāmānuja's house. From Nampi, Rāmānuja received instruction in the *Vyāsa Sūtra* and learnt the meanings of the hymns of *NDP* with the exception of the *Tiruvāymŏḻi*.[221] One day, Rāmānuja asked his wife to get a Śrīvaiṣṇava who had brought an offering of oil, something to eat. She said there was nothing in the house. Doubting her, Rāmānuja sent her away on an errand, went inside and found some *appam*,[222] which he brought the hungry man. Needless to say, he was distressed with her indifference to Śrīvaiṣṇava tenets. Soon after, she quarrelled, in Rāmānuja's absence, with Pĕriya Nampi's wife over the use of the well, claiming the superiority of her *brāhmaṇa* sub-sect over Nampi's. Pĕriya Nampi too scolded his wife,[223] but they left immediately for Srirangam without taking leave of their host. This proved the last straw for Rāmānuja. Deciding that his wife was not fit to be his *dharmapatnī*, he sent her on a ruse to her natal home and took *sannyāsa*.[224] Eventually, he left Kāñcī for Srirangam, 'even as a bride leaves her natal home to go to her marital one'.[225]

Āḷavantār had arranged that five of his disciples should teach the intricacies of the faith and the philosophy to Rāmānuja; accordingly, he had 'placed' a part of his immense learning in each of them. Pĕriya Nampi advised Rāmānuja to learn the *rahasya granthas*, i.e. the meanings

[219] A temple town; not a *divya deśa* however.

[220] Here the texts elaborate that Pĕriya Nampi gave Rāmānuja the *pañca samskāras*.

[221] Rāmānuja learnt the meanings of the *Tiruvāymŏḻi* from Tirumalaiyāṇṭān, another of Yāmuna's special students. See Chapter 2-x of the present work.

[222] A filling, fried snack.

[223] Of course, the *Gpps* see no need to be apologetic about patriarchal behaviour on the part of the *ācāryas*! In this particular case, it seems Pĕriya Nampi's sub-sect is definitely considered inferior to Rāmānuja's and he may have felt his wife was responsible for breach of propriety. An excellent example of how, in the very process of negating caste hierarchies within the Śrīvaiṣṇava fold, they are reinforced.

[224] *Agpp/Mgpp*, Iḷaiyāḻvār/Ĕmpĕrumāṉār *vaibhavam*.

[225] This was again mediated by another of Āḷavantār's disciples, Tiruvaranga-p-Pĕrumāḷ Araiyar. TP Araiyar was an accomplished singer-performer of the *NDP*, and did so at the shrine of Varadarāja. Pleased, the lord asked him to choose a boon, upon which Araiyar asked for Rāmānuja, to take with him to Srirangam. Lord Varadarāja regretted his rash promise, but had no choice. *Agpp, Mgpp*, Iḷaiyāḻvār/Ĕmpĕrumāṉār *vaibhavam*.

of the *carama śloka* and the *tirumantra*,[226] from Tirukkoṭṭiyūr Nampi.[227] Accordingly, Rāmānuja went to TirukKoṭṭiyūr, only to be refused by the *ācārya* who wished to be certain of his sincerity of purpose. Seventeen times journeyed Rāmānuja fruitlessly to TirukKoṭṭiyūr, for Nampi believed that the *rahasyas* could only be imparted to one truly deserving. The eighteenth visit was, however, occasioned by Tirukkoṭṭiyūr Nampi's own invitation. Though Rāmānuja was specifically asked to come alone, he took along with him to the temple town, his close disciples, Kūrattāḻvā<u>n</u> and Mutaliyāṇṭā<u>n</u>, though he left them behind when he went to meet the preceptor. In the *Mgpp* version, Rāmānuja is said to have been accompanied by a third disciple as well—Naṭātūr Āḻvā<u>n</u>.[228] Before instructing him, Nampi made Rāmānuja promise to never disclose the esoteric meanings to anyone. However, the very next day, in an unthinkable transgression of the teacher's injunction, Rāmānuja expounded the special meanings to a gathering of Śrīvaiṣṇavas in the presence of the deity in the shrine of TirukKoṭṭiyūr. Hearing of this blatant disregard of his express instructions, Nampi summoned Rāmānuja and asked him if he knew the fruit of disobeying a guru. Rāmānuja explained that he had disobeyed knowing it would lead him straight to hell—but that his punishment would be worthwhile for securing the salvation of millions. Nampi came to appreciate the generosity of Rāmānuja's act, and not only forgave him, but also blessed him saying that the doctrine would be known by his name forevermore.[229]

In popular retellings, this story acquires more dramatic presentations such as Rāmānuja announcing the *rahasyas* from the top of the temple *gopuram* for not just initiated Śrīvaiṣṇavas, but the whole world to hear![230] It is worthwhile considering why it is among the best known of all the anecdotes about Rāmānuja.

Another anecdote seems simply to say that no pollution arises from contact with a person of low caste. The great preceptor would go to the Kaveri for his bath holding Mutaliyāṇṭā<u>n</u>'s hand, but he would return

226 Also known as the *dvayamantram*; see Chapter 3-ii of the present work.

227 TirukKoṭṭiyūr is a temple town south of Srirangam. The *ācārya's* name indicates where he stayed—the significance emerges from the story.

228 Both Kūrattāḻvā<u>n</u> and Mutaliyāṇṭā<u>n</u> are counted as Tĕ<u>n</u>kalai *ācāryas*, while Naṭātūr Āḻvā<u>n</u> is a Vaṭakalai *ācārya*. Sectarian politics is evident!

229 *Agpp, Mgpp*, Iḷaiyāḻvār/Ĕmpĕrumā<u>n</u>ār *vaibhavam*.

230 As the tower above the gateway to the temple, the *gopuram* marks the threshold of the sacred and lay spaces. The text, however, actually has Rāmānuja say that he would never disclose the *rahasya* to *nāstikas*, unbelievers, but could not possibly keep it from anyone devoted to the lord.

holding onto Piḷḷai Urankāvilli Dāsar, a low-born follower. On being asked by his disciples, Rāmānuja explained that Dāsar was a superior being free of the pride in birth. But even the egalitarian Rāmānuja is shown to have had occasional doubts about disregard of *varṇāśramadharma*, doubts which were dispelled by the example of other *ācāryas*. When Pĕriya Nampi performed the funeral rites for Māra<u>n</u>eri Nampi, an outcaste disciple, Rāmānuja is said to have remonstrated with him, asking if it was proper that he should be giving Vedic *samskāras* to an *antyaja* and creating divisions at a time he was trying to reform the world and pave the way to heaven. Nampi is said to have countered that he wasn't greater than Rāma of the Ikṣvākus who had performed the *brahma-medha samskāra* for Jaṭāyu or Dharmaputra who had honoured Vidura thus. Needless to say, Rāmānuja was convinced.[231] If, in this story, Rāmānuja needs convincing of the egalitarian mission of Śrīvaiṣṇavism, the following exchange, recorded in the *Vārttāmālai* of Pi<u>n</u>pa<u>l</u>akiya Pĕrumāḷ Cīyar, shows the preceptor as himself taking the lead in establishing the centrality of the lower caste followers in the religious community. On being asked by his nephew and disciple, Mutaliyāṇṭān, about the difference between himself and Piḷḷai Urankāvilli Dāsar, Rāmānuja is said to have explained the difference between the *cāttāta mutalis*[232] and the *Vaidikas* thus: '*Ācāryas* have a duty towards their fellow men, to carry out social amelioration and therefore must involve themselves in society, but the *cāttānis* have no such duties and may naturally devote themselves entirely to god.' Rāmānuja further elaborated, 'We have worries about *brāhmaṇyatva*, *gotra*, *sūtra* and *kuṭi* (lineage) and are disturbed. They concentrate only on the relationship between *jīvātmā* and *paramātmā*.'[233] It is easy to see that while Rāmānuja was concerned to establish the worthiness of non-*brāhmaṇa* Śrīvaiṣṇavas in the larger community, the distinction between 'us' and 'them' continues to operate and that the superiority granted to the *cāttānis* is purely in the spiritual sphere.

[231] *Agpp*, pp. 235–40.

[232] Those who do not wear the sacred thread, i.e. of non-*brāhmaṇa* caste. Lester says they include (today) descendants of both *brāhmaṇas* and non-*brāhmaṇas* who followed the anti-caste 'Ā<u>l</u>vār/Bhāgavata Vaiṣṇavism', the *brāhmaṇas* among them renouncing the sacred thread and top-knot, and giving up the performance of Vedic rites, opting for temple service instead. See Robert Lester, 'The Sāttāda Śrīvaiṣṇavas', *Journal of the American Oriental Society*, vol. 114, no. 1, 1994, pp. 39–53.

[233] Pi<u>n</u>pa<u>l</u>akiya Pĕrumāḷ Cīyar, *Vārttāmālai*, ed. S. Krishnaswamy Ayyangar, Puttūr Agrahāram, Tiruchi, 1983, p. 450.

When the hostility of a certain Co<u>l</u>a ruler[234] forced Rāmānuja to flee Srirangam, he made his way with a band of faithful followers to the realm of Biṭṭi Deva in Karnataka. The details in the hagiographies of how they were sheltered by Śrīvaiṣṇava hunters in the forest may have been intended to emphasize both the influence of Rāmānuja in far-flung areas, and his acceptance of people of all communities, but as always, the texts betray the brahmanical moorings of their authors. As we saw, the hunters are said to have brought the escapees honey and raw grain that they could pound and roast themselves, so that they could consume ritually pure food, and eventually escorted them to a *brāhmaṇa* household where they could be properly fed. However, Rāmānuja asked his disciples to secretly watch the cooking, and only when satisfied both on account of its ritual purity and on the housewife's *bhagavat*-bhakti, did he allow them to eat.[235]

Even if one were to insist on the bhakti movement being egalitarian in its fundamental presumptions, a hypothesis I have shown to be questionable, the fact remains that the *ācāryas* were eager to create a relatively non-hierarchical community with the promise of salvation open to all irrespective of birth. Rāmānuja's public exposition of the *rahasyas* at TirukKoṭṭiyūr underlines this determination that the Śrīvaiṣṇava faith was not to be exclusivist in character. The evidence from the Śaiva hagiographies too points to an attempt to establish bhakti as the primary defining characteristic of a person as opposed to the age-old primacy of birth. Epigraphic materials recording the effort to recognize the role of different caste and occupational groups point to the accommodations which were increasingly necessary in the second millennium. An inscription of 1025 CE records a decision of the assembly of Rājarāja-caturvedimangalam relating to the grant of lands and house-sites to gardeners, drummers, potters, garland- makers, torch- bearers and dancing girls of the temple at Rājendraco<u>l</u>a-Viṇṇagar-Ā<u>l</u>vār.[236] Even more tellingly, an inscription dated to 1116 CE from the Naltuṇai Īśvara Temple in Puñcai, Mayūram *tāluk* records the privileges granted by the temple authorities to certain members of the *anuloma rathakāra* castes including blacksmiths, goldsmiths carpenters and stone masons[237] and a similar one dated to 1118 CE from the Ujjīvanāthasvāmi Temple

[234] See Chapter 2-x of the present work.

[235] *Agpp*, Iḷaiyā<u>l</u>vār/Ĕmperumāṉār *vaibhavam*, pp. 241–50.

[236] Mahalingam, 1985, vol. IX, p. 29. Tn 135. Ref.: *ARE*, 1905, no. 107; *SII*, xiv, no. 132, pp. 68–9.

[237] Mahalingam, 1985, vol. VII, p. 283. Tj 1201. Ref.: *ARE* 1925, no. 189.

in Uyyakŏṇṭāṉ Tirumalai, Trichy *tāluk*, records a decision regarding an *anuloma* caste of *rathakāras* and what professions and ritual activities they were allowed and which forbidden.[238] These accommodations became critical with the establishment of Vijayanagara rule and the rise to prominence of new social groups.

Burton Stein has argued that the question of *śūdra* participation in the devotional sects of medieval south India is not an abstract one of reconciliation between the catholicity of bhakti principles and the hierarchies of orthodox Hinduism but whether a powerful and populous section was to enjoy a ritual rank commensurate with its social status.[239] It is indeed this issue that the *ācāryas* too sought to address. It must be remembered that this period was one which saw a creative effort towards what has been called integration of the great and little traditions (Redfield) or Sanskritization (Srinivas). *Brāhmaṇas* became the conscious and wilful agents of a profound, and even radical, modification of the Vedic and Sanskritic elements of their tradition.[240] Though the egalitarian programme of the Śrīvaiṣṇavas did not remain limited to theology and the promise of salvation to all regardless of birth, it never attempted more than a formal and limited critique of caste. The Tĕṉkalai commentaries mounted this critique, questioned established hierarchies, and reinforced this promise. Though the Vaṭakalai position came to stress adherence to *varṇāśramadharma*, it could not entirely repudiate its heritage: the primary structures for reiterating the Śrīvaiṣṇava belief in the fundamental equality of all before the Lord had been laid in the 'life-stories' of the saints.

[238] Mahalingam, 1985, vol. VIII, p. 318. Tp 1441. Ref.: *ARE*, 1908, no. 479; ibid., part ii, para 45, pp. 94–5.

[239] Stein, 'Social Mobility', p. 81.

[240] Nancy Ann Nayar, *Poetry as Theology: The Śrīvaiṣṇava Stotra in the Age of Rāmānuja*, Weisbaden: Otto Harrasowitz, 1952, pp. 5–6.

FIVE

'Whose God is the Greatest of All?' Engaging with Other Faiths

(i) Historiography and Hypothesis

The mutual rivalry between the followers of Viṣṇu and Śiva, with each set claiming pre-eminence for their own lord is too well known to be elaborated. The sectarian *Purāṇas* abound with legends in which the deity revered in each case is shown to have humbled the other beyond recovery. This is a running theme in the Tamil Vaiṣṇava literature too, whether it be the texts produced by the *ācāryas*, or the earlier hymns of the Āḻvārs. A reflection of the same can be found in the Śaiva canon, i.e. the *Tevāram* hymns and *Tirumurai* as well. In fact, the ninth verse of every poem of ten verses of the Nāyaṉār, Sambandar, mocks Brahmā and Viṣṇu by referring to the myth wherein Śiva assumed the form of a fire-*linga* without beginning or end to humble the two gods who were apparently engaged in a vain contest to establish their relative superiority.[1] Champakalakshmi has meticulously elaborated the relationship of the Coḻa state with developments in Śaivism.[2] I have considered earlier in this volume[3] that the contemporaneous development of Śrīvaiṣṇavism in the Coḻa age, when royal patronage was directed largely towards Śaiva institutions centred particularly on the temple at Chidambaram, does suggest the possibility that it was circumstances on the ground which

[1] Indira Vishwanathan Peterson, *Poems to Śiva: The Hymns of the Tamil Saints*, New Jersey: Princeton University Press, 1989, p. 22.

[2] R. Champakalakshmi, 'Introduction', *Studies in History*, vol. 4, no. 2, 1982, p. 165.

[3] See Chapter 1 of the present work.

actually dictated royal policy rather than imperial agency unilaterally influencing developments in the religious sphere. It would, however, be interesting to examine whether the Śaiva-Vaiṣṇava rivalry in the Tamil region was affected by the Co̱las' adoption of the Śaiva faith as a legitimating factor. A comparison of the contexts and ways in which Śiva and his devotees are mentioned in the Āḻvārs' hymns and in the later texts can provide a clue to any shift in this imaging. While a detailed study of the Śaiva canon to reconstruct the image that Śiva's followers had of Viṣṇu and his *bhaktas* is beyond the scope of this work, I will try and examine some of the better known Śaiva legends peculiar to the Tamil region.

Almost as well-known as the stories illustrating the contests between Śiva and Viṣṇu is the legend of the defeat of the Buddhists by Śankarācārya, a Nambūdiri *brāhmaṇa*,[4] in a scholarly debate.[5] It is of course impossible to establish whether Śankara met and debated with the Buddhists, leave alone whether he 'defeated' them. However that may be, what is crucial in this legend is the fact that the *brāhmaṇas* and the Buddhists were involved in a critical battle for patronage. The later history of the subcontinent reveals that the former were largely successful in this struggle, but in the middle and in the second half of the first millennium CE, when merchant groups were lavishly patronizing the sangha, this could well have seemed a desperate battle for survival for the *brāhmaṇas*. Consequently, it is not surprising that medieval Śrīvaiṣṇava literature is replete with vituperative comments on the Bauddhas and the Śramaṇas.

It has been suggested that the ideology of bhakti was suited to the needs of state formation and was used extensively by the important reigning houses of Tamil Nadu during the period of this study.[6] The fact that the efflorescence of the bhakti movement coincided with the rise of the Pallava state in the sixth–seventh centuries does suggest the possibility of some relationship between the two. It has also been argued that 'the Jaina conception of authority and kingship was less adequate than the ritual kingship of the brahmanical tradition'.[7] However, unless

[4] T.V. Mahalingam, *Readings in South Indian History*, Delhi: BR Publishing Corporation, 1977, p. 226.

[5] C. Minakshi, *Administration and Social Life under the Pallavas*, Madras: University of Madras, 1938, pp. 225–6.

[6] Kesavan Veluthat, 'Religious Symbols in Political Legitimation', *Social Scientist*, vol. 21, nos. 1–2, January-February 1993, pp. 23–33.

[7] Burton Stein, *All the King's Mana: Perspectives on Kingship in Medieval South India*, Madras: New Era Publications, 1984, p. 27.

it can be convincingly demonstrated that Buddhism and Jainism (as against brahmanical Hinduism of which bhakti is said to be an agent,[8] and which are said to have been the religions of the towns as against brahmanical Hinduism which was dominant in the agricultural zones), were in any way *unsuitable* to the rise of states, the hypothesis will remain questionable. It is not our concern here to determine whether or not Buddhism and Jainism were actually unsuited to serve as instruments of consolidation for emergent state systems. What I shall attempt to do is to carefully examine exactly how the Jainas and the Buddhists are pictured in the saints' hymns and in the later Tamil and Maṇipravāḷa texts, and compare them. This exercise will be contextualized by the inscriptional evidence for patronage to Buddhists and Jainas in both periods. I will try to discover if the diminished 'threat' of the Buddhists by the early centuries of the second millennium[9] in any way diluted the hostility in their representation in contemporary Śrīvaiṣṇava literature, and, if not, why this was so. It is important to remember that by the thirteenth century, the greatest challenge to the Śrīvaiṣṇavas came not from the 'heterodox' faiths but from the Śaivas.

Ronald Inden has suggested that Buddhism was the religion of the 'Indian imperial kingdoms from the time of Aśoka until the end of the seventh century, during which time Buddhism also became the major cosmopolitan religion of much of Asia'.[10] The earlier *śrauta* rituals such as *aśvamedha* were replaced by the practice of granting *agrahāras* to *brāhmaṇas* by rulers, and the latter practice evolved as a parallel to the Buddhist concept of the *mahādāna*.[11] Land grants to *brāhmaṇas* were not, however, only aimed towards the acquisition of religious merit; they have been linked to the attempt to extend the cultivated area.[12] *Brahmādeyas* were a major institution of agrarian expansion and organization, and have therefore been the focus of all studies in agrarian

[8] See Chapter 4–i of the present work.

[9] Kunal Chakrabarti, *Religious Process: The Purāṇas and the Making of a Religious Tradition*, New Delhi: Oxford University Press, 2001, pp. 110–54.

[10] Ronald Inden, *Text and Practice*, New Delhi: Oxford University Press, 2006, p. 94.

[11] Ibid., pp. 93–4.

[12] Romila Thapar, *Asoka and the Decline of the Mauryas*, New Delhi: Oxford University Press, 1961 (revised and reprinted edition, 1998), pp. 62–3, 67, mentions the practice of *brahmadeya* in Mauryan times and the methods the *Arthaśāstra* recommends to encourage settlement in uncultivated areas.

history, particularly in south India.[13] Besides, land grants were scarcely limited to *brāhmaṇas*; the Sātavāhanas and Kuṣāṇas granted land to officials, and for the establishment of *kaṭakas* or military camps.[14] Inden's arguments do, however, provide some important insights. If the grant of land to *brāhmaṇas* can be seen as a parallel to gift-giving to the Buddhist monk/sangha, a practice recommended by Buddhism in opposition to the violent and destructive Vedic sacrifice and, as productive of religious merit, then the struggle for patronage seen in our period of study takes on a doubly interesting colour. In a study of the Raichur Doab area of Karnataka between the tenth–eleventh centuries CE, it was noticed that whereas the main ruling family members were patrons of Jainism, the local chiefs were strong patrons of Śaivism.[15] Another study of the western Deccan that compared a sample of inscriptions from the reign of the Cālukyas of Bādāmi (sixth–eighth centuries) with one of the Cālukyas of Kalyāṇi (tenth–twelfth centuries) found that in the earlier phase, the royal family were prominent as donors while in the second phase, the names of local chiefs and mercantile communities were significant.[16] It has been pointed out in the same context that temples, in becoming large landowners, began to take on roles traditionally associated with the state, i.e. they began to assign taxes, collect revenues, and get land cultivated.[17] The growth in the politico-economic power of the temple is, thus, clearly not limited to establishments of the Śaiva and Vaiṣṇava faiths, but is something that, in the period of our study, cut across sectarian considerations.

Champakalakshmi has suggested that though the *bhakti* movement was often characterized as a protest against caste hierarchy, it was

[13] R. Champakalakshmi, 'Reappraisal of a Brahmānical Institution: The Brahmādeya and its Ramifications in Early Medieval South India', in *Structure and Society in South India*, ed. Kenneth Hall, New Delhi: Oxford University Press, 2001, (paperback edition, 2004) p. 59.

[14] R.S. Sharma, *Aspects of Political Ideas and Institutions in Ancient India*, Delhi: Motilal Banarsidass Publishers Pvt. Ltd., 1959 (revised edition, 1996), pp. 275–309.

[15] Aloka Parasher-Sen. Personal communication.

[16] A. Aruna, 'Religious Patronage and Identity Formation- A Study of Jaina Inscriptions (6th–12th centuries CE)', in *Kevala Bodhi: Buddhist and Jaina History of the Deccan*, ed. Aloka Parasher-Sen, The BSL Commemorative Volume, Delhi: Bharatiya Kala Prakashan, 2004, pp. 270–4.

[17] Ibid., p. 274.

primarily pitched against the 'heterodox' Buddhist and Jaina sects.[18] Further, 'Appar and Sundarar were propagating *bhakti* in a situation of conflict and rivalry for patronage against the Jainas and Buddhists who were influential in royal and urban centres'.[19] She locates the centres of this conflict between the 'heterodox' and 'orthodox' faiths in the Tamil land in Kāñcīpuram and Madurai, the capitals of the Pallavas and Pāṇṭiyas respectively.[20] M.N. Rajesh suggests that the emergent bhakti cults appropriated some Buddhist and Jaina ideals such as that of equality of all before god and salvation for all irrespective of caste and creed.[21] While it is debatable whether Jaina or Buddhist preceptors ever spelled out the notion of equality of all, leave alone the very notion of 'God' or of 'salvation', it is indeed worth considering that the spread and prevalence of the heterodox faiths among the populace must have made it incumbent upon any competing religious system to jettison, or at least modify, the exclusivity and hierarchy that characterized brahmanical Hinduism. We have already seen—in the case of Śrīvaiṣṇavism—that this was, however, as much a function of the later development of the sect as of the 'bhakti movement' itself.

George Spencer has argued that one can find in the 'fanciful lore' around the bhakti saints, an 'authentic core of these sectarian traditions which preserves memories of a spiritual crisis . . . centred upon the Pallava and Pāṇḍya royal courts where rivalries among religious elites for royal patronage were most intense'.[22] Selecting from the Śaiva hagiographies stories where one or the other Nāyaṉār was involved in conflict with the Jainas, Dehejia argues that the period of the 'bhakti movement' in Tamil Nadu saw the gradual growth of an aggressive and

[18] R. Champakalakshmi, 'The City in Medieval South India; its Forms and Meaning', in *Craftsmen and Merchants: Essays in South Indian Urbanism*, ed. Narayani Gupta, Chandigarh: Urban History Association of India, 1993, p. 17; also R. Champakalakshmi, *Trade, Ideology and Urbanization, 300 BC-1300 AD*, New Delhi: Oxford University Press, 1996, pp. 395–6.

[19] R. Champakalakshmi, '*Patikam Pāṭuvār*: Ritual Singing as a Means of Communication in Early Medieval South India', *Studies in History*, vol. 10, no. 2, July-December 1994, pp. 204–5.

[20] Ibid.

[21] M.N. Rajesh, 'Syncretism, Tamil Forms of Worship and Jaina Influence', in *Kevala Bodhi: Buddhist and Jaina History of the Deccan*, ed. Aloka Parasher-Sen, The BSL Commemorative Volume, Delhi: Bharatiya Kala Prakashan, 2004, p. 308.

[22] George Spencer, 'The Sacred Geography of the Tamil Shaivite Hymns', *Numen*, vol. 17, Fasc. 3, 1970, p. 234.

overbearing attitude on the part of the Jainas.[23] This both overlooks the palpable aggression that the bhakti saints in these tales display towards the Jainas and Buddhists, and is akin to suggesting that the portrayal of Shylock in *The Merchant of Venice* shows that Jews in the Elizabethan age were excessively greedy and inhuman. Further, it assumes that the hagiographies are 'true' accounts' which, I have argued, is far from the case. Rather, I suggest that these stories depict the anxieties of the brahmanical composers of the *Gpps* and the *Pĕriya Purāṇam* regarding the influence of the Jainas which were, considering the circumstances on the ground, in all likelihood, considerably disproportionate to the actual threat.

Lastly, I will also look at the representation of Muslims in Śrīvaiṣṇava literature. Arab traders are known to have established trade links with the Malabar Coast as early as the middle of the first millennium CE; indeed the name, Malabar, itself seems to have been derived from Ma'bar, Arabic for passage.[24] Settlements of Arabs in the littoral tracts of the Tamil region and native converts to Islam date to at least the seventh century.[25] Our examination of the hymns of the Āḻvārs has failed to produce any reference to Islam, but the same cannot be said of the later literature. I suggest that in the bhakti period, the presence of Islam in the Tamil region was too marginal to claim attention. In the early half of the second millennium however, some negotiation with this new faith was called for. An episode in the hagiographical narratives about Rāmānuja gives us a clue to these tensions and the resultant accommodations.[26]

(ii) Evidence of Jaina and Buddhist Presence in Tamil Nadu

Though both the 'heterodox' faiths rose in north India in the sixth century BCE, both seem to have come to the Deccan by at least the third century BCE, if not earlier. The presence of Aśokan edicts in several sites in Karnataka and Andhra would also suggest the interchange of ideas between the regions north and south of the Vindhyas by at least this date. Legends take this history further back: Bavari, a disciple of the Buddha from Kośala is believed to have settled in the region of Aśmaka in present-day Andhra, and brought the teachings of the master to the

[23] Vidya Dehejia, *Slaves of the Lord*, Delhi: Munshiram Manoharlal, 1988, p. 27.

[24] S. Krishnaswami Aiyangar, *South India and her Muhammadan Invaders*, New Delhi: S. Chand & Co. Pvt. Ltd., 1921, p. 70.

[25] Ibid., pp. 69–70.

[26] See Chapter 2–x of the present work.

region. The Mauryan emperor Candragupta is said to have renounced his throne at the instance of his mentor Bhadrabāhu and retired as a Jaina ascetic to Śravaṇabelagola in Karnataka.[27] Even if these legendary accounts are dismissed as ahistorical, other evidence points to Jaina presence in south India at an early date. Tamil Brāhmi inscriptions of the second–first century BCE from Cittaṉavācal in Pāṇṭiyanāḍu refer to donations made to a Jaina monk;[28] indeed, the earliest inscriptions from Tamil Nadu are probably Jaina inscriptions.[29] Verse 72 in the *Naṟṟinai*, a Sangam work, was composed by Iḷam Bodhiyar.[30] The two late Sangam epics, *Cilappatikāram* and *Maṇimekalai*, abound in references to Buddhists and Jainas. In fact, the protagonist of *Maṇimekalai*, a courtesan's beautiful daughter whose favours are sought by the prince of the land himself, rejects a life of 'empty worldliness' to become a Buddhist nun. It also speaks of a *caitya* built by the brother of Kiḷḷivaḷḷavaṉ of the Coḻa dynasty who ruled in Kāñcī in the second century.[31] Ilanko Atikaḷ, the composer of the *Cilappatikāram*, was very likely a follower of Jainism. Buddhadatta, author of the Buddhist work, *Abiddhammāvatāra,* who lived in the fifth century in the Kaveri delta, tells us that he enjoyed the patronage of Accyuta Vikkanta of the Kaḷabhra dynasty.[32] The *Kuntalakeśi*, composed by a Jaina teacher Nādagutta is a *kāvya* dated to the fourth century; the fifth-century *Nīlakeśi* is yet another Jaina work that concerns itself mainly with refuting the former.[33] The tenth-century Jaina work

[27] A ninth century inscription from Śravaṇabelagola graphically describes the advent of Jaina monks to the south. According to it, the last of the Śruta Kevalins, Bhadrabāhu, is said to have foretold a famine in Ujjain and led the whole sangha to the south. The *Bṛhat Kathā Kośam*, written in the tenth century by Harisena relates that Bhadrabāhu sent out emissaries under the leadership of Viśākhamuni to the Coḻa and Pāṇṭiya lands to spread the faith. Ref.: K.V. Raman, 'Jainism in Tondaimandalam', *Bulletin of the Institute of Traditional Cultures, Madras*, vol. 18, no. 1, 1974, p. 13.

[28] Shrinivas V. Padigar, 'Concept and Art: Vicissitudes of Jina Chaityas and Chaityalayas in Karnataka', *Deccan Studies*, vol. 5, no. 1, 2007, p. 63.

[29] A. Ekambaranathan and C.K. Sivaprakasam, *Jaina Inscriptions in Tamil Nadu: A Topographical List*, Madras: Research Foundation for Jainology, 1987.

[30] T.N. Ramachandran, *The Nagapattinam and other Buddhist Bronzes in the Madras Museum. Bulletin of the Madras Govt Museum*, Madras: Government Press, 1954, p. 4.

[31] Ibid., p. 10.

[32] Raman, op. cit., p. 16.

[33] Ramachandran, op. cit., p. 4.

Amṛtasāgara also quotes verses in praise of King Accyuta Vikkanta.[34] The names of the Buddhist philosophers and logicians Digvaga, Dharmapāla and Bodhidharma are connected with Kāñcī.[35] The *Mattavilāsa Prahasana* (early seventh century CE) would not have ridiculed the Buddhists and Jainas if they were not a significant and familiar presence in the social landscape. Indeed, it mentions a Buddhist *vihāra* in the environs of Kāñcī and Buddhist monks in the city.[36] The third verse of the concluding stanzas of *Lokavibhāga*, a Digambara Jaina work, says that it was completed in Śaka 380 (456 CE) in the twenty-second regnal year of King Simhaviṣṇu, lord of Kāñcī.[37] The ruler has been identified with Pallava Simhaviṣṇu II. The *Vīracoḻiyam*, a curious work on Tamil grammar conceived on ultra-Sanskritic lines[38] and apparently composed at the request of Vīrarājendra Coḻa (accession 1070 CE), was the work of a Buddhamitra[39] who calls himself the chieftain of Pŏṉpeṟṟi.[40] Legend has it that Cekkiḻār was goaded into the composition of the *Pĕriya Purāṇam*, the hagiography of the Nāyaṉmārs, by Kulottunga II seeking literary enjoyment in the *Jīvaka Cintāmaṇi*, a secular *kāvya* in Tamil attributed to a Jaina author.[41] Guṇavīra Paṇḍita, another Jaina author, dedicated his work of grammar, *Nemināṭham*, to Neminātha of Tĕṉmayilāpuri.[42] Avirodāḻvār, a Jaina poet of the fourteenth century, has composed 103 verses in praise of the same lord, known also as Mayilaināthar.[43] It is evident that Mylapore in the heart of modern-day Chennai was an important Jaina centre of worship.[44]

Architectural remains also tell a parallel story. Though monumental evidence for the presence of Jainism and Buddhism is scarce in Tamil Nadu per se—with only a few Jaina temples and practically no Buddhist

[34] Raman, op. cit., p. 16.

[35] Minakshi, *Administration and Social life Under the Pallavas*, p. 222.

[36] Ibid., p. 223.

[37] Ibid., p. 229.

[38] K.A. Nilakanta Sastri, *The Cōḻas*, Madras: University of Madras, 1935–7 (revised edition, reprint, 1975), p. 275.

[39] Ramachandran, op. cit., p. 7.

[40] Sastri, *The Cōḻas*, p. 275.

[41] Ibid., p. 655.

[42] Raman, 'Jainism in Tondaimandalam', op. cit., p. 21.

[43] Ibid.

[44] As the site of a major temple to Śiva as Kapālīśvara, it might have been a contested territory. This might be the context for Sambandar's attack on the Jainas in his decad on the Mayilai temple. Or was the Jaina shrine taken over and converted into a Śaiva one?

vihāras, *stūpas* or *caityas* surviving—it is abundant in the Deccan. Construction of stone edifices, which had begun under the Cālukyas of Bādāmi (mid-sixth to mid-eighth centuries CE) became common under the Rāṣṭrakūṭas (mid-eighth to late-tenth centuries CE) and their successors, the Gangas and the Santaras, some of whose members were followers of Jainism.[45] This trend reached its zenith between the eleventh and thirteenth centuries under the Cālukyas of Kalyāṇi and the Hoysalas of Dvārasamudra.[46] From the middle of the twelfth century, however, Jainism experienced persecution at the hands of the Śaivas in northern Karnataka and Śrīvaiṣṇavas in the southern part of the state.[47]

The most important Buddhist epigraphic record in Tamil Nadu is undoubtedly that on the Leiden plates.[48] The Larger Leiden plates dated to the twenty-first year Rājarāja I, i.e. 1005 CE, refer to the (ongoing) construction of the Cūḍāmaṇivarma *vihāra* by Kaḍārattaraiyaṉ (the king of Kaḍāram) in Nāgapaṭṭinam and a large grant of tax-free lands (the village Āṉaimangalam) by the Coḻa ruler for the said *vihāra* and the *paḷḷi* in it. Though the grant came into effect from the year 1005, the construction of the *vihāra* seems to have taken 9 years. The Lesser Leiden Plates were apparently issued by Kulottunga I in favour of the *sangarattār* (Sangha members/administrators) in response to a request by the king of Kaḍāram to record the grants on copper plate. While a Rājendracoḻapĕrumpaḷḷi is mentioned besides the Rājarājapĕrumpaḷḷi, the grants seem to pertain only to the former. It is interesting to note that there is no further inscriptional evidence pertaining to this *paḷḷi*. How long did it continue in existence? A ruined tower-like structure near the seashore in Nāgapaṭṭinam served as a guide for ships in the nineteenth century. In the last quarter of the century, the structure was pulled down by the Jesuits (after several letters had been written to the British Government of India for permission, many of the earlier ones being rejected) to build a school with the material. Fortunately, however, pictorial documentation of the structure is available[49] and all that can be said with certainty about it is that it does not conform to any known architectural pattern of either a Hindu temple or of a mosque. More to the

[45] Padigar, op. cit., p. 64.

[46] Ibid., p. 65.

[47] Ibid.

[48] *Epigraphica Indica*, vol. XXII. Published by the Director General, Archaeological Survey of India, Delhi, 1984, pp. 223–9, 267–81. Larger and Lesser Leiden Plates.

[49] *Epigraphica Indica*, vol. XXII, Illustrated plates.

point is the fact that on demolition, there was found a bronze idol of the Buddha[50] (which was eventually presented to Lord Napier).[51] Can there be any connection between the *vihāra* constructed in the early eleventh century and Tirumankai Āḻvār? Evidently not. But what leaps to the eye is its connection with the story of the Āḻvār which was 'constructed' by the hagiographers. It seems likely that the Buddhist shrine was built by a foreign ruler (the kingdom of Kaḍāram has not been located, nor has Śrīvijaya with any certainty[52]—the king of the latter kingdom is known to have made some donations of jewellery through his agent to the temple of Nāgai-y-aḻakar[53] and has been thought to be the same ruler who had the *vihāra* built)[54] for the merchants of his realm.[55] It is possible that the *vihāra* lost influence and importance under the later Coḻas but continued to exist and function as an 'eyesore' for the proselytizing Śrīvaiṣṇava (and Śaiva) hagiographers and inspired their stories of Tirumankai Āḻvār and Tirujñāṉa-Sambandar.[56]

Specifically Buddhist inscriptions are extremely rare in Tamil Nadu. One epigraphic reference in archaic characters of the seventh century on the pillars of a Śiva temple in Rājendrapaṭṭanam, a village in the Vṛddhācalam *tāluk* of South Arcot district, refers to Sariputta being the disciple of Buddhavarman, Śrī Śāntimati and so forth.[57] Excavations in Kāveripaṭṭinam uncovered a Buddhist monastery and temple (with several archaeological layers of activity) dated to the period between the third and eighth centuries; a Buddhapada and some small bronze icons

[50] Ibid., Illustrated plates.

[51] Ibid., p. 229. According to Ramachandran, op. cit., the site subsequently yielded a very large number (nearly 300) of bronze images. Article summarized in A. Aiyappan, and P.R. Srinivasan, *Story of Buddhism with special reference to South India*, Department of Information and Publicity, Madras: Government of Madras, 1960, pp. 52–8.

[52] K.A. Nilakanta Sastri, *A History of South India*, Madras: Oxford University Press, 1955, pp. 173–5, parenthesises Śrīvijaya as Palembang in the Malay Peninsula.

[53] T.V. Mahalingam, A Topographical List of Inscriptions in the Tamil Nadu and Kerala States, Delhi: ICHR, S. Chand & Co. Ltd., 1985, vol. VII, pp. 359–60. Tj nos. 1545 and 1547; Refs.: *ARE* 1956–7, nos. 164 and 161.

[54] Champakalakshmi, *Trade, Ideology and Urbanization*, pp. 51–2.

[55] Ibid.

[56] Sambandar's contest with the Buddhist monks is set in Kāraikkāl, geographically very close to Nāgapaṭṭinam. See account above.

[57] K.R. Srinivasan, 'A Note on other Buddhist Vestiges in Tamil Nadu', in *Story of Buddhism*, ed. Aiyappan and Srinivasan, op. cit., p. 159.

of the Buddha have been recovered from the site but no inscriptions.[58] A beautiful copper gilt image of the Javanese type, probably of Maitreya, dated to the ninth century, that was found from Melayūr in the Shiyali *tāluk* of Tanjavur,[59] is also said to have been originally collected from Kāveripaṭṭinam.[60] An inscription of 1241 CE from the Varadarāja/Aruḷāla-p-Pĕrumāḷ Temple in Kāñcīpuram refers to an order of Madhurāntaka Pottāppi Cōḻan according to which taxes were levied on all oil merchants in Mummuṭi Coḻa Pĕruntĕruvu in Kāñcīpuram. Stones with the insignia of Gaṇḍagopāla were apparently set up to mark the jurisdiction and Bauddhapaḷḷi is mentioned as one of the places exempted from this tax.[61] Another glancing reference comes from Pallankoyil in Tanjavur district. A set of six copper plates discovered from Vedāraṇyam on the east coast of the Tanjavur district records, in tenth-century Tamil characters, a gift of land in Tanavalippūṇṭi as *bhogam* to the Jaina temple called Sundaracoḻa Pĕrumpaḷḷi with the interesting stipulation that one quarter of the grant should be assigned to female disciples and the rest for male disciples. Among the boundaries of the land is mentioned a Śākyapaḷḷi and the Śākyapaḷḷiyappadari Temple of Kūṭalūr.[62] Navalūr, a village in the Chingleput district is said to have been a *paḷḷiccantam* of the Kaccikku Nāyaṉār Temple of Buddha Kāñcī.[63] A stone slab found on the roof of the *maṇḍapa* of a Śiva temple in TirucCopuram in the North Arcot district bears a Pāṇṭiya inscription recording the gift of land by a Buddhist monk, Sariputra Paṇḍita, in the presence of the *sanghattār* of the place, for worship and offerings on new moon and full moon days.[64]

[58] K.V. Soundara Rajan, *Kaveripattinam Excavations, 1963-73*, Archaeological Survey of India, New Delhi, 1994, pp. 26–9.

[59] P.R. Srinivasan, 'Buddhist Images of South India', in *Story of Buddhism with special reference to South India*, ed. Aiyappan and Srinivasan, op. cit., p. 79.

[60] Soundara Rajan, op. cit., p. 29.

[61] Mahalingam, 1985, vol. III, pp. 187–8, Cg 767. Ref.: *ARE* 1919, no. 607; ibid., part ii, para 56.

[62] K.R. Srinivasan, 'A Note on other Buddhist Vestiges in Tamil Nadu', pp. 160–1.

[63] A. Ekambaranathan, 'Buddhist Vestiges in Toṇḍaimaṇḍalam', *Bulletin of the Institute of Traditional Cultures, Madras*, vol. 21, no. 1, 1977, p. 21, footnote: *ARE*, 13 of 1934–5.

[64] Ibid., p. 20; *SII*, vol. 17, no. 131. Sambandar is said to have debated with and defeated a Buddhist monk named Sariputta. I have argued with the Śrīvaiṣṇava evidence that the hagiographies were carefully constructed using available evidence. The choice of the name Sariputta, for instance, by the Śaiva hagiographers of the twelfth–thirteenth centuries when Buddhism

It must also be remembered that Xuan Zang, who visited the Tamil country around 630 CE, lamented the decline of Buddhism in Kāñcīpuram which he had heard spoken of as a great Buddhist centre in the past.[65] It has been conjectured on the basis of the find of four Buddha figures in the round[66] that the present Kāmākṣī[67] and Kaccapeśvara Temples in Kāñcī were once Buddhist shrines. Three Buddha figures at Paḷḷūr, about 8 miles north-west of Kāñcī, are said to have been brought therein from a nearby mound called Buddhameṭu or Putumeṭu.[68] A Buddha figure and a *dharmacakra* have also been found in Kaṇikiḻuppai, a village adjacent to Pallāvaram.[69] Two headless Buddha images were unearthed in the 1970s in Mylapore in the heart of Madras city.[70]

Among the sculptured panels of the Vaikuṇṭha-p-Pĕrumāḷ Temple in Kāñcī is one of a *caitya*, which has been assigned to the period of Buddhavarman.[71] A few Buddhist images belonging to a later period testify to the tenacity of the Buddhist faith in the Tamil land through the second millennium. A Buddha figure, exquisitely modelled but for the flame on the head which has been left unfinished as a lump, found from a modern temple in Tyāgaṉūr in the Attūr *tāluk* of Salem district is dated to the tenth century.[72] A Buddha seated in *padmāsana* found in Madagaram in Tanjavur district seems to have the characteristic features of Coḻa

was practically invisible in the Tamil land, demonstrates the validity of the argument in the Śaiva case as well.

[65] T. Watters, *On Yuan Chwang's Travels in India*, vol. II, Delhi: Munshiram Manoharlal, 1961, pp. 226–7.

[66] Ekambaranathan, op. cit., p. 21, footnote—Annual Reports of Epigraphy 1908, 1934–5.

[67] T.A. Gopinatha Rao discovered, in 1915, an imposing Buddha image in granite, 7'10" in size, in the innermost *prākāra* of the Kāmākśī temple at Kāñcī. It is tentatively attributed to the early seventh century. The statue can be seen in the Buddhist sculpture gallery of the Government Museum, Madras. Ref: Aiyappan and Srinivasan, *Story of Buddhism*, pp. 70–1. On the basis of the discovery of the above mentioned figure and four other Buddha images, Gopinatha Rao was inclined to believe that the temple itself, or a part thereof, had been originally a Buddhist one. Ref: T.N. Vasudeva Rao, 'Buddhism and Kanchi', *Journal of Indian History*, vol. 53, part 1, 1975, p. 23.

[68] Ekambaranathan, op. cit., p. 18.

[69] Ibid., p. 19.

[70] Ibid.

[71] C. Minakshi, *The Historical Sculptures of the Vaikuṇṭha Perumāḷ Temple, Kāñchī*, Delhi: Government of India Press, Manager of Publications, 1941, p. 51.

[72] Srinivasan, 'Buddhist Images of South India', pp. 92–3.

figures dateable to about 1000 CE.[73] The seated Buddha found near the police station in (Śiva) Kāñcī, and dated to the first half of the eleventh century is, however, of the Javanese type rather than the indigenous Co<u>l</u>a. A slightly damaged, seated Buddha figure from TiruvAtti in South Arcot district may belong to the middle of the eleventh century or slightly later.[74] The Buddha from TiruvAlañculi in Tanjavur district, of about the same period is a rare standing Buddha figure in stone found in the Tamil country.[75] Besides, this figure shares many stylistic features with the bronzes found from Nāgapaṭṭinam.[76] The figure erected on a platform on the bund of a tank called Pa<u>l</u>uppura<u>n</u>i in Jayakŏṇṭaco<u>l</u>apuram in Tiruccirāppaḷḷi district is noteworthy for a beautiful umbrella carved in high relief above the halo representing Śākyasimha Buddha (suggesting his royal status). This umbrella recalls the umbrellas occurring in some seals of the copper plate grants of the time of Rājendra Co<u>l</u>a I and the figure is consequently assigned to the latter half of the eleventh century.[77] Even more interesting is the local name of the figure—Pa<u>l</u>uppar, meaning, one who is ripe. The term is the exact equivalent of Samyak Sambuddha who was the 'most ripened among the wise'.[78] A twelfth-century specimen of Buddha in the *dhyāna* posture has been found from Arikkamedu south of Pondicherry.[79] Of a similar date are two figures, one damaged and another in the *bhusparśa mudrā* in the Karukki<u>l</u>amar<u>n</u>ta Amma<u>n</u> Temple in Kāñcī,[80] another in *bhadrāsana* from Mā<u>n</u>ampāṭi in Tanjavur and the seated figures from Karaṭikuppam, north of Pondicherry, and from Kūvam.[81] The *dharmacakra* found along with the two Buddha images in Kūvam is now worshipped locally as the Sudarśana *cakra* of Viṣṇu by the local populace.[82] The only inscribed stone Buddha—though the writing in the Grantha script is too weathered to be read—comes from Manikandi in Ramanathapuram district and is dated to the thirteenth century.[83] On the inner side of the southern wall of the Ekāmreśvara Temple in

[73] Ibid., p. 93.

[74] Ibid.

[75] Ibid., p. 94.

[76] Ibid.

[77] Ibid., p. 95.

[78] Ibid.

[79] Ibid., p. 98.

[80] The two images in the Karukkilamar<u>n</u>ta Amma<u>n</u> Temple are from the Kāmākṣi Temple, originally discovered by Gopinatha Rao. See footnote above.

[81] Srinivasan, 'Buddhist Images of South India', pp. 98–9.

[82] Ekambaranathan, op. cit., pp. 18–19.

[83] Srinivasan, 'Buddhist Images of South India', pp. 99–100.

Kāñcīpuram are found, carved in relief, seven seated Buddha images in their respective niches, dated to approximately the fourteenth–fifteenth centuries. Even more interesting is a reclining Buddha carved on the outer side of the eastern wall of the same temple which is considered the only specimen of the representation the Buddha's *parinirvāṇa* in south India.[84] An image of Buddha in the *anjali hasta* pose is also found in the outer *prākāra* of the Viṣṇu Temple at TirukKaṇṇamankai in Coḻanāḍu.[85] Scenes from the Buddha's life are also depicted on the balustrades of the great Rājarājeśvara Temple at Tanjavur.[86]

We do know that Buddhist monasteries flourished in the Deccan. Epigraphic evidence points to widespread Buddhist presence in the Andhra region; Buddhist cave shrines and *vihāras* are among the most notable historical–archaeological features of the Western and Eastern Ghats. The rarity of Buddhist monumental remains in Tamil Nadu may therefore be more a function of the neglect of Buddhist institutions from lack of patronage in the second millennium, and from the destruction and building over of Buddhist shrines[87] and monasteries from latter-day indifference to history and from simple pragmatism, as much as due to active hostility. The archaeological record from Tamil Nadu surveyed here also clearly shows that Buddhist motifs and images were incorporated in Puranic worship and in temples dedicated to Puranic gods and goddesses.

[84] Aiyappan and Srinivasan, op. cit., pp. 100–1. Also, T.N. Vasudeva Rao, 'Buddhism and Kanchi', *Journal of Indian History*, vol. 53, part 1, 1975, pp. 23–4.

[85] A. Etirajan, *108 Vaiṇava Divya Deśa Stala Varaḷāru*, Karaikkuti: Vaiṇava Siddhānta Nūrpatippuk Kaḻakam, 2003, pp. 127–33. Since this source is essentially a pilgrims' manual, it does not give any information regarding the date of this sculpture.

[86] Kenneth Hall, *Trade and Statecraft in the Age of the Colas*, New Delhi: Abhinav Publications, 1980, p. 25.

[87] This seems the likeliest explanation for the absence of Buddhist shrines in the Kāñcīpuram region which in Xuan Zang's time seems to have been a flourishing centre of the religion. The apsidal Durga Temple in Paṭṭaḍakal in Karnataka is a good example of the taking over of a Buddhist shrine for Puranic deities. Even though it is commonly held that apsidal shrines were Buddhist, and this shrine has tiny Buddhas carved in low relief along the length of the shrine wall, it is considered to be dedicated to Sūrya since its inner walls and ceiling are extensively carved with Puranic motifs. The temple takes its name from a nearby fort, *durga*. Source—personal visit to the shrine.

The evidence for the existence of Jainism is comparatively abundant. Several historical Jaina shrines remain in worship,[88] and numerous Jaina sculptures of Tīrthankaras, *yakṣas* and *yakṣīs* have been discovered,[89] usually in association with epigraphic evidence. Bronze figures such as those of Parśvanātha, Dharmadevi, Mahāvira and Brahmādeva dated to the twelfth-thirteenth centuries have been discovered at TiruNarunkŏṇṭai in the South Arcot district.[90] More than 500 Jaina inscriptions—from the earliest down to those inscribed in the twentieth century—have been recovered from Tamil Nadu, distributed over the entire state.[91] Of these, 43 inscriptions date to the pre-Christian era, though all but 12 of them have been found in one district. Nine of the latter ten are in one cluster besides. It is, of course, important to remember that these are probably the earliest inscriptions found in the state. Just over 30 inscriptions pertain to the first seven centuries of the Common Era; the distribution of these is however slightly wider.[92] One of these is of particular historical interest. A first-century CE Tamil Brāhmi inscription found on a rock inside a cavern in TirukKōyilūr in the South Arcot district states that Satiyaputo Aṭiyamāṉ Nĕṭumāñci caused an abode to be donated. Satyaputras are mentioned in Aśokan records, and have been identified with the Kŏnku country. Atiyamāṉ Nĕṭumāṉ Añci has been celebrated in Sangam poems by Paraṉar and Auvvaiyār, and has been described as a worshipper of Śiva.[93] It is easy to read this as evidence of 'tolerance', or of 'kings patronizing different religions as a matter of policy'.[94] I believe it is amenable to a different interpretation, which I will discuss shortly.

[88] Tirupparuttikuṉṟam near Kāñcīpuram, for instance. Ref: S. Gurumurthy, 'Jaina System of learning in South India', *Bulletin of the Institute of Traditional Cultures, Madras*, vol. 15, no. 2, 1971, pp. 108–9.

[89] Raman, op. cit., pp. 13–23 and illustrated plates between pp. 13–22.

[90] T. Ganesan, 'Jaina Vestiges of Tirunarungondai in South Arcot District, Tamil Nadu', in *Essays in Indian History and Culture*, ed. Y. Krishan, New Delhi: Indian History and Culture Society, 1986, pp. 148–50.

[91] Ekambaranathan and Sivaprakasam, op. cit. All figures that follow are collated from the said book.

[92] The break-up is: first–second centuries: 5; third–fourth centuries: 18; fifth–sixth centuries: 3; seventh century: 3.

[93] Ekambaranathan and Sivaprakasam, op. cit., p. 360.

[94] Sastri, *The Cōḻas*, p. 643, 'Not only did the kings as a rule tolerate religions and sects other than their own, but they often patronised all persuasions in equal measure'.

The number of inscriptions climbs dramatically from the eighth century onwards; what is true of the larger picture holds for the specifically Jaina case as well. Of the 125 Jaina inscriptions believed to have been engraved in the eighth century, 95 (of the total of 106) found in one site in Kaḻukumalai in the Chidambaraṉār district do not bear any date but may be ascribed to this period owing to the dates of the inscriptions before and after them. It is significant that while this clustering of records in one site indicates the great popularity of this shrine/monastic residence in this period, it also suggests the relatively narrow spread of the religion. The 90-odd records belonging to the ninth century are distributed comparatively widely across the state. Interestingly, two of them mention the exploits of Nandivarman III Pallava (846–69 CE) but neither any contribution nor reference to the temple of Kuntu Tīrthankara despite being inscribed on the inner wall of its *gopuram* near the entrance.[95] In the tenth century, only 45 inscriptions pertain to Jainism/are inscribed close to Jaina *paḷḷis*. The number of epigraphic remains with relation to Jainism is just 27 in the eleventh century, 19 in the twelfth, and 35 in the next two centuries. The situation remains much the same in the fifteenth and sixteenth centuries: a score mentions in the first case and a dozen in the latter.

A very interesting inscription of the early eight century[96] of the Pallava Narasinga-p-potaraiyar Narasimhavarman II Rājasimha from the Kāmākṣi Ammaṉ Temple in Pĕriya Kāñcī must be mentioned here. The epigraph recording a gift of land to the temple of *aṟiver* (*arhat*) mentions that Queen Lokamahādevi was possessed by a *brahmarākṣasa*. It appears that an *ācārya* of the Ājīvika persuasion played some part in alleviating the affliction.[97] Though this does not have a direct bearing on our argument, it bolsters the image of Kāñcī as a highly catholic centre for religious and philosophical debate, besides being significant evidence of the continuity of the Ājīvika *darśana* well into the first millennium CE in the deep south of the country.

(iii) Analysis and Comparison with Evidence from the Hymns

It would be interesting to examine how the Śaiva and Vaiṣṇava belief systems came to dominate the cultural landscape of the Tamil region,

95 Ekambaranathan and Sivaprakasam, op. cit., pp. 215–16.

96 708–9 CE.

97 Mahalingam, 1985, vol. III, p. 115. Cg 480. Ref.: *ARE*, 1954–5, no. 360; Ibid., part ii, p. 16 and plate III facing p. 57.

all but eliminating Jainism and Buddhism. We have seen that the hagiographic literature of both the orthodox sects feature stories of conversions, particularly of prominent conversions of rulers, from the reviled heterodox systems, as also stories of contestations between their own saints and monks of Buddhists and Jaina persuasions. It is perhaps the story of Appar's conversion of the Pallava ruler Mahendravarman I (accession 610 CE), that is reflected in an inscription of the same ruler in a pillar of the rock-cut cave near the summit of the rock-fort hill in Tiruccirāppaḷḷi. The Sanskrit epigraph in florid Pallava Grantha characters states that the river Kaveri is beloved of the Pallava king Guṇabhara (also called Puruṣottama and Śatrumalla in the inscription), who was a worshipper of the *linga* and who 'left hostile conduct to embrace Śaivism'.[98] Mahendravarman Pallava is also known to have composed a satirical play in Sanskrit, *Mattavilāsa Prahasana*, where he ridicules the grasping habits and licentiousness of the monks of the heterodox faiths.[99] As seen earlier in the tales told in the hagiographic texts, the *bhakti* saint or *ācārya* invariably trounces his opponent, and in some cases also goes on to inflict cruel punishment through the agency of his patron- ruler.[100] It has been noted that the *Mahābhārata* is obsessed with the threat of the '*nāstikas*',[101] i.e. those who deny the authority of the Vedas. The hostility of the bhakti saints and *ācāryas* towards Jaina and Buddhist monks can be said to have had the weight of tradition behind it. Indeed, in a system where 'tradition' was revered to the degree that innovations were frowned upon and where new ideas—for new ideas did arise—were claimed to be actually the original interpretation of the ancient texts but which had been clouded by the passage of years, this rivalry had absolutely perfect credentials.

Historians, with the advantage of hindsight, can trace, through texts and inscriptions, the rise to prominence of Śaiva and Vaiṣṇava bhakti cults. But how does one find the answer to *why* an oil presser of Kāñcī or a stone cutter from Srirangam transferred his allegiance from Jainism/Buddhism to Śiva or Viṣṇu? Could one of the reasons be the fundamental atheism of Jainism? Despite the development of the

[98] Mahalingam, 1985, vol. VIII, p. 249. Tp 1122. Ref.: *ARE*, 1888, nos. 63 and 64; *SII* I nos. 33 and 34, pp. 28–30; *EI* I no. 9, pp. 58–60.

[99] Ramachandran, op. cit., p. 9.

[100] Appar's conversion of Mahendravarman Pallava; Rāmānuja's conversion of Biṭṭi Deva of Karnataka and subsequent impaling of several 1,000 Jainas; Sambandar's conversion of Kūṉ Pāṇṭiya and impaling the Jainas.

[101] Personal communication from Dr Naina Dayal.

practice of veneration of the Jinas, the emphasis in Jainism remained on self-discipline to avoid the accretion of bad karma. More pertinently, was it a question of transferring allegiance from one faith to another as the hagiographies of both the Śaivas and Vaiṣṇavas seem to imply?[102] It has been noted that all Hindu worship is not soteriological in intent; that 'in fact, most Hindus perform worship out of devotion to their god, not out of deference to the theology of *samsāra*'.[103] Perhaps the bhakti focus on a benevolent god, willing to intervene in the lives of his devotees when appealed to, was more comforting for the lay worshipper? This loving god was moreover easily approachable in shrines throughout the Tamil land.[104]

There was, of course, the important factor that the bhakti hymns were composed in the language of the ordinary folk. While drawing on a classical tradition of literature, which continued to carry prestige in the Tamil land, the poetry of the bhakti saints moved from the rather erudite idiom of the Sangam anthologies to the vernacular, and incorporated folk motifs to enhance its appeal. That the bhakti hymns were not 'written' for an elite readership but were intended to be sung is clear from literally hundreds of the hymns. The signature verses of the majority of the poems, which double as *phalaśrutis*, claim to bring special blessings—here and hereafter—to those who *recite*, or better still *sing*, the said verses in praise of the lord.

Tirumankai Āḻvār claims, 'Those who sing this lovely garland of words of Kaliyaṉ, ruler of Mankai, in praise of the Lord of TiruMaṇikkūṭam in Nānkūr where mansions touch the moon will rule this earth surrounded by the oceans and reach the heaven crossing *sūryaloka* (the abode of the sun).'[105]

[102] Speaking of the ninth-century Rāṣṭrakūṭa ruler Amoghavarṣa, Sastri, *A History of South India*, p. 155 says, 'By temperament, Amoghavarṣa was a religious man who loved literature more than fighting. He is said to have retired from his court more than once to spend time in the company of Jaina monks. It is doubtful, however, whether he formally renounced Hinduism, though a small Jaina catechism entitled *Praśnottara-ratna-mālikā* is attributed to him'. It is unclear how one can 'renounce' Hinduism unless one specifically adopts some other religion which prescribes exclusive initiatory rites. I will argue that one did not need to be exclusively Jaina or Bauddha but could combine worship of Puranic deities with revering Buddhist and Jaina ones.

[103] John D. Smith, 'Review of '*The Hindu Temple: Its Meaning and Forms*' by George Michell', *Modern Asian Studies*, vol. 13, no. 2, 1979, p. 351.

[104] See Chapter 6 of the present work.

[105] *Pĕriya Tirumŏḻi* 4.6.10.

Elsewhere he says, 'Kaliyan̲, lord of Mankai of rich fields surrounded by strong ramparts has praised the Lord of Kaṇṇapuram in sweet Tamil. Those who sing it with music will have no sorrow.'[106]

Āṇḍāḷ: 'Those who recite these ten verses in pure Tamil by Kotai, daughter of the lord of Villiputtūr of the Veyar clan, describing her dream of marriage to the cowherd Lord, will rejoice with good offspring.'[107] Again, concluding the *Tiruppāvai*, 'Those who sing without fault this garland of thirty songs—which describes the boons that maidens lovely as the moon received on singing the praises of the beautiful, red-eyed, four-armed, auspicious Tirumāl, of Keśavan̲, of Mādhavan̲, who churned the Bay of Bengal,[108]—by Bhaṭṭar-Pirān̲'s Kotai, of Putuvai where lotuses bloom in cool waters, shall find eternal joy everywhere'.[109]

Nammāl̲vār: 'Those who recite these ten hymns of the flawless thousand of Caṭakopan̲ on the Lord Mādhava will be freed from rebirth.'[110]

And the song with which the *NDP* opens, the *Pallāṇṭu*, the benediction that Pĕriyāl̲vār calls upon the gem-hued almighty lord himself: 'These words blessing the pure Lord who wields the invincible Sāṛnga bow (are) lovingly spoken by Viṣṇucittan̲ of Villiputtūr. *Pallāṇṭu*! Blessings in this good year on them too who sing (this) with joy and surround the Lord at all times chanting "*namo Nārāyaṇa*".'[111]

Cutler has pointed out that *phalaśrutis* relate the audience of the poems, i.e. the devotees, with the preceding text, much of which documents the poet's personal experiences and relationship with the lord. Through this

[106] *Pĕriya Tirumŏl̲i* 8.7.10.

[107] *Nacciyar Tirumŏl̲i* 7.10.

[108] *Vanga-k-kaṭal* literally means the 'Bengal Sea'. As a resident of Śrīvilliputtūr, almost equidistant from the three seas, Āṇḍāḷ may have been familiar with all three, the Arabian Sea, the Bay of Bengal and the Indian Ocean, and thus made this distinction. On an irreverent note, if the mythic ocean that was churned, i.e. Tiruppārkaṭal, is merely the prosaic Bay of Bengal, perhaps Vaikuṇṭha, the celestial residence of Viṣṇu, can be located on a map too!

[109] *Tiruppāvai* 30.

[110] *Tiruvāymŏl̲i* 1.6.10.

[111] *Pĕriyāl̲vār Tirumŏl̲i* 1.1.12 Owing to this remarkable poem where the human Āl̲vār blesses the lord and each of his aspects with everlasting glory, he is described in the hagiographies as having become father to the great lord himself, due to his overflowing parental concern. *Pallāṇṭu* literally means 'live long'.

concluding stanza, the poet sets himself up as a model for other devotees, whom he invites to relive his own experience.[112]

Who were these devotees? If the Āḻvārs and Nāyaṉmārs were struggling to establish their respective gods as the only one(s) worthy of worship, were they addressing an audience composed largely of Buddhists and Jainas? Is that the reason why their comments on the preachers and mendicants of these faiths are so much harsher than their references to each other? I will address the second question a little later. Noting that Sambandar set aside the tenth verse of each of his extant 400 hymns for denouncing the Buddhists and Jainas, Dehejia concludes that such constant censure and condemnation could only have been occasioned by the 'obvious power and influence of these sects in the era of the Tamil saints'.[113] We have already seen that Jainism and Buddhism were well established in the Tamil region by the early centuries of the Christian Era. It remains impossible, in the present state of our knowledge, to even guess at the numbers of followers of the two 'heterodox' faiths, or even their approximate percentage in the entire population. Numerous references in the Sangam poems make it evident that *brāhmaṇas* and brahmanical ways of worship were known in the Tamil land by the beginning of the Christian Era, but it is equally clear that indigenous forms of worship, of Murukaṉ/Cĕyyoṉ, and Māyoṉ were very deeply entrenched. The early centuries of the Christian era saw the emergence of Puranic religion as an outcome of a complex dialogue between the Vedic/Sastraic religious complex and hundreds of local cults across the country.[114] The absorption of Murukaṉ into Śiva's 'family', and identification of Māyoṉ with Kṛṣṇa, the cowherd god of the Vṛndāvana region, and the identification of both these with the overarching deity Viṣṇu-Nārāyaṇa, their brahmanization as it were, were part of this same process. This ensured the acceptability of the new Puranic gods to the Tamil populace. New forms of worship would have followed in its train. While these new forms of worship would have sought to establish the *brāhmaṇa* priest as the central intermediary between worshipper and deity, it would be erroneous to assume that these changes emanated from any one source. Rather, these methods of worship themselves evolved over centuries, affecting and in turn being affected by socio-political developments. With the older method of legitimizing kingship, such as the public sacrifice, losing

[112] Norman Cutler, 'The Devotee's Experience of the Sacred Tamil Hymns', *History of Religions*, vol. 24, no. 4, 1984, p. 93.

[113] Dehejia, op. cit., p. 21.

[114] Chakrabarti, op. cit., pp. 44–72.

currency,[115] partly due to the influence of Buddhism and Jainism with their stress on ahimsa, new mechanisms of legitimation developed, such as fabrication of genealogical tables for emerging ruling dynasties, and royal patronage to temples. Kings established authority not merely by conspicuous 'Gifts of Power',[116] but also by establishing themselves as the chief or first worshipper and thus establishing their proximity to the divine.[117] The three-pronged relations of ruler, priesthood and laity evolved through complex interactions, with differences in every part of the country reflecting specific regional socio-political circumstances.

We have already seen that the Kaḷabhras were supposed to have been patrons and followers of the heterodox faiths. The ascendancy of Brahmānical religion from the sixth–seventh centuries led to them being pictured as fanatics who abrogated *devadāna* and *brahmadeya* rights.[118] I do not believe that the specific religious persuasion of a ruling dynasty can lead to a complete eclipse of other religious belief systems in society at large. Rather, development, change and evolution in the 'other' belief systems would have also continued apace irrespective of the availability of patronage or lack thereof from the rulers. It remains true, however, that active intervention of the ruling class in the affairs of a particular religion or sect can have significant consequences as is seen in the case of Śaivism under the Co<u>l</u>as.

If the Kaḷabhras have been abused as evil kings for their apparent patronage of Jainism and Buddhism, the Co<u>l</u>as have been extolled for their broad vision. The inscriptional evidence relating to the heterodox faiths has been cited frequently and in exhaustive detail to speak of the sectarian harmony or 'tolerance' in Co<u>l</u>a times,[119] or to stress the importance of the heterodox faiths in the Tamil land.[120] It has been used to argue that the bhakti saints were fighting the challenge of the

[115] See above, reference to Inden.

[116] I have borrowed the phrase from the title of James Heitzman's monograph.

[117] David Shulman, 'Poets and Patrons in Tamil Literature and Literary Legend', in *Powers of Art: Patronage in Indian Culture*, ed. Barbara Stoler Miller, New Delhi: Oxford University Press, 1992, pp. 100–1.

[118] See Chapter 1-i of the present work.

[119] V. Balambal, 'Patronage of the Imperial Colas to Jainism', in *Kevala Bodhi*, ed. Aloka Parasher-Sen, pp. 285–90; also Sastri, *The Cō<u>l</u>as*, p. 643, 'A progressive king like Rajaraja even made it a point to give clear expression to his general attitude to religion by including in decoration of the Great Siva Temple at Tanjore themes from Vaisnavism and even Buddhism'.

[120] Rajesh, op. cit., pp. 308–17; Dehejia, op. cit., pp. 25–8.

heterodox sects.[121] While the latter claim is indisputably borne out by the evidence, I believe that it needs to be refined. The first matter to be considered is that compared to the several thousands of inscriptions[122] found from Tamil Nadu, the number of Jaina and Buddhist inscriptions is miniscule indeed. A careful perusal reveals that even this numerical data can be misleading; many of these inscriptions are classified as Jaina for no other reason that they have been found in the vicinity of a Jaina *paḷḷi* (shrine). Nor do all the others indicate patronage—many are, as in the case of Śaiva or Vaiṣṇava temple inscriptions too, records of sale of land or repair of dams, inscribed simply in the most prominent place in the neighbourhood. Meanwhile, we have also seen that the presence of Śramaṇas[123] and Bauddhas is distinctly marked in Tamil literature. This suggests that along with the *brāhmaṇas* and indigenous elite, monks subscribing to either of the two faiths may have constituted the majority of the literate section of the populace. It is again this literate section that would have distinguished the different philosophical bases of the different religious systems. For the common people, however, who were by and large inherently polytheistic, Śiva and Viṣṇu as much as Buddha and the Tīrthankaras might have been welcome additions to the older pantheon of Māyōn̲, Cĕyyōn̲, Vendan̲, Varuṇan̲, Kŏr̲r̲avai and the numberless martyred heroes whose memorial stones were regularly worshipped. Thus, the *Cilappatikāram*, an epic with a pronounced Jaina inclination, includes songs in praise of Murukan̲ and Kṛṣṇa.[124] It is my contention that it was the religious elite which recognized fundamental differences between the brahmanical and the non-Vedic religious systems, foresaw the possibility of polarization, and eventually contributed to it, while also making adjustments whenever necessary. This recognition would underlie the integration of traditional and folk forms of worship by both brahmanism and the heterodox faiths in an attempt to concentrate support and patronage in their own hands. This absorption, albeit in altered forms, of indigenous forms of worship and

[121] Champakalakshmi, '*Patikam Pāṭuvār*', pp. 199–215.

[122] Mahalingam, 1985, vol. I, p. vii, informs us that at least sixteen thousand inscriptions dated from the earliest times up till 1300 CE have been recovered from the states of Tamil Nadu and Kerala. (The number is naturally likely to be substantially larger if we count the inscriptions from the fourteenth to the nineteenth centuries as well.) Of course, a great number of these inscriptions are secular.

[123] Generally used in Tamil to refer to Jaina monks.

[124] Dehejia, op. cit., pp. 25–6.

cults, was to alter the 'great traditions' as we well know. More crucial in our present context is the fact that the leaders of the different religious systems self-consciously exalted their own god(s) over that/those of the others. However, even as late as the early eleventh century, it was possible for a person to simultaneously make substantial gifts of land to a Jaina temple *and* to those of Viṣṇu, Śiva, Uttarādevi and Durgā, and to consecrate the images of the deities in all these shrines to 'ensure the protection of the city of Salukki'.[125] I believe this is an instance not of mere 'tolerance', but of deep-set polytheistic suspicion that the neglect of any deity can lead to calamitous consequences irrespective of the blessings of others. An offended god can wreak vengeance, and the best that another god, however powerful and however well-pleased with the devotee's worship, can do is to mitigate the suffering. Curses, as anyone who is familiar with Hindu mythology knows, are irreversible; they can merely be softened. Since the wrath of supernatural beings is best avoided, it is advisable to not ignore any godling, unless known to be specifically subordinate to a higher god and thus automatically propitiated when the overlord is worshipped. Thus, the Pallava, Pāṇṭiya and Coḻa rulers may have made their gifts to different religious establishments partly in order be seen as patrons by all sections of their populace, but also because of what I shall term *ideal polytheism*.

A corollary of this hypothesis is that new, and at least semi-independent, gods must regularly emerge to explain away the minor and major tragedies that inevitably visit every individual despite the most dutiful performance of all prescribed rituals. Some recent examples are the emergence of the cult of Santoṣī mā in the 1970s, and the brand new, twenty-first century ritual of appeasing Saturn on Śani *amāvasya*. The new gods are, however, usually given a cloak of immense antiquity; their worship is supposed to have been merely reinstituted after having been inexplicably forgotten over the ages.

The brahmanical religious elite, however, did not subscribe to ideal polytheism. Perceiving the fundamental agnosticism, if not actual atheism, of the heterodox faiths, despite the worship of the Tīrthankaras and eventually *yakṣas* and *yakṣīs* in the Jaina case, that of the Buddha and the Bodhisattvas in the Buddhist, and numerous goddesses in both, not to speak of their rejection of Vedic authority, the brahmanical religious elite rejected the possibility of accommodation of their deities even as inferior gods in their pantheon. Already by the seventh century, they

[125] Ekambaranathan and Sivaprakasam, op. cit., p. 250. Ref: *ARE*, 474/1920; *South Indian Temple Inscriptions*, vol. 1, part 1, no. 123.

were asking their followers to reject those they termed 'false gods'. Related to this was the fact that a number of deities came to be considered subordinate to certain 'great Gods', (such as the *gaṇas* and the family of Śiva), or to be considered their *avatāras* (especially in the case of Viṣṇu), or forms other than *avatāras* (such as Mohinī).

The heterodox religious elites, with their more clearly defined philosophical systems, seem to have exercised greater discretion in the adoption of deities. A clear distinction can be drawn between 'indigenous' cult practices without brahmanical sanction that were absorbed in the emergent pantheons of Buddhism and Jainism, and the patented high gods of brahmanical Hinduism. The *Cilappatikāram* features an episode where a Jaina nun, Kavunti Aṭikaḷ, listens patiently to a discourse by a *brāhmaṇa* about gods to be worshipped and the benefits that would accrue. She finally replies, 'O Brahmin of good conduct learned in the *Vedas*! I have no desire to go on your path for realising the ends you have described. . . . You go ahead and worship the gods you love. We shall also go on our way.'[126]

The brahmanical religions were self-consciously Vedic, however different their actual praxis were from the Vedic system which they claimed to inherit. As a result, Śaivism and Vaiṣṇavism revered a common body of sacred texts, though each sect claimed to be the only true interpreter. Thus, while competition was inevitable between the two, it was formulated in very different terms from the way it was articulated with reference to the heterodox faiths which explicitly rejected the authority of the Vedas. While Indra, Brahmā, numerous other named and clusters of unnamed deities could be easily subsumed under the overarching power of the Supreme God, Śiva or Viṣṇu, it was important to show that the god claimed as Supreme in his own right by the rival sect was not quite so. In fact, the growth of bhakti, deep, emotionally charged devotion to a personal god, can also be related to this complex meshing of 'monotheism'[127] with polytheism. Unflinching devotion to the chosen god came to be considered superior to worshipping sundry divinities.

[126] Cited in Dehejia, op. cit., p. 25.

[127] Here I am using monotheism with rather different connotations from what it means in the Semitic religions. It is the overarching superiority of one god over all others—who are recognized as gods. L.S.S. O'Malley, *Popular Hinduism: The Religion of the Masses*, 1935, says, '...the great majority of Hindus are theists believing in one personal god, though they are at the same time polytheistic in their religious observances'. Cited in Chakrabarti, op. cit., p. 53.

Pěriyāḻvār sings, 'Becoming the supreme Lord of all creation, He came as Hṛṣīkeśa to churn and destroy the clans of *asuras* and *rākṣasas*. Come, break your old clannish ties and join the groups of devotees, revere His feet, chant His thousand names, and sing "*Pallāṇṭu*".'[128]

And Kulaśekhara Āḻvār says, 'I do not mix with those who are not [His] devotees, nor do I wish to live like a great lord. My lord of Arangam, the Lord of the immortals,[129] is my master for seven lives.'[130]

Tirumaḻicai Āḻvār says that though the devotees of the lord may forget his names, they would never stoop to worship godlings.[131]

Tirumankai asks if there is any god— the three-eyed one (Śiva), the four-headed one (Brahmā), or the one with a white elephant (Indra) who aren't formed of the matter he swallowed and emitted.[132] 'Devotees! When the dark ocean swelled and the worlds disappeared, all were contained in the stomach of Him who bears the discus. Don't you know? How can you worship another god? Do not waste your good deeds, worship Him alone.'[133]

The rewards of such devotion are frequently stressed in the hymns.

In Pěriyāḻvār's words, 'He gives me good rice with ghee, excellent attendants, ornaments for my hands, neck and ears, fragrant sandal paste and cleanses my soul. I sing *Pallāṇṭu* (glory) to Him who has the foe of snakes, Garuḍa, on His banner.'[134] And Nammāḻvār rejoices, 'My red-lotus eyed, sugar-like Lord, my mountain of nectar entered me on my merely calling, "Mādhava", and promised to protect me forever. Govinda destroys my sins.'[135] And very simply, 'Uproot all thoughts of you and yours. Merge with the Lord; there is no greater fulfilment.'[136]

I must add a caveat here. While a number of verses do speak of the grace of the lord and the blessings that flow from devotion to him, the poems do not by any means constitute a 'promotional campaign'. Much of the *Nālāyira Divya Prabandham* is simply rich poetry and, as in any

128 *Pěriyāḻvār Tirumŏḻi* 1.1.5.

129 Reference to the *devas* who have drunk the nectar of immortality.

130 *Pěrumāḷ Tirumŏḻi* 3.5.

131 *Nāṉmukaṉ Tiruvantādi* 68.

132 *Pěriya Tirumŏḻi* 11.6.3.

133 *Pěriya Tirumŏḻi* 11.6.1.

134 *Pěriyāḻvār Tirumŏḻi* 1.1.8 Pěriyāḻvār's specific advantages may stem from his having been the priest of the temple at Śrīvilliputtūr.

135 *Tiruvāymŏḻi* 2.7.3.

136 *Tiruvāymŏḻi* 1.2.3.

good poetry, a range of emotions finds expression.[137] In fact, though many hymns in the mode of lover speaking to/of her beloved, and a great number of the 'pilgrimage poems'[138] are stacked with stereotypical imagery, many of the *viraha* (separation) poems are startlingly intense. We have already seen the Śrīvaiṣṇava insistence on the salvific power of the lord and, indeed, his ardent desire to save his devotees. The legends of Nārāyaṇa descending to save the world from tyrannical *asuras* in his many *avatāras* or of coming to the assistance of his devotees when summoned (as by Draupadi in the well-known episode of her disrobing by Duḥśāsana in the *Mahābhārata*) reinforce the grace of the benevolent lord.

The story of Tirumaḻicai Āḻvār's fire-raising contest with Śiva[139]—underlined by the Āḻvār's doing so from his toe in contrast with Śiva opening his famed third eye in the middle of his forehead—is a fairly naked myth demonstrating the rivalry between the Vaiṣṇavas and the Śaivas. It is also interesting to remember that this 'fiery' battle is sparked off by Śiva's offer of a boon to the Āḻvār, who is initially disinterested and then asks, challengingly, to be granted *mokṣa*. Significantly, in this Vaiṣṇava myth, Śiva is reduced to admitting that the desired boon is beyond his powers; only Viṣṇu is capable of granting liberation. A much later source,[140] the *sthalapurāṇa* of Tañjai-mā-maṇi-k-koyil quoting the authority of the *Brahmāṇḍa Purāṇa*[141] tells of three *asuras*, Tañjakaṉ,

[137] Friedhelm Hardy, *Viraha Bhakti: The Early History of Kṛṣṇa Devotion in South India*, New Delhi: Oxford University Press, 1983, p. 245, says, 'It is only to be expected that in a large corpus like the *Prabandham*, we should find much poetry that is no better than mediocre. Yet some of the poems found here belong to the best that were written in India in connection with Kṛṣṇa *bhakti*'.

[138] Most of the *Pĕriya Tirumŏḻi* can be considered pilgrimage poetry.

[139] See Chapter 2-ii of the present work. Verse 25 of *Nāṉmukaṉ Tiruvantādi*, attributed to this Āḻvār, says, 'That I worship none else will be borne out by the mat-haired Śiva'. In Verse 66 from the same work, he says he would never contemplate on nor circumambulate Śiva or Brahmā. And in Verse 84, he declares that Śiva is no match for him. These might have formed the basis for the story of Tirumalicai refusing to acknowledge Śiva as he passed overhead, and the contest between them that followed.

[140] Approximately fourteenth–sixteenth centuries. David Dean Shulman, *Tamil Temple Myths: Sacrifice and Divine Marriage in the South Indian Śaiva Tradition*, Princeton: Princeton University Press, 1980, pp. 29–39.

[141] Chakrabarti, op. cit., pp. 44–72, has shown that such quotations from supposedly authoritative sources may be entirely fictitious but were frequently used to bolster the claims being made in the said text.

Daṇḍakan̲ and Gajamukhan̲, who meditated upon Śiva to acquire immortality. Śiva, appearing before them, promised that he would not be the agency of their death, but that their wish could only be granted by Pĕrumāḷ.[142] This notion was expressed earlier by Pĕriyāl̲vār, 'None knows the cure for the sickness of rebirth, not the bull-bannered one (Śiva), not Brahmā, Indra, nor anyone else.[143] Oh dark-gem coloured Lord who appeared as the healer [Dhanvantari who rose from the milk ocean when it was churned for nectar]! Cut asunder my bonds of rebirth and lead me to your temple, oh my father in TiruMāliruñcolai!'[144] And Peyāl̲vār asks if even fair-faced Indra, lotus-seated Brahmā, and mat-haired Śiva can fully comprehend the glories of the Lord who bears a lotus on his navel.[145] Tirumal̲icai Āl̲vār declares, 'Nārāyaṇa created the four-faced Brahmā who in turn created Śankaran̲'.[146]

The *Agpp* carries the following story about the preceptor Nāthamuni who is credited with having rediscovered the hymns of the Āl̲vārs. Once, the ruler in Gangaikŏṇṭacol̲apuram (incidentally, a town which came into existence more than a century after the purported time of Nāthamuni) came to Vīranārāyaṇapuram to worship at the temple of Man̲n̲anār, where Nāthamuni served as priest. When leaving, the king placed his foot on the head of his *sāmanta* (feudatory) to climb onto the royal elephant. Nāthamuni watching this wondered if that was how Pĕrumāḷ stepped on Brahmā and Rudra to climb onto Garuḍa's back.[147] This entirely gratuitous insert—for it bears no relation to the tale before or after it—scarcely needs explanation.

Chidambaram is a sacred site for both Vaiṣṇavas and Śaivas, both the Āl̲vārs and Nāyan̲mārs having sung of their respective god enshrined therein. While this is true of many towns such as Kāñcīpuram and Kumbhakoṇam/Kuṭantai, there being numerous temples dedicated to different gods in these sacred sites, both gods in Chidambaram are

[142] The myth follows the usual pattern whereby the three *asuras*, drunk on their newly acquired power, start harassing people including devotees of the lord, to protect whom, Viṣṇu finally finishes them off. In this case, the dying wish of Tañjakan̲ was that the site should take his name, thus, Tañjakan̲-ūr = Tanjavur.

[143] It is interesting how the bhakti saints have internalised the Buddhist concept of life/birth being essentially suffering, and freedom from the cycle of rebirths as the end of their devotions.

[144] *Pĕriyāl̲vār Tirumŏl̲i* 5.3.6.

[145] *Mūn̲rām Tiruvantādi* 97

[146] *Nān̲mukan̲ Tiruvantādi* 1.

[147] *Agpp*, Nāthamunikaḷ *vaibhavam*, pp. 120–5.

enshrined in the same temple.[148] There is no gainsaying the fact that Chidambaram is almost the greatest of all Śiva temples in Tamil Nadu, even if one discounts the special patronage of the Co<u>l</u>as to this temple. Śiva in Chidambaram is Naṭarāja who dances the *Ānandatāṇḍava* and is, too, the Unseen One.[149] Did the Ā<u>l</u>vārs sing of Viṣṇu in this site[150] to assert Vaiṣṇava presence in the holiest of Śaiva sites? Or, was it in order to establish the independent sovereignty of Viṣṇu here? The *Puṇḍarīkapura Mahātmya* is said to mention the visit of Viṣṇu to Chidambaram to witness Śiva's delightful dance;[151] being a *sthalapurāṇa*, however, it is likely to be a late source. Māṇikkavācakar refers to Viṣṇu lying in front of Naṭarāja, absorbed in the contemplation of Śiva's foot raised in cosmic dance and supplicating him for a vision of his other foot[152] as well. And earlier, Appar singing of him in Tillai-Ci<u>rr</u>ambalam[153] is ecstatic at having seen him whom even Aya<u>n</u> (Brahmā) and Māl (Viṣṇu) could not see despite worshipping Him everyday with flowers, incense and sandal

[148] This is, however, not unique. One of the 108 *divya kṣetras* of the Śrīvaiṣṇavas is a small shrine of Viṣṇu in the Ekāmbaranāthar Temple in Kāñcīpuram. Viṣṇu is called Nilātinkaḷtuṇṭam here. Source: Personal visit. Also, Sastri, *The Cō<u>l</u>as*, p. 643, tells of a brick shrine of Varadarāja-p-Pĕrumāḷ (originally built by Kocco<u>l</u>a and rebuilt in stone in the short reign of Adhirājendra), in the precincts of the temple of Candramaulīśvara at TiruvAkkarai which was, according to inscription *SII*, 205 of 1904, rebuilt in stone by Cĕmpiya<u>n</u> Mahādevi.

[149] Naṭarāja is the *utsava mūrti* in Chidambaram. The *mūla* deity is the *ākāśa linga*, i.e. the *linga* of ether and, consequently, invisible. If Śiva's dance is celebrated in legend and poetry, it is not more so than the *Cidambara rahasya*—the palpable and yet unseen presence of Śiva.

[150] *Pĕriya Tirumŏ<u>l</u>i* 3.2.1–10; 3.3.1-10 and *Pĕrumāḷ Tirumŏ<u>l</u>i*, 10.1–10.

[151] T. Satyamurti, *The Nataraja Temple*, New Delhi: Classical Publications, 1978, p. 24.

[152] *Tirukkovaiyār*, verse 86. The composer of the *Tirukkovaiyār* is the ninth century saint-poet Māṇikkavācakar, not included in the list of the 63 Nāya<u>n</u>mārs, being later than Sundarar whose *Tiruttŏṇṭat-tŏkai* forms the basis for the list elaborated by Cekki<u>l</u>ār in the *Pĕriya Purāṇam*, but highly revered as a saint-poet among Tamil Śaivas. His compositions are included in the Śaiva canon, the *Tirumurai*.

[153] Chidambaram may be derived from the Sanskrit *cit+ ambaram*, indicating the character of the deity here, i.e. of the essence of space/sky. Or, it may be a corruption of the Tamil Ci<u>rr</u>ambaḷam= *ci<u>rr</u>u+ ambaḷam*, i.e. little hall. The reference may be to the hall of Siva's dance. See Peterson, *Poems to Siva*, p. 99, 145 where it is read in the latter sense. See also B.G.L. Swamy, *Chidambaram and Nataraja: Problems and Rationalization*, Mysore: Geetha Book House Publishers, 1979, pp. 15–16, where the etymologies are discussed and the latter disputed.

paste.[154] It is significant that the Āḻvārs (and following them, orthodox Śrīvaiṣṇavas to this day) speak of the site neither as Ciṟṟambalam nor as Chidambaram, but as Tillai-TiruCitrakūṭam,[155] i.e. Citrakūṭa of the *Rāmāyaṇa*. Equally significantly, they entirely refrain from any mention of Śiva in the context of TiruCitrakūṭam, as though he did not exist.

The *sthalapurāṇa* of TiruNaraiyūr, a *divya deśa* to which Tirumankai Āḻvār has devoted a hundred verses, gives an interesting story about the Coḻa king whom Tirumankai mentions worshipping at this shrine.[156] King Koccĕnkaṇāṉ,[157] a Coḻa ruler credited by the Āḻvār with raising 70 temples to Śiva,[158] is said by the *sthalapurāṇa* to have been exiled from his kingdom after defeat in war. As he was wandering about in despair, he was advised by some sages to worship Pĕrumāḷ on the banks of the river Maṇi-Muktā.[159] He did so, and as he emerged after a bath in the holy river, there appeared in his hands, a divine sword with the help of which he was able to defeat all his enemies and regain his kingdom. He then became a Viṣṇu *bhakta* as well, granted land to the temple, and had a *tirumaṇa maṇḍapa* and a *vimāna* built for it.[160] It is significant that the ruler Cĕmpiyaṉ Koccĕnkaṇāṉ, portrayed as a devotee of Viṣṇu by Tirumankai Āḻvār, is also known from the hymns of the *Tevāram* trio and is associated with the Śaiva sacred shrine of Āṉaikkā;[161] indeed, he is one of the 63 canonized Nāyaṉmārs. All three *Tevāram* poets celebrate the king for his temple building activities. The central motif of the tale in the *sthalapurāṇa* is, of course, that of a *bhakta* of Śiva turning to Viṣṇu in his time of need, and finding succour from the latter. Tirumankai's words express the recognition that Koccĕnkaṇāṉ's patronage extended to both Śaivas and Vaiṣṇavas. One wonders, however, if the *Tevāram* poets were aware of this king's catholicity of faith when they were claiming him for their own, or believed him to be as single-minded as themselves in his devotion to their chosen deity, Śiva.

154 Appar, IV.80. Translated by Peterson, *Poems to Siva*, op. cit., p. 107.

155 Tillai, another Tamil name for Chidambaram, seems to derive from the tree *tillai*, Latin: Exoecaria agallocha, that grows profusely around here. But this etymology is disputed. Swamy, op. cit., p. 18.

156 *Pĕriya Tirumŏḻi* 6.6.3–9.

157 See Chapter 1-iii of the present work.

158 *Pĕriya Tirumŏḻi* 6.6.8.

159 The name of the river near Nācciyār Koyil/Tirunaraiyūr.

160 Etirajan, op. cit., pp. 107–12.

161 Peterson, *Poems to Siva*, p. 147 and p. 196.

Tirumankai Āḻvār has devoted ten hymns to a shrine called Nandipura Viṇṇagaram.[162] We know that the Vaikuṇṭha-p-Pĕrumāḷ Temple in Kāñcī was built by Nandivarman II Pallavamalla; it is probable that this shrine was also built by the same ruler.[163] The *sthalapurāṇa* of TiruNandipura Viṇṇagaram,[164] however, recounts the following myth to explain the etymology of the site. Śiva's *vāhana*, Nandi, in his usual arrogance[165] bypassed Viṣṇu's *dvārapālakas* on his way to meet the lord. The slighted *dvārapālakas* cursed him to suffer with *agni* constantly burning within him. The distraught bull sought Śiva's help, but he said that the word of Viṣṇu's *dvārapālakas* was equivalent to that of the lord himself. He advised Nandi to meditate on Viṣṇu and obtain his grace. Nandi performed penance and was finally rid of his suffering by Tirumāl who also granted that the site would take his name.[166] Clearly, the contestation between the two sectarian religions did not abate with time. The latter myth might, however, be of greater antiquity than the hagiographies, and may have evolved at any time after the original reason of the shrine's name had been forgotten.[167]

In the hagiography of Tirumankai Āḻvār, it is not the gods who are pitted against each other, but their devotees. Kaliyaṉ's vanquishing Sambandar in a poetic contest in the latter's birthplace[168] is clearly another attempt to establish the superiority of the Vaiṣṇavas over the Śaivas. The *DSC* version which pictures the meeting of the two saints in a more friendly spirit than the *Gpps* also, however, takes care to establish the superiority of the Āḻvār's merit by portraying Sambandar as honouring Parakāla with a poem in his praise while Parakāla sings only of Viṣṇu. The said legend is, however, equally significant in its accent, on this meeting having been brought about by Sambandar's desire to meet the Āḻvār who was apparently covered in glory after vanquishing the

162 *Pĕriya Tirumŏḻi* 5.10.1–10.

163 Tirumankai has devoted *Pĕriya Tirumŏḻi* 2.9.1–10 to the Kāñcī temple which he calls Parameccura Viṇṇagaram; in fact, this strengthens the possibility of Nandipura Viṇṇagaram taking its name from the same ruler.

164 Viṇṇagaram can be translated as *nagara* of Viṣṇu. It is also translated as heavenly *nagara*, *viṇ* in Tamil meaning the celestial realm.

165 Traditionally called '*Adhikāra* Nandi' as one is supposed to take permission for entry from Śiva's bull.

166 Etirajan, op. cit., pp. 159–61.

167 See discussion of site myths in Chapter 6-ii of the present work.

168 See Chapter 2-viii of the present work.

Bauddhas.[169] Clearly, Sambandar's reputation as a foe of Bauddhas and Jainas was well established and familiar in Vaiṣṇava circles as well.[170]

If Sambandar's and Tirumankai's was a mere contest of poetic talent, the hagiography of Rāmānuja leaves no room for doubt that it is the philosophical system of Viśiṣṭādvaita that is to be considered superior to Advaita. The stories of the conversions of Yādava Prakāśa, Yajñamūrti, and Rāmānuja's cousin, Govinda Bhaṭṭar, are framed very carefully. Yādava is shown to have repeatedly erred in his interpretation of Vedānta. Moreover, these errors are shown to be fundamental to his belief system.[171] He is also portrayed as a fairly unprincipled character, capable of plotting a disciple's death, rejoicing inwardly when Rāmānuja disappears in the forest, though shedding crocodile tears, and then drawing Rāmānuja's cousin into the Śaiva fold though a trick, presumably to estrange him from his cousin's beliefs and prevent his publicising his evil intentions. His conversion is thus not merely philosophical/ religious, but also of character for, after taking 'refuge in Rāmānuja's feet', he devotes himself to serious scholarship.

Govinda is passionate. He wholeheartedly embraced the Śaiva faith on receiving what he clearly perceived as an omen, just as he had previously been devoted to Rāmānuja. He remained steadfast in his adopted faith despite the engagement with Pĕriya Tirumalai Nampi on scholastic matters, but dramatically moved to the Śrīvaiṣṇava fold on hearing the emotionally charged hymns of Nammāḻvār. Here, it is the richness of the *Tiruvāymŏḻi* that is the catalyst, underlining the special character of bhakti that can triumph over intellectual beliefs.

Yajñamūrti is said to have been on his way to *digvijaya*, establishing his philosophical system without rival. To trounce such a scholar was undoubtedly a matter of great prestige. An inset within the story is telling. Rāmānuja praying to Peraruḷāḷar asks if the lord wishes to engage in *līlā* (sport) to wipe away, through a falsifier, the (only) correct *darśana.* This echoes Śrīvaiṣṇava, and indeed, brahmanic understanding of the

[169] See Chapter 2-viii of the present work.

[170] Sastri, *The Cōlas*, p. 636 says, 'Impossible as history, this beautiful legend enshrines the belief in the common mission of Śaivism and Vaiṣṇavism, entertained by the Tamil Vaiṣṇavas of the eleventh-twelfth centuries. In stemming the tide of anti-Vedic heresy, the *ālvārs* and *nāyaṉārs* had laboured together in the past, and what was more natural for their successors than to bring together the great Śaiva antagonist of Jainism and the equally great Vaiṣṇava opponent of Buddhism'.

[171] Note that he fears Advaita would be endangered by Rāmānuja's interpretations.

Buddha. It has been shown that the incorporation of the Buddha as an *avatāra* of Viṣṇu was a brahmanical device to undermine the popularity of Buddhism.[172] Śrīvaiṣṇavas explain that the lord took birth as Buddha to spread falsehood and hasten the end of the world so that he could come to redeem it as he did in his previous births.[173] Indeed, the Advaitins are often reviled as *pracchanna Bauddhas*[174] (Buddhists in disguise) by Śrīvaiṣṇavas, for denying the qualities of the Supreme Brahmān.[175]

There are numerous instances of these attempts at mutual one-upmanship that the Vaiṣṇavas and the Śaivas were constantly engaged in. One of the most familiar motifs in the Āḻvārs' hymns is the grace of Viṣṇu towards Śiva. As Brahmā was growing excessively vain, Śiva cut off one of his five heads to humble him. But this brought upon him the grave sin of *brāhmaṇa-hatyā* (decapitating a *brāhmaṇa)* as a result of which the skull stuck to Śiva's palm.[176] Śiva wandered across the worlds looking for someone who could bestow enough grace on him to relieve him of his curse. It was finally Śrī, consort of Nārāyaṇa, who filled his begging bowl and released him. Just as the Śaiva saints emphasize the greatness of their lord to whom Rāma prayed at Rāmeśvaram before setting out across the sea to Lanka, and to the humbling of Brahmā and Viṣṇu by the infinite fire-*linga*, the Āḻvārs frequently refer to the above legend to establish the greatness of their own god.[177]

Another popular legend that is frequently alluded to in the hymns is Kṛṣṇa's contest with Bāṇāsura.[178] The *asura*, having obtained the boon

[172] Chakrabarti, op. cit., pp. 109–54.

[173] Personal communication from Śrīvaiṣṇava scholars, Professors N.S. Sadagopan and (late) J. Parthasarathi.

[174] Personal communication from Professors N.S. Sadagopan and (late) J. Parthasarathi. Also see, *Paramata-bhangam* of Vedānta Deśika, stanzas 22–3.

[175] Carman, *The Theology of Rāmānuja*, p. 53, says 'The four later Vaiṣṇava commentators, Rāmānuja, Nimbārka, Vallabha and Madhva, all insisted on the heterodox character of Śankara's interpretation and sometimes (especially Madhva) charge him with being a crypto-Buddhist. There is no doubt that Śankara, like his predecessor Gauḍapāda, made use of the weapons of the later Buddhist logic in order to challenge the dominant intellectual position of Buddhism'.

[176] Śiva is thus known as Kapālīśvara, the Lord with a Skull.

[177] *Pĕriyāḻvār Tirumŏḻi* 1.9.9; *Tiruccanta Viruttam* 11, 53, 113; *Amalanadipiran* 6; *Pĕriya Tirumoli* 1.4.8, 1.5.8, 2.3.1; *Iraṇṭām Tiruvantādi* of Pūtattāḻvār, 17, 63; *Nāṉmukaṉ Tiruvantādi* 31, *Tiruvāymŏḻi* 4.10.4, etc.

[178] *Nāṉmukaṉ Tiruvantādi* 56; *Tiruccanta Viruttam* 70, 71; *Pĕriya Tirumŏḻi* 5.1.7, etc.

of protection from Śiva, proceeded to tyrannize all creatures. The story reaches its climax with Aniruddha, grandson of Kṛṣṇa, falling in love with and wishing to marry the *asura's* daughter Uṣā against the wishes of her father. In the ensuing battle, Kṛṣṇa proceeds to cut Bāṇa's thousand arms, but graciously spares his life and that of Śiva and his retinue who were committed to protecting the *asura*. Besides demonstrating the greater might of Nārāyaṇa, the myth also clarifies that he takes care to not falsify a promise made (rashly) by Śiva to his devotee, and crucially establishes him as a god of mercy.

The great deeds of the 'other' god are sometimes attributed to one's own.

Nammāḻvār speaks of Viṣṇu as the one who burnt the three cities.[179]

Peyāḻvār sings that the lord reclining on the serpent bears the bull-rider, Śiva, on his frame.[180] Tirumaḻicai proclaims, 'You are the entire universe with all its sentient beings. You are Brahmā, the austerity-practising Śiva, fire, the mountains, the eight quarters, the sun and the moon.'[181] And, 'the *kāyā*-flower coloured One himself became the three (Brahmā, Viṣṇu, Śiva)'.[182]

Often of course, the Āḻvārs state in various ways that Śiva, Brahmā, Indra and the hordes of celestials offer worship to Nārāyaṇa.[183] Equally common is the claim that Brahmā and Śiva (and sometimes Indra) specifically, and 'all the gods' generally, bow to Nārāyaṇa in a designated shrine (Venkaṭam/Srirangam, etc.) to obtain some boon or favour, or his intervention against some *rākṣasas*.[184]

Sometimes the contest is expressed more subtly: 'The city of Khaṇḍam of my Lord Puruṣottama who grew and touched the sky and filled the sun and moon with awe stands on the banks of the Ganga whose waters sparkle with the *kŏṉrai* flowers from Śiva's matted hair and *tulasi* from the feet of Nārāyaṇa.'[185] Or: 'The city of Khaṇḍam of my Lord Puruṣottama—

179 *Tiruvāymŏḻi* 1.1.8. The reference points to Śiva as Tripurāntaka.

180 *Mūṉṟām Tiruvantādi* 31.

181 *Nāṉmukaṉ Tiruvantādi* 20.

182 *Pĕriya Tirumŏḻi* 2.2.8.

183 *Pĕriyāḻvār Tirumŏḻi* 2.8.1, 4.1.5; *Pĕrumāḷ Tirumŏḻi* 1.6, 4.3; *Pĕriya Tirumŏḻi* 2.10.9, 5.7.2; *Tirucchanda Viruttam* 7, 9; *Nāṉmukaṉ Tiruvantādi* 42, 43, 89, etc.

184 Numerous sites derive their sanctity from such legends. See, for example, the *sthalapurāṇa* of Kaṇṭiyūr where Viṣṇu is said to have rid Śiva of the curse of the *kapāla* (skull) attached to his hand, or of Tañjai-mā-maṇi where he appeared to defeat three *asuras* who were getting out of hand.

185 *Pĕriyāḻvār Tirumŏḻi* 4.7.2. The verses are from a poem praising one of the sacred sites of Viṣṇu.

who wields the sonorous conch and radiant discus and who makes the heads of *asuras* roll—stands on the bank of the Ganga whose water flows from Brahmā's hands, over Trivikrama's feet and through Śiva's matted hair, washing radiant gems along its course.'[186] And: 'Was it not beautiful when the lotus-born Brahmā washed the feet of the Lord with the waters which became the Ganga?'[187] Further: 'Praising Him with Vedic chants, Brahmā washed His lotus feet with water from his pot when He measured the world. This was the water that flowed down onto the head of Śiva'.[188] These stanzas would have immediate resonance for devotees familiar with the practices of offering obeisance by touching the feet of elders/ teachers/revered persons with their foreheads/hands, prostrating before the deity enshrined in the temple, and reverently drinking the *pādatīrtha*, water with which the Lord's feet have been washed in the temple. The superiority of Nārāyaṇa is doubtlessly established.

Tŏṇṭaraṭippŏṭi Āḻvār avers that Śiva and Brahmā perform penance in age after age to see the lord and stand disappointed. But the Lord took pity on the elephant that called out to him in distress, and appeared forthwith to release him from the jaws of a crocodile.[189] Apart from, of course, extolling the majesty of Viṣṇu with respect to Śiva, this hymn underlines the important point that the great lord is accessible to the humblest devotee if only approached with love—perhaps the most distinctive feature of bhakti.

Nammāḻvār asks if he should address Kṛṣṇa as crescent bearing Śiva, as four-faced Brahmā, or as the lord who made them and is worshipped by them.[190] While the second half of the stanza seems to suggest the Āḻvār's wish to establish the superiority of Viṣṇu over Śiva and Brahmā, the first section actually expresses a deep monotheism—the one lord taking numerous forms, and yet remaining undiluted in his essence. This monotheism, which seems almost a foundational belief for Nammāḻvār,[191] finds reflection in some hymns of Tirumankai too. In a poem celebrating the deity enshrined in Aḻuntūr, the Āḻvār addresses the lord as Nara,

[186] *Pĕriyāḻvār Tirumŏḻi* 4.7.3. The reference is to Viṣṇu's *avatāra* as the dwarf, Vāmana, who grew to straddle the universe in three strides, hence Tri-vikrama. Brahmā is said to have washed the lord's feet after this cosmic act with water from his *kamaṇḍalu* (ritual pot).

[187] *Peyāḻvār Tiruvantādi* 6.

[188] *Nāṉmukaṉ Tiruvantādi* 8.

[189] *Tirumālai* 44.

[190] *Tiruvāymŏḻi* 3.4.8.

[191] *Tiruvāymŏḻi* 1.3.6; 1.3.7; 1.1.1-10; 1.5.4; 9.3.2; 10.10.11.

Nārāyaṇa, lord of Naraiyūr,[192] Mādhava, Madhusūdana, Hara[193] and Ādivarāha.[194] In another hymn, he says, 'He becomes everything and everyone, the *Vedas*, the Three and the first One'.[195] Nammāḻvār says, 'Let each one worship as he deems fit, and each shall attain his god's feet. Our Lord, who stands above all these gods accepts the offerings made to them and bids them deliver the fruit'.[196] In another hymn, he declares that the lord worshipped by Brahmā, Śiva and Indra is father, mother and self, and yet apart from all.[197] The identification of the Self with the lord is telling—the Lord is One, apart, but simultaneously the entire known universe too. This idea finds repeated illustration in the motif of the lord who swallowed the worlds and lay as a baby on a banyan leaf floating in the boundless ocean. But the Āḻvār warns his fellows, in the same stanza as above, to not fall into fear and confusion by worshipping unworthy godlings. Clearly, there is an unresolved tension between competing notions of an all-embracing god and a pantheon with gods ranged hierarchically. The Āḻvārs reflect it by using sharply polemic language sometimes and granting, at others, that prayers addressed to any god reach Tirumāl.[198] This is remarkably in consonance with the *Gītā*'s pronouncement that even those who worship other gods with devotion are in reality worshipping the *bhagavat*.[199]

This leverage was evidently impossible with respect to the deities of the Buddhists and Jainas. Tales of contest between any two religions invariably end with the defeat of the 'other' by the party whose followers are the authors of the particular text under consideration. But while in the contests between Śaivas and Vaiṣṇavas, the defeated party merely accepts the superiority of the other faith, in the outcome of contests with Śramaṇas or Bauddhas, the hapless monks are usually impaled, burnt or ground to powder en masse.[200] In the Vaikuṇṭha-p-Pĕrumāḷ Temple in Kāñcī, there is actually a sculpture portraying a person being impaled. Clearly, the religious policy of the later period of Pallavamalla was not one

[192] Both Aḻuntūr and Naraiyūr are temple towns.

[193] Śiva.

[194] *Pĕriya Tirumŏḻi* 7.7.4.

[195] *Pĕriya Tirumŏḻi* 4.1.2.

[196] *Tiruvāymŏḻi* 1.1.5.

[197] *Tiruvāymŏḻi* 3.6.9.

[198] *Tiruvāymŏḻi* 3.9.6.

[199] *Bhagavad Gītā*, IX.23- 24. Cited in Suvira Jaiswal, *Origin and Development of Vaisnavism*, Delhi: Munshiram Manoharlal, 1980, p. 215.

[200] See Chapter 2-x—2-xv of the present work.

of uniform tolerance.[201] It is clear from the *Pĕriya Purāṇam* examples that most of the stories featuring Jainas are simply gratuitous—the stories of the three minor Nāyaṉmārs, Mūrti, Taṇṭiyaṭikaḷ and Naminandi,[202] seem to have no purpose other than reviling the Jainas. Again, the episodes from Sambandar's hagiography seem excessively vituperative. There are fewer mentions of the Buddhists—and this is interesting. We have already seen that Sambandar pours abuse on the heterodox faiths in every one of his hymns; the stories in the *Pĕriya Purāṇam* may, therefore, have been designed to explain the same.

The Āḻvārs seem to have comparatively lesser to say of the followers of the heterodox faiths, though the scattered verses where they do speak of them are drenched in abhorrence. Tirumaḻicai Āḻvār declares, 'The Śramaṇas are ignorant, the Bauddhas are confused, and the Śaivas small-minded. Those who don't praise the adorable wonder-Lord, Mādhava, are insignificant now.'[203] Tŏṇṭaraṭippŏṭi Āḻvār says to the lord of Arangam, 'The Śākyars who do not believe in destiny and the hate-filled Śramaṇas and Muṇḍas shall suffer for their irresponsible words about you. I shall chop their heads off if I get the opportunity.'[204] Tirumankai Āḻvār, whom hagiography credits with a 'victory' over the Buddhists, having sung, in a hymn to the lord of Venkaṭam, with assurance, 'In the temples of the Bauddhas and Śramaṇas who worship the *pīpal* and *aśoka* trees, our Lord of beautiful eyes became their god',[205] goes on, in the very next stanzas of the same poem, to heap scorn. 'The shaven-headed, saffron-robed Śramaṇas fall over each other to gobble food and grow fat',[206] and 'Steer clear, o heart! of the curd-rice-gulping Śramaṇas who have nothing but arguments'.[207] He extols his listeners to Viṣṇu worship, 'The *Veḷḷiyār* (Pāśupatas) *Piṇṭiyār* (Jainas) and *Bodiyār* (Bauddhas) quote false texts. If you realize that, then learn to sing the glory if TiruVallavāḻ'.[208] In another poem, he says, 'The Lord of grace has none for the saffron-robed

[201] Minakshi, *The Historical Sculptures of the Vaikuṇṭha Perumāḷ temple*, pp. 49–50.

[202] See Chapter 2-xiii, xiv, xv of the present work.

[203] *Nāṉmukaṉ Tiruvantādi* 6. This kind of polemic may be responsible for the hagiographic account of this Āḻvār having studied the 'other' philosophies for considerable lengths of time and rejecting them in favour of Nārāyaṇa bhakti.

[204] *Tirumālai* 8.

[205] *Pĕriya Tirumŏḻi* 2.1.5.

[206] *Pĕriya Tirumŏḻi* 2.1.6.

[207] *Pĕriya Tirumŏḻi* 2.1.7.

[208] *Pĕriya Tirumŏḻi* 9.7.9.

Bauddhas and impure Śramaṇas...'[209] And in yet another, 'They roam about without shame, without fear or knowledge, with peacock feather in their hand, like corpse-eating *piśācas*'.[210] The Digambara practice of going naked was clearly revolting to the saint, but to compare the *ahimsā*-devoted Jaina monks to corpse-eaters lays open not merely their disgust but also perhaps such prejudice that these saints saw little need to actually familiarize themselves with the tenets of the other faiths.[211] Nammāḻvār calls upon 'Bauddhas, Jainas, and those who quote the *Linga Purāṇa*' to cease arguing endlessly and offer, instead, praise to the god of Kurukūr, assuring them that 'He is you and all your gods'.[212] Indeed, he suggests that those who 'desolately worship lowly gods' have been relegated to this only because if liberation were given to all—no doubt a certainty for all Nārāyaṇa-worshippers—there would be no world for the lord's sport.[213] While the *ācāryas* might take up fine philosophical points of debate, it seems that in the popular realm, the heterodox faiths were scorned and reviled less because of what they actually stood for than for the simple 'sin' of not worshipping the Puranic gods.

While Jaina presence in Tamil Nadu continued in the second millennium, the Buddhists had practically disappeared. Interestingly, Jaina accounts also claim 'credit' for this; apparently a Jaina monk, Akalanka, confuted the Buddhist monks of Kāñcī and procured their expulsion from south India.[214] It was, therefore, important for the hagiographers to concentrate on the Jainas who, by their very existence, however marginal, seemed to pose the threat of potential expansion while a passing mention of the Buddhists may have sufficed to gloss, as it were, their share of abuse in the Nāyaṉmārs' or Āḻvārs' hymns.

In the Śrīvaiṣṇava *Gpps*, however, one of the important stories about Tirumankai Āḻvār has to do with his robbing a Buddhist shrine. The difference in texture is, however, noteworthy. There is no contest of superiority or any attempt to humiliate the Buddhists; they are simply cheated. Evidently, the authors of the *Gpps* saw no need to justify a

[209] *Pĕriya Tirumŏḻi* 5.6.8.

[210] *Pĕriya Tirumŏḻi* 2.4.8.

[211] However, Indira Vishwanathan Peterson, 'Śramaṇas Against the Tamil Way: Jains as Others in Tamil Śaiva Literature', in *Open Boundaries: Jain Communities and Cultures in Indian History*, ed. John Cort, Albany: State University of New York Press, 1998, p. 169, shows that the descriptions of Jainas and Buddhists in the Nāyaṉār Sambandar's verses reveal his close knowledge of these groups.

[212] *Tiruvāymŏḻi* 4.10.5.

[213] *Tiruvāymŏḻi* 4.10.6.

[214] Raman, op. cit., p. 15.

blatantly dishonourable act; like Kṛṣṇa in the *Mahābhārata*, Tirumankai of the hagiographies regularly acts on the premise that the ends justify the means. The Buddhists clearly are fair game. It is, in fact, the *DSC* which comes out, in this context, strongly against worship of non-Vedic deities.[215] Can it be argued that as an earlier text, it was more familiar with the actual practices of Buddhism unlike the *Gpps*, for whom perhaps, Buddhist practices, in the Tamil region specifically, were more a matter of memory?

One departure from the usual pattern of Śaiva–Vaiṣṇava rivalry is the story of the persecution of the Śrīvaiṣṇavas at the hands of Kṛmikaṇṭha Co̱la̱n. We have seen that the inscriptions at Srirangam do not reveal any marked break in patronage that might correspond to the reign of any particular Co̱la king. Yet, the prominence given to this narrative in all accounts, and Rāmānuja's long exile to Karnataka, which is not of a piece with the general tenor of the hagiographies, makes it impossible to dismiss the whole account. I believe that there must have been a period of severe sectarian tension at the very least for such a tale to have arisen. Moreover, if the temple at TiruNārāyaṇapuram had merely to be sanctified by association with Rāmānuja, he could have been sent there (by the hagiographies) in the course of his several pilgrimages. That the Śrīvaiṣṇavas do not emerge with any particular credit after this confrontation, except perhaps the Pyrrhic satisfaction of knowing that the evil king died suffering, reinforces the likelihood of there being some historicity to the narrative. It is to the period of this king's reign that the destruction of the Vaiṣṇava shrine at Chidambaram is also imputed. Co̱la adoption of Śaivism as a 'royal cult'[216] has been mentioned before. It is possible that there was a period of severe polarization. It might also explain the fervour with which the Vijayanagara rulers, who succeeded the Co̱las, patronized Vaiṣṇava temples.

Some residues of the hostility of Rāmānuja's period seem to have coloured Śaiva–Vaiṣṇava relations in the subsequent period as well. At least one long inscription of the thirteenth century (from Pudukkottai district) gives indisputable evidence of disharmony between a Śiva and a Viṣṇu temple and their eventual reconciliation. The epigraph has been found on a rock-cut shrine in the Satyagirīśvara Temple in TiruMĕyyam village, TiruMĕyyam *tāluk*. The record of 1245 CE enumerates various points of settlement arrived at by a grand assembly comprising the

[215] *DSC*, *sargaḥ* 14, verses 79–88.

[216] R. Champakalakshmi, 'Introduction', *Studies in History*, vol. 4, no. 2, 1982, p. 165.

nāḍus, the *nagarams*, the villages and *samaya mantrīs* of Kāṉanāḍu alias Virutarājabhayankara vaḷanāḍu, the *araiyakaḷ* who policed the *nāḍu*, the Śrī Rudramaheśvaras of the same *nāḍu*, Śrīvaiṣṇavas of Pāṇṭināḍu, Śrīvaiṣṇavas and Śrīmaheśvaras of TiruMĕyyam, Śrī Rudramaheśvaras of the temple of TirukKoṭṭunkuṉṟam in the Tirumalai nāḍu and the Vaiṣṇava Anusandhāṉam in the presence of one of the (named) *daṇḍanāyakas* of the Hoysala Vīra Someśvara. The first item of settlement was the long standing quarrel concerning the sharing of the *kaṭamai* dues from the village between the Śiva and Viṣṇu temples in the village. It was resolved that two-fifths of the *kaṭamai* should go to the Śiva temple and the remainder to the Vaiṣṇava temples. The other items were a mutual exchange of *devadāna* lands of the two temples, the compound wall common to both temples, the fixation of boundaries by Tirucūlakkal and Tiruvaḻikkal, the sharing of a tank and a well, the lands belonging to each temple, the habitation sites belonging to the two temples, and proprietary rights of individuals and the erasure and re-engraving of old inscriptions of both the temples. Many officials attest the record.[217] Another inscription, from the Vaikuṇṭha Nārāyaṇa-p-Pĕrumāḷ Temple in Akkūr in Māyavaram *tāluk*, seems to indicate strained relations if not actual discord with the local Śiva temple. This epigraph of 1231 CE records a grant by the *kūttapĕrumakkaḷs* (officers) of the village administration of tax-free land for opening a road to the river Kaveri to carry the image of Rājarāja Viṇṇagar Ĕmpĕrumāḷ for the sacred bath on festive occasions as the authorities of the temple of Tiruttāṉtoṉri-māṭamuṭaiyār refused permission for the deity's sacred bath as usual in the tank belonging to the latter temple.[218] An interesting inscription of 1160 CE in the Amṛtaghaṭeśvara Temple in TirukKaṭaiyūr in Māyavaram *tāluk* records a decision of the *mahāsabhā* of TirukKaṭavūr in Akkūr *nāḍu*, assembled in the Kulottungacoḻaṉ-*tiruveṭuttukkaṭṭi* (hall) of the temple of Kālākāladevar, to confiscate to the temple, the properties of those *maheśvaras* who, contrary to their tenets as the custodians of the Śiva temple and its observances, mingled freely with the Vaiṣṇavas and wore (or sold) lotuses grown for the god.[219]

[217] Mahalingam, 1985, vol. VI, pp. 205–6. Pk 838. Ref: IPS no. 340; *ARE*, 1906, no. 387.

[218] Mahalingam, 1985, vol. VII, Tj 947. Ref.: *ARE*, 1925, no. 231. The latter temple was dedicated to Śiva. It is also clear that the village administration stepped in to avoid or resolve a confrontational situation.

[219] Mahalingam, 1985, vol. VII, p. 299, Tj 1267. Ref.: *ARE*, 1925, no. 257; ibid., part ii, p. 84.

One wonders if the rule to avoid mingling with Vaiṣṇavas was a general one or specific to this temple—or perhaps to this period. Can we see in this, a reflection of the hostility that according to the Śrīvaiṣṇava hagiographies led to Rāmānuja's fleeing to the western country? Or was this injunction passed essentially because of the misconduct of the *maheśvaras* with regard to temple property—the flowers meant for the lord in this case—where the solecism of socializing with Vaiṣṇavas was elevated to the status of a crime? From Srirangam itself, however, an inscription dated to 1198 CE in the Ranganātha Temple that refers to a negotiation with the important neighbouring Śaiva temple of Tiruvāṉaikkā seems untouched by hostility. It seems that the river Kolliṭam had eroded into the lands belonging to the two temples. Resettlement of the proper boundaries was carried out by arbitration under orders of King Aṉṉavāyiluṭaiyāṉ Gangeyarāyar (Kulottunga III) in his twentieth year and 213th day through the *puravuvāri nāyakaṉ cĕyyār* officers in consultation with the representatives of both temples, representatives from the *sabhā*, accountants of the two villages, and the superintendents of both temples. Account was taken of the holdings of the two temples as they were before their erosion in the nineteenth year of the king (1197 CE) and the actual enjoyment rights of both the parties and by suggesting suitable exchange of lands in some cases. It is recorded that the award satisfied both parties and they demarcated their respective portions by planting *tiruvāḻi* (*cakra*) and *śūla*.[220]

Last, I shall consider briefly the sole episode which indicates familiarity and negotiation with Islam. Let us first look at the variations in the narrative in the different texts. The *DSC* is entirely innocent of Muslims and Delhi. Its ambit does stretch to northern India—after all, nearly 10 of the 108 places of pilgrimage elaborated in Śrīvaiṣṇava scriptures are in Vaṭanāḍu or the northern land. Besides, Yādava Prakāśa is said to have taken his disciples to Kāśi. On the other hand, the *Agpp*, which is believed to have been composed in the late thirteenth-early fourteenth centuries, does send Rāmānuja to Dillipuram to recover the lost idol. Clearly, Malik Kafur's invasion of Srirangam had made a deep impact. Stray stories about the general's other campaigns and possibly those of other 'Turuṣka' rulers of Delhi to other parts of the Deccan must have contributed to the making of legends that were then posited back to Rāmānuja's times. All the same, the *Agpp* and *Mgpp* draw a very civil

220 Mahalingam, 1985, vol. VIII, pp. 208–9. Tp 955. Ref.: *ARE*, 1938-39, no. 113; *SII* xxiv, no. 142.

picture of the Sultan,[221] a man who, despite having looted these icons, (in the eyes of the Śrīvaiṣṇava hagiographers, possibly from ignorance of their sanctity?) is perfectly ready to return them to the faithful, and even to escort Rāmānuja to his daughter's chambers where the ascetic believes the icon to be present. Clearly, the image of Muslims as iconoclastic marauders had not yet developed.[222] The later versions of the story are equally interesting. It is in later texts that the story of the Muslim Goddess, known as Tulukka Nācciyār or Sultāni,[223] is elaborated, which suggests that though the presence of Muslims was not significant in the early days of the development of the Śrīvaiṣṇava community, it had become important enough by the fifteenth century to call for engagement.

Ranjeeta Dutta has considered the phenomenon of the Muslim Goddess in Śrīvaiṣṇavism in some detail,[224] in order to show how different communities were integrated into the ritual framework of the temple through this legend. It is true that the Maṇipravāḷa texts were consciously engaged in building a community, and this tale, like several others, was important for constructing a community wherein the privileges and rights of different groups in the temple and its ritual, usually commensurate with their wealth and status as patrons, was spelt out. A question which has, however, not been addressed is, 'Why a *Muslim* Goddess?' Why couldn't a low caste one, or a 'tribal' woman do as well? After all, in a very great number of Viṣṇu shrines, the lord is married to a girl from a prominent local community besides his principal, brahmanical wives. It is also clear from the evidence Dutta presents[225] that the rituals into which the different groups that are drawn in through

[221] The hagiographies do not use the word, Sultan. It is used here in a general fashion, as these hagiographies are contemporaneous with the Delhi Sultanate.

[222] Richard H. Davis, *Lives of Indian Images*, Princeton: Princeton University Press, 1997, p. 119, points out that 'Hindu literature engaged with the threat of Muslim rule in India... denotes the invaders as ethnically distinct *turuṣkas* (Turks) or *pārasikas* (Persians), and classifies them in terms of foreign origin, *mleccha* and *yāvana*... Never do Hindu texts of this period use terms denoting religious affiliation for the Turks, who understood themselves to be members of the Islamic community.'

[223] V.N. Hari Rao, ed. and tr., *Kōil Oḻugu: The Chronicle of the Srirangam with Historical Notes*, Madras: Rochouse and Sons, 1961, pp. 24–7.

[224] Ranjeeta Dutta, 'The Politics of Religious Identity: A Muslim Goddess in the Śrīvaiṣṇava Community of South India', *Studies in History*, vol. 19, no. 2, pp. 157–84.

[225] Ibid.

the Tulukka Nācciyār myth are not involved in worship at this goddess's shrine. Rather, they come to participate in the wider ritual structure of the temple. Such general incorporation and legitimation could have been easily achieved by very different narrative strategies than the one actually adopted. What, then, are the possible sources of this particular legend and the reasons for its significance?

Arab trading settlements are known from the seventh-eighth centuries onwards at several places on the Indian coast.[226] By the late thirteenth century, a number of ports flourished on the east coast, among them Kāyal, an agency for a booming trade in horses.[227] These ports became the nuclei of various Muhammadan settlements of Arabic character in all the seaport towns.[228] Over the next few centuries, some Muslim settlements seem to have come up in the interior as well. I quote S. Krishnaswami Aiyangar:

> In the course of his description of Malik Kafur's campaign in the Tamil country, Amir Khusru says that the army met near Kandūr, some Mussalmans who were subjects of the Hindu 'Bir' [Vira Ballala]. They were half Hindus, but as they were able to repeat the *kalima*, the Malik of Islam spared their lives.... This shows that at Kandūr, which I have identified as Kaṇṇaṉūr, near Srirangam, there was a settlement of Mohammedans quite different from the northern Mussalmans who came with the invaders.[229]

The shrine of the Tulukka Nācciyār or Bībī Nācciyār in Srirangam is located in the north-eastern corner of the Rājamahendraṉ enclosure of the Ranganātha Temple.[230] The Srirangam temple has seven concentric enclosures and the *Koyil Ŏluku* details the construction of the same. Tirumankai Āḻvār is said to have undertaken the repair and construction

[226] Aiyangar, op. cit., pp. 69-71.

[227] Ibid.

[228] Ibid., p. 73.

[229] Ibid., p. 72.

[230] The shrine itself is rather unique: essentially a mural on the far corner of the shrine wall depicting a stylized female form in a long, full skirt—the attire itself supposedly 'northern'. While murals and paintings are seen in a number of temple walls and roofs, some dating from the Coḻa period and others from the Vijayanagara and even later, this one derives its special character from the consciousness among the temple functionaries that it is a substitute for an idol. During a visit to the temple, on enquiring for directions to this particular shrine from some temple priests, I inadvertently asked—in Tamil—where I could find the *vigraha* of the Tulukka Nācciyār. The shocked priests carefully corrected me explaining that it was forbidden to make images of Muslims, and that the Nācciyār was therefore represented only by a *citra* (painting)!

of the *gopuram*, some *prākāras* (enclosures), *maṇḍapas* (pavilions), a kitchen, and a storehouse.[231] However, it must be kept in mind that the *Ŏluku's* record of events before the thirteenth century do not stand up to historical scrutiny. Clearly, the texts wished to endow the very walls around the temple with sanctity by attributing their construction to the most enterprising (in legend) and prolific (in fact) of the Āḻvārs. It is evident, however, that the temple complex continued to grow through the centuries around the central shrine of which eleven of the twelve Āḻvārs sang.[232] In the course of this expansion, it is likely to have laid claim to an area which might have been sacred to local Muslims—perhaps a grave-shrine of a local saint of a type common throughout the subcontinent. It is possible that this shrine was thus incorporated within the temple structure not only in a physical sense, but also in its ritual and its body of myth, albeit in a fashion that accommodated various other groups of stakeholders. There is evidence for such practice from the Śrīvaiṣṇava scriptures too. Apparently the garden that Tŏṇṭaraṭippŏṭi Āḻvār used to tend fell in the line of the *prākāra* that Tirumankai Āḻvār was constructing around the temple. He accordingly moved the wall to accommodate the garden from which *tirumālai*[233] had been prepared.[234] I am not suggesting that this was historically true; what is clear from the story is that both accommodation and inclusion were envisaged in the creation of the larger physical and ritual spaces of the temple.

It must be remembered that the Muslims of south India in this period were largely traders, and social and political stability is of utmost importance to the mercantile class. It has been pointed out that acceptance of some local beliefs and practices makes it easier for traders

[231] Hari Rao, op. cit., pp. 11–12. *Agpp* and *Mgpp*, Tirumankai Āḻvār *vaibhavam* also speak of Tirumankai's building activities at the Srirangam Temple.

[232] There is evidence in some places, for example, at Mahabalipuram, that the shrine which is today considered the *divya kṣetra* is probably not the one of which the Āḻvārs sang. In the case of Srirangam, however, it appears that the central shrine is very old as the stucco image of the reclining Lord in the sanctum sanctorum is mentioned in the *Cilappatikāram* among others. Also, Madhurakavi Āḻvār is the only one not to speak of any shrine of Viṣṇu. His entire devotion is directed towards Nammāḻvār.

[233] *Tirumālai* literally means holy garland—which Tŏṇṭaraṭippŏṭi Āḻvār used to prepare daily for the lord; it is also the name of one of Tŏṇṭaraṭippŏṭi's two compositions.

[234] *Agpp*, Tirumankai Āḻvār *vaibhavam*.

to be accommodated in the local trading diaspora.[235] It can be postulated that the 'surrounding' community similarly adopts aspects of the beliefs and practices of the newer settlers. A hypothetical reconstruction of the situation, when the temple walls came to encroach on a local Muslim shrine can give us a picture of tensions which were perhaps sought to be contained by the more powerful local community, i.e. the Śrīvaiṣṇava. It allowed the worshippers of the grave-shrine continued access, and also accorded to the object of their reverence, the so-called Muslim goddess, a place of privilege within the ritual of the temple. Scriptures eventually sought to legitimize it by elaborating on a 'lost and found' motif, weaving in aspects of the remembered history of the temple with fantasy and simultaneously bringing in diverse local groups into the larger ritual functioning of the temple.

(iv) The Integration

It need hardly be pointed out that the socio-political situation of the sixth to ninth centuries in Tamil Nadu was vastly different from that of the eleventh to the fourteenth. The first period was one of consolidation of Pallava rule after an era of relative political instability of which little is known.[236] While kings/kingdoms are spoken of even in the Sangam period—the Cera, Coḻa and Pāṇṭiya *mūventar*—as ruling in the fertile tracts of the Kerala region and the plains irrigated by the Kaveri, Vaigai and Tāmralipti, even though the more general political structure was of chieftains at war with one another for control of prosperous regions and for booty capture, establishment of kingdoms on a mature basis seems to have begun only with the Pallavas. This period of early state formation contrasts strongly with the second phase, one of established state structures, with the Coḻa state in particular extending its reach in terms of both external expansion and internal consolidation. Again, the first period was one where several religious systems of northern origin—brahmanism,[237] Buddhism and Jainism—all of which had been known in

[235] Romila Thapar, *Somanatha: The Many Voices of a History*, New Delhi: Viking-Penguin India, 2004, p. 36.

[236] The so-called dark ages of the Kaḷabhras.

[237] It is far from clear, however, which aspects of what is loosely called Hinduism are 'brahmanical' in their inspiration (other than those that can clearly be traced to the Vedas and their appendices) and which may actually be of Dravidian origin. While K.A.N. Sastri would argue for most aspects of this religious system, especially those that in the perspective of the Hindu

the Tamil country for some centuries, were all represented to a greater or lesser degree, and were negotiating in their different ways with the older Tamil religious complex. I have argued that the development of these cannot have caused sharp distinctions to emerge between lay followers of each of these faiths among the populace. It is also likely that patronage was not restricted to any one or two of the several religious ideologies, though contestation for the same seems to have developed, undoubtedly for the lion's share if not for monopoly of this patronage. This can explain the derogatory references to the Śramaṇas and the Bauddhas in the hymns of the Āḻvārs and Nāyaṉmārs.

It might have been interesting to see if the Jainas and Buddhists in Tamil Nadu also produced such literature condemning the Śaivas and Vaiṣṇavas, or for that matter, each other. But what has survived of the pens of the Buddhists and Jainas are epics like the *Cilappatikāram* and *Maṇimekalai*, Tiruvaḷḷuvar's famed book of aphorisms, the *Tirukkuraḷ*, the grammars *Naṉṉūl*[238] and *Tŏlkāppiyam*, etc.; indeed, even these were only rediscovered in the nineteenth century after ages of having been consigned to oblivion. It remains true even today when a variety of sources are being tapped to understand the past that most, if not all, history is that which was written by the victors.

For reasons that are yet to be fully explained, the brahmanical religions seem to have succeeded in establishing themselves in a dominant position in the emergent socio-political framework. Was it because the gods of the Buddhists and Jainas didn't lend themselves to the kind of intense personal devotion characteristic of bhakti that they were gradually marginalized in the age of the singing saints? The prestige of brahmanism in the north, its established role as a legitimizer of political authority and its capacity to absorb local cults are, of course, important factors. Certainly by the ninth–tenth centuries, the brahmanical religions fashioned through the medium of bhakti had come to dominate the religious landscape of Tamil Nadu. While Buddhism seems to have nearly died out, Jainism continued rather quietly. In 610 CE, the Pallava king, Mahendravarman I, had a rock-cut shrine inscribed, 'This brick-less, timber-less, metal-less and mortar-less temple which is a mansion for Brahmā, Īśvara and Viṣṇu was made by king Vicitracitta'. This is

---

nationalist historian would count as 'positive', being 'brahmanical' in origin, George Hart sees the same complex as owing far more to Dravidian than to northern elements.

238 A twelfth-century text composed by Pavanandi. Ref.: K.K.A. Venkatachari, *The Śrīvaiṣṇava Maṇipravāḷa/The Maṇipravāḷa Literature of the Śrīvaiṣṇava Ācāryas: 12th to 15th Centuries* AD, Bombay: Anantacharya Indological Institute, 1974, p. 9.

the same king who is said to have embraced Saivism at the instance of Appar and who ridiculed the Śramaṇas in his *Mattavilāsa Prahasana*. Some centuries later, Śaivism, as is well known, achieved pre-eminence as the royal cult of the Co̱ḻas.

The hagiographies are a product of this second period, and while they mirror the concerns of their age, they are careful to weave in the hymns of the saints. Thus, Jainism with its continuing visibility and popularity came in for much greater vilification in the *Gpps* and in the *Pĕriya Purāṇam*, whereas Buddhism which was perhaps all but forgotten except for its tenets which might have been taught in *āśramas* for the express purpose of refuting them, had ceased to be a real enemy. So Sambandar's almost equal condemnation of the Jainas and Buddhists[239] gets a very unequal treatment in the hagiographies, while Tirumaḻicai or Tirumankai Āḻvārs' scornful mentions of Buddhist monks is woven into their 'life-stories' in the form of creeds that they studied and discarded as false, or as shrines they plundered and believers they fooled.

But the 'heterodox' faiths had a much greater contribution to make to the social landscape of Tamil Nadu than their strictly religious intervention might suggest. Familiarity of the populace with these religious systems which did not place any great premium on caste status would have posed a challenge to brahmanic religious ideology with its sharp hierarchies. R.S. Sharma refers to 'some heterodox sects such as Vaiṣṇavism' which tried to improve the position of the lower orders.[240] Whether the Buddhist and Jaina monks themselves did try to improve the lot of the lower castes or not, they did certainly offer a glimpse of a world which was not as strictly exclusive as the brahmanical, and made it incumbent upon the leaders of the Śaiva and Vaiṣṇava religious movements, as they consolidated themselves in the early second millennium, to negotiate the demands of caste orthodoxy with a comparatively egalitarian societal framework to create more inclusive communities.

[239] There are some instances where Sambandar specifically rails against Jainas: in a cycle of hymns dedicated to the Śiva temple at Ālavāy, he alludes to debates with Jaina monks and ordeals faced by him at their hands; in *Tevāram* III: 305 and 366, he asks for Śiva's help in defeating Jainas in debate; in *Tevāram* III: 297, he assures the Pāṇṭiya queen of his ability to defeat them; in *Tevāram* III: 309, he prays that the flame kindled by the Jainas to burn him should consume the Pāṇṭiya king instead. Ref: Peterson, 'Śramaṇas against the Tamil way', p. 168.

[240] R.S. Sharma, 'The Kali Age: A Period of Social Crisis', in *Feudal Social Formation in Early India*, ed. D.N. Jha, Delhi: Chanakya Publications, 1987, p. 55.

SIX

Bathing in Every *Tīrtha*
Patterns of Worship, Pilgrimage and the Saint Poets

(i) *Historiography and Hypothesis*

We have seen that the Śrīvaiṣṇava tradition argues powerfully for an unbroken link from the Āḻvār saints who sang, between the sixth and ninth centuries, their devotional songs to Viṣṇu, and the sectarian religious system that was consolidated between the eleventh and fourteenth centuries and continues, albeit with important changes and developments, to present times. We have seen too that some modern scholars largely support this view,[1] while others see a perceptible break between the Āḻvār bhakti tradition and the religious system that was formulated by the *ācāryas*.[2] Both the development of the pilgrimage itinerary as we now know it, and the apotheosis of the saints, appear to be facets of the project of consolidation of the sectarian community, a concern of the later tradition. However, there is also overwhelming

[1] John Carman and Vasudha Narayanan, *The Tamil Veda: Piḷḷāṉ's Interpretation of the Tiruvāymoḻi*, Chicago: The University of Chicago Press, 1989; Nancy Ann Nayar, *Poetry as Theology: The Śrīvaiṣṇava Stotra in the Age of Ramanuja*, Weisbaden: Otto Harrassowitz, 1992; Steven Paul Hopkins, *Singing the Body of God: The Hymns of Vedāntadeśika in their South Indian Tradition*. New Delhi: Oxford University Press, 2002.

[2] Friedhelm Hardy, *Viraha Bhakti: The Early History of Kṛṣṇa Devotion in South India*, New Delhi: Oxford University Press, 1983.

evidence for both the pilgrimage tradition in the Tamil land and the worship of the saints in iconic form in the period before the *ācāryas*.

The Tamil land is dotted with several hundred historic shrines dedicated to numerous deities, among which the temples to Śiva and Viṣṇu are the most prominent. A significant number of these shrines date back over a thousand years though most of the temples have acquired their modern forms in later centuries. It is, of course, a moot point that several shrines which were in worship in earlier ages have now fallen into ruin; inscriptions from such dilapidated structures often help to reconstruct some aspects of their past.[3] A surprisingly large number of temples, however, continue to remain in worship and are sites of popular pilgrimage. Most of these shrines claim a unique status—as the locus of the world, as the site of some significant event in the Sanskrit epics or the *Purāṇas*, or of some other specific act of the chief deity, Śiva or Viṣṇu, derived from local mythology. Many at least of these myths and their associations with specific shrines go back to ancient times, as is seen from references to these stories and shrines in very early literature,[4] in the hymns of the saints,[5] and in inscriptions[6] as well. Composition of *sthalapurāṇas* which detail the origin myths, specific glories and chief legends associated with each shrine, and the benefits that would accrue to the pilgrim visiting it, began in the medieval

[3] T.V. Mahalingam, *A Topographical List of the Inscriptions in the Tamil Nadu and Kerala States*, vol. I, Delhi: ICHR and S. Chand & Co., 1985, pp. 24–31, records over forty inscriptions from a ruined Viṣṇu temple in the Arakkoṇam *tāluk* of the North Arcot district. The god is called Pĕrumāṉaṭikaḷ of Govindappāṭi and also Niṉṟaruḷina Pĕrumāṉaṭikaḷ. The earliest inscriptions here are dated to the reign of Parāntaka I, accession *c.* 907 CE.

[4] *Nālaṭiyār* v 39 speaks of Viṣṇu as *niṉṟāṉ, iruntāṉ, kiṭantāṉ. Cilappatikāram* XI, 11.41–51 describes the standing form of Viṣṇu at Venkaṭam. Cited in R. Champakalakshmi, *Vaiṣṇava Iconography in the Tamil Country*, New Delhi: Orient Longman, 1981, pp. 37–8.

[5] *Pĕriya Tirumŏḻi* 2.6.9, 7.3.2; *Tirukkuruntāṇṭakam* 19.

[6] Mahalingam, 1985, vol. VI, p. 426, Sm 55. Ref.: *ARE*, 1960–61, no. 292; *EI*, xxxvi, no. 18 (B), 137. An eighth-century CE inscription from the Ranganātha Cave Temple in Nāmakkal, Salem district, gives a list of names of gods, demigods and *asuras* associated with the principal deity in the *śayyā gṛha*, obviously referring to the figures carved on the walls of the sanctum around the reclining Viṣṇu: Mārkaṇḍeya, Parṇa (Suparṇa, i.e., Garuḍa), Varuṇa, Brahmā, Īśa, Dakṣa, Śaśi, Surya, Tumbur, Nārada, Guru, Bhṛgu, Sāṛnga, Kaumodaki (Cakra), Nandaka, Pāñcajanya, Śrī, Madhu and Kaiṭabha.

period.[7] This activity, spurred as it was by the competitive composition of similar *sthalapurāṇas* in numerous shrines, was clearly situated in a religious system that privileged pilgrimage, and was in turn aware of the importance of glorification of the specific site to which a particular *sthalapurāṇa* pertained above all others. This 'henotheistic' character extends beyond individual shrines to clusters of shrines as well.[8] Taking the Śaiva example, one may point to the set of eight shrines which are venerated as the *aṭṭavīrattāṉam* (Sanskrit *aṣṭavīrasthānam*, the eight sites of heroic deeds of the lord) or the five *bhūtalinga* shrines (where the *linga* is claimed to be a natural representation of the deity in one of the five fundamental elements: earth, water, fire, wind and ether/*ākāśa*).[9] One of the most important ways in which this henotheistic pilgrimage tradition has elevated certain shrines above others is through the association of a few hundred of the temples with the Āḻvārs and Nāyaṉmārs. The *Tevāram* can almost be considered pilgrimage literature as the majority of the poems of the Śaiva *mūvar*, i.e. Appar, Sundarar and Sambandar, are associated with individual shrines;[10] a significant number of poems in the *Nālāyira Divya Prabandham* too praise the sacred sites of Viṣṇu. Nammāḻvār underlines this multiplicity of sacred centres, 'The Lord of the *tulasi* garland, a radiant form of knowledge, by his wondrous glory appears in many famous spots and sports on earth, then swallows Śiva, Brahmā and all else in a trice'.[11]

The conception of the sacred site embraces the larger settlement in which the shrine is situated.[12] The Śaiva sacred spots, the *pāṭal pĕṟṟa talam*, i.e. the 'sites which have been sung of', number 274 in Tamil Nadu and its surrounding regions. These are distributed thus: Coḻanāḍu: 190; Tŏṇṭaināḍu: 32; Naṭunāḍu: 22; Pāṇṭiyanāḍu: 14; Kŏnkunāḍu: 7; Vaṭanāḍu: 8; Ilanāḍu (Sri Lanka): 2; Tuḷuvanāḍu: 1; Malaināḍu: 1. Another 263 shrines

[7] Dating based on David Dean Shulman, *Tamil Temple Myths: Sacrifice and Divine Marriage in the South Indian Śaiva Tradition*, Princeton: Princeton University Press, 1980, pp. 29–39. The sixteenth–seventeenth centuries have been called a 'veritable golden age of Puranic composition in Tamilnad'. See also, Richard H. Davis, *Lives of Indian Images*, Princeton: Princeton University Press, 1997, p. 137.

[8] I am borrowing the term from religious systems with numerous divinities wherein the god being venerated at a particular moment is elevated above all the others.

[9] Personal visit.

[10] Shulman, *Tamil Temple Myths*, op. cit., pp. 12–13.

[11] *Tiruvāymŏḻi* 3.10.9.

[12] Indira Viswanathan Peterson, *Poems to Śiva: The Hymns of the Tamil Saints*, New Jersey: Princeton University Press, 1989, p. 145.

are mentioned in passing in the hymns. The addition of these latter, the *vāyppu talam*, brings the number of Tamil centres sacred to Śiva to 537. The Vaiṣṇava tradition claims 108 *divya kṣetras*. This number is, however, arrived at by an artificial calculation, no doubt because of the holiness attributed to the number itself. Several Āl̲vārs have praised one or more of the holy places of Viṣṇu either by dedicating hymns to the shrine or by mentioning them in passing.[13] Nammāl̲vār has sung of 27 holy places besides mentioning seven more;[14] the hymns praising sacred centres are, however, randomly scattered through the *Tiruvāymŏl̲i*. The only Āl̲vār to have systematically sung of sacred spots is Tirumankai.[15] In all, the Āl̲vārs sang of/mentioned 97 shrines of Viṣṇu in the Tamil region and its immediate environs (including 13 in present-day Kerala and 2 in present-day Andhra Pradesh). These, along with the hymns dedicated to, or references in the hymns to remoter northern sites such as Badari, Ayodhya, Mathura and Dvaraka, sacred in the mythology of Viṣṇu, make another nine sites, while the holy number, 108, is arrived at by adding the two other-worldly residences of the lord—TirupPārkaṭal, the milk ocean where he reclines on his serpent bed, and Vaikuṇṭha. Many of the legends that are elaborated in the early medieval commentaries and late medieval *sthalapurāṇas* find reflection in earlier sources—largely in the hymns of the saints themselves, but also sometimes in epigraphs.

It is clear then that the ritual of pilgrimage was significant in the Vaiṣṇava saints' conception of the religious life, but it does not appear, except in the case of Tirumankai, to have been the central focus. It would be more accurate to say that the bhakti of the Āl̲vārs was temple-oriented, in that their devotion was primarily directed not to a transcendent god but to a deity enshrined in a temple, who was nevertheless imaged as the transcendent lord who had incarnated in several forms and performed numberless cosmic acts. The emphasis on pilgrimage, which is likely to

[13] It might be said that the Śrīvaiṣṇava tradition does not distinguish between the '*pāṭal pĕr̲r̲a talam*' and the '*vāyppu talam*' as does Śaiva terminology.

[14] These 34 include the 2 northern sites, Dvārakā (Tuvārai) and Mathurā (Vaṭa Maturai). They also include his mention of Vaikuṇṭam/Tiruvaikuṇṭam which has been elaborated as a pilgrim centre named Śrīvaikuṇṭham. See Table II d.

[15] The *Pĕriya Tirumŏl̲i* is systematically arranged as a pilgrims' progress from the northern sites to the southern, taking an upward curve in the clockwise direction after reaching the southernmost shrine. It is tempting to conjecture that this emphasis on pilgrimage is the reason the *ācāryas* attributed the *Pĕriya Tirumaṭal*, one of the unsigned works in the *NDP* which reads almost like a list of pilgrimage sites, to Tirumankai. See also, Tables II c and II e.

have strengthened in the later part of the bhakti period, was elaborated upon and consolidated in the subsequent age. Both scriptural and epigraphic references attest to the growing importance of pilgrimage to these venerated shrines. I shall argue that while the Śrīvaiṣṇava notion of pilgrimage, as it was shaped under the guidance of the *ācāryas*, did mark important changes, it also displayed strong continuities from the older bhakti tradition. Since there is evidence that some shrines lost their importance or were abandoned in subsequent centuries, it will be interesting to examine the reasons for the same.

Śrīvaiṣṇava tradition attributes the introduction of the Āḻvārs' hymns in the temple ritual to Nāthamuni. Related to this is the apotheosis of the saints; it is tempting to ascribe the latter to the agency of the *ācāryas* of the early second millennium. Inscriptional evidence suggests, however, that both these practices may have a longer history than the commentarial and hagiographical traditions suggest. We have already seen how the hymns of the saints, both Āḻvārs and Nāyaṉmārs, were considered by their respective traditions as lost and rediscovered, and also examined the epigraphic evidence that clearly points to the popularity of the hymns from at least the early tenth century.[16] It is interesting that while the claims of the Śrīvaiṣṇava tradition in this specific instance must be refuted, the larger claim of continuity is actually bolstered. I will examine some of the ways in which the hagiographies contributed to the development of the pilgrimage movement, the cult of saints and the consolidation of the forms of worship by their reconstruction of the very lives of the saints.

The notion of continuity is powerfully articulated in the hagiographies through the presentation of the preceptorial lineage. The original teacher in Śrīvaiṣṇava understanding was Viṣṇu, who taught the lore to Śrī, who in turn instructed Viśvaksena, the divine commander, and who further transmitted it to Nammāḻvār. The accent on flawless transmission of scriptural knowledge from the Supreme Lord to the contemporary leaders of the Śrīvaiṣṇava religious community may account for the centrality of the story of Nāthamuni being miraculously granted apprehension of the *Tiruvāymŏḻi* and, indeed, of the entire corpus of the poetry of the Āḻvārs, upon meditative repetition of Madhurakavi's *Kaṇṇinuṇciruttāmpu*.[17] However, it is clear from the hagiographical accounts that Rāmānuja was not a direct disciple of Yāmuna, grandson of Nāthamuni. This break is smoothed over in the traditional accounts

[16] See Chapter 1–iii of the present work.

[17] Ibid.

by the stories of Rāmānuja's discipleship under five teachers, to each of whom Yāmuna had entrusted a part of his knowledge.[18] The earlier rupture, i.e. between Nāthamuni and Nammāḻvār, and the mythology around it, may indicate more than just a 'break' in tradition. Rather, it suggests the appropriation of a deeply rooted regional tradition, that of bhakti of the Āḻvārs, by a brahmanical Vaiṣṇava one and the consequent consolidation of an integrated Śrīvaiṣṇava tradition. This, indeed, is my central thesis.

I have so far argued that the hagiographies were carefully constructed in the period between the twelfth and fourteenth–early fifteenth centuries in order to serve a variety of purposes such as the consolidation of a broad-based community and the transmission of important theological, social and sectarian concerns of the leaders. However, the examination of the hagiographical accounts has made it abundantly clear that they were not simply works of imaginative fiction, as the *ācāryas* subjected the hymns of the Āḻvārs to close analysis before constructing the 'life-stories' of the saints. All the same, there is little hymnal corroboration from the corpus of the *NDP* for numerous episodes in the lives of the saints that are elaborated in the hagiographies. It would appear, then, that these episodes are fictional, and woven into the stories of the saints for the purposes discussed earlier. Again, however, the evidence does not always permit us this confidence. I have long wondered as to why the stories of the three *mutal* Āḻvārs are so brief, almost skeletal in fact, while that of Tirumaḻicai[19] is as complex as it is, considering that these are all 'ahistorical' persons. Why did the *ācāryas* refrain from creating elaborate bildungsromans for the three earliest Āḻvārs as they did for Tirumaḻicai— rich with motifs that might help further their theological or social agenda? While I have no clear answers to these questions, I would like to examine the constraints within which the *ācāryas* recreated these stories. I use the word 're-create' rather than simply 'create' since the inscriptional evidence suggests that popular legends regarding the saint-poets might have circulated in oral form for some centuries before the hagiographies were composed.

(ii) Saints, Stories, Meanings

There is considerable scholarly literature on the histories of image worship and pilgrimage in the Tamil context. Friedhelm Hardy argued

[18] See Chapter 2–x of the present work.
[19] See Chapter 2–ii of the present work.

that the immobile *arcā vigraha* (the idol in the temple) had to be a northern concept for, in Tamil religious understanding, the divine is not only envisaged within the confines of concrete reality but is also dynamic and mobile. The Āḻvārs resolved this tension by conceptualizing a mystically active but physically immobile god. As Māyoṉ was envisaged as active in the Tamil land, the *sthalapuraṇās* were born.[20] George Hart, however, has shown that the basic orientation of Tamil religion since earliest times has been towards deities that inhere in a place, or are immanent rather than transcendent.[21] David Shulman concludes from his analysis of the Tamil *Purāṇas* that the myths are imbued with the belief that sacred presence is revealed in individual localized manifestations.[22] Indira Peterson points out that 'the shrine is a centre in more senses than one: it is situated at the centre of the sacred landscape in a palpable manner; it is, at the same time, identified with the centre or navel of the universe, the spot through which passes the *axis mundi* linking heaven, earth, and the nether regions'.[23] The Census of India, 1911, rather perceptively points out, 'It seems not unlikely that the virtue of a pilgrimage arises mainly from the sacred character attaching to the place itself and not so much from the desire to honour the deity whose shrine it is'.[24] Though most scholars would agree with this evaluation of the centrality of the geographical site per se, the importance of the deity enshrined therein cannot be lost sight of in the Tamil context with its well-developed tradition of devotion to a personal god.

Burton Stein places the beginning of the 'great age of religious pilgrimage in the Tamil country' in the twelfth century.[25] He argues that the rise of temples was the result of religious developments of the medieval period; brahmanical centres became religious centres with respect to a group of villages and other institutions as a result of the 'Hindu revival' which made the brahmanical temple the most significant institution for bhakti worship. Temples became economic as well as

[20] Hardy, *Viraha Bhakti*, pp. 468–9.

[21] George L. Hart, *The Poems of the Ancient Tamil: Their Milieu and their Sanskrit Counterparts*, Berkeley, California, 1975, pp. 130–3.

[22] Shulman, op. cit., p. 88.

[23] Peterson, *Poems to Śiva*, p. 143.

[24] R.V. Russell, in *Census of India, 1911, Vol. XIII, Central Provinces Report*, Pt. 1, p. 91, cited in Agehanand Bharati, 'Pilgrimage in the Indian Tradition', *History of Religions*, vol. 3.1, 1963, p. 136.

[25] Burton Stein, 'Circulation and Historical Geography of the Tamil Country', *Journal of Asian Studies*, vol. 37, no. 2, 1977, p. 288.

religious centres. Temple worship and pilgrimage were important aspects of the new sect religions. Popular temple-centred religious activity encouraged the growth of pilgrimage centres which also became market centres of importance.[26]

The role of bhakti in making the temple an institution of central importance in the socio-economic structure of Tamil Nadu has been well-documented and analysed. It also seems clear that temple building activity was spurred in the later Pallava and the Co<u>l</u>a periods by the ideology of bhakti: shrines of which the Ā<u>l</u>vārs and Nāya<u>n</u>mārs sang expanded into great temples with elaborate ritual structures as a result of royal and community patronage.[27] The fact that Rājarāja I commissioned the composition of a hymnal work to glorify the great temple at Tanjavur[28] attests to the importance of the saints' hymns in sanctifying a particular shrine. The A<u>n</u>bil plates of Parāntaka I praise Āditya I for erecting in stone, a number of lofty and impregnable temples to Śiva on the banks of the Kaveri, along its whole course from the mountains to the sea.[29] It is likely that many of these were temples sung about by

[26] Burton Stein, 'The State, the Temple and Agricultural Development: A Study in Medieval South India', in *All the Kings' Mana: Papers on Medieval South Indian History*, ed. Burton Stein, Madras: New Era Publications, 1984, p. 175, pp. 201–2.

[27] Mahalingam, 1985, vol. VIII, pp. 240–1. Tp 1085. Ref.: 1911, no. 277; *SII*, viii, no. 126, pp. 262–3. The above inscription and several others (from Tp 1083 to Tp 1101) of the early tenth century testify that Pūti Ādittapiṭāri, wife of Parāntaka I, had the temple of Candraśekhara in Tiruccĕnturai, Tirucciráppaḷḷi *tāluk* built in stone and made several grants for celebration of various festivals. Mahalingam, 1985, vol. VIII, pp. 297–8. Tp 1347. Ref.: *ARE*, 1914, no. 123: *SII*, xiii, no. 50, pp. 22–3 registers sale of land by the Pĕrunkuri *sabhā* of Srikaṇṭha *caturvedimangalam* and the *ūr* of Ĕrumpiyūr as *devadāna* to Pipīlikeśvara Temple in Tiruvĕrumpūr. The record is dated to c. 953 CE. Mahalingam, 1985, vol. II, pp. 3–4. SA 14. Ref.: *ARE*, 1888, no. 18; *SII*, iv, no. 223 records that Nakka<u>n</u> Pāvai, the *āṇukki* of the king purchased some lands and assigned the *melvāram* dues of the lands in the twenty-fourth regnal year of Co<u>l</u>a Rājendra I, i.e. *c.* 1036 CE, to the Naṭarāja Temple in Chidambaram. Mahalingam, 1985, vol. IX, pp. 33–4. Tn 154. Ref.: *ARE*, 1916, no. 402 records the grant of *kārā<u>n</u>mai* of certain lands by the *nagarattār* of Vintanūr to the Gopālasvāmi temple in Ma<u>nn</u>ārkoyil, Ambāsamudram *tāluk* in 1209 CE.

[28] Karuvūr Tevar's *Tiruvicaippā* is dedicated to the Lord Rājarājeśvara.

[29] *Epigraphica Indica*, vol. XV, p. 50.

the Nāyaṉmārs.[30] While many temples were *rebuilt* in stone,[31] there were others which were built for the first time directly in stone. Some poems in the *Tevāram*, in fact, refer to certain temples as *kaṟṟaḷi* (structures of stone).[32] Mahendravarman I's boast, recorded in the early seventh century, of having constructed a temple without brick, timber, metal or mortar is well known. It appears that stone temples were probably rare in the pre-Coḻa period, as they require great resources which could be harnessed in appreciable measures only with the establishment of an imperial structure like that of the Coḻas. The majority of the temples sung about by the saint-poets must, therefore, have been brick shrines, or indeed, made of even more perishable materials. Indeed, the very fact that some temples are specifically described as *kaṟṟaḷi* points to the rest not being so.

The architectural, sculptural and social aspects of the south Indian temples and the *sthalapurāṇa* literature have been studied to understand the antiquity of the shrines,[33] of the diverse means employed for political legitimation,[34] of the consolidation of social relationships and

[30] C. Minakshi, *Administration and Social Life under the Pallavas*, Madras: University of Madras, 1938, p. 174. Also see, Indira V. Peterson, 'Singing of a Place: Pilgrimage as Metaphor and Motif in the Tēvāram Songs of the Tamil Śaiva Saints', *Journal of the American Oriental Society*, vol. 102, no. 1, 1982, p. 81.

[31] Mahalingam, 1985, vol. II, p. 372. SA 1600. Ref.: *ARE*, 1900, no. 123; *EI* vii, no. 20 (K) is an eleventh-century record of the dilapidated brick structure of the central shrine of the Trivikrama-p-Pĕrumāḷ Temple in TirukKoyilūr having been rebuilt in granite. Mahalingam, 1985, vol. VII, p. 99. Tj 430. Ref.: *ARE*, 1931–32, no. 134 is a record from the Prāṇeśvara Temple in Tiruppĕnturai, Kumbhakoṇam *tāluk*, dated to the reign of Coḻa Kulottunga III (accession 1178 CE). It purports to be a copy of an inscription engraved on stone when the original brick temple of Tiruppĕnturai-uṭaiyār was converted into a stone temple in the reign of Karikāla Coḻa, where the inscriptions previously engraved on door jambs and caves of stone were copied on the temple walls.

[32] B.G.L. Swamy, 'The Date of the Tevaram Trio: An Analysis and Reappraisal', *Bulletin of the Institute of Traditional Cultures, Madras*, vol. 19.1, 1975, p. 147.

[33] Vidya Dehejia, *The Namakkal Caves*, State Department of Archaeology, Government of Tamil Nadu, 1977.

[34] C. Minakshi, *The Historical Sculptures of the Vaikuntha Perumal Temple, Kanchipuram*, Memoirs of the ASI, no. 63, Manager of Publications, Delhi: Government of India Press, 1941.

hierarchies,[35] or of messages embedded in the site myths.[36] However, one aspect which is overlooked even in dense temple studies is the physical distance between the different sacred places. It is not just that modern means of transport reduce travelling time and alter conceptions of distance; the density of settlements along the way and the network of connections and pathways are likely to have been very different five or ten centuries earlier. Most historians are, naturally, likely to factor in these important differences and assume that a journey which takes about six hours today might have been a week's expedition in older times. The converse of this is what interests me, however. Most modern studies fail to remark on the extreme nearness of some of the sacred shrines celebrated in the hymns.[37] Let me illustrate this with some prominent examples. There are eleven *divya deśas* in Tirunānkūr/Tiruvāli— of which six are not more than a few hundred metres from one another while the other five, besides two more[38] are comparatively further, between four and eight kilometres distant[39]—and all are celebrated in the hymns of Tirumankai Āḻvār.[40] Modern Kāñcīpuram houses thirteen Śrīvaiṣṇava *divya deśas*, among which some are scarcely a five minutes' walk from one another while others are scattered at slightly greater, nevertheless, walking distances. In fact, as pilgrims' guidebooks conscientiously inform pilgrims, the three *divya deśas* of Nīrakam, Kārakam and Kārvāṉam are supposed to be incorporated in a single temple, that of Ūrakam

[35] Rajan Gurukkal, 'Temples as Sites of Social and Religious Interaction', in *History of Science, Philosophy and Culture in Indian Civilization*, ed. B.D. Chattopadhyaya, Delhi: Centre for Studies in Civilisation and Pearson Longman, 2009, pp. 199–210.

[36] Shulman, op cit; Dennis Hudson, 'The Śrīmad Bhagavat Purāṇa in Stone: The Text as an Eighth Century Temple and its Implications', *Journal of Vaishnava Studies*, vol. 3, no. 3, 1995, pp. 137–82.

[37] Peterson, 'Singing of a Place', pp. 69–90, notes that during a field trip to the Śaiva pilgrim shrines, she found that most of the shrines in the Tanjore region were within 10 to 15 km. of one another.

[38] Adding the *divya deśas* of KāḻicCīrāma Viṇṇagaram (modern Cīrkāli) and Tiruvāli to the Nānkūr eleven would actually give us thirteen temples in close proximity to each other. I have followed the conventional pilgrims' manuals in enumerating eleven Nānkūr *divya deśas*.

[39] Personal visit. Most pilgrims' guides-cum-*sthalapurāṇas* do specify that the eleven Nānkūr *divya deśas* are within a few kilometres of each other. See, for example, A. Etirajan, *108 Vaiṇava Divya Deśa Stala Varaḷāru*, Kāraikkuṭi: Vaiṇava Siddhānta Nūrpatippuk Kaḻakam, 2003, pp. 188–236.

[40] Tirumankai claims in several of his signature verses to belong to Āli.

in Kāñcī where the central shrine houses a majestic stucco image of Ulakaḷanta Pĕrumāḷ (the Lord who measured the earth, as Vāmana-Trivikrama). Temple functionaries helpfully point out sculptured niches in the *prākāra* walls as the other *divya deśas* to anxious, '108-oriented' pilgrims.[41] Similarly, several of the nine *divya deśas* (now designated the *nava-Tiruppati*) sung by Nammāḻvār in the Tirunelveli region around his hometown, TirukKurukūr/Āḻvār Tirunagari, are within two to three kilometres of each other; indeed, two of them are within a minute's walk of one another.[42]

I have some very tentative explanations for this peculiar, though by no means rare phenomenon.[43] An interesting pattern emerges when one plots the sacred shrines on a map of the Tamil region.[44] Both the Āḻvārs and the Nāyaṉmārs have sung about a large number of sacred places in certain areas such as Kāñcīpuram and its immediate environs, the Kaveri delta, the Kumbhakoṇam–Tanjavur–Tiruccirāppaḷḷi region and the Madurai–Tirunelveli region. There are almost no Vaiṣṇava shrines which have been 'sung about' in the modern districts of Vellore, Dharmapuri, Salem, Erode, Coimbatore, Dindigul and Theni.[45] Other than this clustering of shrines along the eastern coastal belt— 'never broader than about sixty miles', in Hardy's words[46]—there is a further smattering in Malaināḍu or modern Kerala.

It is fairly evident that some of the above-mentioned temples are so close to each other that it is not the expansion of modern towns that has resulted in several of them now falling within the limits of the same municipality/township but that, even six or seven centuries earlier, each of these shrines could scarcely have been the locus of a separate settlement. It is also equally apparent that the maximum concentration

41 Personal visit.

42 Personal visit.

43 Nearly 160 of the 274 Śaiva *pāṭal pĕṟṟa talam* are located along the lower Kaveri basin, roughly between the Tanjavur district and the mouth of the river. This implies a similar density of sacred centres.

George Spencer, 'The Sacred Geography of the Tamil Shaivite Hymns', *Numen*, vol. 17, Fasc. 3, 1970, p. 236, says that the Tanjavur district alone houses 160 shrines but the map included with the article on p. 237 is inaccurate. Also, Peterson, 'Singing of a Place', pp. 69–90, mentions 160 shrines along the Kaveri.

44 See Hardy, *Viraha Bhakti*, pp. 256–61, including maps.

45 I suspect that this holds largely true for Śaiva *pāṭal pĕṟṟa talam* too. Spencer, op. cit., pp. 236–8, also points to the concentration of temples in certain districts.

46 Hardy, *Viraha Bhakti*, p. 258. However, the band is approximately 150 km. wide around Madurai and tapers southwards.

of temples is in and around the most fertile, rice-cultivating regions of the Tamil country. Temples are said to have been central in the organization and expansion of agriculture,[47] an argument that needs to be nuanced considering the extreme proximity of a number of these shrines and their concentration in regions which are among the earliest agrarian centres of the Tamil land.

Let us recall here the legend of Tirumankai Āḻvār's poetical contest with the Nāyaṉār Sambandar. Apparently, the Āḻvār's 'speech could not flower' in a town where there was no *vigraha* of Viṣṇu. It was only after he had worshipped the Viṣṇu idol that a *bhāgavata* woman/*arcaka* had in her/his keeping[48] that he could compose his poetical tour de force, the *Tiruvĕḻukūṟṟirukkai.*[49] A common Tamil proverb says that one must not live in a town without a temple.[50] There is of course, no reason to assume either that the legend is based on historical fact, or that the proverb is a millennium old. What they may, however, point to is a deeply held Tamil notion that places derive their auspiciousness from the presence of the divine. It follows, then, that the Āḻvārs expressed their belief in the presence of their chosen deity in and around their own hometowns in numerous hymns and in diverse ways, leading to the eventual elaboration of each of these expressions into distinct temples. It is likely, too, that the Āḻvārs sang of the lord in the places they happened to visit, or perhaps stayed at en route to the older and more established shrines such as Venkaṭam and Srirangam. A hymn of Nammāḻvār's in the voice of a lovelorn maiden's mother is telling. 'For her, all temples that house idols of any *deva* are temples of the ocean-hued one'.[51] This undoubtedly expresses the Āḻvār's own feelings since the passion he describes in the 'girl' is patently his own. Autochthonous deities might in this fashion have been absorbed in the Vaiṣṇava or Śaiva pantheon by the hymnists who saw the greatness and omnipresence of their chosen god in every village shrine. Considering the intense emotionality of bhakti in the case of most saints and, additionally, the strong missionary zeal of some such as Tirumankai and Sambandar, this would certainly have served to propagate and spread Puranic religion. While the saint-poets may have worshipped at local shrines in the hamlets where they halted, singing

[47] Kesavan Veluthat, *The Early Medieval in South India*, New Delhi: Oxford University Press, 2003, pp. 62–3.

[48] *Agpp/DSC* versions. See Chapter 2–viii of the present work.

[49] It is an unsigned composition. See Chapter 1–iii of the present work.

[50] '*Koyil illā ūril kuṭiyirukkāte*'.

[51] *Tiruvāymŏḻi* 4.4.8.

impassioned hymns in praise of the lord whose inherent magnificence they perceived even in humble structures, it is even possible that there may have been no physical temple or shrine in at least some of the places when the Āḻvārs actually sang of them; in that sense, they can be said to have literally sung these shrines into existence.[52]

A couple of examples will illuminate this point further. In a poem expressing the despair of separation, Nammāḻvār, in the voice of a lovelorn girl, accuses Māyakkūttaṉ of southern Kuḷantai of having left her, mounted on his bird.[53] Māyakkūttaṉ translates into 'the one who dances the dance of *māyā*'. We saw that the acaryic tradition took care to avoid portraying the lord as *māyiṉ* in order to defend against Advaitin attacks, their conception of a *saguṇa* lord as free from any blemish.[54] 'Māyakkūttaṉ' as a description or attribute of the lord is, accordingly, unacceptable to the Śrīvaiṣṇava tradition which consequently understands Nammāḻvār's adjectival noun as a proper noun, the name of the *utsava mūrti* in the temple at Kuḷantai.[55] The references in the verse are further elaborated in the temple legend and architecture such that Garuḍa is represented as only a processional image,[56] suggesting the potential of his imminent departure. What is equally interesting is that in the said hymn, the lord seems to be described as being in the west as well as in southern Kuḷantai.[57] The image of the lord accordingly faces the west in this temple,[58] which the *sthalapurāṇa* claims as a rarity.

What we have, therefore, is the elaboration of a temple complex to fit with the hymnal tradition. It is certainly possible that in this case, there already was a temple, or at least a small, local west-facing Viṣṇu shrine at Kuḷantai. Noting the hymns devoted to different shrines scattered throughout the *Tiruvāymŏḻi*, Kaylor and Venkatachari point out, 'All of [them] have become now, if they were not already in Nammalvar's time,

[52] I am using the phraseology from A.K. Ramanujan, *Hymns for the Drowning: Poems to Visnu by Nammalvar*, New Delhi: Penguin India Ltd, 1993, p. 107.

[53] *Tiruvāymŏli*, 8.2.4. This is not a poem dedicated to a shrine. Kuḷantai finds only passing mention.

[54] See Chapter 3 of the present work.

[55] Ibid.

[56] Etirajan, op. cit., pp. 494–6. Also, *Navathiruppathi, Temple History: 108 Divya Desams details/9 Temple History*, Chennai: V.R.K. Publications (pamphlet literature). Also, personal visit. Garuḍa's posture indicates his readiness to take off.

[57] *Tiruvāymŏḻi* 8.2.4. Nammāḻvār's wording is cryptic; the only meaning we can access today is mediated through the commentarial tradition.

[58] Etirajan, op. cit., pp. 494–6. East-facing images are commoner.

places of religious pilgrimage'.[59] Tirumankai's hymns praising eleven separate shrines in Tiruvāli-Tirunānkūr give the impression that they were all majestic structural temples.[60] Was there actually so dense a cluster of temples in this area as early as the eighth-ninth centuries? Or, was the Āḻvār in his zeal, projecting the immense popularity of Viṣṇu worship in his hometown, describing wayside shrines as great mansions with the same poetic license that made him sing of the Kaveri washing down gemstones and pearls from the hills[61] and parrots reciting the Vedas in the streets of Tirunānkūr?[62] Considering the bias of patronage towards Śaiva shrines in Coḻa times, it is likely that Tirunānkūr had not acquired impressive structures even till the period of the composition of the hagiographies.[63] Was the abundance of hymns to shrines in Tirunānkūr in the *Pĕriya Tirumŏḻi* responsible for the localizing of the legend of Tirumankai being unable to compose poetry in the absence of a Viṣṇu *vigraha*?[64] In other words, did the hagiographers notice the absence of physical temple structures to correspond with the mansions in the *Pĕriya Tirumŏḻi*, and acknowledge through the legend, the Āḻvār's having sung these shrines into existence?

The famous 'shore temple' at Mahabalipuram that enshrines an image of Viṣṇu in the *śayana* pose seems to have been created in the reign of Narasimhavarman II alias Rājasimha (680–72 CE).[65] Less than a kilometre from the shore is the Talaśayana[66]-p-Pĕrumāḷ Temple, considered a *divya*

[59] David Kaylor and K.K.A. Venkatachari, *God Far, God Near: An Interpretation of the Thought of Nammalvar*, no. 5 (Supplement), Bombay: Ananthacharya Indological Research Institute Series, 1981, p. 34.

[60] *Pĕriya Tirumŏḻi* 3.5.1-10 to 4.8.1-10 (140 stanzas).

[61] *Pĕriya Tirumŏḻi* 5.1.9, 5.4.9, 5.7.10.

[62] *Pĕriya Tirumŏḻi* 3.8.8

[63] The eleven temples of Tirunānkūr and the two others in nearby Cīrkāḻi and Tiruvāli (see footnote no. 38) are rather modest structures even today, and to the untrained eye at least, seem comparatively late. To one familiar with the Vaikuṇṭha-p-Pĕrumāḷ *koyil* in Kāñcīpuram as Tirumankai certainly was and, in all likelihood, the 'shore temple' in Mahabalipuram as well, the Nānkūr temples, even if they had existed in his day—which is highly improbable—could have scarcely seemed impressive.

[64] The site mentioned in the hagiographies is KāḻicCīrāma Viṇṇagaram, i.e. modern Cīrkāḻi, the birthplace of Sambandar. This is within the rough circumference of Tiruvāli/Nānkūr.

[65] C. Sivaramamurti, *Mahabalipuram*, New Delhi: Director General Archaeological Survey of India, 1978, pp. 29–32.

[66] Sanskrit *sthalaśayana*.

deśa. Since the latter is a comparatively recent structure with carving and workmanship dateable to the Vijayanagara period,[67] it could not have been the temple of which Tirumankai Āl̲vār sang.[68] In fact, Tirumankai's description, 'Our Lord-with-the-discus resides along with the Pingala Lord Śiva-who-frequents-the-cremation-ground, in Mallai Kaṭalmallai Talaśayanam where celestials in hordes offer worship',[69] agrees entirely with the layout of the shore temple which houses shrines of both Śiva and Viṣṇu separated by a narrow porch.[70] The description of the lord as Kaṭalmallai Talaśayana (the one who sleeps on land, in Mallai-on-the-sea),[71] is particularly interesting, especially as the location of the temple in Mallai is repeated in the phraseology. Was it the presence of the temple at the very edge of land, almost at the 'twilight' zone of sea and sand, which invited remark? The entire complex of the 'shore temple' was apparently buried under a thick deposit of sand till the middle of the last century.[72] It is impossible to determine with accuracy when the elements effaced the Pallava temple from view, but if this had happened within a few centuries of its construction, it is reasonable to suppose that in the Vijayanagara period, when the pilgrimage network was being consolidated, a new temple was built near the shore to tally with Tirumankai's hymn, and accorded *divya deśa* status. Indeed, this process can be seen to have continued into fairly recent times. The Ranganātha Temple in Vṛndāvana, which too is counted as one of the 108 *divya deśas*, is known to have been constructed some time in the middle of the nineteenth century.[73]

What becomes clear is that the developing Śrīvaiṣṇava tradition elaborated the hymns of the Āl̲vārs not merely in textual commentaries but also in physical space as temples. Let us look at a stanza by Tirumankai:

Oh Lord who are in water, atop lofty mountain peaks, in the soft radiance of the moon! Oh you who are within the prosperous town of Kacciyūr! In the

67 Sivaramamurti, op. cit., p. 29.

68 *Pĕriya Tirumŏl̲i* 2.5.1–10 and 2.6.1–10.

69 *Pĕriya Tirumŏl̲i* 2.6.9.

70 Sivaramamurti, *Mahabalipuram*, op. cit. pp. 29–32. Also, personal visit.

71 The old name of the town is Māmallapuram or Mallai/Māmallai. Kaṭal means ocean.

72 Sivaramamurti, *Mahabalipuram*, op. cit., p. 32.

73 Personal visit, and communication from Srivatsa Gosvami ji, scholar and *guru* of the Caitanya *sampradāya*. In fact, *arcakas* at the temple were fairly clear on both points and didn't see any contradiction in the temple at a sacred shrine mentioned by Āṇḍāḷ [*Nācciyār Tirumŏl̲i* 14.1–10] being only about 160 years old.

ghat of Vĕhkā! In the hearts of those who melt for you! Praised by the world, in the heart of darkness! In the dark skies! Thief! On the southern banks of the beautiful Kaveri which has great fame/name, and forever in my heart! I desire your auspicious feet.[74]

This verse can also be translated very differently, by seeing the descriptive attributes as place names.

Oh Lord in Nīrakam, atop lofty Venkaṭam, in Nilātinkaḷtuṇṭam! Oh you who are in Ūrakam in prosperous Kacci! In the port of Vĕhkā! In the hearts of those who melt for you! In Kārakam praised by the world! In Kārvāṉam! Thief! On the southern banks of the beautiful Kaveri in Perakam, and forever in my heart! I desire your auspicious feet.[75]

The second is, in fact, the more traditional reading. This stanza seems to have generated several *divya deśas*, so much so that three sites mentioned in it have not, despite acquiring *divya deśa* status, 'become' temples even now.[76] Though Ūrakam might have denoted a distinct shrine as the *Tiruccanta Viruttam* speaks of the Lord there in seated posture,[77] it seems doubtful if a separate shrine is intended in the verse quoted above or if the reference is merely to the *ūr* of Kacci (Kāñcī). Besides, the deity at the shrine known as Ūrakam now is not seated but Trivikrama as we saw above,[78] so that the term in the hymn is probably a descriptive as I have argued, and not a reference to the temple that goes by the name today. The *divya deśa* called Nilātinkaḷtuṇṭam is a small subsidiary shrine in the important Śiva temple of Ekāmreśvara in Kāñcī.[79] It is reasonable

[74] *Tirunĕṭuntāṇṭakam* 8. Translation by Kanaka Jagannathan.

[75] Translation by Srirama Bharati. Ref.: *Nalayiradivyaprabandham: The Sacred Book of 4000*, Original Text with English Translations by Srirama Bharati, Chennai: Sri Sadagopan Tirunarayansvami Divyaprabandham Pathasala, 2000, p. 428.

Nīrakam, Venkaṭam, Nilātinkaḷtuṇṭam, Ūrakam, Vĕhkā, Kārakam, Kārvāṉam and Perakam/TirupPer are counted among the 108 *divya deśas*. However, it remains true that some of the phrases which may be read as descriptive are also place names. Per, for instance, is mentioned in *Pĕriyāḻvār Tirumŏḻi* 2.5.1, 2.6.2, and 2.9.4, in *Nāṉmukaṉ Tiruvantādi* 36 and in *Pĕriya Tirumŏḻi* 1.5.4, 5.6.2 etc.

[76] Nīrakam, Kārakam and Kārvāṉam.

[77] *Tiruccanta Viruttam* 63, 64. It would be well to remember here that Hardy considers the *Tiruccanta Viruttam* a late addition to the hymnal corpus. See Chapter 1–iii of the present work.

[78] The four forms of Viṣṇu as sleeping, sitting, standing and walking (or any one or more of these) are mentioned in several hymns, *Mutal Tiruvantādi* 77, *Tiruccanta Viruttam* 63, 64.

[79] The Ekāmreśvara/Ekāmbaranātha Temple is both a *pāṭal pĕṟṟa talam* and one of the five *bhūtalinga kṣetras*.

to conjecture that it might have been one of the numerous sculptures of worshipful deities—in this case, Viṣṇu—that adorn major temple walls to underline the supremacy of the main god, which acquired the status of an independent Vaiṣṇava shrine. It appears that the Śrīvaiṣṇava exegetical tradition projected the above verse, despite its lacking the specificity of the pilgrimage hymns in his *Pĕriya Tirumŏḻi*, as an expression of actual pilgrimage undertaken by Tirumankai Āḻvār.

Similarly, while most Āḻvārs including Nammāḻvār have mentioned Vaikuṇṭham,[80] the heavenly abode of Viṣṇu, two stanzas of Nammāḻvār referring to the lord residing in Vaikuṇṭham[81] are read by the commentators as referring to a terrestrial abode, viz., Śrīvaikuṇṭham, in the Tirunelveli region.[82] Again, it appears that a *divya deśa* has been 'created' in order to make up the requisite numbers.

Our hagiographies indicate that the *Tiruvāymŏḻi* was a spontaneous outpouring of Nammāḻvār's upon being granted a vision of the Supreme Lord. Local legends stress that the deities of various *divya kṣetras* themselves came to TirukKurukūr and had Nammāḻvār sing of them.[83] The legend of his having sat in unbroken meditation till the age of sixteen when he uttered his first words, an esoteric answer to Madhurakavi's esoteric question,[84] also underlines the belief that Nammāḻvār did not actually journey to the various shrines of the lord that he sang about. Nammāḻvār himself seems to suggest in at least one stanza that the power of a pilgrim site is such that merely thinking of it is sufficient to receive its

[80] *Mutal Tiruvantādi* 76, *Tiruccanta Viruttam* 84, *Pĕrumāḷ Tirumŏḻi* 10.10, *Tiruppāvai* 9, *Tiruvāymŏḻi* 9.10.5, etc.

[81] *Tiruvāymŏḻi* 9.2.4 and 9.2.8.

[82] The *sthalapurāṇa* claims that the lord appeared before Brahmā and granted him the secrets of creation which had been lost. Since he had arrived directly from Vaikuntha, Brahmā requested him to assume the same form here as he took in his divine abode. Ref.: Etirajan, op. cit., pp 475–477. Also, *Navathiruppathi, Temple History*, op cit., (pamphlet literature).

[83] The legend was recited by several *arcakas* in the 'Nava-Tiruppati' temples, a cluster in the Tirunelveli region around the Āḻvār's hometown. (See Table II d, nos. 13–21). It is also mentioned in the *sthalapurāṇa* of Āḻvār Tirunagari. This is now re-enacted in an annual festival where (the processional images of) the deities of the nine shrines arrive at Āḻvār Tirunagari to visit Nammāḻvār. The same legend is responsible for the interesting feature that none of these temples possess either a shrine or an image of Nammāḻvār though almost all of them house images of the other Āḻvārs in a group, often along with Rāmānuja and some other *ācārya*.

[84] See Chapter 2–ix of the present work.

rewards.[85] 'Even as I said, "Tirumāliruñcolai", Tirumāl entered my heart, filled it entirely'.[86] This is not to suggest that Nammāḻvār composed *all* his hymns on various shrines based merely on hearsay though I believe it may be true of Venkaṭam and Vĕhkā since he has not sung of any other place north of Coḻanāḍu, whereas an actual journey to either of these shrines in the ninth century would have entailed halts at several other shrine-centres en route. On the other hand, since most of the Śrīvaiṣṇava *divya deśas* in modern Kerala are known only from Nammāḻvār's hymns,[87] it is likely that he travelled to Malaināḍu. It remains possible, however, that some of these were established local-regional pilgrimage centres and that he could have heard of them owing to their proximity to his hometown. In fact, the tenor of many of the hymns addressed to the lord in the Malaināḍu shrines suggests a wish to visit these places rather than a record of an accomplished pilgrimage.[88] It is equally important that the Śrīvaiṣṇava tradition itself did not firmly hold that the holy places of the lord sung of by the Āḻvār were necessarily material, physical spaces.

Description of the sacred residences of the lord through hearsay is not uncommon in the *NDP*. When Āṇḍāḷ asks to be taken to Mathura,[89] the banks of the Yamuna,[90] Bhaktavilocanam,[91] Govardhana[92] and Dvārakā,[93] it is not to identifiable physical locations but to the mythological ones associated with Kṛṣṇa. In fact, the tenor of this poem clearly indicates the speaker's obsession with the divine hero's mythical exploits. Pĕriyāḻvār's decad on Khaṇḍam (Devaprayāg) could be about any site but for the qualifier, 'on the banks of the torrential Ganga'.[94] It is generally accepted by modern historians that actual pilgrimages were probably not undertaken by any of the Āḻvārs to the northern sites[95] mentioned

85 Kaylor and Venkatachari, op. cit., p. 55.

86 *Tiruvāymŏḻi* 10.8.1.

87 Nammāḻvār has sung of 12 shrines in Kerala of which three have also been sung by Tirumankai.

88 *Tiruvāymŏḻi* 5.9.1–11 on TiruVallavāḷ; 6.1.1–11 on TiruVaṇvaṇṭūr; 7.8.1–11 on TiruvĀṟanviḷai; 8.3.7 on TiruVaṇparicāram; 9.7.1–11 on TiruMūḻikkaḷam; 9.8.1–11 on TiruNāvāy.

89 *Nācciyār Tirumŏḻi* 12.1.

90 *Nācciyār Tirumŏḻi* 12.5.

91 *Nācciyār Tirumŏḻi* 12.6.

92 *Nācciyār Tirumŏḻi* 12.8.

93 *Nācciyār Tirumŏḻi* 12.9.

94 *Pĕriyāḻvār Tirumŏḻi* 4.7.1.

95 See for example, Hardy, *Viraha Bhakti*, p. 424, where he speaks of Āṇḍāḷ's imaginary pilgrimage to Mathurā, Gokula, Vṛndāvana, Dvārakā etc.

in the hymns[96] as the descriptions of the northern sites are either formulaic or patently notional. Tirumankai Āl̲vār, for instance, describes flamboyantly, the lush forests of Piriti where pepper vines twine about the trunks of *venkai* trees, evidently unaware of and indifferent to the fact that pepper, a plant extremely fastidious about its habitat, would never survive in the Himalayan regions.[97] There can be little doubt that Tirumankai transferred the floral landscape of the Western Ghats with which he was familiar to the northern mountains which he knew only through hearsay.

The trend seems to continue in the hagiographical literature as well. The stories of most Āl̲vārs carry some motifs of their travels to different holy centres; indeed, it is only Tiruppāṇāl̲vār and Tŏṇṭaraṭippŏṭi who are supposed to have remained steadfastly in Srirangam, no doubt because their hymns themselves are entirely oriented to the lord of Srirangam. It is, however, not merely in these general descriptions of peregrinations in the hagiographies that we find the idea of pilgrimage reinforced but in specific tales that knit in verses of the Āl̲vārs with specific experiences attributed to them. Tirumankai's verses on Aṭṭabuyakaram[98] describe various aspects of Viṣṇu and end with the refrain, 'Who could it be?' and the answer, 'I am the Lord of Aṭṭabuyakaram'. This stylized way of singing of the lord is woven into the story of the Āl̲vār having met the lord of Aṭṭabuyakaram disguised as an old Vaiṣṇava while the former was journeying to Venkaṭam.[99]

Considering the intensity with which the saints praised the locales in which the lord supposedly dwelled, including perhaps many where there was no temple of any note, why did they not sing of certain shrines which we know to have been in existence from the sixth–seventh centuries? A Sanskrit inscription of circa 610 CE from a pillar in front of a cave shrine[100] tells us that the temple of Murāri named Mahendra Viṣṇugṛha was excavated out of the rocks on the banks of the Mahendra

[96] *Pĕriya Tirumŏl̲i* 1.2.1–10, 1.2.1–10, 1.4.1–10, 1.5.1–10 and 1.6.1–10 are dedicated to Piriti (Jośīmaṭha), Badari (two decads), Śāligrāma and Naimiśāraṇya respectively, all in the Himalayan region.

[97] *Pĕriya Tirumŏli*, 1.2.2–9. Venkai is identified as Pterocarpum marsupium.

[98] Sanskrit: Aṣṭabhujakara; *Pĕriya Tirumŏl̲i* 2.8.1–10.

[99] See Chapter 2-viii-b of the present work.

[100] I have used the term cave temple/shrine to refer to shrines excavated out of living rock. These are not necessarily natural caverns, nor particularly deep. The central image in these shrines is, similarly, carved out of the living rock, and is usually in relief, not in the round. The structural part of the temple is often elaborated with free-standing architecture that projects from the hill or

taṭākai in the city of Mahendrapura.[101] The Lakṣmīnarasimha Temple and the Ranganātha Temple in Nāmakkal *tāluk*, Salem district,[102] are both cave temples of some antiquity. Two eighth-century Sanskrit inscriptions in the Grantha script from the Ranganātha cave temple record the excavation of this shrine, called the Atiyanātha Viṣṇugṛham, by King Guṇaśīla of the Atiya *kula*.[103] Several caves in Mahabalipuram are sculpted with Vaiṣṇava motifs, notable being the Mahiṣāsuramardini cave and the Varāha cave. Another temple known as the Mukunda Temple also belongs to the period of Rājasimha.[104] The Cinka-p-Pĕrumāḷ Koyil,[105] about forty kilometres south of modern Madras/Chennai, is also another cave temple that dates from Pallava times.[106] Why did the Āḻvārs not compose any hymns in praise of these temples, whose existence they could scarcely have been unaware of, considering the familiarity of Tirumankai and Pūtam with Māmallai and the fact that the Cinka-p-Pĕrumāḷ Temple is only a minor detour from the straight route (today) between several sacred shrines in and around modern Madras and modern Kāñcī? This peculiarity has been noted with respect to the Śaiva context as well. Appar, known for bringing Mahendravarman to the Śaiva faith, failed to sing of a single temple consecrated by the king.[107] Sundarar and Sambandar have similarly ignored cave temples in the vicinity of temples they have sung of. To quote B.G.L. Swamy, 'There appears to be an opinion in some quarters [not published as far as I know] that the *āgamas* prescribe only structural temples worthy of consecration and worship of Śiva and not rock-cut cave shrines; and that for this reason,

---

boulder face. In all the cases, the hillock or boulder out of which the shrine has been carved can be perceived.

101 Mahalingam, 1985, vol. I, p. 10. NA 46. Ref.: *ARE*, 1896, no. 13; ibid., 1943–44, no. 83.

102 The older Salem district has been subdivided since 1985 into others. In speaking of the near-absence of *divya deśas* in Salem district (among others) above, I intended the current political division.

103 Mahalingam, 1985, vol. VI, p. 426. Sm 52 and 53. Ref.: *ARE*, 1960–1, no. 291; *EI* xxxvi, no. 18 (A), 137 and *ARE*, 1906, no. 7; *EI* xxxvi, no. 18(D), 138.

104 Sivaramamurti, op cit., p. 34.

105 Tamil Cinka= Sanskrit Simha. Temple of the lion-god, i.e. Narasimha.

106 Personal visit and observation.

107 K.R. Srinivasan, *Cave temples of the Pallavas*, Madras: Archaeological Survey of India, , 1964.

In fact, this casts serious doubt on the hagiographical account of the conversion itself, and is further reason to revise the dates of the three principal Nāyaṉmārs.

the [*Tevāram*] trio did not visit the Pallava-founded temples'.[108] Swamy dismisses this as a sentimental explanation,[109]suggesting instead that the Nāyaṉmārs be dated to the tenth century when a large number of structural temples were in existence.[110] Apart from the fact that this still fails to answer the apparent neglect of cave temples by the hymnists, his solution is incompatible with both the larger socio-economic picture and the abundant inscriptional evidence of the hymns being recited in the ninth and tenth centuries.[111]

The earliest of the *Pāñcarātra Samhitās*, the *Jayākhya*, is dated, on account of some architectural elements it contains, between 600 and 850 CE by Gonda.[112] An eighth-century inscription from the Sundaravarada-p-Pĕrumāḷ Temple in Uttiramerur, Chingleput *tāluk*, in Sanskrit/Pallava Grantha, records that the said shrine was built by 'truthful and dexterous' Parameśvara Takṣaka of Pāṭaka, in conjunction with the *āgamikas* of the village versed in the Āgamic principles and practice.[113] This Āgamic literature is mainly concerned with the construction of temples and images, the rules of rituals, in short, the rules of religious praxis.[114]

108 Swamy, op. cit., p. 148. The opinion seems to be shared by Professor R. Champakalakshmi—personal communication.

109 Swamy, op. cit., p. 148.

110 Ibid., pp. 119–80. R. Champakalakshmi, 'Religious Conflict in the Tamil Country: A Reappraisal of Epigraphic Evidence', *Journal of the Epigraphic Society of India*, vol. 5, pp. 69–81, has presented a convincing argument against Swamy's dating. While agreeing that Swamy's dating is too late to be plausible, I feel that there is a strong case for downward revision of the accepted dates for the Śaiva *mūvar* by about a century or two. If Mahendravarman Pallava were indeed Appar's protégé and convert as the hagiographies maintain, why does he never mention the temples he built to Śiva? I have outlined other reasons for a later dating of the Nāyaṉmārs in the introductory chapter.

111 See Chapter 1–iii of the present work.

112 M. Matsubara, *Pāñcarātra Saṁhitās and early Vaiṣṇava Theology*, Delhi: Motilal Banarsidass Publishers Pvt. Ltd., 1994, p. 19.

113 Mahalingam, 1985, vol. III, p. 259, Cg 1049. Ref.: *ARE*, 1898, no. 50; *SII* vi, no. 333.

114 Matsubara, op. cit., p. 35.

Also, R. Champakalakshmi, 'Śankara and Puranic Religion', in *Ancient to Modern: Religion, Power and Community in India*, ed. Ishita Banerjee-Dube and Saurabh Dube, New Delhi: Oxford University Press, 2009, p. 50, points out, 'Later Purāṇas followed new modes of legitimation of the brahmanical order (*varṇa*) whenever and wherever this order was threatened. In the process, the *Āgamas/Tantras* came to be recognized as an important source of authority in religious matters, particularly temple worship, rituals and sectarian practices'.

Prescriptive texts are not created in a vacuum but evolve through practice.[115] It seems, thus, unlikely that worship in cave temples could have been prohibited by the *Āgamas* in so early a period as the sixth–seventh centuries. Second, if there did already exist at this date such a prohibition (which I doubt), would it not have served to discourage the mobilization of resources towards making such temples? What seems probable is that as structural temples came to vastly outnumber cave temples, the latter came to be considered insufficiently sacred in the prescriptive literature. The relative abundance of bhakti poetry in praise of structural temples—brick-and-mortar, as well as stone—in comparison to those glorifying rock-cut shrines would have contributed to the crystallization of this position.

The assumption that cave temples were not considered worthy of hymns by the saint-poets is brought into question by significant exceptions such as the Tāyumāṉavar shrine in Tiruccirāppaḷḷi,[116] the Puṇḍarikākṣa-p-Pĕrumāḷ Temple in Tiruvĕḷḷarai[117] and the Śiva and

[115] J.A.B. van Buitenen, *Āgama Prāmāṇyam of Yāmuna* (Sanskrit Text and English Translation with Introduction), Madras: Ramanuja Research Society, 1971, p. 5, points out that the 'Pāñcarātra texts abundantly demonstrate that they had grown out of temple service and recorded practices that had been observed since long'.

[116] The Tāyumāṉavar shrine in Tiruccirāppaḷḷi is a cave temple dedicated to Śiva built high up on a hillock (called the Rock-fort). Personal visit. Appar and Sambandar have devoted one *patikam* each to the shrine. The upper levels of the hill have yielded stone beds of Śramaṇas with traces of obliterated writing dated to the seventh century, probably names of monks and titles of Pallava kings. Other Jaina epigraphs in natural caverns in the same hill are dated to the third–fourth centuries CE. Ref.: A. Ekambaranathan and C.K. Sivaprakasam, *Jaina Inscriptions in Tamil Nadu. A Topographical List*, Madras: Research Foundation for Jainology, 1987, pp. 444–8.

[117] A temple to Viṣṇu carved out of whitish rocks near Srirangam. Personal visit. Tirumankai has dedicated a decad to the shrine, *Pĕriya Tirumŏḻi* 5.3.1–10.

Mahalingam, 1985, vol. VIII, p. 104. Tp 486. Ref.: *ARE*, 1905, no. 541; *SII* xii, no. 40, p. 16; *EI*, xi, no. 16, pp. 154–8 is a Tamil inscription of the fifth regnal year of Pallava Dantivarman, i.e. 805 CE, from this temple. Dantivarman is said to have been born in the Pallavatilaka family which sprang from the Bhāradvāja *gotra*. The inscription records the digging of a great well at Tĕṉṉūr, a suburb of Tiruvĕḷḷarai, by a private individual and a verse on the transient nature of worldly life, enjoining all to do charitable deeds, before they are caught in the clutches of old age, so as to perpetuate their name.

Viṣṇu temples in TiruMěyyam.[118] Most surviving rock-cut shrines are situated in Tŏṇṭaimaṇḍalam and Pāṇṭimaṇḍalam.[119] In Mahabalipuram, Tirumankai seems to have neglected the cave shrines with Vaiṣṇava themes while hymning the shore temple. Considering his celebration of eleven temples in Nānkūr, this is intriguing. Are there other hymned structural temples—Śaiva or Vaiṣṇava—in the vicinity of neglected cave shrines? I present here, a conjectural hypothesis which needs to be corroborated by further intensive field research and superimposed mapping of rock-cut shrines with *divya deśa* temples. The evidence I have presented earlier establishes that there may not always have been physical structures when the Āḻvārs sang of a sacred spot of Viṣṇu, that many of the 'hymned temples' came into being in a later period, and that the Śrīvaiṣṇava tradition itself recognizes that the Āḻvārs' pilgrimages may sometimes be more notional than real. On the other hand, there are also 'unsung' old cave temples, sometimes proximate to comparatively newer ones which have been hymned. It seems probable, then, that the later tradition, being strongly influenced by the *Āgamas*, neglected the cave temples mentioned by the saints and preferred to invest more recent, structural temples that agreed with Āgamic architectural prescriptions with the sanctity of the *NDP* hymns wherever possible.[120]

[118] Personal visit. The two temples are nearly adjacent to one another and carved out of the same hill. The Śiva temple is a *vāyppu talam* mentioned by Appar while the Viṣṇu temple has been mentioned by Tirumankai in *Pěriya Tirumŏḻi* 2.5.8; 3.6.9; 5.5.2; 6.8.7; 8.2.3; 9.2.3; 10.1.5 and 11.7.5. Interestingly, the name of Śiva here is Satyagiriśvara and that of Viṣṇu, Satyamūrti. The Tamil word *měy* (from which the place name is derived) means truth.

Inscriptional evidence shows that the cave temple was in existence by at least the early eighth century. Mahalingam, 1985, vol. VI, p 205. Pk 834. Ref.: *ARE*, 1906, no. 402; IPS no. 13; Ibid. (Trans), pp. 14–15 is written in archaic Tamil of the second half of eighth century CE on a parapet slab in the west *prākāra* of the central shrine in the Satyagirinātha-p-Pěrumāḷ Temple. It records a renovation, probably of the temple, by a lady, and the gift to the central shrine (*uṇṇaḻikaippuram*) of the temple of lands including cultivation and proprietary rights (*kārāṇmai* and *mīyāṭci*).

[119] The topography of much of Coḻanāḍu is plains irrigated by the Kaveri. Two of the above-mentioned, 'living' cave temples are, however, in the heart of Coḻamaṇḍalam.

[120] I am not familiar with the primary source texts of the *Āgamas*, but have not come across any specific injunction against cave temples in any of the secondary literature describing the rules of *caryā* and *kriyā*. Perhaps this supposed Āgamic prohibition of worship in such temples is merely derivative.

Where patronage may not have been forthcoming for the construction of structural temples, where the descriptions of the temple-structure or the lord within by the saint-poets was far too specific to allow imaginative interpretations, or where an older local tradition of worship in and pilgrimage to the cave shrine was strongly established, the older cave shrines came to be counted within the standardized scheme.

Finally, it is also possible that the Śaiva and Śrīvaiṣṇava pilgrimage networks deliberately chose to underline Śaiva and Vaiṣṇava presence in Jaina strongholds.[121] In fact, Champakalakshmi has argued that Śaivas may have appropriated the old Jaina site of Tiruccirāppaḷḷi around the seventh century when Mahendravarman Pallava recorded, in the same hill, his conversion from Jainism to Śaivism.[122] I suggest a similar process in the case of the rock-cut shrines at TiruMĕyyam; it is possible that Śaiva and Vaiṣṇava symbols were either superimposed on Jaina ones at this site, or obliterated and replaced them.[123] I further suggest that this process was one that was not limited to the high-point of the bhakti

---

Āgamic rituals prescribe clockwise circumambulation of the shrine, always keeping it to one's right, since this is supposed to confer auspiciousness and power on it. I wonder if cave temples were frowned upon or regarded as insufficiently sacred as circumambulation of the central shrine therein is often not possible as in the case of structural temples where a *prākāra* encircles the *garbha gṛha*.

[121] TiruMĕyyam in the Putukkoṭṭai district, a little south of the Tanjavur-Kumbhakoṇam zone, is very close to Cittaṉavācal, Nārttāmalai and several other Jaina centres. The earliest inscriptions from Cittaṉavācal date from the second-first centuries BCE. Continued Jaina presence here up till at least the thirteenth century and in several neighbouring sites is attested by inscriptions. The hilly area of Ammācatram in the same district was the site of an important Jaina monastery and temple, the Tiruppaḷḷimalai, which received endowments in the late ninth century (*ARE*, 1941–2, nos. 209–10). Seven inscriptions from various temples in the TiruMĕyyam *tāluk* itself, dated to different periods, recording grants of land refer to (Jaina) *paḷḷiccantam* land being excluded from the said grant. Ref.: Ekambaranathan and Sivaprakasam, op. cit., pp. 462–4. Finally, an undated inscription that mentions Guṇasena (probably a Jaina monk) enunciating the art of playing the *parivādini*, a musical instrument, has been found to the left of the entrance of the above rock-cut temple itself. Ref.: Ekambaranathan and Sivaprakasam, op. cit., pp. 313–14. Also Mahalingam, 1985, vol. VI, p. 660. Pk 660. Ref.: *ARE*, 1940–1, no. 221; *IPS*, no. 4 Ibid. (Trans), pp. 10–11.

[122] Champakalakshmi, 'Religious Conflict in the Tamil Country', p. 71. However, the reading of the inscription remains controversial.

[123] An analogous example is Badarinath, an important centre of Vaiṣṇava pilgrimage, where the image of the deity in the central shrine is clearly that

movement alone as argued earlier but may have been carried out even in the second millennium, in the course of consolidation of pilgrimage networks.[124] Āgamic reservations regarding cave temples could probably be overlooked in the larger battle against the heterodox faiths.

The relationship of the pilgrimage tradition with the hymnal one is delineated by an interesting example of a kind different from those considered earlier here. We have seen instances where several *divya deśas* are incorporated in the same temple, partly because the hymns had traditionally been read to signify shrines where they may not have been intended by the saints, and failed eventually to be successfully elaborated in architectural form. The reverse is the case with the Tañjai-mā-maṇi-k-koyil in Tanjavur.[125] Three separate temple structures separated by a few hundred metres from one another are said to together constitute one *divya deśa*.[126] None of the four references to this shrine in the hymns of Pūtam and Tirumankai specify the form of the deity or temple. We have seen that the Tanjavur region in the heart of the fertile Kaveri basin has perhaps the highest concentration of temples in the Tamil country. I suggest that more than one patron decided, probably at different points of time, to consecrate the hymns on Tañjai-mā-maṇi as temples, and

of Buddha. Personal communication from Professor Narayani Gupta, after her visit to the temple.

124 An inscription in tenth-century Sanskrit Grantha characters from Chitaral in Kanyakumari district records the setting up of a stone entrance to the shrine of the goddess/*yakṣī* Varasundari. A later inscription, in Tamil, dated to 1250 CE, from the same place, refers to the same shrine as that of Bhagavati. Ref: Ekambaranathan and Sivaprakasam, op. cit., pp. 124–5, Ref.: *TAS*, vol. IV, no. 41, and *TAS*, vol. I, p. 194. Clearly, the takeover of old Jaina shrines was a widespread phenomenon.

An aside: Not far from the Arjuna's Penance panel in Mahabalipuram is a realistic sculpture from living rock of a group of three monkeys, the mother picking lice out of the child's head. The monkeys unmistakeably bear Śrīvaiṣṇava *nāmam* (caste marks) on their foreheads! Are these caste marks as old as the Pallava sculptures themselves? Or, given the reverence in which monkeys are generally held due to their association with Hanumān, were they etched by some zealous Śrīvaiṣṇava(s) in later centuries?

125 Tañjai-mā-maṇi= great gem of Tañjai, i.e. Tanjavur. The shrine is hymned in *Pĕriya Tirumŏḻi* 1.1.6; 2.5.3; 7.3.9, and *Iraṇṭām Tiruvantādi* 70.

126 Personal visit. The *sthalapurāṇa* recites how three demons were killed, two by the Lord Viṣṇu which explains two of the temples and the third by Devi, who also has a related shrine in Tanjavur. The third temple that constitutes the Vaiṣṇava *divya kṣetra* is supposed to signify the site of the lord's original appearance in response to the gods' plea for help against the demons.

deference to the politically, economically or socially powerful patrons caused all three temples to be considered embodiments of the hymns.

It has frequently been noted that bhakti introduced a deeply emotional form of worship that privileged simple devotion expressed through offerings of flowers, leaves, water, etc., in place of the older, Sanskritic forms.[127] The word *pūjā* is said to derive from the Tamil *pū-cĕy*, i.e. to 'do' with flowers.[128] Jarl Charpentier has, however, derived the word from the Tamil *pūcu*, meaning, to smear or daub, and concluded that the most characteristic feature of *pūjā* is washing or sprinkling the image with water, honey or curds, or daubing it with red paint in lieu of earlier blood sacrifices.[129] Both anointing the image of the deity with ash, vermillion and sandal paste and offering flowers, fragrant substances and betel nut to the deity appear, from the Āḻvārs' hymns, to have been established forms of worship in the second half of the first millennium CE. It also appears that certain temple rituals which are assumed by the Śrīvaiṣṇava tradition and its literature to have been in existence from times immemorial may have had their beginnings in the seventh–eighth centuries. The ritual of waking the god with the singing of the *Tiruppaḷḷiyĕḻucci*[130] in the temple at Srirangam is today replicated in most temples, sometimes with *Suprabhātams* composed for the specific deity enshrined therein.[131] It seems from an examination of the ten stanzas of the *Tiruppaḷḷiyĕḻucci* that there was a pre-existing tradition of ritually opening the temple in the morning with offerings of flowers and garlands—easily imagined as the temple demarcates sacred space from profane space.[132] Tŏṇṭaraṭippŏṭi's addressing a hymn to the lord describing the beauties of dawn and the eagerness of both humans and celestials to worship him with music thus created and elaborated a pattern of ritual to which additions and variations accrued over the centuries.

[127] Suvira Jaiswal, *Origin and Development of Vaiṣṇavism*, Delhi: Munshiram Manoharlal, 1980, p. 114.

[128] Personal communication from Professor J. Parthasarathi—attributed by him to Suniti Kumar Chatterjee.

[129] Jaiswal, op. cit., p. 138 (footnote no. 4: Jarl Charpentier, *Indian Antiquary*, 1927, p. 98).

[130] The 'wake-up' song composed by Tŏṇṭaraṭippŏṭi.

[131] A good example is the *Venkaṭeśa Suprabhātam* for the lord of Tiruppati which is perhaps the most popular of the genre.

[132] I have borrowed the contrastive terminology from the title in Larry Shiner, 'Sacred Space, Profane Space, Human Space', *Journal of the American Academy of Religion*, vol. 40, no. 4, 1972, pp. 425–36.

In fact, we find at least two inscriptional records of the performance of *śrībali* and *tiruppaḷḷiyĕḻucci* ceremonies from the tenth century itself. The earlier record comes from the Sundaravarada-p-Pĕrumāḷ Temple in Uttiramerūr (968–9 CE).[133] It is tempting to conjecture that the ritual involved singing Tŏṇṭaraṭippŏṭi's hymn since it is a Viṣṇu temple. The second record comes from the Karkoṭakeśvara Temple in Kumarasavalli, Uṭaiyārpālayam *tāluk* (979 CE).[134] References to such ceremonies in the eleventh–twelfth centuries become substantially greater.

It is clear that already by the ninth–tenth centuries, many of the ritual practices and festivities associated with temples had a fair degree of currency and popularity in the Tamil country. In the Vallīśvara Temple in Mānkāṭu, Sriperumbudur *tāluk*, an inscription of Pallava Nandivarman III's reign, dated to *circa* 863 CE, records some provision made by the Ceḻivāṇiyar (merchant community) of Kuṉṟattūr in Puliyūrkkuṭikoṭṭam for offerings in the local temple on the Tiruvātirai, new moon (*talaivuvā*) and full moon (*tinkal nilavu*) days, throughout the *sabhā* of Tiruvĕḷḷikīḻ.[135] A record from the Lakṣminārāyaṇa Temple in Kāvāntaṭalam, Chingleput *tāluk*, dated to the eighteenth regnal year of Pallava Kampavarman, i.e. *circa* 887 CE, records a gift of gold with which the *sabhaiyār* of the *caturvedimangalam* in Tamaṉūr *nāḍu* undertook to maintain (among other things), the celebration every year of the *Cittirai Tiruvoṇam* festival for 7 days, providing daily 100 lamps, engaging 16 drummers (*taṭṭaḷi kŏṭṭikaḷ*), performing the sacred bath (*snāpanam*) of the god and offering sacred food offerings for 7 days.[136] From the Puṇḍarikākṣa-p-Pĕrumāḷ Temple in Tiruvĕḷḷarai,[137] Lālkuṭi *tāluk*, an inscription of 978 CE registers a gift of 20 *kaḻañcu* of gold for offerings to the deities Kṛṣṇa and his consort, Rukmiṇi-pirāṭṭiyār, in the Pĕriya Śrīkoyil (big temple) at Tiruvĕḷḷarai by Irāyiraṉdevi Ammaṉār, wife of Uṭaiyār-āṉaimeṟṟuñciṉār (Rājāditya). The offerings (4 *nāḻi* of rice) were to be given on the days of full moon and new moon, *aṣṭami*, and *sankrānti*, and another gift of gold was made

133 Mahalingam, 1985, vol. III, pp. 280–1. Cg 1115. Ref.: *ARE*, 1898, no. 49; *SII* ii, no. 194.

134 Mahalingam, 1985, vol. VIII, p. 334. Tp 1510. Ref.: *ARE*, 1914.

135 Mahalingam, 1985, vol. III, p. 447. Cg 1758. Ref.: *ARE*, 1929–30, no. 352; *SII* no. 53.

136 Mahalingam, 1985, vol. III, p. 207. Cg 848. Ref.: *ARE*, 1901, no. 208; *SII* vii, no. 421.

137 Cave temple mentioned earlier.

for a lamp.[138] Donations for offerings on *sankrānti*,[139] feeding devotees on the occasion of Māci Makam festival,[140] celebrations of Mārkaḻi Tiruvātirai and Vaikāci Tiruvātirai (auspicious days: Tiruvātirai asterism of the months of Mārkaḻi and Vaikāci) with the performance of *Cākkai kūttu* dances,[141] consecration of the image of Goddess Umā Bhaṭṭāraki (adopted as a daughter by the donor, a woman) in the local temple and celebration of her marriage with the god,[142] establish the elaboration of the temple culture by the first millennium.

An inscription from the Varadarāja-p-Pĕrumāḷ Temple in Kāñcī dated to 1135 CE records a gift of bathing with 81 pots of water Lord Aruḷāla-p-Pĕrumāḷ who was pleased to take his stand at TiruvAttiyūr.[143] This inscription assumes significance as it was for the daily bath of this deity in this temple that Rāmānuja is supposed to have performed the *nitya kainkarya* of bringing pots of water. Since Rāmānuja was well-established by this time as the *darśana pravartaka* in Srirangam—indeed, he would have been 118 years old if the standard dating of his life is correct—repetition of a ritual performed by the great *ācārya* in his youth might have been considered a particularly meritorious act.

The hagiographic legend of Pĕriyāḻvār and Āṇḍāḷ demonstrates the integration of such cultic practices through their sanctification as practices of the revered saint-poets. That Pĕriyāḻvār was a temple priest in Śrīvilliputtūr[144] and particularly attached to the form of Kṛṣṇa as a child is fairly evident from his own hymns.[145] The episode of Pĕriyāḻvār's debate with scholars of other persuasions and his eventual victory

[138] Mahalingam, 1985, vol. VIII, p. 108. Tp 507. Ref.: *ARE*, 1905, no. 534; *SII* vii, no. 132, pp. 278–9.

[139] Mahalingam, 1985, vol. VIII, p. 363. Tp 1644. Ref.: *ARE*, 1924, no. 399. Sundareśvara temple, Melappaḻuvūr, 996 CE.

[140] Mahalingam, 1985, vol. VIII, p. 265. Tp 1192. Ref.: *ARE*, 1903, no. 266; *SII*, no. 571, p. 291. Dārukavaneśvara Temple in Tiruppālatturai, Tiruccirāppaḷḷi *tāluk*, 1009 CE.

[141] Mahalingam, 1985, vol. VIII, pp. 336–7. Tp 1521. Ref.: *ARE*, 1914, no. 65; ibid., part ii, para 22. Karkoṭakeśvara Temple, Kamarasavalli, Uṭayar pālayam *tāluk*, 1041 CE.

[142] Mahalingam, 1985, vol. VIII, p. 165. Tp 771. Ref.: *ARE*, 1936–7, no. 151. Agnīśvara Temple, Kumāravayalūr, Tiruccirāppaḷḷi *tāluk*, 985 CE.

[143] Mahalingam, 1985, vol. III, p. 161. Cg 655. Ref.: *ARE*, 1919, no. 471.

Aruḷāla is the Tamil equivalent of Varadarāja, and Attiyūr or Hastigiri is the old name for this temple.

[144] *Tiruppallāṇṭu* 11.

[145] *Pĕriyāḻvār Tirumŏḻi* 1.2.1–10, 1.3.1–21, 1.4.1–10, 1.5.1–10, 1.6.1–11, etc.

replays the motif of the *ācāryas*' debates with Advaitins and reiterates the superiority of the Vaiṣṇava faith. Equally significant is the finale to the story—the lord's appearance in all his glory before the Āḻvār, which serves various purposes. For one, it explains the composition of the unique poem, the *Tiruppallāṇṭu*. This hymn of eleven stanzas that has given birth to an entire genre of hymnal literature called the *mangalāśāsana* is extraordinary in that a human being—the Āḻvār—bestows blessings on the Supreme Lord, wishing him, his consort and his accoutrements everlasting[146] life and glory.[147] Also, it underlines the Śrīvaiṣṇava belief that the lord is himself attached to his devotee and can scarcely bear separation from the latter. Finally, it outlines celebratory rituals which came to feature prominently in temple festivities: the lord's appearance among his human devotees in secular spaces beyond his divine realm is re-enacted in the regular procession of the *utsava mūrti* with music and chanting of Sanskrit and Tamil hymns in the streets immediately around the temple walls, and on various specified occasions, even further beyond.

The story of Āṇḍāḷ has Pĕriyāḻvār reciting the glory of the different places where the lord resides; this, indeed, seems to be the occasion when the concept of 108 *divya deśas* is first articulated. However, none of the three hagiographies, the *DSC*, *Agpp* and *Mgpp*, actually describes more than a few places in this context even though they all agree that Āṇḍāḷ chose the lord of Srirangam after hearing about all 108. In fact, the three hagiographies send Tirumankai Āḻvār and the *ācāryas* Nāthamuni and Rāmānuja on pilgrimages to places other than the standard 108 too. Though the date of the enumeration of the *pāṭal peṟṟa talankaḷ* in the Śaiva tradition cannot be accurately established, there can be no doubt that by the twelfth–thirteenth centuries, when the earliest Śrīvaiṣṇava hagiographies were composed, the fact that several hundred of Śiva's beloved places had been hallowed by the hymns of the Nāyaṉmārs was reasonably well known. This is especially significant since the last two or three centuries would have seen the elaboration of a great number of these shrines into structural temples under the aegis of the Coḻa monarchs.

146 Strictly speaking, many crores of hundred thousand years.

147 The theme is reiterated in several of his poems addressed to the baby Kṛṣṇa, especially one where Yaśoda urges the child to come so that she can perform the rites to ward off the evil eye. See *Pĕriyāḻvār Tirumŏḻi* 2.8.1–10. This solicitousness towards the lord is almost unique to Pĕriyāḻvār though other Āḻvārs have also sung of the lord as a child.

I suggest that since the Śrīvaiṣṇava *ācāryas* would have known—from their careful examination of the *NDP*—that the number of shrines dedicated by the Āḻvārs to Viṣṇu were markedly lesser, they decided upon 108, a number traditionally considered sacred. A preliminary delineation of the sacred geography is also seen in the elaboration in the *DSC*, put in Śaṭhakopa's words, in the context of Godā's *svayamvara*, of the number of shrines in Coladeśa, Pāṇḍyadeśa, Keraladeśa, Toṇḍīr, Madhyadeśa and the north.[148] While the residences of the lord of which the Āḻvārs sang might have been identified with specific sites, and a few score temples might already have come to be elevated as especially revered shrines by the thirteenth century, the actual elaboration of a specifically Śrīvaiṣṇava pilgrimage network took place later; indeed, it was a process that was carried out over several centuries.

The concept of *tīrtha* and the practice of *tīrthayātrā* as acts of piety are first mentioned in the *Viṣṇusmṛti*, a work of the third century.[149] Hazra's proposal of dates between 700 and 1400 CE for the Puranic chapters on holy places[150] should be seen in the context of the bhakti evidence of journeys to different sacred sites. Epigraphic evidence is not wanting either. In 1012 CE, a grant was made in the Aḻakiya Narasimha-p-Pĕrumāḷ Temple, Ĕṉṉāyiram, Viḻuppuram *tāluk* for, among other things, feeding 1,000 Vaiṣṇavas and *dāsas* who came to witness the festival of Āṉi-Aṉulam. Two inscriptions from the Vīrattāṉeśvara Temple in Tiruttaṇi dated to 1013 CE register sale of land to a private individual for feeding pilgrims going to and returning from Venkaṭam.[151] Even the notion of pan-Indian pilgrimage seems to have been established by the early medieval centuries as seen from a fascinating inscription dated to 1050 CE from the Ammaināṭha Temple in the Ambāsamudram *tāluk* of Tirunelveli district in the deep south of India which registers a gift from Yogadeva and Somadevi, belonging to Kaśmīradeśam, for burning a perpetual lamp in the temple of Kayilāyamuṭaiya Mahādeva at Nigarilicoḷa-caturvedimangalam, a *brahmadeya* in Muḷḷināḍu.[152]

[148] Since this episode features in the *DSC*, I have used the *DSC*'s Sanskritized versions here for Coḻanāḍu, Pāṇṭiyanāḍu, Malaināḍu, Toṇṭaināḍu, Naṭunāḍu, and Vaṭanāḍu. *DSC, sargaḥ* 12, verse 18.

[149] R.N. Nandi, *Social Roots of Religion in Ancient India*, Calcutta: KP Bagchi & Co., Calcutta, 1986, p. 46.

[150] Ibid., p. 47.

[151] Mahalingam, 1985, vol. III, p. 495. Cg 1959 and 60. Ref.: *ARE*, 1905, nos. 429, 430.

[152] Mahalingam, 1985, vol. IX, p. 53. Tn 244. Ref.: *ARE*, 1916, no. 613; *SII* xiv, no. 197, p. 112.

The twin emphases on pilgrimage and on numerous shrines of each god would have served to accommodate local deities and pre-existent sacred centres, in fact, as early as the period of the saint-poets of both Śaiva and Vaiṣṇava persuasions, 'elevating' the local shrine to the status of the great god of the brahmanical pantheon and, on the other hand, making the latter accessible. This would of course have larger implications as well—the role of the Āḻvārs and Nāyaṉmārs in popularizing brahmanical worship and the socio-economic consequences of the same have been discussed by several scholars.[153] I suggest that beside these well-known reasons, pilgrimage could also be an attempt to accommodate the essential polytheism of the masses. Indeed, the monotheism of the Tamil saint-poets incorporates a deeper polytheism: the Āḻvārs singing of Narasimha, Vāmana–Trivikrama, Rāma and Kṛṣṇa may be explained as expressions of the *vyūha* concept,[154] but acceptance of these as incarnations of Viṣṇu is itself a historic process of accommodation and integration.[155] Further, I suggest that the Āḻvārs and Nāyaṉmārs, like the majority of the people among whom they lived, were also imbued with 'ideal polytheism'[156] which, however, due to their focus on and deep devotion to a particular god, found expression by imaging him in different forms.[157] Their singing of their chosen lord, whose heroic, amatory and compassionate deeds they praise in shrine after shrine, is also an expression of this polytheism. The acaryic tradition, in the Śrīvaiṣṇava case at least, gave pattern, over a period of several centuries, to this old polytheistic culture through its formalization of the pilgrimage network and, in the process, also wove in more contemporary communitarian concerns. Meanwhile, local legends and origin myths found a larger area of circulation and came to claim Puranic status through their absorption

[153] See Chapters 4 and 5 of the present work.

[154] Hudson, 'The Śrīmad Bhagavat Purāṇa in Stone', pp. 137–82. Also see, Dennis Hudson, 'Āṇḍāḷ Āḻvār: A Developing Hagiography', *Journal of Vaishnava Studies*, vol. 1, no. 2, 1993, pp. 27–61, and Dennis Hudson, 'Bathing in Krishna: A Study in Vaiṣṇava Hindu Theology', *Harvard Theological Review*, vol. 78, 1980, pp. 539–66. Hudson reads the hymns of the Āḻvārs as expositions of Pāñcarātra philosophy.

[155] See Jaiswal, op. cit., pp. 32–87 and 118–32; see also, Kesavan Veluthat, 'Ideology and Legitimation: Early Medieval South Asia', in *Mind over Matter: Essays on Mentalities in Medieval India*, ed. D.N. Jha and Eugenia Vanina, New Delhi: Tulika Books, 2009, p. 3.

[156] See Chapter 5 of the present work for a discussion of this concept.

[157] Śiva is imaged as Dakṣiṇāmūrti, Lingodbhavamūrti, etc.

into the brahmanical temple just as locally important communities found representation in its ritual activities.

The distinct identities and attributes of the *mūla* and *utsava mūrtīs* in each temple both reinforce 'ideal polytheism' and signify the successful integration of local myths and communities. The *mūlavar* in the temple at Śrīvaikuṇṭham[158] in the Tirunelveli district is called Śrīvaikuṇṭhanāthan̲ and the *utsavar* Kaḷḷapirān/Coranāthan̲.[159] The *sthalapurāṇa* attributes its origin myth to the *Brahmāṇḍa Purāṇa*. When Brahmā's *satyaloka* was inundated with water during the *pralaya*, the demon Somakāsura stole the *rahasya granthas* pertaining to creation. Brahmā meditated at this spot and pleased Viṣṇu who retrieved the *granthas*. Since the lord had appeared here directly from Vaikuṇṭham, the site is known as Śrīvaikuṇṭham. The second story in this *sthalapurāṇa* bears an uncanny resemblance to some of the legends about Tirumankai Āl̲vār. A thief called Kālatūcan̲ always prayed to the lord in the above temple before setting out on his robbing expeditions and offered a generous share of the booty to the temple. Caught when robbing the royal palace once, he prayed to the lord who took the form of the devotee and appeared before the king. When the king questioned him, the lord showed him his heavenly form and admonished him for not discharging his kingly duties properly. The penitent ruler asked him to remain in the temple in the form he had appeared before him— as the lord of thieves. It must be noted that the local *kaḷḷar* community has an important ritual presence in the temple and the chief of the *kaḷḷars* is entitled to specific honours during various temple festivities.[160]

With the development of the pilgrimage tradition, sanctity came to be attributed to and claimed by different temples not only because of their localization of pan-Indian Puranic myths and even specifically Tamil ones, but also because of their claim to association with one or more of the Āl̲vārs or Nāyan̲mārs. Thus, the temple tank of Kavittalam (Sanskrit: Kapisthalam) is claimed to be the site of Gajendramokṣam,

[158] The temple has *divya deśa* status through two mentions by Nammāl̲vār which may simply refer to the lord's cosmic station, i.e. Vaikuṇṭha. 'Reclining in Puḷinkuṭi, seated in Varaguṇamankai, standing in Vaikuṇṭha ...' *Tiruvāymŏl̲i* 9.2.4 and 'You who are in TirupPuḷinkuṭi of mansions which touch the moon/O Lord of Tiru-Vaikuṇṭha...', *Tiruvāymŏl̲i* 9.2.8.

[159] Both the Tamil and Sanskrit names mean 'the Lord of Thieves'.

[160] See Friedhelm Hardy, 'Ideology and Cultural Contexts of the Śrīvaiṣṇava Temple', *The Indian Economic and Social History Review*, vol. 14, nos. 1–2, 1977, pp. 119–51, for a discussion of community integration through this myth.

i.e. where Nārāyaṇa killed a crocodile to save his elephant-devotee.[161] Tirumaraiyūr derives its uniqueness from (among other things) being the only shrine where the *vigrahas* of all 108 *divya deśas* can be worshipped. The deities of all the temples apparently came here to oblige an aged *bhakta* who desired to see them but was unable to make the pilgrimages. The *sthalapurāṇa* of TiruvĀtaṉūr demonstrates how the shrine derives its special character from association with an Āḻvār. Once, when Tirumankai Āḻvār was engaged in the construction of the *prākāra* walls of the Srirangam Temple, he ran out of money and asked the lord to bail him out. Taking the form of a merchant (*vaniya*) with a merchant's headdress and carrying a *marakkāl* (a measure/a large measuring vessel), the lord of Srirangam appeared before the Āḻvār saying that Ranganātha had directed him to help the Āḻvār. Tirumankai asked the merchant why he had then come with an empty *marakkāl,* upon which he replied that if one prayed sincerely to Ĕmpĕrumāṉ, submitting in *śaraṇāgati* thrice, one could get whatever one wanted. The Āḻvār said he wanted the workmen paid. The 'merchant' proceeded to measure out the sands on the banks of the river, saying that the *marakkāl* would convert the sands into gold for those who had worked sincerely, but would give out only sand to shirkers. The onlookers were angered at what they presumed was a ruse to short-change them. The merchant fled but Tirumankai Āḻvār gave chase on his horse. He finally took refuge in Ātaṉūr and is, accordingly, enshrined there. Since he had picked up, en route, an *olai* (palm leaf) to write some accounts, that village is known as Olaippāṭi. The lord in Ātaṉūr is represented in the *śayana* pose, with a *marakkāl* under his head and holding a palm leaf in his hand.[162] This delightfully absurd story has no basis in the more authoritative hagiographies.[163] Ātaṉūr is enumerated in a long list of sacred spots in the *Pĕriya Tirumaṭal.*[164] The poem distinguishes or qualifies the lord in each locale in a phrase or two; in the context of Ātaṉūr,[165] it praises him as 'measurer of time/

[161] Etirajan, op. cit., pp. 81–3.

[162] Ibid., pp. 88–94.

[163] Other motifs woven into the story, such as the centrality of *śaraṇāgati* and the caste in which the lord chose to appear, and which he continues to represent through the iconography by the unusual accoutrements of *olai* and *marakkāl* underline other concerns of the community which were discussed in Chapters 3 and 4 of the present work.

[164] Ascribed to Tirumankai.

[165] *Pĕriya Tirumaṭal* 71/130. (There are two systems of counting the *Ciriya* and *Pĕriya Tirumaṭals.*)

master of all three phases of time'.[166] It is possible that this esoteric hymnal reference gave rise to the unique iconography in this temple and the above legend.[167] It is equally likely that this imaging of the lord as a merchant marked significant patronage from the mercantile community; the *sthalapurāṇa* eventually accounting for this sculptural curiosity through a story featuring the most enterprising Āḻvār of the hagiographies. In another instance of association, the *varaḷāru* of Kuṭantai[168] claims that the temple chariot was the gift of Tirumankai.[169] Similarly, the *sthalapurāṇa* of TirupPer Nagar claims that the site has salvific properties being the *kṣetra* of Nammāḻvār's last temple decad[170] and hence, of his *mokṣa*.[171]

Indeed, with the growth in the numbers of temples, such associations might have been stratagems employed by different temples to establish themselves as unique and as capable of conferring special blessings, merit, relief from specific ailments, etc. The legend of the lord favouring an Āḻvār or Nāyaṉār in a particular shrine would have helped to enhance its popularity. Such associations with Ranganātha of Srirangam are naturally numerous: Tiruppāṇāḻvār and Āṇḍāḷ were both absorbed into him by his divine grace; he was the focus of the worship of Tŏṇṭaraṭippŏṭi. Nammāḻvār, singing of the lord in Kumbhakoṇam, described him as Ārāvamutaṉ,[172] nectar that never satiates,[173] a phrase that, despite

[166] Srirama Bharati, op. cit., p. 738; Vankipuram Navanītam Vedānta Deśikaṉ, (Text with Tamil commentary and English Translation), *Āḻvār Tiruvuḷḷam: Iyarpā*, Madras: Śrī Viśiṣṭādvaita Research Centre, 1994, pp. 762–3.

'*aṉṉavaṉai Ātaṉūr āṇṭu aḷakkum aiyaṉai*'. Kanaka Jagannathan tentatively suggests these alternate readings: 'The Lord who rules, measures Ātaṉūr'/'The Lord of Ātaṉūr who rules with measure'.

[167] Sponsorship of this temple by local merchants might be another reason for the depiction of the deity as one.

[168] *Sthalapurāṇa* of Kuṭantai, Vaiṣṇava name for Kumbhakoṇam.

[169] Etirajan, op. cit., p. 98.

[170] *Tiruvāymŏḻi* 10.8.1–10.

[171] Etirajan, op. cit., pp. 69–71.

[172] Nammāḻvār describes the lord as Ārāvamuta elsewhere too, see *Tiruvāymŏḻi* 2.5.4 and 2.5.5. The decad beginning with this word addressed to the lord in Kumbhakoṇam is supposed to be the one recited by the pilgrims in Viranārāyaṇapuram. Nāthamuni is said to have given the name Ārāvamutaṉ (i.e. transformed a descriptive phrase into a proper noun) to the lord at Kumbhakoṇam. See *Mgpp*, Nāthamunikaḷ *vaibhavam*.

[173] The Sanskrit translation, *aparyāptāmṛta*, fails to capture the nuances and richness of the Tamil.

having become familiar as the given name of the lord in the said temple, never fails to amaze by its beauty. The iconography of the *garbha gṛha* in Kumbhakoṇam has associations with Tirumaḻicai Āḻvār.[174] Some of these associations may, however, be secondary in that the shrines which claim special or miraculous relationships with individual Āḻvārs or Nāyaṉmārs may have also been already revered shrines. Thus, the Śiva temple in TiruvŌṟṟiyūr (a suburb north of modern Madras) where Śiva is said to have facilitated the marriage of the Nāyaṉār Sundarar to his lady love, Cankili,[175] also has hoary associations with the serpent deity.[176]

An important sacred centre known from the late Sangam works *Pĕrumpāṇāṟṟupaṭai* and *Paripāṭal* is Vĕhkā in modern Kāñcī.[177] The early Āḻvārs— Pŏykai, Pey and Tirumaḻicai (though not Pūtam)— have sung of the lord reclining in Vĕhkā/Kacci-Vĕhkā.[178] An interesting aspect of the iconography at Vĕhkā is that Viṣṇu is represented here as reclining with his head supported on his left hand (and consequently, with his head to the right hand of the viewer) which is exceedingly unusual. According to the *sthalapurāṇa*, Sarasvatī in the form of the river Vegavatī repeatedly foiled Brahmā's attempts to perform a *yajña* in the holy site of Kāñcī by sweeping away the sacrificial site with her torrential waters. Brahmā prayed to Viṣṇu for help; the lord accordingly lay down on his serpent bed across the path of the furious river and tamed (and shamed) her. The site is said to derive its name from a corruption of Vegavatī.[179] The peculiar posture of the lord in the site is explained by a legend which draws in one of the early Āḻvārs.[180] Before examining the myths, however, let us try and situate the oddity as it were. Considering that

[174] See Chapter 2-ii of the present work.

[175] G. Vanmikanathan, *Periya Puranam by Sekkizhaar: Condensed English Version*, Madras: Sri Ramakrishna Math, 2004, pp. 98–106, 115–30.

[176] Shulman, op. cit., p. 119.

[177] Hardy, *Viraha Bhakti*, p. 230, 607.

[178] *Mutal Tiruvantādi* 77; *Mūṉṟām Tiruvantādi* 26, 62, 64; *Nāṉmukaṉ Tiruvantādi* 36.

Vĕhkā is probably the first temple referred to in Tamil literature. Ref.: Hardy, 'Ideology and Cultural Contexts of the Śrīvaiṣṇava Temple', pp. 121, 144, footnoting *Pĕrumpāṇāṟṟupaṭai* line 373.

[179] This myth seems to be a very old one as there are at least two inscriptions dated to 944 CE and 1032 CE in the Yathoktakāri temple that refer to the lord who lay as an anicut (dam/bridge) at TiruVĕhkā. Mahalingam, 1985, vol. III, pp. 153–4. Cg 628. Ref.: *ARE*, 1921, no. 21; ibid., part ii, p. 95 and Mahalingam, 1985, vol. III, p. 155. Cg 635. Ref.: *ARE*, 1921, no. 23.

[180] See Chapter 2–ii of the present work.

the image in question is six to eight feet long,[181] and can be presumed to have taken a fair amount of time to create and the involvement of several artisans as well, the possibility of it being a 'mistake' can be discounted. The second possibility is that both left-facing and right-facing Viṣṇus were familiar in an earlier period before *śilpa* and *āgama* prescriptions standardized the correct posture as the left-facing one, and that few other examples of the latter have survived. An example from the parallel Śaiva tradition will illuminate this argument. Śiva in the *Ānandatāṇḍava* is invariably represented with his right foot on the ground (trampling the demon Apasmara) and the left one upraised. I am told that there exists a bronze sculpture of the *Ānandatāṇḍava* in the Mīnākṣi Temple at Madurai where Śiva stands on his left leg.[182] According to a popular story that explains this peculiarity, two sages devoted to Śiva overcome by solicitude for the lord begged him to rest his right leg which had been eternally bearing his weight in the dance. Śiva immediately obliged his devotees by shifting to the other foot, and the sculpture is said to be a representation of this act of grace. This story naturally belongs to a period when the standardization of the iconographic form of the *Ānandatāṇḍava* had already taken place. Bronze sculptures of this form of Naṭarāja became common from the middle of the tenth century and were created with further elaborations in iconographic details through the eleventh century.[183]

There can be several reasons why this particular statue differed from the norm. Some temples may choose to enshrine a peculiar iconic form or adopt an out-of-the-way pattern of worship as a special feature to attract pilgrims in a competitive environment. The temple in question should, however, be one that has a reasonable degree of confidence in being able to carry off the exception without inviting censure from more orthodox elements.[184] Artisans can also be mischievous/they may wish to express their individual creativity in surprising ways.[185] This explanation may have more substance than appears at first sight. Among the hundreds

[181] Personal visit; the observation on size is approximate.

[182] Personal communication from Professor N.S. Sadagopan.

[183] Vidya Dehejia, *Art of the Imperial Cholas*, New York: Columbia University Press, 1990, pp. 39–47.

[184] This explanation was suggested to me by Professor John Stratton Hawley. He quoted the example of the Banke Bihari temple in Bṛndāvana which accentuated its uniqueness sometime in the middle of the last century by shortening to a few minutes at a time, the deity's revelation of himself to worshippers. This brevity enhanced the excitement of *darśana* dramatically.

[185] This explanation was suggested by Professor Vijaya Ramaswamy.

of sculptures in a pillared hall of the Viṭṭhala Temple in Hampi are two portrayals of Narasimha breaking out of a pillar in Hiraṇyakaśipu's netherworld palace in response to the devotion of the child Prahlāda. At much the same height from the ground, on two nearly adjacent pillars, these two remarkably different sculptures project either the individual visions of two different craftsmen or, the creative endeavour of the same sculptor to explore and interpret a given theme in distinct ways.[186] A third possibility is that at a particular juncture in history, a politically or ritually powerful group may decide to invest a particular iconographic form with legitimacy and choose to suppress those that go against the norm thus established.[187] Considering that Śiva is represented dancing (not necessarily the *Ānandatāṇḍava*) on the left leg as often as on the right in stone sculptures on temple walls in the eighth–ninth centuries[188] and that the Coḻa rulers adopted the Naṭarāja form as almost their dynastic deity in the tenth, this could be equally valid.

Let us try and see if any of the explanations for the unique Naṭarāja fit the unique sleeping Viṣṇu. Since Vĕhkā is among the earliest-known Viṣṇu shrines in the Tamil country, and since commissioning a massive new stone icon to replace an old and familiar one suggests almost insuperable obstacles, the first explanation cannot fit. The second is only partly convincing as the image in question is unlikely to have been independently executed by a single individual. On the other hand, it must be remembered that the iconic representations of Viṣṇu in a majority of the *divya deśas* are said to possess some distinguishing features.[189] While the bronze *utsava mūrtis* (processional images) are largely standardized,[190] Viṣṇu invariably represented standing, usually flanked by Śrīdevi and Bhūdevi, also standing, and sometimes accompanied also by an additional

[186] Personal visit.

[187] This explanation was suggested by Dr P.K. Basant.

[188] C. Sivaramamurti, *Nataraja in Art, Thought and Literature*, New Delhi: National Museum, 1974, photographs passim.

[189] Personal observation from pilgrimages.

[190] Art historians would, however, be able to distinguish differences in styles—indeed, one of the methods of dating bronzes from Tamil Nadu is by identifying the style. The Naṭarāja figure, for example, despite a certain standardization, evolved from the mid-tenth through the twelfth centuries. See Dehejia, *Art of the Imperial Cholas*, pp. 40–6, with photographs.

There are exceptions, of course. For instance, the face of the *utsava mūrti* named Peraruḷāḷaṉ in the Varadarāja Temple in Kāñcīpuram is badly pocked and pitted. This is said to be the result of the lord having emerged from Agni during a great sacrifice performed by Brahmā.

set of seated consorts, the *mūla mūrtis* made of stone, stucco or wood, are specific to the site despite conforming to a general norm. In the seated posture, for example, Viṣṇu may be shown as Narasimha (again, with variations as *ugra* or *yoga*, in the act of killing Hiraṇyakaśipu or with Lakṣmi in his lap) or 'at home'[191] enthroned upon the coils of Ananta. There is similar variety in the reclining posture, the lord portrayed as Padmanābha with a lotus bearing Brahmā issuing from his lap, solitary in *yogaśayana* or surrounded by his consorts and select devotees in *bhogaśayana*, resting the head on an arm and gazing towards the viewer/ worshipper or with outstretched arm and face turned upwards. Most of these are, however, elaborated within a basic formulation, i.e. the left-facing one. The most likely explanation, then, is that the Vĕhkā image belongs to a period before the standardization of the *śilpa* norms. Perhaps other Viṣṇus resting the head on the left hand were executed in more perishable materials. This explanation is bolstered by the fact that the *mūla mūrti* in Tiruvāṭṭāṟu[192] is a right-facing Viṣṇu. Interestingly, the *sthalapurāṇa* of this *divya kṣetra* elaborating the origin myth makes no mention of the posture of the lord except to state that the rays of the evening sun fall upon his face.[193] We know that the Vaikhānasa and Pāñcarātra Āgamas were never really accepted in Kerala;[194] considering that it is the Āgamic literature that prescribes only the right-facing position as proper for the reclining Viṣṇu, it is no surprise that the Tiruvāṭṭāṟu image did not give rise to any legends explaining its oddity. The silence of all the Āḻvārs who have mentioned Vĕhkā regarding the

[191] '*Vīṟṟirunta Pĕrumāḷ*', a specific description of the seated lord.

[192] This is one of the sacred shrines in the Kerala region sung by Nammāḻvār.

[193] *108 Vaiṣṇava Divya Deśa Vaibhavamum Purāṇa Abhimāna Stalankaḷum: A Pilgrims' Guide*, Madras: The Little Flower Company, 1984, revd. edn. 2002, pp. 103–4.

[194] The *sthalapurāṇa* of TirukKurunkuṭi says that during a pilgrimage to TiruvAnantapuram, Rāmānuja attempted to systematise worship in the temples there according to *Pāñcarātra* doctrine but was entirely unsuccessful. Apparently, the Nambūdiri priests of Kerala tried to harm Rāmānuja, and the lord, either out of consideration for him or heeding the prayers of his priests in the temple, had Garuḍa bodily lift Rāmānuja and deposit him in TirukKurunkuṭi while he slept at night. John Carman, *The Theology of Ramanuja: An Essay in Inter-Religious Understanding*, Bombay: Ananthacharya Indological Research Institute, 1981, p. 43, mentions a slightly different version told in the late Sanskrit text, *Prapannāmṛta*. The *DSC*, *Agpp*, *Mgpp* and *Rāmānujārya Divya Caritai* do not feature either version. Was it the Sanskrit text that borrowed the legend from the *sthalapurāṇa* or the other way round?

unusual posture suggests that it did not appear as peculiar to them as it does to us.[195] However, of the five Āḻvārs who have mentioned this shrine, Nammāḻvār may not have actually visited it as he mentions only two sites north of Kuṭantai–Viṇṇakar, viz., Tiruppati and Vĕhkā, both of which may have been honoured by him simply as old centres of Viṣṇu worship. Again, even if he did actually journey to Vĕhkā,[196] he may not have found the right-facing image strange, being familiar with a similar one at Tiruvāṭṭāṟu.[197] Tirumankai refers to Vĕhkā twice[198] and the lord as reclining in Kacci once;[199] in any case, the right-facing image did not excite comment from him any more than from the early Āḻvārs who, it has been suggested, belonged to a different devotional milieu from the later ones.[200]

The myth of the tamed river suggests that Kāñcī was perhaps the cult-centre of a powerful goddess who was eventually subjugated by the male god Viṣṇu. It also carries suggestions of older, autochthonous patterns of worship that were resistant to brahmanical forms such as the performance of Vedic sacrifices. That Kāñcī continued to be an important centre of goddess worship and to be considered one of the *śakti pīṭhas*, as the site of the goddess' sexual power (Kāmākṣi) indicates that the subordination of the goddess was never entirely successful though she was clearly forced to relinquish important spaces, both physical and ritual, to brahmanical deities.[201] An examination of this process is beyond the scope of this work, however.

[195] This is significant since the Āḻvārs often describe the image of the lord in his different beloved places carefully, remarking on any feature that distinguishes one standing, sitting or reclining Viṣṇu from another. See Chapter 2–ii of the present work for the Āḻvār's association with the slight peculiarity of the image in Kuṭantai.

[196] *Tiruviruttam* 26 mentions celestials worshipping the lord in Vĕhkā.

[197] *Tiruvāymŏḻi* 10.6.1–10.

[198] *Pĕriya Tirumŏḻi* 2.6.5, and *Tirunĕṭuntāṇṭakam* 8.

[199] *Pĕriya Tirumŏḻi* 10.1.7.

[200] Hardy, *Viraha Bhakti*, pp. 281–93.

[201] Kāñcī is metaphorically divided into Ci<u>nn</u>a (small) Kāñcī also known as Viṣṇu Kāñcī and Pĕriya (great) Kāñcī which is Śiva Kāñcī. A third section, slightly removed geographically, is Jina (Jaina) Kāñcī. This division roughly corresponds to the spatial distribution of temples in Kāñcī though there are some important Vaiṣṇava *divya deśas* in Pĕriya Kāñcī. Ci<u>nn</u>a Kāñcī is dominated by the Varadarāja-p-Pĕrumāḷ Temple which was the locus of the *ācāryas* of the Sanskritic school of Śrīvaiṣṇavism and benefited from patronage during the

What is relevant for us is that the subordination of the cult of the goddess by the worship of Viṣṇu had already been achieved by the period of the late Sangam texts and, even if the iconography did not invite comment in the earlier period, it had begun to call for justification by the time the explanatory legend was composed. It is tempting to credit the Śrīvaiṣṇava hagiographers with the construction of this myth, especially since we have seen how the stories about the Ā̱lvārs blend information available from their hymns with much that cannot be proved. Indeed, I have argued that the hagiographies served as another, perhaps more popular, mode of exegesis beside the comparatively dense commentaries and philosophical works. Since a corollary of this position might be that the hagiographies were merely purposive fiction, I would like to modify it. While the genre of hagiography might be thought to have allowed the *ācāryas* greater freedom in articulating their vision of the Śrīvaiṣṇava community, they were not by any means entirely free to tell a story as they wished. The second myth related to TiruVĕhkā, indeed, the one mentioned in the Śrīvaiṣṇava hagiographies,[202] finds inscriptional corroboration well before the composition of the earliest among them. The earliest of these epigraphs, dated to 1075 CE, is found in the Pāṇḍava-p-Pĕrumāḷ Koyil in Pĕriya Kāñcī. The record registering a grant of some land to the above temple mentions buying the same from the *ūr* of Orirukkai.[203] The latter happens to be a village in the outskirts of Kāñcī and claims to derive its name from a corruption of *ŏru-rāvu-irukkai* meaning, one-night's stay. The next two inscriptions come from the Yathoktakāri[204] temple itself. Dated to 1090 CE and 1104 CE, they record orders of the Co̱la king, Kulottunga I, granting two and three *velis* of land respectively for the temple of TiruvAnekatangāta-paṭamuṭaiya

---

Vijayanagara period. The goddess has been completely relegated to Śiva Kāñcī where, despite being mistress of her own temple as Kāmākṣi, she is usually considered the spouse of Śiva as Ekāmreśvara.

202 See Chapter 2–ii of the present work.

203 Mahalingam, 1985, vol. III, pp. 133–4. Cg 549. Ref.: *ARE*, 1893, no. 17; *SIT* iii, no. 68.

204 'He who Did as Told'. This is the name of the lord in the said temple since he is said to have rolled up his serpent-mat and left the village as his devotee asked him to.

Benjamin A. McClintic suggested that there might have been a popular memory of some *guru*/teacher/preceptor having moved away and been recalled. Over time, it might have changed to the lord moving away and returning.

Mahādeva,[205] i.e. the lord who does not stay more than one (night) and (rests under) the canopy of the serpent.

The dependence of the hagiographers on hoary oral traditions is seen again in the case of the *mutal* Āl̲vārs. Even though only two of the three Āl̲vārs who are said to have huddled together during the storm in an *iṭaikal̲i* (passageway) have mentioned TirukKovalūr in their hymns,[206] the hagiographies, usually so careful in using the evidence from the hymns, are clear about the poets of the three *Tiruvantādis* having come together. The correspondence is emphasized by the *ācāryas* glossing the first stanza of each of the three *Tiruvantādis* as a record of the particular divine experience.[207] To a 'secular' reader, however, there seems little connection between the verses in question and the experience they are supposed to refer to. Pŏykai does, however, speak of being granted a vision of the lord in an *iṭaikal̲i* in the context of Kovalūr.[208] In fact, Tirumankai, a later Āl̲vār, also refers to the lord of Kaṇṇamankai as the One who appeared in an *iṭaikal̲i* in Koval.[209] An inscription from the Trivikrama-p-Pĕrumāḷ Temple in TirukKovalūr dated to 1008 CE, recording donations for the conduct of a *tirumañjana* ceremony on the days of *uttarāyaṇam* and *dakṣināyaṇam* refers to the deity as TiruvIṭaikal̲i Āl̲vār[210] (the sacred–passageway–Lord). Three other inscriptions dated to the eleventh and twelfth centuries from the same temple speak of

[205] Mahalingam, 1985, vol. III, pp. 156–7. Cg 640–1. Ref.: *ARE*, 1890, nos. 24 and 22; *SII* ii nos. 77 and 78.

[206] Pŏykai, *Mutal Tiruvantādi*, 77 (mentions Kovalūr), and 86 (mentions *iṭaikal̲i*). Pūtam, *Iraṇṭām Tiruvantādi*, 70 (mentions Kovalūr).

[207] Pŏykai, *Mutal Tiruvantādi* 1, 'The earth is my lamp, the ocean my oil, the radiant sun the flame. I offer this garland of songs at the feet of the discus-bearing Lord to cross the ocean of misery'. Pūtam, *Iraṇṭām Tiruvantādi* 1, 'Love is my lamp, eagerness the oil, my heart the wick. Melting, I light this lamp and offer this Tamil garland of knowledge'. Pey, *Mūn̲rām Tiruvantādi* 1, 'I have see Tiru, I have His golden frame! I have seen His radiant complexion. I have seen Him of the lovely discus and the right-whirled conch'. Translation by Kanaka Jagannathan.

Tiru= Sanskrit Śrī and can be read both as a proper noun and as auspiciousness. The Śrīvaiṣṇava *ācāryas* interpret this reference to Tiru as indicative of the inseparability of the lord and Śrī—a theological concept of central importance.

[208] Pŏykai, *Mutal Tiruvantādi* 86.

[209] *Pĕriya Tirumŏl̲i* 7.10.4.

[210] Mahalingam, 1985, vol. II, p. 371. SA 1596. Ref.: *ARE*, 1900, no. 129; *SII* vii, no. 142.

the deity by this name.[211] The popular name of the deity in this temple evidently preserves memories of an old myth, possibly a local legend which, however, had gained sufficiently wide currency by the eighth century for Tirumankai to refer to it. Clearly then, there were older popular traditions about the Āḻvārs that the hagiographers could at best embellish and embroider with some details; if these older narratives provided them with a stock of colours with which to paint their canvases, they also circumscribed the final picture. In other words, it was within very well-defined limits that these hagiographical accounts could be articulated.

The account of Tŏṇṭaraṭippŏṭi Āḻvār allows an excellent demonstration of this kind of re-creation. Though at one level, it is a fairly typical trope on the dangers posed by women to spiritual aspirants, the specifics of the story show how the hagiographers knitted in references in the hymns of Tŏṇṭaraṭippŏṭi with contemporary reality. His speaking of himself in the signature verses as one who makes *tulasi* garlands for the lord[212] and as a flower-basket-bearer[213] indicates that he was a temple functionary, very likely a *brāhmaṇa*. The possibility is reinforced by his expressing regret at his 'forfeiting the rights of priesthood and the acts of feeding the three fires'.[214] It is not clear whether this is merely a stereotyped expression of lowliness or if the Āḻvār was actually penalized for some misdeed by revocation of priestly rights; the hagiographical tradition evidently read this along with several laments about the times he was caught in the 'net of fish-eyed women/women with long tresses'[215] and the time he was a thief, keeping company with rogues[216] to create a plausible story. In this context, some inscriptions of the thirteenth century acquire great interest. An inscription of the reign of Rājarāja III from the Tanjavur region records the calumny of some *Śivadrohins*. Two Śaiva *brāhmaṇas* are said to have stolen a jewel from the goddess and given it to a concubine, and committed further atrocities by confining to a dark cellar in the temple, a temple servant who claimed his due

[211] Mahalingam, 1985, vol. II, pp. 372–3. SA 1601. Ref.: *ARE*, 1900, no. 118; *EI* vii, no. 20(L), p. 146; Mahalingam, 1985, vol. II, p. 372. SA 1600. Ref.: *ARE* 1900, no. 123; *EI* vii, no. 20 (K); Mahalingam, 1985, vol. II, p. 375. SA 1609. Ref.: *ARE*, 1921, no. 349.

[212] *Tirumālai* 45.

[213] *Tiruppaḷḷiyĕḻucci* 10.

[214] *Tirumālai* 25.

[215] *Tirumālai* 16, 33, 36.

[216] *Tirumālai* 16.

share of food. They also apparently maintained false accounts, flouted royal orders, purloined temple paddy and hid one of the temple icons. The record details the remedial and punitive actions the Śivamaheśvaras took.[217] Another inscription of Māravarman Kulaśekhara's reign records the misdeeds of a temple manager who brought and kept as his concubine a *brāhmaṇa* widow from a foreign land, used the cooked offerings of the temple for himself, misused the treasury, took bribes and felled the trees in the *devadāna* land. The punishment meted him is not known as the rest of the record is damaged.[218] No doubt, misuse or purloining of temple property by temple functionaries was an ever-present anxiety and a story incorporating such elements would have found resonance among its listeners. Whether the composer of the *Tirumālai* and the *Tiruppaḷḷiyĕḻucci* was actually a reformed thief or not is beside the point. What is important is that the hagiography manages to enunciate a clear 'moral' in a story that seamlessly weaves in the saint-poets' own words and expresses contemporary concerns.

The inscription from the Caurirāja-p-Pĕrumāḷ Temple in Tiruk-Kaṇṇapuram, Naṉṉilam *tāluk* dated to 1128 CE that refers to the deity as 'Cauri-p-Pĕrumāḷ sung by Tirumankai Āḻvār'[219] may not be remarkable, for the tradition of singing the hymns of the Āḻvārs and Nāyaṉmārs was clearly well established much earlier. What is interesting is that far more elaborate traditions regarding the saint-poets had been already either constructed or existed by this time, for an inscription of 1127 CE from the Aṣṭabhujakaram Temple in Kāñcī records a donation for the requirements of worship on the 13 *keṭṭai* days of every year, *keṭṭai* being the birth *nakṣatra* of Pŏykaiyāḻvār and Pūttatāḻvār.[220] A Kotai-Āṇḍāḷ *nandavanam* (garden) is referred to in an inscription of 1126 CE from Srirangam.[221] An inscription of 1188 CE from the Srirangam Temple registers a gift of land by a resident (name lost) of Malli *nāḍu* for rearing a flower garden called

217 *South Indian Inscriptions*, 1927, no. 297. Cited in K.V. Soundara Rajan, 'The Kaleidoscopic Activities of Mediaeval Temples in the Tamil Nad', *Quarterly Journal of the Mythic Society*, vol. 42, 1952, pp. 94–5.

218 *South Indian Inscriptions*, 1908, no. 125. Cited in Soundara Rajan, ibid., pp. 94–5. *South Indian Inscriptions* nos. 308 and 225 of 1927 are also said to deal with similar cases of fraud and misappropriation of temple property.

219 Mahalingam, 1985, vol. VII, pp. 438–9. Tj 1890. Ref.: *ARE*, 1922, no. 509.

220 Mahalingam, 1985, vol. III, pp. 159–60. Cg 650. Ref.: *ARE*, 1893, no. 33; *SII* iii, no. 80.

221 Mahalingam, 1985, vol. VIII, p. 202. Tp 929. Ref.: *ARE*, 1948–9, no. 39; *SII* xxiv, no. 114.

Cūṭikŏṭuttāḷ, and for the supply of a garland to the god.[222] The use of the name Cūṭikŏṭuttāḷ[223] and the combination Kotai-Āṇḍāḷ are significant. Even if we assume that the *DSC*,[224] was being composed or had recently been composed by this time, it is very unlikely that a purely textual construction of brahmanical *ācāryas* would have immediately found resonance in popular discourse. Again, therefore, it appears that there was an older tradition around which the hagiographical narratives were constructed. Two *taṉiyaṉs* (free standing stanzas of praise) composed by Pĕriya Nampi and Tirumalai Nampi, both disciples of Yāmuna, speak of Tiruppāṇāḻvār as *munivāhana.*[225] Was there an oral tradition revolving around an outcaste saint that these early *ācāryas* absorbed,[226] and transferred to the unknown poet of the *Amalaṉādipirāṉ*?

The dependence on oral traditions might explain the incompleteness of some stories and the entirely miraculous and unrealistic one of Tirumaḻicai. This begs the question of whether the narratives of Kulaśekhara and Tŏṇṭaraṭippŏṭi also have some basis in oral traditions. It is not possible to give a satisfactory answer with the available evidence. A perusal of the hagiographical accounts of the Āḻvārs (and for that matter, even the *ācāryas*) shows that many of them[227] seem largely believable, with just a hint of magic to the realism. Perhaps some of the episodes in the accounts that cannot be substantiated by the hymnal evidence can be traced back to popular narratives. This might also explain why the accounts of the *mutal* Āḻvārs are so brief: perhaps the composers of the hagiographies simply did not have enough to work on.

The installation of images of the Nāyaṉmārs in Rājarāja's great temple at Tanjavur at the beginning of the eleventh century attests to their

[222] Mahalingam, 1985, vol. VIII, pp. 207–8. Tp 951. Ref.: *ARE*, 1938–9, no. 119; *SII*, xxiv, no. 138.

[223] 'She who gave what she had worn', a reference to Āṇḍāḷ.

[224] See Chapter 1–iii of the present work for arguments regarding the dating of the *DSC*.

[225] A reference to his having been carried into the sanctum of the Srirangam Temple by the priest, Lokasārangamuni. See Chapter 2–vii of the present work.

[226] The example of the 63 Śaiva Nāyaṉmārs is illuminating. Even from the elliptical references in the *Tiruttŏṇṭartŏkai*, it is evident that Sundarar was drawing on oral traditions about old devotees of Śiva. Many details in the stories that have finally come down to us through the medium of Cekkiḻār's *Pĕriya Purāṇam* may, however, owe to the circumstances and contexts of the latter composition.

[227] Eight of twelve accounts.

apotheosis at least some time earlier.[228] There are two earlier references dated to 995 and 997 CE, of gifts for offerings in 'the shrine of Nampi Ārūra̱n (Sundarar) who composed the *Tiruppatiyam*' from the Āmravaneśvara Temple in Kūkūr, Kumbhakoṇam *tāluk*.[229] The epigraphic evidence from the Vaiṣṇava stream is, as usual, less abundant, and later in time. A shrine to Kulaśekhara-p-Pĕrumāḷ was set up by a private individual in the Gopālasvāmi Temple in Mannārkoyil, Ambāsamudram *tāluk* in 1021 CE.[230] A gift made to the shrine of Tirumankai Āḻvār in the Caurirāja-p-Pĕrumāḷ Temple in TirukKaṇṇapuram, Na̱ṉilam *tāluk*, in 1082 CE, shows the Āḻvār was already apotheosized. It is believed that Tirumankai was the first of the Āḻvārs to be represented in iconographic form.[231] The earliest epigraphic evidence for an image of Tiruppāṇāḻvār seems to be the one dated to 1275 CE from the Vaikuṇṭha-p-Pĕrumāḷ Temple in Tiruvĕṇṇainallūr, TirukKoyilūr *tāluk*.[232] Arguing that non-*brāhmaṇa* temple participation in the case of Vaiṣṇavism became significant only after Rāmānuja,[233] Champakalakshmi says,

> the worship of the twelve Āḻvārs, including the *śūdra* Nammāḻvār and the bard Tiruppāṇāḻvār was, [to an extent], the result of liberalism in temple worship introduced by Rāmānuja—who tried to bring about a synthesis between the Vedic and Tamil traditions, between the metaphysical severity of *Vedānta* and the personal and emotionally powerful *bhakti* and between the *varṇa* basis of Vedic social division and the sectarian orientation of *bhakti* in south India.[234]

While we do not possess early epigraphic evidence for the apotheosis of the archetypal low-caste saints, Nammāḻvār and Tiruppāṇāḻvār, the

[228] Mahalingam, 1985, vol. VII, pp. 598–619, Tj 2636 to 2732 are from the great temple at Tanjavur; a number of these inscriptions refer to the installation of the images of the Nāya̱ṉmārs.

[229] Mahalingam, 1985, vol. VII, p. 21. Tj 96. Ref.: *ARE*, 1917, no. 299. and Mahalingam, 1985, vol. VII, pp. 21–2. Tj 97. Ref.: *ARE*, 1917, no. 275.

[230] Mahalingam, 1985, vol. IX, pp. 28–9. Tn 134. Ref.: *ARE*, 1916, no. 400; ibid., part ii, para 2.

[231] Champakalakshmi, *Vaiṣṇava Iconography*, pp. 240–1.

[232] Mahalingam, 1985, vol. II, p. 432. SA 1859. Ref: *ARE*, 1921, no. 500; *SII* xii, no. 242.

[233] R. Champakalakshmi, 'Peasant State and Society in Medieval South India: A Review Article', *The Indian Economic and Social History Review*, vol. 18, 1981, nos. 3–4, p. 421.

[234] R. Champakalakshmi, 'Religion and Social Change in Tamil Nadu AD 600–1300', in *Medieval Bhakti Movements in India: Sri Caitanya Quincentenary Commemoration Volume*, ed. N.N. Bhattacharyya, Delhi: Munshiram Manoharlal, 1989, p. 171.

late-tenth century Ukkal inscription referring to Tiruvāymŏḻi-deva is significant.[235] Also, though we have already seen the role of the acaryic tradition in shaping a comparatively egalitarian community, it needs to be asked whether it was the *ācāryas*/Rāmānuja who liberalized temple worship or if they were themselves inheritors of a complex temple tradition that involved the larger community and were essentially providing scriptural justification for the same.

Hardy has suggested that though the temple culture—which he deems a northern introduction—was stimulated and developed in the south through the ecstatic devotion of the saint-poets, temple ritualism and Tamil devotionalism remained 'separate and potentially antagonistic entities' such that the 'elitism of the institution and its refusal to permit certain sections of the populace... to participate in its ritual events... meant that certain members of the Tamil devotional movement were excluded from the source of its own religion [the entrancing sight of the god in his temple]'.[236] Apart from the fact that this view is incompatible with some invaluable suggestions he himself has made elsewhere[237] regarding the history of Āḻvār bhakti, it falls into the common error of regarding the story of Tiruppāṇāḻvār as representative of the period of the bhakti movement.[238] My point is not to argue that temples were highly egalitarian and open to members of all castes in the late first millennium; brahmanical orthodoxy was firmly enough established to rule that possibility out. Rather, it appears that the temple culture[239] exhibited, even as it evolved, features derived from and grounded in the bhakti tradition. This points to a role of the larger community, including several non-*brāhmaṇa* castes, in the shaping of the institution which was, however, in all likelihood, dominated by *brāhmaṇas.* It was to this institution that Rāmānuja succeeded, so to speak. His 'reforms' must, therefore, be seen not so much as liberalizing temple worship as an attempt to acquire wider brahmanical sanction for unorthodox customs

[235] Mahalingam, 1985, vol. I, p. 105. NA 456. Ref.: *ARE*, 1893, no. 20; *SII* iii, no. 2.

[236] Friedhelm Hardy, 'Tiruppāṇ Āḻvār: The Untouchable who Rode Piggy Back on the Brahmin', in *Devotion Divine: Bhakti Traditions from the Regions of India*, ed. D.L. Eck and Francoise Mallison, Groningen: Egbert Forster, 1991, pp. 129–30.

[237] These will be discussed shortly below.

[238] This is particularly surprising since Hardy was among the earliest to point out the ascription of authorship to the unsigned compositions by the acaryic tradition.

[239] Considering the early evidence of the hymns of the Āḻvārs and Nāyaṉmārs as well as the inscriptional evidence, there seems little reason to speak of the temple *culture* as we know it to be a northern introduction into the south.

established in the Tamil land which probably were disapproved of by the more conservative *smārta* establishment. I will return to this point shortly.

Our hagiographies suggest that both the worship of the Ālvārs and the recitation of their hymns were customs of hoary antiquity.[240] In fact, they attribute the initiation of the custom of reciting the hymns over a period of 20 days in the month of Mārkaḻi to Tirumankai Āḻvār. We have seen, however, that the hymns were believed to be lost till they were rediscovered by Nāthamuni who set them to music and re-established the practice of singing them in temples.[241] The epigraphic evidence does point to an older tradition of reverence for both the saints and their hymns. Besides, it is likely that the hymns of at least Pĕriyāḻvār and Āṇḍāḷ, closely related to popular worship practices, and often with a folksong-like quality, were adopted by the ordinary masses in their daily and life cycle rituals.

(iii) The Integration

It is clear that the Śrīvaiṣṇava tradition, believing in an ancient tradition of worship of the Āḻvārs and tracing its spiritual-preceptorial lineage to them, was faced with an awkward gap in the *guruparamparā* which it resolved by the tale of Nāthamuni's miraculous apprehension of the hymns of the saint-poets and his hailing them as the *Drāviḍa Veda*. Let me point out again here that the claim of Vedic status for the *Tiruvāymŏḻi* had been made already in the *Kaṇṇinuṇciruttāmpu*. In fact, the tensions inherent in this claim can be seen in the Tamil poem itself, for Madhurakavi says that though scholars versed in the four Vedas consider him low and impure, Caṭakopan is his father, mother and master.[242] That this claim needed reiteration even later, by the *brāhmaṇa*-led Śrīvaiṣṇava movement, is brought out by the hagiographic tale of Madhurakavi having to subject the *Tiruvāymŏḻi* to the Sangam test in which, needless to say, he was vindicated. Further, Madhurakavi is said to have had an image of Nammāḻvār consecrated as an *arcā* and

[240] See Chapter 2–viii–c, d, e of the present work.

[241] Nāthamuni is also said to have learnt of the forgotten practice of performing the *adhyayanotsava* in the month of Mārkaḻi and re-instituted it along with such ancient rituals as having the processional image of Nammāḻvār being brought to the Srirangam Temple for the same. See *Agpp*, *Mgpp*, Nāthamuṉikaḷ *vaibhavam*.

[242] *Kaṇṇinuṇciruttāmpu* 3:

arranged for the performance of rituals and worship to the same.[243] In the absence of epigraphic evidence for the worship of the Āḻvārs in image form before the late tenth century, it is tempting to dismiss this as a fabrication meant merely to underline a long tradition of revering Nammāḻvār. However, certain aspects of the larger story compel us to consider this legend with care. For instance, the fundamental break between the Āḻvārs and the acaryic tradition *could* have been glossed entirely by describing Nāthamuni as a descendant or direct disciple of Madhurakavi whom the hagiographies regard as a *brāhmaṇa*. That the hagiographical literature chooses rather to retain the 'gap' is significant. Over forty years ago, J.A.B. van Buitenen noted:

> ... the fact stands out that Nāthamuni had to go to the common people in order to collect the hymns of the Ālvārs that had been rejected by the orthodox authorities. Although the Tamil scriptures had not received official sanction for use in temple worship, they were current among the people and certainly also in use at their devotional worship. What Nāthamuni in effect did was to incorporate the scriptures, henceforth known as Dravida Veda, into the temple worship at Śrīrangam.[244]

Walter Neevel built on Buitenen's path-breaking insight through analysis of the role of the four earliest *ācāryas* in the integration of originally non-Vedic popular movements, not only of *Pāñcarātra* but also the bhakti of the Āḻvārs into the classical Vedic tradition.[245] Hardy furthered the argument by suggesting that the legend of Nāthamuni's recovery of the hymns indicates the acquisition by a *brāhmaṇa* family of the Coḻa country of the knowledge of Nammāḻvār's works and their acceptance as the Tamil Vedas.[246] Hardy also argued that Madhurakavi was

[243] See Chapter 2–ix of the present work.

[244] J.A.B. van Buitenen, op. cit., p. 3. Though this observation is of fundamental significance for understanding the formation of Śrīvaiṣṇavism, the statement that the hymns of the Āḻvārs had been rejected by the orthodox authorities presumes an earlier 'confrontation' in which the Tamil hymns were rejected. Besides, the epigraphic evidence points to the gradual growth of the influence of bhakti devotionalism with its attendant features, including singing of the saints' songs in temples from the ninth century itself, particularly in the Śaiva case where a revolutionary intervention such as Nāthamuni's is not known.

[245] Walter G. Neevel, *Yamuna's Vedanta and Pancaratra: Integrating the Classical with the Popular*, Missoula: Scholars Press, 1977, p. x.

[246] Friedhelm Hardy, 'The Tamil Veda of a Śūdra Saint: The Śrīvaiṣṇava Interpretation of Nammāḻvār', in *Contribution to South Asian Studies*, ed. Gopal Krishna, New Delhi: Oxford University Press, 1979, pp. 29–87.

probably not a direct disciple of Nammāḻvār's, but a devotee of the Āḻvār who had been apotheosized in a temple in his native TirukKurukūr.[247] I have shown this to be untenable[248] but Hardy's curious dating does not impact the analysis that follows.

It seems fairly clear that—whether Madhurakavi was merely a devotee of Nammāḻvār's separated from him by several generations and who had inherited the tradition of reciting his hymns or, whether the two were actually master and disciple, and Nāthamuni met in TirukKurukūr descendants of Madhurakavi who had preserved a tradition of reciting the hymns of the master— there was, by the mid-tenth century, a strong local tradition of worship of the saint-poet, possibly as a separate cult centred around the *sthalavṛkṣa*[249] outside the main Viṣṇu temple of the village. Some resistance on the part of at least some sections of the *brāhmaṇa* community to the apotheosis of the saint and the claim of Vedic status for his hymns seems likely[250] especially as this cult seems to have had little regard for the hierarchies of the orthodox caste order.[251] It must be remembered too that this was a Vaiṣṇava community; the hymns of Nammāḻvār are clearly focussed on Viṣṇu as the Supreme Lord and are frequently polemical with regard to other deities.[252] The bhakti of the Āḻvārs (and Nāyaṉmārs) had always a strong communitarian aspect to it; it was not an introverted meditative devotion—whatever the hagiographies might say about Nammāḻvār— but one which exuberantly called out to fellow men and women to join in the worship of the chosen deity. This is evident not only in the *phalaśruti* verses but in numerous stanzas throughout the corpus of the *NDP* as well. Kulaśekhara Āḻvār says of the lord of Arangam, 'The crowds of His devotees sing and dance and

[247] Ibid., pp. 41–2.

[248] See Chapter 1, footnotes 154 and 155 of the present work.

[249] The tamarind tree under which Nammāḻvār is supposed to have meditated for 16 years is evidently an ancient one of impressive dimensions (Personal visit). Temple functionaries say that the leaves of the tree do not 'sleep', i.e. close at night unlike normal tamarind trees'—which I could not verify— and that this tree flowers and fruits but that the fruits do not ripen. The branches were heavily laden with tamarind pods; I cannot distinguish unripe pods from ripe ones, but with better-informed pilgrims visiting the shrine throughout the year, this account would be difficult to maintain if untrue.

[250] See reference to *Kaṇṇinuṇciruttāmpu* 3 cited above.

[251] Nammāḻvār says in *Tiruvāymŏḻi* 3.7.9, 'The servant's servant of even a *caṇḍāla* among lowly *caṇḍālas* below the four *jātis* is my master if he is a true devotee of my gem-hued Lord who bears the discus'.

[252] See Chapter 5 of the present work.

call out 'Rangā!' When will I join them?'[253] Āṇḍāḷ invites her girlfriends to join in the performance of the *pāvai nompu*.[254] Pĕriyāḻvār urges people to name their children after the Lord Dāmodara-who-smote-the-cart, and exult,[255] and, in the voice of Kṛṣṇa's mother, invites the cowherd women to admire her wonderful baby.[256] 'Come and offer worship with fresh flower garlands and hearts filled with love in TirukKurunkuṭi where sharp-beaked egrets rejoice with their mates in fields filled with water birds', says Tirumankai.[257]

Nāthamuni, by all accounts, seems to have belonged to a priestly *brāhmaṇa* family[258] deeply influenced by the *Pāñcarātra*, a cult which accepts the supremacy of Viṣṇu. Indeed, it is even possible that he belonged to the community that called itself Śrīvaiṣṇava—an inscription from Srirangam dated to 945 CE mentions Śrīvaiṣṇavas as the recipients of a gift of gold for the deity's bath.[259] The community is mentioned by name in Tiruppati in an inscription of 966 CE,[260] and in another tenth-century inscription from a ruined Viṣṇu temple in Arakkoṇam.[261] The Śrīvaiṣṇavas appear in almost all these early epigraphic records as important temple functionaries[262] and may have been largely

253 *Pĕrumāḷ Tirumŏḻi* 2.1.

254 *Tiruppāvai* 1–30.

255 *Pĕriyāḻvār Tirumŏḻi* 4.6.6.

256 *Pĕriyāḻvār Tirumŏḻi* 1.3.1–21.

257 *Pĕriya Tirumŏḻi* 9.6.8.

258 R. Champakalakshmi, 'From Devotion to Dissent and Dominance', in *Tradition, Dissent and Ideology*, ed. R. Champakalakshmi and S. Gopal, New Delhi: Oxford University Press, 1996, p. 145, cites George Hart III, *The Poems of the Ancient Tamils: Their Milieu and their Sanskrit Counterparts*, Berkeley, California, 1975, pp. 51–8, 'There were several kinds of *brāhmaṇas* in the Tamil land, each showing different degrees of assimilation of the indigenous culture'. Hierarchies in status between these different groups meant that Nāthamuni as a temple priest was more likely to have been receptive to the folk culture represented by Āḻvār devotionalism than a Smārta *brāhmaṇa*.

259 Mahalingam, 1985, vol. VIII, p. 175. Tp 820. Ref.: *ARE*, 1892, no. 71; *SII*, iv, no. 518, p. 150; *SII* xxiv, no. 6.

260 Vasudha Narayanan, *The Vernacular Veda: Revelation, Recitation and Ritual*, Columbia, SC: University of South Carolina Press, 1994, p. 2.

261 Mahalingam, 1985, vol. I, p. 31. NA 133. Ref.: *ARE*, 1906, no. 329; *SII* xiii, no. 105.

262 There are at least six epigraphic mentions of Śrīvaiṣṇavas from the first decade of the eleventh century and several more thereafter. Mahalingam, 1985, vol. I, p. 35. NA 152. Ref.: *ARE*, 1906, no. 322; Mahalingam, 1985, vol. III, pp. 284–6. Cg 1126, Cg 1127, Cg 1131, Cg 1132, Cg 1133; Mahalingam, 1985, vol. II, p. 372. SA

brāhmaṇas. Was this community in general and Nāthamuni's family in particular influenced by the bhakti of the Āḻvārs, and if so, to what degree? Considering the popularity of *Tiruppatiyam* singing in temples in the tenth century,[263] and the strong temple-orientation of a number of the bhakti saints, it is likely that Nāthamuni would have been aware of bhakti devotionalism and its widespread popular appeal. In any case, he did learn of the cult around Nammāḻvār—possibly through pilgrims from Nammāḻvār's native Kurukūr who visited his temple as the hagiographies have it—and set about incorporating this worship system into the brahmanical Vaiṣṇava one. I believe that the hagiographies record a historical fact when they speak of his sojourn to TirukKurukūr to learn the 'thousand' stanzas[264] of the *Tiruvāymŏḻi*. The recitation of Nammāḻvār's hymns and probably even Madhurakavi's *Kaṇṇinuṇciruttāmpu* was, in all likelihood, a living tradition in the saint's hometown. Further, I suggest that Nāthamuni's subsequent pilgrimage (which seems rather restricted by the usual standards of the *guruparamparās*) was made with the specific purpose of recovering other hymns of Vaiṣṇava saints.

This appropriation of an older and well-established tradition would have generated its own tensions and demanded certain accommodations from the Śrīvaiṣṇava community. One of the ways in which this was articulated was the acknowledgement of Vedic status for the hymns of the Tamil saints, something which was accepted within the Tamil cult itself long before it was recognized by a brahmanical tradition. Indeed, the *Kaṇṇinuṇciruttāmpu's* declaration that Caṭakopaṉ rendered the inner meaning of the Vedas in Tamil[265] only makes explicit what seems implicit in the verses of several other Āḻvārs.[266] The sanctity of Tamil is, of course, emphasized in a number of hymns where the signature stanza mentions the rewards to be got from recitation/singing of the *Tamil* poem.[267] More significant is the parallelism between the Tamil songs and Sanskrit Vedas suggested in several hymns. Kulaśekhara describes the

---

1599. Ref.: *ARE*, 1900, no. 128; *SII* vii, no. 141; Mahalingam, 1985, vol. VIII, p. 182. Tp 849. Ref.: *ARE*, 1892, no. 15; *SII* xxiv, no. 58; Mahalingam, 1985, vol. IX, pp. 55–6. Tn 226. Ref.: *ARE*, 1911, no. 539; *SII* xiv, no. 199, pp. 11–114.

[263] See inscriptional evidence in Chapter 1–iii of the present work.

[264] The *Tiruvāymŏḻi* comprises 1,102 hymns but the eleventh stanza of most decads have as their refrain, 'These ten of a thousand...'

[265] *Kaṇṇinuṇciruttāmpu* 8, 9.

[266] A parallel claim can be seen in some hymns of the Nāyaṉmārs Appar and Sambandar too.

[267] *Nācciyār Tirumŏḻi* 6.10, *Tiruppāvai* 30, *Pĕrumāḷ Tirumŏḻi* 2.10, etc.

Lord of Srirangam as sweet Tamil songs and as the northern tongue.[268] Tirumaḻicai Āḻvār says, 'The name of the red-eyed lord is sweet to the ear. Know that it is the refuge of men. I have found it excellent substance for my poetry. It is the very substance of the Vedas.'[269] Tirumankai Āḻvār sings, 'The lord resides with joy in Aḻuntūr where meritorious *brāhmaṇas* adept in reciting *pure Tamil and northern* works[270] perform fire sacrifices whose smoke clouds the skies'.[271] He praises the lord as himself the five elements, Tamil poetry and northern works, the sun, the moon, the four quarters, and the essence within the Upanisads.[272] Nammāḻvār's repeatedly saying that the lord 'Himself sings His own praises in His own words through him'[273] suggests that his songs are to be considered *śruti* like the Vedas. Indeed, Nammāḻvār's mystic pronouncements often indicate his identification with the Supreme Lord, an aspect noted and recognized by the post-tenth century Śrīvaiṣṇava tradition, and probably well before that by the Tamil cult around the poet-saint. Yāmuna's *Āgama Prāmāṇya* that argues for the Vedic validity of the *Pāñcarātra* was a further step in this process of accommodation. It has been argued that it was only under the *ācāryas* Yāmuna and Rāmānuja that the 'northern schemata of Viṣṇu and his *avatāras*, and of *ParaVāsudeva* and his *vyūhas* and *vibhūtis* replace[d] the more archaic and simple conceptions of the south'.[274] This argument is scarcely tenable considering the deep familiarity of almost all the Āḻvārs with the various *avatāras* of Viṣṇu and the complex ways in which they conceive the lord, identifying the temple *arcā* with the various *avatāras* and with the supreme cosmic lord as well. While I do not believe, unlike Hudson,[275] that the entire corpus of poetry of several Āḻvārs is essentially an exposition of Pāñcarātric principles, his argument does establish the Āḻvārs' awareness of these concepts. The influence of *Pāñcarātra* on the temple cult appears, from the inscriptional evidence itself,[276] not to speak of the way the saints imaged the temple in their hymns, to have been substantial. Nāthamuni's appropriation of the Tamil cult of worship of the Āḻvārs in temples had

[268] *Pĕrumāḷ Tirumŏḻi* 1.4.
[269] *Nāṉmukaṉ Tiruvantādi* 69.
[270] The words are, '*cĕṉtamiḻum vaṭakalaiyum tikaḻnta nāvar...*'.
[271] *Pĕriya Tirumŏḻi* 7.8.7.
[272] *Tirunĕṭuntāṇṭakam* 4.
[273] *Tiruvāymŏḻi* 7.9.1–10; 10.7.5.
[274] Hardy, *Viraha Bhakti*, p. 221.
[275] Hudson, 'Bathing in Krishna', pp. 539–66.
[276] See early references to various temple rituals above.

been essentially articulated in a vernacular idiom. The composition of Sanskrit treatises by his grandson was essential to legitimize it in a brahmanical framework. However, the *Pāñcarātra Āgama* texts have no place in Vedānta or Uttara Mimāmsa[277] and the Vedic compatibility of the Āḻvār tradition remained a sectarian viewpoint.

The second 'break' in the preceptorial lineage, between Yāmunācārya and Rāmānuja, and the latter's writing exclusively in Sanskrit has led to much theorizing about Rāmānuja's relationship to the entire Āḻvār tradition. Robert Lester has disputed the authorship of the three *Gadyas* and the *Nityagrantha* where Rāmānuja displays a ritualistic attitude not seen in his major philosophical works.[278] John Carman and Vasudha Narayanan have taken pains to point out that whether the account of Tirukkurukaip-Pirāṉ Piḷḷāṉ writing the first commentary on the *Tiruvāymŏḻi* at Rāmānuja's explicit wish is historically accurate or not, the former's use of phraseology is close to and sometimes identical with the language of Rāmānuja. Spelling out the question of the extent of the unacknowledged influence of the entire Āḻvār tradition on Rāmānuja's writings which are exclusively in Sanskrit and silent over the Tamil hymns, they believe that the key to this may lie in the works of his immediate disciples.[279] Hardy's argument about the erasure of emotionalism from the Āḻvārs' hymns in the commentarial tradition assumes a fundamental shift in the religious conception that occurred from the Āḻvārs to the *ācāryas*. I agree that important shifts and changes did take place but I see them as the function of the coming together of three diverse streams than as changes in the course of the evolution of a unitary tradition.[280]

Let us briefly review relevant aspects of the hagiography of Rāmānuja. Our texts are unanimous in portraying his paternal family as a Vedic *brāhmaṇa* one. The choice of Yādava Prakāśa, an Advaitin, as guru for the boy is indicative of its Vedantic moorings. On the other hand, the

[277] C.J. Bartley, *The Theology of Rāmānuja: Realism and Religion,* London: Routledge Curzon, 2002, p. 3.

[278] See Chapter 3-ii of the present work.

[279] Carman and Narayanan, op. cit., pp. xi–xii. Also see Nayar, op. cit., for demonstrating this continuity through the works of two other disciples of Rāmānuja's, Kūreśa and Bhaṭṭar.

[280] There naturally occurred further and important changes over the next several centuries in the evolution of a 'unified' tradition in response both to changes in the socio-political situation and the internal dynamics of the sectarian religious community. I have considered some of them in the previous chapters.

association of Rāmānuja's maternal uncle, Pĕriya Tirumalai Nampi, with the Viṣṇu temple at Tiruppati underlines the Vaiṣṇava orientation of the family. The well-known episodes of disagreements between Rāmānuja and his teacher over the interpretation of various Upanisadic passages indicate the growing perception in the young scholar's mind that his devotional orientation was incompatible with the teachings of *Advaita Vedānta*. His final break with Yādava and subsequent exposition of *Viśiṣṭādvaita* as a philosophical system were crucial for establishing the devotionalism of the Āḻvārs and the religious system it had generated as a valid one in the pan-Indian, Sanskritic-brahmanical context. Thus, far from disputing Rāmānuja's reverence of the Tamil saint-poets, I suggest that Rāmānuja entered the Śrīvaiṣṇava 'movement' in order to legitimize its fundamental religious conceptions which, by the eleventh century, were a composite of a Tamil tradition of bhakti deriving from and deifying the Āḻvārs, and a brahmanical Vaiṣṇava one. The hagiographical tradition is not far from the truth in suggesting that Rāmānuja was not a direct disciple of Yāmunācārya but the lesson there is *not* that Rāmānuja was indifferent to the Āḻvārs.[281] In fact, as one observes the hagiographies bending over themselves in trying to establish that Rāmānuja was the true spiritual heir of Yāmunācārya, having acquired all the learning he would have from the master himself through the medium of his five disciples— and I might add, wondering where the 'catch' is— one tends to overlook a far more critical point; a point, moreover, so obvious as to scarcely need 'discovery': the Vedantin Rāmānuja *adopted* the latter's school as being more compatible with his own religio-philosophical ideas.[282] According to the hagiographical accounts, Rāmānuja composed his important philosophical works after he came to head Yāmuna's school as its most influential *ācārya*. There can be little doubt, however, that the germ of the ideas elaborated in the *Śrībhāṣya* and other texts was already present when he finally broke with Yādava; indeed, the differences between student and teacher were over

[281] Bartley, op. cit., p. 2, perceptively points out, 'Rāmānuja was an agent of Vedanticisation in what was originally a non-Vedic tradition. He sought to harmonise the tenets of his *bhakti* cult with those of the classical Vedantic tradition....' I differ from Bartley in his explanation for Rāmānuja's silence on the Tamil Veda. 'For him, *bhakti* is a contemplative and an intellectual rather than an emotional phenomenon.' Ibid., p. 3.

[282] Rāmānuja's 'entry' into the tradition is critical for the additional reason that unlike Nāthamuni and his grandson Yāmuna, he belonged to the more orthodox Smārta *brāhmaṇa* group and was, thus, uniquely in a position of arguing Vedic compatibility for the Tamil tradition.

interpretations regarding the nature of the supreme soul— Rāmānuja's being a theological one as opposed to Yādava's insistence on a *nirguṇa* Brahmān.

The account of Rāmānuja's discipleship under five of Yāmuna's pupils underlines his attempt to fully understand and integrate the older tradition with his philosophical principles eventually elaborated as Viśiṣṭādvaita. Śrīvaiṣṇavism, thus, came to denote from the period of Rāmānuja onwards, a religious system that revered a set of Tamil saint-poets and their hymns, and the Vedantic philosophical system of Viśiṣṭādvaita. It took its distinctive name from the brahmanical community which had appropriated the Tamil cult and which paved the way for it to acquire a pan-Indian Sanskritic legitimacy. In the process of this integration, the old community of Śrīvaiṣṇavas necessarily shed its exclusive brahmanism, initially integrating those non-*brāhmaṇa* groups who had been the original custodians of the fundamental religious beliefs of the sect and accommodating, over the next few centuries, numerous others.

Though Viśiṣṭādvaita was formulated as the philosophical basis for the bhakti of the Āḻvārs, the older tradition, nourished on different impulses, could not always fit neatly into the Vedantic framework. One can scarcely put it better than Kaylor and Venkatachari:

> Later Śrīvaiṣṇava *ācāryas* follow the general Hindu tendency to systematize and regularize the religious experience, and they incorporate Nammāḻvār's hymns into their system which is only partly derived from it... Nammāḻvār's hymns reflect primary religious experience; as such, they are pre-philosophical and pre-theological and pre-prescriptive; though they certainly contain philosophy and theology and ritual indications, they are not expressed for the purpose of prescribing in any of these areas, and they are resistant to later attempts to find in them normative thought and normative action.[283]

The resultant tensions, doctrinal as well as social, necessitated continuous interpretation and elaboration of the older tradition of the Āḻvārs, which was carried out through the composition of hagiographies, commentaries, praise-poems and philosophical works.

[283] Kaylor and Venkatachari, op. cit., p. 67.

Appendices

TABLE I: *Nālāyira Divya Prabandham*

Parts		*Composer*	*Composition*	*No. of Hymns*
Book I			Mutal Āyiram	
	1	Pěriyāl̠vār	*Pěriyāl̠vār Tirumŏl̠i*	473
	2	Āṇḍāḷ	*Tiruppāvai*	30
	3	Āṇḍāḷ	*Nācciyār Tirumŏl̠i*	143
	4	Kulaśekhara	*Pěrumāḷ Tirumŏl̠i*	105
	5	(Tirumal̠icai)	*Tiruccanta Viruttam*	120
	6	Tŏṇṭaraṭippŏṭi	*Tirumālai*	45
	7	Tŏṇṭaraṭippŏṭi	Tiruppaḷḷiyěl̠ucci	10
	8	(Tiruppāṇ)	*Amalan̠ādipirān̠*	11
	9	Madhurakavi	*Kaṇṇinuṇ Ciruttāmpu*	10
Book II			Iraṇṭam Āyiram	
	10	Tirumankai	*Pěriya Tirumŏl̠i*	1,084
	11	Tirumankai	*Tirukkuruntāṇṭakam*	20
	12	Tirumankai	*Tiruněṭuntāṇṭakam*	30
Book III			Tiruvāymŏl̠i	
	13	Nammāl̠vār	*Tiruvāymŏl̠i*	1,102
Book IV			Iyarpā	
	14	(Pŏykai)	*Mutal Tiruvantādi*	100
	15	(Pūtam)	*Iraṇṭām Tiruvantādi*	100
	16	(Pey)	*Mūn̠r̠ām Tiruvantādi*	100
	17	(Tirumal̠icai)	*Nān̠mukan̠ Tiruvantādi*	96
	18	Nammāl̠vār	*Tiruviruttam*	100
	19	(Nammāl̠vār)	*Tiruvāciriyam* (71 lines)	7
	20	(Nammāl̠vār)	*Pěriya Tiruvantādi*	87
	21	(Tirumankai)	*Tiruvěl̠ukūr̠r̠irukkai* (46 lines)	1
	22	(Tirumankai)	*Ciriya Tirumaṭal*	77.5
	23	(Tirumankai)	*Pěriya Tirumaṭal*	148.5
TOTAL				4,000

NOTE:

Brackets indicate only traditional ascription.

TABLE II(a): *Shrines mentioned in the earliest five sets of hymns*

Regions	*(Pŏykai)* *Mutal Tiruvantādi*	*(Pūtam)* *Iraṉṭām Tiruvantādi*	*(Pey)* *Mūṉṟām Tiruvantādi*	*(Tirumaḻicai)* *Nāṉmukaṉ Tiruvantādi*	*(Tirumaḻicai)* *Tiruccanta Viruttam*
	Pārkaṭal 16, 42	Pārkaṭal 3	Pārkaṭal 11	Pārkaṭal 3, 36, 54, 89	Pārkaṭal 81
	Vaikuṇṭha 76		Vaikuṇṭha 32, 61	Vaikuṇṭha 19, 65, 73, 75, 79, 89	Vaikuṇṭha 84
Vaṭanāḍu	Venkaṭam 26, 27, 37, 38, 39, 68, 76, 77, 82	Venkaṭam 25, 26, 27, 28, 33, 45, 46, 48, 53, 54, 72, 75	Venkaṭam 14, 26, 30, 32, 39, 40, 45, 58, 59, 62, 68, 69, 70, 71, 72, 73, 75, 89	Venkaṭam 34, 39, 40, 41, 43, 44, 45, 47, 48, 53, 54, 90	Venkaṭam 60, 81
Tŏṇṭaināḍu		Pāṭakam 94	Pāṭakam 30		Pāṭakam 63, 64
	Vĕhkā 77		Kacci-Vĕhkā 64/ Vĕhkā 26, 62, 76	Vĕhkā 36	Vĕhkā 63, 64
		Māmallai 70	Kaṭal 30		
			TiruvAllikeṇi 16	Mayilai-TiruvAllikeṇi 35	
		TiruNīrmalai 46	Aṭṭabuyakaram, 99	TiruĔvvuḷ 36	Ūrakam 63, 64
		Taṇkāl 70	Kacci 26		
		Attiyūr 95, 96	Kaṭikai 61		
			Viṇṇagaram 62		
			Veḷukkai 26, 34, 62		

(Contd.)

Table II(a) (*contd.*)

Naṭunāḍu	Kovalūr 77 Iṭaikaḻi, 86	Koval 70			
Coḻanāḍu	Arangam 6	Arangam 28, 46, 70, 88	Arangam 62	Arangam 3, 36, 60	Arangam 21, 49,51, 52, 53, 54, 55, 93, 119
		TirukKoṭṭiyūr 46, 87	TirukKoṭṭiyūr 62	TirukKoṭṭiyūr 34	
		Kuṭamūkku 97 Kuṭantai 70	Tĕn-Kuṭantai 62 Kuṭantai 30	Kuṭantai 36	Kuṭantai 56, 57, 58, 59, 60
		Tañjai, v 70		TirupPer 36	Kurunkuṭi, v 62
				Aṉbil 36	
Pāṇṭiyanāḍu		Māliruñcolai 46, 54			
Regionwise distribution					
(Pŏykai)	Vaṭanāḍu: 1	Tŏṇṭaināḍu: 1	Naṭunāḍu: 1	Coḻanāḍu: 1	Pāṇṭiyanāḍu: 0
(Pūtam)	Vaṭanāḍu: 1	Tŏṇṭaināḍu: 5	Naṭunāḍu: 1	Coḻanāḍu: 5	Pāṇṭiyanāḍu: 1
(Pey)	Vaṭanāḍu: 1	Tŏṇṭaināḍu: 9	Naṭunāḍu: 0	Coḻanāḍu: 3	Pāṇṭiyanāḍu: 0
(Tirumaḻicai)	Vaṭanāḍu: 1	Tŏṇṭaināḍu: 3/5	Naṭunāḍu: 0	Coḻanāḍu: 6/7	Pāṇṭiyanāḍu: 0

NOTES:

Pārkaṭal, the ocean of milk, and Vaikuṇṭha are notional.

The only site in Vaṭanāḍu mentioned in these five works is Venkaṭam.

Brackets indicate that the ascription is only traditional. Common authorship of the *Nāṉmukaṉ Tiruvantādi* and the *Tiruccanta Viruttam* seems doubtful.

TABLE II(b): *Shrines mentioned by Kulasekhara, Pĕriyāl̲vār, Āṇḍāḷ and Tŏṇṭaraṭippŏṭi*

Regions	*Kulaśekhara* Pĕrumāḷ Tirumŏl̲i	*Pĕriyāl̲vār* Pĕriyāl̲vār Tirumŏl̲i	*Āṇḍāḷ* Tiruppāvai (TP) *and* Nācciyār Tirumŏl̲i (NT)
	Pārkaṭal 2.8, 4.4	Pārkaṭal 2.6.6, 5.2.2	Pārkaṭal *NT* 3.8, 5.7
	Vaikuṇṭha 10.10	Vaikuṇṭha 2.7.9. 4.7.9	Vaikuṇṭha *TP* 9, *NT* 3.10,
Vaṭanāḍu		Mathurā 3.6.3, 4.7.6, 9	Mathurā *NT* 4.6, 6.5, 7.3, 12.1
		Āyppāṭi 3.6.7	Āyppāṭi *TP* 3, *NT* 12.2
		Dvārakā 4.1.6, 4.7.8, 4.7.9	Dvārakā *NT* 1.4, 4.8, 12.9
		Khandam 4.7.1–11	Bhaktavilocanam *NT* 12.6
		Śaligrāma 4.7.9	Bhaṇḍirāvata *NT* 12.7
		Badari 4.7.9	Govardhana *NT* 12.8
			Bṛndāvana *NT* 14.1–10
	Ayotti 8.6, 8.7, 10.1	Ayotti 4.7.9	
	Venkaṭam 4.1–10	Venkaṭam 1.5.3, 2.6.9, 2.7.3, 2.9.6, 3.3.4, 5.4.1	Venkaṭam *NT* 1.1,3, 4.2, 5.2, 8.1–10, 10.5,8
Col̲anāḍu	Arangam 1.1–10, 2.1–10, 3.1–10	Arangam 1.4.9, 2.7.2, 2.7.8, 2.9.11, 3.3.2, 4.8.1–10, 4.9.1–11, 4.10.1–10	Arangam *NT* 11.1–10
	Ālinagar 8.7		
	Tillai-TiruCitrakūṭam 10.1–10		
	Kaṇṇapuram 8.1–10	Kaṇṇapuram 1.6.8	Kaṇṇapuram *NT* 4.2
		TirupPer 2.5.1, 2.6.2, 2.9.4	
		Tirukkoṭṭiyūr 1.2.1, 1.2.10, 2.6.2, 4.4.1–11	

(*Contd.*)

Table II(b) (*contd.*)

		Vĕḷḷarai 1.6.8, 2.8.1–10	
		Kuṭantai, 1.4.7, 1.7.4, 2.6.2, 2.6.6, 2.7.7	Kuṭantai *NT* 13.2
Pāṇṭiyanāḍu		Māliruñcolai 1.6.8, 3.4.5, 4.2.1–11, 4.3.1–11, 5.3.1–10	Māliruñcolai *NT* 4.1, 9.1–10
		Villiputtūr 2.2.6	Villiputtūr NT 5.5
		Kurunkuṭi 1.6.8	
Malaināḍu	Vittuvakkoṭu 5.1–10		
		Body as temple 5.2.1–10, 5.4.9	

Regionwise distribution

Kulaśekhara	Vaṭanāḍu: 2 Malaināḍu: 1	Toṇṭaināḍu: 0	Co<u>l</u>anāḍu: 4	Pāṇṭiyanāḍu: 0
Pĕriyā<u>l</u>vār	Vaṭanāḍu: 8	Toṇṭaināḍu: 0	Co<u>l</u>anāḍu: 6	Pāṇṭiyanāḍu: 3
Āṇḍāḷ	Vaṭanāḍu: 8	Toṇṭaināḍu: 0	Co<u>l</u>anāḍu: 3	Pāṇṭiyanāḍu: 2
Tŏṇṭaraṭippŏṭi	Vaṭanāḍu: 0	Toṇṭaināḍu: 0	Co<u>l</u>anāḍu: 1	Pāṇṭiyanāḍu: 0

NOTES:

Pārkaṭal, the Ocean of Milk, and Vaikuṇṭha are notional.

Other than Venkaṭam, the Vaṭanāḍu sites mentioned here are in north India and, despite being geographically identifiable, probably notional.

Each row does not necessarily feature the same site.

Tŏṇṭaraṭippŏṭi's *Tirumālai* and *Tiruppaḷḷiyĕ<u>l</u>ucci* are devoted exclusively to Arangam.

TABLE II(c): *Shrines Mentioned by Tirumankai Ālvār in the Iraṇṭam Āyiram*

(Pěriya Tirumŏli)

Regions		*Main dedication*	*References*
Vaṭanāḍu	1	Piriti 1.2.1–10	
	2	Badari 1.3.1–10, 1.4.1–10	
	3	Saligrāma 1.5.1–10	
	4	Naimiśāraṇya 1.6.1–10	
	5	Singavel-kuṉṟam 1.7.1–10	
	6	TiruVenkaṭam 1.8.1–10; 1.9.1–10; 1.10.1–10; 2.1.1–10	Venkaṭam 4.3.8; 6.8.1; 7.1.3; 7.3.5; 7.10.3; 8.2.3; 9.7.4; 9.9.9; 10.1.2
	7		Mathura 6.8.10
Toṇṭaināḍu	8	Ěvvuḷ 2.2.1–10	
	9	TiruvAllikeṇi 2.3.1–10	
	10	TiruNīrmalai .2.4.1–10	TiruNīrmalai 2.7.8; 5.2.8; 6.8.4; 7.1.7; 8.2.3; 9.2.8; 10.1.1
	11	Kaṭalmallai talaśayanam 2.5.1–10; 2.6.1–10	Kaṭalmallai 3.5.8; 7.1.4
	12	TiruvIṭaventai 2.7.1–10	Iṭaventai 1.8.4
	13	Aṭṭabuyakaram 2.8.1–10	
	14	Parameccura-Viṇṇagaram 2.9.1–10	
	15		Pātakam 6.10.4
	16		Ūrakam 1.5.4
	17		Kacci [Věhkā] 2.6.5; 10.1.7
	18		TiruNiṉṟavūr 7.10.5
	19		Puṭkuḻi 2.7.8
	20		Kaṭikai 8.9.4, 9
	21		Taṇkā 5.6.2; 10.1.2
Naṭunāḍu	22	TirukKovalūr 2.10.1–10	Kovalūr 2.4.1; 5.6.2; 6.10.5; 7.3.2; 7.10.4
	23	TiruvAhīndrapuram 3.1.1–10	
Coḻanāḍu	24	Tillai-TiruCitrakūṭam 3.2.1–10, 3.3.1–10	

(Contd.)

Table II(c) (*contd.*)

25	KāḻicCīrāma-Viṇṇagaram 3.4.1–10	
26	TiruvĀli 3.5.1–10; 3.6.1–10, 3.7.1–10	TiruvĀli 2.4.1; 6.8.2; 8.9.6,8; 10.1.3
27	Nānkūr-Maṇimāṭakkoyil 3.8.1–10	
28	Nānkūr- Vaikuṇtha-Viṇṇagaram 3.9.1–10	
29	Nānkūr- Arimeya-Viṇṇagaram 3.10.1–10	
30	Nānkūr- TirutTevanārtŏkai 4.1.1–10	
31	Nānkūr- Vaṇpuruṣottamaṉ 4.2.1–10	
32	Nānkūr- Cĕmpŏṉceykoyil 4.3.1–10	
33	Nānkūr-TiruTĕṟṟiyampalam 4.4.1–10	
34	Nānkūr-TiruMaṇikkūṭam 4.5.1–0	
35	Nānkūr- Kāvaḷampāṭi 4.6.1–10	
36	Nānkūr- TiruVĕḷḷakuḷam 4.7.1–10	
37	Nānkūr- Pārttaṉpaḷḷi 4.8.1–10	
38	Intaḷūr 4.9.1–10	
39	TiruVĕḷḷiyankuṭi 4.10.1–10	
40	Puḷḷampūtankuṭi 5.1.1–10	
41	Kūṭalūr 5.2.1–10	
42	TiruVĕḷḷarai 5.3.1–10	Vĕḷḷarai 10.1.4
43	Arangam 5.4.1–10; 5.5.1–10; 5.6.1–10; 5.7.1–10; 5.8.1–10	Arangam 1.8.2, 3.7.6; 6.6.8; 7.3.4; 8.2.7; 9.9.2
44	TirupPer 5.9.1–10	TirupPer 1.5.4; 5.6.2; 7.6.9; 10.1.4
45	Nandīpura-Viṇṇagaram 5.10.1–10	
46	TiruViṇṇagar 6.1.1–10; 6.2.1–10; 6.3.1–10	10.1.8

(*Contd.*)

Table II(c) (*contd.*)

	47	Naraiyūr 6.4.1–10 to 7.3.1–10 (100 stanzas)	Naraiyūr 2.4.1; 6.3.3; 8.2.2; 10.1.5
	48	TirucCerai 7.4.1–10	10.1.6
	49	A̲luntūr 7.5.1–10; 7.6.1–10; 7.7.1–10; 7.8.1–10;	10.1.7
	50	Cirupuliyūr Jalaśayanam 7.9.1–10	
	51	Kaṇṇamankai 7.10.1–10	Kaṇṇamankai 7.6.5; 10.1.1
	52	Kaṇṇapuram 8.1.1–10 to 8.10.1–10 (100 stanzas)	
	53	TiruKaṇṇankuṭi 9.1.1–10	
	54	TiruNākai 9.2.1–10	
	55		Koḻi 9.2.5
	56		Tañjai māmaṇi 1.1.6; 2.5.3; 7.3.9
	57		Karampan̲ūr 5.6.2
	58		Talaiccankanān̲matiyam 8.9.9
	59		Kuṭantai 1.1.2, 1.1.7, 1.5.4; 2.4.1; 3.6.5,8; 5.5.7; 6.8.9; 6.10.1; 7.3.3; 7.6.9; 8.9.5; 9.2.2; 10.1.6 ; 10.10.8; 11.6.9
Pāṇṭiyanāḍu	60	TirupPullāṇi 9.3.1–10; 9.4.1–10	
	61	TirukKurunkuṭi 9.5.1–10; 9.6.1–10	Kurunkuṭi 1.5.8; 2.4.1;5.6.2; 6.3.3
	62	Māliruñcolai 9.8.1–10; 9.9.1–10	Māliruñcolai 1.8.5; 2.7.7; 7.3.6; 7.9.7; 9.2.8; 10.1.8
	63		Mĕyyam 2.5.8; 3.6.9; 5.5.2; 6.8.7; 8.2.3; 9.2.3; 10.1.5; 11.7.5
	64		Kūṭal 9.2.5
	65	TirukKoṭṭiyūr 9.10.1–10	TirukKoṭṭiyūr 7.1.3; 10.1.9
Malainādu	66	TiruVallavāḻ 9.7.1–10	
	67		TiruMūḻikkaḷam 7.1.6
	68		TiruNāvāy 10.1.9

NOTE:
68 shrines are mentioned in the *Pĕriya Tirumŏli* of which 51 have hymns dedicated to them; there are references to 17 shrines of these 51 in other hymns as well. Reference alone is made to 17 other sites.

Tirukkuruntāṇṭakam (*TKT*) and *Tirunĕṭuntāṇṭakam* (*TNT*)	
Vaṭanāḍu	
Venkatam	*TKT* 7, *TNT* 16
Tŏṇṭaināḍu	
Kacci	*TKT* 19, *TNT* 9, 15
Nīrakam	*TNT* 8
Kārvānam	*TNT* 8
Mallai	*TKT* 19, *TNT* 9
Nilātinkaltuṇṭam	*TNT* 8
Taṇkā	*TNT* 14, 17
TiruNīrmalai	*TNT* 18
Ūrakam	*TNT* 13
Vĕhkā	*TNT* 8, 13, 14
Kārakam	*TNT* 8
Naṭunāḍu	
Kovalūr	*TNT* 6, 7, 17
Colanāḍu	
Aluntūr	*TNT* 15, 26
Arangam	*TKT* 7, 12, 13, 19 *TNT* 11, 12, 14, 18, 23, 24, 25
Kaṇṇapuram	*TNT* 16, 27
Kaṇṭiyūr	*TKT* 19,
Kuṭantai	*TKT* 6, 14, *TNT* 17, 19, 29
TiruNaraiyūr	*TNT* 16
TirupPer	*TKT* 17, 19, *TNT* 8, 9, 19
TiruvĀli	*TNT* 12, 22
TiruViṇṇagaram	*TNT* 29
Pāṇṭiyanāḍu	
Mĕyyam	*TKT* 19
Malainādu	
TiruMūlikkaḷam	*TNT* 10

NOTE: 23 shrines in *Tirukkuruntāṇṭakam* and *Tirunĕṭuntāṇṭakam* of which five are not mentioned in *Pĕriya Tirumŏli*. TOTAL: 73.

Regionwise distribution

Vaṭanāḍu: 7
Toṇṭainādu: 14+4
Naṭunāḍu: 2
Colanāḍu: 36+1
Pāṇṭiyanāḍu: 6
Malaināḍu: 3

TABLE II(d): *Shrines Mentioned by Nammālvār in the* Tiruvāymŏli (TVM) *and the* Tiruviruttam

Regions		*Main dedication*	*Only reference*
Vaṭanāḍu	1		Dvārakā *TVM* 4.6.10; 5.3.6
	2	Mathura *TVM* 9.1.3-10	Mathura *TVM* 7.10.4; 8.5.9;
	3	Venkaṭam *TVM* 3.3.1-11; 6.10-1-11	Venkaṭam *TVM* 2.7.11; 3.9.1; 4.5.11; 8.2.1; 8.2.8; 9.3.8; *Tiruviruttam* 8, 10, 15, 31, 50, 60, 81
Toṇṭaināḍu	4		Vĕhkā *Tiruviruttam* 26
Co<u>l</u>anāḍu	5	Kuṭantai *TVM* 5.8.1-11	Kuṭantai *TVM* 8.2.6; 10.9.7
	6	TiruViṇṇagar *TVM* 6.3.1-11	
	7	TiruArangam *TVM* 7.2.1-11	TiruArangam, *Tiruviruttam* 28
	8	Kaṇṇapuram *TVM* 9.10	
	9	TirupPer *TVM* 10.8	
Paṇṭiyanāḍu	10	TiruMokūr *TVM* 10.1	
	11	Māliruñcolai *TVM* 2.10; 10.7	Māliruñcolai *TVM* 10.8.1
	12	Kurunkuṭi *TVM* 5.5	Kurunkuṭi *TVM* 1.10.9; 3.9.2
	13	Kurukūr *TVM* 4.10	
	14	Srivaramangalanagar *TVM* 5.7	
	15	Tolaivillimangalam *TVM* 6.5	
	16	TirukKoḷūr *TVM* 6.7	Koḷūr *TVM* 8.3.5
	17	TirupPerai *TVM* 7.3	
	18	TirupPuḷinkuti *TVM* 9.2	Puḷinkuṭi *TVM* 8.3.5
	19		Varaguṇamankai *TVM* 9.2.4
	20		Vaikunta/ Tiruvaikunta *TVM* 9.2.4, 9.2.8

(Contd.)

Table II(d) (*contd.*)

	21		TiruKuḷantai *TVM* 8.2.4
	22		Vāṉamāmalai *TVM* 5.7.6
Malaināḍu	23	TiruVallavāḻ *TVM* 5.9.	
	24	TiruVaṇvaṇṭūr *TVM* 6.1	
	25	TiruvĀṟaṉviḷai *TVM* 7.10	
	26		TiruVaṇparicāram *TVM* 8.3.7
	27	TirucCĕnkuṉṟūr *TVM* 8.4	
	28	TirukKaṭittāṉam *TVM* 8.6	
	29	TirupPuliyūr *TVM* 8.9	
	30	TirukKāṭkarai *TVM* 9.6	
	31	TiruMūḻikkaḷam *TVM* 9.7	
	32	TiruNāvāy *TVM* 9.8	
	33	TiruvAṉantapuram *TVM* 10.2	
	34	TiruVāṭṭāru *TVM* 10.6	

Regionwise distribution

Tiruvāymŏli:

Vaṭanāḍu: 3 Coḻanāḍu: 5 Paṇṭiyanāḍu: 13 Malaināḍu: 12

Tiruviruttam:

Vaṭanāḍu: 1 (Venkaṭam- 7 mentions)
Tŏṇṭaināḍu: 1 (Vĕhkā- 1 mention)
Coḻanāḍu:1 (TiruArangam- 1 mention)

TABLE II(e): *Shrines Mentioned in the* Ciriya Tirumaṭal *and* Pĕriya Tirumaṭal

Regions		*Ciriya Tirumaṭal*	*Pĕriya Tirumaṭal*
Vaṭanāḍu			
	1	Āyppāṭi	
	2	Badari	
	3	Vaṭa Maturai (Mathurā)	
	4	TiruVenkaṭam	Venkaṭam
Toṇṭaināḍu			
	5	Kacci Ūrakam	Ūrakam
	6	Nīrmalai	Nīrmalai
	7	Taṇkāl	Taṇkāl
	8	Vĕhkā	Vĕhkā
	9	Iṭaventai	Iṭaventai
	10	Kaṭalmallai	Kaṭalmallai
	11	Kaṭikai	
	12		Kacci-Veḷukkai
	13		Pāṭakam
	14		Puṭkuḻi
	15		Aṭṭabuyakaram
Naṭunāḍu			
	16	TirukKovalūr	Kovalūr
Coḻanāḍu			
	17	Arangam	Arangam
	18	Kuṭantai	Kuṭantai
	19	Perāli/TiruvĀli	Āli
	20	Naraiyūr	Naraiyūr
	21	Kaṇṇapuram	Kaṇṇapuram
	22	Viṇṇagaram	Viṇṇagar
	23	Perakam	Per
	24	Kaṇṇamankai	Kaṇṇamankai
	25	Vĕḷḷarai	Vĕḷḷarai
	26	Cerai	Cerai
	27	TiruvAḻuntūr	Aḻuntūr
	28		Intalūr

(*Contd.*)

Table II(e) (*contd.*)

	29		Tillai-TiruCitrakūṭam
	30		Nānkūr-Maṇimāṭakkoyil
	31		Ātanūr
	32		Talaiccankaṉāṉmatiyam
Pāṇṭiyanāḍu			
	33	Māliruñcolai	Māliruñcolai
	34	TiruMokūr	
	35		Koṭṭiyūr
	36		TiruMĕyyam
	37		Kurunkuṭi
	38		Puḷḷāni
Malaināḍu			
	39	TirupPuliyūr	
	40		Vallavāḻ
	41		Mūḻikkaḷam

NOTE:
24 shrines are mentioned in the *Ciriya Tirumaṭal* and 35 in the *Pĕriya Tirumaṭal.*

Shrines Mentioned in the Other Compositions of the Nālāyiram

The *Amalaṉādipirāṉ* is devoted to the lord of Arangam and also mentions Venkaṭam twice.

Madhurakavi's *Kaṇṇinuṇciruttāmpu*, being devoted to Nammāḻvār, does not mention any shrine.

The *Tiruvāciriyam* and the *Pĕriya Tiruvantādi* do not mention any shrine.

The *Tiruvĕḻukūṟṟirukkai* mentions only Kuṭantai.

Bibliography

Primary Sources in Tamil

Ācārya Hṛdayam of Aḻakiya Maṇavāḷap Pĕrumāḷ Nāyaṉār, with the commentary of Maṇavāḷa Māmuni, ed. P.B. Annangaracārya, Śrīmad Varavara Munīndra Granthamāla, 1966.

Āḻvār Tiruvuḷḷam: Iyarpā, Text with Tamil commentary and English Translation by Vankipuram Navanītam Vedānta Deśikaṉ, Madras: Śrī Viśiṣṭādvaita Research Centre, 1994.

Ārāyirappaṭi Guruparamparāprabhāvam of Piṉpaḻakiya Pĕrumāḷ Cīyar, ed. S. Kiruṣṇasvāmi Ayyankār, Tirucci: Puttūr Agrahāram, 1975.

Bhagavad Viṣayam, ed. Vai. Mu. Gopalakrsnamācāriyār, A. Vi. Narasimhācāriyār, 10 vols., Tiruvellikeni, 1925. Contains 600, 9000, 12000 and 24000, *Īṭu* with *Arumpatavurai.*

Divya Sūri Caritam of Garudavāhana Paṇḍita, Translated into Hindi by Paṇḍita Mādhavācārya, ed. T.A. Sampath Kumaracharya and K.K.A. Venkatachari, Bombay: Ananthacharya Research Institute, 1978.

Mūvāyirappaṭi Guruparamparāprabhāvam (Vaṭakalai) of Tṛtīya Brahmatantra Svatantra Cīyar, ed. K. Śrīnivāsācārya, Madras: The Little Flower Company, 1968.

Nālāyiradivyaprabandham—The Sacred Book of 4000, Rendered in English with Tamil Original by Srirama Bharati, Chennai: Sri Sadagopan Tirunarayansvami Divyaprabandham Pathasala, 2000.

Rāmānujārya Divya Caritai of Piḷḷai Lokāṉ Cīyar.

Śrī Tivyapirapantam, 4 vols., ed. Tamil Scholars, Madras: Murray & Co., 1956.

Tiruvāymŏḻi, Text with Tamil commentary and English translation by V.N. Vedanta Desikan, Madras: Srivisistadvaita Research Centre, 1994.

Vārttāmalai of Piṉpaḻakiya Pĕrumāḷ Cīyar, ed. S. Krishnaswamy Ayyangar, Tirucci: Puttūr Agrahāram, 1983.

Yatirāja Vimśati of Varavaramuni, ed. Satyamurti Svami, Gwalior, 1972.

Primary Sources in Sanskrit and Tamil in English Translation

Āgama Prāmāṇyam of Yāmuna, Sanskrit Text and English Translation with Introduction by J.A.B. van Buitenen, Madras: Ramanuja Research Society, 1971.

Mumukṣuppaṭi of Piḷḷai Lokācārya with Maṇavāḷamāmuni's Commentary, Translation by Patricia Y. Mumme, Bombay: Ananthacharya Indological Research Institute Series no. XIX, 1987.

Nalayiradivyaprabandham—The Sacred Book of 4000 Rendered in English with Tamil Original by Srirama Bharati, Chennai: Sri Sadagopan Tirunarayansvami Divyaprabandham Pathasala, 2000.

Sri Thirumazhisai Piran's *Nanmukan Thiruvandadi* (Text with a free Translation and Commentary) by Dr N. Ranganathan, Published by Sri N. Rajagopalan, Madras, 1999.

The Śrīvacanabhūṣaṇa of Piḷḷai Lokācārya, ed. and tr. Robert Lester, Madras: The Kuppuswami Sastri Research Institute, 1979.

Srivacana Bhusanam by Pillai Lokacarya and Yatiraja Vimsati of Srimad Varavaramuni, An English Glossary by Sri Satyamurthi Swami, Gwalior, A Publication of Sri Ram Nam Yogashram, Ayodhya, Faizabad, 1972.

Tevaram Hymnes Sivaites du Pays Tamoul, ed. François Gros and T.V. Gopala Iyer, no. 68.1, Pondichéry: Publications de l'Institut Français d'Indologie, 1984.

Vedārthasamgraha of Rāmānuja, ed. and tr. J.A.B. van Buitenen, Deccan College, Poona, 1956.

Vāraṇamāyiram and *Tirukkuruntāṇḍakam*, Translation and commentary by Dr V.K.S.N. Raghavan, Madras: Visishtadvaita Pracharini Sabha, 1995.

Modern Sources in Tamil

Etirajan, A., *108 Vaiṇava Divya Deśa Stala Varaḷāru*, Kāraikkuṭi: Vaiṇava Siddhānta Nūrpatippuk Kaḻakam, 2003.

Navathiruppathi, Temple History: 108 Divya Desams details/ 9 Temple History, Chennai: V.R.K. Publications (Pamphlet literature).

Sri Nrisimhapriya, A Monthly Publication of The Nrisimhapriya Trust, Chennai, 2003–9.

108 Vaiṣṇava Divya Deśa Vaibhavamum Purāṇa Abhimāna Stalankaḷum: A Pilgrims' Guide, Madras: The Little Flower Company, 1984 (revd. edn. 2002).

Epigraphic Sources

Ekambaranathan, A., and C.K. Sivaprakasam, *Jaina Inscriptions in Tamil Nadu: A Topographical List*, Madras: Research Foundation for Jainology, 1987.

Epigraphica Indica, vols. XV, XXII, XXV, Published by the Director General, Archaeological Survey of India, Delhi,1984.

Mahalingam, T.V., *A Topographical List of Inscriptions in Tamil Nadu and Kerala States*, ICHR and S. Chand and Co., Delhi, vols. I–IX, 1985.

South Indian Inscriptions, vols. I, II, III, XII, XIII, XIV, Archaeological Survey of India, New Delhi/ Mysore, 1984–7.

Secondary Sources in English

Adluri, Sucharita, 'Śruti and Smṛti in Rāmānuja's Vedānta', *Journal of Vaishnava Studies*, vol. 15, no. 1, 2006, pp. 193–219.

Aiyangar, K.V. Rangaswami, 'Govindarāja', *Annals of the Bhandarkar Oriental Research Institute*, vol. 23, 1942, pp. 30–54.

Aiyangar, S. Krishnaswami; see Ayyangar, Rao Saheb S. Krishnaswami.

Aiyappan, A. and P.R. Srinivasan, eds., 1960, *Story of Buddhism with special reference to South India*, Madras: Department of Information and Publicity, Government of Madras.

Aiyar, K.G. Sesha, 'Tirumangai Azhwar and Danti Durga', *Quarterly Journal of the Mythic Society*, vol. 13, no. 2, 1923, pp. 580–8.

Appadorai, A., *Economic Conditions in South India 1000-1500* AD, 2 vols, Chennai: Madras University Historical Series.

Appadurai, Arjun, 'Right and Left Hand Castes in South India', *The Indian Economic and Social History Review*, vol. 11, nos. 2–3, 1974, pp. 216–59.

———, 'Kings, Sects and Temples in South India, 1350- 1700 AD', *The Indian Economic and Social History Review*, vol. 14, nos. 1–2, 1977, pp. 47–74.

———, 'Gastro-Politics in Hindu South Asia', *American Ethnologist*, vol. 8, no. 3, 1981a, pp. 494–511.

———, 'The Past as a Scarce Resource', *Man*, New Series, vol. 16, no. 2, 1981b, pp. 201–19.

———, *Worship and Conflict under Colonial Rule*, Delhi: Orient Longman, 1983.

Appadurai, Arjun and Carol A. Breckenridge, 'The South Indian Temple: Authority, Honour and Redistribution', *Contributions to Indian Sociology*, vol. 10, no. 2, 1976, pp. 187–211.

Ate, Lynn, *Yasoda's Songs to her Playful Son, Kṛṣṇa: Periyāḻvār's 9th Century Tamil Tirumoḻi*, Woodland Hills, California: South Asian Studies Association, 2011.

Arunachalam, M., 'The Siddha Cult in Tamil Nadu', *Bulletin of the Institute of Traditional Cultures, Madras*, vol. 21, no. 1, 1977, pp. 85–118.

Ayyangar, Rao Saheb S. Krishnaswami, *South India and her Muhammadan Invaders*, Delhi: S. Chand & Co. Pvt. Ltd., 1921.

———, 'Tirumangai Alvar and Danti Durga', *Quarterly Journal of the Mythic Society*, vol. 12, no. 3, 1922, pp. 261–7.

———, 'Tirumangai Alvar and Danti Durga', (reply to criticism of previous article by K.G. Sesha Aiyar, see above), *Quarterly Journal of the Mythic Society*, vol. 13, no. 3, 1923, pp. 695–8.

Ayyangar, S. Satyamurthi, *Tiruvaymoli English Glossary, Volumes I & II*, Bombay: Ananathacharya Indological Research Institute, 1981.

Ayyangar, S.V. Varadaraja, 'The Date of Tirumangai Ālvār', *Journal of Indian History*, vol. 26, no. 2, 1948, pp. 131–4. See also Iyengar.

Ayyar, P.V. Jagadisa, 'Periyapurana or the Lives of the Great Saiva Devotees', *Quarterly Journal of the Mythic Society*, vol. 12, no. 2, 1923, pp. 194–202; vol.13, no. 3, pp. 645–64.

Bailey, G.M. & Ian Kesarcodi-Watson, *Bhakti Studies*, New Delhi: Sterling Publishers, 1991.

Bakker, Hans, ed., *The History of Sacred Places in India as Reflected in Traditional Literature: Papers on Pilgrimage in South Asia*, Leiden: EJ Brill, 1990.

Balambal, V., *Studies in Cola History*, Delhi: Kalinga Publications, 1998.

Balasubhramaniam, S.R., *Early Cola Temples*, Delhi: Orient Longman, 1971.

———, *Middle Cola Temples*, Faridabad: Thompson Press India Ltd, 1975.

———, *Late Cola Temples*, Madras: Mudgala Trust, 1979.

Bartley, C.J., *The Theology of Rāmānuja: Realism and Religion*, London: Routledge Curzon, 2002.

Basant, P.K., 'Book Review: R.S. Sharma, Early Medieval Indian Society: A Study in Feudalisation', *Studies in History*, vol. 19, no. 1, 2003, pp. 139–43.

Basham, A.L., *The Wonder that was India*, Delhi: Rupa, 1954, repr. 1994.

———, *The Cultural History of India*, Oxford: Clarendon Press, 1975.

Beck, Brenda E.F., 'The Authority of the King: Prerogatives and Dilemmas of Kingship as Portrayed in a Contemporary Oral Epic from South India', *Kingship and Authority in South Asia*, ed. J.F. Richards, New Delhi: Oxford University Press, 1998, pp. 189–215.

Beteille, A., 'Social Organization of Temples in a Tanjore Village', *History of Religions*, vol. 5, no. 1, 1965, pp. 74–92.

Bhandarkar, R.G., *Vaisnavism, Saivism and other Minor Religious Systems*, Strassburg: Karl J. Trubner, 1963.

Bharadwaj, K.D., *The Philosophy of Ramanuja*, Delhi: Sir Shankar Lall Charitable Trust Society, 1958.

Bharati, Agehananda, 'Pilgrimage in the Indian Tradition', *History of Religions*, vol. 3, no. 1, 1963, pp. 135–67.

Bhardwaj, S.M., *Hindu Places of Pilgrimage in India: A Study in Cultural Geography*, Delhi: Surjeet Publications, 1989.

Bhatt, S.R., *Studies in Ramanuja Vedanta*, New Delhi: Heritage Publishers, 1975.

Breckenridge, Carol Appadurai, 'Scale and Social Formations in South India, 1350- 1750', in *Studies of South India*, ed. G.W. Spencer, Madras: New Era Publications, 1985.

Brown, C. Mackenzie, 'Purana as Scripture: From Sound to Image of the Holy Word in Hindu Tradition', *History of Religions*, vol. 26, no. 1, 1986, pp. 68–86.

Buck, M.M. and G.E. Yocum, eds., *Structural Approaches to South Indian Studies*, Chambersburg: Wilson Books, 1974.

Buitenen, J.A.B. van, 'On the Archaism of the *Bhāgavata Purāṇa*', in *Krishna: Myths, Rites and Attitudes*, ed. Milton Singer, Honolulu: East-West Centre Press,

1966, pp. 23–40; (also in J.A.B. van Buitenen, *Studies in Indian Philosophy and Literature*, Delhi: Motilal Banarsidass, 1981, pp. 223–42).

———, *Āgama Prāmāṇyam of Yāmuna*, Sanskrit Text and English Translation with Introduction, Madras: Ramanuja Research Society, 1971.

———, '*Kapyāsam Puṇḍarīkam*', in *Studies in Indian Philosophy and Literature*, ed. J.A.B. van Buitenen, Delhi: Motilal Banarsidass, 1981, pp. 147–56.

Bryant, Edwin F., *Krishna: The Beautiful Legend of God (Śrīmad Bhāgavata Purāṇa Book X)*, New York: Oxford University Press, 2003.

———, ed., *Krishna: A Sourcebook*, New York: Oxford University Press, 2007.

Carman, John, *The Theology of Rāmānuja: An Essay in Interreligious Understanding*, New Haven and London: Yale University Press, 1974; Bombay: Ananthacharya Indological Research Institute, repr. 1981.

———, 'Conceiving Hindu Bhakti as Theistic Mysticism', in *Mysticism and Religious Traditions*, ed. Steven Katz, New York: Oxford University Press, 1983.

———, *Majesty and Meekness: A Comparative Study of Contrast and Harmony in the Concept of God*, Grand Rapids, Michigan: William B. Eerdsman Publishing Company, 1994.

Carman, John and Frederique Marglin, eds., *Purity and Auspiciousness in Indian Society*, International Studies in Sociology and Social Anthropology 43, Leiden: EJ Brill, 1994.

Carman, John and Vasudha Narayanan, *The Tamil Veda: Piḷḷāṉ's Interpretation of the Tiruvāymoḻi*, Chicago: The University of Chicago Press, 1989.

Carpenter, J.E., *Theism in Medieval India*, London, 1921.

Census of India, 1911, vol. XIII, Central Provinces Report, Pt. 1.

Chakrabarti, Kunal, 'Review Article: The Sacred and the Profane in Ancient Indian Myth and Literature', *Studies in History*, vol. 5, no. 1, 1989, pp. 143–58.

———, 'Recent Approaches to History of Religions in Ancient India', in *Recent Perspectives of Early Indian History*, ed. Romila Thapar, Bombay: Popular Prakashan, 1995, pp. 185–245.

———, 'Cult Religion: The *Purāṇas* and the Making of the Cultural Territory of Bengal', *Studies in History*, vol. 16, 2000, pp. 1–16.

———, *Religious Process: The Purāṇas and the Making of a Religious Tradition*, Delhi: Oxford University Press, 2001.

Champakalakshmi, R., 'Vaiṣṇava Concepts in Early Tamil Nadu', *Journal of Indian History*, vol. 50, no. 3, 1972, pp. 723–54.

———, 'Archaeology and Tamil Literary Tradition', *Puratattva (ASI)*, vol. 8, 1975–6.

———, 'Religious Conflict and Persecution in the Tamil Country', *Proceedings of the Indian History Congress*, Thirty-seventh Session, 1976.

———, 'Religious Conflict in the Tamil Country: A Reappraisal of Epigraphic Evidence', *Journal of the Epigraphic Society of India*, vol. 5, 1978, pp. 69–81.

———, 'Growth of Urban Centres in South India: Kuḍamūkku-Paḻaiyarai, the Twin City of the Colas', *Studies in History*, vol. 1, no. 1, 1979, pp. 1–30

———, *Vaiṣṇava Iconography in the Tamil Country*, New Delhi: Orient Longman, 1981a.

———, 'Peasant State and Society in Medieval South India: A Review Article', *The Indian Economic and Social History Review*, vol. 18, nos. 3–4, 1981b, pp. 411–26.

———, 'Introduction', *Studies in History*, vol. 4, no. 2, 1982, pp. 161–6.

———, 'Urbanisation in South India: The Role of Ideology and Polity', Presidential Address, *Proceedings of the Indian History Congress*, Forty-seventh Session, Srinagar, 1986.

———, 'Religion and Social Change in Tamil Nadu AD 600-1300', in *Medieval Bhakti Movements in India, Sri Caitanya Quincentenary Commemoration Volume*, ed. N.N. Bhattacharyya, Delhi, Munshiram Manoharlal, 1989.

———, 'Urban Process in Early Medieval Tamil Nadu', in *The City in Indian History*, ed. Indu Banga, Delhi: Manohar, 1991.

———, 'The City in Medieval South India: Its Forms and Meaning', in *Craftsmen and Merchants. Essays in South Indian Urbanism*, ed. Narayani Gupta, Chandigarh: Urban History Association of India, 1993.

———, '*Patikam Pāṭuvār*: Ritual Singing as a Means of Communication in Early Medieval South India', *Studies in History*, vol. 10, no. 2, July-December 1994, pp. 199–215.

———, 'From Devotion to Dissent and Dominance', in *Tradition, Dissent and Ideology*, ed. R. Champakalakshmi and S. Gopal, New Delhi: Oxford University Press, 1996a, pp. 135–62.

———, *Trade, Ideology and Urbanisation: South India 300 BC- 1300 AD*, New Delhi: Oxford University Press, 1996b.

———, 'Puranic Religion: The Evolution of the Tamil Saiva Tradition', in *Traditions in Motion: Religion and Society in History*, ed. Satish Saberwal and Supriya Varma, New Delhi: Oxford University Press, 2005.

———, 'Śankara and Puranic Religion', in *Ancient to Modern: Religion, Power and Community in India*, ed. Ishita Banerjee-Dube and Saurabh Dube, New Delhi: Oxford University Press, 2009, pp. 49–85.

Champakalakshmi, R. and Usha Kris, *The Hindu Temple*, New Delhi: Roli Books, 2002.

Chandra, Pramod, ed., *Studies in Indian Temple Architecture*, Delhi: American Institute of Indian Studies, 1975.

Chattopadhyaya, B.D., *The Making of Early Medieval India*, Delhi: Oxford University Press, 1994.

———, *Representing the Other? Sanskrit Sources and the Muslims*, Delhi: Manohar, 1998.

Chetty, Rao Bahadur V. Ranganadham, *History of Triplicane and the Temple of Sri Parthasarathi Svami*. Madras, 1948.

Clooney, Francis X., 'Divine Word, Human Word: The Srivaisnava Exposition of the Character of Nammalvar's Experience as Revelation', in *In Spirit and In Truth: Festscrift for Ignatius Hrudayam*, Madras, 1985.

———, '"I Created Land and Sea": A Tamil Case of God Consciousness and its Srivaisnava Interpretation', *Numen*, vol. 35, 1988.

———, 'Nammāḻvār's Glorious Tiruvaḷḷavāl: An Exploration in the Methods and Goals of Śrīvaiṣṇava Commentary', *Journal of the American Oriental Society*, vol. 111, no. 2, 1991, pp. 260–76.
———, *The Art and Theology of Srivaisnava Thinkers*, Madras: TR Publications, 1994.
———, 'Book Review: Patricia Mumme's The Srivaisnava Theological Dispute: Manavalamamuni and Vedanta Desika', *Journal of the American Oriental Society*, vol. 114, no. 2, 1994, pp. 319–20.
———, *Seeing through Texts: Doing Theology among the Srivaisnavas of South India*, Delhi: Sri Satguru Publications, Indian Books Centre, 1997.
———, 'For Bhakti is Synonymous with Upāsanā: Rāmānuja's Understanding of Upāsanā particularly as exemplified in the Commentaries of *Tiruvāymoḻi*', *Journal of Vaishnava Studies*, vol. 6, no. 1, 1998, pp. 117–39.
———, 'Restoring "Hindu Theology" as a Category in Indian Intellectual Discourse', in *The Blackwell Companion to Hinduism*, ed. Gavin Flood, Oxford and Malden: Blackwell Publishing Limited, Indian repr. 2003, pp. 447–77.
———, 'Śrīvaiṣṇavism in Dialogue, c 1900: Alkondavilli Govindacharya as a Comparative Theologian', *Journal of Vaishnava Studies*, vol. 13, no. 1, 2004, pp. 103–24.
———, 'Ramanuja and the Meaning of Krishna's Descent and Embodiment on This Earth', in *Krishna: A Sourcebook*, ed. Edwin F. Bryant, New York: Oxford University Press, 2007.
———, *The Truth, the Way, the Life: Christian Commentary on the Three Holy Mantras of the Śrīvaiṣṇava Hindus*, Belgium: Peeters Publishers; Grand Rapids, Michigan: William B. Eerdmans Publishing Company, 2008.
Clothey, Fred, ed., *Images of Man: Religion and Historical Process in South Asia*, Madras: New Era Publications, 1982.
———, *Rhythm and Intent: Ritual Studies from South India*, Madras: Blackie and Son, 1983.
Clothey, Fred and Bruce Long, *Experiencing Śiva: Encounters with a Hindu Deity*, Delhi: Manohar, 1983.
———, 'On the Study of Religion in South India', in *Studies in South India: An Anthology of Recent Research and Scholarship*, ed. R.E. Frykenberg and P. Kolenda, Madras: New Era Publications, 1985.
Colas, Gerard, 'History of Vaisnava Traditions: An Esquisse', in *The Blackwell Companion to Hinduism*, ed. Gavin Flood, Oxford and Malden: Blackwell Publishing Limited, Indian repr. 2003, pp. 229–70.
Coleman, Tracy, 'Suffering Desire for Krishna: Gender and Salvation in the Bhāgavata Purāṇa', *Journal of Vaishnava Studies, vol. 10*, no. *2*, 2002, *pp. 39-50.*
Cort, John E., 'Bhakti in the Early Jain Tradition: Understanding Devotional Religion in South Asia', *History of Religions*, vol. 42, no. 1, 2002, pp. 59–86.
———, ed., *Open Boundaries: Jain Communities and Cultures in Indian History*, Albany: State University of New York Press, 1998.
Cutler, Norman, 'The Devotee's Experience of the Sacred Tamil Hymns', *History of Religions*, vol. 24, no. 2, 1984, pp. 91–112.

———, *Songs of Experience: The Poetics of Tamil Devotion*, Bloomington: Indiana University Press, 1987.

———, 'Tamil Bhakti in Translation', *Journal of the American Oriental Society*, vol. 111, no. 4, 1991, pp. 768–75.

———, 'Tamil Hindu Literature', in *The Blackwell Companion to Hinduism*, ed. Gavin Flood, Oxford/ Malden: Blackwell Publishing Limited, Indian repr. 2003, pp. 145–58.

Cutler, Norman and J.P. Waghorne, eds., *Gods of Flesh, Gods of Stone*, Chambersburg: Anima Publications, 1985.

Cutler, Norman and Paula Richman, *A Gift of Tamil: Translations from Tamil Literature in Honour of K Paramasivam*, New Delhi: American Institute of Indian Studies, 1992.

Damodaran, G., *Acarya Hrdayam: A Critical Study*, Tirupati: Tirumalai Tirupati Devasthanams, 1976.

Daniels, E.V., *Fluid Signs: Being a Person the Tamil Way*, Berkeley: University of California Press, 1984.

Davis, Richard H., *Lives of Indian Images*, Princeton: Princeton University Press, 1997.

———, 'The Story of the Disappearing Jains: Retelling the Śaiva-Jain Encounters in Medieval South India', in *Open Boundaries: Jain Communities and Cultures in Indian History*, ed. John Cort, Albany: State University of New York Press, 1998, pp. 213–24.

———, 'A Muslim Princess in the Temples of Viṣṇu', *International Journal of Hindu Studies*, vol. 8, nos. 1–3, 2004, pp. 137–56.

Dayalan, D., 'Hymns of the Nayanars and the Tripurantaka Episode in the Big Temple, Tanjavur', in *Indian Archaeological Heritage (K.V. Sounderarajan Festshrift)*, ed. C. Margabandhu, K.S. Ramachandra, A.P. Sagar, D.K. Sinha, Delhi: Agam Kala Prakshan, 1991.

———, *Early Temples of Tamil Nadu: Their Role in Socio- Economic Life; c AD 550-925*, New Delhi: Harman Publishing House, 1992.

De, S.K., *The Early History of the Vaisnava Faith*, Calcutta, 1961.

Deccan Studies (Journal), Special Issue on Jainism, vol. 5, no. 1, Hyderabad: Centre for Deccan Studies, January-June 2007.

Dehejia, Vidya, *The Namakkal Caves*, State Department of Archaeology, Government of Tamil Nadu, 1977.

———, *Looking Again at Indian Art*, Publications Division, New Delhi: Ministry of Information and Broadcasting, 1978.

———, *Slaves of the Lord: The Path of the Tamil Saints*, Delhi: Munshiram Manoharlal, 1988.

———, *Andal and her Path of Love*, Albany: State University of New York Press, 1990 a.

———, *Art of the Imperial Cholas*, New York: Columbia University Press, 1990 b.

———, *The Sensuous and the Sacred: Chola Bronzes from South India*, New York: American Federation of Arts, in association with Ahmedabad: Mapin Publishing, 2003.

Desai, P.B., *Jainism in South India and Some Jaina Epigraphs*, Sholapur: Gulabchand Hirachand Doshi Jaina Samskṛti Samrakshaka Sangha, 1957.

Desmet, Richard, 'Ramanuja: Pantheist or Panentheist?', *Annals of the Bhandarkar Oriental Research Institute*, vols. 58–9, 1977–8, pp. 561–71.

Devanathachariar, K., 'Srivaisnavism and its Caste Marks', *The Quarterly Journal of the Mythic Society*, vol. 5, 1914–15, pp. 125–39.

Dirks, N.B., 'The Structure and Meanings of Political Relations in a South Indian Little Kingdom', *Contributions to Indian Sociology*, vol.13, no. 2, 1979, pp. 169–204.

Durga, P.S. Kanaka and Y.A. Sudhakar Reddy, 'Kings, Temples and Legitimation of Autochthonous Communities: A Case Study of a South Indian Temple', *Journal of the Economic and Social History of the Orient*, vol. 35, 1993, pp. 145–66.

Dutta, Ranjeeta, 'Imaging the Goddess: A Process in the Identity Formation of the Śrīvaiṣṇava Community', in *Invoking Goddesses: Gender Politics in Indian Religion*, ed. Nilima Chitgopekar, New Delhi: Har- Anand Publications, 2002, pp. 112–39.

———, 'The Politics of Religious Identity: A Muslim Goddess in the Śrīvaiṣṇava Community of South India', *Studies in History*, vol.19, no. 2, 2003, pp. 157–84.

———, 'Community Identity and Sectarian Affiliations: The Śrīvaiṣṇavas of South India from the Eleventh to the Seventeenth Century AD', Unpublished Ph.D. Thesis, New Delhi: Jawaharlal Nehru University, 2004.

Eck, D.L., 'India's Tirthas: Crossings in Sacred Geography', *History of Religions*, vol. 20, no. 4, 1981, pp. 323–44.

Eck, D.L. and Francoise Mallison, *Devotion Divine: Bhakti Traditions from the Regions of India*, Groningen: Egbert Forster, 1991.

Edholm, Erik Af and Carl Suneson, 'The Seven Bulls and Krsna's Marriage of Nila/ Nappinnai in Sanskrit and Tamil Literature', *Temenos: Studies in Comparative Religion*, vol. 8, 1972, pp. 29–53.

Ekambaranathan, A., 'Buddhist Vestiges in Toṇḍaimaṇḍalam', *Bulletin of the Institute of Traditional Cultures, Madras*, vol. 21, no. 1, 1977, pp. 17–21.

Ferro-Luzzi, Gabriella Eichinger, 'Ritual as Language: The Case of South Indian Food Offerings', *Current Anthropology*, vol. 18, no. 3, 1977, pp. 507–14.

Flood, Gavin, ed., *The Blackwell Companion to Hinduism*, Oxford and Malden: Blackwell Publishing Limited, Indian repr. 2003.

Forsthoefel, Thomas A. and Patricia Y. Mumme, 'The Monkey-Cat Debate in Śrīvaiṣṇavism: Conceptualizing Grace in Medieval India', *Journal of Vaishnava Studies*, vol. 8, no. 1, 1999, pp. 3–33.

Frykenberg, R.E., 'Constructions of Hinduism at the Nexus of History and Religion', *Journal of Interdisciplinary History*, vol. 23, no. 3, Religion and History, 1993, pp. 523–50.

Frykenberg, R.E. and P. Kolenda, eds., *Studies of South India: An Anthology of Recent Research and Scholarship*, Madras: New Era Publications, 1985.

Fuller, C.J., *The Camphor Flame: Popular Hinduism and Society in India*, Princeton: Princeton University Press; India: Penguin Books, 1992.

Ganesan,T., 'Jaina Vestiges of Tirunarungondai in South Arcot District, Tamil Nadu', in *Essays in Indian History and Culture*, ed. Y. Krishan, New Delhi: Indian History and Culture Society, 1986.

Ghose, Rajeshwari, *The Lord of Ārūr,The Tyāgarāja Cult in Tamilnāḍu: A Study in Conflict and Accommodation*, Delhi: Motilal Banarsidass Publishers Pvt. Ltd., 1996.

Glushkova, Irina, '*Dharma* and *Bhakti*: Marital Conflicts in the Vārkarī Tradition', in *In the Company of Gods: Essays in Memory of Günther-Deitz Sonthheimer*, ed. Aditya Malik, Anne Feldhaus, Heidrun Brückner, New Delhi: IGNCA, Manohar, 2005.

Gnanambal, K., 'Srivaisnavas and their Religious Institutions', *Bulletin of the Anthropological Survey of India*, vol. 20, no. 3, July-December 1971, pp. 97–187.

Goldman, Robert, 'A City of the Heart: Epic Mathurā and the Indian Imagination', *Journal of the American Oriental Society*, vol. 106, no. 3, 1986, pp. 471–83.

Gonda, Jan, *Aspects of Early Viṣṇuism*, 1954; repr., Delhi: Motilal Banarsidass, 1969.

———, *Viṣṇuism and Śivaism: A Comparison*, London: Athlone Press, 1970.

———, *Selected Studies*, vols. II, IV, VI pt. 1, Leiden: EJ Brill, 1975.

———, *Medieval Religious Literature in Sanskrit: A History of Indian Literature*, vol. II, fasc I. Wiesbaden: Otto Harrassowitz Verlag, 1977.

Gopalan, L.V., *Sri Vaisnava Divyadesams (108 Tirupatis)*, Madras: Visistadvaita Pracharini Sabha, 1972.

Gopalan, R., *History of the Pallavas of Kanchi*, Madras: University of Madras, 1928.

Gopinath Rao, T.A., *The History of the Srivaisnavas*, Madras: Madras University, 1923.

Goswami, Kunja Govinda, 'Vaiṣṇavism', *Indian Historical Quarterly*, vol. 31, 1955, pp. 109–33.

Goudriaan, T., 'Vaikhanasa Daily Worship according to the Handbooks of Atri, Bhrgu, Kasyapa and Marici', *Indo- Iranian Journal*, vol. 12, no. 1, 1970, pp. 162–215.

Govindacarya, Alkondavilli, *Sri Bhagavat Gita with Ramanujacarya's Visistadvaita Commentary*, Madras: Vaijayanti Press, 1898.

———, *The Divine Wisdom of the Dravida Saints*, Madras: CN Press, 1902.

———, *Holy Lives of the Azhwars*, Mysore: GE Press, 1902.

———, *The Life of Ramanujacharya*, Madras: S. Murthy & Co., 1906.

———, 'The Artha Pancaka or the Five Truths by Pillai Lokacarya with an introduction by G.A. Grierson', *Journal of the Royal Asiatic Society*, July 1910a, pp. 565–608

———, 'The Astadasa Bhedas or the Eighteen Points of Doctrinal Difference Between the Tengalais (Southerners) and Vaḍagalais (Northerners) of the

Viśiṣṭādvaita Vaiṣṇava School in South India', *Journal of the Royal Asiatic Society*, October 1910b, pp. 1103–12.

———, 'The Pancaratras or Bhagavan Sastra', *Journal of the Royal Asiatic Society*, October 1911, pp. 935–61.

Gros, Francois, 'Towards Reading the Tevaram', in *Tevaram Hymnes Sivaites du Pays Tamoul*, ed. F. Gros and T.V. Gopala Iyer, no. 68.1, Pondichéry: Publications de l'Institut Français d'Indologie, 1984.

Gros, Francois and T.V. Gopala Iyer, eds., *Tevaram Hymnes Sivaites du Pays Tamoul, Volumes I and II*, no. 68.1, Pondichéry: Publications de l'Institut Français d'Indologie, 1984.

Gurukkal, Rajan, 'Aspects of the Reservoir System of Irrigation in the Early Pandyan State', *Studies in History (new series)*, vol. 2, no. 2, 1986, pp. 155–62.

———, 'Forms of Production and Forces of Change in Ancient Tamil Society', *Studies in History*, vol. 5, no. 2, 1989, pp. 159–76.

———, 'Towards the Voice of Dissent, Trajectory of Ideological Transformation in South India', *Social Scientist*, vol. 21, nos.1–2, 1993, pp. 2–22.

———, 'The Beginnings of the Historic Period: The Tamil South', in *Recent Perspectives of Early Indian History*, ed. Romila Thapar, Bombay: Popular Prakashan, 1995, pp. 237–65.

———, 'Temples as Sites of Social and Religious Interaction', in *History of Science, Philosophy and Culture in Indian Civilization*, ed. B.D. Chattopadhyaya, Centre for Studies in Civilization, Delhi: Pearson Longman, 2009, pp. 199–210.

Gurumurthy, S., 'Jaina System of Learning in South India', *Bulletin of the Institute of Traditional Cultures, Madras*, vol. 15, no. 2, 1971, pp. 92–112.

———, 'Buddhist System of Learning in South India', *Bulletin of the Institute of Traditional Cultures, Madras*, vol. 18, no. 2, 1974, pp. 73–84.

Hall, Kenneth R., *Trade and Statecraft in the Age of the Colas*, New Delhi: Abhinav Publications, 1980.

———, 'Peasant, State and Society in Cola Times: A View from the Tiruvidaimarudur Urban Complex', *Indian Economic and Social History Review*, vol. 18, no. 3, 1981, pp. 393–5.

———, ed., *Structure & Change in South Indian Society. Essays in Honour of Noboru Karashima*, Delhi: Oxford University Press, 2001.

Hall, Kenneth R. and George W. Spencer, 'The Economy of Kāñcīpuram, A Sacred Center in Early South India', *Journal of Urban History*, vol. 6, no. 2, 1980, pp. 127–51.

Hardy, Friedhelm, 'Ideology and Cultural Contexts of the Śrīvaiṣṇava Temple', *The Indian Economic and Social History Review*, vol. 14, nos. 1–2, 1977, pp. 119–51.

———, 'The Philosopher as a Poet: A Study of Vedāntadeśika's *Dehalīśastuti*', *Journal of Indian Philosophy*, vol. 7, 1979a, pp. 277–325.

———, 'The Tamil Veda of a Śūdra Saint: The Śrīvaiṣṇava Interpretation of Nammāḻvār', in *Contribution to South Asian Studies*, ed. Gopal Krishna, Delhi: Oxford University Press, 1979b, pp. 29–87.

———, 'Diary of an Unknown Indian Girl', *Religion*, no. 10, 1980, pp. 165–82.
———, *Viraha Bhakti: The Early History of Kṛṣṇa Devotion in South India*, New Delhi: Oxford University Press, 1983a.
———, 'Viraha in Relation to Concrete Space and Time', in *Bhakti in Current Research, 1979-1982*, ed. Monika Thiel-Horstman, Berlin: Dietrich Reiner Verlag, 1983b, pp. 143–53.
———, 'Tiruppāṇ Āḻvār: The Untouchable who Rode Piggy Back on the Brahmin', in *Devotion Divine: Bhakti Traditions from the Regions of India*, ed. D.L. Eck and Francoise Mallison, Groningen: Egbert Forster, 1991, pp. 129–54.
———, 'The of Śrīvaiṣṇava Hagiography of Parakāla', in *The Indian Narrative: Perspectives and Patterns*, ed. Christopher Schakle and Rupert Snells, Wiesbaden: Otto Harrassowitz, 1992, pp. 81–116.
———, *The Religious Culture of India: Power, Love and Wisdom*, Cambridge, 1995.
———, 'The Formation of Śrīvaiṣṇavism', in *Charisma and Canon: Essays on the Religious History of the Indian Subcontinent*, ed. Vasudha Dalmia, Angelika Malinar and Martin Christof, New Delhi: Oxford University Press, 2001, pp. 41–61.
———, 'A Radical Reassessment of the Vedic Heritage: The Ācāryahṛdayam and its wider Implications', in *Representing Hinduism: The Construction of Religious Traditions and National Identity*, ed. Vasudha Dalmia and Heinrich von Stietencron, 1995; reproduced in Vasudha Dalmia and Heinrich von Stietencron, eds., *The Oxford India Hinduism Reader*, Delhi: Oxford University Press, 2007, pp. 29–49.
Hari Rao, V.N., ed. and tr., *Kōil Oḻugu: The Chronicle of the Srirangam Temple with Historical Notes*, Madras: Rochouse and Sons Pvt Ltd, 1961.
———,'Vaisnavism in South India in the Modern Period', in *Studies in Social History (Modern India)*, ed. O.P. Bhatnagar, Allahabad, 1964.
———, *The Srirangam Temple: Art and Architecture*, Tirupati: The Sri Venkateswara University, 1967.
Hart, George, 'Women and the Sacred in Ancient Tamil Nadu', *Journal of Asian Studies*, vol. 32, 1973, pp. 233–50.
———, *The Poems of the Ancient Tamils: Their Milieu and their Sanskrit Counterparts*, Berkeley, California, 1975a.
———, 'Ancient Tamil Literature, Its Scholarly Past and Future', in *Essays on South India*, ed. Burton Stein, New Delhi: Vikas Publishing House, 1975b.
———, 'The Nature of Tamil Devotion', in *Aryan and Non-Aryan in India, Michigan Papers on South and Southeast Asia, No. 14*, ed. Madhav M. Deshpande and Peter Edwin Hook, Ann Arbor: University of Michigan, 1979.
Hawley, John Stratton, 'Images of Gender in the Poetry of Kṛṣṇa', in Richman *Gender and Religion: On the Complexity of Symbols*, ed. Caroline Walker Bynum, Steven Harrell and Paula, Boston: Beacon Press, 1986.
———, 'Author and Authority in the Bhakti Poetry of North India', *The Journal of Asian Studies*, vol. 47, no. 2, 1988, pp. 269–90.

———, 'The Bhakti Movement: Since When?', Lecture delivered at the India International Centre, 23 March 2009.

———, 'The *Bhāgavata Māhātmya* in Context' , in *Patronage and Popularisation, Pilgrimage and Procession: Channels of Transcultural Translation and Transmission in Early Modern South Asia; Essays in Honour of Monica Horstmann*, ed. Heidi Rika Maria Pauwels, Wiesbaden: Harrasowitz Verlag, 2009, pp. 81–100.

Hawley, John Stratton and Donna Marie Wulff, eds., *The Divine Consort: Rādhā and the Goddesses of India*, Delhi: Motilal Banarsidass, 1984.

Hawley, John Stratton and Donna Marie Wulff, eds., *Devī: Goddesses of India*, Berkeley and Los Angeles: University of California Press, 1996.

Hawley, John Stratton and Vasudha Narayanan, eds., *The Life of Hinduism*, Berkley: University of California, 2007.

Hegewald, Julia A.B., 'Jaina Temples in the Deccan: Characteristics, Chronology and Continuity', *Deccan Studies*, vol. 5, no. 1, 2007, pp. 9–38

Hegde, Rajaram, 'The Jaina Tradition and the Regional Society in Early Kannada Literature', *Deccan Studies*, vol. 5, no. 1, 2007, pp. 39–61.

Heitzman, James, 'Temple Urbanism in Medieval South India, 850-1280', *The Journal of Asian Studies*, vol. 46, no. 4, 1987a, pp. 791–826.

——— , 'State Formation in South India', *The Indian Economic and Social History Review*, vol. 24, no. 1, 1987b, pp. 35–61.

———, 'Ritual Polity and Economy: The Transactional Network of an Imperial Temple in Medieval South India', *Journal of the Economic History of the Orient*, vol. 34, 1991, pp. 23–54.

———, *Gifts of Power: Lordship in an Early Indian State*, Delhi: Oxford University Press, 1997.

Hobsbawm, Eric J., 'Introduction: Inventing Traditions', in *The Invention of Tradition*, ed. E.J. Hobsbawm and Terence Ranger, Cambridge: Cambridge University Press, 1983.

Hooper, J.S.M., *Hymns of the Alvars*, Calcutta: Association Press, 1929.

Hopkins, Steven Paul, 'In Love with the Body of God: Eros and the Praise of Icons in South Indian Devotion', *Journal of Vaishnava Studies*, vol. 2, no. 1, 1993, pp. 17–54.

———, 'Singing in Tongues: Poems for Viṣṇu by Vedāntadeśika', *Journal of Vaishnava Studies*, vol. 4, no. 4, 1996, pp. 159–87.

———, *Singing the Body of God: The Hymns of Vedāntadeśika in their South Indian Tradition*, Delhi: Oxford University Press, 2002a.

———, 'Loving God in Three Languages: Vedas of Vedāntadeśika', *Journal of Vaishnava Studies*, vol. 10, no. 2, 2002b, pp. 51–79.

———, 'Sacred Narratives of Vedāntadeśika: The Bell of Tirupati: Miracles, Love of God and a Touch of Politics in the Sacred Narratives of Vedāntadeśika', *Journal of Vaishnava Studies*, vol. 15, no. 2, 2007, pp. 207–20.

———, *An Ornament for Jewels: Love Poems for the Lord of Gods by Vedāntadeśika*, Oxford University Press, 2007a.

———, 'Sanskrit from Tamil Nadu: At Play in the Forests of the Lord: The Gopalavimshati of Vedantadeshika', in *Krishna*, ed. Edwin F. Bryant, New York: Oxford University Press, 2007b, pp. 285–306.

Hopkins, Thomas J., 'The Social Teaching of the *Bhāgavata Purāṇa*', in *Krishna Myths, Rites and Attitudes*, ed. M. Singer, Chicago: University of Chicago Press, 1966, pp. 3–22.

———, *The Hindu Religious Tradition*, Encino, California: Dickenson Publishing Incorporated, 1971.

Hospital, Clifford, 'Bhakti and Liberation in the Bhagavat Purana', *Studies in Religion/Science Religieuses*, vol. 12, no. 4, 1983, pp. 397–405.

Hudson, D. Dennis, 'Śiva, Mināksi and Viṣṇu—Reflections on a Popular Myth in Madurai', *The Indian Economic and Social History Review*, vol. 14, nos. 1–2, 1977, pp. 107–18.

———, 'Bathing in Krishna: A Study in Vaiṣṇava Hindu Theology', *Harvard Theological Review*, vol. 73, nos. 3–4, 1980, pp. 539–66.

———, 'Pinnai: Krishna's Cowherd Wife', in *The Divine Consort: Rādhā and the Goddesses of India*, ed. John Stratton Hawley and Donna Marie Wulff, Berkeley: Religious Studies Series, 1982, pp. 238–61.

———, 'Violent and Fanatical Devotion among the Nāyaṉārs; A Study in the *Periya Purāṇam* of Cēkkiḻār', in *Criminal Gods and Demon Devotees: Essays on the Guardians of Popular Hinduism*, ed. Alf Hiltbeitel, Albany: SUNY Press, 1989, pp. 373–404.

———, 'Āṇṭāḷ Āḻvār: A Developing Hagiography', *Journal of Vaishnava Studies*, vol. 1, no. 2, 1993a, pp. 27–61.

———, 'Vāsudeva Kṛṣṇa in Theology and Architecture: A Background to Srivaisnavism', *Journal of Vaishnava Studies*, vol. 2, no. 1, 1993b, pp. 139–70.

———, 'Vraja among the Tamils: A Study of the Bhāgavatas in Early South India', *Journal of Vaishnava Studies*, vol. 3, no.1, 1994, pp. 113–40.

———, 'The Śrīmad Bhagavat Purāṇa in Stone: The Text as an Eighth Century Temple and its Implications', *Journal of Vaishnava Studies*, vol. 3, no. 3, 1995, pp. 137–82.

———, 'Antal's Desire', *Journal of Vaishnava Studies*, vol. 4, no. 1, 1995–6, pp. 37–76.

———, 'A New Year's Poem for Kṛṣṇa: The Tiruppallāṇṭu by Villiputtūr Viṣṇucittan ('Periyāḻvār')', *Journal of Vaishnava Studies*, vol. 7, no. 2, 1999, pp. 93–129.

———, 'Rādhā and Piṉṉai: Diverse Manifestations of the Same Goddess?', *Journal of Vaishnava Studies*, vol. 10, no. 1, 2001, pp. 115–53.

———, 'Early Evidence of the Pancaratra Agama', in *The Roots of Tantra*, ed. Katherine Ann Harper and Robert L. Brown, Albany: State University of New York Press, 2002, pp. 135–60.

Hudson, D. Dennis and Frederique Appfel Marglin, 'Who has the Potency?', *Journal of Vaishnava Studies*, vol. 11, no. 1, 2002, pp. 111–21.

Inden, Ronald, *Text and Practice*, Delhi: Oxford University Press, 2006.

Iyengar, Pandit M. Raghava, 'The Date of Sri Āṇḍāḷ', *Journal of Oriental Research* vol. 1, no. 2, 1927 pp. 156–66.

———, 'The Kalabhras in South India', *Journal of Indian History*, vol. 8, 1930a, pp. 74–80.

———, 'The Kalabhras in South India', *Journal of Indian History*, vol. 8, 1930b, pp. 294–6.

Iyengar, Rao Saheb Dr S. Krishnaswami. see Ayyangar, S Krishnaswami.

Iyengar, S.V. Varadaraja, 'The Date of Tirumangai Ālvār', *Journal of Indian History*, vol. 26, no. 2, 1948, pp. 131–4 (see also Ayyangar).

Jacobsen, Knut A., *Pilgrimage in the Hindu Tradition: Salvific Space*, Oxon, UK: Routledge, 2013.

Jagadeesan, N., *History of Srivaisnavism in the Tamil Country, Post Ramanuja*, Madurai: Koodal Publishers, 1977.

———, 'The Araiyar', *Bulletin of the Institute of Traditional Cultures, Madras*, vol. 11, no. 1, 1967, pp. 46–52.

Jagannathan, Sarojini, *Impact of Sri Ramanujacarya on Temple Worship*, Delhi: Nag Publishers, 1994.

Jaiswal, Suvira, *The Origin and Development of Vaiṣṇavism*, Delhi: Munshiram Manoharlal, 1980.

Jha, D.N., 'Temples as Landed Magnates in Early Medieval India', in *Indian Society, Historical Probings: In Memory of D.D. Kosambi*, ed. R.S. Sharma, New Delhi: ICHR and People's Publishing House, 1974.

———, 'Temples and Merchants in South India: c. AD 900-1300', in *Essays in Honour of Prof. S.C. Sarkar*, New Delhi: People's Publishing House, 1976.

———, 'Relevance of Peasant State and Society to Pallava-Cola Times', *Indian Historical Review*, vol. 8, no. 2, 1981, pp. 74–94.

——— 1984. 'Validity of the Brahmana- Peasant Alliance and the Segmentary State in Early Medieval South India', *Social Science Probings*, vol. 1, no. 2, pp. 270–96.

——— , ed., *Feudal Social Formation in Early India*, Delhi: Chanakya Publications, 1987.

———, *Economy and Society in Early India: Issues and Paradigms*, Delhi: Munshiram Manoharlal, 1993.

———, ed., *The Feudal Order: State, Society and Ideology in Early Medieval India*, Delhi: Manohar, 2000.

Jha, Makhan, ed., *Dimensions of Pilgrimage: An Anthropological Appraisal*, New Delhi: Inter Alia Publications, 1985.

Kamalakar, G., ed., *Vishnu in Art, Thought and Literature*, Hyderabad: Birla Archaeological and Cultural Research Centre, 1993.

Kanakasabhai, V., *The Tamils Eighteen Hundred Years Ago*, 1904; repr., New Delhi: Asian Educational Services, 1979.

Karashima, Noboru, *South Indian History and Society: Studies from Inscriptions. AD 850-1800*, Delhi: Oxford University Press, 1984.

———, 'The Prevalence of Private Landholding in the Lower Kaveri Valley in the late Cola Period and its Historical Implications', in *Feudal Social Formation in Early India*, ed. D.N. Jha, Delhi: Chanakya Publications, 1987, pp. 113–29 (also reproduced in D.N. Jha, ed., *The Feudal Order: State, Society and Ideology in Early Medieval India*, Delhi: Manohar, pp. 121–34).

———, *Towards a New Formation: South Indian Society under Vijayanagar Rule*, Delhi: Oxford University Press, 1992.

———, *History and Society in South India: The Colas to Vijayanagar*, Delhi: Oxford University Press, 2001.

Kaylor, R. David, 'The Concept of Grace in the Hymns of Nammālvār', *Journal of the American Academy of Religion*, vol. 44, no. 4, 1976, pp. 649–60.

Kaylor, R. David and K.K.A. Venkatachari, *God Far, God Near: An Interpretation of the Thought of Nammalvar*, no. 5 (Supplement), Bombay: Ananthacharya Indological Research Institute Series, 1981.

Kennedy, R., 'Status and Control of Temples in Tamil Nadu', *Indian Economic and Social History Review*, vol. 11, nos. 2–3, 1974.

Kosambi, D.D., 'Social and Economic Aspects of the Gita', in *Myth and Reality: Studies in the Formation of Indian Culture*, D.D. Kosambi, Bombay: Popular Prakashan, 1962, repr. 2000

Krishnan, K.G., *Inscriptions of the Early Pandyas, c. 300 BC–AD 984*, Delhi: ICHR and Northern Book Centre, 2002.

Kulke, H., 'Fragmentation and Segmentation versus Integration? Reflections on the Concepts of Indian Feudalism and the Segmentary State in Indian History', *Studies in History*, vol. 4, no. 2, 1982, pp. 237–64.

———, ed., *The State in India, AD 1000-1700*, Delhi: Oxford University Press, 1995.

Kumar, Savitri V., *The Puranic Lore of Holy Water Places*, Delhi.

Kumarappa, Bharatan, *The Hindu Concept of the Deity as Culminating in Ramanuja*, London: Luzac, 1934; reprinted as *The Hindu Conception of the Deity*, Delhi: Inter-India Publications, 1979.

Kurosawa, Akira, *Rashomon* (Japanese film), 1950.

Lakshamma, G., *The Impact of Ramanuja's Teachings on Life and Conditions in Society*, Delhi: Sandeep Prakashan, 1990.

Lester, Robert C., 'Rāmānuja and Śrī-Vaiṣṇavism: The Concept of Prapatti or Śaraṇāgati', *History of Religions*, vol. 5, 1966, pp. 266–82.

———, *Rāmānuja on the Yoga*, Madras: Adyar Library and Research Centre, 1976.

———, 'The Sāttāda Śrīvaiṣṇavas', *Journal of the American Oriental Society*, vol. 114, no. 1, 1994, pp. 39–53.

Lorenzen, David, 'The Life of Sankaracarya', in *Experiencing Siva: Encounters with a Hindu Deity*, ed. Fred Clothey and Bruce Long, Delhi: Manohar, 1983.

Lott, Eric, *God and the Universe in the Vedantic Theology of Ramanuja*, Madras: Ramanuja Research Society, 1976.

———, 'Iconic Vision and Cosmic Standpoint in Ramanuja Vedanta', in *Proceedings of the Seminar on Temple Art and Architecture*, K.K.A. Venkatachari, series no. 10, Bombay: Ananthacharya Indological Research Institute, 1980, pp. 30–46.

Ludden, David, 'Patronage and Irrigation in Tamil Nadu: A Long Term View', *Indian Economic and Social History Review*, vol. 16, no. 3, 1979, pp. 347–65.
———, *Peasant Society in South India*, Princeton: Princeton University Press, 1985.
Lynch, O.M., *Divine Passions: The Social Construction of Emotion in India*, Delhi: Oxford University Press, 1990.
Madan, T.N., ed., *Way of Life: King, Householder and Renouncer*, Delhi: Motilal Banarsidass, 1982.
Mahadevan, Iravatham, 'From Orality to Literacy: The Case of Tamil Society', *Studies in History*, vol. 11, no. 2, 1995: pp. 173–88.
Mahalakshmi, R., 'Outside the Norm, Within the Tradition: Karaikkāl Ammaiyār and the Ideology of Tamil Bhakti', *Studies in History*, vol. 16, no. 1, 2000, pp. 17–40.
Mahalingam, T.V., *South Indian Polity*, no. 2, Madras: Madras University Historical Series, 1954.
———, 'The Nagesvara Svami Temple', *Journal of Indian History*, vol. 45, no. 1, 1967, pp. 1–94.
———, *Kanchipuram in Early South Indian History*, Bombay: Asia Publishing House, 1969.
———, *Report on the Excavation in the Lower Kaveri Valley*, Madras: University of Madras, 1970.
———, *Readings in South Indian History*, Delhi: BR Publishing Corporation, 1977.
———, *Inscriptions of the Pallavas*, Delhi: ICHR and Agam Prakashan, 1988.
Malik, S.C., ed., *Indian Movements: Some Aspects of Dissent, Protest and Reform*, Simla: Indian Institute of Advanced Studies, 1978.
Marr, John R., 'The Folly of Righteousness: Episodes from the Periya Purāṇam', in *The Indian Narrative: Perspectives and Patterns*, ed. Christopher Schakle and Rupert Snells, Wiesbaden: Otto Harrassowitz, 1992, pp. 117–35.
Matsubara, M., *Pāñcarātra Saṁhitās and Early Vaiṣṇava Theology*, Delhi: Motilal Banarsidass, 1994.
Meenakshisundaram, K., 'A Brief Study of the Marriage System of the Kongu Vellala Gounder Community', *Bulletin of the Institute of Traditional Cultures, Madras*, vol. 18, no. 1, 1974, pp. 1–12.
Michell, G., ed., *Temple Towns of Tamil Nadu*, Bombay: Marg Publications, 1993.
———, ed., *Eternal Kaveri: Historical Sites around South India's Greatest River*, Bombay: Marg Publications, 1999.
Miller, Barbara Stoler, 'Radha: Consort of Krsna's Vernal Passion', *Journal of the American Oriental Society*, vol. 95, no. 4, 1975, pp. 655–71.
———, ed., *The Powers of Art: Patronage in Indian Culture*, Delhi: Oxford University Press, 1992.
Minakshi, C., *Administration and Social Life under the Pallavas*, Madras: University of Madras, 1938.
———, *The Historical Sculptures of the Vaikuṇṭha Perumāḷ Temple, Kāñchī*, Memoirs of the ASI, no. 63, Manager of Publications, Delhi: Government of India Press, 1941.

Mukherjee, S.N., ed., *Indian History and Thought: Essays in Honour of A.L. Basham*, Calcutta: Subarnarekha, 1982.

Mukta, Parita, *Upholding the Common Life: The Community of Mirabai*, Delhi: Oxford University Press, 1994.

Mumme, Patricia Y., 'Jīvakartṛtva in Viśiṣṭādvaita and the Dispute over Prapatti in Vedanta Deśika and the Tenkalai Authors', in *Prof. Kuppuswami Sastri Birth Centenary Commemoration Volume, Part 2*, ed. S.S. Janaki, Madras: The Kuppuswami Sastri Research Institute, 1985, pp. 99–118.

———, 'Grace and Karma in Nammalvar's Salvation', *Journal of the American Oriental Society*, vol. 107, no. 2, 1987, pp. 257–66.

———, *The Śrīvaiṣṇava Theological Dispute: Maṇavāla Māmuni and Vedānta Deśika*, New Era Publications, Madras: 1988.

———, 'Haunted by Śankara's Ghost: The Śrīvaiṣṇava Interpretation of *Bhagavad Gītā* 18:66', in *Texts in Context: Traditional Hermeneutics in South Asia*, ed. Jeffrey R. Timm, Albany: SUNY Press, 1992, pp. 69–84.

———, 'Rules and Rhetoric: Caste Observance in Śrīvaiṣṇava Doctrine and Practice', *Journal of Vaishnava Studies*, vol. 2, no. 1, 1993, pp. 113–38.

———, 'Ramayana Exegesis in Tenkalai Srivaisnavism', in *Many Ramayanas: The Diversity of a Narrative Tradition in South Asia*, ed. Paula Richman, Delhi: Oxford University Press, 1994, pp. 202–16.

———, 'Review of Nancy Ann Nayar's Poetry as Theology: The Śrīvaiṣṇava Strotra in the Age of Rāmānuja', *Journal of Asian Studies*, vol. 55, no. 4, 1996, pp. 1044–5.

———, 'History, Myth, and Śrīvaiṣṇava Hagiography: Lessons from Biblical Scholarship', *Journal of Vaishnava Studies*, vol. 5, no. 2, 1997, pp. 157–84.

Mumme, Patricia Y. and Thomas A. Forsthoefl, 'The Monkey-Cat Debate in Śrīvaiṣṇavism', *Journal of Vaishnava Studies*, vol. 8, no. 1, 1999, pp. 3–33.

Nagasvami, R., 'South Indian Temple as an Employer', in *Studies in Ancient Tamil Law and Society*, ed. R. Nagasvami, Institute of Epigraphy, State Department of Archaeology, Madras: Government of Tamil Nadu, 1978a.

———, ed., *South Indian Studies*, Madras: Society for Archaeological, Historical and Epigraphical Research, 1978b.

———, *Art and Culture of Tamil Nadu*, Delhi: Sundeep Prakashan, 1980.

Nambudiri, P.P. Narayanan, 'Bhakti Cult in Kerala', *Proceedings of the Indian History Congress*, Bodhgaya, vol. 42, 1981, pp. 157–62.

Nandi, R.N., *Religious Institutions and Cults in the Deccan*, Delhi: Motilal Banarsidass, 1974a.

———, 'Origin and Nature of Saivite Monasticism: The Case of Kalamukhas', in *Indian Society, Historical Probings. In Memory of DD Kosambi*, ed. R.S. Sharma, New Delhi: ICHR and People's Publishing House, 1974b.

———, 'Some Social Aspects of the Nalayira Divya Prabandham', *Proceedings of the Indian History Congress*, Thirty-seventh Session, 1976.

———, *Social Roots of Religion in Ancient India*, Calcutta: KP Bagchi & Co., 1986.

Narasimhachari, M., *Contributions of Yāmuna to Viśiṣṭadvaita*, Madras: Prof. M Rangacharya Memorial Trust, 1971.

Narayanan, M.G.S., and Kesavan Veluthat, 'Bhakti Movement in South India', in *Indian Movements; Some Aspects of Dissent, Reform and Protest*, ed. S.C. Malik, Indian Institute for Advanced Studies, Simla, 1978; also reproduced in D.N. Jha, ed., *Feudal Social Formation in Early India* , pp. 348–75, and D.N. Jha, ed., *The Feudal Order: State, Society and Ideology in Medieval India,* pp. 385–410.

Narayanan, M.G.S. and Kesavan Veluthat, 'The Temple in South India. Paper presented in the Symposium on the Socio-Economic Role of the Religious Institution in India', *Proceedings of the Indian History Congress*, Bodhgaya, 1981.

Narayanan, Vasudha, 'The Goddess Sri: The Blossoming Lotus and Breast Jewel of Viṣṇu', in *The Divine Consort: Rādhā and the Goddesses of India*, ed. John Stratton Hawley and Donna Marie Wulff, Berkeley: Religious Studies Series, 1982, pp. 224–37.

———, 'The Two Levels of Auspiciousness in Srivaisnava Ritual and Literature', in *Purity and Auspiciousness in Indian Society*, ed. John Carman and Frederique Marglin, International Studies in Sociology and Social Anthropology 43, Leiden: EJ Brill, 1985a.

———, 'Hindu Devotional Literature: The Tamil Connection', *Religious Studies Review*, vol. 12, 1985b, pp. 12–19.

———, 'Arcavatara: On Earth as He is in Heaven', in *Gods of Flesh, Gods of Stone*, ed. Norman Cutler and J.P. Waghorne, Chambersburg: Anima Publications, 1985c.

———, *The Way and the Goal: Expressions of Devotion in the Early Śrī Vaiṣṇava Tradition*, Institute for Vaishnava Studies, Harvard University: Washington DC and Cambridge Massachusetts Centre for the Study of World Religions, 1987.

———, 'Oral and Written Commentary on the *Tiruvāymoḻi*', in *Texts in Context: Traditional Hermeneutics in South Asia*, Albany: SUNY Press, 1992, pp. 85–108.

———, 'The "Sacred Utterance" of the Silent Seer: Speech and Sight in the Revelation of the Tamil Veda', *Journal of Vaishnava Studies*, vol. 2, no. 1, 1993, pp. 79–111.

———, *The Vernacular Veda: Revelation, Recitation and Ritual*, Columbia, SC: University of South Carolina Press, 1994a.

———, 'The Rāmāyaṇa in the Theology and Experience of the Śrīvaiṣṇava Community', *Journal of Vaishnava Studies*, vol. 2, no. 4, 1994b, pp. 55–89.

———, 'Singing the Glory of the Divine Name: Parāśara Bhaṭṭar's Commentary on the Viṣṇu Sahasranāma', *Journal of Vaishnava Studies*, vol. 2, no. 2, 1994c, pp. 85–98.

———, 'The Realm of Play and the Sacred Stage', in *The Gods at Play: Lila in South Asia*, ed. William Sax, New York: Oxford University Press, 1995a, pp. 177–203.

———, 'Tiruvenkaṭam in the Fifteenth Century', *Journal of Vaishnava Studies*, vol. 3, no. 3, 1995b, pp.91–108.

———, 'Renunciation and Gender Issues in the Śrī Vaiṣṇava Community', in *Asceticism*, ed. Vincent L. Wimbush and Richard Valantasis, New York: Oxford University Press, 1995c.

——— , 'Music and the Divya Prabandham in the Śrīvaiṣṇava Tradition', *Journal of Vaishnava Studies*, vol. 4, no. 2, 1996a, pp. 37–56.

———, 'Sri: Giver of Fortune, Bestower of Grace', *Devī: Goddesses of India*, ed. in John S. Hawley and Donna Marie Wulff, Berkeley and Los Angeles: University of California Press, 1996b.

———, 'Śrī Vaiṣṇava Festivals and Festivals Celebrated by Śrī Vaiṣṇavas', *Journal of Vaishnava Studies*, vol. 7, no. 2, 1999a, pp. 175–94.

———, 'Brimming with Bhakti, Embodiments of Shakti: Devotees, Deities, Performers, Reformers, and Other Women of Power in the Hindu Tradition', in *Feminism and World Religions*, ed. Arvind Sharma and Katherine K Young, Albany: SUNY Press, 1999b, pp 25–77.

———, 'Casting Light on the Sounds of the Tamil Veda: Tirukkōneri Dāsyai's "Garland of Words"', in *Women and Textual Tradition in India*, ed. Laurie, L. Patton, New York: Oxford University Press, 2002, pp. 122–36.

———, 'Selections from the Poetry of Āṇḍāḷ and Nammāḻvār', *Journal of Vaishnava Studies*, vol. 12, no. 1, 2003a, pp. 67–85.

———, 'Gender in a Devotional Universe', in *The Blackwell Companion to Hinduism*, ed. Gavin Flood, Oxford and Malden: Blackwell Publishing Limited, Indian repr. 2003b, pp. 569–87.

———, 'Tamil Nadu: Weaving Garlands in Tamil: The Poetry of the Alvars', in *Krishna*, ed. Edwin F. Bryant, New York: Oxford University Press, 2007, pp. 187–204.

Natarajan, B., *The City of the Cosmic Dance: Chidambaram*, Southern Art Series 2, Delhi: Orient Longman, 1974.

Natarajan, D., 1974. 'Endowments in Early Tamil Nadu', *Bulletin of the Institute of Traditional Cultures,Madras*, vol. 18, no. 2, pp. 101–18.

Nayar, Nancy Ann, *Poetry as Theology: The Śrīvaiṣṇava Stotra in the Age of Rāmānuja*, Weisbaden: Otto Harrassowitz, 1992a.

———, 'The Other Āṇṭāḷ : Portrait of a Twelfth Century Śrīvaiṣṇava Woman', in *Vaisnavi: Women and the Worship of Krishna*, ed. Steven J. Rosen, Delhi: Motilal Banarsidass, 1992b.

———, 'The Śrīvaiṣṇava Stotra: Synthesizing the Tamil and Sanskrit Vedas', *Journal of Vaishnava Studies*, vol. 2, no. 1, 1993, pp. 55–77.

———, *Praise-Poems to Viṣṇu and Śrī: The Stotras of Rāmānuja's Immediate Disciples*, Bombay: Ananthacharya Indological Research Institute, 1994a.

———, 'The Tamilizing of a Sacred Sanskrit Text: The Devotional Mood of Rāmānuja's Bhagavadgītā-bhāṣya', in *Hermeneutical Paths to the Sacred Worlds of India*, Katherine K. Young, Atlanta: Scholars Press, 1994b, pp. 186–221.

———, 'The Bhagavad-gītā and Śrīvaiṣṇavism: Multilevel Contextualization of an Ancient Hindu Text', *Journal of Vaishnava Studies*, vol. 3, no. 2, 1995, pp. 115–41.

———, 'After the Āḻvārs: Kṛṣṇa and the Gopis in the Śrīvaiṣṇava Tradition', *Journal of Vaishnava Studies*, vol. 4, no. 5, 1997a, pp. 201–22.

———, 'Idols, Icons and Incarnations: A Catholic Perspective on the Śrīvaiṣṇava Worship of Images', *Journal of Vaishnava Studies*, vol. 5, no. 2, 1997b, pp. 97–127.

———, 'Āḷavantār's *Catuḥsloki* with the Commentary by Periyavāccān Piḷḷai: An Introduction and Translation', *Journal of Vaishnava Studies*, vol. 12, no. 1, 2003, pp. 213–38.

Neevel, Walter G., *Yamuna's Vedanta and Pancaratra: Integrating the Classical with the Popular*, Missoula: Scholars Press, 1977.

Oddie, G., 'Sectarian Conflicts within Srivaisnavism: Tengalais and Vadagalais in the Kaveri Delta c 1800–1902, in *Bhakti Studies*, ed. G.M. Bailey and Ian Kesarcodi-Watson, New Delhi: Sterling Publishers, 1991, pp. 82–98.

Orr, Leslie, 'The Vaisnava Community at Srirangam: The Testimony of Early Medieval Inscriptions', *Journal of Vaishnava Studies*, vol. 3, no. 3, 1995, pp. 109–36.

———, 'Women's Wealth and Worship: Female Patronage of Hinduism, Jainism and Buddhism in Medieval Tamilnadu', in *Faces of the Feminine in Ancient, Medieval and Modern India*, ed. Mandakranta Bose, New Delhi: Oxford University Press, 2000, pp. 124–47.

———, 'Jain and Hindu 'Religious Women' in early Medieval Tamilnadu', in *Open Boundaries: Jain Communities and Cultures in Indian History*, ed. John Cort, Albany: State University of New York Press, 1998, pp. 187–212.

Padigar, Shrinivas V., 'Concept and Art: Vicissitudes of Jina Chaityas and Chaityalayas in Karnataka', *Deccan Studies*, vol. 5, no. 1, 2007, pp. 62–100.

Padmaja, T., *Temples of Krishna in South India: History, Art and Traditions in Tamil Nadu*, Delhi: Abhinav Publications.

Padmanabhan, Seetha, *Parasara Bhatta: His Contribution to Visistadvaita*, Madras: Sri Visistadvaita Research Centre, 1995.

Pandeya, B.K., 'The Cola Temple and its Privileges', *Proceedings of the Indian History Congress*, Thirty-ninth Session, Hyderabad, 1978.

———, 'The Brahmadeya and Devadana Land during the Cola Period', *Proceedings of the Indian History Congress*, Forty-second Session, Bodhgaya, 1981.

Pankaja, N., 'A Note on Some Epigraphs of Srivilliputtur Temple', in *Indian Archaeological Heritage (KV Sounderarajan Festshrift)*, ed. C. Margabandhu, K.S. Ramachandra, A.P. Sagar, D.K. Sinha, Delhi: Agam Kala Prakashan, 1991.

Parameswaran, Mangalam R., *Studies in Srivaishnavism*, Winnipeg, Canada: Larkuma, 2005.

Parasher- Sen, Aloka, ed., *Kevala Bodhi: Buddhist and Jaina History of the Deccan: The BSL Commemorative Volume* (in 2 volumes), Delhi: Bharatiya Kala Prakashan, 2004.

———, 'Renunciation and Pilgrimage in the Jaina Tradition: Continuity and Change in the Deccan', *Deccan Studies*, vol.5, no. 1, 2007, pp. 157–76.

Pariti, Aruna, 'Women Patrons of Jaina Religion: Glimpses from the Chalukyan Inscriptions', *Deccan Studies*, vol. 5, no. 1, 2007, pp. 127–37.

Parpola, Asko, 'The Encounter of Religions in India', *Temenos: Studies in Comparative Religion*, vol. 12, 1976, pp. 21–36.

Parrinder, Geoffrey, *Avatar and Incarnation*, London: Faber and Faber, 1970.

Parthasarathi, J., 'Sri Andal's Bridal Love as seen in her Poems', *Sri Ramanuja Vani*, vol. 26, Jan-Apr.

———, 'Vaisnavism and Tamil Literature', Manuscript.

———, 'Nayanmar Saints and their Compositions', Manuscript.

———,'Alvar Saints and their Compositions', Manuscript.

Pauwels, Heidi, 'Review of *The Goddess Lakshmi: The Divine Consort in the South Indian Vaisnava Tradition* by P. Pratap Kumar', *Journal of the American Academy of Religion*, vol. 66, no. 4, 1998, pp. 955–8.

Peterson, Indira Viswanathan, 'Singing of a Place: Pilgrimage as Metaphor and Motif in the Tēvāram Songs of the Tamil Śaiva Saints', *Journal of the American Oriental Society*, vol. 102, no. 1, 1982, pp. 69–90.

———, 'Lives of the Wandering Singers: Pilgrimage and Poetry in Tamil Śaivite Hagiography', *History of Religions*, vol. 22, no. 4, 1983.

———, *Poems to Śiva: The Hymns of the Tamil Saints*, New Jersey: Princeton University Press, 1989.

———, 'In Praise of the Lord: The Image of the Royal Patron in the Songs of Saint Cuntaramūrtti and the Composer Tyāgarāja', in *The Powers of Art: Patronage in Indian Culture*, ed. Barbara Stoler Miller, New Delhi: Oxford University Press, 1992.

———, 'Śramaṇas Against the Tamil Way: Jains as Others in Tamil Śaiva Literature', in *Open Boundaries: Jain Communities and Cultures in Indian History*, ed. John Cort, Albany: State University of New York Press, 1998, pp. 163–86.

Pillai, J.M. Somasundaram, *The Great Temple at Tanjavur*, The Tanjore Temple Devasthanams, 1935.

Pillai, S. Vaiyapuri, *History of Tamil Language and Literature*, Madras, 1956.

Pillai, V.R. Parameswaran, *Temple Culture in South India*, New Delhi: Inter-India Publications, 1986.

Pillay, K.K., *The Sucindram Temple*, Madras: Kalakshetra Publications, 1953.

———, 'The Temple as a Cultural Centre', *Journal of Oriental Research*, vol. 29, 1959–60, pp. 83–94.

———, *A Social History of the Tamils*, vol. I, Madras: University of Madras, 1975.

Preston, James J., 'Sacred Centres and Symbolic Networks in India', in *The Realm of the Sacred: Verbal Symbolism and Ritual Structures*, ed. Sitakanta Mahapatra, Calcutta: Oxford University Press, 1992.

Raghavan, V.K.S.N., *History of Visistadvaita Literature*, Delhi: Ajanta Publications, 1979.

Rajagopal, S., ed., *Kaveri: Studies in Epigraphy, Archaeology and History. Professor Y. Subbarayalu Felicitation Volume*, Chennai: Panpattu Veliyiittakam, 2001.

Rajam, V.S., 'AṆANKU: A Notion Semantically Reduced to Signify Female Sacred Power', *Journal of the American Oriental Society*, vol. 106, no. 2, 1986, pp. 257–72.

Ramachandran, T.N., *The Nagapattinam and other Buddhist Bronzes in the Madras Museum*, Bulletin of the Madras Government Museum, Madras: Government Press, 1954.

Ramakrishnananda, *Life of Ramanuja*, Madras: Sri Ramakrishna Math, 1959.

Ramamurti, Rajam, Sept. 'On the Themes of Divine Immanence and Localization', *Tamil Civilization: Quarterly Research Journal of the Tamil University*, Tanjavur, 1983.

Raman, K.V., *Some Epigraphical Gleanings on Vaisnava Acaryas. Professor Nilakanta Sastri Felicitation Volume*, Professor Nilakanta Sastri Felicitation Committee, Madras, 1971.

———, 'Jainism in Tondaimandalam', *Bulletin of the Institute of Traditional Cultures, Madras*, vol. 18, no. 1, 1974, pp. 13–23.

———, *Sri Varadarajasvami Temple—Kanchi: A Study of its History, Art and Architecture*, New Delhi: Abhinav Publications, 1975.

———, Presidential Address, *Proceedings of the Indian History Congress*, Forty-sixth Session, Amritsar, 1986.

———, 'Tamil Historiography: Some Glimpses from a Pioneer's Work', in *Kaveri: Studies in Epigraphy, Archaeology and History. Professor Y. Subbarayalu Felicitation Volume*, ed. S. Rajagopal, Chennai: Panpattu Veliyiittakam, 2001, pp. 286–98.

Raman, K.V., et al., eds., *Srinidhih: Perspectives in Indian Archaeology, Art and Culture. KR Srinivasan Festschrift*, Madras: New Era Publications, 1983.

Ramanujam, B.V., 'Divya Suri Charitam', *Journal of Indian History*, vol. 13, no. 2, 1934, pp. 181–203.

———, *History of Srivaisnavism in South India upto Ramanuja*, Annamalainagar: Annamalai University, 1973.

Ramanujan, A.K., *The Interior Landscape*, New Delhi: Oxford University Press, 1967, repr. 1995.

———, 'Karma in Bhakti with special reference to Nammalvar and Basavanna', Paper presented in the *ACLS/ SSRC Workshop on Karma in Post- Colonial Texts*, Pendle Hill, Pennsylvania, 1980.

———, 'On Women Saints', in *The Divine Consort: Rādhā and the Goddesses of India*, ed. John Stratton Hawley and Donna Marie Wulff, Religious Studies Series, Berkeley, 1982, pp. 316–26.

———, *Hymns for the Drowning: Poems to Visnu by Nammalvar*, New Delhi: Penguin India Ltd., 1993.

———, *Collected Essays*, New Delhi: Oxford University Press, 1999.

Ramanujan, A.K. and Norman Cutler, 'From Classicism to Bhakti', in *Essays on Gupta Culture*, ed. Bardwell L. Smith, Delhi: South Asia Books, 1983.

Ramanujan, A. Appan, 'The Śāttāda Śrivaishnavas', *Bulletin of the Institute of Traditional Cultures, Madras*, vol. 22, no. 1, 1976, pp. 1–4.

———, 'Non Vedic Base of Srivaisnavism', *Bulletin of the Institute of Traditional Cultures, Madras*, vol. 26, no. 1, July–December 1982, pp. 45–48.

Ramaswamy, Vijaya, 'Review Article: Peasant State and Society in Medieval South India', *Studies in History*, vol. 4, no. 2, 1982, pp. 307–20.

———, *Walking Naked: Women, Society and Spirituality in South India*, Shimla: Indian Institute of Advanced Studies, 1997.

Rangachari, K., *The Sri Vaisnava Brahmans: Bulletin of the Madras Government Museum*, New Series, General Section, vol. II, Superintendent of the Government Press, Madras, 1931.

Rangachari, V., 'The Successors of Rāmānuja and the growth of Sectarianism among the Srī-Vaishṇavas', *Journal of the Bombay Branch of the Royal Asiatic Society*, vol. 24, 1914–15, pp. 102–36.

———, 'The Life and Times of Vedānta Deśika', *Journal of the Bombay Branch of the Royal Asiatic Society*, vol. 24, 1914–15, pp. 277–312.

———, 'The History of Shri Vaisnavism from the Death of Sri Vedanta Desika to the Present Day', *Quarterly Journal of the Mythic Society*, vol. 7, no. 2, January 1917, pp. 106–18; April 1917, pp. 197–209.

———, 'Historical Evolution of Srivaisnavism in South India', in *The Cultural Heritage of India*, ed. H. Bhattacharyya, vol. 4, Calcutta: Ramakrishna Mission Institute of Culture, 1956, pp. 163–85.

Rangaswami, J., 'Sri Varadarajasvami Temple in Kancipuram as the Centre of Vatakalai Srivaisnavism', *Tamil Civilization: Quarterly Journal of the Tamil University*, vol. 7, nos. 2–4, 1989, pp. 18–28.

———, *Śrīvacana Bhūṣaṇam of Piḷḷai Lokācārya. Translation and Commentary of Manavāḷamāmuni; Critical Evaluation of the Theo-Philosophy of the Post-Rāmānuja Śrīvaiṣṇavism*, Delhi: Sharada Publishing House, 2006.

Rangaswamy, M.A. Dorai, *The Religion and Philosophy of Tevāram, with special reference to Nampi Ārurār*, 4 vols. in 2 books, Madras: University of Madras, 1958–9.

Rao, T.N. Vasudeva, 'Buddhism and Kanchi', *Journal of Indian History*, vol. 53, no. 1, 1975, pp. 17–24.

———, *Buddhism in the Tamil Country*, Annamalainagar: Annamalai University, 1979.

Raychaudhuri, Hemchandra, *Materials for the Study of the Early History of the Vaisnava Sect*, Delhi: Munshiram Manoharlal, 1920, repr. 1975.

Reddy, D. Narasimha, *A Study of Some Minor Temple Festivals according to Pāñcarātra and Vaikhānasa Āgamas*, Tirupati: Padmasri Publications, 1983.

Richman, Paula, ed., *Many Ramayanas: The Diversity of a Narrative Tradition in South Asia*, New Delhi: Oxford University Press, 1994.

———, *Extraordinary Child: Poems from a South India Devotional Genre*, Honolulu: University of Hawai'i Press, 1997.

Rosen, Steven J., ed., *Vaisnavi: Women and the Worship of Krishna*, Delhi: Motilal Banarsidass, 1992.

———, ed., *Vaisnavism: Contemporary Scholars Discuss the Gaudiya Tradition*, Delhi: Motilal Banarsidass, 1994.

Roy, Kumkum, 'Of Theras and Therīs: Visions of Liberation in the Early Buddhist Tradition', in *Re-searching Indian Women*, ed. Vijaya Ramaswamy, Delhi: Manohar, 2003.

Ryan, James, 'Erotic Excess and Sexual Danger in the Cīvakacintāmaṇi', in *Open Boundaries: Jain Communities and Cultures in Indian History*, ed. John E. Cort, New York: SUNY Press, 1998 pp. 67–84.

Sahu, B.P., 'The Brahmanical Model viewed as an Instrument of Socio-Cultural Change—an Autopsy', *Proceedings of the Indian History Congress*, Forty-sixth Session, Amritsar, 1986.

Sampath, R.N., 'The Pith of the Upaniṣads vis-a-vis Rāmānuja Siddhānta', *Journal of Oriental Research*, vols. 47–55, 1977–86, pp. 223–33.

Sankar, K.G., 'The Date of Tiruppavai', *Journal of Oriental Research*, vol. 1, no. 2, 1927, pp. 167–9.

———, 'Contemporaries of Pĕriyālvār', *Journal of Oriental Research*, vol. 1, no. 4, 1927, pp. 336–49.

Sarma, B.N. Krishnamurti, 'The Sūtras of Bādarāyaṇa', *Annals of the Bhandarkar Oriental Research Institute*, vol. 23, 1942, pp. 398–404.

Sarma, I.K., 'Beginnings of Temple Architecture at Kanchipuram, Raw Materials and Religious Impacts', in *Archaeology and History. Essays in Honour of A Ghosh*, ed. B.D. Chattopadhyaya and B.M. Pande, Delhi: Agam Kala Prakashan, 1987.

Sastri, K.A. Nilakanta, *The Cōḻas*, University of Madras, Madras, 1935–7; rsvd. edn., repr. 1975.

———, *A History of South India*, Madras: Oxford University Press, 1955.

———, *A History of South India from Prehistoric Times to the Fall of Vijayanagar*, New Delhi: Oxford University Press, 1958.

———, *Development of Religion in South India*, Delhi: Munshiram Manoharlal, 1963, repr. 1992.

———, *The Culture and History of the Tamils*, Calcutta: Firma KL Mukhopadhyay, 1964.

Sastri, P.P.S., 'Commentators on the Rāmāyaṇa in the Fifteenth, Sixteenth and Seventeenth Centuries', *Annals of the Bhandarkar Oriental Research Institute*, vol. 23, 1942, pp. 413–4.

Satyamurti, T., *The Nataraja Temple: History, Art and Architecture*, New Delhi: Classical Publications, 1978.

Sax, William, ed., *The Gods at Play: Lila in South Asia*, New York: Oxford University Press, 1995.

Schalk, Peter, 'The Oldest Buddhist Artefacts Discovered in Tamiḻakam', in *Being Religious and Living through the Eyes: Studies in Religious Iconography and Iconology, A Celebratory Publication in Honour of Professor Jan Bergman*, ed. Peter Schalk, Uppsala: Acta Universitatis Upsalensis, 1998, pp. 307–28.

Schrader, F.O., *Introduction to the Pancaratra and the Ahirbudhnya Samhita*, Madras: The Adyar Library and Research Centre, 1995.

Seshadri, K., 'The Substance of Ramanuja's Sribhasyam' (in seven parts), *Journal of Indian History*, vol. 25, nos. 1–3; vols. 26, nos. 1–3; vol. 27, no. 1, 1947–9.

Seshadri, R.K., *Abiding Grace: A History of Sri Vaishnavism in South India with particular reference to the parallels in some other Religions*, Tirupati: Tirumala Tirupati Devasthanams, 1988.

Sharma, Krishna, *Bhakti and the Bhakti Movement: A New Perspective*, New Delhi: Munshiram Manoharlal, 1987.

Sharma, R.S., *Aspects of Political Ideas and Institutions in Ancient India*, Delhi: Motilal Banarsidass, 1959; rsvd. edn. 1996.

———, 'The Kali Age: A Period of Social Crisis', in *Feudal Social Formation in Early India*, ed. D.N. Jha, Delhi: Chanakya Publications, 1987, pp. 45–64.

———, 'How Feudal was Indian Feudalism?' in *Feudal Social Formation in Early India*, ed. D.N. Jha, Delhi: Chanakya Publications, 1987, pp. 165–97.

Shiner, Larry E., 'Sacred Space, Profane Space, Human Space', *Journal of the American Academy of Religion*, vol. 40, no. 4, 1972, pp. 425–36.

Shrimali, K.M., ed., *Essays in Indian Art, Religion and Society*, Indian History Congress, Delhi: Munshiram Manoharlal, 1987.

———, 'Religion, Ideology and Society', Presidential Address, Ancient India Section, *Proceedings of the Indian History Congress*, Forty-ninth Session, Dharwad, 1988.

Shulman, David, *Tamil Temple Myths: Sacrifice and Divine Marriage in the South Indian Śaiva Tradition*, Princeton: Princeton University Press, 1980a.

———, 'On South Indian Bandits and Kings', *The Indian Economic and Social History Review*, vol. 17, no. 3, 1980b, pp. 283–306.

———, 'Divine Order and Divine Evil in the Tamil Tale of Rāma', in *Temples, Kings and Peasants: Perceptions of South India's Past*, ed. G.W. Spencer, Madras: New Era Publications, 1987.

———, 'The Poetics of Tamil Devotion: Melting Pot or Battleground', Review Article, *History of Religions*, vol. 29, no. 1, 1989, pp. 74–76.

———, ed., *Syllables of Sky: Studies in South Indian Civilization. Essays in Honour of Velcheru Narayana Rao*, New Delhi: Oxford University Press, 1995.

———, *Wisdom of Poets, Studies in Tamil, Telugu and Sanskrit*, New Delhi, 2001.

Singer, Milton, ed., *Krishna: Myths, Rites and Attitudes*, Honolulu: East–West Centre Press, 1966.

Singh, R.L. and Rana P.B. Singh, *Trends in the Geography of Pilgrimages: Homage to David E Sopher*, The National Geographic Society of India, Varanasi: Banaras Hindu University, 1987.

Singh, Satyavrata, *Vedanta Desika: His Life, Works and Philosophy*, Banaras: Chowkhamba Sanskrit Series, 1958.

Sivaramamurti, C., *Nataraja in Art, Thought and Literature*, National Museum, New Delhi, 1974.

———, *Mahabalipuram*, Director General Archaeological Survey of India, New Delhi, 1978.

Smith, Bardwell L., ed., *Hinduism: New Essays in the History of Religions*, Leiden: EJ Brill, 1982.

———, *Essays on Gupta Culture*, Delhi: South Asia Books, 1983.

Smith, Brian K., ed., *The City as a Sacred Centre*, Leiden: EJ Brill, 1987.

Smith, Daniel, *Vaiṣṇava Iconography*, Madras: Pāñcarātra Pariśodhana Pariṣad, 1969.

———, 'A Typological Survey of Definitions: The name 'Pāñcarātra'', *Journal of Oriental Research*, vols. 34–5, 1964–5, pp. 102–17.

———, 'Pancaratra Literature in Perspective', *Journal of Ancient Indian History*, vol. 12, 1978–9, pp. 45–58.

Smith, John D., 'Review of "The Hindu Temple: Its Meaning and Forms" by George Michell', *Modern Asian Studies*, vol. 13, no. 2, 1979, pp. 350–2.

Solomon, Ted J., 'Early Vaiṣṇava Bhakti and its Autochthonous Heritage', *History of Religions*, vol. 10, 1971, pp. 32–48.

———, 'The Message of Place in Hindu Pilgrimage', *National Geographic Journal of India*, vol. 33, no. 4, 1972, pp. 353–69.

Soundara Rajan, K.V., 'The Kaleidoscopic Activities of Mediaeval Temples in the Tamil Nad', *Quarterly Journal of the Mythic Society*, vol. 42, 1952, pp. 87–101.

———, *Kaveripattinam Excavations 1963-73 (A Port City on the Tamil Nadu Coast)*, Archaeological Survey of India, New Delhi, 1994.

———, 'Divya Prabandham of Alwars as a Socio Cultural Source', *Journal of Indian History*, vol. 41, no. 1, 1963, pp. 177–90.

———, 'Determinant Factors in the Early History of Tamil Nadu', *Journal of Indian History*, vol. 45, no. 1, 1967, pp. 647–72.

Spencer, G.W., 'Religious Networks and Royal Influence in 11th century South India', *Journal of the Economic and Social History of the Orient*, vol. 12, no. 1, 1969, pp. 42–56.

———, 'The Sacred Geography of the Tamil Shaivite Hymns', *Numen*, vol. 17, fasc. 3, 1970, pp. 232–44.

———, *The Politics of Expansion: The Chola Conquest of Sri Lanka and Sri Vijaya*, Madras: New Era Publications, 1983.

———, ed., *Studies of South India*, Madras: New Era Publications, 1985.

———, ed., *Temples, Kings and Peasants: Perspectives of South India's Past*, Madras: New Era Publications, 1987.

Sri Andal. Her Contribution to Religion, Philosophy and Literature, Madras: Sri Ramanuja Vedanta Centre, 1985.

Srinivasa Chari, S.M., *Fundamentals of Visistadvaita- Vedanta: A Study Based on Vedanta Desika's Tattva-mukta-kalāpa*, Delhi: Motilal Banarsidass, 1988.

Srinivasacari, P.N., *The Philosophy of Visistadvaita*, Madras: Adyar Library, 1943.

Srinivasan, C.R., *Kanchipuram Through the Ages*, Delhi: Agam Kala Prakashan, 1979.

Srinivasan, K.R., *Cave Temples of the Pallavas*, Archaeological Survey of India, New Delhi, 1964.

———, *Temples of South India*, New Delhi: National Book Trust, 1972.

Srinivasan, P.R., 'Buddhist Images of South India', in *Story of Buddhism with special reference to South India*, ed. A. Aiyappan and P.R. Srinivasan, Madras: Government of Madras, 1960.

Sri Ramanuja Vani, A Quarterly Journal of the Visistadvaita Vedanta, Madras: Sri Ramanuja Vedanta Centre, 1980–2000.

Stein, Burton, ed., 'The Economic Functions of a Medieval South Indian Temple', *Journal of Asian Studies*, vol. 19, no. 2, 1960, pp. 163–76.

———, 'Brahman and Peasant in Early South Indian History', *The Adyar Library Bulletin*, vols. 31–2, 1967–8, pp. 229–69.

———, 'Integration of the Agrarian System of South India', in *Land Control and Social Structure in Indian History*, ed. Robert E. Frykenberg, Madison: University of Wisconsin Press, 1969 pp. 173–215.

———, *Essays on South India*, New Delhi: Vikas Publishing House, 1975.

———, *South Indian Temples: An Analytical Reconsideration*, New Delhi: Vikas Publishing House, 1976.

———, 'Circulation & the Historical Geography of the Tamil Country', *Journal of Asian Studies*, vol. 37, no. 2, 1977a, pp. 7–26.

———, ed., 'Temples in the Tamil Country, AD 1300–1750', *Indian Economic and Social History Review*, vol. 14, no.1, 1977b, pp. 11–46.

———, 'The Segmentary State in South Indian History', in Richard G. Fox (ed.), *Realm and Region in Traditional India*, Delhi: Vikas Publishing House, 1977c.

———, *Peasant, State and Society in Medieval South India*, New Delhi: Oxford University Press, 1979.

———, 'Mahanavami: Medieval and Modern Kingly Ritual in South India', in *Essays on Gupta Culture*, ed. Bardwell L. Smith, Delhi: South Asia Books, 1983.

———, *All the Kings Mana: Papers on Medieval South Indian History*, Madras: New Era Publications, 1984.

———, 'Social Mobility and Medieval South Indian Hindu Sects', in *Social Mobility and the Caste System in India: An Interdisciplinary Symposium*, ed. James Silverberg, Mouton, Paris, 1985a, pp. 78–94.

———, 'Vijayanagar and the Transition to Patrimonial System', in *Vijayanagar—City and Empire: New Currents of Research*, ed. A.L. Dallapiccola and S.L. Lallemant, Weisbaden: Franz Steiner Verlag, 1985b.

Studies in Rāmānuja: Papers Presented at the First all-India Seminar on Śrī Rāmānuja and his Social Philosophy at Śrīperumbūdūr, Madras: Sri Ramanuja Vedanta Centre, 1979.

Subbarayalu, Y., *Political Geography of the Chola Country*, State Department of Archaeology, Government of Tamil Nadu, 1973.

———, 'The Cola State', *Studies in History*, vol. 4, no. 2, 1982, pp. 265–306.

———, *South India under the Cholas*, New Delhi: Oxford University Press, 2012.

Subrahmanian, N., 'Bhaktism in Medieval Tamilnad', in *Medieval Bhakti Movements in India, Sri Caitanya Quincentenary Commemoration Volume*, ed. N.N. Bhattacharyya, Delhi: Munshiram Manoharlal, 1989.

Subhrahmanya Sastry, Sadhu, ed., *Early Inscriptions (1930-38)*, TTD vol. I; repr., Delhi: Sri Satguru Publications, 1984.

Subramaniam, V., 'The Origins of Bhakti in Tamil Nadu: A Transformation of Secular Romanticism to Emotional Identification with a Personal Deity', in *Bhakti Studies*, ed. G.M. Bailey and Ian Kesarcodi-Watson, New Delhi: Sterling Publishers, 1991 pp. 11–52.

Swamy, B.G.L., 'The Four Saivite Samayacaryas of the Tamil Country in Epigraphy', *Journal of Indian History*, vol. 50, no. 1, 1972, pp. 95–128.

———, 'The Date of the Tevaram Trio : An Analysis and Reappraisal', *Bulletin of the Institute of Traditional Cultures, Madras*, vol. 19, no. 1, 1975, pp. 119–80.

———, '"Kaḷabhra Interregnum"—A Retrospect and Prospect', *Bulletin of the Institute of Traditional Cultures, Madras*, vol. 20, no. 1, 1976, pp. 81–148.

———, *Chidambaram and Nataraja: Problems and Rationalization*, Mysore: Geetha Book House Publishers, 1979.

Talbot, Cynthia, 'Temples, Donors and Gifts: Patterns of Patronage in Thirteenth Century South India', *Journal of Asian Studies*, vol. 50, no.2, 1991, pp. 308–40.

Tatachariar, Thiru Mahamahopadyaya Agnihotram Ramanuja, 'Vaisnava Tradition', *Bulletin of the Institute of Traditional Cultures, Madras*, vol. 20, no. 2, 1976, pp. 43–62.

Thangappa M.L. and A.R. Venkatachalapathy, *Red Lilies and Frightened Birds: Muttolayiram*, Delhi: Penguin Classics, 2011.

Thapar, Romila, *Asoka and the Decline of the Mauryas*, New Delhi: Oxford University Press, 1961; rvsd. and repr. edn. 1998.

———, 'Imagined Religious Communities', *Modern Asian Studies*, vol. 23, no. 2, 1989, pp. 209–31.

———, ed., *Recent Perspectives of Early Indian History*, Bombay: Popular Prakashan, 1995.

———, *Somanatha: The Many Voices of A History*, New Delhi: Viking and Penguin India, 2004.

Thiruvengadathan, A., 'The Tamil Movement in Srivaisnavism', in S.S. Janaki (ed.), *Prof. Kuppuswami Sastri Birth Centenary Commemoration Volume*, pt. 2, Madras: The Kuppuswami Sastri Research Institute, 1985, pp. 119–30.

Thompson, M.S.H., 'The Agastya Selection of the Tamil Saivite Hymns', *Bulletin of the School of Oriental Studies, University of London*, vol. 4, no. 4, 1928, pp. 761–8.

Tirumalai, R., 'Visistadvaita and Mystical Experience', *Journal of Oriental Research*, vols. 47–55, 1977–86, pp. 192–205.

Tiruvenkatachari, S., 'The Trivikrama Avatara in Mahabalipuram', *Journal of Indian History*, vol. 22, no. 1, 1943, pp. 7–15.

Trautmann, Thomas R., 'The Study of Dravidian Kingship', in *Aryan and Non-Aryan in India, Michigan Papers on South and Southeast Asia, No. 14*, ed. Madhav

M. Deshpande and Peter Edwin Hook, Ann Arbor: University of Michigan, 1979.
Turner, Victor, 'The Centre Out There: Pilgrims' Goal', *History of Religions*, vol. 12, no. 3, 1973, pp. 191–230.
Vaidya, C.V., 'The Date of the Bhagavata Purana', *Journal of the Bombay Branch of the Royal Asiatic Society*, New Series 1, 1925, pp. 144–61.
Vanmikanathan, G., *Periya Puranam by Sekkizhaar. Condensed English Version*, Madras: Sri Ramakrishna Math, 2004.
Varadachari, K.C., *Alvars of South India*, Bombay: Bharatiya Vidya Bhavan, 1970.
———, 'Bhaktisara Yogi and his Philosophy of Religion', *Journal of Indian History*, vol. 21, nos. 1–2, 1942a, pp. 83–116.
———, 'Some Contributions of Alvars to the Philosophy of Bhakti', *Annals of the Bhandarkar Oriental Research Institute*, vol. 23, 1942b, pp. 621–32.
Varadachari, V., *Agamas and South Indian Vaisnavism*, Madras: Prof. M. Rangacarya Memorial Trust, 1982.
———, *Yamunacharya*, Madras: Prof. M. Rangacharya Memorial Trust, 1984.
Varadacharya, V., 'Prapatti', *Journal of Oriental Research*, vols. 42–6, 1972–7, pp. 46–56.
Vasantha, R., 'The Colas and the Introduction of Srivaishnavism in Karnataka', *Quarterly Journal of the Mythic Society*, vol. 64, 1973, pp. 32–6.
———, *The Narayanasvami Temple at Melkote*, Mysore: Mysore Directorate of Archaeology and Museums, 1991.
Vaudeville, Charlotte, 'Evolution of Love Symbolism in Bhagavatism', *Journal of the American Oriental Society*, vol. 82, no. 1, 1962, pp. 31–40.
Veliath, S.J. Cyrill, *The Mysticism of Ramanuja*, Delhi: Munshiram Manoharlal, 1993.
Vēlupiḷḷai, Ālvāpiḷḷai, 'The Vision of Civa̱n in Tamil Caivam', in *Being Religious and Living through the Eyes: Studies in Religious Iconography and Iconology, A Celebratory Publication in Honour of Professor Jan Bergman*, ed. Peter Schalk, Uppsala: Acta Universitatis Upsalensis, 1998, pp. 361–72.
Veluthat, Kesavan, 'The Socio-Political Background of Kulasekhara Alvar's Bhakti', *Proceedings of the Indian History Congress*, Thirty-eighth Session, Bhuvanesvar, 1977, pp. 137–45.
———, 'Royalty and Divinity: Legitimation of Monarchical Power in South India', *Proceedings of the Indian History Congress*, Thirty-ninth Session, Hyderabad, 1978.
———, 'The Temple Base of the Bhakti Movement in South India', *Proceedings of the Indian History Congress*, Waltair, pp. 185–94, 1979; also reproduced in K.M. Shrimali, ed., *Essays in Indian Art, Religion and Society*, Indian History Congress, Delhi: Munshiram Manoharlal, 1987.
———, 'Religious Symbols in Political Legitimation', *Social Scientist*, vol. 21, nos. 1–2, January–February 1993a, pp. 23–33.
———, *The Political Structure of Early Medieval South India*, Delhi: Orient Longman, 1993b.

———, 'The Role of Nadu in the Socio-Political structure of South India (*c.* AD 600–1200)', in *The Feudal Order: State, Society and Ideology in Early Medieval India*, ed. D.N. Jha, Delhi: Manohar, 2000 pp. 179–96.

———, 'Imagining a Region: Kerala in Medieval Literature and Historiography', Paper presented at the Centre for Historical Studies, Jawaharlal Nehru University, 18 March 2009a.

———, *The Early Medieval in South India*, New Delhi: Oxford University Press, 2009b.

———, 'Ideology and Legitimation: Early Medieval South Asia', in *Mind over Matter: Essays on Mentalities in Medieval India*, ed. D.N. Jha and Eugenia Vanina, New Delhi: Tulika Books, 2009c, pp. 3–14.

Veluthat, Kesavan and M.G.S. Narayanan; see Narayanan, M.G.S.

Venkatachari, K.K.A., *Śrīvaiṣṇava Maṇipravāḷa/ The Maṇipravāḷa Literature of the Śrīvaiṣṇava Ācāryas: 12th to 15th Centuries* AD, Bombay: Anantacharya Indological Institute, 1978.

———, ed., *Proceedings of the Seminar on Temple Art and Architecture*, Bombay: Anantacharya Indological Research Institute, 1980.

———, *Nappinnai, Consort of Krsna: Study of Tamil Tradition*, Unpublished Manuscript, 1981–2.

———, ed., *Proceedings of the Seminar on Symbolism in Temple Art and Architecture*, Bombay: Anantacharya Indological Research Institute, 1981.

———, ed., *Agama and Silpa. Proceedings of Seminar held in December 1981*, Bombay: Anantacharya Indological Research Institute, 1982.

———, 'The Srivaisnava Agamas and the Indigenous Tradition of India', *Oriental Journal, Sri Venkatesvara University*, vol. 37, nos. 1–2, January–December 1994.

———, *Tamil as a Vehicle of Revelation*, Manuscript.

———, *Ritual and Symbolism in Srivaisnava Pratistha Ritual and the Conversion of Symbol into the Supreme*, Bombay: Anantacharya Indological Research Institute.

Venkataraman, K.R., 'The Vaikhanasas', in *The Cultural Heritage of India*, ed. H. Bhattacharyya, vol. 4, Calcutta: Ramakrishna Mission Institute of Culture, 1956.

Venkatasubramanian, T.K.V., 'Social Roots of Tamilian Religious Ideology', *Proceedings of the Indian History Congress*, Thirty-ninth Session, Hyderabad, 1978.

———, 'Bhakti Ideology vis-à-vis Saivite Hymns of Nāyanmārs', *Proceedings of the Indian History Congress*, Gorakhpur, 1990.

Venkatesan, Archana, 'Āṇṭāḷ and her Magic Mirror: Her Life as a Poet in the Guises of the Goddess. The Exegetical Strategies of Tamil Śrīvaiṣṇavas in the Apotheosis of Āṇṭāḷ', Unpublished Ph.D. thesis, University of California, Berkeley, 2004.

———, 'The Gift of a Garland: The Āṇṭāḷ Story in the Guruparamaparā Prabhāvam 6000 and the in the Śrī Villiputtār Sthala Purāṇa', *Journal of Vaishnava Studies*, vol. 15, no. 2, 2007, pp. 189–205.

———, *The Secret Garland: Āṇṭāḷ's Tiruppāvai and Nācciyār Tirumoḻi*, Translated with Introduction and Commentary, New York: Oxford University Press, 2010.

———, 'A Different Kind of Āṇṭāḷ Story: The *Divyasūricaritam* of Garunavāhana Paṇḍita', *The Journal of Hindu Studies*, vol. 6, no. 3, 2013, pp. 1–54.

Venkatraman, R., 'The Date of Tirumular: A Reassessment', *Proceedings of the Indian History Congress*, Thirty-eighth Session, Bhuvanesvar, 1977.

Verghese, Anila, *Archaeology, Art and Religion: New Perspectives on Vijayanagara*, New Delhi: Oxford University Press, 2000.

Vidyarthi, P.B., *Sri Ramanuja's Philosophy and Religion. A Critical Exposition of Visistadvaita*, Madras: M. Rangacarya Trust, 1977.

Visistadvaita: Philosophy and Religion, A Symposium by Twenty Four Erudite Scholars, Madras: Ramanuja Research Society, 1974.

Warder, A.K., 'Feudalism and Mahayana Buddhism', in *Indian Society, Historical Probings. In Memory of DD Kosambi*, ed. R.S. Sharma, New Delhi: ICHR and People's Publishing House, 1974.

Watters, T., *On Yuan Chwang's Travels in India*, Delhi: Munshiram Manoharlal, 1961. (First Indian Edition). (Originally published in 1904).

Welbon, G.R. and Glenn Yocum, *Religious Festivals in South India and Sri Lanka*, Delhi: Manohar, 1982.

Werner, Karel, ed., *Love Divine: Studies in Bhakti and Devotional Mysticism*, Richmond, Surrey: Curzon Press, 1993.

Yocum, Glenn E., 'Shrines, Shamanism and Love Poetry: Elements in the Emergence of Popular Tamil Bhakti', *Journal of the American Academy of Religions*, vol. 41, no. 1, 1973, pp. 3–17.

———, 'Sign and Paradigm: Myth in Saiva and Vaisnava Bhakti Poetry', in *Structural Approaches to South Indian Studies*, ed. M.M. Buck and Glenn Yocum, Chambersburg, PA: Anima Books, 1974, pp. 184–206.

———, 'Tests of Devotion among the Tamil Saiva Nāyanmārs', *Journal of Oriental Research*, vols. 42–6, 1972–7, pp. 66–71.

———, *Hymns to the Dancing Siva: A Study of Manikkavacakar's Tiruvacakam*, New Delhi: Heritage Publications, 1982.

Young, Katherine, 'Dying for Bhukti and Mukti: The Srivaisnava Theology of Liberation as a Triumph over Death', *Studies in Religion/ Science Religieuses*, vol. 12, no. 4, 1983a, pp. 389–96.

———, 'Beloved Places (Ukantaruḷinanilankaḷ): Praise of Tamil Nadu and the Making of Indic Civilization', Unpublished Manuscript, 1978.

———, 'The Spirit and the Bride say "Come!" Continuing a Hindu–Christian Dialogue', *Journal of Vaishnava Studies*, vol. 6, no. 1, 1998, pp. 99–116.

———, '*Om*, the Vedas, and the Status of Women with Special Reference to Śrīvaiṣṇavism', in *Women and Textual Tradition in India*, ed. L. Patton Laurie, New York: Oxford University Press, 2002, pp. 84–121.

———, 'Śankara on the Salvation of Women and Śūdras', in *Goddesses and Women in Indic Religious Tradition*, ed. Arvind Sharma, Leiden and Boston: Brill, 2005, pp. 131–66.

Young, Katherine and Alaka Hejib, 'Etymology as a Bridge Between Text and Sectarian Context: A Case Study of Parāśarabhaṭṭar's Commentary', in *Hermeneutical Paths to the Sacred Worlds of India*, ed. Katherine K. Young, Atlanta: Scholars Press, 1994 pp. 222–30.

Younger, Paul, 'Singing the Tamil Hymn Book in the Tradition of Rāmānuja', *History of Religions*, vol. 20, no. 2, 1982; also reproduced in G.W. Spencer, ed., *Temples, Kings and Peasants: Perceptions of South India's Past*, Madras: New Era Publications, 1987.

———, *Playing Host to Deity: Festival Religion in the South Indian Tradition*, New York: Oxford University Press, 2002.

Zvelebil, Kamil, *The Smile of Murugan: On Tamil Literature of South India*, Leiden: EJ Brill, 1973.

———, *Tamil Literature*, Leiden: EJ Brill, 1975.

———, 'The Beginnings of Tamil Bhakti in South India', *Temenos: Studies in Comparative Religion*, vol. 13, 1977, pp. 223–57.

———, *Tamil Traditions on Subrahmanya-Muruga*, Madras: Institute of Asian Studies, 1991.

Index

abhiśekha 98
Ācārya Hṛdayam 44, 150, 155–6, 158
Accyuta Vikkanta 6, 184–5
acit 73
adhikāri 62
adhyayanotsava 70–1, 270
ādi 149
ādi-prapanna 74
Ādiśaiva 30
Ādivāhakan 60
Advaita 76, 79, 81, 99, 120, 208, 277
Advaitin 75, 83, 120, 209, 236, 252, 276
Āgama(s) 97–8, 100–1, 148, 167, 243–6, 259, 261, 275–6
Āgama Prāmāṇya 98, 148
Agamic 130, 244, 246–8, 261
Agastya 17
agrahāras 180
Ahobila 82
Ājīvika 193
akam 2, 4, 17
Aḻakiya Maṇavāḷaṉ 57–8, 69–71, 83, 114
Aḻakiya Maṇavāḷa-p-Pĕrumāḷ Nāyaṉār 44, 149, 151, 155–6
Āḷavantār 33, 47, 77–8, 80–1, 107, 172–3
Ālināḍu (*also see* TiruvĀli) 62, 144
Ālinagar 67, 140, 284
Ālināṭan 64
Allaudin Khilji 9, 86
Aḻuntūr 29, 211–12, 275, 288–9, 292
Āḻvār TiruNagari 29, 71, 73, 82, 234, 240
Amalaṉādipirāṉ 27, 61, 116, 137, 161, 209, 267, 281, 294
amśa 48, 53–4, 58–9, 62, 73
anādi 149
Ānandatāṇḍava 205, 259–60
Ananta 33, 52, 54, 72, 75, 85, 89, 125, 261
Aṉbil 32–3, 231, 283
Āṇḍāḷ 13, 17, 21, 26, 32, 37, 42, 45, 55–8, 64, 78, 95–7, 101, 106, 110–12, 114–17, 124–5, 135, 146, 161–2, 196, 238, 241, 251–2, 257, 267, 270, 273, 281, 284–5
Andhra 3, 7, 9, 183, 191, 227
anga(s) 38, 64, 73, 163
Aniruddha 33, 210
Āṉporuṉai 141
antādi(s) 24–6, 49, 136
Āṇṭāṉ, see Mutaliyāṇṭāṉ
antima kula, 61
aṇu 73
anubhava grantha(s) 97, 125, 150
Appar 11–15, 28–30, 74, 90–1, 159, 168, 170, 182, 194, 205–6, 223, 226, 243–6, 274
apsarā 50, 62, 145
Arab/(ic) 183, 219
Arabian Sea 196

Arangam, see TiruvArangam
Ārāvamutan̲ 52, 257
Ārāyirappaṭi 13, 41, 98, 150
arcā 53, 71, 108–9, 111, 116, 123, 149, 151, 270, 275
arcaka 67, 89, 235, 238, 240
arcaka mukhena 151, 172
arcāvatāra 149, 151
arcā vigraha 52, 65, 74, 230
areca-nut(s) 66
Arjuna 109, 248
Arthaśāstra 180
Aruḷāla-p-Pĕrumāḷ Ĕmpĕrumān̲ār 81, 83, 188, 251
Aruḷmāri 64
Aśoka 10, 76, 180, 183, 192
āśrama(s) 223
Aṣṭabāhu Narasimha 69
Aṣṭabhuja 8, 69, 242, 266
aṣṭākṣaram 64, 110
asura(s) 163, 202–4, 209–11, 225
Āsuri Keśava-p-Pĕrumāḷ 75
aśvamedha 48, 180
Atharvan 74
Atiyanātha Viṣṇugṛham 243
ātmā(m) 73, 102
Aṭṭabuyakaram 31, 242, 282, 286, 292
Attul̲āy 88
Auvvaiyār 192
avaidika(s) 67
Avan̲inārāṇam 8
avatāra(s) 2–3, 13, 48, 53, 59, 68, 85, 89, 96, 103, 108–9, 111, 116, 123, 125, 149, 201, 203, 209, 211, 275
avayava 71, 142
avayavī 71, 142
Ayodhya 73, 82, 140, 142, 227
ayonija 49, 135
Ayotti 140, 284
Āyppāṭi 82, 113, 284, 292

Badari 82, 227, 242, 247, 284, 286, 292
bāla-līlā 55
bamboo worker 50, 137
Bauddha(s) 14, 19, 50, 179, 195, 199, 208–9, 212–14, 222
Bauddhapaḷḷi 188
Bay of Bengal 196
Bhagavad Gītā 10, 95, 99, 101, 110, 148, 152, 156, 212
Bhagavad Gītābhāṣya 3, 81, 100, 102, 109
Bhagavad Viśayam 144, 149, 152–5
bhāgavata(s) 52–3, 60, 62–3, 72, 83, 138, 151, 235
bhāgavata apacāra 52
Bhāgavata Mahātmya 15
Bhāgavata Purāṇa 95, 111, 152
bhagavat bhakti 85, 172, 176
bhakta(s) 6, 14, 31, 60, 97, 120, 122, 125–6, 130, 138, 140, 145, 147, 170, 179, 206, 256
Bhaktavatsala 122
Bhaktavilocanam 241, 284
bhakti āndolan 15
Bhāṣyakāra 82
Bhaṭṭar (Parāśara) 3, 45, 79, 98, 105, 109, 119, 153–4, 157, 160, 276
Bhaṭṭar Pirān̲ 55, 196
Bhīṣma 60
Bhṛgu 50, 225
Bhūdevi 260
Bhūmi (devi)/pīrāṭṭi(yār) 56, 62, 75, 110, 133
bhū-pradakṣiṇā 79
bhūta 48
bhūtalinga 226, 239
Bhūta Sūri 13, 48
Biṭṭi Deva 85, 176, 194
Bodhāyana 81, 99
Bodhimankai 92
Bodhisattvas 200
Bodiyār 213
Brahmā 48, 50, 75, 80, 103, 137, 161, 163, 178, 201–5, 209–12, 222, 225–6, 240, 255, 258, 260–1
brahmadeya(s) 6, 23, 84, 164, 180–1, 192, 198, 253

Brahmāṇḍa Purāṇa 203, 255
brahmarākṣasa 59, 77, 193
Brahmasūtras 79
Bṛhadāraṇyaka Upaniṣad 10
Buddha 11, 19, 65–6, 68, 183, 187–91, 199–200, 209, 248
Buddhism 194, 197–8, 201, 208–9, 215, 221–3

caitya(s) 184, 186, 189
cakra 52, 62, 82, 190, 217, 225
Cālukya(s) 7–9, 28, 166, 181, 186
caṇḍāla(s) 61, 87, 138, 151, 158, 161–2, 164, 272
carama śloka 110, 121, 174
Caṭakopaṉ 29, 38, 70, 72, 74, 196, 270, 274
Catuḥślokī 78, 105
Cekkiḻār 15, 38, 185, 205, 267
Cĕlva Nampi 54–5
Cĕlvappiḷḷai 87
Cera(s) 6, 17, 53, 130, 138–40, 221
Ceramāṉ Pĕrumāḷ 13
Cĕyyoṉ 2, 197, 199
Chidambaram 30–1, 90, 141, 168, 178, 204–6, 215, 231
Cilappatikāram 2, 7, 12, 16, 26, 114, 184, 199, 201, 220, 222, 225
Cinka-p-Pĕrumāḷ Koyil 165, 243
Ciriya Tirumaṭal 24, 27, 39–40, 64, 147, 256, 281, 292–3
Cīrkāḻi 64–5, 233, 237
Ciruttŏṇṭar 28, 168
Cittaṉavācal 184, 247
Coḻa(s) 6, 8–9, 11–12, 17, 20–2, 28–30, 33–4, 51, 62–3, 71, 83–4, 86, 88–90, 125, 132–3, 138, 141, 144, 159–60, 165–6, 168, 176, 178–9, 184–90, 192, 198, 200, 205–6, 215, 219, 221, 223, 23–2, 237, 252, 260, 263, 271
Coḻamaṇḍalam 165, 246
Coḻaṉ 88, 90, 188, 215
Coḻanāḍu 25–6, 82, 136, 141, 191, 226, 241, 246, 253, 283–4, 286, 289, 290–2
Curuppārkuḻal 55
Cūṭikŏṭutta(ḷ) 56, 267

Dantidurga 8, 31
darśana 81, 86, 106, 193, 208, 259
darśana pravartaka 77, 148, 172, 251
darśārtha 80
Daśaratha 95, 142
Dāśarathi 154
Deccan 181, 183, 186, 217
Dehalīśastuti 49, 121
Delhi 42, 86–7
Deśika, *see* Vedānta Deśika
deva(s) 19, 63, 162, 202, 235
devadāna 6, 84, 164, 198, 216, 231, 266
Devadevi 58–9, 123, 125
Devaki 75, 95, 142
devālaya 63
Devanāyaka 109
Devaprayāg 82, 241
devaraṭiyār 23
dharma 25, 59, 121, 145
Dharmaśāstra/ic 135–6
Dharmasena 90
digvijaya 81, 208
dīkṣitar 75
Dillipuram 86, 217
divya deśa(s) 53, 64, 68, 82, 141–2, 173, 206, 233–4, 238–41, 243, 246, 248, 252, 255–6, 260, 262
divya kanyā 62
divya kṣetra 65, 69, 90, 205, 220, 227, 240, 248, 261
divyarūpa 74
divyasūri(s) 70
Draupadi 203
Drāviḍa Veda 38, 70, 73, 149, 270–1
Durvāsa 96
Dvāpara 31, 46, 48, 50, 73
Dvārakā 112, 227, 241, 284, 290
Dvārāvatī 82
dvaya(m)/(mantram) 72, 110, 174

Eastern Ghats 191

ekadaṇḍa 79
Ekāmreśvara 190, 239, 263
Ĕmpār 80
Ĕmpĕrumāṉ 55, 256

Gadyas/Gadyatrayi 4–5, 81, 99–100, 104
gandharva vivāha 145
Ganga (river) 77, 82, 153, 210–11, 241
Gangaikŏṇṭacolapuram 204
Gangas 7, 186
gaṇikā 145
Garuḍa 54–5, 75, 118, 151, 202, 204, 225, 236, 261
Garuḍavāhana Paṇḍita 41
ghāt 60, 76, 239
Gītā, see Bhagavad Gītā
Gītābhāṣya, see *Bhagavad Gītābhāṣya*
Gītārthasamgraha 99, 102, 148
Godā 58, 253
gopī(s) 105, 111, 113, 121, 145, 172
Gopinatha Rao 31, 33, 189, 190
gopuram(s) 71, 174, 193, 220
goṣṭhī 54, 77
gotra 33, 62, 145, 171, 175, 245
Govardhana 2, 82, 241, 284
Govinda 112, 202
Govinda (Bhaṭṭar) 75, 76, 77, 80, 81, 208
Govinda Cīyar 80
Grantha 165, 190, 194, 243–4, 248
Guṇabhara 26, 194
guru 19, 43, 74–6, 79, 154, 174, 238, 263, 276
Guruparamparāsāram 21, 158

Hampi 9, 260
Hanumān 76, 248
Hari-Hara 25, 69, 136
Hastigiri 115, 251
Hayagrīva 82, 163
Hiraṇyakaśipu 2, 96, 260–1
Hoysala(s) 9, 85, 186, 216
hunter(s) 5, 50, 64, 76–7, 85, 137, 169–70, 176

ideal polytheism 200, 254–5
Ikṣvāku(s) 152, 158, 175
Iḷaiyāḻvār 19, 75, 98, 171–4, 176
Iḷam Bodhiyar 184
Īḻanāḍu 226
Ilanko Atikaḷ 184
Indra 50, 80, 201–2, 204, 210, 212
Iraṇṭām Āyiram 23–4, 49, 95, 209, 248, 264, 281–2
Iraṇṭām Tiruvantādi 24, 49, 95, 209, 248, 264, 281–2
Īśvara 10, 222
iṭaikaḻi 49, 264, 283
Itihāsas 149
Īṭu 3, 44, 144, 149, 152–3
Iyarpā 23–7, 136, 281

Jagannātha 82
Jainism 7, 11–12, 93, 148, 180–1, 184–6, 192–5, 197–8, 201, 208, 221–3, 247
Jalauka 10
Janaka 55–7
Jaṭāvarman 32, 37
Jaṭāyu 152, 175
Jaṭila Parāntaka Nĕṭuñcaṭaiyan 32
jīva/jīvātmā 44, 106, 175
Jivaka Cintāmaṇi 185
jñāna(m) 56, 75, 95, 102, 115, 124
jñānayoga 102, 132
Jñānasāra 81

kadamba tree 163
Kaḍāram 186–7
Kailāśanātha 26
kainkarya 54, 58, 77–9, 122–3, 171–2, 251
Kaiśika 61
Kaiśika Purāṇa 59
Kākaṭiyas 9
Kaḷabhra(s) 6–7, 10, 12, 184, 198, 221
Kālahasti 77, 80, 169
KāḻicCīrāmaViṇṇagaram 64–5, 67, 233, 237, 287
Kalikaṉṟi 63

Kālinagara/Kālipura 67
Kaliyaṉ 31, 64, 195–6, 207
Kali yuga 31, 53–5, 58–9, 62, 71, 73
kaḷḷar 129, 135, 255
Kāma 51, 112, 114
kāma 25, 145
Kāmākṣi 189–90, 193, 262–3
Kamalanayana Bhaṭṭar 75
Kāmasūtra 145
Kāñcī/Kāñcīpuram 7–8, 23, 25–6, 31, 44, 48, 51, 63, 69, 75–9, 83–4, 115, 119, 136, 148, 150–1, 166–7, 171–3, 182, 184–5, 188–94, 204–5, 207, 212, 214, 233–4, 237, 239, 243, 251, 258, 260, 262–3, 266
Kaṉikaṇṇaṉ 50–1
Kaṇṇaki 16, 114
Kaṇṇaṉ 56
Kaṇṇaṉūr 219
Kaṇṇappa(r) 169–70
Kaṇṇapuram, *see* TiruKaṇṇapuram
Kaṇṇinuṇciruttāmpu 14, 30, 38, 74, 98, 143, 146, 149, 228, 270, 272, 274, 281, 294
Kantalūr Śālai 39
Kapālīśvara 92–3, 185, 209
Kāraikkāl 92, 168, 187
Kāri 38, 72, 74
karma 59, 95, 102, 105, 119, 123, 151, 155, 195
karmayoga 102
Karnataka 3, 15, 42, 86–8, 93, 176, 181–4, 186, 191, 194, 215
kaṟṟaḷi 232
Kārttikai 59, 70
Karūr 141–2
Kāsārayogi 13, 48
Kāśi 81, 217
kāśāya 84–5
Kaṭalmallai 238, 282, 286, 292
Kaṭhopaniṣad 10
Kaumudiki 48
Kausalyā 75
Kaustubha 53
Kaveri 9, 26, 28–9, 60–1, 68, 116, 130, 141–2, 154, 174, 184, 194, 216, 221, 231, 234, 237, 239, 246, 248
Kavunti Aṭikaḷ 201
kāvya 41, 56, 63, 184–5
Kerala 20, 58, 115, 138–42, 199, 221, 227, 234, 241, 253, 261
Keśavaṉ 196
Koccĕnkaṇāṉ 28–9, 63, 206
Kolanār kuḻal 39
Koḻi 53, 138–9, 288
Kŏḷḷi(nagar) 53, 138
Kŏḷḷiṭam 60, 68, 217
Kŏnku(nāḍu) 138–9, 192, 226
Kŏṟṟavai 64, 199
Kotai 13, 55–6, 58, 113, 196, 266–7
Kovalaṉ 16, 114
Kovalūr, *see* TirukKovalūr
koyil 115, 235
Koyil Ŏluku 42, 70, 87, 219
Kṛmikaṇṭha 88, 215
Kṛṣṇa 2, 17, 54, 56, 61, 105–6, 108–13, 116, 121, 142, 145, 156, 162, 172, 197, 199, 203, 209–11, 215, 241, 250–2, 254, 273
Kṛṣṇāvatāra 55, 111, 142, 155
kṣatriya 129, 134–5, 158
Kukkuṭakuṭa 53
kula 6, 13, 61–2, 145
kuladeva 86
Kulaiccirai(yār) 12, 91
Kuḷantai 118, 236, 291
Kulaśekhara 36–7, 53–4, 95, 110, 118, 123, 129, 135, 138–42, 146, 161–2, 202, 266–8, 272, 274, 281, 284–5
Kulottunga I/II/III 9, 83–4, 90, 165–6, 185–6, 216–17, 232, 263
Kumbhakarṇa 96, 111
Kumbhakoṇam 26, 35, 52, 204, 232, 234, 247, 257–8, 268
Kumudavalli 62, 68, 71, 145
Kūṉ Pāṇṭiyaṉ 91, 194
Kūrattāḻvāṉ 78, 81, 84–5, 88, 103, 154, 160, 171, 174

Kūreśa 105, 109, 119, 276
Kurosawa 46
Kurukāpuri 58, 71
Kurukūr, *see* TirukKurukūr
Kurukūr Nampi 14, 25, 74
Kuṣāṇa(s) 181
Kūṭal 53, 138–9, 287–8
Kuṭamūkku 26, 283
Kuṭantai, *see* TirukKuṭantai

Laghu Bhāskarīya Vyākhyā 140
Lakṣmaṇa 75
Lakṣmī 61, 124, 261
Lakṣmīnarasimha Temple 243
Lanka 67, 76, 122, 141, 209, 226
Leiden plates 186
līlā 55, 81, 86, 96, 208
linga 77, 80, 169–70, 178, 194, 205, 209, 226
Linga Purāṇa 214
Lokasārangamuni 60–1, 138, 267

Mādhava(n̲) 196, 202, 212–13
Madhurakavi 14, 21, 25, 30, 32, 38, 47, 71, 73–5, 98, 129, 135, 143–4, 146, 149, 170, 220, 228, 240, 270–2, 274, 281
Madhuramangalam 75
Madhurāntakam 36, 78, 173
Madhva 102, 209
Madurai 32, 54–6, 74, 91–3, 114, 138–9, 182, 234, 259
Mahābali 163
Mahabalipuram 26, 220, 237–8, 243, 246, 248
Mahābhārata 151, 156, 164, 194, 203, 215
Mahadāhvaya Sūri 13, 49–50
mahātmya(s) 15, 53, 205
Mahendravarman 11, 15, 28–9, 91, 194, 222, 232, 243–4, 247
Mahendra Viṣṇugṛha 26, 242
Mahisāra 50
Malaināḍu 82, 115, 141–2, 226, 234, 241, 253, 285, 288–9, 291, 293
Māl 2, 11, 16, 205
Mal̲icai, *see* TiruMal̲icai
Malik Kafur 9, 44, 86, 217, 219
Māliruñcolai, *see* TiruMāliruñcolai
mallāṇṭa 32
Māmallai/Mallai 31, 238, 243, 282
Māmallapuram 48, 238
Maṇavāḷa Māmun̲i 43
maṇḍapa(m)/(s) 37, 54, 71, 165, 188, 206, 220
mangalāśāsana(s) 55, 252
Māṇikkavācakar 111, 205
Maṇimekalai 7, 12, 184, 222
Maṇipravāḷa 4, 21, 41–2, 48, 65, 102, 125, 150, 157, 180, 218
Mankaiyarkkaraci 91
Man̲n̲anār 29, 204
mantra(s) 72, 77–8, 104, 110, 152, 158, 174
mantrārtham 72
mantrī 53, 165, 216
Mār̲an̲ 32, 38, 72, 74
Mār̲an̲eri Nampi 175
Mārkal̲i 35, 56, 58, 70–1, 113, 251, 270
maṭha(s) 19, 44, 83–5, 132
Mathura 82, 111, 227, 241, 284, 286, 290, 292
Mattavilāsa Prahasana 185, 194, 223
Maurya/(n)/(s), 10, 180, 184
māyā 18, 50, 106, 117–18, 120, 236
Māyakkūttan̲ 118, 236
Māyan̲ 56, 114
Māyāvādīs 83
Mayilai/Mayilāpūr 48, 92–3, 167, 185, 282
Mayilaināthar 185
Māyin̲ 117, 120, 236
Māyon̲ 2, 25, 197, 199, 230
mediatrix 3, 105, 121, 125
Melkote 87
Mimāmsa 101, 105, 165, 276
mleccha 62, 218
mokṣa 25, 48, 51, 106, 110, 145, 203, 255, 257

Mukundamālā 54
mūla mantra 158
mūla mūrti 57, 261
mūlavar 57, 255
mullai 2
Muṇḍakopaniṣad 10
munivāhana 161, 267
Mūṉṟām Tiruvantādi 24, 49, 69, 82, 204, 210, 258, 264, 281–2
Murukaṉ 2, 11, 16, 197, 199
Muslim(s) 9, 42–3, 66, 86–7, 183, 217–21
mutal Āḻvār-s/*kaḷ* 13, 24, 26, 48–9, 51, 135, 229, 264, 267
Mutal Āyiram 23, 281
Mutaliyāṇṭāṉ 85, 107, 154, 174–5
Mutal Tiruvantādi 24, 31, 49, 69, 95, 239–40, 258, 264, 281–2
Muttŏlāyiram 17
mūvar 30, 226, 244
Mūvāyirappaṭi 13, 41
Mylapore 48, 93, 185, 189

Nācciyār 56, 63
Nācciyār Tirumŏḻi 13, 37, 97, 110–14, 117, 196, 238, 241, 274, 281, 284
Nāgapaṭṭinam 65–7, 184, 186–7, 190
Nagara Nampi 143, 170
Nagarāṉ 143
Naimiśāraṇyam 82, 242, 286
Nālāyira Divya Prabandham 3, 17, 20, 39, 55, 112, 118, 128, 133, 202–3, 226, 281
Nālāyira(m) 24, 38, 54, 97, 139, 294
Nālu-kavi-p-pĕrumāḷ 64–5
Nālūrāṉ 84
Nāmakkal 225, 232, 243
Nambūdiri 179, 261
Naminandi 94, 213
Nammāḻvār 1, 3–4, 14, 17, 21, 24–7, 29–30, 32, 36, 38, 41, 47, 52, 58, 64, 70–5, 81–2, 89, 95–8, 108–10, 115, 117–20, 124, 128–9, 134–5, 141–4, 146–7, 149–50, 152–3, 155–6, 162, 170, 196, 202, 208, 210–12, 214, 220, 226–9, 233–7, 240–1, 255, 257, 261–2, 268, 270–2, 274–5, 278, 281, 290, 294
Nampāṭuvār 59
Nampi Āṇṭār Nampi 30, 39
Nampi Ārūrāṉ 143, 268
Nampiḷḷai 152
Nañcīyar 153
Nandagopa 111
Nandakam 48
Nandaṉar 129
Nandipura Viṇṇagaram 207, 287
Nandivarman 8, 31, 34, 193, 207, 250
Nānkūr, *see* TiruNānkūr
Nāṉmukaṉ Tiruvantādi 24, 27, 52, 118–19, 136–7, 202–4, 209–11, 213, 239, 258, 275, 281–3
Nappiṉṉai 56, 105, 110–11, 145
Nārada 15, 60, 225
Narasimha 35, 69, 116, 234, 254, 260–1
Narasimhavarman I/II 28, 31, 193, 237
Nārāyaṇa 2, 33, 35, 50, 55, 69, 103, 119, 136–8, 158, 196–7, 203–4, 209–14, 256
Naṟṟinai 184
Naṭarāja 205, 231, 259–60
Naṭātūr Āḻvāṉ 174
Nāthamuni(kaḷ) 4, 29, 30, 32–3, 39, 47, 52, 97–100, 115, 119, 148, 172, 204, 228–9, 252, 257, 270–5, 277
Naṭunāḍu 82, 226, 253, 283, 286, 289, 292
navīna daśāvatāra 158
Nāyaṉmārs 2, 3, 5, 7, 11–14, 17, 21, 24, 28–30, 34, 37–8, 40, 47, 70, 91, 106, 123, 128, 131–2, 149, 157, 159, 167–8, 170, 185, 197, 204–6, 213–14, 222, 226, 228, 231–2, 234, 243–4, 252, 254–5, 258, 266–9, 272, 274
Nĕṭiyoṉ 16
Neṭumāraṉ 12, 91
Nĕṭuñcaṭaiyaṉ 32
Niculāpuri 68

Nilātinkaḷtuṇṭam 205, 239, 289
Nimbārka 102, 209
Nīlā/Nīlādevi 54, 110
Nīla-nirattar 62
nirguṇa 10, 81, 120, 278
Nityagrantha 99, 276
nityakarma(s) 172
nityakarmānuṣṭhānam, 60
nityasūris 96
nompu 56, 113, 273

Om namo nārāyaṇāyaḥ 110, 158
Orirukkai 52, 166, 263
outcaste 59–60, 135, 175, 267

Palghat 140
Pallāṇṭu 13, 32, 35, 54–5, 196, 202, 251–2
Pallava(s) 7–8, 10–11, 15, 25–6, 28–9, 31, 34, 51, 56, 91, 132–3, 141, 159, 164, 179, 182, 185, 189, 193–4, 200, 221–2, 231, 238, 243–5, 247–8, 250
Pallavamalla 8, 31–2, 207, 212
Pallavarāyaṉ 51
paḷḷi 22, 186, 193, 199
paḷḷiccantam 188, 247
Pāṇanātha Sūri 61
pāṇar 13, 129, 135, 161
Pāñcajanya 48, 225
pañcama (caste/*varga*) 59, 116, 127, 134
Pāñcarātra 98, 100–1, 108, 245, 254, 261, 271, 273, 275
Pāñcarātra Āgama(s) 97–8, 100–1, 148, 261, 276
Pāñcarātra Samhitā(s) 98–9, 108, 244
pañcasamskāra(s) 62
Pāṇṭimaṇḍalam 21, 26, 246
Pāṇṭiya(s) 6–7, 9, 11–12, 15, 17, 22, 25, 31–2, 35, 37, 55, 57, 91, 130, 133, 138–9, 141, 143, 182, 188, 194, 200, 221, 223
Pāṇṭiyanāḍu 25–6, 55, 73, 82, 93, 141, 143, 184, 226, 253, 283, 285, 288–9, 290–1, 293
pāpa 67
para bhakti 56, 115, 124
para jñāna 56, 115, 124
Parakāla(ṉ)/Sūri 13, 58, 62–4, 66–70, 207
Pārkaṭal 196, 227, 282–5
parama bhakti 56, 115, 120, 124
paramapada 19
paramapada vācal 71
paramātmā 44, 175
Parāntaka 29, 32–3, 35, 164, 225, 231
Parāśara 79
Parāśara Bhaṭṭar 45, 98, 109, 157, 160; *also see* Bhaṭṭar, Parāśara
paratva 104, 109, 144, 149
Paravādi-matta-gaja 64–5
Paripāṭal 11, 16, 25–6, 258
Pārvati 51
Pāśupatas 213
pāṭal pĕṟṟa talam 226–7, 234, 239, 252
Patikam 159, 245
pāvai 56, 111, 113, 273
Peraruḷālar 63, 76–9, 81, 208, 260
Pĕriya-Koyil Nampi 89
Pĕriyāḻvār 13, 26, 32, 35, 54–8, 64, 73, 95, 114, 124, 129, 135, 142–4, 146, 161–2, 196, 202, 204, 241, 251–2, 270, 273, 281, 284–5
Pĕriyāḻvār Tirumŏḻi 13, 32, 37, 55, 95, 124–5, 144, 170, 196, 202, 204, 209–11, 239, 241, 251–2, 273, 281, 284
Pĕriya Nampi 78–80, 85, 88, 161, 172–3, 175, 267
Pĕriya Pĕrumāḷ 57, 60–1, 77
Pĕriya Pirāṭṭi(yār) 72, 75
Pĕriya Purāṇam 14, 47, 90–1, 93–4, 117, 127, 133, 144, 161, 170, 183, 185, 205, 213, 223, 267
Pĕriya Tirumalai Nampi 75, 80–1, 208, 277
Pĕriya Tirumaṭal 24–5, 27, 39–40, 64, 147, 227, 256, 281, 292–3
Pĕriya Tirumŏḻi 8, 25, 28–9, 31, 37, 62–5, 70, 119, 124, 146–7, 163–4, 195–6,

202–3, 205–7, 209–10, 212–14, 225, 227, 237–40, 242, 245–6, 248, 262, 264, 273, 275, 281, 286, 289
Pĕriya Tiruvantādi 27, 74, 281, 294
Pĕriyavāccāṉ Piḷḷai 44, 46, 105, 110
Pĕrumāḷ Tirumŏḻi 37, 54, 95, 118, 128, 138–9, 140–2, 161–3, 202, 205, 210, 240, 273–5, 281, 284
Pĕrumpāṇāṟṟupaṭai 258
Pĕrumpuḷiyūr 52
Pĕrundevittāyār 76
Pey(āḻvār) 13, 24, 27, 48–9, 82, 135, 204, 210–11, 258, 264, 281–3
phalaśruti(s) 21, 195–6, 272
Piḷḷai Lokācārya 44, 87, 99, 106, 108, 150–1
Piḷḷai Lokāṉ Cīyar 44
Piḷḷaittamiḻ 142
Piḷḷai Urankāvilli Dāsar 175
Piṉṉai, *see* Nappiṉṉai
Piṉpaḻakiya Pĕrumāḷ Cīyar 41, 44, 110, 160, 175
Piṇṭiyār 213
Pirāṭṭi 58, 60, 72, 75, 133
piśāca(s) 80, 85, 214
Pŏlintu-niṉṟa-pirāṉ 72
Pŏykai 13, 24, 27, 31, 48–9, 135, 258, 264, 266, 281–3
Prabandham, see Nālāyira Divya Prabandham
prabandha(s) 58, 64–5, 143
pracchanna Bauddha(s) 19, 209
pradakṣiṇā patha 82
prākāra/(m)/(s) 65–6, 71, 189, 191, 220, 234, 246–7, 256
prakṛt 73
Prākṛt 4
Prameyasāra 81
praṇava 158
prapanna(s) 74,104–5,121,123,125,151,158
prapatti 104,116,121–2,124,151–5
prasāda(s) 35
praśasti 33, 40
pravartaka 77,148, 172, 251
Premāgrahāra 33
preta 48–9,75
Pukār 16,114
pulaiya(s) 164
puṇya 68
Puṇyakoṭi *vimāna* 76
Puri 100
puram 2, 16–17
Purāṇa(s) 16, 55, 149, 178, 225, 230, 244
puruṣakāra 105
Puruṣasūkta 55
pūrvaśikhā 73
Puṣkaram 82
Pūtam 13, 24, 27, 48, 135, 243, 248, 258, 264, 281–3
Pūtattāḻvār 48, 135, 209
Putuvai 114, 196

rahasya(s) 72, 174, 176, 205
rahasya granthas 35, 81, 173, 255
Rahasyatrayasāram 104, 158
Rājarāja (Coḻa) 9, 30, 35–6, 39, 86, 159, 166, 176, 186, 198, 231, 265, 267
Rājasimha 7, 193, 237, 243
Rājendra (Coḻa) 34, 190, 231
rākṣasa(s) 25, 53, 152, 202, 210
Rāma 2, 53, 67, 75–6, 96, 108, 121–2, 142, 152, 169, 209
Rāmānuja Nūṟṟantādi 25, 40, 89
Rāmānujārya Divya Caritai 44, 87, 261
Rāmapriya 86
Rāmāyaṇa 53, 81, 96, 121–2, 154
Ranganātha 33, 57–8, 64, 68, 70, 77, 83, 114, 116, 123, 154–5, 217, 219, 225, 238, 243, 256–7
Rāṣṭrakūṭa(s) 7–8, 186, 195
Rāvaṇa 2, 96, 111, 122, 152, 162
Ṛk 74, 136
rudrākṣa 80, 93

sabhā 22, 35, 54, 164–5, 216–17, 231, 250
saguṇa 10, 81, 236
saguṇabrahma 99, 120

Śaiva Siddhānta 127, 160
Śākya(r)/(s) 50, 83, 190, 213
Śākyapaḷḷi 188
Śāligrāma 82, 242, 284, 286
samādhi 68, 79
sāmanta 204
Sāmaveda 73–4, 165
Sambandar, *see* Tirujñāna Sambandar
sampradāyagrantha(s) 41
samskāra(s) 75, 173, 175
Sāndipani 61
Sangam 1–2, 4, 7–8, 11–12, 15–18, 26, 28, 74, 138–9, 141, 167, 184, 192, 195, 197, 221, 258, 263, 270
Śankara (ācārya) 19, 99, 101–2, 120, 179, 209
sangha 179, 181, 184, 186, 188
śankha 62, 82
sannyāsa 79, 173
sansārin 104
Santoṣī mā 200
Saptavati 67
śaraṇāgati 44, 64, 104, 121, 256
Śaraṇāgati Gadyam 4, 104
Sarasvatī 82, 258
śarīra-śarīrī 104
Śārnga 62, 196, 225
śastra(s)/ic 62, 69, 80, 162, 172, 197
Sātavāhana(s) 180
Śaṭhakopa 58, 70, 253
Saturn 200
satyam 75
saulabhya 103–4, 109
senāpati 22, 72, 166
Śeṣa 75, 90
śeṣa 105, 124
śeṣi 105, 124
seva(i) 106
Siam 8
siddhānta 50, 81, 127, 160
simhāsanādhipatis 90
Simhaviṣṇu 7, 185
Sītā 45, 53, 55, 76, 96, 122
smārta 270, 273, 277
Smṛti(s) 55, 297
Śramaṇa(s) 50, 83, 137, 179, 199, 212–14, 222–3, 245
śrauta 180
Śravaṇabelagola 184
Śrī 3, 49–50, 56–7, 72, 74–5, 99, 104–5, 121, 125, 146, 163, 209, 225, 228, 264
Śrībhāṣya 3, 81, 99, 149, 171, 277
śrīkāryam 35
Śrīkūrma 82
Śrīnātha 33
Śrīnivāsadāsa 99
Sriperumbudur 75, 85, 104, 250
Śrīranga Gadyam 4, 104, 109
Srirangam 2, 11, 16, 25, 33, 36, 41–2, 53–4, 57–60, 65, 67–8, 70–1, 73, 77–90, 102, 107, 109, 113–16, 119, 123, 125, 136–8, 141, 148, 150, 152, 154–5, 159–62, 166–7, 171–4, 176, 194, 210, 215, 217, 219–20, 235, 242, 245, 249, 251–2, 256–7, 266–7, 270–1, 273, 275
Śrīvacana Bhūṣaṇa 44, 108, 151–2
Śrīvaikuṇṭham 129, 227, 240, 255
Śrīvaramangalam 32, 290
Śrīvatsa 59, 123
Śrīvijaya 187
Śrīvilliputtūr 13, 54–5, 57, 101, 112, 114, 196, 202, 251, 285, 315
Śrīyaḥpati Nārāyaṇa 50
śruti 38, 82, 149, 275
sthalapurāṇa(s) 4, 16–17, 44, 62–3, 87, 122, 203, 205–7, 210, 225–7, 230, 232–3, 236, 240, 248, 255–8, 261
sthalavṛkṣa 272
Sthāṇu 139–40
stotra(s) 4, 49, 70, 97, 109, 119, 121
Stotraratna 78, 99
stūpa(s) 186
Sudarśana *cakra* 52, 190
śūdra 50, 52, 62, 71, 129, 134–5, 144, 158, 165, 177, 268
Sugrīva 121
Sultan(ate) 9, 171, 218

Sultāni 218
Sundarabāhustava 103
Sundarar 13–14, 28, 30, 159, 168, 170, 182, 205, 226, 243, 258, 267–8
Sūrya 75, 191, 225
svapaca 61, 152
svayamvara 58, 115, 253
Śvetāśvatara Upaniṣad 10

Tai 50, 113–14
Taittiriya Upaniṣad 75
tamarind tree 52, 72–3, 156, 272
Tāmralipti 221
ta<u>n</u>iya<u>n</u>(s) 97, 161, 267
Tanjai 203, 210, 248, 283, 288
Tanjakan 203–4
Tanjavur 22, 31, 124, 143, 159, 188–91, 204, 231, 234, 247–8, 265, 267–8
Taṇṭiyaṭikaḷ 93–4, 117, 213
Telugu 8–9, 30
Tĕnkalai(s) 40, 43, 45–6, 68, 70, 88–90, 98–100, 104–6, 115, 121–2, 134–5, 148, 151, 153, 155, 157–8, 160, 174, 177
Teṭṭaruntiral 36
Tevāram 14, 28–9, 31, 39–40, 70, 93, 133, 159, 162, 178, 206, 223, 226, 232, 244
Theragāthā, Therīgāthā 146–7
Ticai-āyiratti-ainnū<u>rr</u>uva(n)/(r) 133, 165
Tilakavatiyār 166
Tillai 141, 168, 205–6, 284, 286, 293
tīrtha 16, 87, 211, 253
Tīrthankara(s) 23, 192–3, 199–200
tīrthayātrā 253
Tiruccanta Viruttam 24, 27, 39, 52–3, 117, 136–7, 209, 239–40, 281–3
TirucCenku<u>n</u>ūr 153
Tiruccirāppaḷḷi 68, 190, 194, 231, 234, 245, 247, 251
TiruCitrakūṭa(m) 90, 141, 206, 284, 286, 293
Tirujñā<u>n</u>a-Sambandar 11, 13–14, 28, 30, 40, 64–7, 91–3, 143, 159, 168, 170, 178, 187–8, 197, 207, 213, 223, 226, 235, 237, 243, 245, 274
Tirukkacci Nampi 78–9, 171–2
TirukKaṇṇapuram 112, 123, 141, 196, 268, 284, 288–90, 292
TirukKolūr 73, 290
TirukKoṭṭiyūr 19, 25, 35, 115, 154, 174, 176, 283–4, 288, 293
Tirukkoṭṭiyūr Nampi 78, 81, 110, 174
TirukKovalūr 13, 35, 49, 264, 283, 286, 289, 292
TirukKoyilūr 35–6, 49, 192, 232, 268
Tirukkulattār 87
TirukKuraiyalūr 71
Tirukkuruntāṇṭakam 64, 147, 225, 281, 289
Tirukkurukaip-Pirā<u>n</u> Piḷḷā<u>n</u> 41, 98, 150, 157, 160, 176
TirukKurukūr 29, 71, 74, 141, 214, 234, 240, 272, 274, 290
TirukKurunkuṭi 59, 72, 261, 273, 283, 285, 288, 290, 293
TirukKuṭantai 26, 52–3, 65, 82, 112, 136, 204, 257, 262, 283, 285, 288–90, 292, 294
Tirumāl 112, 196, 207, 212, 241
Tirumalai 16, 22, 80–1
Tirumālai 59, 162, 211, 213, 220, 265–6, 281, 285
Tirumalainallā<u>n</u> 85
Tirumālaiyāṇṭā<u>n</u> 81, 107, 173
Tiruma<u>l</u>icai 13, 24, 26–7, 48, 50–3, 117, 124, 128, 135–6, 138, 146, 161, 202–4, 210, 223, 229, 258, 267, 275, 281–3
TiruMa<u>l</u>icai 48
TiruMāliruñcolai 16, 21, 26, 56, 82, 103, 112–15, 165, 204, 241, 283, 285, 288, 290, 293
TiruMālirunku<u>nr</u>am 16, 115
Tirumañjanam 70, 264
Tirumankai 8, 11, 13, 24, 27–9, 31, 36, 58, 66–7, 70–2, 95, 110, 122–3, 125, 129, 135, 141, 144–7, 162–4, 187,

195, 202, 206–8, 211, 213–15, 219–20, 223, 227, 233, 235, 237–8, 240–3, 245–6, 248, 252, 255–7, 262, 264–6, 268, 270, 273, 275, 281, 286
tirumantram 72, 174
TiruMĕyyam 215–16, 246–7, 288–9, 293
Tirumurai 30, 178, 205
Tirumuraikaṇṭapurāṇam 30
Tirumurukāṟṟupaṭai 11, 15–16
TiruNagari 29, 62, 71, 73, 82, 234, 240
TiruNānkūr 62, 144, 163, 195, 233, 237, 246, 287, 293
TiruNaraiyūr 28–9, 62–3, 125, 206, 212, 288–9, 292
TiruNārāyaṇapuram 42–3, 86–8, 215
Tirunāvukkaracar 13, 90–1, 143
Tirunĕlveli 37, 129, 234, 240, 253, 255
Tirunĕṭuntāṇṭakam 36, 64, 147, 239, 262, 275, 281, 289
Tirunīlakaṇṭayāḻppāṇar 13, 160
Tiruppallāṇṭu, see Pallāṇṭu
Tiruppaḷḷiyĕḻucci 36–7, 59, 162, 170, 249–50, 265–6, 281, 285
Tiruppāṇāḻvār 25, 26, 27, 59, 60, 61, 97, 116, 122, 125, 127, 129, 134, 135, 137, 138, 146, 161, 242, 257, 267, 268, 269, 281
TirupPārkaṭal, *see* Pārkaṭal
Tiruppati 16, 80, 82, 90, 99, 144, 234, 240, 249, 262, 273, 277
Tiruppatiyam 22, 26, 34–6, 39–40, 268, 274
Tiruppāvai 32, 36–7, 105–6, 110–14, 162, 196, 240, 273–4, 281, 284
Tiruttŏṇṭar Tŏkai 14
Tiruvāciriyam 27, 74, 281, 294
TiruvAhīndrapuram 109, 286
TiruvĀlināḍu 62, 144
TiruvĀli-TiruNagari 62, 71, 233, 237, 287, 289, 292, 341
TiruVallavāḻ 213, 241, 288, 291, 293
TiruvAnantapuram 261, 291
Tiruvantādi(s) 24, 27, 31, 49, 52, 69, 74, 82, 95, 118–19, 136–7, 202–4, 209–11, 213, 239–40, 248, 258, 264, 275, 281–2
TiruvArangam 25, 36, 125, 136, 202, 213, 272, 283–5, 287, 289, 290–2, 294
Tiruvaranga-p-Pĕrumāḷ Araiyar 78, 81, 173
Tiruvarangattu Amutaṉār 89
TiruvĀrūr 93–4
Tiruvāymŏḻi 3, 23, 25, 29, 34–6, 38, 41, 52, 69–70, 72–4, 80–1, 97–8, 107, 117–20, 142–44, 149–50, 153–5, 162–3, 173, 196, 202, 208–12, 214, 226–8, 235–6, 240–1, 255, 257, 262, 269–70, 272, 274–6, 281, 290–1
Tiruvāymŏḻideva 36
TiruVĕhkā 51–2, 83, 136, 239, 241, 258, 260–3, 282, 286, 289–92
TiruVĕḷḷarai 245, 250, 285, 287, 292
Tiruvĕḻukūṟṟirukkai 27, 64–5, 147, 235, 281, 294
Tiruvĕmpāvai 111
TiruVenkaṭam 16, 25, 69, 80, 82, 99, 112–17, 122, 136–7, 140, 210, 213, 225, 235, 239, 241–2, 253, 282–6, 289–92, 294
Tiruvenkaṭamuṭaiyāṉ 80, 82
TiruViṇṇagar 282, 287, 289–90, 292
Tiruviruttam 74, 143, 262, 281, 290–1
TiruVittuvakkoṭu, *see* Vittuvakkoṭu
TiruvOṟṟiyūr 92, 166, 258
Tŏṇṭaimaṇḍalam 10, 25–6, 28, 130, 246
Tŏṇṭaināḍu 82, 115, 136, 226, 253, 282, 286, 289–92
Tŏṇṭanūr 85
Tŏṇṭaraṭippŏṭi 25, 37, 58–9, 72, 123, 125, 129, 135, 145–6, 161–2, 211, 213, 220, 242, 249–50, 257, 265, 267, 281, 285
tridaṇḍa 84–5
tridaṇḍi 79
Trikavi 65, 67
Triśanku 107, 151, 158

Trivikrama 53, 116, 211, 234, 239, 254
Trivikrama-p-Pĕrumāḷ Temple 35, 232, 254, 264
Tṛtīya Brahmatantra Svatantra Cīyar 41, 43
tulasi 49, 55–6, 86, 156, 162, 210, 226, 265
Tulukka Nācciyār 218–19
Tuḷuvanāḍu 226
Turuṣka 42–3, 86, 217–18

ubhaya Vedānta/Vedantin(s) 38, 41, 149–50
Ulakaḷanta Pĕrumāḷ 234
Uḷḷankai Kŏṭunta Nāyaṉār 80
Umāpati Śivācārya 30
Upaniṣad(s)/(ic) 10, 75, 99, 101, 120, 275, 277
upāya, upeya 105
ūr 23, 52, 166, 204, 231, 239, 263
Uraiyūr 53, 59, 138–9
Ūrakam, 233, 239, 282, 286, 289, 292
ūrāḻvār 23
ūrdhva puṇḍra 69
Ūrvaśi 75
Uṭaiya-nānkiyār 72
Uṭaiyavar 75
utsava 74
utsava mūrti(s) 30, 57, 86, 90, 118, 205, 236, 252, 255, 260
utsavar 57, 86–7, 90, 255
utsava vigraha 87
Uttara Badarīkāśrama 82
Uttara Mimāmsa 101, 276
uṭukkai 22, 165
Uyyakŏṇṭār 172

vaibhavam 13, 19, 29–30, 48–50, 53–5, 58–9, 62, 68–71, 75, 97–8, 122, 124, 170–4, 176, 204, 220, 257, 270
Vaidehi 53
vaidya 62, 145
Vaigai 74, 92, 221
vaikhānasa(s) 34, 36, 261
Vaikuṇṭha(m) 61, 74, 90, 96, 108–9, 115, 123, 145, 196, 227, 240, 255, 282–5
Vaikuṇṭha Gadyam 4, 104, 108
Vaikuṇṭha-p-Pĕrumāḷ 8, 31, 189, 207, 212, 237, 268
Vairamegha 8, 31
vaiśya 78, 93, 135, 171–2
Vaitaraṇi 60
Vākulābharaṇa 75
valanāḍu 84, 143, 216
Vallabha 102, 209
Vallabhadeva 54
Vaḻuti-vala-nāṭan 143
Vāmana 57, 112, 116, 211, 234, 254
vamśa 33, 73
Vañci/Vañcikalam 53, 141
vaṇiya(s) 164, 250, 256
Varadarāja 44, 63, 76, 83, 108, 165, 167, 171–3, 188, 205, 251, 260, 262
Varadarāja Pañcāśat 123
Varaguṇamankai 32, 255, 290
Varaguṇavarman 32
varaḷāru 257
Varanasi 76, 82
Varavaramuni 19, 44
varga 59
varṇa 62, 127, 130, 134, 156, 158, 244, 268
varṇāśramadharma 20, 132, 153, 171, 175, 177
Vārttāmālai 44, 175
Vaśiṣṭha 50, 158
Vāsudeva 54, 62, 275
Vaṭakalai 19, 43, 45, 68, 88–90, 98–100, 105, 115–16, 121–2, 148, 151, 153, 157–8, 160–1, 174, 177
Vaṭakku-Tiruvīti-Piḷḷai 44, 149
Vaṭanāḍu 141, 217, 226, 253, 282–6, 289–92
Vaṭapatraśāyi 54–5
Vaṭapĕrunkoyil-uṭaiyāṉ 54
Vātāpi 28
Vaṭṭĕḻuttu 23

vāyppu talam 227, 246
Vedabāhya mata 69
Vedādhyāyana 52
Vedānga(s) 54, 58, 64
Vedānta 75, 78, 81, 100–2, 151, 208, 268, 276–7
Vedānta Deśika 4, 19, 21, 43, 49, 99, 104–5, 108–9, 120, 123, 153, 158, 209
Vedāntadīpa 81
Vedānta Sūtras 81, 99, 102
Veda pārāyaṇa 70
Vedārthasamgraha 81, 124
Veda Vyāsa 156
Vĕhkā, *see* TiruVĕhkā
veḷāla(s) 90, 129, 131, 133–5, 164, 168
Veḷḷiyār 213
Velvĕṭṭi Nampiyār 152
Venkaṭam, *see* TiruVenkaṭam
Veyar 13, 54, 114, 196
vibhava 103, 108
Vibhīṣaṇa 121, 152
Vicitracitta 222
Vidura 152, 175
vidvān(s) 55
vidyā(s) 50, 54, 62, 73, 78
vigraha(s) 52, 64–5, 71, 74, 87, 219, 230, 235, 237, 256
vihāra(s) 65–6, 185–7, 191
Vijayālaya 29, 83
Vijayanagara 9, 159–60, 177, 215, 219, 238, 263
Villiputtūr, *see* Śrīvilliputtūr
vimāna 66, 76, 206
vīṇa(i) 60–1
Vināyaka 30
Vindhya 76, 183
Viṇṇagar, *see* TiruViṇṇagar
Vipranārāyaṇa 58–9, 123
viraha 18, 56–7, 106, 113, 117, 203
Vīranārāyaṇapuram 29, 97, 148, 204, 257
viśeṣa kaṭākṣa 77, 79, 171
Viśiṣṭādvaita/ic 24, 76, 80–1, 97, 99, 119, 125, 149, 208, 257, 277–8
Viṣṇucitta/(n)/(r) 13, 54–6, 101, 114, 196
Viṣṇusmṛti 253
Viṣṇu Vardhana (Rāya) 85–6
Viṣvaksena 72, 167, 228
Viśvāmitra 107, 158
Viṭṭhala Deva Rāya 85
Viṭṭhala Temple 260
Vittuvakkoṭu 118, 141–2, 285
Vittuvakoṭṭagrahāram 141–2
vrata(m) 56, 111
Vṛndāvana 82, 112, 121, 197, 238, 241
vyākhyāna(s) 41, 44, 79, 128
Vyāsa 79, 156
Vyāsa Sūtra 173

Western Ghats 191, 242

Xuan Zang 189, 191

Yādava/Yādava Prakāśa 75–80, 120, 171, 208, 217, 276–8
yajña 48, 52, 78, 258
Yamuna 111, 241
yakṣas/yakṣīs 192, 200, 248
Yajñamūrti 81, 208
yajñopavīta 79
Yajurveda/Yajus 54, 58, 74, 136
Yāmunācārya 4, 33, 75, 77–9, 98–9, 102, 105, 107, 110, 115, 148, 161, 172–3, 228–9, 245, 267, 275–8
Yaśodā 95, 142, 156, 252
Yathoktakāri 52, 258, 263
Yatidharma Samuccaya 80
Yatīndramatadīpikā 99
Yatirāja Vimśati 19, 44
yoga 10, 25, 261
yogābhyāsa 50
yogaphala 52
yogaśayana 261
Yudhiṣṭhira 152